So
Much to Give

So Much to Give

A Story of America's Greatest Generation

Carlton Randolph Crane

ReadersMagnet, LLC

DEDICATION PAGE

I dedicate this book to my grandchildren:

Colton Randolph Crane
Grayson Avery Crane
Staley Anne Crane
Brooke Lynn Fouts
Harper Ryan Nelson
Jordyn Ivy Crane
Cole Randolph Crane

So that they will know that once upon a time a generation of Americans lived that believed in Love, Family, Honesty, Honor, and Integrity. And that generation, and their children, built the greatest nation the world has ever seen.

Carlton Randolph Crane

CONTENTS

PART ONE: THE BEGINNING

PART TWO: THE STAND

PART THREE: THE END

The Beginning

*They were so very young and there was so much
to understand*

The Hill

About five miles southeast of the junction of State Highway 60 and Farm-to-Market road 1055 is located the small town of Coalville, Texas. It, and its 4,000 inhabitants, is nestled in the pine tree country of deep East Texas. The nearest city of any size is Dallas, which is about one hundred and ten miles to the northwest. The nearest small town is Athens, which is due north about fifty miles.

Old abandoned coal mines dot the surrounding hills and are Coolville's only claim to fame. For, at one time, the town was a booming coal mine center of about 15,000 people. But, as the hard rock black coal slowly died away, so did the town. Those that could not return to the farm went to the nearby population centers of Dallas or Athens to try and find work. Coalville slowly returned to being a farming community with its population showing a small loss each year.

Like most small towns in this part of Texas, Coalville has a town square with a courthouse in the center. Positioned all along the square are the small businesses that keep the town functioning. From time to time, many of the stores go out of business and then back in again. The movie theater, named the Texan, on the north side of the square holds the record for going in and out of business. It has been in and out of business ten times in the last five years. Right now, it is in business. Located on the west side of the courthouse lawn is the statue of a Civil War soldier. This statue is unlike other Civil War statues in this part of Texas, because it is a statue of a Union soldier. During the Civil War, Coalville residents had remained loyal to Sam Houston and fought on the side of the Union. There is a graveyard south of Coalville down near Huntsville, Texas where 2,000 Texas Union troops are buried. Most of today's residents boast of relatives buried there.

To most people the image of Texas is that portrayed in the western movies. But the eastern part of Texas is nothing like that. It has rolling hills, thick pine tree forests, low lying swamps, and spring fed creeks. In this part of Texas, all four seasons of the year prevail: cold winters, wet springs, dry hot summers, and cool beautiful falls. The weather is extremely tricky and given to quick changes. It was actually recorded that it rained, hailed, sleeted, and snowed all in the same day, and all of this was preceded by a dust storm. The spring produces violent thunderstorms, tornadoes, and flash-floods. In the summer, there is heat in excess of one hundred degrees with little rain. The winter produces Texas Northers, cold wind, ice, and snow. Fall is the most beautiful and peaceful time of the year when very few bad things happen.

It is in this part of Texas that Coalville exists, hidden in the tall pine trees and rolling hills. The low pine tree-covered hills that surround the town make it appear to be in a small shallow valley. However, these hills, when compared to hills in other parts of the country, are not very impressive. Strangely, no one lives on the hills that surround Coalville. People live in the town itself or past the hills on the farm land. It is as though homage is being paid to the old coal mines. The mining companies long ago gave up their leases on the hills and ownership returned to private individuals across the state, because, strange as it may seem, no one in Coalville owned any of the land in the hills. The hills are now used mostly for hunting leases, and hunters from all over the state are drawn to the hills to hunt deer, wild boar, dove, and quail. That is, all of the hills except for one.

This one hill, for some reason, has no game. The deer do not roam onto this hill; nor do the wild boar. Dove and quail do not nest on this hill. The reason for this has no explanation. At least, there is not a reasonable explanation. There are several stories about hunters getting lost on the hill and falling into some of the old abandoned mine pits. Other stories say that people have gone up on this hill and have never come down again. Yet, there has never been any proof to any of these stories. Old men in town tell the story of a mine cave-in that buried thirty-five men many years ago during the prime of the coal mining era. The story says the ghosts of these buried men roam the hill keeping all living things away. There is no record however of a mine cave-in in any of the mining company records.

Maybe it's because of the stories, or maybe it's because there's not any game, but nobody ever goes up on this one hill. All of the old miners' trails leading up the hill have slowly been lost to the undergrowth and dense trees. Thick under growths of bush weeds and small mesquite trees cover the hill and are towered over by tall and closely packed pine trees. At its base is a small dirt road that travels five miles in a complete circle around the hill. The height from the dirt road to the top of the hill is about five hundred feet, rising at about a thirty-degree angle. The dirt road is not exactly at the base of the hill. There is a sharp drop measuring about twenty feet from the edge of the road into a ravine that runs along with the road most of the way around the hill. The ravine is dry and dusty most of the year. But during the spring heavy rains can cause it to become a raging river because of the water runoff from the hill.

In relation to Coalville, this hill is due south of town. All of the other hills line themselves east and west of town. This seems to create a natural wind tunnel that blows in from the north and straight in on the hill. On a calm day in town, the pine trees on the hill can be seen swaying in the constant breeze. Stories told by the old men in town say that the moaning of the wind in the tall pines is the sound of the thirty-five lost miners crying for release.

Over the years, this hill became known in Coalville as Lonesome Hill. Lonesome Hill holds many mysteries. This story is of one of those mysteries. Yet, to this day, nobody ever goes up on Lonesome Hill, or so the old men in town say.

CHAPTER ONE

Short Cut

March 1918

The Lawrence farm lay south of Coalville just beyond Lonesome Hill. The farm was small and not very profitable, but that didn't matter because the farm was not the main source of income for the Lawrence family. Jerry and Norma Lawrence were teachers at Coalville High School. Jerry taught math and Norma, music. They were an odd couple as Jerry was tall, unassuming, and quietly spoken and Norma was short, straightforward, and energetic. Both were in their twenties, but seemed older. They didn't have children of their own yet, but it seemed they always had children at their house. Norma was a gifted pianist and taught piano in her home for a small fee. The fee, though small, was more than most people in the Coalville area could afford. Times were slow in Coalville and there was a great war raging in Europe. Most of Coalville's young men had gone off to fight the Kaiser. As a result, not many people took piano lessons from Norma Lawrence.

Lois Homes could afford the lessons. Lois was a tall handsome woman of thirty-two. She had auburn red hair and bright green eyes. Her mouth was small and dainty under a nose that was slightly turned up at the end accenting a beautiful face. Lois had a full firm figure that caused the men in Coalville to turn and look as she walked by. She was married to Lester Homes, the president and chairman of the board of the Coalville National Bank. As a result, Lois had the money to do just about anything she wanted.

The war in Europe had been a boon to the Coalville National Bank. Now Lois and Lester were wealthier than ever and still increasing. Being able to afford the piano lessons from Norma Lawrence wasn't a concern. The lessons, however, weren't for Lois but for her six-year-old daughter Bobbie. Bobbie was a gifted child when it came to music. It was for this reason that Lois sought out Norma for special lessons for Bobbie. Every Tuesday and Thursday at six o'clock, Lois would gather up Bobbie and drive the ten miles to the Lawrence farm for Bobbie's special lessons.

Instead of going out on the main highway, Lois would take the short cut around Lonesome Hill saving her a good fifteen minutes. The trips were well worth the drive and the money well spent, because Bobbie, for a child so young, was doing extremely well. Only last week, Lois and Lester had attended a special recital by Bobbie at which she played some very difficult musical pieces. Lester was proud of his daughter beyond words. Even now, at her young age, Lester was planning for the finest musical school he could afford.

On this day, Thursday, Lois sat in the living room of the Lawrence home talking to Jerry while waiting for Bobbie to finish her lessons.

"I hope they finish the lesson soon, that sky is looking mean," Lois said.

Jerry got up and walked to the window. "It sure is," he said. "I'll check and see how much longer they'll be."

With that, he walked out of the living room. Lois went to the window and looked up at the sky. There was a real Texas thunderstorm on the way. She needed to start home now! These storms came up fast and could be dangerous. A tornado could even be in the making. As she was thinking these things, Jerry came back into the room.

"They're finished, just a few more minutes to get her homework set."

"That's fine; may I just pay you now so we can leave immediately?" She asked.

"Sure, that's no problem. That'll be ten dollars and I'll give you a receipt," Jerry replied. He was writing the receipt as Bobbie and Norma came into the room.

"She did really well today," Norma said.

"That's great," exclaimed Lois as she grabbed Bobbie and gave her a big hug.

Bobbie hugged her mother back and laughed, "I'm going to be famous Mrs. Lawrence says."

"I'll bet you are too," Lois laughed. "But we need to head home; it's already starting to rain."

By the time they got in the car it was raining hard. As she turned out of the Lawrence's driveway and onto the small Farm-to-Market road, the wind started to blow with strong gusts. Lois drove down the road wondering why she had left the Lawrence house in the first place. It would have been smarter to wait this one out. However, it was too late now; she was committed. Lois Homes was soon to make her second bad decision.

As she reached the main highway cutoff, she had to decide whether to take the main highway or use her short cut around Lonesome Hill. She decided on the short cut thinking she could beat the main part of the storm by saving time. However, after only a few minutes onto the dirt road around Lonesome Hill, the wind and rain became fierce. Her windshield wipers could not keep up with the downpour. Though, she couldn't see her watch, she knew it must be nearly eight o'clock as the lessons only lasted about an hour. She slowed the car to help her vision but all she could see in her headlights were sheets of rain. Suddenly a bright flash of lightning danced across the sky, lighting up the entire road. The sight she saw pushed her to near panic. She had only come about half way around the hill. Water was running down the hill and across the small dirt road at an alarming rate. After braking the car to a slow stop, she clasped her hands together and sat back to think.

"Mommy, is it bad?" came a small voice beside her.

God, she had forgotten about Bobbie. She mustn't show her panic to Bobbie.

"Oh, it's bad but it'll stop in a minute and then we'll head on home," she said as calmly as she could. "Why don't you climb in the back seat there and just lay down until we get home, okay sweetheart?"

"Okay, Mommy," Bobbie replied as she climbed into the back seat. Her voice had sounded a bit calmer.

Lois had decided to just stay parked in the road until the rain stopped and then try to continue. She left the car running and the headlights on just in case someone else should come up the road. She doubted that would happen but she did it anyway. The rain had not slowed even a little and it had even started to hail. The hail stones pounding the car made a loud and frightening sound. She turned around to give Bobbie assurance again, but the child was curled up in the back seat fast asleep.

The next flash of lightning struck fear into her heart. Sheets of blowing rain and pounding hail continued to assault the car, and now the water running down the hill had become a small river. Water ran down the hill, across the road and then made a small waterfall as it poured off the other side of the road and down into the ravine. Lois now became completely stricken with fear. Tears formed in her eyes and rolled down her cheeks onto clenched hands she held at her lips. She had started to pray when suddenly she felt the front of the car move. Her eyes widened and her hands grabbed the steering wheel. She couldn't see because of the dark and rain, but she felt the car move again.

The next flash of lightning showed her a terrible sight. The raging water was actually moving the car across the road to the far edge. If the car fell off the road and down into the ravine, she and Bobbie could very well be killed. Still, she waited for the rain to stop. It had been pouring down for nearly an hour it seemed. She had lost track of time, but it should stop raining soon she thought. The debate raged in her mind about whether to try to drive on or continue waiting. She decided she must try to drive or soon they would be swept off the road. Slowly she put the car in gear and eased off the clutch, and, to her alarm, the car did not move. She stopped for a minute and then tried again. This time the back of the car began to slide toward the far edge of the road as the wheels spun uselessly in the water and mud. Quickly, she removed her foot from the accelerator. Now there was no choice but to wait. The car was setting almost cross ways in the road and the back wheels were dangerously close to the far edge of the road. The front of the car now faced the raging torrent of water running down the hill. Water began to flood in on the engine and it sputtered and died. Now, only her headlights still worked and they looked directly at the torrent of water. She could feel the car slowly moving backwards toward the edge.

In panic, she climbed into the back seat and picked up Bobbie in her arms. It was imperative to get out of the car. She had to take her chances in the storm, because the car was sure to slip over the edge of the road at any time. With Bobbie in her arms, she turned the latch and opened the back door. She pushed it open, but the wind and rain slammed it shut again. Again she tried, but she couldn't hold Bobbie and keep the door open at the same time. Tears streaming down her face and anger overcoming her fear, she tried again. This time the door opened all the way and she held it open with her foot. Blowing rain hit her in the face. Bobbie was awake now and crying. Slowly she inched herself out of the door with her legs and one free hand. She almost made it. Just as she got one foot on the muddy ground, the car slipped over the edge. Lois clutched Bobbie tightly in her arms until it didn't matter anymore.

CHAPTER TWO

The Beginning

June 1919

The day on Lonesome Hill was coming to an end, and the evening sunset had turned the sky into a blazing display of gold, orange, and red. A man moved cautiously down the steep slope of the hill. He followed an almost invisible trail that was covered in thick bushes and undergrowth. His experienced steps took him around the dangerous old mine pits. He stooped over in an effort to avoid low hanging mesquite tree branches. On his lanky six-foot frame, he wore a tattered old suit with a well-stained dress shirt. The suit jacket had no buttons and the pockets were torn. The belt in the suit pants was pulled tight to hold the pants on his thin frame. On his head, he wore a beat-up old dress hat. His shoes were loose on his feet and he wore no socks. In his back pocket, he carried a bottle of whiskey. Underneath his hat, his full head of dark brown hair was showing gray streaks. His eyes were light brown and set in a drawn and unshaven face. He was only in his mid-thirties, but he appeared much older.

Slowly he made his way down the hill. Finally, he emerged from the trees and bushes onto the ring road around Lonesome Hill. He stood there for a minute and stretched his muscles. Reaching into his back pocket, he pulled out his bottle and took a long deep drink. He glanced at the bottle and shook it. The liquid in the bottle splashed around revealing the bottle to be less than half full. After taking another long drink, he again placed the bottle into his back pocket. Carefully, he looked up and down the road as though he was expecting someone. Then, he walked across the road to the far edge and looked down into the ravine. The ravine was dry and dusty as it was summer and there had been little rain the last few months. He kicked a rock at the edge of the road and watched it tumble down into the ravine. Once again he looked up and down the road, and then he turned toward the east and started walking along the road.

He had only walked a short distance when he heard a sound. Quickly, he darted into the bushes where the hill met the road. He sat quietly for several minutes. Again the sound came. Afraid to move, he continued to sit quietly waiting for someone to appear. But no one appeared. Slowly, he moved out of the bushes and back onto the road taking care to look all around. Again the sound came. This time he followed the noise. As he walked around a bend in the road, he saw a small basket on the edge of the road nearest the ravine. The sound was coming from the basket. Slowly and carefully he approached the basket continually looking around him as he walked. Upon reaching the basket, he knelt down and looked inside. There, to his complete astonishment, was a baby. He moved the blankets that covered the baby so he could get a better look. Nervously, he constantly looked around for someone. The baby was smiling and kicking. It made little laughter-like sounds. It seemed to smile up at him. He smiled back and put his finger to the baby's chin.

"What've we got here?" He said in a soft smooth voice. The baby laughed at his touch, and he responded with a low laugh of his own.

"Where did you come from? Why are you here all by yourself on this road?" Of course the baby didn't answer.

"I wish you could talk 'cause this doesn't make any sense." Again, he looked all around trying to find someone. No one would leave a baby all alone on this road! But he could see or hear no one. He returned his attention to the baby. The only reason that came to his mind was that someone must have abandoned the child.

"But why would someone want to get rid of somethin' as cute as you? And why would they want to get rid of you this way?" He whispered down to the baby. The baby looked up at him and gurgled as if it were trying to talk.

"Unless someone knows about me, and I'm supposed to find you." He reached up and rubbed his unshaven chin while continuing to study the baby.

"But the only people that know about me wouldn't do anythin' like this." The baby continued to smile up at him. It seemed to enjoy his voice. He stood up and walked around the basket. His glance continually went between the basket and all directions around him. Still, he couldn't see anyone and the only sound he heard was that being made by the baby. He seemed to be fighting a battle inside himself as to what to do. Whoever left the baby here must have expected someone to pick it up and he was sure he wasn't the one they expected. And are they still watching from somewhere? Finally, he knelt down and looked at the baby again. The baby smiled back at him.

"You know, I've been alone for a while now. No one wants me either," he said. "Why don't you come and live with me? I ain't got much and the place where I live ain't so great, but I think we could make a good team. We could be two people nobody wants, but we could want each other."

The baby only smiled and laughed up at him. He stood up and again looked up and down the road. No one was in sight. This was a very strange thing. He couldn't reason out why anyone would do this. He wondered if someone intended for him to find this baby. But nobody knew he was here, except for one person, and she didn't have a baby. Maybe the baby was intended to be found by someone else. But why put it here on this lonely road that is rarely used? Finally, he gave up trying to understand what this was all about. Quickly, he glanced around one more time. Then, he grabbed the basket and darted into the bushes and started making his way back up the hill.

He moved swiftly and surely as only someone who was experienced in traveling on the hill could. Even the extra burden of carrying the basket didn't slow him. After a short while, he stopped and knelt down. He checked to see if anyone had followed him, but he saw no one. Once or twice during his run up the hill, he thought he had heard voices. But now, as he listened closely, the only sounds he heard were the sounds of the hill. He looked into the basket to check the baby. The baby was lying quietly with its eyes wide open. Once happy that no one was following him and that the baby was okay, he continued his journey.

Shortly, he came to a huge open pit. The pit had once been the opening to a coal mine. It was nearly fifty feet deep with sharp protruding ledges. Now, it was over grown with bushes and branches from low standing mesquite trees. Tall pine trees surrounded the pit blocking out any sunlight making it almost invisible. An inexperienced person could have easily blundered into the pit. He stopped at the edge and slowly started making his way around the upper perimeter. Soon, he had traversed about half of the perimeter and had reached the opposite side. There, hidden in the pine trees, stood a small cabin. The logs with which the cabin was built blended in with the surrounding environment. Anyone who didn't know the cabin was there could miss seeing it entirely.

He entered the cabin and set the basket on a small table that stood in the middle of the main room. There were two other small rooms attached to the cabin. One served as a bedroom and the other as a junk room. The kitchen was part of the main room and was near the fireplace which dominated the east wall. The main room contained the table, three wooden chairs around the table, a large rocking chair near the fireplace, a large chest-of-drawers, one small end table, several cabinets in the kitchen area, a wood-burning stove in the kitchen area, and two bookshelves attached to the south wall. There was no indoor plumbing and, as a result, the toilet was in a small outhouse about twenty yards directly behind the main cabin. The cabin had two entrances: the front door off the main room and a back door off the junk room. There was no electricity. Light was provided by kerosene lanterns. The main room had two lanterns and there was one each for the other rooms. Since there was no running water, drinking water was brought in and stored in a large barrel that stood over the sink in the kitchen area. The water was obtained from a small spring that bubbled up at the bottom of the pit. Buckets of water had to be carried up the steep pit wall to the cabin. This was a major chore so this job was done once a week all at one time. This required several trips to the bottom of the pit and back to the cabin. It usually took five or six trips to fill the barrel in the kitchen.

He picked up the kerosene lantern on the table and walked to the fireplace. There, he lit the lantern with matches he kept on the mantel above the fireplace. He turned the lantern up high to light the entire main room, and then went back and set the lantern on the table. "Well, let's see exactly what we got here," he said, as he picked the baby up out of the basket. As he lifted the baby up, a piece of paper fell to the cabin floor. Holding the baby in one arm, he reached down and retrieved the paper with his free hand. He held the paper close to the lantern and read the note aloud to himself.

"Please take care of my baby. I can't keep her. She is four months old. On the back of this note is the formula she requires for feeding and how to make it. In the basket are three bottles already made up and several diapers. Please love her."

He looked down at the baby in his arms. "So, you're a girl huh! Your mom must be in a lot of trouble to have to get rid of you. You're an awful good girl. You haven't cried a bit or made any kind of fuss."

Still holding the baby in one arm, he searched through the basket with his other hand. He found the bottles and the diapers. He picked up the note again and looked on the backside. There, written neatly, was the formula for making the baby's bottles.

"I suppose I can get this stuff, but I'll surely need some advice on how to care for you. I need to know when I can stop givin' you milk formula and start feedin' you real food and other things like that. But, I'll work it all out. Don't you worry? And it'll just be me and you up here all by our lonesome. We won't need anybody else. I'll teach you book learnin' and everythin' you need to know. Now, what can I call you? You've got to have a name. I just can't call you baby!"

He studied the baby for several minutes but could not think of a name immediately. "Well, I guess your name can wait for a while 'cause it's goin' to take some thought. It has to be just the right name. I'll come up with a good name for you. Then you'll have a good name and a good home."

As he said these things, the baby started to cry. It was a quiet whimper at first, then a loud scream. Out of normal reaction, he picked up a bottle and put into the baby's mouth. Immediately the baby stopped crying and started nursing the bottle. Then silence fell over the cabin on the hill. They sat there in the soft light of the lantern looking at each other as the baby nursed quietly on the bottle in the arms of a strange man. Slowly, the baby's eyes closed as it drifted off to sleep.

As darkness settled over the hill, a strange pair rested in the lantern light. He would still be sitting there when dawn arrived the next day.

CHAPTER THREE

The Twins

June 1920

The year was 1920. Summer was just beginning and it was already getting hot. It was during this time of year, June, in which Mrs. James T. Collie gave birth to fraternal twins. The girl she decided to name Cheryl. Cheryl had always been a favorite name to Mary Collie. Why, she didn't know, but it had. So the girl's name was Cheryl Jean Collie, born one minute and ten seconds after the boy.

The boy was named Daryl. Mostly because it sounded like Cheryl, and Mary believed twins should have names that sounded alike. So the boy was named Daryl Gene Collie simply because it rhymed with Cheryl Jean Collie and for no other reason.

James Collie accepted the names with little debate. He didn't particularly like the name Daryl but he gave into Mary's wish, as he did most of the time. First of all, James didn't expect twins. When the nurse came up to him with a huge smile on her face and announced, "Mr. Collie, you have a beautiful set of twins. A boy and a girl," he almost passed out. He could hardly believe it. The doctor hadn't said anything about twins. Wasn't the doctor supposed to know these things? None-the-less, he had two instead of one and now he would have to figure his expenses over again. Somehow it didn't seem right that he should be worrying about expenses at a time like this, but he couldn't help himself. After all, he wasn't the richest man in Coalville and having two at once like this could cause problems. His small fertilizer business kept him and Mary going fine, but now it would have to keep four of them going. He thought about it silently for a long time. Times were hard in Coalville and it worried him, but he knew he could make it. He always seemed to make it when in a tight spot. His main concern now was for Mary. She was so small to be having twins. But Doc Jewel had said she was fine and for him not to worry.

James was a determined but quiet man standing just over six feet tall. He had dark black hair and deep brown eyes. At twenty-five years of age, his face still held a youthful look. It was unusual in Coalville for a man so young to have his own business. But James had laid the basis for his business before he went to war in 1917. He had been one of the first men to leave the coal mines and try another line of work.

James was an only child, which was rare in this time of large families. As a result, his father had left him the house in town in which he now lived. His mother and father were both dead. His father died at an early age due to a combination of hard work and bad health that came from heavy cigarette smoking. Upon his father's death, James tried to quit school and help with the house and farm but his mother would have none of that. They sold the farm and moved permanently into the house in town. With the money from the sale of the farm and a small life insurance policy his father left, James finished high school. His mother wanted him to go to college, but there was just no way so he went to work in the coal mines. Shortly after that, his mother died. He worked in the mines for a while but decided not to have the short life his father had. So, with what money he had, he bought a store on the town square and started his fertilizer business. He had just gotten started when the war broke out. However, without hesitation, he enlisted in the army. Being twenty-two years old at the time, he was the old man in his unit.

He met Mary Jo Gutsman from Athens, Texas at a dance in Dallas just before he shipped out to France. She was very different from him. She was relatively short being just over five feet tall. Her hair was a light sandy blond, and her eyes were water blue. She had a beautiful fair face with a narrow chin and dainty straight nose. Her slim full figure even made her look smaller than she was. Even though she was the same age as he, she had just graduated from Baylor University in Waco, Texas with a degree in English Literature. Her family was German and had come to Texas with the first Anglo-American settlers that came with Stephen F. Austin. She was the third of four children with the youngest being her brother and two older sisters. Her ancestors had died at the Alamo and fought at San Jacinto. Her grandfather had ridden with the First Texas Union Calvary in the Civil War and was buried in the Texas Union cemetery near Huntsville. How a girl with such rich heritage and education could have fallen in love with him, James could never understand. But she did and it was almost love at first sight. They were married three days before he left for France.

Somehow, he survived the war. Many of the men in his unit didn't. He came home to a hero's welcome, but he didn't feel like a hero. He just felt lucky to be alive. It was always a mystery to him why men standing next to him died but he never got a scratch. His store was still there waiting for him as was Mary. He had been gone just under two years, but Coalville had changed.

Coalville was a dying town and James knew it. The coal that kept the town going for so long had run out. Now the town was just a meeting place for farmers that lived nearby. James had seen the coal going and had gone into the fertilizer business. This proved to be a wise move, for after the coal mines closed, people turned back to their real livelihood, the farm. When they did, James was there with his fertilizer, seed, and other farm needs.

James Collie was still in the fertilizer business and probably would be until the day he died. However, his children would not. He would see to it that they had every chance to be whatever they wanted to be. Every chance he could give them. And so, Daryl and Cheryl Collie entered the world on the twenty-fourth day of June. The year of our Lord was 1920, a little after three o'clock in the morning.

CHAPTER FOUR

Dee and Cherrie

October 1926

Mary Collie was rushing around getting lunch ready for her husband. As she hurried around, Cheryl sat at the table and watched silently. Cheryl had the same features as her mother. The sandy blond hair and eyes of water blue. At her young age of six years, her hair was much blonder than her mothers. She had the same fair skin, however, now it had a deep tan. Her body was small, but not too small. She was a tomboy in every sense of the word. She could run, climb, and fight as good, if not better, than most boys.

"Cherrie, go out and find your brother, lunch will be ready in a minute," Mary said without stopping her work. Cheryl remained seated.

"Cherrie!"

Cheryl jumped off her chair and ran out the kitchen door letting the door slam with a bang.

"Oh, Cherrie!" she heard her mother yell behind her.

Cheryl thought by slamming the door she had gotten revenge for being sent out to look for Daryl. In the mind of a six-year-old, this revenge was enough. Anyway, how did she know where Dee was? He might be anywhere. She stopped to think for a second. He was probably in that dumb old tree house of his down by the Jordan land. She went skipping down the path until she came to the fence that separated Jordan land from Collie land. There, just on the Collie side was a tall oak tree. She shaded her eyes against the noonday sun, and looked up to see the tree house about halfway up the tree.

"Dee," she yelled. No answer came. "Dee Collie, I know you're up there." Still, no answer came. "Dee Collie, you better answer me. Mom says to come to lunch."

A small blond head appeared at the door of the tree house. Daryl had the same features as his twin sister, except his eyes were a darker blue and his tan was much deeper. His body was not as small and he looked every inch the outdoor type. His eyes sparkled with mischief.

"Okay, I'm comin' you don't have to yell."

"I knew you'd come if I told you it was lunchtime," Cheryl said with a big, I-knew-you-were-there-all-the-time smile on her face.

"Shut up and don't be so smart," was his reply as he swung to the ground.

"Come on let's get to the house before Dad gets home," with that Cheryl darted up the path. Daryl was right behind her stepping on her heels.

They entered the house in a rush, but a little late. James and Mary were already seated at the table waiting calmly. After washing up, they took their places at the table. James said grace and then looked up at Daryl and then to Cheryl. He didn't speak, but he didn't have to. They knew he was angry. When James was angry, it was plain to see in his eyes.

Lunch went on without much conversation. James told Mary about Lester Homes being elected president of the Chamber of Commerce. He said it was because he was rich and not for any other reason. Cheryl knew Lester Homes was rich, because he lived in the big house at the end of Main Street. She had been by his house many times on her way to school. It was surrounded by a big iron fence and it sat far back off the road. In fact, it sat so far back that Cheryl had never seen it up close. She thought that someday she might go up to Lester Homes' house and look around. But Lester was a strange man and if he caught her around his house he would probably tell her dad. Then she would be in real trouble.

As she sat there thinking about all this, she watched Dee eat. She thought he must eat more than anybody in the world. When he wasn't eating a regular meal, he was sneaking in the kitchen and stealing food. Someday he might explode, she thought seriously. Cheryl was brought out of her deep thought by Rachael's clearing off the table.

Rachael was the family's Negro maid. She was short and heavy set with large legs and arms. Rachael was in her middle thirties, but already had gray in her dark black hair. Her skin was light brown with darker freckles across her face. She had been around ever since Cheryl could remember. She was just like a second mother to Cheryl and Daryl. Rachael didn't live in Negro Town like the rest of the black people, but lived out behind the Collie house in a small house of her own. James let her live there mainly because Mary insisted. He didn't like Rachael living there because he thought it could cause trouble. Many white people in town didn't like a black living among them. But Mary wouldn't have it any other way, so Rachael had been living out back for as long as Cheryl could remember.

"Well, dopey, you goin' to sit there all day?" A loud voice from behind her said. She turned around to see Daryl standing there grinning from ear to ear.

"We better get outside and hide before Rachael or mom finds somethin' for us to do," he said. Cheryl agreed with this and they both bolted out the door and down the path. When they came to the oak tree, Daryl immediately started climbing up to his tree house.

"Dee, how come you spend all your time in that dumb old tree house?"

"I got secrets up here," he replied.

"What kinda secrets you got?"

"Just secrets."

"Dee, can I come up too?" She was almost afraid to ask.

"You're a girl, crazy. Girls don't climb trees."

"I can climb as good as you," she shot back.

"Sure you can Cherrie, but if you were to fall and get hurt, Dad would beat the putty outa me."

"I'm not gonna fall. Dee, I'm comin' up." She hadn't finished talking before she was climbing the tree.

"Cherrie, you better not! Girls don't climb trees!"

She kept climbing with determination.

"Cherrie!" But before he could say anymore, she was sitting on the limb beside him.

"I wanna see your secrets," she said calmly.

"I'm not gonna show 'em to you, so just get down outa my tree," he ordered.

"I'm not goin' 'til I see your secrets," she yelled back.

"Get the hell out of my tree," he screamed.

Cherrie's eyes widened and her mouth dropped open. Dee had said a bad word right in front of her.

"Daryl Gene Collie, I'm goin' to tell Mom." She started climbing down as she spoke. "Boy Dee, you're really gonna be in trouble now," she yelled back.

He didn't say anything. After she had gone, he climbed inside his tree house.

She ran up the path to the house and burst in the back door. Then she ran to her room and shut the door. She fell on the bed and started to cry. Big tears rolled down her cheeks and into her mouth. She couldn't tell on Dee because if Dad knew he had said a bad word he'd whip the tar out of him. But she was so angry because Dee wouldn't let her in his tree house or let her see his secrets. She wondered what his secrets were. The more she wondered the more she cried. Why did she have to be a girl? It seemed boys had all the fun. She made her mind up then and there that she would sneak back to Dee's tree house when he wasn't around. Then she'd find out what his secrets were.

That night when they were in bed and the house was quiet, Cherrie heard Dee call her from his bed. "What do you want?" She asked, trying to sound tired.

"How come you didn't tell on me?" He asked softly.

"I don't know, just because I guess."

"'Cause why?"

"Just 'cause," she said sounding irritated.

"Just 'cause why?" He persisted.

"'Cause Dad would've whipped you good, that's why."

Things were quiet for a while.

"Cherrie?"

"What?" She was getting irritated now.

"I'm sorry for what I said to you today," he said softly.

She didn't say anything.

"Did you hear me?" He asked.

"Yes, go to sleep, Dee."

"Night," he said.

"Night," she answered.

Cherrie rolled over and pulled the covers up to her chin. She felt good now. She went to sleep with a smile on her face.

CHAPTER FIVE

Dee's Secrets

March 1930

By the time they were in the fifth grade, Dee and Cherrie had begun to trust each other a lot more than before. They weren't like most brothers and sisters, because instead of fighting all time, they got along nicely together. Even though they shared almost everything now, Cherrie still hadn't been inside Dee's tree house, nor had she discovered his secrets. Sometimes it bothered her and she wondered about it, but she had other things to occupy her mind. The thing occupying her mind now was Dick Jordan.

Dick Jordan lived next door to the Collies with his mother. He was tall and skinny with full head of sandy brown hair. His eyes were dark brown and set under thin high eyebrows. He was somewhat of a loner at school. Because of his good grades, he was thought to be the smart kid by many of his classmates. His father had been killed in the Great War and was thought of as a dead hero in Coalville. Dick was two years older than Cherrie and two grades ahead of her in school. But he didn't seem any older to Cherrie, because he was always nice to her. Sometimes they would sit for hours at night and talk. He would tell her things she could only dream about. After all, he was in the seventh grade and was quite a bit smarter than she. Cherrie looked upon Dick as her boyfriend. It seemed in school that every girl must have a boyfriend, so Cherrie chose Dick.

The girls at school would laugh and say, "He's twelve years old. He's not your boyfriend." But when he walked home with her one evening after school, they stopped laughing.

A few times Dick even asked Cherrie over to his house for supper and she had gone. Cherrie was proud of this because the Jordan family lived mostly to themselves and outsiders were frowned upon. Cherrie was the only person invited into the Jordan house since Mr. Jordan had been killed. Cherrie treasured every moment with Dick. She announced to the world that someday she would marry Dick Jordan.

Dee, on the other hand, didn't like Dick Jordan at all. He didn't like him first because of the way Cherrie followed him around, and he didn't like him second because Dick was two years older than him. Dee didn't like him third simply because he was Dick Jordan. From his tree house, Dee would watch Cherrie and Dick sometimes. They would talk for hours and sometimes Dick would hold her hand. Dee knew some things about the Jordan's he hadn't told anybody. Dee had some secrets. Things he had seen from his tree house. In his tree house, Dee had a telescope his dad had given him to study the stars. Dee studied the stars and other things also. Yes, Dee had some secrets. Secrets he hadn't told anybody.

That night Dick Jordan stopped by the Collie house and asked Cherrie to come over to his house after supper. Cherrie said she would. After supper, Dee caught Cherrie before she left.

"Cherrie, do you think you ought to go over to the Jordan house tonight?" He asked.

"Sure, why not?"

"Well, Dick is two whole years older than you, and anyway you're only ten years old. Anyway, I don't think you should go over to his house so much." He stood back and waited for her reply.

"Dee Collie, I don't care if Dick is a hundred years old, I still like him. And what's the matter with the Jordan's anyway?"

"They're just funny that's all," he said.

"What're you talkin' about? How're they funny?"

"They just are!" He exclaimed.

"Oh, you're crazy, Dee!" With that she ran out the door. Dee watched her go down the path and out of sight. Dee then went out the back door and down the path.

When Cherrie got to Dick's house, he was sitting on the back porch. As she walked up, he asked, "That you Cherrie?"

"Yeah," she answered.

"I'm glad you could come over, 'cause I'm goin' off for a while and I wanted to tell you 'bye," he said.

"Where're you goin', Dick?"

"Dallas," he answered.

"Dallas!"

"Yeah, we could be there for a whole month or more."

"Why're you goin' to stay so long?"

"I don't know for sure. It has somethin' to do with my Dad's insurance."

"I'll miss you Dick, but you'll probably have a good time in Dallas. Dad says Dallas has got more than two hundred thousand people. It's got a zoo and all kinds of other big city things to do." When she finished, she felt as though she had given him some new knowledge.

"Dallas ain't so big. You ever heard of New York?"

"Yes, of course I have. We studied about New York in school," she answered.

"Well, we might even go to New York and it's got millions of people," he proclaimed.

"Isn't New York a long way north?" She asked.

"Sure it is, but it's got millions of people and things you ain't ever seen before."

"Millions," she wondered.

"Millions," he said pointedly.

"I don't know Dick; millions is an awful lot of people."

"Yeah, I know, but it's true and we might go there."

"That's an awful long way off Dick. You might be gone a long, long time." Then after a short pause, "I'll sure miss you." She didn't have to pretend to be sincere because she was.

"I'll miss you too, Cherrie, but I'll be back after a while and I can go on being your boyfriend. I've got to go now, Cherrie. Mom wants me to help her pack things. But remember, I'll be back 'fore long." With that, he leaned over and kissed her on the cheek and then turned and ran into the house.

Cherrie sat there for a minute in a state of shock. It was the first time a boy had kissed her. She got up from the porch, turned around, and started up the path in a daze. She got to the house before she came out of her daze.

Mary saw her daughter come in the front door. "What's wrong Cherrie?" She asked.

"Nothin', Mom," she said. "Where's Dee?"

"I think he's out back somewhere. Why?"

"Nothin', I just wanted to talk to him. Well, good night, I'm goin' to bed."

"Night sweetheart," her mother said. Cherrie went to her room and went to bed.

Dee had seen the whole thing from his tree house. He didn't know what they were saying, but he saw Dick Jordan kiss his sister. He decided right then and there that he would have to tell Cherrie one of his secrets. Dick Jordan had kissed his sister, and Dee didn't like it. He didn't like it mainly because he simply didn't like Dick Jordan. Yes, he decided firmly, he would have to tell Cherrie one of his secrets.

That morning at breakfast, Cherrie told the family about the Jordan family's trip to Dallas and maybe even New York. However, the news was no surprise to her father. He said he had known about it for some time. This almost brought tears to Cherrie's eyes. She had so hoped to tell the family some news only she knew. Having her dream shattered, she listened to her father explain the trip.

According to James, Ruth Jordan was going to Dallas to see about the late Mr. Jordan's insurance. Mr. Jordan's body was never found and he was listed as missing in action. The insurance company, which did not like to pay war claims, in the first place, would not pay the death claim without a body. The government had been giving Mrs. Jordan money every month, but the private insurance company, with which Mr. Jordan had a policy, had never paid. Finally, after twelve years, the government had declared Mr. Jordan dead and the insurance company was going to have to pay the claim. So, Ruth Jordan was going to Dallas to sign some papers and collect the money. As for going to New York, James knew nothing of that.

"How much do you reckon she'll get, dad?" Dee asked.

"Lester Homes says she'll probably get somewhere around five thousand dollars. He should know, he's got his hands in things like that," James answered.

"They're gonna get five thousand dollars!" Cherrie exclaimed. "Does that mean Dick's goin' to be rich?"

"Well, I guess Ruth and Dick Jordan will be right well off," James said. "I've got to get to town and back to work. Can I drop you kids at school?"

"Dad," Dee said, teasingly. "Today is Saturday."

"So it is. I work so much I don't even know what day it is."

After James had gone and Rachael had cleared the table, Cherrie and Dee went outside. They sat on the porch for a while wondering what to do on this nice Saturday. Dee had reconsidered telling Cherrie his secret. If the Jordan family was going to be gone for a while, he didn't have to worry about Dick. But still, Cherrie thought a lot of Dick.

"Cherrie?"

"What?"

"How would you like to go up in my tree house?" He asked.

"Why?"

"I want to show you somethin'," he said.

"How come you want me in your tree house all of a sudden? You never wanted me there before." She said suspiciously. "I don't care about your dumb old tree house. I'm thinkin' about not goin'."

"Okay," Dee said as he started down the path.

"But I will," she yelled quickly and followed him down the path.

They walked down the path without talking. When they got to the tree Dee climbed up and then helped Cherrie up.

"I want you to know that you're the only person I've ever let come up here," he said seriously. "You've got to promise not to tell anyone about anything you see or hear unless I give the okay."

"Okay, I promise," she said.

"Cross your heart and hope to die, stick a needle in your eye?" He asked seriously.

"Cross my heart and hope to die, stick a needle in my eye," she repeated the serious oath.

"Okay, come on in."

Cherrie followed Dee into the small house. At first it didn't seem like so much, but then she began to notice things. She saw a telescope sticking out of a hole in the roof. There was a big box with a padlock sitting in the corner. In the middle of the house was a wooden box that served as a desk. On top of the padlocked box were a number of quilts and blankets. In the opposite corner, was a cardboard box filled with empty soda pop bottles. There was paper everywhere. A stack of old newspapers stood by the door and another stack on the desk. It was so crowded, Cherrie could hardly turn around. Then she saw the pictures on the wall. There were pictures of the moon, sun, stars and other heavenly bodies. But she stared at the three pictures over the padlocked box. They were pictures of naked women. Cherrie stared at them for a minute.

"Daryl Gene Collie, where did you get those nasty pictures? What if Mom or Dad saw those? You're dirty Daryl Gene Collie!" Dee knew Cherrie never used his full name unless she really wanted to get a point across.

"Cherrie, don't look at 'em," he said calmly.

"Where'd you get those things, Daryl Gene Collie?"

"At school," he said coolly.

"At school!" she yelled.

"Yep, at school," he repeated.

"Daryl Gene Collie, you . . ."

"Cheryl Jean Collie will you shut up a minute," he screamed at her before she could finish what she was about to say. "Now, follow me," he said, lowering his voice to a whisper. Cherrie started to say more about the pictures but decided against it.

"Okay," she said, "I'm comin'." Dee stood up on the desk and climbed through the hole in the roof. Cherrie followed him and soon they were both sitting on the roof of the tree house.

Dee pointed in the direction of the Jordan house and said, "What do you see there?"

"I see the Jordan house," she replied.

"Right, now, what do you see over yonder?" Dee had swung around and was pointing toward the hills.

"Do you mean Lonesome Hill?" She asked.

"Right."

"So what?" She asked. Dee didn't answer; he was adjusting his telescope toward Lonesome Hill. "What're you doin' Dee?" She pressed.

"Now don't touch anything, just look through the scope and tell me what you see," he instructed her. Putting her hands behind her back, she peered through the scope. "What do you see?" He asked.

"I see an old run down house," she answered.

"Right."

"So what?" Her voice was loud and strained because she was getting tired of this game. What was he doing? "Are you goin' to tell me what this is all about?"

"Well," he started slowly. "Why is it every Saturday night Ruth and Dick Jordan sneak out the back way and go to that shack on Lonesome Hill?" He stopped to let it sink in with a look of pride in his eyes.

Cherrie looked at him for a long while then said, "Why?"

"I don't know, why," he exclaimed.

Cherrie looked from the Jordan house to Lonesome Hill and then to Dee. "You mean Ruth and Dick go up there on Lonesome Hill every Saturday night?"

"Yep," he replied simply.

"I don't get it," she said.

"I don't get it either. I told you they're funny people. I don't like you messin' around them and lettin' him kiss you and everythin'."

Cherrie jumped as if she had been hit. "Daryl Gene Collie, you been spyin' on me," she yelled.

"I just happened to see you by mistake. I was really lookin' for Dick and Ruth."

"You make me so mad!" She said.

"Well, anyway they're funny. I'm not goin' up on Lonesome Hill to find out why they go up there, but you can bet there's somethin' funny goin' on."

"How long they been doin' it, Dee?" She had forgotten her anger and was completely interested in the strange happenings.

"Long time," he stated.

"How come you don't tell somebody?" She asked.

"'Cause, no reason. They're not doin' anything wrong I don't guess. They're just funny is all I can figure. Anyway, it's my secret and you promised not to tell."

Cherrie relaxed and sat down on the roof. Her brain was working hard trying to make something out of the story she had just heard. Dee sat across from her and looked at her but did not say anything. They both just sat there for a short time. "You got any more secrets up here?" She asked softly.

"None you can see, and don't go tellin' anybody about those pictures," he ordered.

"I should, but I'm not. Those are dirty, Daryl Gene Collie."

"Okay! Okay! Let's get down," he said. On the way back to the house, Cherrie couldn't help but wonder about Ruth and Dick Jordan. What was up on Lonesome Hill and why did they have to sneak up there? However, like Dee, she wasn't about to go up on Lonesome Hill to find out.

CHAPTER SIX

The Return

September 1931

Over a year passed before Ruth and Dick Jordan returned, but when they did return, they did it in style. The Jordan family made their return appearance to Coalville a big event. They drove down Main Street in a brand new car. The new Ford was driven by a stranger to Coalville. The stranger's name was Jim Upter, and he was said to be Ruth Jordan's driver and handyman. Jim Upter stayed at the Jordan house in an extra room. This raised quite a few eyebrows in Coalville. For an unmarried man and woman to stay in the same house was unheard of, especially with a young boy in the household. However, Ruth Jordan stated that Jim Upter was an employee of hers and nothing more. She simply ignored the rumors and gossip. Ruth, Dick, and Jim Upter would attend church services together each Sunday. After a while, most of the town came to forget the whole thing.

Jim Upter was a big man at near six feet six inches tall and weighed over two hundred and twenty pounds, and none of the weight appeared to be fat. He had dark brown hair and light brown eyes that were set close together in a long narrow face. His hair was cut short almost in a crew cut. He was very quiet and kept mostly to himself except when doing chores for the Jordan household. He didn't make any friends in town and didn't seem to want any. No one knew how much salary Ruth Jordan paid Jim, and it became a major topic of conversation at many a town gathering.

James Collie said that Ruth had collected more than ten thousand dollars on Mr. Jordan's insurance. Why they had stayed gone so long, he didn't know. To Cherrie, the return of Dick Jordan didn't have the meaning she thought it would. First, she found she had forgotten about him in a year. Second, he had seemed to change. He was not the same friendly boy he was when he left Coalville. Dick was different now and Cherrie could see it. It was not something she could identify or put her finger on or touch, but it was there and she could not change it. She was sorry in a way, but in another way it didn't seem to matter. They were still friendly and they still talked to each other, but the feeling was gone. At least, she felt it was gone. There were times when the old feeling would rise in her and she would feel a strange longing to be his girlfriend again. Somewhere deep inside of her, the feeling for Dick still burned. At times, she felt that he had the same feeling and that he was trying to hide it. It didn't matter because they just weren't the same anymore. One year had made more of a difference than Cherrie had ever thought it could.

Dee had also noticed how the Jordan family had changed. But they hadn't changed in one way. They still made their trips to Lonesome Hill. Only now, not just Ruth and Dick went to Lonesome Hill, but Jim Upter went with them. On Saturday nights, Dee would go to his tree house and wait for them to start their trip. They would go at different times, but mostly they started their trips between ten and eleven o'clock. Friday and Saturday nights were the two nights that Dee was allowed to stay up late. But his mother usually wanted him in the house by nine o'clock. It took some pleading and a little intervention from his dad to get his mother to agree to let him stay out in his tree house pass dark. But Mary Collie finally gave in and allowed him to stay out, but only if he stayed in his tree house and didn't go wandering off into the night.

So, each Saturday night, Dee would position himself in his tree house with his telescope and wait. Since Ruth and Dick had been back, Dee had only missed one Saturday night watching for them. That one Saturday night, he and Cherrie had gone to the picture show. Ruth and Dick, and now including Jim Upter, had not missed a single Saturday night.

The desire to know what was going on between the Jordan family and Lonesome Hill began to grow inside of Dee. Each Saturday, the desire got hotter and hotter. Added to this desire was the burden of keeping the entire thing secret. He began to feel the need to share his secret with someone else. His first thought was to bring Cherrie back to the tree house and share the whole thing with her. After all, she already knew about the trips. But she didn't know about the trips since Ruth and Dick returned. After the Jordan family had left town, he and Cherrie never talked about the secret again. Cherrie was true to her word, because she never breathed a word to anyone about what she had seen from Dee's tree house, or, for that matter, what she had seen inside the tree house. Anyway, Dee observed that she didn't seem very interested in Dick Jordan at the present time. Dee was pleased to see that Dick Jordan was no longer the love of her life. The main thing to Dee was that Cherrie was a girl and he needed another boy with whom to share this secret. Although Dee trusted and respected Cherrie, he needed someone that could take action with him. For that, to him, meant he needed a boy.

Dee was unsure as to what course of action to take. He wanted to tell Cherrie, but then again he didn't. She would probably want to get their parents involved and that was something Dee didn't want to do. He felt very protective of his secrets. However, he also knew that he couldn't continue to keep this secret to himself much longer. He had to take someone into his confidence. Just who that would be he didn't know.

But Dee had reached a couple of decisions. One, he now knew he was going to share his secret with someone else. Two, Dee had decided the time had come to find out about the Jordan family and Lonesome Hill. Next Saturday night he would make his first trip to Lonesome Hill.

CHAPTER SEVEN

Deep Void

November 1931

Lester Homes drove down Main Street toward the Coalville city limits. As he did every Thursday, Lester had left his office early to tend to personal business. Lester Homes was a tall man measuring just over six feet. He was only fifty years of age, but he looked much older. His hair was almost completely gray with only a few streaks of his natural black. He did, however, retain a full head of hair. His skin was dark and his body was in good trim. He wore a pair of small glasses that he needed only for driving. Lester would be a handsome man, according to most ladies, if it were not for his face. Not that his face was ugly or deformed, but his face never smiled. His eyes never showed love, happiness, hate, or anything for that matter. They only showed a deep void.

As Lester passed the city limits, he started looking for the next driveway. When he reached it, he turned the car into the opening. He passed through the entrance into the Coalville Cemetery. The Coalville Cemetery was located just outside of Coalville on a large spread of open land. It was a well-kept, beautiful place. Lester parked the car in the parking area and got out. He opened the back door of the car and took out a setting of yellow roses from the back seat. He closed the car door and started walking slowly up the path leading to the graves. A large chain link fence surrounded the grave area and a gate was located just at the end of the entrance path. As he reached the gate, he opened it and walked in.

Searching through the graveyard was not required; Lester knew exactly where to go. The same place he had gone every Thursday for the last eighteen years. He approached his destination and stopped. He looked down at the two tombstones that stood side by side. One was normal size and the other was very small. He took the yellow roses and divided them into two bunches and placed one bunch at the base of each tombstone. He then sat on the ground facing the two stones and removed his glasses. The stones read:

LOIS LONDON HOMES	BOBBIE JOE HOMES
LOVING WIFE OF LESTER	LOVING DAUGHTER OF
DEVOTED MOTHER OF BOBBIE	LOIS AND LESTER
BORN AUGUST 10, 1886	BORN JANUARY 22, 1912
DIED MARCH 15, 1918	DIED MARCH 15, 1918

Just as every Thursday, his eyes began to fill with tears as he began to speak. "Well Lois, things are not going very well for us. The bank isn't doing so well since the war. Some of our loans are bad. I've not done so well without you and Bobbie. I don't know how much longer I can keep the bank open. The folks just don't have any money to put in the bank. And even if they did, they don't trust banks anymore. I guess we won't be so bad off though. We got the house and it's paid for. Then there are the cars and they're paid for. We own a lot of land. Our stocks aren't worth much, but that's not so bad because we didn't have that many anyway."

He stopped and looked down at the ground for a while, then raised his head and started talking again. "How's Bobbie today? I hope she is still working hard on her piano. You make her keep at it now! She's going to be great and famous someday. I sure wish I could see her. You know, she was so little when you left. I just didn't get a chance to spend the time with her the way I could have if you hadn't left." He stopped talking again as the tears now poured from the deep void in his eyes, down his cheeks and dropped onto his business dress shirt. He fought to get control of his voice as the tears caused him to choke on his words. Clasping his hands together tightly, he turned his head from side to side. He seemed nervous and afraid.

After gaining control of himself, he continued. "You know Lois; I've been doing some other things that I'm not sure you would like. No, it's not another woman. You should know better than that. I've never even looked at anyone else. No, there are some other things that have to do with business. You never got into my business anyway so it's no big deal. It's just that these things aren't things I would normally do, you know! But with the bank on the down slide and all, I just started out on these things. I'm not going to tell you about them now, but I may need your advice later on. Will that be okay? Good! Good! I thought it would. These other things have kind of got me trapped. I don't know how to explain it except that I'm not sure of myself anymore. I got lots of pressure, Lois. I mean lots of pressure. You see if you were here and if Bobbie were here, I wouldn't be doing these things. I'm sure of that. Yes, I'm real sure of that!"

He had gained control of his emotions now, but he was still tense and nervous as if he were trying to explain something that he didn't understand himself. Getting to his feet, he started walking around the graves in a circle. As he walked, his mood seemed to change from sorrow to anger. He jammed his hands deep in his pockets and stomped around the graves. "You see, you left with Bobbie and left me here alone." He was yelling now. "But you know I love you and Bobbie. Yes, you know it. So, I wouldn't do anything to hurt you two. But you have to understand that these things I'm doing, well, they just have to be done. You shouldn't get mad at me and upset Bobbie. Now, you have to understand. Please understand." His voice dropped to a whisper and all of his anger was gone. "Please understand these things," he cried.

He sank to his knees between the tombstones and placed a hand on each stone. "We will be together again," he whispered. "I'm not sure how long it'll take. But I'm sure that I cannot, and will not; continue on without the two of you. When these things are finished, we will all be together again." He was talking in a normal tone and voice now. He looked straight up into the sky with his eyes wide and unblinking. "You see, you have to be dead to be happy. We all have to be dead. Maybe everyone should have to be dead."

Getting to his feet once again, he turned back toward the gate. He started walking away from the graves. Then, he stopped, turned and looked back. He stared at the graves with his empty eyes and a smile spread across his face. "I'll see you same time next week," he said, as he turned and walked out the gate.

CHAPTER EIGHT

Friendships

May 1932

Doctor Julius J. Jewel sat and watched, as Moonbeam studied the checker board. Dr. Jewel and Moonbeam sat across from each other over a small wooden table. Dr. Jewel was a small man just over five feet tall. A full head of gray hair matched a thin mustache below his nose. He was a little chubby around the waist line, but sixty-six years of age had earned that. He always dressed sloppily. Now, he wore a pair of old loose fitting dress pants being held up by a bright pair of yellow suspenders. The suspenders came across the top of a bright red T-shirt. On his feet he wore a pair of slippers without any socks.

Looks, however, can be deceiving in many cases. Dr. Jewel had been a doctor in Coalville for forty years, and a good one. Dr. Jewel had been in Coalville through its boom and now in its depression. At one time, there were several doctors in Coalville, but now only he and one other remained. Most of the town's children were brought into the world by Dr. Julius Jewel. He always understands that he is a small town doctor. He never tries to handle a case beyond his abilities. At the first sign of real trouble, Dr. Jewel sends his patients to more qualified doctors in Dallas.

"Okay, you old black fart, when are you goin' to move?" He asked in an irritated voice.

"I's goin' ta move when I has it figured out," came the slow reply.

"What's to figure? You don't have a move and you know it. Why don't you just give up?"

"I ain't sure yet," Moonbeam replied to the greater irritation of the doctor.

Moonbeam stood tall and skinny with skin as black as coal. His hair was a bright gray. Moonbeam's hair was his dominant feature. It wasn't just gray, it was bright silver. At night, with a moon in the sky, Moonbeam could be seen from a great distance because of the reflection of the moonlight on his hair. It makes for a strange sight. Moonbeam, himself, can't be seen because of his black skin. All that can be seen is this patch of glowing silver light moving down the street.

The story of how he came to be called "Moonbeam" is not generally known, but it is believed to have something to do with his hair. Thomas Jefferson Washington, better known as Moonbeam, had been arguing with and irritating Dr. Jewel for all his forty years in Coalville. Moonbeam had come to work for Dr. Jewel soon after the good doctor opened his practice in Coalville. Moonbeam was a young man at that time. In Coalville, in those days, a young black man didn't have a lot of good opportunities.

When Dr. Jewel hired Moonbeam to do odd jobs and cleanup work around his clinic, it was a job sent from heaven for him. Moonbeam had no education to speak of, so any type of job was a good job. Moonbeam had lived in Negro Town and worked for Dr. Jewel through the Coalville boom and through the death of Dr. Jewel's wife. That period covered about twenty years. When Dr. Jewel's wife died, it was a terrible blow to him. Only the town's need for him kept him going during that period. It was that need and his growing friendship with Moonbeam. It was shortly after the death of Maxine Jewel that Moonbeam moved into a small house next to the clinic. Dr. Jewel owned the house, which was really a part of his own house. It was much easier having Moonbeam close by to help him with the clinic. That was the reason most people believed, but mostly it was good to have him close for his company.

To a stranger, Dr. Jewel and Moonbeam would appear to hate each other. But nothing could be further from the truth. They consistently argued over everything. As they grew older, it got worse. It was one grumpy old man fighting with the other. But they would not know what to do if they were separated. Now, at their age, the fun of one picking at the other was a source of great pleasure.

"Jesus Christ, you're slower than Christmas! You know you're beat, why don't you just say so. If you don't hurry up and move, I'm goin' down to the newspaper office and tell them the story about how you got that stupid name, 'Moonbeam'. Ha! How would you like that you old black fart?"

"Ya can calls me anythin' ya want, but ya had better stop usin' the name of the Lord in vain," Moonbeam replied. "And I doesn't care who ya tell that story to."

"If we have to wait until you move, I suspect you'll die at this table. And if you do, I win."

"I has my mind on other things. I been given great thought ta goin' over and askin' Miss Rachael Lowell ta go ta preachin' with me on Sunday," Moonbeam said, without raising his head from the checker board.

"Why, you old black fart, what makes you think a nice woman like Rachael Lowell is goin' to go anywhere with you?"

"Me and Miss Rachael has feelin's for each other," the black man stated.

"You better be careful of what kind of feelin's? She's twenty years younger than you. I'm a doctor and I'm tellin' you that you're too old to have those kind of feelin's. Why! If you went to bed with her, you'd probably die in bed of a heart attack." Dr. Jewel threw back his head and laughed an exaggerated laugh.

"Why, you dirty old white trash," Moonbeam brawled. "The good Lord is goin' ta strike you down one day. I means it. He will."

"Yeah, well, not before you move. Just think what it's goin' to look like to Jesus, when he makes his second comin' and you're still studyin' this checker move." Dr. Jewel laughed aloud again.

At that moment, Moonbeam started to rise from the table. His knee hit the leg of the table and knocked the checker board and all of the checkers onto the floor. "Oh! My Lordy, look what I has gone and done," he exclaimed.

"You did that on purpose," Dr. Jewel yelled. "You cheated. You can't stand to lose can you? You old pile of black shit. That's what you are you know, is a pile of black shit with a lot of little silver flies on top."

"I's goin' ta walk down toward the Collie house and see is I can visit with Miss Rachael," Moonbeam said with a smile. "We can play another game of checkers later if ya want."

"Go on out there you crazy old man. I hope you get laid and it kills you!"

Moonbeam was on his way out the front door and Dr. Jewel was right behind yelling and screaming, when the Reverend John Tuney and his daughter Bob Ann appeared at the door. "What's all of this yellin' about?" Reverend Tuney asked with a look of wonder on his face.

"Aw, it's just this old black fart and his cheatin' ways," Dr. Jewel yelled.

"There's no need to yell, Jay, and there is certainly no need to use that type of language," the Reverend said softly.

Moonbeam had already walked out the door and was on his way up Main Street. He turned and waved to Dr. Jewel with a big smile on his face. Dr. Jewel closed the door and, when Moonbeam couldn't see him, smiled and laughed to himself.

Dr. Jewel then turned to his new visitors. "John, Bob Ann, y'all come on in. What brings you two here? I'll be at church Sunday, I've already given my offerings, and you can't be sick or you'd be at the clinic. Now, with all that said, what's up?"

"Does anything have to be up for me to come and visit, Jay Jay?" The Reverend smiled.

John Tuney's smile looked like a crack in his face. John was a few years younger than Dr. Jewel but he looked older. His hair was thin and white leaving most of the front of his head bald. He was shorter than his daughter and they made a strange pair when walking together. He had bright sharp blue eyes that always looked straight at you. When he preached a sermon, he always appeared to look at each and every person in the congregation. He was dressed in black and always wore a small black hat.

"No, I guess not. Come on in and sit," Dr. Jewel replied, as he directed them into the sitting area of his small house. After they were seated, Dr. Jewel asked, "Can I get y'all somethin' to drink? I'm goin' to have a beer myself."

"No thank you, nothing for me, Jay Jay."

"I'll have somethin' cold," said Bob Ann. "But I'll go get it, and your beer. You sit down. Dad wants to talk with you." With that Bob Ann pushed Dr. Jewel into a chair and turned to walk to the kitchen.

As she turned to walk toward the kitchen, Dr. Jewel had to admire her. Even at his age, he could feel the sexual stirring she caused. She was tall for a woman about five feet seven and had long black hair that hung down to the middle of her back. She had one of those sweet looking faces with all of the features perfect. The best thing about Bob Ann was her body. It was the classic hour glass figure with long well-shaped legs. She had breasts that stood out firm and bounced when she walked. Many men in Coalville said she had the best set of *jugs* in East Texas. At thirty-one, she was without a doubt, the best-looking woman in Coalville. She was also married and the preacher's daughter. What a woman to be a preacher's daughter, Dr. Jewel was thinking when he realized he had been staring.

He quickly turned his head back toward John Tuney and asked, "Did you want to talk with me, John?"

"Yes, I did, Jay Jay," he replied. "You remember our little secret don't you?"

"Yes, John, I remember," Dr. Jewel replied slowly. As Dr. Jewel spoke Bob Ann returned to the room carrying Dr. Jewel's beer and a coke for herself. She handed him his beer and then went back and sat by her father.

"Certain things have been happening that lead me to believe that our secret may not be a secret anymore." John Tuney spoke slowly and precisely. "I was just wondering. Well, I mean . . .'

He never finished his sentence before Bob Ann interrupted.

"What dad is tryin' to ask is have you told anyone or could anyone have got into your files?" Bob Ann asked pointedly.

Dr. Jewel looked at them both for a long minute. "No, John, I haven't told anyone. You should know better than to ask that. As for my files, no one has been in my files. And if they had, they wouldn't find anything they could understand." There was a long silence with all of them just sitting there looking at each other.

"Well, okay Jay Jay, I'm sorry if this seemed like something it wasn't. I guess we'll be going now." John Tuney got up and Bob Ann followed him. They started walking toward the front door.

"John," Dr. Jewel called after him. "What is this all about? Why are you askin' me this now?"

"What do you think of me, Jay Jay?" John asked, as he turned back to face the doctor.

"To be truthful, I don't think of you very much at all. If you mean what kind of man do I think you are? Well, I don't know. I'm not much for goin' to church, but I hear you're a fair to good preacher and you've done a lot of good for the people in this town. But we were friends once and I can't forget how that ended. But the truth is John, I still love you and I think you're a good man." With that Dr. Jewel stopped talking and looked down at his beer.

"Thanks Jay Jay. Now, you come to church, you hear." John Tuney said, pointing his finger at Dr. Jewel. Then, he and his daughter turned and walked out the door and closed it behind them.

After they had gone, Dr. Jewel walked back into his living area and sat in his easy chair. He was deep in thought as he took a long drink of his beer. He held the bottle up and looked at it. It was nice to have beer again. After years of prohibition and drinking homemade beer, he could now have a real beer. Smiling to himself, he finished off the beer. He wondered why people tried to enforce their own moral codes on others. Beer was something he enjoyed and he didn't understand why it should bother anyone else. It's not like he was a drunk or anything. People should be concerned with their own morals and not so interested in other people's.

Dr. Jewel got up and went to the kitchen. Opening the refrigerator, he took out another beer. He picked up the opener on top of the refrigerator and opened the bottle. He then took a fast long drink as if he were challenging someone to stop him. Satisfied with himself, he returned to his easy chair in the living area. Thoughts raced through his mind about the visit from John Tuney and his daughter. Now there was a couple that should examine their own morals.

For forty years John Tuney and Dr. Jewel had been best friends. Dr. Jewel had brought Bob Ann into the world. As hard as he tried, he had been unable to save Thelma Tuney. The internal damage had been too bad and he had been unable to stop the internal bleeding. The loss of Thelma had hurt John badly, but he went about being both father and mother to Bob Ann. The problem was, as Dr. Jewel saw it, he had not only been father and mother, but Bob Ann's preacher as well. It had been hard on Bob Ann, but she grew up loving and respecting her father. John had never remarried. He never even made the attempt to find a wife for himself or a mother for Bob Ann. He seemed satisfied to have a family of just Bob Ann and himself.

But things changed between John Tuney and Dr. Jewel. They were no longer close friends. They spoke to each other and there were no open hostilities, but the true friendship had died. Dr. Jewel guessed that it had been a question of morals in a certain way. Now, John had come back checking on him. Why? What had happened to cause the good reverend to worry about their deal? Dr. Jewel turned his bottle up and finished the beer. He put the empty bottle on the floor next to his chair. He leaned back in his easy chair and closed his eyes. Soon he was fast asleep.

CHAPTER NINE

Just Colored Folks

May 1932

Rachael Lowell was busy cleaning up the Collie kitchen when she heard someone call her name. Looking around the kitchen, she didn't see anyone. Then, she heard it again and it sounded as if it were coming from outside. She walked to the kitchen window and looked out. There, standing next to the window, was Thomas Jefferson Washington. "Hello, Miss Rachael," he smiled.

"Thomas, what are ya doin' outside of this here window?" She asked, trying to sound angry.

"Well, I come ta see ya Miss Rachael. But I surely wish ya wouldn't call me Thomas. Most folks just call me Moonbeam."

"Do ya mean ta tell me you'd have folks call you Moonbeam; instead of your given name?"

"Yes, I surely would. I don't like Moonbeam so much, but I don't like Thomas Jefferson at all," he replied.

"Okay, Moonbeam, what's it I could do ya for?"

"Well, Miss Rachael I come ta ask ya to go ta preachin' with me come Sunday. I knows you're a God fearin' woman and all. There's goin' ta be one of them revivals in a tent over by the main highway. They brung a preacher all the way from Birmingham, Alabama to preach at us. And just colored folks is allowed. I was goin' ta go myself and I just thought I'd ask if ya would kindly join me. I feel it's goin' ta be a great experience and lots of colored folks will be comin' ta Jesus."

"That's real nice of you Moonbeam, I believe I will be inclined to go with you," she replied in her kindest voice.

The smile on Moonbeam's face grew much larger. "That's good Miss Rachael. I'll come by here just 'fore nine o'clock Sunday morning to walk with ya ta the highway."

"No, don't come here. Come out back by my place. I'll be a waitin' for ya there," she said.

"Sure nuff," he answered. "I'll see ya then."

Rachael watched as Moonbeam walked off down the road. She watched him until he disappeared from view. "Why, does that old man like me," she wondered aloud to herself. "But I got to be nice ta him, it's the Christian thing ta do."

Rachael finished cleaning the kitchen and started looking for Mary Collie to tell her she was finished. She walked into the Collie living room where she found Mary trying to listen to the radio. "Mrs. Collie, I'm all done now. I's goin' out ta my place if ya got nothin' else for me."

"That's fine Rachael, I got nothin' else. I'll see you tomorrow morning. Good evenin'."

Rachael waved and went out the back door and onto the path in the back yard; the same path that Dee used to go to his tree house. She walked the short distance to her small house and went in. Rachael kept a spotlessly clean house. Everything was in place and in order. On the walls of the house were pictures of her late mother and her late husband. Her mother had died when she was small but she remembered a great loving relationship with her mother. Rachael was the only girl among six children. As a result, she got special treatment from her mother. Her five brothers had all left home when she was very young. Slowly, she lost contact with all of them. Rachael's husband had died a year after they were married. He had been killed in a farming accident when he got caught in a cotton bailer. She had never remarried; instead she turned her life to God. The fulfillment in her life came from her church activities.

She had been working for the Collie family ever since her husband died. Mary Collie had hired her shortly after the birth of the twins. Those two kids were Rachael's pride and joy. She treated them exactly as if they were her own. In a way, she believed them to be her own. The twins, in turn, loved Rachael. It was Rachael that gave the twins their nick names. Daryl she called Dee because his name started with the letter 'D'. Cheryl she called Cherrie because the child was always asking her for cherries on her ice cream. Rachael used the nick names all the time and finally the entire family started using them and then everyone else.

Rachael had moved into her house five years ago when Mary decided it would be easier and better for everyone if Rachael could live close by instead of all the way out in Negro town. At first Rachael didn't like the idea, but after moving in and getting set up, she liked it. It allowed her to be close to her family and work. The Collies were good to Rachael and she loved them more than anyone else in the world. She had no other family except the Collies.

Rachael moved around her house getting things ready for tomorrow morning. She always laid out her clothes and had everything prepared for the morning. After she was all finished with her organizing, she went and picked up her Bible. She sat down in her comfortable rocking chair and started to read. Rachael read at least ten chapters each night out of her Bible. Her Bible was her most prized possession. It had been given to her by her mother when she was very small. Every night, Rachael can be seen sitting, rocking, and reading her Bible.

She read until her eyes got too heavy to read anymore. Then, she closed her Bible and placed it back in its special place on her chest-of-drawers. The special place had a picture of her mother on the wall just above the Bible. She got undressed and climbed into bed with a smile on her face, because she was thinking of going to preaching with Moonbeam on Sunday.

CHAPTER TEN

Into the Night

Dee had thought about going up on Lonesome Hill plenty of times. However, he never found a cause great enough to lift his courage high enough to go. But now, he thought the time had come, but he needed help. Who could he get to help him? Not Cherrie; she was a girl. Not any of the kids at school, because they didn't like the idea of going up on Lonesome Hill. Besides that, he had to find someone he could trust with his secrets. He thought on the problem for a long time and came up with no one.

Then, he thought of Billy Bob Barnett. The Barnett family lived in the hills east of town. In fact, they lived less than two miles from Lonesome Hill. Billy Bob would probably know how to get up on Lonesome Hill, and he may have even been up on the hill. Anyway, Billy Bob was Dee's best bet and Dee knew it. Dee decided to ask Billy Bob about the adventure today at school. He would have to be careful about asking Billy Bob to help him. He might start talking and spoil the whole thing. But Dee had to trust someone and Billy Bob was his best hope for getting up on Lonesome Hill.

On their way to school that day, Dee didn't talk much to Cherrie. He was in deep thought making plans for tomorrow night. Tomorrow night was Saturday night and Ruth, Dick, and Jim Upter would make their trip to Lonesome Hill. Dee walked along in deep thought stumbling over everything in his path.

"What's the matter with you, Dee?" Cherrie asked.

"Huh?"

"What's the matter with you?" She repeated.

"There's nothin' the matter with me, what're you talkin' about?" He asked.

"I mean, how come you're walkin' along like you're asleep or somethin'?"

"I'm thinkin'," he answered.

"So, what're ya thinkin' about?"

"Oh, just school and things. I got a test in math today and I'm kind of worried," he replied.

"You're good in math, you'll make it okay," she said.

"Yeah, I guess I will."

They entered the school yard and there they split up. Dee had math his first class and Cherrie had spelling class. Dee waved a short goodbye and started up the steps that led to his math room. Cherrie walked on around the building to the rear where her spelling and homeroom classes were.

As Dee walked in the math room, he looked around for Billy Bob. The room was about half full when Billy Bob came in. Billy Bob was dressed as usual, in his faded blue jeans and plaid cotton shirt. His long blond hair was uncombed, also as usual. His high top tennis shoes were untied and the strings flopped as he walked along. He always dressed a little sloppy, but unlike some of the people that lived near the hills, he was always clean. The Barnett family didn't have much, but what they did have, Sally Barnett always kept clean and decent.

Billy Bob's freckled face broke into a broad grin when he saw Dee waving. He walked up to Dee with his hands in his pockets and his grin exposed two missing upper teeth. "Hi, Dee, ready for the test?"

"Yeah, I guess. Say, Billy Bob, I need to talk with you durin' recess," Dee said.

"Yeah, whata we gonna talk about?" Billy Bob asked.

"It's somethin' special I need you to help me with," Dee replied.

"Okay, but what's it about anyway?" But as he spoke the bell rang and they all took their seats.

Dee could hardly concentrate on his math for thinking about his plan. He didn't know for sure how he did on his math test and he didn't care at the present time. After Math came Art class, then Spelling, and then recess. Dee thought recess would never come, but finally the bell rang and he was free. They had hardly gotten outside before Dee pulled Billy Bob off behind the baseball backstop and started talking.

"Look, Billy Bob. I need your help," Dee said.

"How can I help?" Billy Bob asked with a look of wonderment on his face.

"Have you ever been up on Lonesome Hill before?"

"No, I sure haven't," Billy Bob replied firmly.

"Well, do you know a good way to get up there?" Dee asked almost quietly.

"What do you want to go up there for? You know what they say about that hill. It gives me the creeps anyway," Billy Bob answered sincerely.

Dee explained to Billy Bob about Dick and Ruth Jordan and their trips up on the hill. He told him how long he had been watching them and how they only went on Saturday nights.

"Come on, Dee, you sure about all that? I barely live two miles from Lonesome Hill and I ain't ever seen anybody up there," Billy Bob said.

"Yes, I'm sure, I saw them go there a hundred times, I tell you," Dee said irritated. "Now are you goin' with me or not?"

"I ain't sure Dee. I mean, I couldn't help you much 'cause I never been up there."

"You could help me some and besides I don't want to have to go by myself."

"Dee, they say that hill is haunted and it sure is spooky lookin'. Especially goin' up there at night is really scary."

"You don't believe in ghosts do you? And anyway if Ruth and Dick Jordan can go up there and come back, then why can't we?" Dee argued.

"Ruth and Dick Jordan ain't me, and I ain't so sure about ghosts either," Billy Bob answered firmly.

"Aw, please Billy Bob. You're not goin' chicken on me are you?"

"I ain't chicken, Dee," said Billy Bob showing some hurt.

"Well then, why won't you go with me?"

"I ain't said I wouldn't go have I?" Billy Bob asked in a hurt tone.

"Then you'll go?" Dee asked smartly.

"Yeah, I guess so," he said. "But if I get killed my old lady's gonna be plenty mad."

"Okay, look, come into town with your dad tomorrow and spend the night with me. Then we'll sneak out when it gets dark and go to my tree house. We'll wait until Ruth and Dick go and then we'll follow them. It'll be easy as fallin' off a log."

"Well, it sounds easy enough. I'll be over ta your house right after lunch tomorrow 'cause Dad always eats at home," Billy Bob said.

"Okay, let's go play a little catch," Dee said.

But before they could join the rest of the boys the bell rang and they went back inside. To Dee, it seemed like the afternoon would go on forever before school let out. After the last bell, Dee met Cherrie out in front of the building and they started home together. Again Dee was in deep thought about his plan, as he had been all day.

"How'd you do on your test?" Cherrie asked.

"What?"

"I asked you how you did on your test. Can't you hear anything today?" She yelled.

"Yes, I can hear. Stop yellin' so loud."

"Well, don't act so dumb," she said.

"Oh, shut up and hurry up. We got to get home," Dee said as he picked up the pace.

"What's the hurry? We got plenty of time before supper."

"Aw, Cherrie, you're so slow all the time," Dee said. With that they both became silent and walked along without a word. They passed Lester Homes' house and reached their own yard a little later. They went in the house and let the door slam as usual.

"Who's there?" Mary Collie yelled from the kitchen.

"It's just me and Dee," Cherrie yelled back and started toward the kitchen.

"You got in a little early today didn't you?" their mother asked.

"Yeah, Dee almost ran all the way home, and I had to stay up with him."

"What's his hurry? Supper won't be ready for a while yet."

"I don't know. He wouldn't say. I bet he goes to that dumb old tree house of his first thing," Cherrie said. As she spoke, Dee when out the back door and down the path toward his tree house.

Saturday dawned clear and bright, as Dee had hoped it would. During the previous night, he had a hard time sleeping with Lonesome Hill on his mind. He could hardly wait until Billy Bob arrived in the afternoon so they could start planning the trip up the hill.

It seemed forever before Billy Bob arrived at one o'clock that afternoon. But Billy Bob wasn't alone. Tagging along behind him was his sister Sue Ann.

Sue Ann was a year younger than Billy Bob but acted much older. She, like Billy Bob, had golden blond hair. She was tall for an eleven-year-old girl and a little on the skinny side. But overall she was a fairly good looking girl in Dee's opinion. Sue Ann was dressed neat and orderly compared to Billy Bob. She wore a pair of new looking blue jeans that were rolled up to just below her knees. She wore a pair of low black flats and no socks. Her hair was in a neat pony tail hanging down to the middle of her back and she had on one of her brothers long white cotton shirts. The two, Billy Bob and Sue Ann, made a strange comparison as they came up to the front porch.

"Hey! Dee," yelled Billy Bob as he approached. "Dad says ta ask Mrs. Collie if it's okay for us to stay first."

"I already asked her," Dee answered. "She said it was okay."

Harry Barnett sat in the car waiting for Billy Bob to confirm that he could stay. Harry was a big muscular farmer. He was tall and lean with short blond hair. He had clear blue eyes with small blond eye brows. His hands were large and strong from hard farm work. It was easy to see that Billy Bob was his son because Billy Bob was just a smaller version of Harry.

Harry heard Dee yell the okay, and then he waved and drove on down the road. Billy Bob picked up his little hand bag and started on toward the Collie front porch with Sue Ann close behind.

"Mom wouldn't let me come 'less I brought my Sunday clothes and 'less I brought sis," Billy Bob exclaimed in disgust. "She wants ta visit with Cherrie."

"That's okay," Dee said, "Cherrie's inside."

They went in the house and put Billy Bob's things in Dee and Cherrie's room, and then they went into the living room.

"Mom, I'd like for you to meet Billy Bob and Sue Ann Barnett. They live east of town near the hills," Dee said as he introduced his visitors.

"I've seen the Barnett family at church," Mary Collie said and shook their hands.

"Yes Ma'am," said Billy Bob, a little flushed.

"Well, we want to go down to the tree house. Mom, will you see if you can find Cherrie for Sue Ann?"

"Sure. Run on. But be back in time for supper."

As she spoke, Dee ran out the back door dragging Billy Bob behind him. They ran down the path in the backyard, and out of sight.

"Well," Mary said turning to Sue Ann. "I think Cherrie is in the bathroom. She'll be out in a minute. Why don't you come on in the kitchen with me until she does?"

Sue Ann nodded and followed Mary into the kitchen.

"Are you in Cherrie's class at school?" Mary asked.

"No Ma'am, Cherrie's one grade ahead of me. But we play together a lot during lunch period. We have a lot of fun," was the reply.

"Well, we're glad y'all could come over to spend the night with Dee and Cherrie," Mary said politely.

"Mom wouldn't let Billy Bob come 'less I got ta come too." Then after a short pause, "Billy Bob and Dee are planin' somethin'," Sue Ann said in a matter-of-fact tone.

"What?" Mary asked.

"What? What?" Sue Ann asked.

"What are Billy Bob and Dee planin'?" Mary pressed.

"I don't know what. Somethin' dumb most likely," Sue Ann replied.

Just then Cherrie came walking into the kitchen zipping up her blue jeans. "Hey, Sue Ann, I didn't know you were comin' over with Billy Bob!"

"Neither did Billy Bob. But I told mom how Billy Bob was always goin' places and how I never got ta go anyplace. So, she let me come with him," Sue Ann explained smiling.

"Good," said Cherrie. "Come on into my room. I got a brand new Sears and Roebuck catalog and it's got all kinds of new toys in it."

"Hey! I'd like ta see that," yelled Sue Ann. They stormed out of the kitchen and into Cherrie and Dee's room.

As supper time neared, Dee and Billy Bob had not returned. Mary Collie wasn't worried, but she wanted everyone at the supper table at the same time. Latecomers always made more work for her and Rachael. So, as usual, she decided to send Cherrie out to find Dee. She went into Dee and Cherrie's room to get Cherrie. As she walked in, she found Cherrie and Sue Ann still reading the catalog. "Cherrie, I want you to go out and find Dee and Billy Bob for supper."

"Aw, Mom they'll be here in time."

"Just go find them, Cherrie," Mary said flatly.

"Yes Ma'am. Come on with me Sue Ann. They're probably in the tree house anyway," Cherrie said and got up to leave. But before they could leave, Dee and Billy Bob came in.

"Well, it's about time y'all got back," Mary said. "Go get cleaned up for supper."

Throughout supper, Cherrie watched Billy Bob eat. She hoped no one saw that she was watching, but she couldn't help looking. Cherrie had always thought Dee ate more than anybody, but Billy Bob was second to none. He not only ate a huge amount, but he ate at blinding speed. Rachael had refilled his plate three times and his glass four. It seems the Barnett children were only allowed to have milk at their meals, so the iced tea was a special treat for them. The

Collie children, on the other hand, were allowed to have tea for supper. Billy Bob was taking full advantage of the time and place. As Cherrie sat there and watched, Billy Bob started his fifth glass of tea.

After supper, Cherrie and Sue Ann helped Mary with the dishes while Dee and Billy Bob vanished again. They didn't appear again until after dark. "Where y'all been, Dee?" Cherrie asked.

"Just outside messin' around," Dee answered casually.

"Well, you and Billy Bob are goin' to have to make a bed on the floor 'cause I'm sleepin' in my bed and Sue Ann is sleepin' in yours," Cherrie announced with a big smile on her face.

"OK," Dee said. "Come on Billy Bob, let's get some quilts and make a bed on the floor." With that the two boys walked out of the living room and into the bedroom down the hall.

Cherrie stood there for a minute in shock that Dee hadn't said a word in argument. She thought surely he'd be mad about sleeping on the floor while Sue Ann took his bed. "Somethin' is goin' on," Cherrie said thoughtfully.

"Yeah, I know," Sue Ann said looking at Cherrie.

"I don't know what, but somethin' is goin' on. You can bet on it," Cherrie repeated. "'Cause Dee's sure been actin' dumb and he's really not too dumb 'cept when he wants to be."

"Well, Billy Bob's dumb all the time. He just naturally ain't smart. So you don't have to worry 'bout him," Sue Ann stated with a look of sincerity.

"Oh! I'm not worrin' 'bout neither one. I was just wonderin' that's all. Just wonderin'," Cherrie said with a strange look in her shiny blue eyes. "Anyway, we have to get ready for bed. Come on, the boys probably already got their bed down."

By the time Cherrie and Sue Ann had changed into their pajamas and made their way to the bedroom, the boys had already curled up inside their bed on the floor.

"Y'all sure got to bed in a hurry," Cherrie commented suspiciously.

"Yeah, well, turn out the light and go to bed yourself will ya," Dee answered.

"Sure," Cherrie said. "But if somebody steps on you tonight it'll probably be me goin' for some water or to the bathroom."

"Cherrie, if you don't shut up, I'll goin' ta brain ya."

"Okay. Okay. Good night," she said smiling.

"Good night!"

After the goodnights were said all around, the room fell silent. The only sounds heard were the sounds of the crickets, and the only light was the light of the moon that shone through the window. The quietness was almost too much for Dee to bear, as he lay there waiting for time to pass. However, the waiting didn't seem to bother Billy Bob, for he had fallen sound asleep.

Dee's head slowly rose up from under the covers and peered around the room. The moonlight allowed him some fairly good sight. Cherrie and Sue Ann appeared to be sound asleep. Dee reached over and shook Billy Bob. "Billy Bob. Hey, Billy Bob," Dee whispered.

"OK, I'm awake," he replied softly.

"Let's get dressed," Dee said. "But be quiet, very quiet."

They crawled out of the covers and started dressing. When they were dressed, Dee went over to the closet and brought out his air rifle.

"What're you gettin' that for?" Billy Bob asked in a high whisper.

"Just in case," Dee whispered.

"Just in case what?" Bill Bob asked in a high whisper.

"Just in case period," Dee replied in a frustrated whisper.

As they talked, Dee lowered the barrel and all the BBs rolled down to the end of the gun cutting the quietness like a knife. Both boys looked toward the girls, but they still seemed to sleep.

"This way," Dee said and started for the window.

As he gripped the window to raise it, he heard a voice behind him say, "Daryl Gene Collie!"

"Oh! No," Dee said in a long breath. "Cherrie, why aren't you asleep?" Dee was almost in tears.

"'Cause I knew somethin' was goin' on," Cherrie whispered. "Now, where're y'all goin'?"

"Cherrie, please go to sleep and be quiet," Dee pleaded.

"Tell me what's goin' on Dee or I'll wake up mom and dad."

"Me and Billy Bob are goin' to Lonesome Hill," he said flatly.

Cherrie sat there on the bed and thought for a minute. "It's Ruth and Dick Jordan, isn't it?" She said simply.

"Yes," Dee said. "Don't tell mom or anybody. Please let us go! Please Cherrie!"

"I won't tell 'cause I'm goin' too," Cherrie said getting out of bed.

"Cherrie, you can't go, stupid!"

"Why?" She asked as she got into her blue jeans.

"I guess if we don't let you come, you'll wake mom and dad?" Dee asked, although he was sure of the answer.

"That's about it," she smiled.

"Hey, don't leave me," Sue Ann said getting up.

"Oh no," Dee exclaimed. "Now it's both of 'em."

"Maybe we better wait until some other time Dee," Billy Bob said.

"No, we got to go tonight," Dee said flatly. Then he turned to the girls, "If y'all are comin' you better come on 'cause we're leavin'."

Dee opened the window and climbed out into the night. He was followed by Billy Bob, Cherrie and Sue Ann. Sue Ann slipped on her shoes as she climbed out the window. They all got out the window and ran down the back path. They didn't stop until they reached Dee's tree house. By the time they reached the tree house, each one was out of breath.

"Y'all stay down here. I'll go up and see if I can see the light through my telescope," Dee said.

Dee climbed up the tree and for several long quiet moments no sound was heard. Cherrie was about to call out when Dee yelled down, "The light's on up there all right. But we're too late to follow anybody. We'll have to go on our own."

"Dee, you said we would follow Ruth and Dick," Billy Bob said concerned.

"We got started too late. I guess they left a little earlier than usual anyway," Dee said as he dropped to the ground. "Well, let's go." Dee started walking into the night.

"Wait for me, Dee," Cherrie said and ran up by his side. Billy Bob and Sue Ann followed close behind. They walked for a long way before anyone spoke. It was almost as though they were afraid to speak.

"Dee," Billy Bob said at last.

"Yeah," Dee whispered.

"I been thinkin'," he said.

"You have," Dee said sarcastically.

"We should've spent the night at my house. We wouldn't have had ta walk so far," Billy Bob said.

"Maybe, but we wouldn't have had the telescope. Anyway, we'll be at the foot of the hill in a minute," Dee said.

There was a deep ravine just below the road at the foot of the hill. They went down into the ravine and up the other side and then climbed onto the dirt road. They stood on the road and looked up the slope of the hill, but it was dark and hard to see. The willow trees that grew all over the hill were low and twisted, giving an eerie, haunting look. Short and stubby mesquite bushes grew all up and down the slope. As they stood there gazing up the hill and straining to see, the moon went behind a cloud and they were put into total darkness.

"Hey, Dee," a voice from the dark called.

"What?"

"Man, it's really dark. You think we better wait 'til another time?" Billy Bob asked with a tone of worry in his voice.

"No," Dee said simply.

"You sure ya know the way to that shack?" Billy Bob asked.

"Sure," Dee answered, not really sure at all. "Come on and stay close together."

Dee didn't have to tell Cherrie to stay close. She was so close behind him that if he turned around he would have knocked her down.

They made their way up the steep slope of Lonesome Hill, walking through the thick mesquite bushes and slumping Weeping Willow trees. The trees almost completely blotted out the moon, or what moonlight escaped through the clouds that now began to fill the sky.

There was no trail at all. Dee had thought he might find the trail that Ruth and Dick used but he couldn't, and now he was not sure where he was. He thought for sure the shack was near the top of the hill and to the right of his tree house. But now he didn't know if he was right or left of his tree house. He did know, however, that they were nearing the top of the hill. The slope was becoming less steep and the bushes were thinning out.

Dee stopped and looked hard and long into the darkness. He stood there thinking with his index finger in his mouth. Then, he turned to the others to speak. To his surprise, he turned too quickly, knocking Cherrie into a nearby mesquite bush. The crash she made falling cut the quietness like a rifle shot. They all froze where they were.

Finally Dee spoke. "Get up Cherrie," he said.

"I am. But you nearly killed me," she answered.

"Where are we anyway?" Sue Ann asked.

"I'm not sure," Dee said thoughtfully.

"I don't reckon ya are either," stated Billy Bob in disgust.

"Now look, Billy Bob. I . . ." But Dee didn't finish his sentence because the sound of voices caused him to cut his sentence short. Dee signaled and they all dropped to the ground and strained to hear.

"Not here," the voice said.

"Why not, I can't think of a better place?"

"But we'll be accomplishin' nothin' if we do it here. We need to do it where the rest of them can see it. Then they'll understand we mean business," the first one stated.

"I'm tellin' you we'll get the same results by doin' it here and then dumpin' the body somewhere in town," the second one argued. The voices faded a little as the wind, which had begun to blow, carried the sound the other way.

Dee turned to the others and said, "Come on, this way." He started toward the voices at a low run. The others followed more out of fear than because of Dee's command.

Dee signaled a halt behind some mesquite bushes. They lay down on their bellies and peered into a small clearing in which sat the mysterious shack.

The clearing was full of men dressed in white robes and hoods. They stood in a circle around a fire that was whipped around by the increasing wind. Also, in the middle of the circle, was a Negro man tied and gagged lying on the ground. His eyes were wide with fear, but he made no effort to free himself.

Suddenly Cherrie realized who the Negro man was. "Hey, that's Moonbeam," she said in a surprised low whisper. She had jumped up to her knees as she spoke.

"Cherrie," Dee cried and grabbed her by her hair and pulled her back down.

"Ouch!" She grunted as she fell back. The wind had covered the noise, as it began to whistle strongly through the trees.

All of the men stood quietly as the two men who were talking argued. "Let's take a vote," the first man was saying.

"No, we'll wait for the Wizard," the second man said.

"Okay, but let's go inside and wait. It looks like rain," the first man said. With that they all went into the shack dragging the Negro man behind them.

Dee and the others lay still for a minute without talking. "Who was that colored man?" Dee finally asked.

"That was Moonbeam. Doc Jewel's handyman," Cherrie whispered. "What were they doin' to him, Dee?"

"I don't know. But they're not up to nothin' good," Dee said.

"Where's Ruth or Dick Jordan?" Billy Bob asked. "I ain't seen them at all."

"They could be wearin' hoods like everybody else," Dee said.

"You mean you think Ruth Jordan is in on the KKK?" Billy Bob asked.

"Could be," Dee answered.

"What's the KKK?" Sue Ann asked.

"It's the Ku Klux Klan crazy," Dee stated.

"The Ku Klux Klan," yelled Sue Ann. Realizing she had yelled; she placed her hand over her mouth. Then she removed her hand and whispered very low, "The Ku Klux Klan?"

"Yeah, the Ku Klux Klan," Dee said again.

"Ain't they bad?" Sue Ann asked.

"They're sure bad for colored folks," Dee said.

"What'd Moonbeam do?" Cherrie asked.

"I don't know but we better beat it before we get caught," Dee said.

They got up and turned to leave, but before they had taken a step, they were forced back into their hiding place by the sound of new voices. Four people approached the clearing from the side nearest Dee and the others. They walked within twenty feet of Sue Ann who was lying on the far side of Billy Bob. They stopped to talk outside the shack, but their words were inaudible because of the wind, which now was blowing at a solid rate. But Dee didn't need words to recognize two of them. One was Ruth Jordan and the other was Dick Jordan. Dee didn't know the other two.

One of the people he didn't recognize had on a black robe and hood with the letters 'KKK' across the front in gold letters. The other man was a short, middle-aged looking man. He had a beard of about a week's growth and shabby clothes. He wore an old tattered hat and shoes with the soles loose and flopping. In the back pocket of his loose hanging slacks was a bottle of whiskey. The shaggy dressed man seemed to be listening as Ruth Jordan talked to the hooded man. The man in black then turned and knocked on the door of the shack. A white hooded man opened the door and all four went inside.

"Let's get out of here," Dee said. But something made Dee turn and look back, and he stopped.

"Come on, let's go," Cherrie urged.

"Look," Dee said pointing to the shack. They all looked toward the shack to see a strange figure gazing in the window of the shack. It was a young girl.

"Who is it?" Cherrie asked.

"I don't know," Dee said. "I've never seen her before."

Billy Bob and Sue Ann nodded the same.

The girl stood slightly crouched peering into the shack, as the wind-whipped fire outside caused shadows to dance around her. The tricky light made it difficult to tell much about her. She wore no shoes and her dress was old and ragged. Her long black hair waved in the wind and her eyes shone in the dark reflecting the fire light. She couldn't have been much older than him, Dee thought, but she was tall and lean and may have appeared older than she really was.

"Come on Dee, let's go," Cherrie urged again.

"Okay," Dee answered.

They all got to their feet and started moving slowly and quietly away from the clearing. Dee was looking back when he tripped over a tree root and fell with crash into a mesquite bush. Cherrie and the others were ahead of him and stopped and waited for him to get up. But Dee didn't get up right away; he lay there for almost a full minute.

"Dee," Cherrie called. "Come on, stupid."

Dee jumped to his feet and ran after them. It seemed to take them an eternity to get down the hill. The wind was blowing and drops of rain were starting to fall. They finally reached the dirt road at the base of the hill and stopped to rest.

"She saw me," Dee said suddenly. "She saw me when I fell. We just looked at each other a minute and then she ran off and I ran off too."

"You reckon she'll tell?" Billy Bob asked.

"I think she was afraid of the people in the shack too," Dee said, "probably just as much as us."

"What about Moonbeam?" Cherrie asked.

"It's not any of our business," Dee said. "We'll just go back and say nothin."

Cherrie searched for the right words to say and finally said, "But they were talkin' like they were goin' to hurt him."

"Maybe just scare him," Dee replied. "Anyway, we need to hurry and get back. If dad finds out we came up here, he'll skin us alive."

Cherrie wasn't ready to give up. She tried one more time. "But, Dee, they might hurt him?" Cherrie pleaded.

"So what, he's just a nigger," Billy Bob broke in.

Dee spun around as though hit by something. Nigger was a word that was not allowed in the Collie household. Dee's love for Rachael made the word even more distasteful. But he didn't speak. He stood silently looking at Billy Bob. For now, he saw Billy Bob in an entirely different light. Suddenly the difference between Billy Bob and Dee became more than the difference between living in town and living near the hills.

"Hey! What's wrong with you?" Billy Bob asked backing up.

"Billy Bob, don't you ever use that word around me again," Dee said with gritted teeth.

"What word?" Billy Bob asked, as he continued to back away from Dee.

"Stop it, Dee," Cherrie said stepping in between the two boys. "We don't have time for this now."

"What did I say?" Billy Bob asked in frustration.

Dee looked at Billy Bob and realized that Billy Bob really didn't know what he had said to make Dee mad. He really didn't understand. He just simply didn't understand. Then, Dee looked back at Cherrie. He could see the pleading in Cherrie's eyes.

"What're you goin' to do Dee?" Cherrie asked. She stared straight into Dee's eyes for a long painful moment.

Unsure of himself, Dee finally said, "Nothin', let's hurry and get back before it rains.

CHAPTER ELEVEN

Missed Appointment

Rachael stood on the front porch of her small house with her arms folded across her breast. As she paced up and down the small distance, a look of worry covered her face. "Where is that old black pile of bones?" She muttered to herself. "He should've been here thirty minutes ago."

"Rachael," a call came from a distance.

Rachael looked up to see Mary Collie standing in her back yard waving to her. "Rachael," she yelled again.

"Yes, Ma'am," Rachael yelled back.

"We're almost ready to leave for church. Can we drop you anywhere; at your church maybe?"

"No Ma'am. Thank ya anyway, but I'm waitin' for Moonbeam. We goin' ta preachin' together as soon as he gets here," Rachael replied. "He's late, but I'll just wait a little longer."

"OK, see you after services."

The Collies and the Barnett children all piled into the car. The children all sat in back dressed in their Sunday best. Rachael watched as they backed out into the street and drove away. "Now, where can that man be?" She muttered again.

As the car moved down the street, Mary turned around to face the children in the back and said, "Y'all sure are a quiet group this morning. Nobody talked much durin' breakfast. Is somethin' wrong?"

"No, Ma'am," said Dee. "It's just this Sunday suit. It makes you not want to move or talk."

"That's the truth," commented Billy Bob.

"Sunday is only once a week. It doesn't hurt you any," Mary replied as she turned back around to face the front.

After Sunday school was over, Dee and Cherrie walked outside with the other children to wait for church services to start. There was usually about fifteen minutes between Sunday school and the regular sermon given by Reverend Tuney. Cherrie pulled Dee away from the others to a quiet place behind some large oak trees.

"Did you hear Rachael this mornin'? She said Moonbeam was supposed to have come by her place to go to church," she whispered in a high voice.

"I heard," Dee said looking down at the ground.

"Well, what'd you think?"

"I don't know," he said, shrugging his shoulders. But his eyes still did not meet hers.

"Dee, what if somethin' has happened to Moonbeam? We saw those men."

"We didn't see anythin' happen to Moonbeam. Did we?" He challenged her.

"No, but you know somethin' happened or he would've been at Rachael's this mornin'."

"Come on Cherrie, we don't know anything for sure and we're not sayin' nothin' to nobody. I already made Billy Bob swear to keep his mouth shut and he said he would. You go and get Sue Ann to do the same. We're not goin' to get into whatever is goin' on. I'm sorry I ever started this Jordan thing. I never thought it would lead to anythin' like this."

"Dee, I think we ought to tell Dad," Cherrie stated flatly.

"Tell him what?" Dee asked. "Are you ready for all the trouble we'll get into?"

"Tell him what we saw! He may want to tell the Sheriff. I mean, after all Dee, we know the Ku Klux Klan is here!"

"Answer my question, Cherrie. Are you ready for all the trouble we'll get into?" Dee pressed.

"Yeah, Dee, I think I am."

People started going back into the church. Cherrie looked long and hard at Dee. "Are you sure that's the way you want it, Dee?"

"That's the way I want it," he replied. Cherrie turned and walked back to church. Dee stood and watched her walk away. Somehow, Dee didn't feel he stood quite as tall in Cherrie's eyes as he once did.

Back inside the church everyone was taking their seats for the sermon. Dee looked across the aisle to where Billy Bob and Sue Ann were sitting. A knowing look passed between them. Cherrie had told Sue Ann to keep quiet. Both Billy Bob and Sue Ann were now sworn to keep the secret. As they sat next to each other, Dee reached over and took Cherrie's hand and held it. Cherrie looked at Dee with hurt in her eyes. The look in Cherrie's eyes made him feel unsure of himself. He loved Cherrie and always wanted to be her big brother. He always wanted her to look up to him and trust him. Now, he was feeling that maybe he had lost all of that. But, as he was having these feelings, he felt Cherrie squeeze his hand and he felt better.

After church, Billy Bob and Sue Ann went home with their parents. Dee watched them drive away. His feelings for Billy Bob had changed. His feelings about many things were changing and they would never be the same again.

───

Meanwhile, Rachael was changing out of her best Sunday dress into her work clothes. She had missed preaching this Sunday all because she had stood around waiting for some old fool. "A missed appointment," she said to herself in a discussed tone. "A gentleman should never miss an appointment with a lady. Well, it won't happen again. That old fool can go by his own self next time. My Lordy, there's no excuse for a missed appointment!

CHAPTER TWELVE

The Example

Doctor Jewel walked down the south side of the town square toward the courthouse. It was Sunday morning and the square was completely empty. Not a soul was in sight. Everyone was preparing for church, Doc Jewel speculated, as he walked along. He had stopped by the Sheriff's house earlier, but had been told the Sheriff had gone to the courthouse to pick up some personal items before going to church. The urgency of his mission showed in his quick step and long stride. This combination was difficult for Doc Jewel, because he was a rather short man. His hair was loosely combed. He was dressed entirely in his black Sunday best.

He had been dressed in his Sunday best earlier in the morning when he found Moonbeam, who was hanging by his neck from the rafters in Doc Jewel's garage. As Doc walked in to get his car for church, he saw Moonbeam swing ever so slowly to and fro. His lifeless eyes were staring, unseeing into space. For a man who had seen death many times before, Doc Jewel was shocked almost out of his senses. With his mouth hanging open, he stood there staring not knowing what to do. His first reaction was to get Moonbeam down and he started to do just that, but then his senses returned and he stopped. The Sheriff would want things left just the way they were. He did reach up to check Moonbeam's pulse to make sure he was dead, although Moonbeam's face and swollen tongue left no doubt of that.

Doc Jewel then got into his car to drive to the Sheriff's house. But his car would not start so he set out walking. Now, as he neared the courthouse, he was confused as to what had really happened. He was just now discovering the realization of what he had seen. Moonbeam was really dead. But why! Who would want to kill Moonbeam and for what reason? No answer came to him and he wondered more. Could it be suicide? No, Moonbeam would not do that!

He walked into the courthouse and up the stairs to the Sheriff's office. Sheriff Thomas Clark was searching through his desk drawer as Doc arrived. "Hello Doc. What're ya doin' here this time of mornin'?"

"You better come with me Tom. There's been a killin'," Doc said calmly and to the point.

Sheriff Clark was a big man. He stood close to six feet five and weighed better than 240 pounds. None of his weight was fat. He had long brown hair with matching brown eyes. He had a dark tan from hours out in the sun walking around town. Sheriff Clark was only thirty years of age and many people in Coalville thought him too young to have his job. Also, he was not born in Coalville. He came to Coalville to run for Sheriff from Athens where he had been a police officer. Since he was young, and since he was not from Coalville, most didn't think he had a chance to win the election for Sheriff. But he did win. His victory was attributed to the fact that the business men in town wanted new and young blood in the office. That had been two years ago. The general opinion around Coalville was that Tom Clark was doing a good job.

Sheriff Clark looked at Doc for a long minute, "A killin', who?"

"My handyman, Moonbeam," Doc answered, remaining calm.

"Moonbeam," the Sheriff said thoughtfully. "How do ya know it's a killin'?"

"'Cause I'm sure Moonbeam wouldn't hang himself," Doc said quietly.

"Hanged," the Sheriff said in an unbelieving tone, "you mean he was hanged?"

"Yeah, that's want I said. Do you mind if I use your phone to call an ambulance to pick up his body?" Doc asked.

"Go ahead, but tell them not to move the body or touch anythin' 'til I get there."

"Sure," Doc said picking up the phone. As Doc dialed the number, Sheriff Clark reached in his desk drawer and got out his gun and holster. He buckled on the holster and checked his gun for bullets. By the time he was ready to go, Doc was hanging up the phone.

"You ready to go?" Doc asked.

"In just a minute," the Sheriff replied. "Let me call Lou to meet us there."

Sheriff Clark took the phone from Doc and dialed the number of Louis Lee Mailer. Louis was Sheriff Clark's one and only deputy. Louis handled most of the dirty work that the Sheriff didn't want to get involved with. The phone rang for several times before someone answered.

"Hello," an irritated sounding voice came over the line.

"Lou, this is Sheriff Clark. We got a problem over to Doc Jewel's place. I need you to meet me over there right away."

"What's up? I was just getting' ready to leave for church with Evie."

"Sorry, but I need you. Go ahead and drop Evie by church then you go on over to Doc's."

"Come on, Tom, what's goin' on?" Lou asked with excitement building in his voice.

"I ain't goin' to talk about it over the phone. Just hurry on over there and wait for me and don't touch or move anythin' 'til I get there," the Sheriff ordered sharply.

—◦◦◦—

After hanging the phone up, Lou yelled for his wife. "Hurry up Evie; I got official business to tend to."

Lou moved his heavy frame quickly around the bedroom to finish dressing. He was a short heavy set man in his early thirties with light brown hair and matching brown eyes. His eyebrows were thin and high upon his narrow forehead.

Lou groaned as he finished tying his shoe laces. His weight had always been a problem for him. Even as a child in school, he could never stay up with the other boys because of his weight. Nothing he did would help him lose weight. It wasn't that Lou was really fat, he was just overweight. His weight problem had, however, kept him out of the army during the big war. As far as education, Lou was fairly intelligent even though he had never finished high school. He dropped out of school in the tenth grade to work in the mines.

He had become the deputy in Coalville through his friendship with Tom Clark. Tom had known Lou's wife in Athens and a natural friendship had developed between Tom and the Mailer family when Tom had moved to Coalville. Then, when Tom had gotten approval for a deputy, he asked Lou to take the job.

Lou jumped at the chance as he was unemployed at the time. He liked his job as deputy because it made him feel important, and Lou liked feeling important. Sometimes he was a little too enthusiastic about his job and Tom had to pull him back into line. Lou was not very popular in town because of the way he pushed himself upon people. But Tom stuck with Lou and kept him out of any real trouble.

"Evie, did you hear me? We have to go. Are you ready yet?" Lou yelled from the bedroom.

"Yeah, I'm ready," she answered from the bathroom. "I just need to finish my hair. What's the big rush anyway?"

As she spoke, Evie came walking into the bedroom to join Lou. She was short and thin with sandy blond hair that hung down to the middle of her back. Her eyes were dark brown set into a small thin face with a high forehead. She had a pointed chin and an unusually long neck. Evie was not ugly, but she had a plain unattractive look. Her well-shaped body didn't seem to go with her facial features. Evie's real name was Eve Von Norris and she came from Clinton, a small town outside of Athens. She had gone to school in Athens as Clinton was too small to have its own school system. It was there she met Tom Clark and graduated high school with him. She had met Lou during the war when he worked at a defense plant in Dallas. They seemed like an unlikely couple, but most of the men were overseas at the time and somehow they ended up getting married.

"I asked you what the big rush is." She said pressing him again. As she talked, she joined him in the bedroom.

"I don't know. The Sheriff just asked me to meet him at Doc Jewel's right away.

I'll drop you by church and I'll pick you up after the services."

"It must be somethin' important for him to call you on a Sunday before church," she said puzzled.

"I don't know, but let's go." He took her by the hand and they hurried out to their car.

Meanwhile, the Sheriff and Doc Jewel were walking out of the Sheriff's office. "I wonder who would want to kill Moonbeam," the Sheriff was saying. "He was as harmless as they come." Then as they walked along and after a short pause, "You know what I mean, Doc?"

"I know he was. That old black fart never hurt anybody," Doc Jewel said as the tears started rolling down his cheeks at last.

The news of Moonbeam's death hit Coalville like a bomb. It was the first killing Coalville had in twenty years when a fight between two miners had resulted in one being killed. It was on everyone's tongue. Not so much the killing as the warning note that came with it. The note had been tied around Moonbeam's neck and it read, "He is an example."

The note was unsigned, but everyone was talking Ku Klux Klan. Sheriff Clark tried to kill the rumors by saying he had no proof to involve any one person much less the Ku Klux Klan. He tried to reassure everyone that he was taking care of everything, but still the rumors ran wild and no one really knew for sure. Outside of the ones involved, only four people knew for sure, and they were children.

Dee and Cherrie had heard the rumors and the talk. They heard people take sides in the issue. They listened and heard all these things but they said nothing. Billy Bob and Sue Ann said nothing, mostly out of respect for the promise made to Dee. Anyway, the death of a nigger didn't upset the Barnett household one way or the other. Most people were indifferent in the same way. After all it wasn't as though a white person had been killed, just a nigger.

Although Dee hid his young twelve-year-old feelings behind the veil of indifference, he couldn't help a different feeling, a feeling he wasn't sure about. A feeling he didn't like. He could remember the look in Cherrie's eyes when she had said, "Are you sure that's the way you want it, Dee?" Cherrie could see into Dee's mind, it seemed. Cherrie wasn't like other girls. She seemed to be different to Dee. Not just because she was his twin sister, but other things Dee couldn't explain; things that caused Dee to respect Cherrie as much as a twelve-year-old could respect anybody.

Cherrie had feelings too, feelings that went beyond indifference. Her feelings were more for Dee than for Moonbeam. She had always looked up to Dee even though they were the same age. Usually, she accepted his judgment with no fear of his being wrong. She had always trusted Dee to be right, no matter what. Now, for the first time, she wasn't sure. She wasn't sure Dee was right about remaining silent, but still she trusted him. Even if he was wrong, she would still trust him and do as he said. More than one time Cherrie had seen Dee defend her from boys who were picking on her without asking who was at fault. More than once, Cherrie had been at fault. But Dee never asked. He only helped her. She felt Dee deserved to be trusted all the way.

So Cherrie and Dee remained silent, each acting as one. Dee not really knowing what to do, and Cherrie accepting whatever decision he made. Two children not really knowing what form of hate killed Moonbeam; not really knowing the power of the secret knowledge they held. Knowing only that they had seen something they thought to be wrong, but not knowing what to do about it.

Meanwhile Sheriff Clark was trying his best to find out anything he could about the murder. "That's all you know about it, uh?" He was asking Doc Jewel.

"That's it, Tom, just like I told you. I didn't leave anything out," Doc assured him.

"Do you know if Moonbeam had been doin' anythin' strange or different lately?"

"No, not to my knowledge, but then I'm not sure what strange or different would be for Moonbeam. He's been livin' out back for years and I never saw him hurt anybody or do anything that would cause someone to want to kill him," Doc said.

"I don't think it's anythin' he did, Doc. If that was it, they'd just have killed him, not hang him and leave a note like they did. But damn it, I don't get it." Sheriff Clark slammed his big fist down on the desk. Then, looking at Doc intently he said, "Do you think there's anythin' to this damn Klan rumor?"

"I don't know. I hope not," Doc said. "We sure don't need any damn Ku Klux Klan around here causin' hell with the colored folks."

"Do you know of any problems with niggers in town?" The Sheriff asked.

"No, and I'm sure you meant to say colored people and not *nigger*," Doc replied stressing the ugly word.

"I didn't mean it the way it sounded, Doc," the Sheriff said quickly. "It just came out kind of natural."

"If you want some advice from an old man, you better stop bein' natural then. With things like they are in town, you better be careful what you say and how you say it."

"Point well taken, Doc," the Sheriff nodded. "Well, I've got to go. The town council has called a meeting and I have to be there. James Collie, Lester Homes and John Tuney will all be there, you want to come along?"

"Might as well," Doc said.

They left the Sheriff's office and went outside to Sheriff Clark's patrol car. It was only a five minute drive to Lester Homes' house where the meeting was being held. Everyone was there when the Sheriff and Doc Jewel arrived including Louis Mailer. They walked in and took a seat as Lester Homes took his place at the center of the gathering.

"Okay, gentlemen this meeting' of the Coalville Town Council is in session," Lester began. "Now, is there any new business?"

"You know damn well there's some new business. Now cut the bullshit and get to it," one of the members shouted.

"Okay, keep calm, everybody keep calm," Lester said. "Now, it seems some of us want to call in the State Police or the Texas Rangers on this hanging."

Sheriff Clark shot to his feet. "You don't think I can handle it?" He asked.

"It's not that, Tom. It's just that this is a murder and you might need some help," John Tuney said softly.

"I tell you we better keep it to ourselves for a while. Do you want the whole damn state to know about it? Why, they'll be down here in everybody's business before you know it," Sheriff Clark said. "I tell you I can handle it if you'll just give me a chance."

"I think Tom's right," Lester said. "We don't want the whole state on us."

"But what if the Klan is here like some folks are saying?" John Tuney asked. "Can you handle that, Tom?"

"That's just a rumor, nobody knows for sure. Do you want to call in the Rangers on a rumor?" The Sheriff asked.

"But what if it's not a rumor?" Doc Jewel asked quietly.

Sheriff Clark turned and faced Doc. His face looked as though he had been betrayed. "If it's not and I can't handle it, then call in anybody you want. But remember this, if it is the Klan it must have members right here in town. The Klan just doesn't move an army in. It has members in the town. With that said, if it was the Klan that did this, and I said *if*, then probably the people who committed this crime are your own neighbors and friends. It may even be someone in this room. But I said *if* it's the Klan. So, before you go off halfcocked callin' in the state you better think a minute and give me a chance to see what is what."

"Damn it, he's right and you all know it." The person now speaking was Louis Mailer. "This thing could get real sticky. And anyway, it ain't fair to the Sheriff not to give him a chance. The Sheriff, and me, can handle this thing. I'm damn sure we can."

"Lou, it's not a question of being' fair or not being' fair. It's a question of being' able to deal with all the possibilities," Doc said softly but firmly.

"Well, if you ask me none of the possibilities are too good," Lou replied. "We may have the Klan and then again maybe we don't. Maybe the killer, or killers, is someone we know and then again maybe they're not. We don't know enough at this point to take this away from the Sheriff and me. I don't know why we're even thinkin' about it." Lou's voice had taken on an angry sound.

"Lou," Sheriff Clark said, as he reached over and touched Lou on the shoulder. "Take it easy. They have the right to be worried and they have the right to express their fears. But we won't get anywhere if we start yellin' at each other."

"The thing is," the Sheriff continued, looking around the room at each person. "I can only promise to do my best. But everyone should understand that I will try and get to the bottom of all this."

Everyone was quiet for a while. Each man looked to the other as if looking for an answer. Finally James Collie, who had thus far remained silent, spoke. "Everythin' you say is true, Tom. But friends or no friends, isn't a crime, a crime?"

"You're damn right it is. I've already heard some talk that we'll probably take it easy because it was a colored man killed. But you better believe this, it ain't so with me. Black, white, brown, yellow, or what have ya, there's been a killin' and I'm goin' to do my best to get the one or ones responsible. That goes for one person, or the Klan. I ain't any lover of colored folks, but there'll be no killings like that around here while I'm the Sheriff." Sheriff Clark noticed that he was standing and shouting. He looked around at the other men a little embarrassed.

"Okay Tom, it's Okay with me to leave it to you, if it's Okay with the rest," James Collie said.

"Then we'll take a vote," said Lester.

They voted and the vote was all for the Sheriff. They all started leaving with mumbled words to one another. James stopped before he went out the door and turned to Sheriff Clark. "I hope it comes out all right, Tom," he said.

"So do I," Sheriff Clark said firmly. "But if it doesn't, y'all can call in the Rangers. Better still, I'll call them in myself," Sheriff Clark said.

"Okay," James said and walked out the door.

James Collie left the meeting with renewed confidence in Sheriff Clark. He knew everything the Sheriff said about friends and neighbors was true. If it was the Klan, then the murderers could be one of his own neighbors. So, it stood to reason it would be a good thing to leave it in local hands at least until something more positive was discovered. James Collie went home with a feeling of misgiving about the entire affair.

CHAPTER THIRTEEN

Alone

Everyone had been gone for hours, as Lester Homes sat alone on the patio behind his house. It was a large patio that looked south of town toward Lonesome Hill. The evening was quiet and beautiful. He held a glass of bourbon and water in his right hand. Lester looked tired. His eyes were red and puffy from lack of sleep and his gray hair was rumpled and hanging in his face. Worriedly, he continually ran his hands over his head. His long legs were stretched out in front of him as he slouched low in the patio chair. Lester was still in his daily business suit, although it was wrinkled and his tie hung loose around his neck.

"What in the Hell am I doin'?" He asked himself aloud. His mind ran rapidly over all of the events of the last few days. "Jesus Christ, what have I done?" He continued speaking to himself.

The only sound he could hear was his own voice as he raised his glass to his lips and took a deep drink. He stood up and took a few staggered steps forward and then turned around to face his house. He swayed a little from intoxication but finally stood straight. Raising his empty glass, he threw it at the empty house. The shattering sound of the glass broke the night silence, but quickly the silence returned.

"Son-of-a-bitchin' house," he yelled, "big son-of-a-bitchin' empty house. Lois, I'm alone. Nobody's here, just me. Please help me, Lois. Lois, I've really screwed up this time. I don't think you would like me now." Lester looked at his house, but it didn't answer him. He dropped to his knees and spread his arms wide apart as if to pray. "Lois, what should I do? You shouldn't have left me alone. You and Bobbie left me alone. The house is empty, I'm empty and I need someone." Lester dropped his arms and hung his head on his chest. He stayed this way for some time. When he raised his head to look at his house again, his eyes were filled with tears. "God Lois, I miss you and Bobbie. I wish I knew what I should do now," he begged to the house. He started to get to his feet but staggered and fell full length on the patio. He decided not to try and get up. Slowly, he felt sleep over come him. Lois, Lois," he whispered as sleep pulled him down.

Meanwhile, at another lonely house, Doc Jewel sat at his kitchen table with a beer in his hand staring down at the checker board. Picking up the checkers, he arranged them on the board as if to play a game. He made the first move then leaned back in his chair and took a long drink of his beer. He sat there as if waiting for someone to make an answering move. Several minutes passed and nothing happened.

"Well, are you goin' to move you old black fart?" He asked out loud. His eyes began to water with tears. "I'm sixty-six years old and now I'm all alone again. Damn you, Moonbeam! Damn you! What did you do to make someone want to kill you? What on earth could you've done? How could anybody hate you that much?"

Doc Jewel finished his beer and pitched the empty bottle in the trash can. He picked up the checkers, folded the checker board and put them away neatly in their special place on top of the refrigerator. Then, he slowly walked to his bedroom and went to bed.

Meanwhile, in yet another lonely house, Sheriff Tom Clark walked into his bedroom and started undressing for bed. Sheriff Clark lived in a small one bedroom house about two blocks south of the town square. His house was supplied by the tax payers of Coalville as was his patrol car. The Sheriff actually didn't own anything himself. The house, furniture, car, and gasoline expenses were all part of his salary structure. His actual take home pay was very modest, but then Coalville was not a metropolis either.

He was very tired. Moonbeam's death had caused him many problems. He didn't have any good leads to follow except for the rumor of the Klan. And if it was the Klan he had no leads as to whom they were. Then, to top it all off, he had to fight to keep control of the investigation. He didn't show it to the others, but it hurt his pride to have them make the suggestion of turning the investigation over to the Texas Rangers. This was the first real crime he had ever investigated. Most of his work in Coalville was simply keeping order between the citizens and patrolling the town square after hours. As he thought about it, he guessed it was no wonder they wanted the investigation handled by someone else. But he was determined to get to the bottom of this murder and to stop any more before they happened.

After undressing, he walked into the bathroom and started running his bath water. He made the water as hot as he could stand it. Just as he was about to step into the tub, he heard his telephone ring. "Shit, who in hell could that be at this hour," he cursed to himself. Without covering himself, he quickly ran into the living area to answer the phone. He picked up the phone and sat down, naked, into the chair next to the telephone table.

"Hello, Sheriff Clark here," he said into the telephone mouthpiece with a tired voice.

"Tom, this is Evie," the voice on the receiver said.

"Yeah, Evie, what's up," the Sheriff replied slowly. His face took on a look of alarm.

"Tom, Lou is gone for the night. He won't be back 'til about noon tomorrow."

"Yeah, I know, he told me about goin' out on the river with a few other guys. I'm not expectin' him in the office tomorrow 'til after noon sometime." After the Sheriff finished speaking there was what seemed like, a long silence.

"Well, can you come over?" Evie asked. Her voice revealed an anxious tone.

"I don't know, Evie," the Sheriff answered carefully. "I was just about to get into the tub and I'm really beat. I've had a hard day."

"It's just that we don't get these chances very often," she persisted softly. "And I need you, Tom. Don't you need me anymore?"

Tom Clark held the telephone receiver in one hand and buried his face in his other. He rubbed his eyes and took a deep breath. "Of course I still need you, Evie," he said sincerely. "It's just that I've really been busy with this killin' and all. I ain't had a lot of time for myself."

"Well, then, take a little time for yourself now," she breathed into the telephone. "I'll see to it that you get real relaxed."

He could almost see her smiling on the other end of the phone line. After a short silence, he said, "OK, I'll be over in a few minutes. I'll take a quick bath and clean up. But I can't stay very long. I don't want to take any chances of Lou coming back before I leave. Leave your back door unlocked as usual and turned out all the lights."

"OK Tom, I'll be waitin'," she replied with a laugh in her voice. She hung up and the line went dead.

Sheriff Tom Clark hung up the phone and returned to the bathroom. He felt the bath water and it was still hot. He slowly inched his way into the tub. Soon he was lying in the tub with hot water up to his neck. It felt good. He laid back and stared at the bathroom ceiling.

Evie was becoming a problem. Ever since that first time when he had gone to her when Lou was gone, he had felt that he must be careful and keep control of the relationship. But as time went by, he began to need her more and more. Recently, he had even started sending Lou on trips so that he could be with her. The whole affair was his fault of course. At first, it had been he that encouraged the secret meetings. His desire for her overcame his better judgment.

Now, she had taken control and forced meetings when he didn't want them. He did like her and she was good to him as a companion and as a sex partner. But lately she had become ever bolder. He feared that Lou would find out one day. When that happened, he would surely lose his job. Many times he had asked himself why he did it. She wasn't a beautiful girl by any means, but she fulfilled his needs and he had no one else. In addition, it was no secret between them that Evie didn't love Lou. She never had. But he didn't think she loved him either. She had been a strange girl even in High School back in Athens. He didn't know what Evie really wanted from him, but he was afraid not to keep her satisfied for fear she would tell about their relationship. She had only Lou to lose, but he had everything to lose.

—◦◦◦—

While relaxing in the hot bath water, his mind drifted back to his first meeting with Eve Von Norris. It was during his first days of High School in Athens. He lived with his parents just outside of Athens on a small farm. Normally, he would walk the two or so miles into town to school. But that was when he was in the lower grades. When he entered High School, it was a different matter. The High School was on the far side of town. As a result, he couldn't walk it in time to reach class. That being the case, his father had arranged for him to catch a ride early each morning with Mr. Jonas. Mr. Jonas had a dairy farm about ten miles outside of town and made a trip to town each morning with his daily milk supply. Mr. Jonas usually passed by the Clark place about six o'clock each morning. Tom would jump on the back of the horse-drawn wagon and ride it into town.

It was that first morning when he rode on Mr. Jonas' milk wagon that he met Evie. When he jumped onto the back of the wagon, he saw her sitting sleepily on the back of the wagon with her bare feet dangling over the side. She had her shoes tied together by the laces and they hung around her neck. She was wearing a long and simple farm dress. Her long hair hung down past the middle of her back.

"Hi," she said, after he had settled in beside her.

"Hi," he replied.

"You're Tom Clark, aren't you?" She asked, allowing her eyes to meet his.

"Yeah, I am," he answered. "How'd you know my name?"

"I've seen ya around school. Most of the girls know your name."

"Why is that?" He asked, taking his eyes away from hers.

"Most of the girls think you're handsome," she replied without taking her eyes away from him. She could tell she was making him

82

uncomfortable. "As for me, outside of bein' big, I think you look kind of ordinary."

He returned his gaze to her and looked long and hard into her face. The early morning sun was shining on her face and the soft breeze from the movement of the wagon blew her hair gently across her shoulders. She certainly wasn't overly beautiful, but she did radiate a simple beauty and sexuality.

"Thanks," he finally replied. "I'll remember that. What's your name? Why is it I don't know you? I know most folks around these parts."

"Well, my name is Eve Von Norris, but my friends call me Evie. As for why you don't know me, I guess you just don't pay attention. I live in Clinton, but I've been goin' to school here in Athens most of my life."

"Maybe it's just that I don't know many folks in Clinton," he replied in a sarcastic tone. "Have you been ridin' with Mr. Jonas all this time?"

"Yes, for a long time, but my Dad brings me in sometimes. It's a long walk from Clinton to here. I catch Mr. Jonas when I can, but I can't always make it."

"I'm glad you made it today," he said with his best smile. "I think I'll start payin' better attention."

She looked at him and a smile grew across her face. "I think maybe I'll start payin' a little better attention myself," she said in a more serious tone.

⸻

That was how it had started. He and Evie had become friends and even had dated some. But nothing serious ever grew out of their relationship, at least not from his standpoint. He never knew how to take Evie. She was always very straight forward. She made him uncomfortable with the way she could always seem to know exactly what he was thinking. When they were dating, she was able to get him to do things he didn't really want to do. He didn't like the way she was able to control him. After graduation, they went their separate ways. Evie went to Dallas to work and Tom joined the Athens Sheriff Department. They hadn't seen each other much until Evie showed up in Coalville with Lou Mailer as her husband.

Tom suddenly opened his eyes and wondered how long he had been day dreaming. Slowly, he stood up and stepped out of the tub. He pulled a towel from its rack and dried himself. He reached over and picked up his watch. Checking the time, he quickened his movements. After getting dressed, he went outside and got into his patrol car. It was only a short drive to Lou and Evie's house. He turned his car lights off and parked the car two blocks away in an old unused garage.

Quietly, he got out of the car and locked it. Then, checking carefully in all directions, he darted into the alley behind the abandoned garage. He followed the alley the two blocks to the Mailer house. Soon he was at the back door of the house. Evie had turned out all the lights and it was very dark. He was sure no one had seen him. The back door was unlocked as usual. He took one last look around, and then went inside.

CHAPTER FOURTEEN

Feelings

For several weeks after the death of Moonbeam, the relationship between Dee and Cherrie was strained. For the first time in their young lives, they seemed to have a hard time talking to each other. Most of the problems were on Dee's part, because of the doubt he had in himself. Cherrie, on the other hand, was willing to continue to follow Dee even though she didn't agree with his silence. Finally, Dee could no longer stand the air of tension. One night as they lay in bed ready for sleep, Dee decided to bring everything out into the open and clear things up with Cherrie. He stared up at the ceiling in the darkness of their room and formulated what he was going to say in his head.

"Cherrie, can we talk for a little while?" Dee asked quietly.

"Sure. I'm not all that sleepy anyway," she replied.

"Listen, Cherrie, I can't stand the way things are between us."

"What do you mean?" She asked, pretending not to understand.

"You know what I mean!" He whispered loudly.

He turned in his bed and propped himself up on his elbow. "Things aren't the same since Moonbeam's death. You and I have been actin' different. It's like we can't talk to each other anymore. I don't like it like this, Cherrie. You've always been my best friend. I don't want to lose you as my best friend."

Cherrie pushed herself up in her bed into a sitting position and leaned back against the wall. She looked over to Dee's bed. Even in the dark, she could see his outline. She was quiet for a while, and then spoke. "I know, Dee," she said softly. "I'm sorry, but keepin' this swear is one of the hardest things I've ever had to do in all my life. I just know we're wrong in not tellin' what we know. Somehow I think we're makin' a bad mistake. I just keep waitin' from day to day for somethin' else to happen. I mean somethin' bad. I don't mean to be the way I've been. I'm still your best friend and I always will be, but I don't know what to say to you."

"Can't we just go on like we always have?" Dee pleaded. "Nothin' has changed between you and me, has it?"

"No, nothin' has changed between us, Dee. But I can't believe you don't think other things have changed. As long as it's you and me I'm okay, but other folks are gettin' hurt."

"Maybe nothin' else is goin' to happen," Dee challenged. "We can't do anythin' about what's already happened, can we?"

"Dee, are you goin' to tell me that you think Moonbeam is the last of it?" Cherrie asked in a harsh whisper. "Or are you like Billy Bob and just don't care?"

Cherrie's last question hit Dee hard. He remembered how he reacted when Billy Bob had called Moonbeam a 'nigger'. He didn't see himself as like Billy Bob and he wondered how Cherrie could. Most of all, he was hurt that she would even mention the possibility.

"Cherrie, you mean you think I don't care about what happened to Moonbeam?"

"No, Dee, I don't mean that," she answered in frustration. "Oh! I don't know what I mean!"

"It's been three weeks and nothin' else has happened," Dee explained. "Stick with me a little longer and see if it blows over. If I thought it would help catch the ones that killed Moonbeam, I'd tell everythin' right now. But they were all wearin' hoods and we don't even know who they were."

"But don't you see, Dee? It'd have to help some because we do know that Ruth and Dick Jordan were there. Don't you think that would be a good startin' place for the Sheriff or somebody?"

Dee didn't answer her question right away, because he couldn't. Her logic was always better than his. It made him wonder why he was keeping all of this a secret. He knew his dad would be plenty mad at them if he found out. But Cherrie didn't seem to be worried about their parent's reaction. But she's not the one that would get the whipping, it would be him. Plus, he just hated to let his dad down. His dad always seemed so hurt when Dee or Cherrie disobeyed him. It was like he never expected his kids to be disobedient and when they were, it crushed him.

"OK, maybe you're right," Dee finally replied. "I'll make a deal with you. We'll wait two more weeks, and then I promise we'll go to dad and mom and tell them everything we know."

"Why wait two more weeks?" Cherrie asked in a puzzled voice.

"I'd like more time for things to settle down before I tell dad and I need some time with Billy Bob and Sue Ann to see if they care if we tell," he replied.

"But what if somethin' else happens before two weeks is up?" She asked.

"In that case, we tell dad and mom right away. Is that okay? Can you wait a little longer?"

"Yeah, I guess so," she answered. "But what're ya goin' to say to Billy Bob and Sue Ann?"

"Well, we made them swear to keep quiet and they have. So, it's only fair that we ask them about it before we tell everything. The swear works both ways you know."

"Yeah, that's true," Cherrie said thoughtfully. "How're things with you and Billy Bob anyway? Have you talked to him since the hill?"

"Not much, just school talk. He still thinks I'm mad at him about somethin' and he doesn't know about what. It's goin' to be hard for me to be friends with him again. He believes colored folks are nothin'. It didn't bother him at all about Moonbeam. It's hard to believe it didn't bother him at all, but I don't think it did."

"You know, it's funny, but I don't think Sue Ann is that way," Cherrie added. "I've talked to her at school and she's really scared. And I'll tell you somethin' else, she thinks one of those hooded men was her Dad."

Dee shot straight up in bed. "When did she say that?" He asked, almost in a shout.

"Not so loud, dummy," Cherrie whispered hoarsely. "It was about a week ago at school. We were talkin' about what we had seen and what we thought we ought to do and I noticed she looked scared. I asked her what the matter was. She told me she thought that she heard her dad's voice. She couldn't tell which one, but she was almost sure one of the men was her dad. And, what's more, she said Billy Bob thought so too."

"How come you didn't tell me this?" Dee asked.

"I didn't want to cause you any more problems. Anyway, I figured that if you knew about Mr. Barnett you never would say anythin' about what we saw to anybody."

"Well, what did she say she was goin' to do?" Dee asked.

"She didn't say. I guess they figure we're all just goin' to keep quiet like we swore we would."

"Is she afraid of her dad?" Dee pressed.

"I don't think so, but I'm sure she doesn't want to get him into any trouble," Cherrie stated. "But I know she feels the same way about Moonbeam as we do. She's different from Billy Bob."

"Mr. Barnett one of the Klan. What's goin' to be next?" Dee whispered.

"But, Dee, what if they won't let us break the swear because of gettin' their dad in trouble? What're you goin' to do then? Are we still goin' to tell after two weeks?"

"Gee, I don't know, Cherrie. I never broke a swear before. There's no tellin' what'll happen to us if we break a swear. I think we should all get together after school and talk this thing out tomorrow. Since I'm the one that made everyone swear, maybe they'll break it if I'm the one that wants to."

"Well, I hate to break a swear, but I say we stick to our two-week deal no matter what they say!" Cherrie said firmly.

"OK, I agree with you, but let me try and talk them into breakin' the swear. I hate to chance breakin' a swear without it bein' okay."

"Okay, we talk to them after school tomorrow, but no matter what they say we stick to our two-week deal." Cherrie said pointedly. "Okay, Dee?"

"Okay, I promise to stick to our deal no matter what. But I sure hope they agree. I don't like the idea of breakin' a swear!" Dee exclaimed.

The two were quiet for several minutes; each one thinking too themselves. "OK, I guess we better hit the sack," Dee said at last breaking the silence. "But before we go to sleep, tell me it's OK between you and me Cherrie."

"It's OK, Dee. It always has been," she replied. With that, Dee smiled and lay down and went to sleep.

<hr />

The next day at school things didn't work out as Dee had planned. He had forgotten that Billy Bob and Sue Ann rode the school bus and could not meet after school. The other problem was that Sue Ann was in a grade below the others and didn't have the same class schedule. However, everyone did have the same lunch schedule. So, at lunch Dee grabbed Billy Bob and Cherrie got Sue Ann.

They all met behind the gym and sat on the ground to eat their bag lunches. Billy Bob and Sue Ann didn't know what the meeting was about but they had a fairly good idea. Billy Bob wasn't his normal carefree self. The smile he always wore on his face was gone. He looked suspicious and worried. Sue Ann looked big-eyed and scared.

"What's this all about, Dee?" Billy Bob asked coolly as he bit into a sandwich. "This got somethin' ta do with the hill?"

"Yes, it does," Dee replied. As they talked, each one started eating their lunch.

"Well, whatever it is we don't want any part of it. We're not doin' anythin' else that has ta do with that hill," Billy Bob stated looking over at Sue Ann. Sue Ann nodded her head in agreement but didn't say anything.

"We don't want you to do anythin'." Dee said. "We just want you to let us out of our swear so we can tell our mom and dad about what we saw."

Cherrie sat quietly watching munching on an apple.

Billy Bob and Sue Ann looked at each other and then back to Dee. "Why do ya want to tell anybody anythin'?" Billy Bob asked slowly.

"Cherrie and I have been talkin' and we're afraid that somethin' else might happen and it would be our fault for not tellin' what we know," Dee said in his most reasonable tone.

"What do you think will happen?" Billy Bob asked suspiciously.

"I don't know," Dee replied quickly. "Maybe somethin' like what happened to Moonbeam."

"So what," Billy Bob said sharply.

That was it for Dee. He got up on his knees, reached across the spread out lunches, and punched Billy Bob in the mouth. Billy Bob fell backwards from his sitting position. He rolled over and got to his feet holding his mouth. Dee was on his feet quickly and standing in front of Billy Bob with his fist doubled up.

"Why'd ya do that?" Billy Bob shouted almost in tears.

"I don't like your give-a-shit attitude," Dee growled with his teeth clenched. "Come on, make some other wise-ass remark!"

Cherrie dropped her apple in shock. She didn't know Dee used that kind of language. Quickly, she got to her feet and jumped in between the two boys. "You two stop it!" She shouted. She pushed Dee back and turned to face Billy Bob. "All we want is for you to let us out of the swear so we can tell our parents about what we saw."

"No, I ain't lettin' you out of our swear," Billy Bob shouted back. He sounded hurt and afraid. He wasn't the same smart, sure person he was when the conversation started.

"Come on, Billy Bob, why not?" Cherrie pleaded.

"'cause, I just ain't," Billy Bob shot back. "We did our part of keepin' quiet. We kept the swear. Now just because you want ta break the swear it supposed ta be okay. Well, it ain't."

Billy Bob was near tears and a small trickle of blood had started running from his mouth down his chin.

"That's not it, Billy Bob!" Cherrie pleaded. "We just don't want anybody else to get hurt."

"Oh, stop tryin' to talk to him. He's too dumb to understand," Dee shouted.

Suddenly everyone stopped shouting and just looked at each other, not speaking. Finally, Sue Ann stepped forward. She was holding her hands to her mouth. Tears were forming in her eyes. She looked as though she was fighting a great battle inside herself. Slowly she walked up to the others. They turned and looked at her. So far she had said nothing. Billy Bob had done all of the talking for them both. She walked up to Billy Bob and looked up at him.

"Let 'em out of the swear," she said softly.

"Sue Ann!" Billy Bob pleaded. "What if it really was Dad? What then?"

"Let 'em out of the swear," Sue Ann repeated slowly pronouncing each word clearly. Then, she put her arms around Billy Bob's waist and pulled herself to him and buried her face in his chest. Billy Bob placed his hand on top of her head and patted it gently.

"Okay, you're out of the swear," he said quietly as he looked up at Dee. "Come on, Sis, let's go."

Billy Bob and Sue Ann gathered up their remaining lunch and discarded paper, and then they turned away from Dee and Cherrie and walked off toward the school yard.

"Thanks, Sue Ann," Cherrie called after them. But they didn't look back.

After they had gone, Cherrie turned to Dee and said, "Well, we're out of the swear."

"Yeah, we're out of the swear," Dee repeated in a lonely voice.

"Now what's the matter with you? Isn't that what you wanted?"

"Yeah, that's what we came for," he said.

"Then, why do you look so gloomy? You're not thinkin' of backin' out on our two-week deal are you?" Cherrie asked sharply.

"No, I'm not goin' to back out," Dee stated. "It's just this didn't turn out the way I thought it would. I never thought it would hurt them so much and for some reason I never saw Billy Bob and Sue Ann to be so close. They're always fightin' and fussin' with each other. They're so different. I never expected to see them hug each other and help each other."

"What did you expect? They're brother and sister," Cherrie stated in a matter-a-fact tone.

"I'm not sure what I expected," Dee said. "Come on we better pick up this stuff and get back to class."

As they started back to class, Cherrie looked over to Dee and asked, "When did you start using words like 'give-a-shit' and 'wise-ass'?"

"Not long ago," Dee replied smiling.

"I wouldn't smile if I were you," she said. "I don't think Mom or Dad would like that kind of language."

"I don't think they would either. That's why I never use it in front of 'em."

"Yeah, sure," Cherrie said sarcastically.

The rest of the day in school, Dee couldn't get the scene at lunch out of his head. He felt bad about hitting Billy Bob and had made up his mind to apologize tomorrow. But the thing that bothered Dee the most was the fact that he had thought less of the relationship between Billy Bob and Sue Ann than he had of himself and Cherrie. For some reason, he had never believed that Billy Bob could feel about his sister as Dee felt about his, or that Sue Ann could feel about her brother as Cherrie felt about him. The realization that Billy Bob and Sue Ann could have feelings just like his and Cherrie's made him see them in a different light. Earlier, he had decided he didn't like Billy Bob anymore because of his attitude toward colored people. But now he found that he had things in common with Billy Bob of which he had been unaware and that Billy Bob's attitude toward colored people was probably not his fault.

Dee had always had colored people around him and he was taught to respect everyone. Billy Bob and Sue Ann obviously had not had that kind of environment. Dee decided that he should spend more time with Billy Bob. He wanted to patch up their friendship.

Another thing that surprised Dee was the fact that Cherrie was not surprised at all at the way Billy Bob and Sue Ann acted. It had seemed to her a normal way for brother and sister to act. She didn't make anything big about it because she thought it was a normal reaction. She just assumed that all brothers and sisters cared for each other deep down. He wondered if that was the same way Billy Bob thought about colored people. It seemed to be a normal reaction for him to disregard them. Just as Cherrie had grown up in an environment of love and trust in her brother, Billy Bob had grown up with an environment of disregard for colored people. As a result, each one believed their actions to be normal. Billy Bob and Sue Ann were obviously raised in an environment that taught them to care for one another. Because, even though it rarely showed on the surface, they had a deep feeling for each other as brother and sister.

Dee had been very impressed by Sue Ann. Even though he was only one year older than her, he had always thought of her as just a little kid. She had been scared, but she did the right thing anyway. And the simple and direct way she convinced Billy Bob to give in was something he would never forget. She was somebody he would like to get to know better. He wanted time alone with Sue Ann when Billy Bob and Cherrie were not there. Anyway she was kind of cute even if she was just a kid.

Another thing that pressed upon his mind was the fact that of the four of them only the girls seemed not to fear punishment. It was Cherrie, not Dee, who had been willing to accept their parent's punishment for going up on the hill. And it was Sue Ann who pushed Billy Bob into dropping the swear not knowing what effect it would have on her Dad, or for that matter, her entire family. He had always been so sure what courage and bravery were. It was a simple matter for him to think of those two things in terms of strength, or being strong. Things that boys have and girls do not have. But now he was not so sure anymore. Maybe courage and bravery don't have to be thought of only in terms of strength. Courage and bravery must come from something inside a person. He was concerned because it appeared that Cherrie and Sue Ann had that something inside and he did not.

Dee thought about all of these things in his twelve-year-old mind. Not all of the things he thought about were completely clear to him, but he decided one thing. That the way you react to certain things is something you are taught and not something that comes natural. Billy Bob was the way he is because he simply didn't know any better. But in the end that didn't matter either because people were being hurt. Not knowing any better couldn't be an excuse for hurting people. That much he knew. His Mother had told him and Cherrie both that the main reason they went to school was not only to get a good education, but also to learn how to make good decisions. The more you knew, the better was your ability to make correct judgements. Up to this point, Dee didn't feel he had made very many good decisions.

CHAPTER FIFTEEN

The Surprise

The sun had just set in the early evening as Sheriff Tom Clark pulled his patrol car into the driveway at the Mailer house. Earlier in the day, Louis Mailer had invited him to dinner. Sheriff Clark had reluctantly accepted. He didn't really want to have dinner with the Mailers. He felt very uncomfortable being with Evie and Louis at the same time, but Louis had pressured him by saying he had an important announcement that they all should share. Try as he may, the Sheriff couldn't get Louis to reveal his announcement. Louis insisted on the Sheriff coming over for dinner at which time the announcement would be made. Finally, the Sheriff had agreed to come.

Sheriff Clark finished parking the car and turned off the engine and lights. He sat in the darkness for a short while looking at the house. It was a small house with two bedrooms. It was, however, larger than the Sheriff's house. The people of Coalville didn't pay for the deputy's house as they did for the Sheriff's. Knowing this, it amazed Sheriff Clark that Louis could afford the mortgage payment on his small salary. Lester Homes' bank held the mortgage on the house. This was not unusual as Lester's bank held the mortgage on most everyone's house. On the other hand, Louis was allowed a city paid patrol car just like the Sheriff's.

A small dim light lit the front porch and doorway. The Sheriff could see activity in the house through the two front windows that were positioned on either side of the door. He took a deep breath and got out of the patrol car. He walked up the front steps and knocked on the door. He had only waited a few seconds when Evie came to the door.

"Hello, Tom. I'm so glad you could come. Come on in," Evie said as she allowed him into the house.

"Well, thank you for havin' me. It's not too often a single man like me gets some good home cookin'," the Sheriff laughed.

"Hey, Tom, come on in this house," Louis yelled from the kitchen. "I'm gettin' us a couple of beers. I'll be right there."

"Come on over and set down. Lou'll be here in just a minute," Evie said as she led the way into the living area.

Sheriff Clark followed Evie into the living area and sat down in a nearby chair. Evie sat down across from the Sheriff on the divan. She was dressed in a loose fitting light brown colored skirt that hung to just above her ankles. The skirt was made of thin cotton that clung to her body as she walked. When she sat down, she crossed her legs and adjusted the skirt to just above her knees exposing smooth bare legs. She wore a white sleeveless blouse that fit snug to her body accenting her breasts but making her long neck appear even longer. The top two buttons were loose exposing a small amount of cleavage. On her feet, she wore simple flat-heeled black shoes. Still, as was her nature, she wore no makeup causing her plain features to be more visible. Her hair was pushed back into a pony tail that added youth to her look. As Sheriff Clark looked across at her, he thought he had never seen her look so lovely.

Just then, Louis came walking into the room laughing and carrying two bottles of beer. "Hey, Tom boy, are ya ready for some good grub."

"You can bet on that," the Sheriff replied taking his eyes away from Evie and looking at Louis. He took the beer Louis handed him and then watched as Louis sat down by his wife. "Now, what's this big announcement anyway? I've been wonderin' about it all day."

"Oh no, not so fast," Louis replied. "We gotta eat first."

"Jesus, Lou. That ain't fair," the Sheriff moaned. "You can't keep me waitin' any longer."

"Hell, I can't," Louis laughed. "Anyway, I'm goin' to let Evie make the announcement." Louis put his arm around his wife and pulled her to him. He placed a kiss on her cheek as she playfully tried to pull away.

"Lou, don't act like this in front of company," she said pulling away and standing up. "I'll go set the table. We'll be ready to eat in a jiffy." With that, she hurried out of the room.

"She looks good, don't she?" Lou asked as he turned the beer bottle up and took a long drink.

"Yeah, she does, Lou," the Sheriff answered simply.

"Okay, y'all come and get it," Evie called from the kitchen. The two men came into the kitchen and took seats at the table. Evie brought two more beers for the men and then joined them at the table. The kitchen table was small but it was covered with food. There were chicken fried steaks, big fluffy biscuits, pan gravy, mashed potatoes and a variety of vegetables. The food smelled delicious. Lou started to reach across the table for the biscuits, but his hand received a hard slap from Evie. "Hold your horses," she demanded. "We haven't said Grace."

"Ouch!" Lou yelled, jerking his hand back.

"Lou, as the man of the house, would you lead us in grace?" Evie's question was more of an order than a request. Lou nodded as everyone bowed their heads.

"Dear Heavenly Father, please bless this food of which we are about to partake. Thank you for our blessings and our friends. Amen." Lou looked up at Evie and smiled. "Now is it okay to eat?"

"Dig in!" She replied.

The meal proceeded with a lot of small talk, mostly about the death of Moonbeam and the progress being made in the case. It was concluded by all that not much progress had been made and that the threat of the Klan was real.

"Well, I for one think it is the Klan," Lou said pushing himself back from the table. "Who else would do somethin' like that and leave that kind of note?"

"Yeah, you're probably right," Tom replied pushing his plate away from him. "That was really good, Evie. But, I don't think I could eat another bite."

"Oh, but you've got to," Evie stated. "I've got fresh apple pie warming in the oven."

"Jesus no, Evie," Tom moaned. "Where am I goin' to put pie?"

"We'll go set in the livin' room for a while 'til your dinner has settled, then I'll dish up the pie after I've sent Lou out for ice cream," she said smiling.

"Ice cream, too?" Tom asked holding his stomach.

"Hey, why do I have to go out for ice cream? Why didn't you tell me earlier?" Lou demanded.

"Because I didn't know if the pie was goin' to be ready or not," she replied smiling at Lou.

"Then Tom is goin' with me!"

"Oh, no he's not. Tom is our company and he's stayin' right here and relaxin'," she shot back at Lou.

"I really don't mind, Evie," Tom interjected.

"I'll not discuss it anymore," she said, closing the subject. "You two go on in the livin' room while I clean up the kitchen. It'll only take me a few minutes then I'll join you. Do you want another beer to take with you?"

"Not if I'm goin' to have pie and ice cream," Tom stated as he got up from the table slowly still holding his stomach. He turned and started walking toward the living room with Lou close behind him. "And when am I goin' to hear this announcement?" He shouted over his shoulder.

"As soon as Evie finishes and can join us," Lou said pushing Tom from behind.

Tom and Lou located themselves in the living room and sat quietly for short time. Then Lou spoke. "She's a great cook ain't she?"

"You can say that again. That's the best meal I've had in a long while."

"I think I got me a great girl, don't you Tom?"

"Yeah, Lou, I think you really do," Tom answered slowly not looking directly at Lou.

"I mean she's a good cook, she takes good care of me, and she's great in bed," Lou said, winking his eye. "Man, I'm a lucky guy."

"Some guys get all the luck," Tom said with a small smile on his lips.

"When're you goin' ta find you a wife?" Lou asked seriously. "Ain't it about time ya found you somebody?"

"Lou, you're not goin' to fix me up again are you?" Tom asked lowering his voice so Evie couldn't hear. "That last girl from Dallas that you fixed me up with was a real strange one. She was like a bitch in heat. I couldn't keep up with her."

"What's wrong with that?" Lou asked laughing. "That's the kind of girl most guys want."

"It's not that. It's just that if I'm lookin' for a wife, I'd like us to have a few more things in common."

Lou threw his head back and laughed. "You son-of-a-bitch, you sure are choosey."

"You might be surprised," Tom said, laughing along with Lou.

"Anyway, I think you should find you a wife. Then you could be happy like me," Lou said seriously.

"Yes, when are you goin' to find you a woman?" Evie asked as she walked into the room. She had obviously finished in the kitchen and then gone to the bathroom to freshen up. She looked just as good now as she had when Tom had first arrived.

"You two don't know everythin'," Tom said. "I may have some things goin' on that y'all don't know about."

Evie set down on the divan by Lou. Again, she made sure her dress was adjusted above her knees as she crossed her legs. She moved close to Lou so he couldn't see her face. Then she looked at Tom with knowing and smiling eyes. Pushing back against Lou, she said, "That's interestin', Tom. Maybe you should fill us in."

"No, I don't think so," Tom replied. "But I do think you two can make your announcement now. We've waited all day and through dinner. So, here we all are just as you planned. Now, how about it? What's up?"

"OK! Evie, tell him," Lou said with a huge smile on his face.

Evie pulled away from Lou and set up straight uncrossing her legs. She clasped her hands together and put them in her lap. She leaned forward and looked straight into Tom's eyes. "I'm pregnant. I'm goin' to have a baby," she said bluntly.

Tom was stunned. For a minute he was so shocked, that he couldn't hear Lou's laughter. Lou had grabbed Evie and pulled her to him in a big bear hug. While she was being hugged by Lou, her eyes stayed locked on Tom's.

"Well, what do you think?" Lou asked happily. "I'm goin' ta be a daddy!"

"That's great, Lou," Tom said, regaining his composure. "I must admit this takes me completely by surprise." Evie had stopped looking at Tom and pulled herself away from Lou's bear hug. She stood up and walked behind the divan and stood behind Lou placing her hands on his shoulders. Again, she looked hard at Tom.

"It was a surprise to me to," Lou said. "I just found out this week. I've been dyin' ta tell you, but Evie wanted to surprise you like this."

"Well, it's sure a surprise," Tom said carefully. "Are you sure about it?"

"I'm sure," Evie said quietly. "Doc Jewel just confirmed it on Monday."

"Are you happy for us?" Lou asked.

"You know I am. If this is what y'all want, then I'm really happy for you. I just didn't know y'all were tryin' to have a baby." Tom's last sentence slowly tapered off.

"To tell the truth, I wasn't even thinkin' about it. It just happened," Lou stated.

"I guess it's just one of those things that happen," Evie said softly. "You don't plan for them, but there they are." Evie moved back around to the front of the divan and looked down at Lou. "Okay, you future daddy, run out and get that ice cream while I keep the pie warm."

"I'm on my way. Should only take me about twenty minutes," Lou said, jumping to his feet. Tom started to get up from his chair but Lou pushed him back down. "You just stay put and take it easy. I'll be right back." With that, he started for the door. Evie followed close behind him not looking back at Tom.

She watched as he went out and got into his patrol car. He waved as he drove away and out of sight. Evie pushed the door closed and turned around to face Tom. She leaned back against the door and stared at him. They looked at each other without talking. Her lips were turned upward in a smug smile. She pushed herself away from the door and walked into the kitchen. She checked the oven and pie, then, adjusted the flame down lower so the pie would stay warm but not burn. Tom had followed her and was watching quietly. He was standing in the kitchen doorway when she turned away from the oven. "Are you afraid?" She asked, as she walked passed him into the living room.

"Should I be?" He responded, as he followed her again.

Evie walked over to the divan and kicked off her shoes. She climbed up on the divan with her bare feet and knelt down on the soft pillows. "It's hot in here," she said as she lifted her skirt to fan herself exposing herself all the way to her waist. She wasn't wearing any underwear.

"Stop it!" Tom yelled. "I asked you a question; should I be?"

"I don't know, Tom," she answered softly. "I guess it depends on what you're afraid of. Are you afraid of Lou or are you afraid this is your baby, or are you afraid of both?"

"I get the feelin' you're tryin' to make me think that the baby is mine," he answered. He moved over to the divan and stood looking down at her.

"It probably is," she replied. "If I had to guess, I'd say it was. Lou and I, well, we just don't do that well in bed."

"Well, he thinks you do."

"Yeah, I know. He thinks he's a great lover."

"So, what do I do? Sweat it out for nine months to find out if it's mine." He continued to tower over her as he talked.

"You don't ever have to know if you don't want to," she answered.

"Won't it be obvious when the baby is born? I mean the way it looks and its blood type and all."

"Maybe," she said shrugging her shoulders, "but still only Doc and me will know for sure and he won't say anything. If you don't want to know, I won't tell you." She looked up at him softly.

"But I'll know! One way or the other, I'll know!" He was almost shouting. "And probably Lou will know too," he said, lowering his voice.

"Lou will never know if we don't want him to. He's not that smart and anyway he's so happy about being a daddy he won't notice anything. He'll only know if I tell him." She continued to look up at him as she spoke.

"But if it's mine, what'll I do?" He asked softly. "I can't just let it go. I'll want you and the baby, but Lou is my friend and you know what this'll do to him!"

Evie stood up on the divan and faced him. She now towered over him. His face came to just below her breast. She reached out and took his head in her hands and pulled it to her breast. He allowed her to hold him tight. Then, as if losing control, he slid his hands under her dress and up her bare legs until he reached her hips. She caught her breath as he squeezed her hips hard enough to hurt.

"You know I don't love Lou," she breathed. "I'll do anythin' you ask me to do. I'll have this baby and let Lou think it's his if that's what you want. And I'll live with him the rest of my life if that's what you want, or I'll take this baby and leave Lou and come be with you if that's what you want. I'll do whatever you want me to do except one thing. I won't stop seein' you. I don't ever want to stop seein' you."

"But Jesus, Evie, what about Lou?" He whispered with his head still pressed against her breast. "I can't do this to Lou." He gathered all his emotional strength and pulled away from her. He turned his back to her and continued. "Every time I sneak over here I feel like dirt. I hate doin' this."

"Then why do you do it?" She asked simply as she stepped down from the divan and walked up behind him. Tom turned around to face her. He reached out and grabbed her by her ponytail and pulled her to him. His grip was so tight that she was forced to stand on her tip toes.

"Because I need you," he growled, "because I need your body. I like bein' between your legs. I like bein' with you. You make me feel good all over. I can't say I love you, but I damn sure need you." When he finished talking, he released her hair but she didn't move. She stayed pressed up against him. Then, as if he surrendered to something inside of him, he put his arms around her and squeezed her tight. "Will that be enough? Because, I can't promise I love you."

"Yes," she breathed. "I'm here any time you need me or want me. But what are we goin' to do? What do you want me to do?"

"Nothin' for now," he said as if surrendering, "I guess we should wait 'til after the baby is born. Then, I guess things will take their own course."

"Are you sure that's what you want?" She asked. "It may be easier on Lou to tell him now than later."

"Tell him what?" He growled pulling away from her. "Tell him you're not sure it's his baby? Tell him we've been bangin' behind his back? We can't do that now! You're not even sure if the baby is mine or not."

"I told you, I'm almost sure," she answered. Then after a short pause she continued. "OK, I guess you're right. But it won't matter to me if the baby is his or not. After the baby, I'm comin' with you. Can we agree on that?"

"Yeah, we can agree on that. I guess we deserve each other."

As they stood there talking, they heard Lou pull up and park the patrol car. Evie quickly pulled on her shoes and ran into the kitchen. Tom hurried over and sat in his chair. The scene was very normal when Lou came through the front door.

"I got some fresh made vanilla ice cream," he beamed. "Old man Johnson had closed his store, but I got him to open up for me. I told him it was a special occasion."

"Sounds good," Tom said, standing up.

"Where's Evie?" Lou asked.

"I'm in here," Evie yelled from the kitchen. "I'm just gettin' the pie out of the oven. Bring the ice cream and I'll serve it up."

Both men hurried into the kitchen where Evie was cutting the pie. Lou set the ice cream on the kitchen table and walked up behind Evie and wrapped his arms around her. He leaned over and kissed her on the neck. She pulled away from him playfully. "I told you not to do that in front of company." She hurried about putting the pie on plates and topping it with huge helpings of ice cream.

"Man, that looks good," Lou said grinning at Tom.

"It looks like more than I can eat," Tom replied.

"Okay, everybody dig in," Evie said as they all sat down at the table. "This'll be my last time for stuff like this. The Doc told me not to gain any weight, so from now on I better watch what I eat."

"Yeah, you better take care of that boy of mine," Lou laughed.

"What makes you so sure it's goin' to be a boy?" Tom asked.

"Just a feelin' I've got. My family usually has boys."

After the pie and ice cream, Tom stood up patting his stomach. "I've got to go, people," he said. "I'm so full I can hardly walk and I've got to be up early in the mornin'." He walked out of the kitchen and toward the front door. "I'm glad for you and Evie, Lou. I hope everythin' works out for you both." At the door, he turned and grabbed Lou's hand and shook it.

"Thanks for comin' over, Tom," Lou said, shaking Tom's hand sincerely.

"Evie, thanks for the meal, it was great."

"I'm glad you enjoyed it," she said reaching up and kissing him on the cheek.

"Well, I'll see you in the mornin', Lou." With that, Sheriff Tom Clark went out the door and got into his patrol car. He waved to Evie and Lou, who were standing on the porch, as he drove away.

———

Tom drove his car out of sight of the Mailer house and then pulled it over to the side of the road and stopped. He turned out the lights and killed the engine. He leaned back in the driver's seat and ran his hands through his hair. "Damn it," he yelled, slamming his fist against the steering wheel. His mind was racing with a hundred ideas of how to handle this new development. In his heart, he was sure the baby was his. However, he was also sure he didn't really love Evie. He had told her the truth about needing her, and he hated himself for it.

He hated himself for needing Evie just about as much as he hated himself for what this would do to Lou. Not that Lou was a close and good friend, but he just didn't like the dishonesty of it all. He wasn't sure what he would do. One thing he was sure of, when all of this came out, he would surely not be reelected as Sheriff. Then what would he do? This was his life. Evie had said she would continue to live with Lou no matter whose baby it turned out to be, if that's what he wanted. But if it was his baby, he wasn't sure that's what he wanted. He wasn't sure his own sense of manhood would allow him to do that sort of thing. At this point, he was confused and worried. He just didn't know what he wanted to do. Taking a deep breath, he cranked the car and drove on into the night trying to understand how he had gotten himself into this kind of mess.

Meanwhile, Evie was in the bathroom preparing for bed. She was trying to calm herself down after the events of the night. Her mind was not filled with hundreds of ideas of how to handle the situation. There was only one idea, and that was to leave Lou and live with Tom as his wife or otherwise. She wanted Tom and she was determined to have him. She loved him and enjoyed him as a man. The way he handled her filled her with lust. Not like Lou, who didn't know how to please a woman, but like a man who could give a woman pleasure. She knew the baby was Tom's, because she knew her own body and when she had become pregnant. Anyway, she didn't think Lou was man enough to get her pregnant.

"Hey, Evie, when are you comin' to bed?" Lou called to her from the bedroom.

"I'm on my way," she shouted back. She looked at herself in the mirror and smiled. She adjusted her nightgown to look more revealing. Then, she went to the bedroom and got into bed with Lou.

CHAPTER SIXTEEN

Next Example

A tall man dressed in a black robe and hood stood looking out over a congregation of eight men dressed in white robes and hoods. The room, in which they stood, was small and dimly lighted. But then, the shack itself was small. The single light bulb hanging from the ceiling did little to illuminate the dark night. It did, however, cast soft shadows on the hooded figures. Everything was quiet and waiting. Everyone was waiting for the man in black to speak. Finally, he did speak.

"Y'all know why we're here. At this meeting tonight, we will make plans to make ourselves known. We now have the people in town wondering. Is it, or isn't it? Our next step is to let them know. We will let them know we are here and why we are here. We will let them know we are here to protect their constitutional rights, which are being violated. We will let them know that there's still a line between white and black. We will show them that they don't have to remain quiet and sullen while they're being insulted and degraded. They will find their strength through us. Through us they'll be able to show the nigger that this is a white community and will remain so. I will tell you how we will show them all these things."

He stopped and allowed all of this to soak in. His eyes roamed across the congregation checking movements and reactions. Then his gaze fell over to his right where three people sat. The three wore no hoods or robes, but sat completely exposed for all to see. He studied the expression on Ruth Jordan's face. It was an expression of careful thought that showed much concern over the words he had spoken. It also showed much admiration and maybe even love.

He felt confident in Ruth Jordan. The expression on Dick Jordan's face showed nothing that could be read. Dick simply watched the proceedings with little interest. This was a worry to him, because the youth would be needed. He hoped Ruth could keep her son in line. The face of the hobo looking man showed nothing but the need for liquor. A need he frequently quenched by reaching into his back pocket.

The tall black-hooded figure then returned his gaze to the white hoods standing and sitting in front of him. Everyone was quiet, waiting for him to continue. "There are some niggers in this town who don't know their places or who don't care," he started again. "One has been made an example of. But not a total example, for we gave no indication of our reason or cause. Furthermore, we did not show ourselves. The next example will be different."

This caused a slight movement and a few mumbled words. Now he was talking about another example. This would be their next move. They listened for him to speak again in his steady unaccented voice. They could tell he was not from East Texas or even Texas for that matter. His speech was too refined and smooth. He used no big words, but his speech was clear and free of an accent. They were not sure where he was from but he spoke forcefully and, they thought, truthfully. When complete silence returned, he spoke again.

"The next example will be different," he repeated. "We will let our cause, reason, and presence be known. We will need the help of the whole town. We will need unification. We will have to be unified to prevent the law from interfering; the law of the unconstitutional." He stopped again, but only briefly.

"The family of James Collie sees fit to allow a nigger to live on their property in the white community. Who is the guiltier? Is it the nigger for living out of her place in a white community, or is it the white for catering to the nigger? I can tell you it's the white for degrading his neighbors by allowing a nigger to live in their community? Both are at fault and we will make an example of both. But this time we will let it be known who made this example and why. And then the town will respect us and we'll have our strength in unification. For us, it'll be one to protect the other. Now, my plan for the Collies is a simple one . . . "

He talked on, his words stirring the minds and wills of his listeners. They felt strong in their group; one to protect the other.

As they listened to him speak, a figure sneaked away from the window of the shack. It was the figure of a tall and slender young girl, who was shabbily dressed and barefooted. She backed away until she thought it was safe, then turned and ran into the trees. She ran through the trees and undergrowth with the experience of one who knew the hill like it was home. She ran until she reached the slope of the west side of the hill, then she slowed to a walk.

Walking with sure steps, she approached a small cabin hidden deep in the trees. The cabin set back behind a huge hole in the ground that used to be the entrance to a mine tunnel. Trees and undergrowth covered the hole and hid the cabin from view. Someone who did not know their way would surely fall into the hole. She maneuvered her way around the hole and up to the cabin door. She went in and closed the door. Inside the cabin, it was dark as a dungeon. With experienced steps, she went over to a small table and lit a kerosene lantern. The lantern light seemed bright in the dark cabin. The light showed one large room with doors leading to two other rooms. The two attached rooms served as bedrooms.

She went to the fireplace that dominated the main room and piled dry wood into the hearth. Soon she had a roaring fire. As the flames grew, she walked over to a window that was on the west wall. Placing her elbows on the window frame, she looked out into the night. Not long before she had watched the sunset from this very window. By facing west, the window had a view over the other hills that were just to the west. The trees that surrounded the cabin gave way on this side so that a small tunnel view of the remaining hills could be seen.

She always liked to watch the sunset from here. As the sun slowly sank below the line of sight and seemed to settle into the hills, it was beautiful. She could look forever at the yellow and gold bands of light that lit the sky at the sun's place of rest. There was a greenish haze that seemed to hang at the foot of the hills every sunset. The sun sinking behind the hills shot beams of light up to the clouds setting them on fire. Oh, how she loved the colors; yellow, orange, red, and gold, all in the East Texas sunset. But soon it was over; that was the trouble, it only lasted a short while.

She walked away from the window and sat on the cabin floor in front of the fireplace. As she gazed into the flames, she wondered how long it would be before Pa got home. She had seen so little of him lately. Ever since the strange hooded men had been coming up on the hill, he always seemed busy. First, she didn't mind the lady and the boy coming, but now a lot of people came, strange people. People who wore hoods and acted differently from other people she had seen. And her Pa spent a lot of time with them. She hardly ever saw him anymore. Ever since the lady and boy started coming again, it had gotten worse. The lady and the boy had stopped coming for a long time, then they came again. This time others came with them; the hooded men. She didn't like the hooded men nor the lady and the boy for that matter. Why couldn't the hill be nice again?

Of all the people who came to the hill lately, she least understood the boy she had seen a few weeks ago. He had fallen in a bush and laid there. She had stared at him for a minute before she ran. She wondered who he was and why he came to the hill. At first, she had wanted to tell her Pa, but had decided against it. If her Pa found out she had been spyin' on him and the others, he would probably be angry. So she remained silent about it. But who was he and why was he spying on the hooded men? She didn't know. For now, all she wanted was for the hill to return to normal.

She got up and walked over to a bookshelf that stood just to the left of the window on the west wall. Looking through the books, she found the one she wanted. It was the one she had read several times. Over the years, her Pa had taught her to read and write and do arithmetic. Now, she could read better than him and her handwriting was beautiful. Her arithmetic was still not very good, but she didn't work on it much. He also taught her geography and history. For instance, she knew she lived in the State of Texas in the United States of America. She knew the history of the state and the country. She used to get a new book about every month. Sometimes the book was a story book like "Pecos Bill," but most of the time the books were study books. Her Pa would tell the woman which books he needed and she would bring them. When the books came, they would spend hours reading and studying them. Those were really great times. But now, she hadn't had a new book in almost six months. This, she suspected, was also due to the men in the hoods.

She picked out "Pecos Bill" and pulled it from the bookshelf. "Pecos Bill" made her identify with her own situation. As a baby, Pecos Bill had been left in the Wild West Texas plains by himself and was adopted and raised by wolves. She felt a little like that. Her Pa had told her the story many times of how he came to find her in a basket sitting on the road. She had grown up on this hill with only her Father as company. Plus, the woman named Ruth and the boy named Dick who came to visit once a week and bring them supplies. She didn't know who her real father and mother were. But she didn't care now. The father who had raised her from a baby was the one she loved. Obviously, her real mother and father didn't want her.

Many times in the last three years, her Pa had asked her if she wanted to go live in the town with the other people. When she asked him if he would come with her he said no and that she couldn't tell anyone about him. He never told her why he couldn't live with other people. She finally stopped asking. The woman and the boy had offered to have her in their house. But each time her Pa had asked her if she wanted to go, she refused. She said she preferred to stay with him. Anyway, she liked the hill. At least, she did before the men in the hoods came. As she sat there pondering these things, the door opened. "Pa," she said.

"Yeah, it's me," was the reply, as he came in the door.

"Where you been, Pa? It's after sundown." She asked, although she knew the answer.

"I been busy," he said. He moved over to the table and sat in an old wooden chair.

"Do you want somethin' to eat? I'll get ya somethin' if you want?"

"No, no, just look under the sink there and see if I got a bottle under there," he answered.

She went over to the sink and looked under it. She reached in and brought out a full bottle of whiskey.

"Good, good," he said, as he saw the bottle come into sight. "Bring it here."

She took the bottle over and set it in front of him. Then, she backed away. He tore at the seal and finally removed the top. He fumbled with the bottle and placed it to his lips. Taking a long swallow, he leaned back in the chair and relaxed as though the troubles of the world had been taken from his shoulders.

"That's better," he mumbled, "much better."

"Pa, ain't ya goin' ta eat anythin'?" She asked.

"Naw, honey, I don't think so. This'll be okay for me," he said pointing to the bottle.

"Okay," she said, lowering her head. "Pa?" She asked softly.

"Yeah honey," he said, taking another swallow.

"Are we goin' to the lake tomorrow?"

He stopped drinking and looked around the room trying to avoid her eyes. Then, as though he had to force the words out, he said, "No."

"But you promised," she cried. "You promised me!"

"I know honey but . . ."

"No," she screamed. "You promised me!" Tears flowed freely down her cheeks and into her mouth. Her body shuddered as she cried. "You promised, you promised!"

"Look honey, I got business to . . ."

"Business," she interrupted, "business with those people? Those hooded people. Oh Pa! You ain't never around no more. Those people got ya, Pa; they got ya!"

"Ain't nobody got me, nobody. I just got business with them is all," he stated nervously.

"Whata ya do for 'em Pa? They give you that rot gut for somethin'. What is it?"

"Now look here young lady, I told you not to be askin' questions about my business. Now you mind your own business." He stopped to take another drink.

"But Pa, I'm lonesome by myself. You ain't never here anymore. You promised we'd go to the lake tomorrow. Now we ain't goin'. Pa, I'm dyin' by myself. I'm dyin'." She looked up at him with her tear stained face as though pleading.

"We can go to the lake another time," he said, smiling a nervous smile.

"You keep sayin' that, Pa. You keep sayin' that, but we never go. We don't do anythin' anymore." Her body heaved as she cried. She was passed being mad. Now she was heartbroken and sad because everything had changed. Nothing was the same anymore, and somehow she thought it never would be again.

He was shaken by her crying. She never cried much before. She would have to understand that's all there was to it. She would just have to understand. He turned to speak to her but she was gone. "Judy!" He cried. He ran to the door that was now standing open and looked out wildly. "Judy," he yelled, "Judy, honey!" He ran out the door and started running about wildly. He started into the trees, but then stopped and ran back into the cabin. Shortly, he came out the door again. This time he clutched his bottle to his chest. "Judy!" He screamed. "Judy, baby! Please answer me!" He ran into the woods yelling and staggering. "Judy! Please answer me, baby!"

CHAPTER SEVENTEEN

Panic

Ruth Jordan stirred in her sleep. She thought she heard someone at the door. Maybe she was dreaming. No, she did hear someone. Someone was calling her name softly. Climbing out of bed, she put on her robe and house shoes. Carefully, she made her way down the hall and to the front door. She opened the door and stared at the man she saw standing there. "What're you doin' here at three o'clock in the mornin?" She asked, as she pulled him through the door. She looked out the door and glanced up and down the street. It was silent and no one was in sight.

"It's my little girl, Judy. She's run off. I can't find her anywhere. Not anywhere!" The man stammered.

"I told you never to come here," she said, gritting her teeth, "and I meant *never!*"

"But Ruth, Judy's run off. I can't find her anywhere. I looked all night. I can't find her." He sat down on the couch. He was breathing deep and grabbing for air.

"Did anybody see you?" She asked.

"I don't think so. I was careful, Ruth. I was real careful," he said shaking. His eyes began to water and his hands shook uncontrollably. "I can't figure out where she went. She just took off." He was almost crying now. His nerves seemed to be coming apart.

"Oh, shut up blubberin' will you? She'll come back. She's got no place to go."

"She was real upset and cryin' and everythin'. And it was all 'cause I wouldn't take her to the lake. I should've. I should've taken her. She's been real lonely these last months with me gone a lot. I should've taken her." He was crying out loud now and his whole body shook.

"Will you shut up blubberin'? You'll wake Dick! Now I'm tellin' you she'll come back. Like I said, she's got no place to go." She stopped talking and looked at him. "I'll get you a drink," she said at last. She turned and went out of the room.

"No," he shouted, jumping to his feet. "I don't want any more to drink."

"Really, are you sure?" She said, returning to the room holding a glass of whiskey. She held the glass in front of his face. "I think you need it."

"I don't need it," he said, eyeing the glass closely. He turned his head away from the glass. "I've got to find Judy. She might get hurt by herself."

"I doubt she'll get hurt. She knows that hill as good as you, maybe even better. You need a drink to calm you down. Now here, take this." She handed him the glass. "Go ahead and drink it."

He took the glass from her hand and held it in his own. He eyed the glass holding it tight. Then, with a great effort, he threw it across the room. The glass smashed against the wall with a loud crash and broken glass and whisky scattered all over the wall and floor.

"No," he yelled. "No more. No more. I've done everythin' you told me to do. I've done it all for you and your crazy friends. But Judy means more to me than you and all your hate and all your crazy friends." He was panting as though he had run for miles. Sweat rolled down his face and neck. His eyes were wild and confused.

"Does she mean more to you than Dick?" She asked in a quiet voice. His head jerked toward her. His eyes pleaded. "Does she? Does that little bastard mean more to you than Dick?" She was being cruel now. Crueler than she wanted to be, but she feared it was the only way to get him under control.

"Don't . . . don't call her that name," he stammered.

"Answer me," she growled through gritted teeth. "Does she?"

"Ruth, I . . . I mean . . . you shouldn't ask me that. Please don't ask me that."

"She does, doesn't she?" She glared. "That little bastard . . ."

"Don't call her that name," he yelled. "You . . . stop . . . callin' her that name." He was shaking badly now. He looked about the room in confusion. His mind searched for words. "Please Ruth, help me find Judy. Please help me!"

"How can I help? I don't know that hill. She's hidin' someplace, but she'll be back. You need to calm down now. Just take it easy," she said, lowering her tone.

"You say that . . . 'cause you . . . you don't care. You don't care about her. I care . . . I care about her. I brought her up since she was a little thing. She was a real little thing. She's just like . . . like my own kid. This whole thing is your fault. Always wantin' more money and always wantin' to be somebody. Usin' Dick to make me . . . make me do like you say. And my drinkin' . . . you're usin' my drinkin' against me too. And you all treat Judy just like . . . like dirt. But I'm the worst by keepin' her up on that hill because I love her so much. You know, I taught her to read and . . . and write . . . and spell and everythin'. I taught her . . . I taught her God too. I taught her to be God fearin'. She's a . . . a good kid. She's the best. Yes, as good . . . as good as Dick. And you call her names . . . you call her names . . . a girl like Judy and you . . . you call her names! Well, no more drinkin' . . . no more name callin'. No more anythin'. Because I'm goin' to find Judy and when I do we're goin' to live like . . . like people are supposed to. I always thought only of you . . . you and Dick. And now she's gone. But now I want her back more than . . . more than anythin' . . . anythin' in this God Almighty world."

He stood there looking at her, feeling as though he had freed himself. Then, as he moved for the door, she jumped in front of him.

"Think what you're doin'," she challenged. "I'll tell Dick; I'll tell him everythin'." She was breathing heavy now. She was scared for the first time. He had never been this way before. She had to regain control. "They'll put you in jail and then what'll happen to Judy?

I'll tell you what'll happen. They'll put her in a home; a home for bastards. You think she wants that? Do you?" Again, she was being cruel. She didn't like using the word *bastard*, but she knew it had a powerful effect on him.

"I don't . . . I don't know . . . I . . ." He was confused again. His head spun with questions. What to do? "She . . . they won't . . . I don't know," he cried. "I don't know! I got to find her."

His brain was clouded with confusion and he was near panic. She slapped his face once, twice, and three times. He backed away until he fell on the couch.

"Now you listen to me," she said, with all her self-assurance returning. "We'll find Judy. We'll look for her and we'll find her. But you do like I tell you. Do you understand?" He looked up at her and nodded. He was completely defeated. His mind was too tired to work anymore. "Now, you go back up to your cabin. I'll bring Jim and we'll be up after daybreak, and then we'll find Judy. Do you understand?"

He nodded again and got to his feet. As he walked to the door, he stopped and turned to look at her. He stared at her with tired scared eyes long and hard. His face was drawn and he looked old, much older than he really was. "I loved you," he said in a very tired and defeated voice. "I still love you I guess, but someday your greed and hate will kill you. And when it does, I hope I'm not here to see it. I hope I'm somewhere else a million miles away. I want to be somewhere far away, so that what happens to you won't hurt me anymore." With that, he stumbled out the door and into the early morning darkness.

His last statement shook her. She had almost lost control, and all because of Judy Cole. She had never realized just how much he had come to love Judy. The truth was she liked Judy too. The kid was smart and loyal. Then she thought about how he had said he loved her. He did love her, she knew that. But all of that was over for both of them. At least, that's what she told herself. She couldn't believe that she might still love him. Not after what he had done and what he had become. Still, sometimes, a feeling stirred deep down inside of her that scared her. She didn't want to love him anymore. Just to look at him now, made her sure of that fact.

Ruth closed her eyes and shook her head as if to clear all of these thoughts from her mind. She forced herself to concentrate on the immediate problems at hand. They all would have to be more careful from now on. She had nearly lost everything. But everything was under control now. She went into the kitchen to make some coffee; she needed it. As she left, she didn't see Dick quietly slip back to his bedroom. She didn't see the puzzled look on his face as he climbed back into bed.

CHAPTER EIGHTEEN

Confusion

Rachael looked out the kitchen window at the dark evening sky. Storm clouds had been building for the last hour throughout dinner. She was clearing up the dishes after the meal. It had been a rather small meal and she was almost through with her duties. As she stood washing the last of the dishes, she continued to look out the window. The kitchen window was directly over the kitchen sink so she could wash dishes and watch the clouds gather at the same time. She leaned closer to the window and scanned the sky. It was dark and she could hear the rumble of thunder. Short flashes of lightning lit up the Collie backyard. The rain would start soon. She wanted to finish her duties and get to her house before the rain started. With this in mind, she started washing the dishes at a faster pace.

The entire family was in the living room listening to the radio. Tonight was the night for the Jack Benny show and everyone wanted to listen to the latest episode? The voice on the radio was replaced by loud static each time the lightning flashed. Cherrie and Dee were comfortably stretched out on the floor. James was in his favorite easy chair and Mary was relaxed on the divan.

"Dad, can you tune it in better than that?" Dee asked.

"Sorry Son, but the lightning is messin' it up," James replied.

"Gee, I hope we can hear it," Cherrie exclaimed. "I don't want to miss Jack and Rochester."

"I'm sure your dad is doin' the best he can," Mary said. Just as Mary spoke, a flash of lightning caused a loud blast of static to emit from the radio. "Oh, me," Mary laughed.

The noise from the radio came into the kitchen where Rachael could hear it. She was smiling and thinking of Rochester's funny character when she saw the first flames. A flash of lightning had lit up the backyard and she could see her house. She wasn't sure what it was at first, but then she could see the flames leaping from her home. Then she realized her house was on fire and she screamed. "Mister Collie, Mister Collie, my house is a fire. It's burnin'."

Rachael ran into the living room in a state of panic. James was taken completely by surprise. He jumped to his feet and met Rachael as she came running through the door between the kitchen and the living room.

"It's burnin', Mister Collie, my house is a fire." Her eyes were wide with fright and she was trembling.

James pushed her aside and ran through the kitchen and out the back door. By the time he got outside, the flames were leaping high into the sky. He saw he could do nothing by himself. He quickly returned to the house. "Now look," he yelled. "I'll get the water hose from the garage. Mary, you call Sheriff Clark and tell him to get the fire fighters together and get them over here fast. The rest of you just stay in the house out of the way."

"But Mister Collie, my house is burnin'. I got ta do somethin'! I got things dear ta me in that house," Rachael said with a pleading look in her eyes. "I got to do somethin'!"

"Rachael, you stay in the house 'til I get back. There's nothin' you can do now. I've got to get the water hose hooked up and see if I can do any good. Now stay here!"

With that he ran out the back door again and headed for the garage. The rain had started to fall, but not enough to help put out the fire. When he got to the garage, he froze in his tracks. There was a man in a white robe and hood standing at the garage door holding a shotgun and it was pointed straight at James.

"Stand right where you are, James Collie," the man said. "I don't want to kill you, but I will if you don't do everythin' I say."

James didn't move. He had a very great respect for the double-barreled, twelve gauge, sawed-off shotgun that was pointing at him. "Who in the hell are you, and what do you think you're doin'?" He managed to ask, after he regained some of his composure.

"Don't worry about who I am, James Collie. You best worry about yourself. For you see, I brought friends with me."

As the man spoke, many white dressed figures materialized out of the dark. In a matter of seconds, they formed a circle around James.

"Now, James Collie, turn around and walk back to the house."

As the man spoke, he motioned with the shotgun. James could not hide his fear. He reluctantly turned around and walked back toward the house with the white figures following him. The rain had now started to fall harder, but James didn't notice it at all.

Mary had seen the men and her husband approaching through the window. She had just finished calling Sheriff Clark, but there had been no answer. Now, she didn't know what to do next. She watched them come closer. Soon she heard her husband call.

"Mary, come outside and bring Rachael and the kids," he yelled. James looked again at the shotgun and gritted his teeth. He prayed silently that they wouldn't harm his family. He looked at the man holding the shotgun. "If you hurt anyone in my family, I'll find you and I'll kill you. If there's anythin' in your life that you can be sure of, you can be sure of that. I'll find you and I'll kill you," James said with a voice that, itself, could have killed.

The man holding the shotgun moved nervously and held the shotgun tighter. Mary, Rachael, Dee, and Cherrie filed out of the house. They all huddled around James in the backyard in the rain.

"Now, James Collie, we only have a short time before the fire is noticed by someone else and the fire fighters arrive. So we will get right down to business." The man that spoke was not dressed like the others. He had on a black robe and hood with the letters KKK across the front. He talked with a clear, unaccented voice. The man spoke again. "Why, James Collie, have you allowed this nigger to live on your property and in the white community?" As he spoke, he pointed to Rachael, who drew closer to James. Rachael's eyes were wide with fear, for now she realized what was taking place.

At the same time, Dee also realized what was taking place. He realized that these were the same men he had seen on Lonesome Hill. Dee looked over at Cherrie and saw her standing huddled close to his mother. Her eyes showed the same recognition as Dee's.

"Answer me, James Collie!" The man in the black robe demanded.

"Because I want her to," James answered curtly, "it's easier for everybody if she lives out there. It's my house and my property and you'll pay for burnin' it down too."

"I don't think so. I also don't think she'll live there anymore, or anywhere else in the white community." Then turning to face Rachael he said coldly, "will you Rachael?" Rachael looked around the circle of men and then to James. She was confused and scared. She didn't know what to say. "Well, will you Rachael?" The man repeated.

"No sir, no sir, I don't guess so," she said.

"What do you mean, you don't guess so? Don't you . . ." the man didn't finish his sentence before James blew his top.

"Now look, this has gone far enough. You get your stupid group of Halloween players off my property," James yelled. Anger had taken the place of fear. "I don't know who you are but . . ." James stopped abruptly as Rachael broke and ran for the burning house. "Rachael! Stop," James yelled.

"Stop her," the man in black ordered. Several white figures darted out after Rachael. But she had a good lead on them and she reached the burning house well ahead of her pursuers. She ran blindly into the flaming house.

"Rachael, come back! Don't . . ." James never finished the sentence. The man carrying the shotgun brought the butt of the weapon up into James' mid-section. He doubled up and fell to the ground with the wind knocked out of him. He lay there gasping for air as rain pelted his face. Mary ran to his side screaming.

At this, Dee attacked. Dee flew headlong into the man with the shotgun, knocking him to his knees. Cherrie stood looking around at all the confusion. Rachael had run into the burning house. Her father was lying on the ground gasping for air. Her mother was bending over her father screaming. The rain was coming down hard now, and her brother was being grabbed by his hair and slung aside by one of the hooded figures.

She saw Dee hit the ground with a thud and roll over on his side holding his chest. Dee got back to his feet, slipping on the wet ground, he renewed his attack. Again he was roughly tossed aside. This time the man raised his hand to strike Dee. But before he could land the blow, Cherrie drove into him with all the force her small body could generate. The man, taken by surprise, fell and his gun went flying off into the darkness and rain. Angered by his young attackers, he started swinging his fist in all directions. One fist caught Cherrie full in the face. She fell to the ground and lay still.

The man in black now realized the confusion that had set in by Rachael's run for the house. Also, he now heard the sound of approaching cars and trucks. He yelled for the men to regroup. And suddenly, they were gone as silently as they had come.

James struggled to his feet and looked around. Then he remembered Rachael's running into the flaming house. He began to run toward the inferno with some trouble, for he was still short of breath. When he reached the blazing house, Rachael was nowhere in sight. Looking closer, he saw her lying just inside the doorway. He grunted a curse because she was not moving. Rushing up the steps, he ran through the door. The flames were hot and the smoke was almost too much for him, but he managed to reach her. James grabbed her by her dress and pulled, but the dress tore. He then had to go back and pick her up bodily and carry her from the house. After reaching safety, he laid her down on the grass and looked at her.

As the rain beat down on her burned face, there was no doubt in his mind that she was dead. Her hair was almost completely burned away and her skin was a horrible sight. The dress she wore, or what was left of it, smoldered slowly as the rain hit it. Her face was unrecognizable. James removed his shirt and put it over her head before the others could see as Mary, Dee, and Cherrie had gathered around them.

They were all soaked to the skin and still the rain came down. Mary's eyes were filled with tears as she sank to her knees crying. Dee held his chest as he walked slowly over and then stood staring at Rachael. Cherrie stood looking at her father. Her eyes were glazed over. She appeared to be unconscious but standing on her feet. Her jaw was already swelling and blood slowly ran from her mouth mixing with the rain on her face. James went to her and picked her up holding her in his arms. She put her head on her father's shoulder and closed her eyes.

James, Mary, and Dee all looked at the thing Rachael still clutched to her breast. They could see it clearly in flickering light of the burning house. Even though the cover was burnt away, they knew it was her family Bible. The thing she held dear to her above all things. The cover was burned away revealing the first page. As the rain hit the page and the writing started to blur, they could still read what it said. "To: Rachael Lowell my fifth child and only girl. From: Emma May Lowell her loving Mother."

James guided his family back inside the house, as Sheriff Clark and several of the volunteer fire fighters arrived.

CHAPTER NINETEEN

The Truth

"You should've told somebody before," James was telling Dee. "Now you see what's happened. Two people are dead and your sister is hurt. Why in Heaven's name didn't you tell somebody before?"

Dee sat on the divan staring at the floor. He was ashamed to look his father in the face. "I don't know for sure, Dad," Dee said. "It just didn't seem like there was anythin' for me to do. It started out as just somethin' to get Cherrie away from Dick Jordan. Then things happened and I was afraid I would get in big trouble with you and mom. I never thought all of this would happen."

"But after Moonbeam's death, didn't you think about tellin' me what you knew?" James asked.

"I was afraid," Dee replied. "But, Dad, you have to know that it wasn't Cherrie's fault. She wanted me to tell all along. I promised that we'd tell in two weeks. But I guess that was too long."

"You mean all of this happened because you were afraid to come and talk to me?" James asked slowly.

"I had sneaked out to go up on the hill and I knew you'd whip me for sure if you knew about all the things that I had been doin'," Dee stated.

"I guess we got a problem, Dee. If you don't feel like you can talk to your own Dad, I guess I've been doin' somethin' very, very wrong."

"I'm sorry, Dad," Dee said, fighting back the tears. "I don't want you to be ashamed of me."

"I guess I'm more ashamed of myself than I am of you," James said. "I just never imagined that you would ever be afraid of me. Somehow we have to fix that."

"No, Dad, it's not your fault. It's mine. I should've taken my punishment. Cherrie was ready to take it, but I wasn't. I'm ready for a whippin' or any other kind of punishment."

"I don't think so, Dee," James whispered and pulled Dee into his arms. He hugged his son tight. "You and I got a lot of things to talk about and work out. There's not goin' to be any punishment. I think we've all been punished enough already." Father and son held each other for a long time before any other words were spoken.

"Is Cherrie goin' to be okay?" Dee asked softly as he pulled away from his father.

"Yeah, Doc Jewel says she'll just have a bruised jaw and a busted lip. But Rachael won't be okay, she's gone forever."

James hated himself the minute the words came out of his mouth. Blaming Dee for Rachael's death was not the answer and was the wrong thing to do. James turned away from his son and faced the wall. Things were quiet for several minutes. James turned back and looked at his son, who sat nervously rubbing his hands together and biting his lip.

"Now Dee," James finally spoke. "Sheriff Clark is comin' over. I called him back after he left. I want you to tell him everythin' you told me. I mean everythin'. The Sheriff will probably want to talk to the Barnett kids so try and tell everythin' you can remember so your stories won't conflict. And one last time, are you sure about Harry Barnett?"

"No, I'm not sure. That's what Billy Bob and Sue Ann think. I couldn't tell who the ones in the hoods were. The only ones I know about for sure are Ruth and Dick Jordan." Dee sounded scared and frustrated.

"Okay, Dee, let's not talk about it anymore 'til the Sheriff gets here. Just be sure you cover the entire story."

"Yes sir," Dee replied, looking up at last. "Dad, are you sure Cherrie is okay?"

"Yeah, I told you what Doc Jewel said."

"She was helpin' me when she got hit. It looked like that guy hit her mighty hard. Where is she now?" Dee asked.

"She's in your bedroom. Your Mother's with her," James answered.

"Can I go in and see her?" Dee asked, as his eyes met his father's for the first time.

"Sure, go ahead. But Sheriff Clark will be here in a little bit and I want you to be here."

"Yes sir," Dee said as he got up to leave the room.

"Dee," James yelled after him.

"Yes sir?" Dee turned back to face his dad.

"Look, Son. I'm sorry if it sounded like I was blamin' you for what happened to Rachael. 'Cause I'm not," James said shamefully. "I'm just so upset by all of this that I'm sure I didn't mean things the way they sounded. I know you wouldn't do anythin' to hurt anybody on purpose."

"Yes sir," Dee said again and walked out of the room.

No matter what anybody said, he still thought it was his fault. Everything was his fault. Cherrie getting hurt was his fault also. He walked down the hall to their bedroom and stopped at the doorway. He saw Cherrie lying quietly with her eyes closed. Their mother was sitting in a chair beside the bed. After all that had happened, Mary Collie still looked rather calm. Dee stopped at the doorway and watched them for a minute.

"Is she asleep?" He whispered to his mother.

"No, I'm not asleep," the reply came from the bed. With that, Dee walked into the room and went over to stand by his mother. Mary could feel that her twins had things to say to each other, so she got up and started out the door.

"I'll go fix us somethin' to drink," Mary said smiling.

"Okay, Mom," Cherrie said trying to smile through her swollen jaw. Dee sat in the chair by the bed. He looked at Cherrie with a worried expression.

"How do you feel?" He asked.

"I feel awful. And don't look at me like that," she answered. "I can't stand it when you have that sorry-for-you look on your face."

Dee felt a little better, because it was clear she was still herself. "Boy, that guy really put one on you, didn't he?" Dee observed.

"You better believe it! And it's your fault, too," she barked. "Runnin' in there and gettin' thrown around like a rag doll. I'm surprised you got any hair left on your head at all! That guy was bouncin' you off the ground like a basketball. By the way, how do you feel?"

"Aw, I'm just fine. Just a little sore in the side is all. But I wanted to tell you I'm real thankful and proud of the way you came to help me," Dee said.

"Well, you should be. The way I got clobbered and everythin'," Cherrie answered.

"Did they tell you about Rachael?" Dee asked looking away.

"Yeah, Mom told me for sure. I was kind of knocked out at the time but I knew she was hurt real bad. Have you told them anythin', Dee?"

"Yeah, I told Dad the whole thing. He called Sheriff Clark and he's comin' over. I've got to tell him everythin' just like I told Dad. Boy, I sure messed everythin' up good."

"Did you tell 'im about Billy Bob and Sue Ann?" She asked.

"Yeah, I told 'im everythin'," he replied.

"Even about Billy Bob and Sue Ann thinkin' maybe one of 'em was their Dad?"

"Yeah, that too," Dee answered as he stood up and looked down at his sister. "Well, I just wanted to see how you were and to thank you for helpin' me. If you want anythin', Cherrie, anythin' at all, you just let me know and I'll get it for you. Okay?"

"Okay, Dee, but you don't have to do anythin' for me. I did what I had to do just like you did when you tried to help Dad. Just like when you've helped me a hundred times before."

"Well, anyway, if you need anythin' you know who to ask. Okay?"

"Okay," she said. "Dee," she called after him as he started out the door. He turned around and looked at her again. "I'm not mad at you or anythin', Dee," she said with a meaningful look in her eyes. "I stuck with you because I wanted to. We always have and we always will be together. I know how you feel, but how do you know if it would've been any different."

Well, maybe we'll know someday. You know what Mom always says, *things always come back around.*"

Cherrie smiled and said, "Yeah, she does say that a lot."

Dee took another long look at his twin sister. She had a swollen jaw, a black eye, and a busted lip. They looked into each other's eyes for several minutes. Then, Dee turned and walked out of the room. He hurried down the hall, into the kitchen and out the back door. Quickly, he ran down the path to the tall oak tree that held his tree house. He climbed up and into his tree house. Now, no one could see him. He was all alone high above everything. He sat in the dark, pulled his legs to his chest, and buried his head against his knees. Then he cried.

CHAPTER TWENTY

Meeting in the Cabin

Ruth Jordan sat quietly in the cabin on Lonesome Hill waiting. She was waiting for the return of the white robed and hooded men. The night had started well enough, but the rain clouds had rolled in and it was now raining with driving force. She left the door leading to the outside open so she could see the clearing in front of the shack. At the same time, she watched the rain pour down. There was little wind so the rain didn't blow into the cabin.

Finally her wait was over. A figure dressed in a black robe came hurrying through the clearing toward the cabin. She had been expecting all the men to return to the cabin, but only the lone figure in black returned. He walked up to the cabin with a quick gait. As he walked into the cabin, he stopped momentarily to look behind him. Seeing no one, he entered the cabin. He immediately started removing the wet robe and hood.

He looked at Ruth for a minute then spoke, "You still here?" He asked.

"Yes, shouldn't I be?" She asked.

"Sure," he said. "I guess so."

"Well, what happened? Where is everyone?" She asked looking around.

He finished removing the robe and hood and threw them into the corner of the cabin. He walked across the room and slammed his fist into the wall. Then he turned back to face Ruth.

"I sent them all home, where you and Dick should be." He had just noticed Dick, who sat in one corner of the cabin by himself. Dick looked up but said nothing.

"Well, what in the Hell happened?" She demanded.

"I think Hell is a good description of what happened. All hell broke loose. Nothing went right tonight. It all turned to shit including this Goddamn weather."

He walked back and forth across the floor of the cabin as he spoke. His face showed worry and anger at the same time. He stopped at the table and leaned down on his elbows holding his head in his hands.

"Well, Goddamn it, will you tell me what happened?" She cried in irritation. She was beginning to get upset, because she knew the news must be bad.

"I'll tell you what happened," he said. "I'll tell you, and it all started with that little bitch, Judy Cole. We spend most of one day trying to find her so we can calm down that drunken bum that I have to deal with. Then guess what? She turns up back at home where she's supposed to be in the first Goddamn place! A whole day shot to shit. Then we all finally get together and head for the Collie house. Then what? It starts to rain. So we add a little more gasoline to the fire to make sure it doesn't go out. As a result, the damn house goes up like a dry forest. Then, that stupid nigger runs into the house. I mean to tell you she ran into that house while it's blazing on fire! At this point, Collie decides to try and play hero, so we had to deck him. Then those two brats of his jumped Barnett. He had to fight his way free of those two crazy kids! Things were so confused after a while that I had to call it off and regroup and leave. When we left, that stupid nigger was still in the burning house, probably dead by now. Collie was still lying on the ground, and that Collie girl was lying on the ground awful still. I don't know if Barnett killed her or what. I tell you Ruth . . ." His sentence was interrupted by a voice from the corner.

"Cherrie! Did you hurt Cherrie?"

"Cherrie? Who in Hell is Cherrie?" Jim Upter asked.

"Cherrie, the Collie girl, did you hurt her?" Dick repeated.

"I don't know how badly she's hurt. I told you Barnett . . ."

"Why did you have to hurt her?" Dick yelled. He was out of the corner and standing directly in front of Jim.

"Hey, what's a matter with you, kid? Ruth, control your kid!" Jim said, as he turned and walked away from Dick.

"Dick, what's wrong?" Ruth asked, showing a little surprise.

"They didn't have to hurt Cherrie!"

"Look, kid. I told you the brat attacked Barnett, he had . . ."

"Don't call her a brat and don't give me a lot of stupid excuses about how it couldn't be helped," Dick cut in at the top of his voice.

"Okay Ruth! I've had it with your kid. Tell him to shut up. I don't have to explain things to him. Shut him up!" Jim screamed with fury in his face.

Ruth was stunned by all the yelling. At first, she was confused as to what to do next. Then she looked at the fury in Jim's face and knew what she must do. "Dick, we'll talk about it later. Okay?" She asked in her most soothing tone.

"No, it ain't okay," Dick replied imitating her tone. "There's a lot of things we need to talk about, don't we, Mother? That drunken old man for instance. I think we should talk about him, don't you, Mother? I think we might have a lot to say about him. Why don't we just go get him right now and have a nice long talk? That would be nice, wouldn't it, Mother? I think . . ."

"Shut up Dick!" Ruth yelled. Her eyes were glaring and her fists were doubled. "I said we'd talk about it later. And that's when we'll talk about it . . . later!"

Dick stood staring into his mother's eyes for a full minute. Then, he turned and looked at Jim again. "If you've hurt Cherrie Collie, you'll pay for it," he screamed pointing his finger at Jim. "I swear you'll pay for it."

With that, Dick ran out the cabin door and into the dark and rain. Jim tried to stop him, but he was too late. Dick made it out the door before they could stop him. Jim started to give pursuit, but Ruth grabbed his arm and held him back.

"Don't worry, he'll just go home. He's a lot like Judy in that respect. He's got no place else to go. Now, just tell me what went wrong at the Collie place," she said, trying to calm down.

"Christ," Jim whispered. "Jesus Christ. One kid runs off and we find her. Now, another kid runs off. We'll probably have to find . . ."

"I said don't worry about Dick," Ruth cut in. "I'll handle Dick. You just handle your own problems. Now, I want to know what happened."

"I don't know if this is going to hold together, Ruth. There're too many things going on! We can't seem to keep our minds on what we're trying to do. The people we got aren't reliable. Barnett is just plain stupid. First, he hit Collie in the belly with the shotgun, and then he couldn't handle the kids. He made things worse instead of better. I can't control these people because I don't think they know why we're doing this. In fact, I don't know why some of them are even involved. I don't even know who a few of these people are! I made it clear that as the Grand Wizard, I should know everyone. But there are two guys that refuse to show their faces to me or identify themselves. They just showed up at our last two meetings. I don't know how they knew about us or anything. I've asked the others who they are but either they really don't know or they're not telling me the truth. I let it go because we need members, but I think I made a mistake. That one guy, the one who killed the old nigger, he is one cold-blooded son-of-a-bitch. I don't think he's here to help with the nigger problem. I think he likes killing. I don't know, Ruth, we may have to rethink this whole thing!"

He stopped talking and they both looked at each other in silence. "If we rethink this whole thing, what does that involve?" Ruth asked in a sarcastic tone.

"It means getting out of here before things get out of control," he stated, "you, me and Dick. We'll head back to New Orleans where I have some influence."

"Things appear to already be out of control," she said quickly. Then thinking about what he had said she added in a softer tone, "You mean you would take me and Dick with you to New Orleans?"

"Yeah, sure I would!" He replied. "Why don't we get started right away? I can have a meeting and tell the group to disband."

"Maybe I'm wrong, but it seems you're not as dedicated to the cause as it seemed at first," Ruth said slowly. "What happened to the big desire to be a KKK leader in Texas? You know the grand army for a just cause."

"Don't make fun of me, Ruth. I don't like it," he said with anger building in his voice again. "It's just that these people aren't ready to be set free yet. They've had niggers among them so much they think it's normal. Now, I don't mind a good fight, but I've never been able to get across to these people what we're fighting about. Maybe I failed, I don't know. But I'm not goin' down for some stupid farmers or a couple of kill crazy people I don't even know. I'll make it plain. You and your kid can come with me if you want, but I'm going to leave as soon as possible. We have a meeting planned for tomorrow night, but I'm going to get as many together as I can tonight. Somebody else can tell the others. I'm going to clean up this cabin and get rid of anything that would prove we were ever here. We need to start out first thing in the morning. I mean right at dawn."

"Okay," Ruth said softly. "I don't want you to leave without me. I'll have to make a few plans, but I'll go with you. As soon as it's light, I'll go to the house and get things ready."

<hr />

Dick Jordan ran down Lonesome Hill in the direction of his house. He was confused as to why he had run away, because he had no place to go except home. But his anger had gotten the best of him. There were so many things on his mind. First, there was Cherrie. Even though he and Cherrie hadn't seen each other much since his return, he still liked her. He could not forget the happy days when he and Cherrie had been boyfriend and girlfriend. A lot of things had happened since then. He was fourteen and she was twelve now, but he remembered the other times. Those had been happy days. Then, there was the drunkard who had come to their house and talked to his mother in such a strange way.

Dick stumbled over a bush and fell flat on his face. Picking himself up, he started again. He would have to pay attention to what he was doing and stop thinking about other things. It would be easy to get killed if he didn't watch where he was going. The rain had slowed somewhat by the time he emerged from the bushes at the base of the hill. Once on the road, he stood and looked around in the dark and rain.

His thoughts returned to the man who had talked so strangely to his mother. What that man meant to his mother he didn't know, but he was going to find out. But right now, he had another mission to attend to. He walked on the muddy road for a short distance. Then, at the proper place that he and his mother had used so many times before, he slipped down into the ravine. Their normal crossing spot was under rushing water. He put his foot into the water and started to wade across. The water was only about knee-deep as he slowly put one foot after the other making sure he had good footing before taking the next step. The water was pouring down into the ravine from off the hill. If the rain continued at its current rate, the ravine would become a river.

He reached the other side of the ravine with no trouble and climbed up onto the opposite edge. He looked around to be sure where he was. Sure of his direction, he started walking toward his house. He looked up at the dark sky. The rain had slacked up again. It seemed the weather didn't know if it wanted to rain hard or just sprinkle. Soon he came to the barbed wire fence that formed the boundary at the back of Jordan land. As he started to enter a small gate that stood hanging loosely on the fence, he halted. In the distant darkness, he could see the glowing light of a fire. It had to Rachael's house, he thought. Dick stood there for a long minute thinking. When he continued, he walked along the fence to the start of Collie land. Then, he climbed over the fence and started for the Collie house.

CHAPTER TWENTY-ONE

The Visitor

The rain had slowed to a steady sprinkle. James Collie stood at the living room window watching the rain drops hit and then run down the window pane. It had only been a few hours since Rachael's death, but it seemed like forever. Everyone in the family was dealing with the events that had happened in their own way. Cherrie was still resting quietly in the twin's bedroom. Mary busied herself around the kitchen, although there was nothing to do. Dee had come back to the house from his tree house and was trying to listen to the radio. He seemed withdrawn and quiet. His eyes were red and puffy revealing what he had done at the tree house.

James could think of nothing to make things better. Dee had told his story to Sheriff Clark. The Sheriff had listened intently and had not said a word. After hearing Dee's story, Sheriff Clark left without saying much, but with a strange worried look on his face.

James went through the kitchen and out the back door. He stepped out into the soft rain. In the short distance up the much used path, he could see the remains of Rachael's house. Although the fire had been put out, the red glow of hot coals still lit the sky. Smoke still drifted into the dark night sky. He pushed his hands into his pockets and lowered his head. His brain was reeling with all that had happened. There was no doubt in his mind that what had happened tonight and what had happened to Moonbeam was connected to the Ku Klux Klan. Sheriff Clark now knew what he faced. They all knew what they faced. He couldn't help but think that from now on things were going to be very difficult for everyone.

Friends were going to face off against each other. New enemies were going to be made. The town was facing the worst test in its history. Maybe even more of a test than the people faced during the Civil War, when most of the town was loyal to the Union but many went and served with the Confederacy. Jim had to force himself to believe that people he grew up with, worked with, went to church with, and lived with could be capable of doing these things. It was not a fact that he liked facing. In his heart he believed there must be an outside influence. This just couldn't begin suddenly. Not between his friends and neighbors. The feel of the rain starting to wet his body brought him out of his deep thoughts. He took a deep breath and went back into his house.

The household tried to return to normal. But no matter how they tried, the fact remained that Rachael was gone. This, every member of the family tried to avoid saying. No one wanted to mention the fact that Rachael would no longer be a member of the family. She would no longer be there to do the house chores. She would no longer be there to tell Dee and Cherrie right from wrong. No longer would she be there to add her *I swanie* and *I do declare* to the conversation. She would just no longer be there. The fact settled on the Collie household, but no one wanted to accept it.

As the family was preparing for bed, a soft knock came at the front door. Dee, still wearing his blue jeans, went to answer the door. He opened the door and stared at the caller.

"I heard Cherrie got hurt and I came to see her," Dick Jordan said.

"Yeah, I guess you did hear," Dee said as he held the door open.

Dee held the door open with his right hand and hit Dick as hard as he could with his left hand. The blow caught Dick full in the face and completely by surprise. Dick staggered backward away from the door, but he didn't fall. Dee followed him out the door and attacked again before Dick could recover. He landed a right to the face and then a left to the face. "You got nerve, comin' here after what happened!" Dee screamed.

Dick opened his mouth to speak but Dee landed another blow before he could say anything. Dick was the larger of the two boys but he wasn't fighting back. With the last blow, Dick went down on one knee. Dee then placed a kick to the head that sent Dick sprawling flat on his back. Dee immediately jumped on top of Dick and started peppering blows to his face. Dick held his hands up to his face to protect himself, but he never hit back.

Suddenly, Dee was being lifted up and pulled away from his adversary. He struggled with the strong hands that held him, but his Father was far too strong for him.

"Okay, young man, you just cool off," James said shaking Dee.

"But Dad . . ." Dee started.

"No buts. Go inside and wait for me," James ordered. As Dee stomped away and into the house, James turned and looked down at Dick. "Are you okay?" He asked reaching down to help Dick up.

"Yes Sir, I'm okay," Dick said, wiping the blood from his face with his shirt sleeve.

"You better come on inside, you're soaked to the bone. We better get in out of this rain."

James took Dick's arm and helped him inside the house. Once inside the house, James looked at Dick and spoke very calmly. "I imagine the Sheriff is lookin' for you and your Mother right now."

"How'd y'all know?" Dick asked. "How'd Dee know?"

"Never mind about that right now. You just go into the bathroom and clean the blood off of you and get out of those wet clothes. I'll bring you some of my old stuff. It won't fit but at least it'll be dry. I'll call the Sheriff and then we'll all talk about it."

"Mr. Collie, I wasn't with 'em tonight. I swear I wasn't. I heard they hurt Cherrie and I came to see how she was. That's the truth, Mr. Collie, it really is." Dick was near tears as he spoke.

"You mean to tell us you came here just to see if Cherrie was okay?" The new voice was that of Mary Collie, who had been standing in the kitchen doorway. Her voice betrayed her disbelief in his statement.

"Yes, Mrs. Collie, it's the truth. I came here for no other reason. I didn't know y'all knew about all that's goin' on. Is she okay, Mrs. Collie?"

"Yes, she's okay, but it could've been worse, and I guess you know Rachael's dead," Mary said, staring Dick in the eyes and showing no mercy in hers.

Dick slumped to his knees. He knelt there quietly as rain water dripped from his soaked hair onto the floor. Slowly, he turned his face up to face Mary and said, "I knew she ran in the burnin' house, but I didn't know she was dead."

"Go on to the bathroom like James told you," Mary said curtly. "I'll bring you the things you need. You're gettin' my floor wet." Mary turned away and disappeared down the hall.

Dick started for the hallway that led to the bathroom, but he stopped at the entrance and turned and faced James and Dee. They looked at him, but said nothing. "Please listen to me," he cried. "There're so many things that I ain't sure about. I'm all mixed up. My mother tells me things are right that don't really look right to me. I know that Cherrie gettin' hurt ain't right! Ain't no way that can be right. She tells how they got to make examples out of some niggers to get the rest in line. But I can't see in line for what! I don't know what they're tryin' to do. All I know is that if it hurts people like Cherrie, it can't be right." Dick stood and looked from James to Dee and then back again begging for understanding.

James studied the boy for a minute. "I don't guess we can blame you much for what your Mother did, boy. But still, people have died and it's not easy to forgive and forget." James walked over and put his hand on Dick's shoulder. "Now go on into the bathroom. When you're done in there, you can see Cherrie. But after that, there'll be questions to answer."

"Yes Sir, Mr. Collie, you'll get your answers, as many as I can give." With that, Dick turned into the hallway and walked down the hall.

As soon as Dick was out of sight, Dee ran over to his father. "Dad, how come you let him in the house? Are you goin' to get the Sheriff?"

"Yes, I'm goin' to call him right now, but don't worry about Dick, he's on our side."

"But Dad, I told you I saw him with those men up on the hill! He and his Mother both." Dee seemed unable to believe his father was allowing Dick to stay in their house.

"Yeah, I know you told me, Dee. But Dick is goin' to tell us some names, I hope, and maybe we can clear this mess up."

"Dad, I don't trust him. He's always been strange to me. Even when we were little kids, he was strange. I still don't trust him." Dee eyed his Father with knowing eyes.

"We'll see, Dee. We'll see," James said as we walked over to the telephone to call the Sheriff.

———

After Dick had finished cleaning up in the bathroom, he walked back out into the hall and went to the twin's bedroom. He stopped at the door and knocked. After a short wait, a soft voice from in the room said, "Come on in." He opened the door slowly and stepped into the room. Cherrie turned her head to see who had entered.

She could hardly believe her eyes. "Dick Jordan!" She exclaimed.

"Hi Cherrie," he said shyly, "how ya feelin'?"

"What's it to you? Does Dad know you're here? Did you sneak in here, Dick Jordan?" She eyed him suspiciously.

"No, Cherrie, I didn't sneak in here. I knocked, didn't I? I had a talk with your Dad and it's goin' ta be okay."

"Well! Then, how come you're dressed in those crazy clothes and your nose looks like it's been bleedin'?" She asked, as she pointed to the shirt Mary had given him to wear.

"Your brother almost killed me, is all," he answered smiling.

"Did you hurt Dee?" She asked sitting up in bed.

"No, I didn't hurt him, but he did a good job on me. Cherrie, I heard you got hurt so I came to see you. I wanted to be sure you were okay." He stopped and looked at her swollen face. "You must've taken a mean lick."

"I guess you did hear. You were probably there with them. You might even be the one that hit me." Her voice was losing some of the anger it had at first.

"I wasn't with 'em, Cherrie, and you know darn well I wouldn't hit you," he said softly.

"I saw you with those men, Dick. I know you're one of them. Dad knows and so does Dee. The Sheriff knows now, because Dee told him, too," Cherrie said, feeling she was warning him more than threatening him.

"Cherrie, please listen. I know they all know. Your Dad has called for the Sheriff already. I don't care about that. I'm goin' to help all I can. I don't know how y'all found out, and I don't care. I don't know when you saw me with those men and I don't care about that either, because it's all over now. I'm goin' to help the Sheriff. I'll tell you again, I wasn't with those men tonight. I just wanted to make sure you were okay. That's all Cherrie. I didn't want them to hurt you. When I found out they had hurt you, I ran off and came straight here to see if you were okay. I didn't know y'all knew about me until your brother tried to beat the daylights out of me. There are so many things I need to find out and so many things I've got to get straight. I don't know what's happenin'. I came here first to see you. Then, I was goin' to start tryin' to find a few things out. But now that y'all know, I guess I'll just have to start with tellin' all I know." He looked down at her. He couldn't tell how she felt. She didn't say anything and her eyes were steady. "Well, do you believe me?"

"I'm not sure," she said. "It's kind of hard to believe you came here just because you were worried about me. Why are you worried about me?"

"Cherrie, you know darn well I like you a lot, so don't go askin' stupid questions," he answered, pushing the words out.

"Dick, you haven't been my boyfriend for two years. You've hardly even looked at me since you returned from Dallas and wherever else you went. How come all of a sudden you like me again?" She looked at him and dared him to lie to her.

"Mother wouldn't let me is why," he yelled back at her. "She said I wasn't to mess with y'all because you had a nigger livin' on your land, and . . ."

"Dick Jordan, you better not say anythin' bad about Rachael. You hear me, Dick Jordan?" Tears came to her eyes and she clenched her fist. She grimaced from the pain in her jaw. "Don't you say anythin' bad about Rachael." She blinked her eyes so she could see through the tears. The thought of Rachael stirred her anger.

"I'm sorry, Cherrie. I forgot . . ."

"Oh! Go away, Dick. Go away and leave me alone. Bein' sorry isn't goin' to bring Rachael back. Bein' sorry isn't goin' to change what all's happened. You were part of it, Dick. You don't care if Rachael is dead or not. You're just like some of the others. Rachael was just a nigger to you. She wasn't a person, just a nigger." Cherrie choked backed the tears. Her face was hurting from the pain brought on by using her jaw so much.

"I told your Mother . . ."

"I don't believe you, Dick. If I wasn't good enough for you when Rachael was here, then I'm not good enough for you now!"

"Cherrie, please . . ."

"Go away, Dick. Just go away," she sobbed. She threw herself down into the bed turning her back on him.

Dick stepped back and looked at her. Then he turned toward the door and slowly walked away. Cherrie turned to watch him leave. He said nothing, but the hurt in his eyes stood out clear. She started once to call him back but stopped herself. He closed the door behind him and he was gone. Cherrie sat up in bed staring at the door. She told herself she had done right. She didn't know why he had come, but she couldn't believe it was because of her. He didn't know he would be caught, because he didn't know they knew about him. He probably thought he would come here and offer his sorrow and everyone would think he was being nice. His mother probably put him up to it. But Dick and his mother didn't know they knew about them. So Dick wasn't fooling anybody. He just got caught, that's all. Cherrie wiped her eyes and lay down to try to sleep. Sleep would come hard this night. This was a day she would remember for the rest of her life.

CHAPTER TWENTY-TWO

Return to the Hill

James Collie had finally gotten his family to bed just before midnight. Everyone seemed not to be able to calm down enough to want to sleep. At last, however, he managed to force everyone into trying to get some sleep. Especially Cherrie needed rest, because she looked drained and exhausted. Later, Dee lay awake in his bed looking at the ceiling through the darkness. He turned his head and looked over to where Cherrie lay sleeping. She was sound asleep now and seemed to be resting nicely, even though she tossed and turned occasionally. Dee returned his stare to the ceiling. Everything seemed to have happened so fast. He really didn't know what all had taken place. Thoughts raced through his mind. He tried to piece them together in his head.

Dick Jordan had told the Sheriff all he knew about what was going on, which wasn't too much. Still, Dick's information implicated his own mother and Jim Upter in murder. There was no doubt now that the Ku Klux Klan was in Coalville and that Ruth Jordan was involved. The Sheriff had told Dick to go home and act as though nothing had happened. Dee considered this to be a bad move, because he still did not trust Dick Jordan. Maybe Dick had told on his own mother, but still Dee couldn't find it in him to trust Dick. Dee didn't know what the Sheriff intended to do now; he wouldn't say. Sheriff Clark only told Dee's father that if he needed his help, he would call on him.

Dee thought of all these things and wondered what would happen next. He knew that it wasn't over, and that there was more to come, there had to be. Dee rolled over and looked at Cherrie again.

She continued to sleep restfully. He looked at her and thought that he would somehow, someway, get revenge for his sister and for Rachael. He wasn't sure how this revenge would come about, but he was sure that somehow it would. His mistake had gotten them into trouble and he was going to try and even the score. There was not much a twelve-year-old boy could do in these circumstances. However, he felt that if he could just get to them. If somehow, he could get to where he could see them, but they couldn't see him. If he could do that, then he could do something to hurt them. And Dee wanted to hurt them very badly.

Suddenly, Dee sat up in bed and looked straight ahead at the wall. He sat there thinking for a minute, and then he quietly climbed out of bed. He put on a pair of blue jeans and an old cotton shirt. He slipped his tennis shoes on and made his way to the window. He looked again to see if Cherrie was still sleeping. She still lay quietly, not moving. Slowly, he raised the window until it was high enough for him to get through. One last time, he looked back at Cherrie. His mind spun with the consideration of what he was about to do. He was already in trouble for going up on the hill once, but now he was planning to go back again. But if he could accomplish something that helped, then any punishment he got would be worth it. Most anything would be better than the hurting he had inside. He fought with the idea of getting back in bed and letting the Sheriff handle the whole thing. Then, he climbed out the window and started down the back path.

This night was different from the night of his first trip to Lonesome Hill. The clouds that had brought the rain were still in the sky blocking the moonlight. Flashes of lightning continued to dance across the sky at intervals. The rain had stopped again, but the ground was wet and muddy. The wind had died down to a slight breeze. He worked his way down the back path, passed his tree house, and reached the ravine. The place where they had crossed the ravine the first time was now under running water. It wasn't very deep but the current was strong. Even though the rain had temporarily stopped, water still drained off the hill, across the road, and spilled down into the ravine. He picked what he thought to be a good spot and waded across the ravine. When he reached the other side, he climbed up the slippery ravine edge and onto the road that ringed Lonesome Hill. Once on the road, he looked down at himself. He was already wet and muddy and the trip was not half over. He was mad at himself for not bringing a flashlight. Without the moonlight, the darkness was almost total. He stopped and stood on the muddy road. Everything was quiet and still except for the breeze. He tried to remember the exact spot where the group had entered the bushes to start their climb on his first visit. He walked up and down the road for several minutes before he decided on what he thought must be the correct entry point.

Dee started up the hill trying to remember the way they had gone before. He wasn't too sure what he was going to do once he found the shack again, but he was sure his plan would fall into place by the time he got there. Dee moved through the trees and mesquite bushes slowly but surely. At last, he reached the spot where he had first heard the voices on his last visit. He stood there for a while trying to decide which way to go. After deciding on a course he thought to be the right one, he started off at a trot. After a short distance, he stopped again and looked around in the darkness. He strained his ears to hear a sound of any kind. No sound came to him. His eyes found nothing that he could remember for sure. He started off again, this time at a slow walk. He knew the shack must be around someplace, but exactly where, he didn't know.

Dee almost ran into the side of the shack before he saw it. There was no fire or light of any kind this time and the hill was in total darkness. Dee stopped and strained to see. His eyes told him he was at the side of the shack where there were no windows. Dee started feeling his way toward the front of the shack. Running his hands along the wall, he reached the corner of the shack. He peered around the corner, but saw nothing.

He dropped to one knee and looked into the darkness around him and then his heart leapt to his throat as someone touched his shoulder. "Does this belong to you?"

Dee spun around and his eyes fell upon Judy Cole. They stared at each other what seemed a long time. "What?" Dee finally asked.

"This BB gun, it's yours, ain't it? You dropped it the last time I saw ya here."

Dee stared at his air rifle. He had forgotten all about it. He must have dropped it when he fell into the bushes and then ran. Moving closer, he strained to see her more clearly in the darkness. "What's your name?" He asked, taking the air rifle from her.

"Judy. Judy Cole," she said. "And your name is Daryl Collie."

"How'd you know my name?"

"It's on your gun," she said pointing to the rifle.

"Yeah," Dee said slowly. Things then got very quiet. They remained there in the dark, Dee down on one knee and her standing over him, neither speaking.

Finally she dropped down beside him. "How come ya come up here? Most folks are afraid to come up here."

"I'm lookin' for somebody," Dee said, after trying to think why he was really here.

"Who're ya lookin' for?" She asked.

"I'm not sure who," Dee said. "But this shack is where they meet."

"Oh, you mean the men in white!" She exclaimed. "Are they why you were here the first time?"

"No. I mean yes the men in white, but no that's not why I was here before. How come ya askin' so many questions? Where do you live anyway? I don't know any Coles in town."

"That's 'cause I don't live in town. I live here on the hill," she stated.

Dee looked at her in disbelief. "Here on the hill, by yourself?"

"No. I live with my Pa in a cabin. It's just over the top of the hill on the other side."

"Holy cow, I didn't know anybody lived up here. How long you been here, anyway?" Dee asked.

She shrugged her shoulders and said, "I guess as long as I can remember."

"If you've been here that long then you must know all about the men in white!" The excitement in Dee's voice caused her to take a step backward.

"Nope, Pa never lets me go near 'em much. I was sneakin' a look the night I saw you."

"But doesn't your Dad know about 'em?" Dee asked.

"Yeah, I guess he does." She was quiet for a minute before speaking again. "They did somethin' bad, didn't they?" She finally asked.

"You mean the men in white?" Dee asked.

"Yeah, the men in white," she responded.

"You can believe that!" Dee said firmly.

"It's goin' ta cause trouble, ain't it?" She asked.

"It's already caused trouble, and I'm sure it's goin' to cause a lot more before it's over."

She dropped her head and her hair fell down across her face. She raised her head slightly and looked at Dee. "I told him they would get him in trouble. I told him a hundred times. But he said he had his reasons for help 'em." She was quiet again. Then, she stood up and looked down at him. "I guess the law's comin', huh?"

Dee looked up at her in the darkness. As close as they were, he couldn't see her face clearly. Her long hair covered her face and hung down to the middle of her back. In the darkness, he could make out her outline. He could see how tall she was and how skinny, but he couldn't make out her features. He didn't have to see her face to tell she was troubled. Her voice sounded weak and slightly scared.

"I guess they are," he answered, standing up. "What're you goin' to do?"

"You think the laws gonna get my Pa?" She asked quietly.

"I don't know. If he's one of them, I guess they will."

"But I don't think he really is. He never wore one of those white robes or anythin'. I think they make him help 'em!" She cried, as though she wanted Dee to believe her more than anything in the world. "Why did you come up here tonight? What're ya tryin' ta do?"

Dee reached into his mind for a good reason, but he came up with nothing. "I don't know why. I thought I could do somethin', I guess. But I'm not sure what it was I thought I could do. I was mad about my sister and I just took off. I don't guess there's anythin' I can do at all."

"Why, were you mad about your sister?"

Dee related the whole story of the night's happenings to her. She stood and listened quietly. Dee still could not tell how she was reacting because he could not see her face clearly. "So, I just got up and came up here," he ended.

"They did all that?" She asked.

"Yeah, they did, and now the Sheriff knows who and why. I don't know what he's planned but you can bet he's planned somethin'."

She started backing away slowly. So slowly, that at first Dee couldn't tell she had moved, but then he noticed her backing away. "Don't leave!" He reached out for her, but she darted off into the darkness before he could stop her. He ran after her yelling, "Hey! Wait a minute."

As he pursued completely blind in the dark, she moved quickly away from him. She knew the hill and he didn't. She knew where she was going and he didn't. She could find her way in the dark and he couldn't. As a result, after a short run, Dee found that he was completely lost and to make matters worse, the rain had started again.

CHAPTER TWENTY-THREE

Missing Person

James Collie was pacing up and down the living room floor like a caged animal, his hands behind his back and his head bent down looking at the floor. He was deep in thought. Just then, a knock came at the front door. James moved to the door as though his life depended on him getting there fast. He opened the door and allowed Sheriff Clark to enter.

"Jim, what the Hell is this about Dee being gone? Jesus H. Christ it's one o'clock in the morning."

"That's just it, he's gone. Cherrie came and got me out of bed a little while ago and told me Dee wasn't in his bed. I looked all over the house and even down to his tree house, but he's no place to be found. And damn it I know what time it is."

"Well, do you think you know where he'd go?"

"I'm not sure, but I'd bet he's gone back up on that damnable hill."

"What!" The Sheriff exclaimed. "Why?"

"I don't know why, but it's somethin' Dee would do. He was awful upset about everythin' that happened. He blamed himself and I guess I didn't help that much either."

"Well, this is just great! Just really great! He'll spoil everythin'. I had planned to go up there tomorrow night. I got some of the deputies from Dallas County together, but we ain't supposed to go until tomorrow night. This is the shits. And another thing, I've been watchin' the Jordan house and Ruth hasn't come back, so I guess she's still up on the hill somewhere. Dick went home and he was still there the last time I checked with my lookout. Now I don't know what to do." The Sheriff looked very upset at having his plans go up in smoke.

James looked at the Sheriff with disbelief. "I don't give a shit about your plans! I'll tell you what we can do! We can go up that hill this very minute. Christ, Tom, Dee might be in trouble."

"But I tell you everythin' is set for tomorrow night. The deputies won't be able to get here on this quick a notice," the Sheriff stated, with a look of complete frustration. "And to top if off, I tried to get hold of Lou to come here with me but Evie said he was spendin' the night with friends of his in Dallas and he was comin' in with the rest of the deputies tomorrow. He didn't tell me nothin' about bein' gone tonight. He better be back here tomorrow night with the rest of the deputies or I'll fire his ass."

"Then, Goddamn it, we'll go without the deputies. And we'll go without Lou. We'll go by ourselves. Jesus, Tom, you've seen what those idiots'll do. I'm not leavin' my son up there with those mental cases." James was very convincing as his voice rose to a shout.

The Sheriff knew James would go, with or without him. "Okay Jim, calm down, we'll go. I guess there's really no other way."

"Damn right there's no other way. And I'll tell you now, Tom, if they've hurt Dee, I'll kill those sons-of-bitches. I'll kill 'em all."

"If there's any killin' to be done I'll do it. Now you calm down or nobody will go anyplace!" The Sheriff's voice shouted back at James.

"We're wastin' time talkin', let's go. I got my rifle ready," James said picking up his gun and shaking it.

"Okay, but do you know the way? I sure don't."

"We'll find our way somehow," James stated in an unsure voice. "We know that there's a cabin up there somewhere and if these kids can find it so can we."

"I can find it again," the voice came from across the room. For the first time, Cherrie had spoken.

Her face was still swollen, and her eye was still a dark black. Everyone was quiet. James and the Sheriff eyed each other but neither spoke.

"Dad, I think I can go right to that old shack and that's probably where Dee went."

Still, there was no reply from anyone. James seemed to be fighting a battle deep inside his soul. He knew it would be wrong to take his daughter into this kind of danger, but he also knew it would probably save them a lot of time.

"No," a new voice entered the conversation. "No, she's not goin' back up on that hill." It was Mary Collie who spoke. She had been standing and listening from the hallway.

"Mom, I can find it. I'm sure I can," Cherrie cried.

"Jim, you can't take her up on that hill. You don't know what to expect," she said, addressing James directly.

James remained silent. His eyes showed an expression of fear and confusion.

"Jim," it was the Sheriff who spoke this time. "She'd save us a lot of time, and time may be important now."

"No!" Mary yelled. "You can't take this child back up on that hill. Not after all that's happened. Y'all must be crazy." Tears began to form in Mary's eyes. She couldn't believe that her husband would even be thinking such a thing. "Those people are crazy. They've killed people. Don't you understand you can't take this child into that kind of danger?"

"It's your decision Jim," the Sheriff spoke again. "But she would be a big help."

James still seemed unable to reach a decision.

"Dad, I can do it and I want to go. Please, Dad!" Cherrie pleaded. She turned and looked at her mother. "I'm sorry, Mom. Please don't be mad at me, but I can do it and they need me. Dee may need me. I know Dee and I know what he's tryin' to do. I can help and I'm just like Dee in that I want to do somethin'."

"Jim, no," Mary put in feebly, as the tears began to flow freely down her cheeks. "Don't take my other child up on that hill."

"We're wastin' time. Come on Cherrie, get your raincoat and keep behind the Sheriff and me. When we need directions, we'll ask you," James ordered. As he spoke, his and Mary's eyes were locked on each other the whole time.

"Jim," was the only pitiful reply from Mary.

"I hate to, Mary, but it's the only way we can do it right now. I'll watch her good, Mary. I swear I will."

They started for the door, but Cherrie stopped and ran back and threw her arms around her Mother. Then, she pulled away and joined her Father and Sheriff Clark who were already heading down the back path. Mary stood in the doorway watching them go. James, her husband, was carrying a rifle under his arm, Cherrie, her daughter, was walking along behind her father looking so small, and the Sheriff was leading the way. The tears rolled down her cheeks and dropped onto her dress. Only yesterday things had been normal. Now, Rachael was dead, Cherrie hurt, and Dee was missing. Her husband was going off with hate in his heart and a rifle in his hands. With him, he took her only daughter. Only she remained behind, unable to help, unable to be of any use.

As she watched them go, the rain started to fall again. The flashes of lightning lit up the sky and she could see them as they got farther and farther away. After a while, she could see them no more. When the lightning flashed, she could see the smoldering remains of Rachael's house. It didn't glow anymore, as the rain had killed the remaining hot coals. The burnt remains made an eerie sight as it was outlined by the flashes of lightning.

To Mary, the ruins looked like a tombstone. A tombstone on Rachael's grave. She stared in the direction of the ruins waiting for the next flash of lightning so she could see. She stood transfixed; her eyes not blinking. In her mind, she could see Rachael standing near her burnt house in the rain. Rachael's face had a look of wonderment, as if she were trying to understand what had happened. What had happened to her and to her house? Mary wanted to call out to Rachael to come in out of the rain, but her voice wouldn't make any sounds. Suddenly, she jumped, as a loud crash of thunder brought her back to reality. She looked around quickly, as if awakening from a dream. Then, she relaxed as her conscious mind took control again.

Mary could feel the dampness of the rain as it started to fall harder. She backed away from the doorway and closed the door. She pressed her head against the cool window pane on the door. After a while, she pushed away from the window and walked to the kitchen table and sat down. There would be no need to try and sleep. She would simply wait here until her family returned.

As she sat at the table, she tried to make her mind stop working. But she couldn't make it stop. She wiped the tears from her eyes with her dress sleeve. It did little good, as new tears replaced the dried ones. This had been the longest day of her life and still it would not end. Through the day, into the evening, and now into the night, this day would not end. She wondered if this day would continue until all that she loved was gone. Why, oh why, was this happening to them?

CHAPTER TWENTY-FOUR

Planned Escape

It didn't take long for Judy to lose Daryl on the hill. She ran through the darkness with knowing skill. She watched as Daryl ran passed her and hopelessly stumbled among the bushes and trees. When she was sure he was lost, she doubled back toward the cabin. Her father had asked her to come to the cabin earlier in the night while they were at their own cabin. That was her destination when she had come upon Daryl. Now she reached the small clearing and approached the cabin for the second time.

She stopped before she went in. For some reason, she was suddenly worried about Dee being lost on the hill. He could get hurt if he was not careful. For one minute, she was tempted to go back and help him find his way down the hill. She looked into the darkness and then up to the sky. The clouds were building again and the rain was starting to come down in force again. This time the rain would be heavy. She shook her head as if to clear it of unwanted thoughts. Daryl would have to take care of himself. She had more important things to deal with.

Ruth Jordan and Jim Upter were sitting calmly at the table talking, when Judy came into the cabin. They looked up, but said nothing. They returned to their talking as Judy crossed over to the other side of the small room where she saw her father sitting quietly. She walked up and knelt down beside him and tugged on his sleeve.

"What is it, Judy?"

She leaned over and whispered to him in a very low voice, "The laws comin'."

His head jerked to face her and his eyes glowed with fear. "How do you know that?" He asked, grabbing her by the shoulders.

"Daryl Collie told me," she said, pulling herself free of his grip.

"Daryl Collie! You been talkin' to Daryl Collie? Where is he?" His voice had gotten louder and now Ruth got up and walked over to where they were.

"What's goin' on?" Ruth asked.

"Uh, she saw . . . she saw somethin' in the dark outside," he stammered. "I'd better go see what it is." With that, he got up and started for the door. "Come show me where you saw it, Judy." They walked out the door and to the edge of the woods that surrounded the cabin. They ignored the rain that pelted down on them. After a short distance they stopped. Then he demanded, "Now, tell me what you're talkin' about."

"I saw Daryl Collie just a while ago right over there by the cabin. I talked to him and he told me the law was comin' to get the men in white."

"How'd they know, how?"

"Daryl's been here before and saw the men in white. I guess he told somebody after they hurt his sister," she answered.

"Judy, I don't understand all this. There's somethin' you ain't tellin' me."

"Pa, there ain't time for all that now! What're you goin' to do about the law? They'll take you away if you're with those men. Then, what'll I do!"

"I don't understand how all this has come about. I wasn't supposed to be involved in anythin' like this. Now I've got more trouble than you know, Judy. I don't want to see the law for more reasons than just the Klan." He ran his hand through his hair and looked about nervously.

"Pa, the reasons don't matter! What're we goin' to do?" She pleaded.

"I need time to think. I need a drink. A drink will help me think."

His hands were shaking and he clasped them together to keep them under control. Then he reached for his back pocket but there was no bottle there.

"No!" She yelled. "No, drinkin'. You help us, Pa. For once, you do somethin' to help."

That seemed to snap him back in control. "Where's the Collie kid now?" He asked.

"I ain't sure. I lost him somewhere in the woods, I think," she replied pointing out into the darkness.

"I wonder what time it is now." He asked mostly to himself.

"I left our cabin a little after midnight," she replied. "But I ain't sure what time it is now. My guess is it's after one."

"That doesn't give us much time 'til day break."

"It doesn't give us much time for what?" Judy asked.

"To plan to get the Hell out of here," he shouted at her.

"You mean we're goin' to run for it, Pa!"

"Yeah, we're goin' ta run for it. But first we've got to get some things from our cabin. We've got to go by there first. Now, Judy, we have to be careful and not let Ruth see what we're up to. We need to be careful of Jim too."

"I like the idea of gettin' out of here. I want to do it fast!" Judy exclaimed excitedly.

"Okay, here's what we're goin' to do. Ruth and Jim are goin' back to Ruth's house early in the morning. We'll get up first and take off. I ain't sure where we'll go just yet, but we'll go anyway. I'll think of someplace tonight. We'll have to be very quiet, because Ruth and Jim are staying in the cabin tonight. Ruth wants us to stay here with them tonight because of all the mess up. She's expectin' you and me to sleep here tonight. That means we won't be able to get back to our own cabin before we leave. So, when we leave, we'll have to go by our cabin first before we leave the hill. That means we'll have to hurry! You got all that?"

"Yeah, I think so," she replied, nodding her head.

"Only thing that worries me is that Collie kid runnin' around up here somewhere," he said with a worried look. "The damn kid could get hurt."

"I can find him if you want," she said. "But it's goin' to start rainin' hard soon. I think there's a big storm buildin' up. So if I'm goin' ta find him, I need to go now!"

"No! No, I want you to stay with me all the time. We'll be getting up early, so you'd best get some sleep. Okay?"

"Okay," she said, and they started back toward the cabin. After a few steps, she stopped and asked, "But what about Daryl Collie? I'm kind of worry about him being out there by his self. He could get hurt real bad. He don't know this hill, Pa."

"I know how you feel," he replied gently. "I don't like it either. But we've got to take care of ourselves first. He got up here by himself and he'll just have to get down the same way."

"I guess so," she said. "But we ain't ever hurt anybody and I don't like thinkin' about what could happen."

"I know," he said gently patting her on the shoulder. "I know. You're a good girl. God, you're a good girl."

As they turned and started for the cabin again, Judy was as happy as she had been in a long time. At last, she was getting her father away from the men in white. As they approached the cabin, she had a big smile on her face.

CHAPTER TWENTY-FIVE

Another Visitor

The rain was starting to fall again, as Lester Homes sat on his patio cleaning the mud from his shoes. He held his arm up to the light coming from a window in the house, so he could see his watch. It was a little after one o'clock in the morning. Four hours had passed since the fiasco at the Collie house. Over to one side of the patio door, lay a wet white sheet. He guessed he had left the hood in the car. Lester banged his shoes together to knock the excess mud away. Then, he placed them back on his feet. Glancing over at the sheet and hood, a small chuckle escaped from his mouth. What a total screw up this whole thing was, he thought. He knew Rachael was dead. The Sheriff had called him soon after it had happened. He had almost not gotten home in time to answer the phone. The Sheriff must be as stupid as the rest of them.

What was going to happen next was the question he had to answer. What did everybody know? Not even everyone at the Klan meetings knew each other. Jim Upter was another stupid one. He thought he was some kind of general or something. All he had really accomplished was getting some poor stupid colored people killed. He certainly didn't have an army. His army mostly consisted of people who didn't have any idea why they were in his army in the first place. It wouldn't last. The whole thing would probably fold up after tonight.

Lester wondered where that would leave him. Upter would surely run for cover and probably take Ruth Jordan and her kid with him. Upter was a brave man when he had a bunch of men in front of him, but he wouldn't stay around and take the heat. Upter knows the people in his army will talk under the first sign of pressure from the law. So, Upter would probably run like a scared rabbit. Now, with two people dead, what was going to happen next? The Sheriff had wanted him to join a group of deputies to go up on the hill tomorrow. But he had begged off, claiming he couldn't stand violence. He needed more information at this point.

Lester walked over and picked up the sheet. He put it under his arm and walked out into the rain. He went over to his car and threw the sheet into the back seat with the hood and then got into the car. He drove through the rain humming, "When We All Get to Heaven." He reached his destination and pulled the car to a stop.

Lights still burned in the house even at this hour. Lester got out and walked up to the front porch of the house. Slowly, he climbed the steps of the porch and went to the front door. He knocked firmly on the door. At first no one came, but after several hard knocks, Mary Collie answered the door.

"Hello, Mary. I'm sorry to come by so late, but I just wanted to see if you and your family were okay. The Sheriff called me and told me about all that's happened. I've just now been able to get away and come over." Lester spoke very softly and with much concern in his voice.

"That's all right Lester," Mary replied. "Come on in out of the rain."

"Thank you, Mary," Lester said, as he stepped into the house. She led him into the living room and offered him a chair.

"Where is everyone? Are they in bed?" He asked, looking around.

"Please, sit down," Mary said, indicating a chair. "No, Lester, they're not in bed. They're not even here. I'm here alone."

"Alone, why alone after all that's happened?"

"Well, Dee's run off somewhere! Jim thinks he went up on that hill again. Jim's gone off to look for him and he took Cherrie with him." She started to cry again thinking of Cherrie up on the hill.

"Did you say Dee's gone up on that hill, *again*?" Lester asked, putting emphasis on the word again.

"Yes, but it's a long story, Lester and I'm not sure I'm up to goin' over the whole thing right now."

"But, you're sayin' Dee's been up on the hill before?"

"Yes, he and Cherrie both have been up there before. That's why Cherrie went along. She thinks she can show them the way."

"You say Cherrie went with *them*. Who all went up to the hill?" Lester asked carefully.

"Oh! The Sheriff went too. It was Jim, the Sheriff, and Cherrie. Jim's carryin' a gun and I'm scared to death at what he might do. Lester, I really don't understand why we're goin' over this now. It's not a good time for me."

"I'm sorry, Mary. I just need to get caught up on what's been goin' on."

"Well, where have you been? All this happened over four hours ago. However, it seems as though it's been years. I've never seen so much happen in one night in all my life. It doesn't seem like it's ever goin' to get over with." Mary put her face in her hands and cried.

"I'm sorry for causing you this trouble right now, Mary. I just would like to know what's been goin' on. I'll go now and we can talk later."

"No, that's all right, Lester. Maybe some company would help me. Would you like some coffee? I could put some on. It's probably goin' to be a long night." Mary wiped her eyes and tried to regain her self-control.

"No thanks, Mary. But I'd really like to know when Dee and Cherrie went up on the hill and what they saw."

"Like I said, it's a long story, but . . ." Mary's sentence was interrupted by a bright flash of lightning and loud crack of thunder. The lights blinked and went out. "Oh for God's sake what's goin' to happen next?" Mary cried. "My family is out in this weather somewhere! It looks like it's goin' to get worst."

She jumped up and ran through the door to the kitchen and over to the window over the sink. She peered out the window trying to see through the rain and darkness. Every now and then, a flash of lightning would light up the sky and she could see. She saw the smoldering remains of Rachael's house and beyond that, to the south, she could see the outline of Lonesome Hill. When she could see it, the sky looked angry.

"My God, it looks like it's goin' to storm!" She declared. Mary was so interested in the scene outside that she didn't notice Lester walk-up behind her. It gave her a start when he spoke.

"You know, Mary, it was a night almost just like this that my Lois and Bobbie died."

Mary turned with a jump. "Damn, Lester, you scared me out of my wits!"

She could only see his outline in the darkness. Then a flash of lightning showed her his face. The look on his face and in his eyes made her uncomfortable. "Are you okay, Lester?"

"Oh, yes, I'm fine. It was raining really hard that night you know. I heard some folks say it rained over four inches in one hour. It turned the ravine around Lonesome Hill into a raging river." His voice was very soft and he talked as if he were speaking to someone else. "They never found out for sure why the car went off the road. They believe it was pushed over by the force of the water running down the hill."

Mary started to move away from the window. "Are you sure you're okay? Why don't we go back into the living room and sit down until the storm blows over?"

"No! Why don't we just stand here and watch out this window? We can see the hill from here. Mary, did you know that I can go straight to the spot where they went off the road? Look over there," he said pointing out the window toward Lonesome Hill. Mary turned her head and looked in the direction he was pointing. "It was right over there," he continued. "But you can't see it very good from here. We're too far away and it's too dark. I could show you. I could take you there."

The thunder cracked loudly as a new flash of lightning lit up the area. The look Mary saw in Lester's eyes truly terrified her. She fought to control her fear. She knew she must use her head and not panic. Lester was obviously not himself, or maybe this was Lester. "Lester, can we please go back into the living room so I can light some candles." Mary said as she started to move again.

This time he didn't stop her. Mary walked passed him and into the living room. He followed her into the living room and sat in a chair. She found the candles that were kept in the living room closet for emergencies such as this. Soon, several candles were lit. The mixture of the candlelight and the flashing lightning gave the room an eerie look. Mary sat in her chair across from Lester. They sat in silence for a short while. Then the rain started to fall harder and it could be heard pounding against the window panes.

Finally Lester broke the silence. "I could take you and show you the exact spot where Lois and Bobbie went off the road." He looked at her intensely from across the room.

"Do you think that's such a good idea in this weather? I mean it's really starting to come down now." Mary tried not to let her voice reveal her terror. "Anyway, I really need to stay here and wait for the rest of my family."

"But, I want to show you, Mary. Don't you see? This night is just like that one. It would be perfect to see the exact spot now. Why, it would be just the same, wouldn't it?"

"Thank you, Lester, but I'd better not," Mary said nervously. She squeezed her hands together and smiled at him through the candlelight.

Lester stood up and walked over to her. He looked down at her. "But, I must insist that you come. I'm tired of always being by myself. Lois would understand that. I've never shown anyone before. I always go there alone. But not tonight, I don't want to be alone there tonight. Please, Mary, I won't take no for an answer." He held out his hand to her.

Mary struggled to decide if she should give in and go, or to insist on staying. She looked up at him and studied his face in the candlelight. The face looked disturbed but at the same time calm. She had no way of knowing what he would do if she refused to go. But on the other hand, she didn't know what waited for her if she went. She decided she may have more control if she didn't get him upset or angry. Her mind made up, she reached up and took his hand. "I must get somethin' to wear for the rain," she said gently.

"Of course," he said, as he released her hand.

"I'd like to leave a note for Jim to tell him where I've gone."

"I understand," he said calmly.

Mary went to the closet and took out her raincoat. She put it on and buttoned it up trying to hide her shaking hands. When she was ready, she went into the kitchen and found a note pad and pencil. She wrote a note and read it aloud so Lester could hear, "Have gone out with Lester Homes to see something. Don't worry. Will be back shortly." Taking a pin from her hair, she attached the note to the front door. Then, she turned to face Lester. "I guess I'm ready," she said slowly.

Lester looked at the note and seemed satisfied. He walked around the room blowing out the candles. Mary was glad she didn't try to put any kind of message in the note. She and Lester then walked out the door and onto the porch. Mary closed the door but did not lock it. Lester guided her to the car by the arm. He opened the door and helped her in. After closing the door, he went around to the driver's side and got in himself.

As they drove along, Mary watched him closely. She watched him too closely. "Why are you looking at me like that?" He asked in a flat unemotional voice.

"I'm sorry I didn't realize I was staring. I was just wonderin' why you do this. Why do you go to this spot?"

"Because I can talk to Lois there," he stated flatly. "I can talk to her at her grave too. Those are the only two places that Lois will talk to me. The funny thing is that Bobbie never talks to me, just Lois. Lois tells me about Bobbie, but Bobbie never talks to me."

"What does Lois say when she talks to you?" Mary asked slowly. She was convinced she was dealing with a crazy man.

"Don't make fun of me, Mary. I'm not crazy. You wouldn't understand anyway."

"I didn't mean for it to sound like that," she said quickly. "It's just, well, maybe I would understand."

She felt certain she must not make him angry. Somehow she must keep him in a good frame of mind.

"No, you wouldn't understand. Nobody would understand. Lois is the only one that understands." His voice softened again as his anger subsided. They didn't talk for the next several minutes as the car pushed on through the rain.

Mary noticed she was perspiring both from fear and from the discomfort of the raincoat. "Can I take this raincoat off; it's getting very hot in here?"

"Sure. Just pitch it in the back seat."

"Thanks," she said, as she struggled to get out of the raincoat.

She freed herself of the raincoat and turned in the seat to put it in the back. Then, she saw the sheet and hood in the back seat. At first, she was stunned. She tried to hide her surprise, as she continued to put her raincoat in the back seat. Not only was she dealing with a crazy man, but he was also one of the Klansmen that had been to her house. She started talking to hide her discovery. "I didn't mean to sound like I didn't believe you, Lester. It's just that I've never done this sort of thing before."

He didn't reply. He just drove on in the rain. The rain was pouring down as they turned onto the old dirt road that ringed Lonesome Hill. After a short drive, Lester began to look about. It was hard to see through the windshield with the rain coming down so hard. Suddenly, she saw a look of recognition on his face as a smile spread across his lips. He pulled the car over to the left near the side of the hill and away from the drop down to the ravine. Mary looked out her window and saw that the ravine was filled with rushing water. The water ran down the side of the hill, across the road, and spilled down into the ravine.

"You see," he smiled. "It's almost just like that other night."

CHAPTER TWENTY-SIX

Remember When

Ruth looked up as the old man and Judy returned to the cabin. "I didn't see anybody," the old man said, as he shook the rain from his hair.

"What did she see?" Jim asked.

"She thought she saw someone out in the woods. But I didn't see anybody. Anyway, it's starting to rain hard again. I doubt anybody will be out in this weather," the old man replied.

"Maybe I should check to be sure," Jim said.

"Be my guest," Clint said pointing to the door.

Jim went to the door and looked out. The rain was coming down steady and hard. He glanced around, but could see nothing. He decided it wasn't worth going out into the rain to investigate. "I'll take a look before I go to bed," he said cautiously.

"Speakin' of goin' to bed, that's exactly where I'm goin'," Ruth stated. "I'll use the side room. Clint, you and Judy can use the back room. Judy'll have to sleep on the floor. There's only a small cot in that room."

"I don't understand why we have to stay here tonight. Why can't we go back to our own cabin?" Clint asked.

"Because I don't trust you," Ruth said simply. "We got lots to do in the mornin' and I don't want to have to be worryin' about what you're doin'." Then she turned and looked at Jim and asked in a softer tone, "Are you comin' to bed?"

"Not right this minute. I'll be there in a little bit. I need to do some more thinking."

"Well, no one has asked us, but we're goin' ta bed," Clint added.

"By all means," Jim replied with a smile.

Clint and Judy disappeared into the back room.

Ruth started for the side room and stopped and turned back toward Jim. "Don't stay up too much longer," she said. "We got a big day tomorrow."

"I'll be there shortly."

Ruth walked into the side room. It was very small and cramped. It had one small double bed pushed into one corner. There was a small window just above the foot of the bed. Rain was driving down against the window pane. Light in the room was provided by a kerosene lamp that sat on a stool next to the head of the bed. The lamp was burning low producing very little light. The bed had old sheets on it that smelled with the dampness of the room. Ruth climbed onto the bed to reach the window. She cracked the window just enough to allow in fresh air but not enough to allow the rain to come in.

With one last look out the window and deep tired sigh, Ruth began to undress. She had no sleeping clothes with her so she was content to sleep in her panties and bra. She crawled onto the bed crossways to look out the window. The rain seemed to come down relentlessly. She pulled the top sheet back and started to climb in between the sheets, but then decided it was too stuffy and she simply lay down on top of the sheets. After a few minutes, she crawled back crossways in the bed and lay on her belly so she could look out the window at the rain. She reached back to the lamp and turned the light out.

Shortly, her eyes grew accustomed to the dark so she could see the trees a short distance away from the cabin. A small breeze blew through the opening in the window and across her face. It felt refreshing. She sat up on her knees in bed and reached behind her back for the snap on her bra. Finding it, she slipped out of the bra. It felt much better without it. The cool breeze blew across her breast and evaporated the sweat that had gathered there. She lay back down on her belly and continued to gaze out the window. She wondered what time it must be. It must be well after midnight, maybe about two o'clock in the morning, she thought. Returning to the head of the bed, she stretched out her full length. She laid her head on the soft feather pillow and closed her eyes. As much as she wanted to sleep, her mind raced with so many thoughts sleep would not come.

Ruth stretched her muscles as much as she could and then relaxed again. She began to think back while lying in this lonely room on a lonely hill in the rain. Her thoughts went back to New Orleans and the first time she had met Jim. She wondered what it was that had attracted Jim to her. Looking down at her almost nude body, she reached a conclusion. Her body was nice and she knew it. She looked much younger than her years, which weren't too many anyway. Jim had told her many times how much he enjoyed looking at her and how beautiful she was. She knew some of it was just talk, but some of it was true. Ruth's eyes closed as she thought about it.

———

Ruth and Dick had gone to New Orleans as a pleasure trip, after getting the insurance money in Dallas. It was the first time Dick had been out of the State of Texas. Ruth had been to Louisiana before, but never to colorful New Orleans. When they arrived in New Orleans, it was gloomy and rainy. In fact, it was raining rather hard. They arrived by train and they were standing all alone in the depot when Jim came to them.

"Can I help you, Ma'am?" The question came from behind her. She turned around to see Jim standing there smiling.

"Well . . . yes. Please do," Ruth stammered. "We need to find a hotel and some transportation."

"Okay, I got the transportation, but the hotel we'll have to work on."

"Oh! I don't have a hotel. I thought I could get one when I got here. I can, can't I?"

"Sure thing, I know a good hotel for you and your little brother," Jim replied.

"Oh, goodness no, he's not my brother. This is my son, Dick."

"He's your son!" Jim said, genuinely surprised. "Is your husband coming later? Mrs. . . ."

"Jordan," Ruth replied. "Ruth Jordan, and no, my husband's not comin' because, you see, I'm a widow."

"There's a cab out front. Come on, I'll carry your bags for you," Jim said, as he started picking up the bags.

"Well, I don't know. I don't even know your name. I don't normally just take off with strangers."

"Oh! I beg your pardon. My name is Upter. Jim Upter. I'm president of the Cab Driver's Union here in New Orleans. That's how I know there's a cab out front."

"Oh! . . . Oh well, okay!" Ruth replied still unsure. "We surely do thank you, Mr. Upter. We certainly are grateful."

That's the way it had happened. More or less a pickup, Ruth thought. She didn't know why she had agreed to keep on seeing Jim. Maybe it was because he had promised to show her New Orleans. But probably, it was because for the first time in a long time a man was giving her his attention. She wasn't sure why she had continued to see Jim but she had and she was glad she did.

Ruth had been in New Orleans for six months before Jim took her to her first Klan rally. She would never forget the burning cross and hooded people. There were hundreds of them. After the meeting that night, Jim was very quiet all the way back to her hotel. It was only after they had entered her room that he began to talk freely.

"Where's Dick tonight?" He asked.

"He's staying with the Butler boy tonight. They're planin' to go sailing in the Gulf first thing tomorrow mornin'," Ruth answered, as she walked over to the liquor cabinet. "What'll you have?"

"I'll just have bourbon on the rocks."

Ruth poured the drinks and handed Jim his. She sat on the divan next to him. She held her glass up in a toast. "A toast to your Klan," she said smiling.

"What did you think about the meeting tonight?" Jim asked, looking at her closely.

"What should I think?"

"I'd hoped you'd be impressed."

"I was . . . I guess," she answered, not looking him in the face.

Jim reached over and placed his hand on her cheek. He tilted her face until their eye's met. "It's important that you understand, because I'm going to ask you to do two things tonight and it'll all depend on your understanding. At least one will."

"What's the mystery?" She asked, trying to sound lighthearted, but the touch of Jim's hand made her fail terribly.

"Ruth, the Klan wants me to go to Texas and start a chapter there," he said. "They'll give me all the help they can."

"You mean start the Klan in Texas? Isn't it already there?"

"Not really. You see, there are people there who want the Klan; they just need organizing. The Klan wants me to go to Texas and start organizing the eastern half of the state. I'll get them organized and I'll be their leader." Jim's eyes glowed as he talked about becoming the leader of the Texas Klan. His excitement boiled over. "They picked me because they think I'm a good leader. My experience as president of the Cab Driver's Union helped them pick me. Plus, my accent is not heavy. I spent a lot of time in the army and I lost most of my accent. This is my chance to do something and be somebody. Just think Ruth, a whole army under my command; under me. It'll be a great army with a just cause. And I'll be their leader." Jim stopped talking and looked long and hard at Ruth, who seemed unsure of the whole thing.

"But how," she asked, "How're you goin' to start a chapter in Texas?"

"Do you love me, Ruth?" He asked softly, looking into her in the eyes.

Ruth lowered her head and stared down at the divan seat. "You know I do, Jim. You know I love you."

Jim pulled her close to him and took her in his arms. He lifted her face up and kissed her long and hard. When their lips had parted, he looked down at her. "Do you love me enough to marry me?" He asked softly.

Her eyes widened and her brain reeled. She felt him kiss her again. Then, she heard him ask her again. She heard herself say yes. Not once, but time after time, as Jim made love to her.

—◦◦◦◦◦—

Ruth opened her eyes to find herself still in the small bedroom in the cabin. Her body had tensed up so much that when she relaxed she exhaled a long sigh. The breeze had stopped blowing through the small opening in the window and she found herself wet with perspiration. The rain had not stopped, as it continued to pound the window pane. She rolled over on her belly again and closed her eyes.

They had decided it would be best not to tell anyone of their marriage. Jim would have a better chance to do his work if no one knew of their relationship. So, they didn't even tell Dick. Jim had assured her that after things got going they would not have to keep it a secret. Anyway, for reasons of her own, Ruth wanted to keep it a secret. Reasons even Jim didn't know. The plan was to start the chapter in Coalville and slowly build into the surrounding areas. And when they thought the time was right, they would move into the larger cities of Dallas and Houston.

Jim dreamed of having a chapter in Dallas. One as large and strong as the chapter he belonged to in New Orleans. They both knew the work would be long and hard and, maybe, even dangerous at times. They each had different reasons for starting out on such a bold venture. Jim, because he believed in it and dreamed of being an important figure in an important movement and Ruth, because she loved Jim and wanted him with her. The Klan was not important to Ruth. Although she never told Jim how she really felt. Jim was the only thing important to Ruth.

Lonesome Hill had presented Jim with the perfect situation. It was a place where no one ever came and a place with a reputation that kept everyone away. It was a place where he could set up his operation without interference. At first, Jim had been reluctant to use Clint to help get the cabin set up as a meeting place. He couldn't understand the relationship between Ruth, Clint, and Judy. Even more, he didn't like Clint's drinking. He believed that drunks were unreliable. More than once he pressed Ruth to explain why she made weekly trips to keep Clint supplied with food and whiskey, but Ruth never clearly explained. She only told him that Clint was a friend that needed her help and that she had promised to give him that help a long time ago. Clint's knowledge of the hill proved valuable in establishing the meeting place. As a result, Jim's questions became less and less frequent. Ruth had managed to keep both Jim and Clint satisfied.

Ruth opened her eyes again. There was a small crack of light falling on her. She rolled over to see Jim standing in the doorway. The light coming from behind him made it hard for her to see him. He pushed the door all the way open so that the light covered her as if she were in a spotlight. He stood there for a long time looking at her. At first, she didn't move. Then, after he had been looking at her for what seemed like several minutes, she put her arms over her head and stretched herself. She pointed her toes and arched her back forcing her breast up as she stretched her muscles to the limit.

Suddenly, he closed the door and the room became dark again. He walked over to the foot of the bed and stood looking down at her in the darkness. She didn't try to cover herself. After all, he was her husband. Her eyes had not readjusted to the dark and she could barely see him. He moved around the foot of the bed and sat on the edge of the bed beside her. She felt him take one of her ankles in each of his hands. He held her ankles for a minute then he started sliding his hands up her legs. His hands traveled up her naked thighs and grabbed hold of her panties. He pulled them down her long legs and then dropped them on the floor.

CHAPTER TWENTY-SEVEN

Reflections

Dick Jordan had left Cherrie's bedroom and gone straight home. He had done everything the Sheriff had told him, and now he didn't know what to do. It was dark outside and the rain was coming down in a steady downpour. Even through the dark and rain, Dick could see the men the Sheriff had left to watch him. There was one parked out front in a patrol car and he knew that someone was watching the back as well. Dick figured they were waiting for his mother to return, more than watching him. He didn't care either way. All that concerned him now was getting out of this mess and still being friends with Cherrie. She still didn't trust him, and he guessed he couldn't blame her. But what really bothered Dick was why he cared so much about her. He had been so upset when he heard she had been hurt. After all, she was still a kid, actually only twelve years old. But still Dick liked her. He liked her more than any of the rest, or maybe more than anybody he knew.

Dick went to bed that night in a deserted house. He had a hard time sleeping, as things kept going over in his mind. He kept remembering things and trying to put them together in his head. Like the day they left Coalville and his saying goodbye to Cherrie. Innocent, but he hadn't forgotten. He had said, "I'll go on being your boyfriend when I get back." But it had not worked out that way after all.

Then the trip to Dallas had come and with that the insurance money. After the money, the trip to New Orleans had come and his mother had met Jim Upter. They had spent nine months in New Orleans. His Mother had met a lot of Jim's friends and they talked and talked. It seemed to Dick that they were always talking. With all their talk, there was little time for Dick in their plans. Then, it was decided to return to Coalville. This change of events made Dick extremely happy, but there was one drawback and that was that Jim Upter was coming with them.

So, they returned to Coalville. Things, however, would be different when they got there. They still made their trips up to Lonesome Hill, but now more often and with more people. Dick had always wondered why his mother had kept Judy Cole and her father in money and supplies. He was a drunk and she was a wild girl. Dick thought that his mother should tell the school board about Judy Cole not going to school. But she had told him not to say anything and to mind his own business. She said when the time came she would tell him all about it. But the time had never come.

Actually, Dick had become good friends with Judy Cole. She was a smart girl and a good person. He had a hard time believing that all her education had come from her drunken father, but he was sure that was the case. Dick had been a friend to everyone until the men in sheets and hoods came. When the Klan moved in on the hill, Judy began to fear everyone, including Dick. Now he hardly ever saw her. Her father would not let her come around the cabin when the Klan was there, which was most of the time. They stayed in their own cabin and Dick saw very little of her.

The Klan had changed everything for Dick. His mother had become distant and completely involved with Jim. Generally, Dick didn't pay much attention to the Klan's doing, but he knew Jim was their leader. In New Orleans, Jim had only been a small ranking member, but here in Coalville he was the leader. Dick didn't know the details but he knew enough now to know that the Klan was wrong.

He rolled over on his back and stared at the ceiling. As his mind remembered all these things, the most puzzling thing of all was the old drunkard. Why had he come to this house and said the things he said? Why had his mother said what she did? What was it that he had threatened to tell Dick? What? Why? He needed to know. There was so much he didn't know or understand.

Dick rolled back over on his side and looked into the darkness. It seemed everything was all mixed up. His mother had some kind of role in the Klan, Jim was one of their leaders, Cherrie hated him, and he had told the Sheriff about his own mother. At the moment, Dick's hopes looked dim. His future, if he had one, appeared even worse.

Dick rolled over on his back again. Then, in a few moments, onto his side again. He couldn't keep his eyes closed. Sleep would not come to Dick Jordan this night.

CHAPTER TWENTY-EIGHT

Decisions

Dee sat huddled under a cluster of willow trees to try and keep out of the rain. It helped some, but still the rain found him and soaked him to the skin. Since Judy Cole had run away, he had spent a short time looking for her but realized that he didn't have a chance of finding her. As Dee saw it, he had three choices. One was to follow the slope of the hill back down to the road and then find his way home from there. Two, was to follow the slope of the hill back to the top and then try and find the cabin again. Three, was to try and find Judy Cole.

Dee knew he couldn't find Judy if she didn't want to be found, so that option was out. He knew the thing he should do was head for home. He didn't know what time it was, but he was afraid it was getting close to daybreak. If his dad found him gone, the results would not be good. His big fear was that his dad had already discovered him gone. If Cherrie woke up and found him gone, or if his mother came to check on Cherrie and found him gone, his dad would know. There were any number of ways his dad could find out he was gone.

Dee made the decision to get back home as fast as possible. He wasn't sure where he was, but if he followed the slope of the hill down, he should find the road eventually. The only problem was that at several points the slope disappeared. That was especially true around some of the old coal pits where the digging had taken place. He would have to be very careful not to step into a pit, and at the same time keep following the slope of the hill. At the moment, he was in an area where the slope was not evident. He was not sure which way to go. After a short pause, he made his best choice and started walking at a fast clip. He was careful not to run, but walked as fast as care would permit.

Once out and walking again, the rain continued to drench him. It didn't matter to him, because he was already soaked through and through. His hair was matted and stuck to his forehead. He had to continually wipe the rain from his face so he could see. After walking what seemed like several minutes, Dee spotted a dim light in the distance. He noticed that the slope of the hill ran up toward the light. This was not the direction Dee had wanted to go. From where he stood, he could easily distinguish the slope of the hill. Making a quick decision, he turned away from the light and started following the down slope. But he had only taken a few steps, when his curiosity got the best of him. He turned back around and started making his way up the slope toward the dim light.

The dim light was not as far away as he had thought. He followed the light and it led to a small cabin. The light was coming from a window on one side of the cabin. Trees allowed Dee protection almost right up to the cabin itself. He reached the cabin and touched it. There was no door or window on this side of the cabin. He felt his way around to the side where he had seen the light. Slowly, he peeked around the corner. The light was dim and the window was small, but in the dark and rain the light was very visible.

Then, he began to understand. This was the same cabin. Dee could see the small clearing in front of the cabin. Now he knew that somehow he had come up from behind the cabin. While he was wondering around, he must have circled the top of the hill and was now at the back of the cabin. This gave Dee some relief; because he was sure he could find his way back down the hill in quick order. He wanted to get back out in the cover of the trees and head for home, but the light in the window attracted him. He had come all this way and now was his chance to see inside the cabin. It would only take a minute. He slid along the side of the cabin toward the window. Reaching the window, he stopped. He lowered himself down on his knees and crawled underneath the window. Then slowly, very slowly, he raised his head to peek into the cabin.

When his eyes got to the level of the window pane, he looked into the cabin and stared directly into another face looking out the window. He couldn't tell who it was because the rain blurred his vision. It didn't matter to him who it was, he ran for the trees as fast as he could.

He heard a voice call from behind him, "Hey! Who's out there?" Dee didn't feel the need to reply.

Jim Upter crashed into the small room where Clint and Judy were sleeping. "Hey, you two, get up. We got problems," he yelled, as he kicked the bed in which Clint lay sleeping.

"What's goin' on?" Clint asked sitting up in bed.

"The Collie kid's somewhere out there on the hill," Jim explained. "We've got to move before he tells someone about us."

"Are you crazy," Clint Shouted, "what would that kid be doin' up here in this weather?"

"I ain't got time to argue with you, old man. You just do what I tell you. Now, move!"

Ruth felt herself being shaken. Finally awake, she opened her eyes and blinked against the lamp light that had been turned up to full brightness. She looked up at Jim standing over the bed.

"Get up, Ruth," he was saying. She looked up at him and tried to focus her eyes. "Come on and wake up, damn it. You haven't been asleep that long. Things are happening."

He grabbed the sheet that covered her and pulled it away. Ruth felt the dampness hit her naked body. She propped herself up on one elbow and squinted up at him. "What time is it?" She asked sleepily.

"It's after two in the morning."

"Is it still rainin'?" She asked, as she glanced at the window.

"Yes, Ruth, it's still raining. If you're finished asking questions, can we get moving?"

"What's happened?" She asked sleepily.

"Well, here's what's happening," Jim said loudly. "I just saw, who I think was the Collie kid, peeking through the window in the other room. I yelled at him but he ran like Hell into the trees. I couldn't catch him in a hundred years. Everything has gone to hell. The best thing we can do now is to get out fast, because the Collie kid sure as Hell will tell somebody. Get up and get dressed. We've got to get goin'."

"Where'll we go?" Ruth asked.

"Someplace where I can think this thing out, if we hurry, maybe we can get back to the house and get the car. If we can't, we'll have to think of something else. Right now we got to get started, come on and get dressed."

"We've got to be sure and get Dick before we go anywhere," Ruth said with conviction, as she swung her long legs off the bed and onto the floor.

"We will. Just hurry up," Jim persisted. "I want you to go on to the house and get anything you need and load it into the car. But please travel light; we haven't got time for a ton of stuff. I'll be along as quick as I can. I'm going to clean things up here and destroy anything that might be used against us. You take that booze drinking son-of-a-bitch and his little bastard with you. We'll leave them at the house. I don't want to leave them alone up here. I don't know what he'll do. After we're gone, he can do whatever to Hell he wants."

Clint had heard Jim's conversation with Ruth. He grabbed Judy and pulled her close to him. "Now listen and don't talk. Just do as I say without any arguments. Okay?" He whispered.

Judy nodded her head in agreement. She had fear in her eyes.

"We'll be headin' for Ruth's house in a few minutes. As soon as we're in the trees, I want you to run. Run down the old miner's path on the north side of the hill. Get to the road and wait for me by the ravine. Be careful, because the rain has filled the ravine and it'll be flowin' like a river."

"What're you goin' ta do, Pa?" Judy asked softly with concern in her voice.

"I'll go with Ruth as far as the road. Then I'll circle around and get you and we'll head for our cabin to get our stuff."

In the other room, Ruth picked up her panties from the floor and put them on. She looked around the room for her bra without success, so she decided to wear her blouse without it. She picked up a brush and started brushing her hair when Jim yelled at her.

"For Christ sakes, Ruth, the rain is going to mess your hair anyway, can you please just get going?" Jim asked with frustration.

Jim finally got all of them together at the cabin door. "Okay, y'all take off and make it as fast as you can. And listen old man, don't you give her any trouble or you'll have to answer to me." Jim reached over and kissed Ruth on the lips and then pushed them all out the door.

Ruth went running out the front door of the cabin slipping her shoes on her feet as she ran. Along with everything else, she had lost her stockings, too. Clint and Judy followed close behind her. The rain hit them as they ran for the trees. Ruth was in the lead as they started working their way through the trees and down the hill. Suddenly, Judy darted away from them and disappeared into the darkness. Ruth never knew Judy had gone. She was too busy watching her step and wiping rain from her face. Without warning, Ruth stepped into a soft muddy spot and fell full length to the ground. She rolled over to get up and saw Clint offering her his hand. Reaching up, she took his hand and pulled herself up. It was then she noticed Judy was not with them.

"Where's Judy?" She yelled through the rain and thunder.

"Never mind about Judy," Clint replied. "Let's just get you down to the road."

"What's goin' on, Clint? Where's Judy? You're not goin' to try anythin' stupid are you?"

"Judy's all right. I'm not tryin' anythin'. I'm goin' as far as the road with you then I'm leavin'. Judy and me are gonna make it on our own. I wish you luck, Ruth."

They both stood there in the rain looking at each other. Ruth's blouse was soaked through by rain, and her breasts showed clearly through the wet material.

"You're still a beautiful woman, Ruth," Clint said admiringly. "I hope you get what you're goin' after and I hope you and Dick find a way to be happy."

"What'll you do, Clint? I promised to take care of you and I will."

"I know you would, Ruth. But I don't want that anymore. You go your way and I'll go mine. Judy and me have gotta do more than live on this hill. I was stupid to think I could ever make that work. It's not been fair to Judy or me. No matter how it all comes out, I guess I'll always love you."

He grabbed Ruth's arm and pulled at her. "Now, come on. We'll drown in this rain, plus we've got to get to your house before the Collie kid alerts somebody."

She didn't move for a minute. Then, she took his hand again and followed him down the hill.

CHAPTER TWENTY-NINE

Sins of the Past

Bob Ann Jackson lay quietly next to her husband in bed. She glanced at the clock next to the bed and saw that it read two thirty in the morning. Jack was sound asleep, but she had not been asleep the entire night. She stared out the window across from her side of the bed. The rain had slowed to a steady drizzle that continued to blur the window pane. Softly, she slipped out of bed. Jack moved and moaned, but continued sleeping. She walked quietly over to the window and looked out into the rainy dark. Her eyes began to water and a lone tear rolled down her cheek. Her brain was filled with memories and thoughts about her life. This kind of night under these kinds of conditions made her emotions work overtime.

She looked again at Jack sleeping calmly. Jack was a good husband and father to their children. She loved him beyond belief. He held a good job as a pharmacist at the Square Pharmacy, where he started working ten years ago straight out of East Texas State Teachers College. Over the last three years, there had been several offers for better paying jobs in Dallas, but he stayed in Coalville. He stayed so Bob Ann could be near her father and because he loved her and wanted her to be happy. She was happy. Happier than she ever thought she could be, or, more truly, happier than she deserved to be. Together they had produced two handsome boys; one was now six and the other four years of age.

These last years had been happy ones for her. She lived close to her father whom she worshiped, she had a husband who she adored, and she had two fine children who she would die for. All of this had helped erase the painful memories of her past. Only recently had those memories began to move back into her brain. The recurrence had been brought on by her father's trips to Lonesome Hill. He didn't know that she knew of his weekly trips to the hill.

She supposed the trips made by her father were to replace the ones normally made by Ruth Jordan. She noticed that the trips started when Ruth left Coalville and stopped when she came back. Her father must have agreed to make the trips for Ruth while she was gone. With all of this happening, she had insisted on going to Doc Jewel and making sure he had not broken their deal. This had only made things worst. Now, this new thing had occurred. Sheriff Clark had wanted to deputize Jack for some sort of police action tomorrow night on Lonesome Hill. Jack had declined, but the question as to why the Sheriff needed deputies for an action on Lonesome Hill was unanswered and it weighed heavily on her mind. There were things on Lonesome Hill that should best be left in the past.

She pressed her head against the window pane and closed her eyes tightly. Now the truth was staring her in the face and threatening to destroy all she had. Past sins were now close to coming back to punish her. But why should they punish her family and her father? Sins can be forgiven, but they seem to never completely go away. Sins for most people are but small events in their lives, but for the preacher's daughter any sin is a major event. Most women would consider beauty such as hers a true blessing, but to a preacher's daughter it was a curse. As a young girl, she was, indeed, beautiful. It had been a joke among all of the boys at school to try and make the preacher's daughter. They all tried to get to her, but none succeeded, at least none that anybody knew about. Yes, she had been a good girl. After all, she was the preacher's daughter.

Bob Ann moved across the room silently to the bedroom door. She opened the door and eased her way into the hall. Once there, she went to the boy's room and peeked in. They were both sleeping soundly. Next, she went to the hall closet and took out her raincoat. Then, she remembered she had no shoes and she was only in her night gown. She started back to the bedroom but decided not to risk waking Jack. As quietly as possible, she slipped on her raincoat, went down the hall to the living room, and then to the front door. Carefully she unlocked the door and slowly swung it open. The door made no sound. She hesitated for a moment and then stepped out into the early morning darkness.

Bob Ann and Jack lived only a few blocks from her father. The Reverend lived in a small house behind the church. She headed in that direction. There were no street lights, so the darkness was complete. Her bare feet touched the wet grass and, at first, gave her a start. Quickly, she ran across her lawn and into the street. Dashing down the street, she slipped several times and had to fight to keep her balance. The drizzle soon had her long coal black hair plastered to her forehead and face. Fortunately the journey was a short one. Soon, she was walking up the front steps to her father's house. She raised her hand to knock, but the door opened before she could complete the action.

"Come in," her Father said. "I've been expecting you."

"Then you know about the Sheriff's intention to go up on the hill tomorrow?" She asked calmly, as she stepped in the door.

"Yes, I know. But it's not tomorrow. It's tonight. You see it's almost three in the morning now. Wait here while I go and get you a towel."

Her Father left the room and then returned with a large bath towel. He handed her the towel and then walked into the living room and sat down in his easy chair. She took off her raincoat and dropped it on the floor near the door. She dried herself off and then wrapped the towel around her head. Her father eyed her closely, paying particular attention to her attire.

"That's kind of a small outfit for traveling isn't it?" He asked, pointing at her.

"Yeah, I guess it is, but I was afraid of waking up Jack. I need to get back soon before he finds me gone, but I wanted to talk to you before all of this happens."

"How'd you know about the Sheriff's intended trip?" He asked.

"Jack told me. The Sheriff wanted to take him along as a deputy, but Jack said he couldn't go. I haven't stopped worryin' since he told me."

"What do you expect to do?" He asked, looking up at her.

"I don't know, Dad. They'll find out. I know they will."

"What can we do? We can't stop the Sheriff. He has a job to do, and a job that needs doing, I might add. Those men who killed the innocent must be caught and punished for their crime. There is no other way. All of this must tie together somehow. I don't know how, but it must."

"I know all of that, but, Dad, what about me? The whole town will find out. What will Jack do? Oh, Dad, what am I goin' to do?"

Bob Ann didn't cry or become hysterical. She remained calm, but afraid. In her mind she had resigned herself as to what must be, but she was trying to find a way to face it.

"Well, child, I'm afraid the time has come for us to face our wrong. We sinned against God and man in doing things the way we did. Now, the time has come for our judgment. We can only hope that mercy will be shown to us. God, I'm sure, has already forgiven us. Jack, if he really loves you, will forgive and understand. But we can only hope the people of town will forgive and understand. We'll soon see if I've done my job in this town. If they're able to forgive, then I've been successful. On the other hand if they can't forgive, then I've failed."

"Oh, Dad, I hope this won't hurt your position in church. I'd rather die than have them blame you."

"It doesn't matter much. This time we'll face this thing together. For you see, they should blame me. It is my fault. I was never fair to you, Bob Ann. You've been more than any father could ever hope for. I was blinded by my personal fear for my position. But those days are gone. Now, I only want to be the father to you that I should've been in the first place. So, come on, I suggest we go tell Jack right now this very minute. It would be much better to have you explain it to him than to have someone else do it. We've done wrong, especially me. All these years it has been wrong. We can't make it right now, but we can make it better by at last letting the truth out. Come on now, we have work to do."

Bob Ann stopped at the door and picked up her raincoat. Her father took it from her and helped her put it on. As he helped her into her raincoat, he took her shoulders in his hands and squeezed them gently. She leaned her head back against his chest.

"Don't worry," he whispered. "God will give you peace and happiness."

The Reverend then got his own raincoat and they went out the door together.

CHAPTER THIRTY

Mistaken Identity

Judy Cole had worked her way down the north side of the hill using the old miner's trail as instructed by her father. Rain was still coming down steadily as she emerged onto the ring road at the bottom of the hill. The road was muddy and slippery. She looked carefully around to make sure no one was nearby, then walked across the road and looked over the edge down into the ravine. Her father had been right. The ravine was raging with water. She wondered how long it would be before her father arrived and exactly where she should be. She looked again down into the ravine and decided that it would be better to wait on the other side of the road by the trail.

Just as she turned to start across the road again, car lights appeared from around the bend in the road. It took her completely by surprise. Without thinking, she took a step backward. The loose, wet mud on the edge of the road gave way. Judy fell backwards into the ravine.

She tumbled down and fell into the rushing water. To her good luck, the water wasn't deep. The water pushed her down the ravine for a short distance, before she was able to grab an exposed tree root that was growing out of the side of the ravine. She grabbed the root and held on for dear life. The water was rushing fast and the root was slippery. She didn't know how long she could hold on. Fighting the current, she pulled herself close to the tree and locked her arms around the root. She interlocked her fingers to try and keep them from slipping. After she had stabilized herself, she looked around to take stock of her situation. She was on the far side of the ravine away from the hill. Even though the water current was strong, she could touch the bottom of the ravine with her feet. The bottom of the ravine was soft and she could dig her feet in. She didn't think she was in danger of washing away, but she wasn't going anywhere either.

Judy scanned the top of the ravine where it touched the road. She noticed the car had stopped and parked at the edge of the road. In the darkness and due to her position in the ravine, all she could see were the headlights. Judy wondered who it could be and why they were here. It didn't matter, she needed help. Yelling for help would do no good. The noise of the rain and rushing water would cover her voice. She decided she must make it to the other side of the ravine and climb up to the road. How to accomplish that task was the problem. There didn't seem to be an immediate solution. She looked around desperately for some means of help, because she was afraid the car would leave without helping her. No solution was immediately at hand.

Then, what at first appeared to be a disaster, turned out to be another lucky stroke. The tree to which she was clinging started to collapse into the ravine. Rushing water had moved enough soil from around the roots that the tree was starting to fall. At first, she was terrified that she was going to drown. But then, she noticed her good luck. The tree was tall enough to span the rushing water. All she had to do was adjust her position so that the tree would not fall on her and force her beneath the water. As the tree slowly gave way, she moved as it moved. Each time the tree would slip lower toward the water; Judy would move higher up the roots and revolve herself to the upper side of the tree. Finally, the tree gave way completely and fell across the ravine. The strong current immediately started to move the tree. But this lasted for only a short distance, as the tree became lodged between the two sides of the ravine. Judy was lying on the upper side of the tree and holding on as tight as she could. She was only about six inches above the flow of water, but she was out of the water and just about one third of the way across the ravine.

After catching her breath, she again looked around to take stock of her situation. The car was still there with its lights on. Even though the rain had slowed, the water continued to rise. Judy noticed that the water was now almost to her stomach as she lay on the trunk. She felt she must go now before she lost any more ground. Slowly, she pulled herself along the trunk. She had to be careful not to slip. As she got to the branches growing out of the trunk, she had to maneuver her way around and over them. She was only a few feet from the other side of the ravine when she felt the tree slip. She stopped and grabbed hold of the tree again. The tree was starting to shift from its position as the water got higher. As the tree started to become completely dislodged, Judy got to her feet and made a desperate jump. She just made it, as she landed on the other side of the ravine half in the water and half out. The tree dislodged and floated down the ravine in the strong current. She clawed her way up the side until she was completely out of the water.

Again, she stopped to catch her breath. She looked up the side of the ravine and started trying to climb out. The mud and clay were so slippery that she would climb two feet and slide back one. By the time she reached the top, she was exhausted, wet, and weak. Unfortunately, she was only able to get her arms over the edge. She could not pull her entire body up onto the road. However, from her position, she could see the car just across the road from her and to her left.

"Hey! Can somebody please help me?" She yelled. "Can anybody hear me? I need help!"

Her voice seemed loud to her, but she did not know if whoever was in the car had heard her. Suddenly a bright flash of lightning lit up the sky. She saw the car clearly now. There seemed to be two people inside. "Hey! Can you help me?" She tried to raise her arm to wave, but when she did, she felt herself slip backwards. Immediately, she dropped her arms and grabbed at the edge of the road again. In the darkness, she thought she heard a car door slam.

"Bobbie? Is that you Bobbie?" It was a man's voice. Suddenly a man was standing over her. "Bobbie! You've come back," the man was saying.

She felt herself being pulled up and into the arms of a strong man. In the dark, it was hard to see who it was, but she was sure it was not her father.

"Oh, Bobbie, I knew if I kept coming here sooner or later you'd come back to me. Thank God. Thank God. You've come back from exactly where you went away."

The man held her tight in his arms. She noticed that he had begun to cry. At first, she was surprised and grateful, but now she was afraid of this man.

"Lester, put her down." It was a woman's voice coming out of the darkness.

"No, I won't lose her again," he replied simply. "This night is just like the other night. She went away and now she's returned. Lois told me she would let Bobbie come back. Lois knows how lonely I've been, that's why she let her come back."

"Please mister, let me down," Judy said slowly as she tried to push herself away from him.

"Lester, put her down. You're goin' to hurt her holding her that tight," Mary said calmly.

"Bobbie, don't be afraid of me. I'm not goin' to hurt you. I'm your dad, I won't hurt you." Lester put Judy down on her feet, but continued to hold her by the shoulders. "Mary, you thought I was crazy didn't you? What do you think now?" His face was a mixture of love and wonderment.

"I don't know Lester, but I guess you were right," Mary answered carefully. "Lester, can I talk to Bobbie for a minute?"

"Of course you can. Everyone will be able to talk to her. You can talk to Mrs. Collie, Bobbie."

Mary reached over and took Judy from Lester's grip. She turned Judy to face her and away from Lester. "Hi. My name is Mary Collie. What's your name?" Mary asked quietly.

"I'm Judy Cole." Judy looked from the woman then back over her shoulder to the man and back again. She tried to hide the fear in her eyes. "Why is he callin' me Bobbie?" She asked softly.

"His little girl was named Bobbie and she died right here on this spot," Mary explained. "He believes you're his little girl. Now, you just stay calm and do as I say. Can you do that?"

"Maybe," Judy replied looking directly into Mary's eyes. "Is he crazy?"

"I don't know," Mary answered. "I really don't know."

Lester reached over and turned Judy around to face him again. "What are you girls talkin' about?" Lester smiled. "Why don't we go back to our house and get you settled in? Your room is just as you left it. I haven't changed a thing. Your clothes and toys are still just as they were." As he spoke, he started guiding Judy toward the car.

Judy's mind was working fast. She was convinced she had jumped from the frying pan into the fire, so to speak. She had escaped the ravine, but now she was with crazy people. The only thing that she could make herself believe was that she must be here at this spot when her father came looking for her. He would be here anytime now. In fact, he should've already been here. "I can't," Judy yelled, as she pulled back from him. "I have to wait here for my Dad."

"Bobbie, you don't have to wait any longer. I'm here! I'm your dad. Please, don't you remember me? We must go home and get out of this rain." Lester's face took on a hurt look.

"You're not my Pa!" Judy yelled. "I don't know who you are, but you're not my Pa. What's wrong with you? I have to wait here 'til my Pa gets here and that's all there is to it."

Mary's heart skipped a beat. Judy was not going along with the plan. She forced herself to hide the fear on her face. She watched Lester closely for his next move. Lester began to look confused. Then his faced clouded over with anger. He started to speak, but Mary interrupted. "Lester, let me talk to her. She must be tired and confused. You can understand that can't you?" Mary tried to make her voice sound kind and convincing.

"Yeah, I guess so," Lester stammered. "Go ahead, but I don't understand why she doesn't know me."

"Just back away for a minute and I'll talk to her," Mary said, pushing him back. "Come on, Lester; give us girls a chance to talk a minute."

She continued to push him away. She kept a smile on her face as she pressed him to back away. Slowly, he began to give ground and the anger disappeared from his face.

"Okay, I'll go wait in the car for you two," Lester said, as he turned and walked through the mud to the car.

As he walked away, he continually looked back over his shoulder at them. When he got to the car, he got inside and stared at them through the windshield. As he watched them, his mind started doing flip flops. Each second his thought processes changed. One second, he was involved with getting Bobbie back and the next second he was wondering why he was here and what he was doing. One part of him was convinced that Bobbie had come back to him, but another part of him questioned his sanity. He gripped the steering wheel and stared at them through the windshield as the struggle in his mind continued.

"Listen to me Judy Cole; I think that man in the car has gone off the deep end. You've got to do like I tell you or I'm not sure what's goin' to happen to us. I don't have time to argue with you about this. Somehow, someway, somewhere, your dad will find us, but right now we have to take care of ourselves. We're goin' over and get in that car and you're goin' to pretend like you're his girl come back home. Do you understand me, girl? We'll go to his house and then I can get help. I can't get help out here! Don't you understand I can't help us out here?"

The urgency in Mary's voice was getting through to Judy but still she was unsure. "How do I know you're not as crazy as he is?" She asked, in a challenging voice.

"I don't guess you do," Mary shouted back. She caught herself and lowered her voice again. "Look, we've got us a real problem here. You've got to trust me. Can't I make you understand?" Mary and Judy looked at each other for a long quiet minute. "Yeah, I understand,"

Judy said, shaking her head quickly, "but I don't know nothin' about his girl. How should I act?"

"Don't say much and call him Dad. Tell him you're tired and want to have a bath and go to bed. That way we can get you out of his sight for a while 'til I can get help."

"Okay, let's do it!" Judy said, trying not to cry. "But can't I leave a note of some kind for my Pa?"

"I don't have anything to write with and it wouldn't last in this wet anyway," Mary replied. Mary nervously looked over to the car. Lester had left the door open so the internal light was on. She could see Lester sitting behind the steering wheel. He was watching them closely and seemed to be getting impatient. He moved as if to get out of the car. Mary quickly took Judy's hand and they walked to the car. Lester saw them coming and got out. He ran around and opened the back door. He had a huge smile on his face.

"Is everything okay now?" He asked pleasantly.

"Yes, she's just tired," Mary replied smiling.

"Yeah, I'm okay now, Dad. Can we go home so I can clean up and get some rest?" Judy asked calmly.

"That's great, that's just great! Jump in and we'll be home in a jiffy."

Mary and Judy climbed into the back of the car. Lester closed the door and ran around and got in the driver's seat. He carefully turned the car around on the slick road and started driving them home. The rain had almost stopped and it would be light soon. The night had been the longest in Judy's young life. She had no idea who she was with or where she was going. She wondered what had happened to her father. He should have been here by now. Something must have happened to keep him from making their meeting. She silently prayed that he was okay and that he would find her. Now, she had to trust the woman named Mary to help her. Judy turned and looked out the back window for one last chance to see her Pa.

CHAPTER THIRTY-ONE

Death on the Hill

After he watched Ruth, Clint and Judy disappear into the darkness, Jim Upter turned back inside the cabin leaving the door ajar. He went and got his black robe and hood from the back room. Next, he spread his robe over the small table in the middle of the main room. Then, going from room to room, he started picking up items and placing them on the robe. He gathered up all the extra white robes and hoods, any papers that were there, and any other signs that would give them away. He stacked them all onto the robe on the table. Taking each corner of the robe, he pulled the corners together to make a sack. After getting the sack created, he tied the top together with his belt. He pulled the full sack from the table and set it in the far corner away from the door.

Jim wasn't sure where he would get rid of the sack, but he was sure he could think of that later. One last trip through the cabin to make sure nothing had been missed. He went into each of the rooms and checked things for one last time. Upon returning to the main room, he reached up and turned out the small dim light. He reached behind him and pulled one of the chairs up and sat down. Things had been happening so fast that he hadn't had time to reflect on what was going on.

Jim sat in the quiet and darkness and thought about what had happened to him. He had lost his dream. He wouldn't become a Grand Wizard of the Ku Klux Klan and it was all because of some kids and a stupid chain of events. It was hard for him to believe that all his plans were coming to an end because of the way things had happened. Most things had gone as he planned them. He had planned, as his first step, to get the niggers out of the white community. This had started out good. The thing with Doc Jewel's nigger had gone just as he had planned and it had the exact affect he had expected. The next step was to have been the Collie nigger. And that had started off okay. But the stupid nigger had run into the burning house. The confusion that set in later was not planned. His men had handled themselves badly. And now this thing with the Collie kid was the final straw. How the Collie kid knew about them he didn't know, but it was the final event of a confused night.

His next step was to have been more recruitment, and he was going to take stronger control of the membership. Not knowing who some of the members were, was something that Jim didn't like. It scared him, because he didn't know how they knew about the meetings and how they knew where the meetings were held. But somehow two of the members knew everything and kept themselves secret. He should've never allowed that. But he had needed members to get started. His intention had been to put a stop to unidentified members. But it was too late now. It was just a matter of time before the law came to the cabin. They soon would know everything about their meetings. He hoped all of the members would keep quiet. As far as he knew, he was the only one that had been recognized. No one else was in danger. In the final analysis, he had failed. His leadership and judgment had not been good. The only thing he had really gotten out of all this was Ruth. He did love Ruth and would make her happy in New Orleans. Once settled in New Orleans, he would look at his future then. He got up from his chair and walked to the far corner to pick up the sack.

"One to protect the other," the voice said.

Jim spun around as if hit by something. He saw a figure standing in the darkness by the door. Even in the darkness, he could see the figure was wearing a white robe and hood. The robe was dirty and wet. Water dripped from the hem of the robe to the floor. The robe completely covered the figure from head to foot, and its arms were concealed inside the oversized sleeves of the robe. The eyes were only dark holes. Jim couldn't identify the figure.

"Who's there?" Jim asked, straining to see.

"One to protect the other," the voice repeated. "Ain't that what you told us?"

"Yes, it is. Who are you, anyway?" Jim started to move toward the robed figured.

"Stay where you are!" The voice demanded.

The figure lifted its left arm and pointed at Jim.

"What?" Jim yelled.

Then he heard the sound of a gun cocking. He couldn't see the gun, but he knew it was there.

"Wait a minute! What is this? Who are you?"

"One to protect the other," the voice repeated.

"Why do you keep saying that?" Jim was shouting now as he neared panic.

"I was just wonderin' if it's one to protect the other. Where're you goin' Jim boy? Are ya leavin' us sudden like?"

"I haven't had time to talk to anyone. Look, things have gone to shit. The law could be here any time now. We've got to get out of here. Don't you understand?" Jim started to move again, but stopped when the gun leveled at him.

"Oh, I understand, Jim boy. You're leavin' and not even sayin' goodbye. I don't think the other boys would like that. Do you, Jim boy?"

"Hey! Nobody knows who we are. I'm probably the only one that's been identified. That's why I've got to go. You and the others have nothing to fear."

"How'd they find out?" The voice became angrier.

"Somehow the Collie kid saw us. I don't know when or how, but he knows about us, but I think I'm the only one he can identify. He was just up here not thirty minutes ago! We couldn't catch him before he ran down the hill. He's sure to bring the law up here. That's why we have to clear out. Especially me! Now, come on and put that gun down. It wasn't my plan to leave without filling y'all in, but you can see how it's worked out!" Jim stopped talking and stared across the small room at the gun.

"What about the organization and our plans?" The voice demanded, but some of the anger had gone.

"They'll have to wait. We can't continue now. Maybe in six months or so we can give it another try, but right now we have to hold off. Now, I'm going to turn around and get that sack over in the corner, and then I'm going out the door. We can't wait any longer. The law may be here any minute!"

The robed figure slowly lowered its arm. "Okay. I guess it'll be okay, but don't come near me when ya leave. I'll be standin' right here by the door watchin' you."

Jim turned quickly and picked up the sack. He held the sack in his arms and started for the door. He stopped and looked again at the figure that was standing next to the door. "You better leave too," he said. "They may not know you now, but if they find you here in that get up you're sure to catch Hell."

The figure nodded its head, but didn't move. Jim walked past the figure and out the door. Suddenly, he felt a sharp deep pain in the middle of his back. Then, he couldn't catch his breath. The strength drained from his arms and legs. He dropped the sack and staggered forward for a few steps and then dropped to his knees. He reached his hand as far as he could around to his back, but he couldn't reach the pain. He opened his mouth to speak but no sound would come out. Slowly, he sank down to his hands and knees trying to understand what had happened. As he tried to get up, he saw the white robed figure standing in front of him. On his hands and knees, he could only see up to the figure's waist. He struggled to stand, but couldn't. He looked down and saw blood gathering on the ground below his face. To his horror, he realized it was coming from his mouth.

The white robed figure walked around to Jim's side and placed its foot on his ribs and pushed. Jim fell completely to the ground on his back. The rain drizzled down onto his face as he blinked his eyes to see. Jim now knew he was dying. He tasted the blood and rain in his mouth and breathing was becoming impossible. Why? Why, was he dying? What had happened? The white robed figure was now kneeling over him. In its hand it held a long bloody butcher knife.

"Sorry, Jim boy," the voice said sincerely. "But I think it would be better if the law found you here. I mean, we need somebody to blame all this on don't we? If you're gone, well, the law may start lookin' for us. On the other hand, if they find you here, they'll probably be happy. You know, you bein' an outsider and all. You understand all this reasonin' don't you, Jim?"

Jim tried to speak but failed. The white robed figure stood up, turned around and started calmly walking away. After a few steps, the figure stopped and turned back and looked at Jim. "One to protect the other," it said again. Then, it ran into the rainy night. After the figure had left, Jim was alone laying on the ground struggling to live. His unblinking eyes stared into the night sky as the rain hit his face. He managed to say one word through the blood that filled his throat. "Ruth," he said. Then he died.

CHAPTER THIRTY-TWO

Reunion

As Dee made his way down the hill, he kept checking behind him to see if anyone was following him. However, he never saw or heard anyone. The trip down the hill was going easily, because he was really getting used to the hill. Even in the darkness, he felt he knew the way. His mind reeled with what to do once he got home. On one hand, he was sure he should tell his dad about the things he had seen, but on the other hand if he did that, he would reveal his trip to the hill. He was bound to get in trouble no matter what he did.

Suddenly, Dee froze in his tracks. He was sure he heard someone talking. He turned to look behind, but the voice seemed to be coming from down the hill instead of up. Standing very still, he listened intently. The voice didn't come again. He started to move but stopped as he heard the talking again. He strained to hear so he could fix the direction of the talking.

"Are you sure about this, Cherrie?"

It was his Dad's voice. Dee listened again to try and make sure of the direction.

"Well, I'm kind of sure," Cherrie said slowly. "I think we need to keep goin' up and around those pits."

"Dad, is that you?" Dee yelled.

James turned from side to side looking in all directions.

"Hey, Dad, is that you and Cherrie?" Dee yelled again.

"Dee! Where are you?"

"Here!" Dee yelled again, as he walked up to his Father. He was next to his Father before James ever saw him.

"Goddamn it, Dee! You scared the livin' shit out of me!"

James handed the Sheriff his rifle and grabbed Dee and pulled him into his arms. He held his son tightly for several minutes. He was trying to decide if he should hug him or whip him here on the spot.

"Why, Dee? Why?" James pleaded. "Why do you do these things to me and your Mom? Your Mother is half crazy. You have me, the Sheriff, and your sister out in the rain at some unbelievable hour of the morning lookin' for you. You've messed with the Sheriff's plans. What can I expect next? Tell me what's next for us, Dee, so I can be prepared."

"I'm sorry, Dad. I guess I'm in real trouble, huh?"

"Yes, you are, Son. You got real trouble. But we'll talk about that later, right now I want to get you kids home. Mary is probably goin' crazy."

"Wait, James," Sheriff Clark spoke. Then, turning to Dee he asked, "Dee, did anybody see you tonight?"

"Yes sir, I saw Judy Cole and talked to her. I saw some people in the cabin, but I'm not sure who they were."

"Did the people in the cabin see you?" James asked.

"Yes sir, they did. One of 'em yelled at me. I thought he was goin' to chase me. I was afraid it was them when I heard y'all."

"What do you think, James?" The Sheriff asked, as he handed James back his rifle. "I don't think we should wait 'til tomorrow. If they saw Dee, they'll probably make a run for it tonight,"

"I can't go after anybody now, Tom. I've got to get these kids home."

"I understand that, but I don't know what to do now!" The Sheriff was confused and worried.

"Maybe we should just go back and wait at the Jordan house. Ruth's sure to show up sooner or later."

"I don't care, first things first, I'm takin' my kids home. Come on Dee and Cherrie; let's get down off this hill and out of this rain." As James finished speaking, he pushed Dee and Cherrie along in front of him.

They had only taken a few steps when they heard the Sheriff yell, "Halt or I'll shoot." James spun around with his rifle at the ready while at the same time knocking Dee and Cherrie to the ground.

"I mean it! Stop or I'll shoot!" The Sheriff demanded again in an excited voice.

James strained to see at whom the Sheriff was yelling, but he couldn't see a thing. The Sheriff had been behind James and up the hill. Now, the Sheriff was holding his rifle steady aiming it up the hill behind them. James hovered over his children trying to be sure they were protected from whatever the Sheriff saw.

"Tom, put that gun down. You don't need that." It was Ruth Jordan who spoke, as she and Clint came into view.

"I ain't sure what I need right now, but I ain't takin' any chances," the Sheriff replied without lowering his weapon. "James, have you got your gun on these two?"

"I do," James answered.

"Come on, Tom, do I look like I'm dangerous?" Ruth asked spreading her arms apart.

Neither man could help but notice Ruth's breast through her wet blouse. James, taking into consideration that his children stood behind him, walked over and took off his raincoat and put it over Ruth's shoulders.

"Thank you, James," Ruth said politely.

"Who's that ya got with you, Ruth?" The Sheriff asked.

"Nobody you know, Tom. He's got nothin' to do with any of this. You can let him go on about his way."

"Oh! I don't think so. Nobody goes anywhere unless I say so. Dee, come over here."

Dee looked at his Father for the okay before moving. He saw his Father nod an okay and he walked over and stood by the Sheriff. "Yes Sir." Dee said.

"Can you tell if that's the man that yelled at you?" The Sheriff asked, pointing his rifle at the man standing by Ruth.

"I don't know for sure, but I don't think so. I think this man is Judy Cole's Dad," Dee explained.

"Tom, I told you this man has nothin' to do with this. He's just a guy we used to do odds and ends for us," Ruth repeated firmly.

"You said *us*, Ruth? Is Jim Upter around here someplace? Is he the one that yelled at Dee? Where is Mr. Upter about now?" The Sheriff asked in quick succession.

"I don't know where Jim is now. He may be at the house," she replied.

Everyone standing there on the hill knew she was lying.

"James, I've got to go and have a look at that cabin. Can you handle taking these two back to town for me, and can Dee come with me to show me where the cabin is?" The Sheriff's voice was firm and decisive. James had never seen Tom Clark in such control as he was now.

"Tom, I told you I have to get these kids home before I do anythin' else," James replied quickly.

"I'll go with him, Dad," Dee spoke up.

"No! No way! We're not startin' this all over again. You kids are goin' home, end of discussion. Tom, I suggest we take what we got and go. We'll get the rest later. As for me, I'm takin' my kids home."

With that, James moved away from Ruth and started toward Cherrie who was still standing alone. As he walked by the man with Ruth, he stopped.

"What did you say your name was?" James asked, looking intently at the man.

"I didn't say," the man replied.

"I think James is right," Ruth said. "Let's get to the house and out of this rain." As she spoke, she moved in between James and the man.

James pushed Ruth back and moved up close to the man's face. "I'll ask you again. What's your name?"

"My name's Morris, Clint Morris," the man replied.

He didn't move and he and James stood staring into each other's face for several minutes.

"Come on y'all, let's go," Ruth urged, as again she tried to move James along.

"Stay where you are, Ruth," the Sheriff ordered. "What's the matter, James?"

"This man's name is Clint all right, but it's not Morris. Sheriff Tom Clark, meet Clint Jordan!" James stepped back and looked at both Ruth and Clint.

"Clint Jordan!" The Sheriff exclaimed. "That can't be. Clint Jordan's been dead for years. He died in the war."

"That's what we all believed," James stated. "But, I'm tellin' you this man is Clint Jordan." Then looking hard at Clint he said, "I know you, don't I Clint?"

"Yeah, I guess you do, James," Clint replied smiling.

"Holy shit," the Sheriff said in amazement. "This just keeps gettin' better and better." "I'm sure the army would be interested to know that Mr. Jordan is still alive, and I'm just as positive that the government would be interested in all those insurance payments you've been gettin', Ruth!"

"Tom, I think we better head back and get this mess all figured out," James said slowly.

"I still want to know where Jim Upter is," the Sheriff demanded firmly. "We still got some missin' pieces."

"I'm sorry, Tom, but I'm on my way back with my kids. I'll help you if you're goin' my way."

"Okay, Okay! We'll go back, but as soon as it's light, I'm comin' back up here and I may need Dee to help me."

"Dee is all done with this, Tom. He ain't comin' back up here and you can't make him," James shouted.

"I'll bring you back, Sheriff," Clint said softly.

"Why would you do that?"

"Because, I've got a problem that I need help with. My daughter, Judy, is waitin' for me to come and get her over on the north side of this hill. Before we go on to town, we need to stop and get her. We can't leave her by herself waitin'."

"How far is it?" The Sheriff asked.

"After we reach the road, it's about two miles," Clint replied.

"Two miles," the Sheriff exclaimed, "it'll take us a half an hour to go two miles in this mud and rain."

"Goddamn it, Tom, we just can't leave the kid. She's expecting her Dad to come and get her!" James yelled.

"Everybody shut up!" This time it was Ruth yelling. "Why don't Tom and Clint go get Judy? I'll go with James to his house and we'll wait there. That way everyone gets what they want. I just want out of this mud and rain."

Everyone looked at each other. Finally, James spoke. "Sounds okay to me," he said softly. "What do you think, Tom?"

Sheriff Clark studied the group for a minute.

"Yeah, it's okay with me, but with one exception. When we go get Judy, we come back over the hill to the cabin. That way I don't have to come back later."

"That's fine with me," Clint said.

"Just one thing you should know, Clint," Sheriff Clark spoke slowly and deliberately. "If you try anythin', anythin' at all, I'll shoot you. I don't care if your kid is there or not, I'll shoot you dead. So, before you make a run for it, you better think about it."

"No need to worry, Sheriff Clark. My runnin' days are over."

As Clint spoke, he looked at Ruth and smiled. Ruth smiled back and walked over and put her arms around Clint and hugged him. Then, the entire group started down the hill. They were muddy, wet, and tired.

CHAPTER THIRTY-THREE

Peace at Last

Mary Collie got out of the shower and dried herself. The shower had felt good. She was almost totally physically and mentally exhausted. She checked the clock in the bathroom and it read five after four in the morning. All that had happened had drained her to the point of collapse. Mary left the bathroom and walked down the hall to Bobbie's old room. She peeked into the room and saw Judy Cole sound asleep on the bed. Judy had showered first and had gone straight to bed. Now, she had to go deal with Lester. Lester had told them to go and clean up. He said Mary could use Lois' room and Judy could use Bobbie's. The rooms were just as if someone lived in them every day. They were clean and well supplied. Mary had taken one of Lois's bathrobes.

She stepped inside the door and walked over to the bed where Judy slept. The child was sleeping soundly. Mary thought that Judy must be as exhausted as she, probably more so. As she stood looking down at Judy, she could not help but wonder about this child. Who was she? How did she fit into all of this mess? Who was her family? Mary couldn't think of any family named Cole that lived in or around Coalville. Who was this girl? Mary continued to watch Judy studying her features as she slept. Judy's dark black hair was dry now and it spread across the soft white pillow. Her eyes were closed gently and her face was relaxed. Judy's facial features and hair looked familiar to Mary but she couldn't place the resemblance. Judy's small turned up nose and sharp facial lines framed by dark black hair reminded Mary of someone else, but she couldn't put a name with the face. She took one last look at the girl and then turned and softly walked away.

Mary quietly closed the door to Bobbie's room, turned and continued down the hall to the head of the stairs. The staircase had a slight curve that ended at the entrance to the study on the bottom floor. Mary had been to this house before, but now it seemed so much bigger and emptier. She started down the stairs, but stopped about halfway down, as she saw Lester standing at the bottom looking up at her. Mary began to feel a little nervous at the way she was dressed, and tried to pull the robe tighter around her. She was in her bare feet and her hair was all tangled and wet from its washing. She wore nothing under the bathrobe. All of her clothes had been wet and dirty, so she had left them in a neat pile on the bathroom floor.

Lester was still in the same wet and muddy clothes. His hair was rumbled and his face looked tired. He had his hands in his pockets as he stood at the foot of the stairs looking up at her. "You're beautiful, Mary. Almost like Lois. You're a little taller and your hair is blonde, but you look about the same."

Turning away, he lowered his head and walked from the stairs into the study where he flopped down into a large chair. He put his elbows on his knees and clasped his hands together. Then, he lowered his head and pressed his clasped hands to his forehead. His hair fell down over his hands. He just sat there saying nothing.

Mary continued down the stairs clutching at her bathrobe until she reached the bottom of the stairs where she paused. There was a phone in the entry way. A temptation to try and make a quick call home overcame her, but she decided against it. She looked into the study at Lester. He seemed totally defeated. She felt sorry for him and at the same time feared him. She had no idea what he might try next. She walked slowly into the study and sat across from Lester in another chair.

"Are you all right, Lester?" She asked softly.

"No, I'm not all right," he answered. "I think I must be crazy, Mary." He started to cry heavily. He pressed the palms of his hands into his eyes. "I don't know what I'm doin' some of the time. Things happen and I don't know why I do them. I know that child isn't

Bobbie. I know it now, but I didn't know it a little while ago. I know you're not Lois, but for an instant on the stairs, it seemed to me you were. What's happening to me? My God, what's happening to me and what have I done?"

"I'm no doctor, but I've always heard that if you're sane enough to think you may be crazy, then you're not crazy," she said slowly and softly. "You obviously know you have a problem, Lester. That says you're okay. We just need to help you work out your problems."

Mary had never seen a man cry so hard. She reached over and put her hand on his head. She pulled his head to her shoulder. He buried his head in her shoulder and cried uncontrollably. She held him for several minutes until his crying subsided. Then, she wasn't sure what she should do next. She couldn't convince herself that Lester was a dangerous man. He obviously has never been able to recover from the loss of his wife and daughter. That was something she could understand, but she needed to know more about the hood and robe she had seen in the back seat of Lester's car. Lester's problems involved more than the loss of his family. If he was involved with the Klan, then he must know something about the death of Moonbeam and Rachael.

"Lester, why don't you tell me about it?" She asked carefully. "Tell me about the Klan and everything." She was surprised when he talked freely.

"There's not much to tell really," he replied pushing away from her and relaxing back into his chair. He stopped crying and looked at her. "I think I'll fix myself a drink. Can I get you anythin'?"

"Yes, I think I could use a little somethin'," Mary replied.

Lester walked over to the liquor cabinet and started mixing two drinks. He talked while he worked at the drinks.

"Jim Upter recruited me. He thought it would be good to have a town father in the Klan. I don't know why I agreed to join. I don't care about colored folks one way or the other. It was one of those times when I thought I could do something about Lois and Bobbie. There're times when I feel like I want everybody dead. If Lois and

Bobbie have to be dead, then I want everybody dead, even myself. I thought I could kill, but I can't. I thought I might be the one to kill Moonbeam, but I couldn't, even if I'd been the one chosen."

He stopped talking and stared up at the ceiling. Soon, he lowered his head and brought Mary her drink. He took a deep drink from his glass and then sat back down in the chair across from Mary. He stared at her across the distance between them.

"Who was chosen to kill Moonbeam?" She asked, returning his stare.

"I don't know," he said, without moving his eyes from her.

"Well, how was the person chosen?" She pressed.

"We were all in our hoods and robes. There were eight of us including Jim Upter. We were all standing around the table in the cabin. All of us accept one. There were only seven of us at first. I don't know who the missing guy was. Anyway, poor old Moonbeam was tied up on the floor and we were goin' to draw straws to see who was goin' to hang him. At that time, I really thought I could do it. I really thought I could kill someone, and what's more, I thought I would enjoy it. Jim wanted Moonbeam hung right in Doc's garage. He felt that would make a big impact, and I guess it did. Jim was breakin' the straws, when this guy walked in. He was our eighth member I guess. You can't always tell who is who in those outfits. Some of the men I'd know no matter what they wear, but some of them, I just have to guess. This guy I couldn't recognize. Anyway, this guy walked up and took all the straws off the table. He crushed them in his hands and threw them on the floor. I remember he pointed at Jim and said, "This nigger belongs to me, Jim boy." The voice sounded familiar, but I couldn't place it. He reached down and grabbed Moonbeam up off the floor and dragged him out the door. I never saw either one of them again. Later, I started feeling bad about what had happened, but I didn't tell anybody."

"You mean to tell me that you don't even know who all was in the group with you?" Mary asked surprised.

"I knew most of them. I mean, after you've been around people for most of your life, you can tell who they are by the way they walk or talk. We always met wearin' our outfits. Jim was the only one who knew who everyone was. At least, I think he did. Sometimes I got the feelin' he didn't know a few of the guys. I don't know how he couldn't. I always assumed he recruited everyone."

Lester had lowered his gaze from Mary's eyes to her legs. During the conversation, she had forgotten about the bathrobe and it had opened up revealing her legs up to the middle of her thighs.

Mary was deep in thought when she noticed Lester looking at her. She began to get worried again. Nervously, she took a sip out of her drink. Then she noticed her exposed legs. Quickly, she put her drink down and stood up pulling the bathrobe together around her. Without hesitating, she walked over to the study entryway. There, she stopped and turned to face Lester. "I think I better call home now, Lester," she said haltingly. "I think James should be home by now."

"Don't worry, Mary, I'm okay now. I'm not goin' to hurt you or the child. But you better call James, because to be truthful, I don't know when I'll go off my rocker again. It's been good to talk to you about all this. I think things will be okay. I know some things about myself now that I didn't know before tonight. I know I can't hurt anybody and I know I've been hoping for things that will never be. I know Lois and Bobbie are gone forever and nothin' I do will change that. All these years of talkin' to Lois, I've just been talkin' to myself. All these years of keepin' their rooms ready was just to keep me hopeful. I'm doomed to be alone for the rest of my life." He spoke softly and dejected.

He seemed defeated. In one last gulp, he finished his drink and set the empty glass on the table next to his chair. He pushed himself out of his chair and walked passed Mary over to the stairs. He stopped at the foot of the stairs and looked at Mary with a lost look on his face. "I'm goin' up to get out of these clothes and clean up. You call James to come get you and the child." With that, he walked slowly up the stairs.

"Lester?" Mary called after him.

"Yes?" He responded without stopping.

"Can you tell me who the other members of the Klan are?" She asked bluntly.

He stopped his ascent of the stairs and turned and looked down at Mary. "Well, you know about me and Jim Upter. That leaves six other people. Of those six, two of them never showed their faces. That includes the one that killed Moonbeam. That leaves four others. I know who they are, but I don't think I'll be tellin' anybody."

"The Sheriff may make you tell," Mary replied.

"He may try," Lester said as he turned and started ascending the stairs again. "He may try."

"Were you at my house tonight with the Klan? Were you there when Rachael died?" She asked coldly.

Suddenly, he stopped his ascent. He seemed to sway as if he were going to fall. He stopped and grabbed the stair rail to steady himself. "Yes, I was," he replied simply and then continued up the stairs.

Mary watched him go. She wanted to say more, to press the issue, but she didn't. The thought of Rachael removed some of the pity she was feeling for Lester. She went to the phone in the entryway, picked up the receiver, and started dialing.

CHAPTER THIRTY-FOUR

Comin' Home

James Collie pushed everyone through the front door to his house. He was glad to get inside out of the weather, although it had just about stopped raining. After everyone was inside, he looked around for Mary. It was strange that she hadn't waited up for them. He went down the hall to their bedroom and found it empty.

"Dad," Cherrie called.

"Yeah," James yelled back as he returned to the living room.

"I found this note in the kitchen," Cherrie said, handing a small piece of paper to him.

James read the note and then flopped down into a nearby chair. "Now what in the Hell is she doin' goin' off with Lester at this time of night. She knew where we were and what's goin' on!"

"Maybe Lester needed some kind of help," Dee helped.

"Jesus, I don't know! What next!" James exclaimed.

"James, I'm goin' home to clean up and talk with Dick," Ruth said, as she started for the door.

"Hold on there!" James shouted. He jumped in between Ruth and the door. "I don't think you're goin' anywhere. I told the Sheriff I'd watch you and that's what I'm goin' to do."

"I won't go anywhere. I need to clean up, but mostly I want to talk to Dick before all this breaks. I can do that, can't I?" She looked at James with tired and lifeless eyes. She looked totally defeated. He thought he could see tears in her eyes, but it could have been the rain. He didn't know what to do.

"You've known me most of my life, James. I give you my word that I just want to talk with Dick."

James went over and looked out the window. The man deputized to watch the Jordan house was still there. He turned back to Ruth. "I guess it'll be all right. But I'll have to go tell the deputy what's goin' on so he can take over for me."

"That's fine with me," Ruth said and then walked out the door without saying anything else.

"You kids get a bath and then go to bed and do it fast," he ordered.

Dee and Cherrie disappeared down the hall. James ran out to the deputy and told him what was going on and then returned to his living room. He sat down and closed his eyes. It was uncomfortably quiet. Ruth had gone home next door, Dee and Cherrie were on their way to bed, and Mary was gone. His eyes opened quickly when he thought of Mary leaving the house and it caused him to worry. Why would she go? It didn't make sense, especially now with her family in danger. He glanced up at the clock on the wall. It was hard to believe it read a little after four o'clock in the morning. Soon, it would be daylight. Something is wrong! Mary would not be gone this long, if at all. He got up and walked over to the door. He opened the door and stared out into the dark. Thoughts ran through his head. Why would Lester come here so late? He was trying to decide what to do, when the phone rang. Hurrying over to the wall phone, he grabbed the receiver.

"Hello," he said quickly.

"James, thank God you're home! Is everyone okay?" Mary cried.

"Yes, we're all fine. Can you please tell me where the Hell you are? What's this note all about?"

"Is Dee okay?" She pressed.

"Yes, yes, I said we're all okay! Now, tell me what's goin' on and where are you?"

"I'm over at Lester's; can you come and get me?" She asked.

She sounded as if she were crying or trying to hold back crying.

"Can't you tell me what's happenin'?" He demanded.

"It's a long story and I'd rather tell you in person. Can you please come and get me?" She sounded urgent.

"Okay, I'm on my way. Just hang on; I'll be there in a few minutes."

Before leaving, James went to check on Dee and Cherrie. They were just getting into bed when James walked into their room. "Your Mom called," he said. "I'm on my way to go get her. When I get back, I expect you two to be right here in bed. Do I make myself perfectly clear?"

"Yes, Sir," they answered in unison.

"I mean it! No more runnin' off. Before you leave this house you better think it over real good."

"Yes, Sir," the double answer came again.

After a last stern look, James left the bedroom, went down the hall, through the living room and out the front door. Before getting into his car, he walked across the street and informed the deputy where he was going. Lester's house was not far, but James, pushed by uncertainty, drove fast and reckless. As he pulled into Lester's driveway, he could see Mary standing under the light on the porch. She seemed to be dressed in a bathrobe. He pulled the car to a halt in the front of the house and got out almost before the car had stopped rolling.

"Mary, are you all right?" He asked, running up the steps to meet her. She met him and threw her arms around him.

"Oh, James, I'm so glad to see you," she cried.

"What's goin' on?"

"Come on in the house and I'll fill you in," she said.

She took his hand and pulled him through the door into the house. They went into the study where they both sat down.

Over the next half hour, Mary relayed her entire story. James sat and listened quietly. He never interrupted her. When she finished, they both sat silently for several minutes.

"Where is Lester now?" He asked, looking around.

"The last time I saw him he said he was going up stairs to clean up. That's been almost an hour ago. Maybe we better go see about him?"

"You say this Judy Cole is upstairs asleep?" He asked.

"Yes, the last time I looked," she responded.

"Do you have any idea who she is? Dee has mentioned her name a couple of times."

"No, I have no idea at all. You don't think Lester is up there with her, do you?" Mary asked with alarm. She shot to her feet. "James, we better go and see what's goin' on. Lester's been gone too long."

"You don't think he would hurt her do you?" James asked nervously.

"No, not really," she answered slowly. "But, please, let's go up and get Judy and go home!"

"Sounds good to me," he said. "You stay down here. I'll go get Judy and check on Lester." James went to the stairs and started up.

"She's in the second room from the end of the hall. It's Bobbie's old room," Mary called after him.

James turned and looked back down at Mary. "Where's the bathroom?" He asked.

"It's all the way to the end of the hall," Mary replied.

James made his way to the head of the stairs. Carefully, he looked around. He didn't think Lester was dangerous, but the way things had been going he didn't feel like taking any chances. As he walked down the hall, he counted the doors. At the end of the hall, he could see the bathroom. A light emitted from under the crack at the bottom of the door. James thought Lester must still be in the bathroom. As he reached the second door from the end, he quietly turned the knob and pushed the door open. He saw a young girl sleeping soundly in a big bed. Silently, he pulled the door shut. His plan was to find Lester, then return for Judy. As he reached the end of the hall, he pressed his ear against the bathroom door and listened.

"Lester? Lester, are you in there?" He called softly. No answer or sound came from the bathroom. "Hey, Lester," he called again, but this time louder. Still, no sound came from behind the door. James knocked firmly on the door. "Lester, are you in there?"

James tried the door and it opened. Slowly, James pushed the door open just enough to put his head inside the bathroom. The room was steamy as if someone had taken a hot bath. James twisted his head from side to side, but couldn't see anything. The bathroom was huge in comparison to the one in his modest house. He pushed the door open wide and walked in. Then, he could see someone lying in the bathtub with the shower curtain pulled. He walked over and pulled the shower curtain back and looked down at Lester Homes.

Lester had probably been dead for some time. He lay in the bathtub with hot water up to his neck. His arms floated beside him. On each wrist there was a clean deep cut. The blood had almost stopped flowing, but still a small trickle could be seen. The tub water was dark red. Lester, himself, looked calm as though he were asleep.

Suddenly, James felt his stomach wretch. He quickly turned and knelt at the toilet where he vomited for several minutes. When he felt he could stand without vomiting, he stood up and moved over to the bathroom sink to wash his face. As he stood in front of the sink, he looked into the mirror at his tired, pale face. It took his eyes a moment to focus on the writing on the mirror. He moved back from the mirror to get a better view. Smeared on the mirror in toothpaste was the message, "ALONE NO MORE." James staggered back to the sink and turned on the cold water. He splashed handful after handful of cold water on his face. James was standing at the sink resting on his elbows when he heard Mary's voice.

"James? Lester?" Mary called.

He rushed to the bathroom door and got there just as Mary was walking in. He met her and pushed her out.

"What's goin' on, James?" Mary demanded, shaking herself free of him. "You look pale as a ghost!"

"Let's get Judy and get out of here," James replied.

"Tell me where Lester is?" She shouted. "We just can't leave without talkin' to him. He may need someone to look after him in the state he's in."

James grabbed Mary by the arm and started down the hall pulling her after him. "Believe me, Mary, Lester's doesn't need anyone to look after him and he's not up to talkin' right now." He guided her up the hall to the second door. "Now, go in there and get Judy. We're goin' home!"

Mary placed her hand on James' cheek. "Stop for a minute, James. Slow down," she said quietly. "Why are you doin' this? Why can't we talk to Lester?"

James looked hard at Mary. He didn't know any other way to say it. "Lester's dead, Mary. He killed himself!"

CHAPTER THIRTY-FIVE

Failed Mission

Sheriff Clark had been right about the time it took to reach the old miners trail on the north side of the hill. The Sheriff and Clint had been walking through mud and slippery clay for almost thirty minutes. Then, suddenly, Clint stopped.

"What's the matter?" The Sheriff asked. "Is this the place? I don't see any trail."

"This is the place," Clint replied.

Clint walked over to the edge of the road and looked up the hill. "Judy!" He yelled. "Judy, I'm here. Come on out!"

"Maybe she's waitin' someplace else, or maybe she got mixed up about where to be," the Sheriff stated as he looked around him.

"No, Judy knows this trail. She should be here. Somethin' must've happened." Clint's voice was becoming excited. He moved off the road and onto the hill.

"Wait a minute," the Sheriff yelled. "Don't go up that hill yet. I don't even see a trail around here."

"The trail's here even if you can't see it. I know it and Judy knows it. She can't be lost, somethin' else has happened." Clint came back down onto the road. He looked around the area intently.

"What're ya lookin' for?" The Sheriff asked.

"I'm lookin' for Judy, you simple ass!" Clint shouted. "If she's not here, maybe she left a note or a clue. She knows this hill too good to not be here. Now, how about helpin' me?"

Sheriff Clark backed away from Clint and started to reply, but didn't. He moved onto the road and started looking around. The Sheriff and Clint spent the next several minutes poking into the bushes and looking around the area. The rain had stopped but the ground was a mixture of mud and water making it very slippery.

"Hey, Clint, come look at this," the Sheriff yelled.

Clint looked up and saw the Sheriff about twenty yards away kneeling down looking at something. Clint hurried over to where the Sheriff knelt.

"Look here at these tracks," the Sheriff said, as he pointed down to the road. "They look like tire tracks where a car pulled off the road and then turned around and headed back the other direction."

"Yeah, and look at these foot tracks," Clint commented, as he studied the ground. "They go over here across the road to the edge of the ravine."

Both men followed the tracks across the road to the edge of the ravine. There, they could tell something had taken place. The ground was all trampled and the edge appeared as though something had been dragged across it flattening it down. They looked over the edge down into the ravine. They could see the tracks where someone had climbed up the ravine to the road.

"I wonder what happened here." The Sheriff breathed. "It looks like somebody pulled somebody else out of this ravine and then they got into a car and drove off. The tracks look like two women and one man."

"Or one woman, one child, and one man," Clint added. "It must have been Judy, who else would've been here?"

"But who're the other two people?"

"I don't know," Clint said. Clint stood up and looked around. Then he sat down in the mud and buried his head in his hands. "Oh Jesus, what's happened to Judy! How can things keep happenin'? When does this ever end? What am I goin' to do now? How can I ever find her?"

Clint was beginning to babble.

"Hey! Get hold of yourself. You can't be much help if you start actin' like a fool," the Sheriff yelled. Sheriff Clark grabbed Clint by the collar and pulled him to his feet. He shook Clint and then pushed him away. "She's probably okay. I don't know, but it looks like somebody picked her up. She may be safe and dry about now someplace in town. I think we need to go on up to that cabin and take care of our business. The sooner we get that done, the sooner we can head for town and try and find out about Judy."

Clint stood looking at the Sheriff wondering what to do. "I don't know maybe we should just wait here for a while."

"I don't think you understand, Clint. I'm not askin' or makin' a suggestion. We're goin' up to that cabin and we're goin' to do it, *now*." The Sheriff gave Clint all the encouragement he needed with a thrust of his rifle barrel into Clint's stomach. Clint staggered back a few steps.

"Now," the Sheriff continued firmly. "Please be so kind as to lead me up this hill to the cabin."

Clint turned and looked up the hill. "We can take the old miner's trail. It'll get us near the top, and then we'll have to circle around to the south to get back where we came from."

"How long do you think that'll take?" The Sheriff asked.

"It shouldn't take us more than twenty minutes. Yeah, I can get us there in twenty minutes," Clint replied nodding his head.

"Okay, let's get started," the Sheriff said, pointing his rifle toward the hill.

The trip up the hill was not nearly as hard as the trip around the hill on the muddy road. They made good time even though it seemed to the Sheriff it was taking forever to get around the pits and through the thick trees and bushes. There was no doubt that this trip would have taken a lot longer without Clint in the lead. Sheriff Clark was sure he would have fallen into a pit if he had been by himself. As they entered a small clearing, the first signs of daylight began to appear. The rain had stopped completely and the clouds were beginning to dissipate.

"There it is," Clint said pointing to the small cabin just passed the clearing.

In the dim morning light, the Sheriff could see the cabin. It looked deserted, but the Sheriff decided to be careful. He and Clint moved along the clearing edge looking for signs of life. After he was sure no one was outside the cabin, the Sheriff yelled a warning.

"Hello, in the cabin. This is Sheriff Tom Clark of Coalville. I'm orderin' you, in the name of the law, to come out of the cabin with your hands in the air." Only silence answered him. "I repeat this is Sheriff Tom Clark of Coalville. I'm orderin' you, in the name of the law, to come out of the cabin with your hands up." Still, only silence answered him.

"I doubt if anyone's there," Clint commented. "I told you the only people there were me, Judy, Ruth, and Jim Upter."

"Yeah, and Judy and Upter are still not accounted for," the Sheriff shot back.

"Well, you can bet Judy's not there, because thanks to you, I'm here instead of bein' out lookin' for her," Clint replied angrily.

"That still doesn't account for Upter!"

"Hell man, he's probably long gone by now," Clint declared.

Sheriff Clark turned away from Clint and stood behind a tall tree. He fired his rifle into the air. The sudden discharge made Clint jump.

"What the hell did you do that for?" Clint yelled. "You scared the shit out of me!"

"If anyone's in there, I want them to know we're armed."

"Christ Almighty, this is ridiculous," Clint said jumping up. He walked into the clearing.

"Hey, you stupid idiot, we don't know if anybody's there or not," the Sheriff yelled after him.

"I'm puttin' an end to this shit," Clint yelled back. "I'll see if anybody's home."

Clint walked on toward the cabin without hesitation. When he was almost to the door, he stopped. He stood looking down at the ground.

"Hey, Sheriff, I think you better get over here," he said calmly without looking up.

"What is it?" Sheriff Clark asked, as he slowly came out from behind the tree.

"Come take a look," Clint said still not looking up. "I think you have one less unaccounted for person."

Sheriff Clark slowly walked toward Clint with his rifle at the ready. As he approached, he could see something on the ground. Soon, he was looking down into the unseeing eyes of Jim Upter. Jim's eyes stared up into the early morning sky. He was lying in a large pool of blood. The Sheriff reached down and felt for Jim's pulse.

"He's dead," the Sheriff proclaimed.

"No shit, Sherlock," Clint said sarcastically.

"Look, I don't need your wise mouth. I'm doin' my job the best I can. I suppose seein' a dead man doesn't mean much to you."

Clint took a deep breath. "I'm sorry, Sheriff. And you're wrong, seein' a dead man does mean a lot to me. I saw a lot of 'em in the war. I've been drunk ever since. This is kind of hard for me to handle sober."

Sheriff Clark looked at the man standing across from him. He looked like a man that had seen a lot of hard times.

"I've been wonderin' about you," the Sheriff said. "How'd you end up in this mess? You don't seem much like the cowardly type to me."

"We'll I may be a coward and I may not. I don't know for sure myself." As Clint talked, he walked away from Jim's body. He pushed his hands deep into his pockets and lifted his face to the sky. He seemed to be fighting the memories that came flooding back into his brain.

"All I know for sure," Clint started. "Is that I did run away. I don't even remember how it happened. All I remember is that after one heavy attack most everyone was dead but me. I woke up lying in a stack of dead bodies. I struggled to free myself from the mangled and broken bodies. Parts of bodies were everywhere and I was soaked in blood. Not my blood, I didn't have a scratch. All I had was a huge bump on my head. After I got free of the bodies, I stood up and looked around. It was the strangest feelin' I've ever had. I was the only livin' thing for as far as I could see. The earth was desolate and scorched. Smoke hung low over the battlefield and fire still burned in the trenches. Dead bodies from both sides were everywhere. Nothin' was alive or movin'. It was the most terrible sight I'd ever seen. I wandered around for a long time. I don't know how long I walked, but I must've walked for miles. I finally came to a French farmhouse that was totally destroyed. I remember an old French couple was pickin' around in the debris. What happened after that is hard for me to remember. The blow on my head must've been worse than I thought, because my memory kept goin' in and out. The next thing I remember for sure is the war bein' over and I was on that tramp steamer headin' for home. Somehow, I swear I don't know how, I was registered as one of the crew. After we docked in New York, I made my way home. I never really knew I was listed as missin' in action 'til I talked to Ruth. Ruth had already gotten some money from the government and didn't want anyone to know about me. That's how the whole thing of me bein' on the hill got started. You know, Sheriff, Dick doesn't even know he's my son. Anyway that's basically my story."

"That's an interesting story. Maybe the army will buy it. But I doubt they're goin' to go along with all this fraud and other stuff," the Sheriff said. "You also haven't explained this daughter of yours we're supposed to be lookin' for."

"That's an entirely different story and not related to any of this," Clint said with a small smile. "And anyway, I didn't know I was supposed to be explainin' anythin'."

"Oh, we'll get to that," the Sheriff said firmly. "We surely will get to that."

Sheriff Clark looked away from Clint and back to body. "I wonder how he died. There seems to be so much blood."

Sheriff Clark bent down and rolled Jim's body over. Then, he could see the large hole in Jim's back. "Well, it looks like he was stabbed in the back. It must've been a big knife like maybe a kitchen butcher knife or somethin' of the like. Do you have any idea who would do this?"

"No," Clint said simply. "It could've been one of the Klan I guess, but I don't know."

"Well, I guess we need to try and make a stretcher of some kind and get him to the funeral home in town. Maybe Doc Jewel can tell us somethin'."

"That's quite a ways for the two of us to carry him," Clint said. "Draggin' him through all this mud is really gonna be a chore."

"Yeah, I know," the Sheriff replied looking up at the sky. "But, it looks like it's goin' to be a beautiful day and we're goin' that way anyhow."

CHAPTER THIRTY-SIX

The Day After

Sheriff Tom Clark sat looking out his office window. His office was on the third floor of the County Court House. Its location gave him a view of the entire town square. He watched people going about their business on this beautiful day. After the rain and storm last night, the day had dawned beautifully in Coalville. The sun was shining, there were no clouds in the sky, and the birds were singing. He glanced up at the clock on the wall above his desk and frowned as he noticed it was nearly two o'clock in the afternoon. He rubbed his face as if to wipe away the fatigue of only three hours of sleep in the last forty hours, but it wouldn't go away.

Sheriff Clark had not gotten into the office until noon, but everything was going on schedule. Louis Mailer had shown up at work early in the morning. Louis had gotten the story about last night's happenings from several different people, but, for him, the story still had a lot missing. Sheriff Clark had not yet spoken to Louis about being unavailable last night, especially for being gone and out of touch without telling him. He had just not found the time yet and he decided it would probably have to wait until everything else had been attended to.

In the meantime, Louis set about trying to get the day organized for the Sheriff. At two o'clock, the Sheriff was to interview Ruth Jordan and start putting all the events that had happened together. Ruth had been informed of Jim Upter's death early this morning. Doc Jewel had to give her a sedative to calm her down. Doc, however, had promised to have her ready to talk by two o'clock. Sheriff Clark felt he had things somewhat under control. Clint Jordan was locked in a cell in the court house basement, Ruth Jordan was under house arrest at her home, Judy Cole was staying with the Collies, and Jim Upter and Lester Homes lay dead at the funeral home. He could still remember his shock when he and Clint arrived at the funeral home with Jim Upter's body to find it already open at that early hour. As it turned out, they had just picked up Lester's body and brought it in.

Sheriff Clark was tired, but the feeling of being in control made him look and feel much fresher. He had bathed, gotten a few hours' sleep, and put on a clean fresh uniform. Taking a deep breath, he got up from his chair and walked over to a small refrigerator that sat by itself in the corner of the office. The door was secured by a huge padlock. Taking a key ring out of his pocket, he thumbed through them until he found the one he wanted. Then, he unlocked the refrigerator door and pulled it open. Inside, stacked very neatly, were several bottles of Blue Bonnet beer. He knew he shouldn't keep beer in his office, but he did just the same. He withdrew a bottle, opened it, and took a long swallow. The taste of the cold liquid was refreshing. He walked back over to his chair and continued to gaze out the window and drink his beer.

At two o'clock sharp, his phone rang. Sheriff Clark put down his beer and picked up the receiver. "Yes," he answered.

"Sheriff, Mrs. Jordan is here to see you." It was Alice, the woman who worked as the secretary for the Sheriff and other officials in the court house.

"Give me five minutes, then send her in and have Lou come in with her," the Sheriff replied.

Quickly, he picked up his empty beer bottle and put it back in the refrigerator. He locked the door again and put the key in his pocket. Returning to his chair, he relaxed and waited.

Ruth came into the office looking tired but much better than she had looked the last time the Sheriff had seen her, except that he couldn't see her breast through her blouse. Louis followed Ruth into the Sheriff's office.

"Sit down, Ruth, and we'll get started," he said, pointing her to a chair.

Ruth sat in the chair indicated. She was holding a handkerchief in her hands and she twisted it nervously. She looked up at the Sheriff. "Can I have some water, Tom?"

"Alice!" Sheriff Clark yelled.

"Yes, Sir," was the reply from the outer office.

"Bring Mrs. Jordan a glass of water, please."

"Yes, Sir," Alice replied.

Shortly, Alice, a short redheaded woman, came into the office carrying a glass of water. She handed it to Ruth and then left. Ruth drank the entire glass and placed it on Sheriff Clark's desk.

"Are you ready to tell me about it now?" The Sheriff asked, looking steadily at Ruth.

Ruth sat up straight in the chair and pushed her hair back with her hand. "Okay, I guess so," she said. "Where do you want me to start?"

"At the beginning, please."

"Well, as you may know, I was pregnant when Clint went to war in January of nineteen-eighteen. Dick was born in April of the same year. A month later, in May, I got a telegram tellin' me Clint was missin' in action. Until the war was over, I kept hopin' they'd find Clint or that he would turn up alive. I kept hopin' and hopin', but it never happened. Clint never came back. At least, he didn't come back right away. The government started giving me a monthly check to help support me and Dick. It wasn't much, but it helped. I took in people's sewin' and washin' to make money. With the money I made and the government check every month, we made it okay. Then, Clint came back. He came to my house one night about two years after the war was over. I couldn't believe he was really alive. I almost died of shock. It took me a while to really believe it was him. But it was, and he wanted money. He told me he was in trouble. As it turned out, Clint was a deserter. In short, he went over the hill. He was afraid if they found him they would shoot him. He'd got back to the states aboard a tramp steamer from France. He wanted to hide here in Coalville."

Ruth stopped talking and looked up at the ceiling for brief moment, and then continued. "So, Clint's been livin' all these years up on Lonesome Hill. I went up there about every Saturday to take him stuff he needed. Dick went with me but he never knew Clint was his father. I made Clint promise not to tell him. I told Clint if he told Dick he was his father, I would turn him in to the army. So, Clint promised not to tell." Ruth stopped and took a deep breath. She looked at the Sheriff, but he said nothing.

"I had forgotten all about the insurance Clint had with this company in Dallas 'til I got a letter from the government tellin' me I could collect my money. The government had forced the company to declare Clint dead and pay me my due. Since the army had listed Clint missing in action and not dead, the insurance company wouldn't pay off, until the government made them do it years later. So, by keeping Clint dead, I got the insurance money and my monthly check from the government. So, I thought it was a good idea, and anyway I didn't want to see Clint shot or hanged. I mean, as long as Clint stayed up on Lonesome Hill and didn't bother anybody, I could collect the money. I didn't see any harm in it. If I had turned Clint in, Dick would've found out about his Father and I would've lost my income. None of that made sense to me. And that's it. That's the story."

"I don't think so, Ruth. It seems you're leavin' out things like Jim Upter, your marriage to said person, the Klan, and Judy Cole. It seems you forgot to tell me about those things, and I really would like to know." The Sheriff leaned back in his chair and looked at Ruth, waiting for her to continue.

"I didn't forget, I was just hopin' you wouldn't ask," she said smiling.

"Why not tell me about you and the Klan first," the Sheriff said.

"Not much to tell about me and the Klan. I just fell in love with Jim and Jim was in the Klan. He came here to start a Klan chapter in East Texas and I was goin' to help him. I had the means to help. I had some money and a place to start. Lonesome Hill was the ideal place because no one ever went up there. Clint could help me because he was up there all the time anyway. So, we just used that old miner's shack up there for a meeting place. I really had very little to do with what they did."

The Sheriff leaned over his desk and studied Ruth. "Tell me, Ruth, why did you ever get mixed up with the Klan, why the Klan?"

"Tom, no man had been interested in me for years before Jim. I never had much time for men 'til I came into the money. I'd been a widow for a long time, or at least as good as a widow. I just couldn't help fallin' in love with Jim and I know he loved me. It had been a long time since a man had held me, kissed me, and made love to me like Jim did. And if the man I loved hated coloreds, then I guess I hated them too. I wanted Jim to be happy here and I'd do anythin' for him. That may not sound like much of a reason to you, Tom, but it's plenty for me. It's plenty for me." Ruth started crying softly. She used her twisted handkerchief to dry her eyes. "How much longer do I have to do this, Tom? I'm not feelin' so good."

"One more thing about this, Ruth, did Upter know that Clint was your husband?"

"No, Jim didn't know."

"Well, did Clint know you were married to Upter?"

"No, he didn't. I told you we kept it a secret from everybody, even Dick. Dick knows now, I spent a lot of time talkin' to him last night. He knows everythin'. He even knows that Clint is his Father."

"So, you kept secrets from Clint and Upter both, uh? The Sheriff said, shaking his head. "You sure had a thing goin', all right."

"Not really, Tom. All there was for me was Jim. Of everythin' else, as far as I'm concerned, it was just me and Jim."

Ruth stopped again and took a deep breath. Her shoulders shook as she tried to hold back tears. "Can I go now, Tom?" She asked softly.

"In just a minute," the Sheriff said waving his hand at her, "now, if you'll just tell me where Judy Cole fits into this whole thing. She's not your child, is she?"

"No, she's not mine. But Judy Cole is another story completely. She has nothin' to do with this whole thing, so couldn't we just leave her out of it?" Ruth spoke with, what seemed to Sheriff Clark, deep feeling.

"I'm afraid not, Ruth," the Sheriff said simply. "People are dead and I have to know all of it. I mean I want the whole story. I know how you must feel, but you're in deep trouble right now. Any help you can give me now may make it easier for you in the long run."

"Do you have any clue as to who killed Jim?" Ruth asked suddenly, trying to change the subject. She looked at Sheriff Clark with sad tear-filled eyes.

"No," Sheriff Clark answered with his head down. "No, I don't have a clue. But if you can fill me in on all the unanswered questions, maybe we can find out. Now, gettin' back to Judy Cole, who is she?"

"Tom, I don't feel I'm the one to tell you about Judy Cole. It's not my place. Ask Clint about her," Ruth answered.

"I have asked Clint," the Sheriff said stiffly. "All he says is that she's his daughter. He won't say anythin' else. He won't tell us who the mother is or where she is. Now, if you know somethin', Ruth, you need to tell me."

"I tell you it's not my place. I don't have to answer any more questions. I've told you all I can, now leave me alone." Ruth was no longer crying and sad, she was getting mad. She stood up and looked down at Sheriff Clark. "I'm tired and I'm hurt. I'm goin' home." She turned quickly and started for the door.

"Ruth," the Sheriff called after her softly. "I don't think you understand that you're under arrest. I only let you stay at home because I was bein' nice. I can put you in a cell down there next to Clint if that's the way you want it, or I can let you go home under house arrest again. It's up to you."

Ruth slowly turned back around and sat back down in her chair. She started to cry again. "What do you want from me? I'm not much of a person I don't guess, but I still have feelings for Clint. He's kept his part of our bargain; I just can't be the one to betray him. Please don't ask me to do that. Leave me with somethin'." Ruth lowered her head into her hands and cried loudly.

"Okay, Ruth, okay. I'm not goin' to beat you or anythin'," the Sheriff said. He got up and walked around his desk to Ruth and put his hand on her shoulder. "I'm sorry for this pressure, Ruth, but I need to know about Judy Cole. Who can tell me about her?"

"I can," said a voice at the office door.

"I tried to stop him, Sheriff Clark, but he pushed on through," Alice was saying quickly.

"It's okay Alice let 'im in."

"I think I can explain Judy Cole's story to you," Reverend Tuney said, as he walked into the office.

"Please do, reverend," the Sheriff said.

"But first, why don't you let this lady go home?" The reverend said turning to Ruth.

Sheriff Clark looked from the reverend to Ruth and back again. Finally he made a decision. "Alice," he yelled.

"Yes, sir," Alice said appearing at the office door again.

"Get someone to drive Mrs. Jordan home and be sure and assign someone to watch her house."

"Yes Sir. If you'll come with me Mrs. Jordan," Alice said, holding the door open.

"Thanks, Tom," Ruth said as she got up. She looked at Reverend Tuney and smiled. "Good luck reverend," she said as she started for the door.

"One last thing, Ruth," the Sheriff called after her. "I would take it very badly if you tried to leave town or anythin' like that."

Ruth gave the Sheriff a tired look and then followed Alice out the door.

"Okay, now reverend, if you please," the Sheriff said as he settled back into his chair again.

"Judy Cole," the Reverend Tuney started. "It's a nice name. Clint gave it to her. Judy, because he thought it was a nice name and Cole because of the old played out coal mines. That's how she got her name, Judy Cole. You see, Tom, Judy is the illegitimate child of my daughter, Bob Ann."

Sheriff Clark rose to his feet and stared at Reverend Tuney. "The illegitimate child of your daughter," the Sheriff breathed.

"Yes, Tom, it's true. Judy Cole is my granddaughter."

"Why? Why, in heaven's name have you allowed her to live on that hill with a deserter and a drunk?" Sheriff Clark asked.

"I wouldn't be so quick to judge Clint. He's done a good job with Judy as far as I can see. Oh! I did wrong. I know that, but that's neither here nor there now. Only the future is important now. God has forgiven me for my sin and now I only hope man can forgive me. You see my daughter had lived the life I set up for her. It's hard to be a preacher's daughter, Tom. People expect you to be a saint. I tried to make Bob Ann into what people expected of her as the preacher's daughter. I didn't allow her the liberties the other kids had. I kept her close and I watched over her like a mother hen. Bob Ann's mother died in childbirth, so I felt I had to make the perfect child for her mother's sake and for mine as well. I didn't think about her at all. I was very selfish about everything. So, as a result, Bob Ann got into trouble."

"She allowed a passing soldier to take her sexually. She did it out of spite for me and, mostly, because the boy had been to France during the war and she thought she loved him. His stories sounded romantic and she gave herself to him. She was a little less lucky than other girls because she became pregnant. When she finally came to me with the truth, she was terrified. Instead of standing by her and helping her, I shamed her and tried to find a way to hide her shame. At my insistence, we told everyone in town that she was going away to Dallas to school for a year, but the truth was she went away to have her baby. I sent her to the farm of an old college friend of mine. After Judy was born, we didn't know what to do with her. We couldn't bring her here. We thought about an orphan's home, but there would be too many questions and Bob Ann didn't want to do that. She wanted to know where her baby was and who its parents would be."

"Then, I remembered how Lois and Bobbie Homes used to drive along the road by Lonesome Hill. After Lois and Bobbie died, I noticed that Lester drove to the spot of their death almost every Friday evening. Bob Ann and I decided to place the baby in a basket and set it by the side of the road and let Lester find it. Lester was the richest man in town, and we thought that if he found the baby, he might keep it to replace Bobbie. If that happened, the baby would have a nice home and, at the same time, be close by for Bob Ann to see. So, we placed the basket at the foot of the hill on the roadside and waited. We had timed it so it would only be a few minutes until Lester came along. We hid in the bushes down by the ravine. But to our surprise, Clint Jordan was the first one to arrive. I didn't know who he was at the time and neither did Bob Ann. We watched as he emerged out of the bushes from the hill and onto the road. He had started walking down the road, when he saw the basket. We watched as he first looked in the basket, and then picked it up and ran up the hill. We were stunned. My first reaction was to follow him onto the hill and get the baby back, but I knew that would be useless."

"Over the next few weeks, Bob Ann was out of her mind with worry and shame. Finally, she talked me into going up on the hill to see what we could find. One Saturday, about two weeks after Clint had taken the basket, Bob Ann and I went on a search of the hill. Naturally, we found nothing. No matter what I said, Bob Ann wouldn't stop insisting on searching. So, about every Saturday we would spend most of our day searching the hill. Finally, one Saturday, we found Clint's shack hidden deep in the woods behind the old pits. That's when we found out Clint's real identity and how he was caring for Judy. For some reason, that only Clint can tell you, he wanted to keep Judy. We agreed he should, but that we would give him supplies and anything else the baby required. That's how Ruth came to know about Judy. We worked out an arrangement with her to take our supplies when she made her weekly trips to see Clint. That's been twelve years ago. Bob Ann never went back to see Judy again. We continued to send supplies, until Bob Ann married Jack. Since she's been married to Jack, she's not been involved with Judy in any way at all. She cut that part of her life loose and went on with her future. It wasn't that she didn't still love Judy. It's just that she had to get on with her own life. Judy was well-taken care of by Clint. While Ruth was gone that one year, I made a deal with her to keep Clint supplied. Ruth sent me the money and I got Clint what he needed. When she got back to town, she took the job back. As far as Judy and what she knows, she doesn't know that Bob Ann is her mother. In fact, she's not seen Bob Ann since she's been old enough to remember. Now I guess Bob Ann's past is coming back."

"Now she has this to go through again, only this time, I'm going to see to it that Bob Ann doesn't have to suffer because of me. I forced Bob Ann to lose her baby because I was afraid of what people might say, because I was afraid for my position in church, and because I thought I could run away from God. But you can't run from God. He sees you everywhere you go, and he sees everything you do. I fooled myself into believing that as long as the people didn't know, it was all right. But God knew, and I knew, and Bob Ann knew. You can't make things better by sinning against God. It's true what they say about two wrongs not making a right. So, Tom, I'm ready to take any punishment that might be called for, but Bob Ann is not to blame for this. I am supposed to be a man of God and I have done a wrong that is not expected of a man of God. All I can say is that I'm at peace with my God, and now I'm ready to answer to society."

The Reverend stopped talking and looked at Sheriff Clark. Sheriff Clark studied the Reverend for a long time. "Does anybody else know about this besides you, Bob Ann, and Clint?" The Sheriff asked.

"Just Ruth Jordan and Doc Jewel," the reverend replied. "Doc Jewel is the one who found out Bob Ann was pregnant. He's kept quiet all these years. He, of course, knows nothing about Judy Cole being Bob Ann's child. He believes we gave the baby away in Dallas. That belief cost me a very good friendship with the good doctor. Jay Jay believes me to be a hypocrite, and I guess he's right. But, as I say, I'm ready to take my punishment."

Sheriff Clark got up from his chair and walked over to his window and looked out at the town. He turned and looked at the reverend with a look of disgust. "I'll tell you the truth, Reverend Tuney; I think your punishment is out of my jurisdiction."

CHAPTER THIRTY-SEVEN

Loose Ends

I t was late evening, when Sheriff Tom Clark walked into his small house. He was very tired. In the last two days, he had only had about four hours sleep. Today had been a long but interesting day. He had finished all of his interviews with the main players in Coolville's big drama. What a tangled mess it had turned out to be. Everyone involved was either in jail, under house arrest, or where he could find them quickly. He had sent Lou to Dallas to arrange for the pickup of Clint and Ruth Jordan by the Federal Authorities. Then, after the interviews, he had gone out to the Barnett farm to talk with Harry. This had to be handled very carefully to avoid getting the Barnett children involved. He didn't mention anything about Billy Bob and Sue Ann believing that Harry had been one of the men they had seen on the hill. Also, he had instructed James Collie not to mention anything about it, and to tell his children to keep it quiet. He had hoped that Harry might confess or volunteer some information with some gentle questioning. But Harry swore ignorance of the entire affair. Tom concluded that there was no use in getting the children involved since he didn't have any kind of proof linking Harry with the Klan much less the murders. However, the worried look on Mrs. Barnett's face during the questioning spoke a lot of unsaid words, especially when Harry was trying to confirm his whereabouts during the time of Moonbeam and Rachael's death. Harry had said he was home, but the look on Mrs. Barnett's face said something different. There was no use in pushing the issue with Harry at this time, but there would be another time. He wasn't ready to give up on Harry Barnett yet. Now, all Tom wanted was to clean up and get some sleep.

Tom unbuckled his gun belt and put the gun and holster into the telephone table drawer. He sat down in his chair next to the phone and pulled off his boots. Dropping his boots by the chair, he leaned back with a sigh. He was about to push himself out of the chair and go run his bath water when he heard a soft knock at the front door. Tiredly, he lifted himself out of the chair and walked slowly over to answer the door. He opened the door to see Evie Mailer standing there. Without saying anything, he stepped out and looked up and down the street. At the same time, he took her arm and pulled her into the house. Seeing no one, he stepped back in the house and closed the door. Evie was standing in the middle of the living room. Her hands were behind her back holding her shoes. She looked like a little girl standing there barefooted and dressed in a blue cotton skirt that came to just below her knees and a bright red blouse that hung loosely from her shoulders. The blouse was worn outside the skirt and hung down below her hips. She had her hair in her favorite pony tail. "Why did you come here?" He asked in a tired voice.

"I wanted to see you," she said simply.

"Do you think that it's a good idea to be seen coming here?"

"I don't know and I don't care," she replied sharply. "I just decided since Lou was gone to Dallas that I'd walk over here. I took off my shoes and walked through the grass most of the way. It felt good. I like walkin' barefooted in cool green grass. Don't you?"

"What do you want, Evie?" Tom's voice showed tiredness.

"Did you send Lou to Dallas so we could be together?" She asked tilting her head to one side in a childish manner.

"No! Believe it or not, I sent him to do an important job. He's takin' all my information to the Feds and he's supposed to come back with them to pick up Clint and Ruth tomorrow."

"Well, anyway, since I'm here, we might as well take advantage of it." She dropped her shoes to the floor and walked to the kitchen. "You got any beer?"

"Evie," he called after her. "I don't think it's a good idea for you to be here. Somebody might see us!"

She was already in the kitchen looking into the refrigerator. "I already told you, I don't care."

"Well damn it, I care," he said keeping his emotions under control. He followed her into the kitchen. "We can't afford a problem now."

In one motion, she turned around holding two beers and kicked the refrigerator door close with her bare foot. Then, she set the beers on the kitchen table and started looking through the kitchen drawers for a bottle opener. "When can we afford a problem, Tom?" She asked without looking at him.

"The bottle opener is on top of the refrig," he said quickly and then continued. "I thought we agreed on all this! We agreed to wait 'til the baby was born!"

"We will wait," she said as she opened the beers. She handed one to Tom and then she took a long drink of the other one. "Man, that's good and cold."

"I thought you were supposed to watch your weight," he said, taking a drink of his own beer. He sat in one of the kitchen chairs and looked up at her as she leaned back against the kitchen counter.

"I am watchin' it. Somethin' every now and then won't hurt me."

"Evie, what're we doin'?" He asked in frustration.

"We're not doin' anythin' yet, but we will before I leave," she smiled, pointing her beer bottle at him. "I'm not goin' to worry about who knows what or whose baby it is. I'm not goin' to tell Lou anythin' 'til after the baby, just like I promised, but I'm not goin' to stay away from you either. I'm goin' to take every opportunity I can get to be with you. Even when I'm big and fat with this baby, I want you to make love to me. And I mean right up 'til the last minute, up 'til I can't stand it anymore." As she talked, she walked over to him and climbed onto his lap. She was facing him and straddling him.

Evie set her beer on the nearby table, then took the beer from his hand and did the same with it. She pressed herself tightly against him and wrapped her arms around his neck. She moved her face to within inches of his. "Then, when I think I can't stand it anymore,

I want you to make me do it again," she breathed. Then, she kissed him deep and hard moving her body against his in an act of passion.

Once again, Tom felt himself lose control and act against his better judgment. His hands went under her skirt and he pulled her tighter against him as his mouth slid from her lips to her neck. He couldn't see the smile on her face as she knew she had won. Evie allowed him to feel her and handled her for several minutes. Then, suddenly, she pushed herself away from him and jumped to her feet. She backed away from him looking at his confusion. He sat there dazed in a state of sexual excitement. She was panting as if she had run for miles. After taking several steps backward and away from him, she stopped. Then, she spread her feet apart, put her hands on her hips, and bent forward at the waist and taunted him. "Do you want me?" She laughed. Her voice was loud and she was still breathing hard.

"What is this, Evie?" He asked getting to his feet and knocking his chair over in the process. "What're you trying to prove?"

"I'm tryin' to prove you're right, Tom. I mean right about needing me. You told me you weren't sure if you loved me, but that you sure as hell needed me. That is what you said, ain't it? Well, how bad do you need me now?" She grabbed the hem of her skirt and waved it around giving him quick glances of what was underneath.

"If you're tryin' to be a bitch, you're doin' a good job," he growled between gritted teeth. He took a step toward her but she quickly moved around to the other side of the kitchen table placing the table between them.

"Yeah, I'm a bitch," she laughed. "But whose bitch am I? Maybe I'm Lou's bitch, or maybe I'm your bitch?"

"I think you're just a bitch," he yelled. "Nobody's in particular: just a bitch." He made a quick move around the table and grabbed at her. But she moved quicker and kept the table between them. He made another move, but again she was able to move around and keep the table between them. "I'm not goin' to chase you all night. It ain't worth it." He straightened up and seemed to relax some.

"Oh, that ain't true, Tom. You know it's worth it. Take a good look at me, Tom. Don't you think it's worth it?" As she spoke, she reached down and unbuttoned her skirt. She pulled the skirt over her head and pitched it behind her onto the kitchen counter. Next, she quickly unbuttoned her bright red blouse and soon it was on the counter with her skirt. Now, she stood dressed only in her panties and bra. All the time she was doing this, she kept herself in the ready position in case he made another move around the table.

"Why are you doin' this to me?" He asked with a puzzled look on his face. "Do you enjoy seein' me lose control of myself?" As he spoke, he leaned on the table with both hands and hung his head between his arms. He didn't want to look at her because he could feel himself being overcome with desire for her.

"Aw come on, are you goin' to cry about it," she taunted. "Before you cry, maybe you better take another look."

He didn't respond. He continued to keep his head down so he couldn't see her. She reached behind her back and unsnapped her bra. She removed the bra and threw it at him. The bra hit him in the head and fell to the table. He stood up and picked up the bra and looked up at her. She remained in her ready position smiling at him. Suddenly, she relaxed and stood up straight displaying her nakedness to him in its fullest.

Tom stood transfixed looking at her. The sight of her nearly naked body excited him. Her small firm breasts were moving up and down with her heavy breathing. He looked down at the bra he held in his hand and then he slung it across the room. She didn't move, but remained standing straight and still. Then, without warning, Tom gripped the table and threw it to one side. The quickness of the move and the sound of the table and chairs crashing caused her to jump back.

Before Evie could move again, he was in front of her. The only direction she could go was backward. She took only a few steps backward when she felt the kitchen counter press into the small of her back. This caused her a moment of fear, but she quickly pushed it aside. Showing fear would defeat her purpose. She groaned in pain as Tom pressed his weight up against her, crushing her between him and the kitchen counter. Pinning her with his weight, he reached around with his left hand and grabbed her ponytail. Savagely, he jerked her head back so that she looked up into his face.

Even with the pain in her back from his pressing weight and the pain in her head from his tight grip on her hair, she smiled up at him with a taunting smile. Her eyes flashed with the knowledge of what she was doing to him. Still holding her tightly by the hair, he stepped back from her. He started walking across the kitchen pulling her along by her hair and kicking turned-over chairs out of his way as he went. His long strides were too much for her and she stumbled and fell, but he retained his tight grip on her hair.

She rolled over on her back and grabbed at his hand gripping her hair trying to ease the pressure on her head. Now, she was being dragged through the kitchen by the hair of her head. She never once yelled out in pain as he dragged her out of the kitchen, down the hall, and into his bedroom. There, he took her ponytail in both hands and lifted her off her feet. He held her in the air with her face level with his. Her toes reached for the floor but it was no use as she dangled in midair. She grabbed at his hands, but they were too strong. Her eyes were shut tight and her lips quivered, but still she made no sound.

He shook her viciously making her body flop around like a fish dangling on a hook. "Open your eyes and look at me," he yelled. Against the pain in her head, she forced her eyes to open. He looked into her eyes for several long seconds. "Is this what you wanted?" He growled at her.

"Yes," she breathed heavily. "It's exactly what I wanted."

He slung her onto his bed. When she hit the bed, she bounced onto her back. She looked up at him as he towered over her and started unbuttoning his shirt. Then he said with conviction, "And to answer your question, you're my bitch."

After it was over, Evie stood in the bathroom looking in the mirror. She had taken a quick bath and cleaned herself up. As she looked into the mirror, she adjusted her skirt and blouse to fit properly. She had taken her hair out of the ponytail before she had taken her bath. Now, she tried to brush her hair and pull it back into the ponytail again. She groaned at the pain caused by the soreness in her head. It seemed even her hair itself was sore. Biting her lip against the pain, she finished arranging her hair into the ponytail.

Evie took one last look at herself. Satisfied with what she saw, she went back to the bedroom where Tom sat propped up in bed. She stopped at the door and looked across at him. "I guess I better get on home," she said softly.

"Look, Evie, I'm really sorry for what I did," he said as he got up and put on his pants. "I know you purposely pushed me to it, but I still should be able to keep myself under control better than that. I could've hurt you. I could've hurt you really bad." His voice was soft and showed real concern.

"I ain't complainin'," she said, smiling her smug smile. "So don't be feelin' sorry." She turned and started up the hallway toward the front door.

"Wait a minute," he yelled after her. "I'll drive you home. It's dark out there." He hurried down the hallway and caught up with her at the front door.

"No," she said, opening the door. "I'll walk." She reached down and removed her shoes. "I like walkin' through the damp grass, it makes me feel good. Anyway, there's less chance of someone seein' us together if I go alone. That's what you want ain't it? You don't want anyone to see us, do you?"

"That's right," he answered lowering his eyes so he wouldn't have to look her in the face. "I don't want anyone to see us."

She glanced out the door into the dark night. It was still and quiet and no one was in sight. She stepped out the door onto the porch and started walking down the steps.

"At least not yet," he whispered after her quickly. "The time will come, but not now."

Evie didn't look back or acknowledge that she heard him. She simply hurried off into the night.

Tom closed the door after she had gone. He went to the bathroom and started running his bath water. While the water was running, he went into the kitchen and picked up the table and chairs that were scattered all around the room. After he had put everything back in its place, he went back to the bathroom. He turned off the water and removed his pants.

Before he got into the tub, he saw himself in the mirror. He stared at himself for a long time. How could he allow Evie to make him lose control? She made him crazy. Maybe he did love her, because surely just sexual desire alone didn't make him act the way he did. He knew he had to make a decision about Evie soon. This couldn't go on until after the baby was born. She was pushing him harder all the time. He hated her for doing this to him, but he also hated the thought of never being with her again.

Soon, it was going to be a decision between Lou's friendship and his career as the Sheriff of Coalville, or Evie. Most of the time he knew what he wanted; except when he was with Evie. When he was with her, she was all he wanted. He stepped into the tub, leaned back and let the hot water surround his body. Taking a deep breath, he closed his eyes. Sheriff Tom Clark needed rest.

Meanwhile, Evie walked quietly home. It wasn't a very long walk, maybe just over a mile. When she could, she stayed off the road and sidewalk and walked in the grass. The grass was cool and damp and she enjoyed the feeling on her bare feet. She smiled to herself as she walked along. She knew she had once again made Tom respond to her. It was only a matter of time now until Tom was hers completely. Then, she would leave Lou and make her life with Tom. Things like she did tonight have to be done, because the only time she was in complete control of Tom was when he was out of control. She smiled to herself as she thought about it. Tom was so big and strong, but she could make him do just about whatever she wanted him to do.

She enjoyed driving him to the point of physically hurting her because it gave her pleasure. For her, making love with Lou was a total waste of time. He was always so soft and so gentle. Always asking her if he had hurt her or if this was okay or that was okay. Sex with Lou was a one way street. Lou got all the pleasure and she got none. She simply went through the motions. But with Tom it was different. Love making was hard, physical, and sometimes violent. He never asked if he was hurting her or anything. Whatever he wanted to do he did, and she loved it. In her mind, she had a right to happiness and pleasure as much as anyone else, and Tom Clark was her means of achieving those goals. She was already carrying his child. Now, it was just a matter of getting him.

Evie was brought out of her thoughts as she neared her house. She stopped for a minute in the front yard and wiggled her toes in the cool damp grass. She felt happy as if everything was going her way. Then, smiling to herself, she went inside.

CHAPTER THIRTY-EIGHT

The Sermon

James Collie looked up from his Sunday morning paper to see Mary enter the room. She was dressed in her Sunday best. As she walked by, she pulled the paper from his hands. "Are you ready?" She asked.

"I've been ready for an hour or more," he laughed.

"Well, let's go then," she said.

"Where're Dee and Cherrie?" He asked.

"They're out in the car where I told them to wait. Now hurry up, Jim, you're so slow." With that, she walked out the front door. James watched her cross the lawn and get into the car. "Hurry up, Jim!" He exclaimed. "Hurry up, Jim! Jesus Christ!" He followed her out to the car. He took his place behind the wheel and turned to study his family. Dee and Cherrie sat in the back seat dressed in their Sunday church clothes.

"Well?" Mary asked.

"Okay, okay, I was just leavin'," he said as he cranked the car.

When they reached the church, the service had already begun. As they drove into the small parking lot, they could hear the chorus to, "When We All Get to Heaven" flowing from the church. James parked the car and they all got out. They hurried to the church and went inside.

The church wasn't big. It had one large room for the sermons and a number of smaller rooms for the Sunday school classes. The Collie family took their usual place on third row from the back, on the right-hand side. They had no sooner taken their seats, when they were asked to all stand and sing number one-twenty-eight. As it turned out, number one-twenty-eight was, "We Shall Gather at The River". James looked around in disgust. He could never sing that song. Why did they always sing that song? He just didn't have the voice for it.

As James looked around, he saw the church was unusually full. It wasn't Christmas or Easter, but nevertheless the church was full. Then, he began to notice faces. In their usual place in front of the Collies sat the Barnett family. Doc Jewell was over in his corner, but he wasn't asleep as he usually was. Then James' eye caught Ruth, Dick, and Clint Jordan. Sitting, directly behind them was Sheriff Tom Clark and Louis Mailer. Evie Mailer was not present. Bob Ann sat near the front with her husband, children, and Judy Cole. James felt a slight tugging on his sleeve. He looked around to see Mary tugging at him. Suddenly, he realized why. He was the only one standing as everyone else had sat down.

Reverend Tuney walked slowly to the rostrum. Today he looked older. His eyes were set back into dark sockets. His forehead was creased with lines of worry. The color in his cheeks was pallid and they sagged. Walking up to the rostrum, he placed his hands on each side and straightened up and stood tall. He allowed his eyes to flow across the faces of the crowd. He seemed to look into each face individually. The silence was sharp, as a complete hush settled over the church. Reverend Tuney cleared his throat and the sound cut the silence like a knife. He lowered his head as if in silent prayer for a long minute. Then, he lifted his head and again gazed out upon the large assembly of people.

"Dear friends," he started. "We all know why we're here today. Not to worship God in God's house as we should, but we're here out of wonderment and contempt. Like vultures here to take what we can from a dying thing; to take our pound of flesh. We are here to sit in judgement of each other. Even though Christ has warned us not to judge lest we be judged, here we are, all gathered here to judge."

"So, I've thrown away my sermon for today and instead I will give you what you want. I'll give you your pound of flesh, for that's what you all came to get. You came to get your pound of flesh. I'll let you make your judgment. I'm sure you've all heard the story by now. About the preacher's daughter who had an illegitimate baby and got rid of it to hide her guilt. The righteous preacher who doesn't practice what he preaches. You all came to see this preacher, and you all came to see the others too. You came to see and hear their stories. You came to take from them. You came to judge them. You came to God's house for this! But I say to you, as did Christ, let he who is without sin cast the first stone."

"But there must be blame! If so, where does the blame go? Surely the blame must go somewhere. Someone must bear the burden of sin and blame. But who should that be? Whom can we blame? Who can bear the blame for Clint Jordan? Clint Jordan destined now to pay back what he took. I tell you none but Clint Jordan can bear his burden. Who will bear the burden for Ruth Jordan? Also, destined now to pay back what she took. I tell you again, none but Ruth Jordan will bear her burden. For those of you who wore hoods and robes to commit murder, who will bear your burden? You may be unknown to man, but you are known to God. So, who will bear your burden? Who will bear the burden of the innocent dead? Can you give back what you took? No, only you can bear that burden. Lastly, who will bear my burden? The answer is the same. No one but me can bear my burden."

"But the heaviest burden of all is not ours to carry. It belongs to Judy Cole, Dick Jordan, Cherrie Collie, Dee Collie and all of our children. They're the ones who will carry the load we have put on them. Then, I ask you where does the blame go? It goes to us all. All of us who allow hate to replace love. All of us who are so selfish that we only take from others and never give. All of us that place pride above all others and all other things. All of us who judge our neighbors but not ourselves."

Reverend Tuney stopped and took a sip from the water glass that stood on the rostrum. Still, the church was deadly quiet. No one stirred. Reverend Tuney again gazed out over the assembly. His eyes were wet with tears and his knuckles were white from gripping the rostrum tightly.

Then, he continued. "All of us will not be punished by man. All of us will not have to face manmade retribution. But we must all live with what we did. So, you've all come to take your pound of flesh! And that, my friends, is our whole problem. It is your problem as well as mine. Yes, mine maybe more than anyone else's. Take! Take! Take! Take! We all want to take something from one another. Take love for ourselves. Take money for ourselves. Take a life out of blind hate. Take freedom from a free man. And worst of all, take the future from a child. Take the future from those whom we love the most. Take all for ourselves. Take so that we can have our own way. Take so that no inconvenience will come our way. Take to protect our own beliefs and our own ways. Not caring who we hurt in the process, as long as we get what we want. Take just for the sake of taking. Take! Take! Take!"

"Did any of us ever think to give? Maybe we could give a little bit of ourselves, or to give a little of our time, or to give a little understanding instead of taking all the time. Did we ever think to give? You all know the story of the two trees in the hurricane down on the Texas coast. Two trees, one a tall straight oak tree, and the other a tall flexible palm tree. A hurricane came roaring through with winds in excess of one hundred and fifty miles per hour. The two trees stood side by side in the terrific wind. The oak tree refused to give with the wind and, instead, chose to stand rigid and straight. As a result, the mighty wind tore it up by its roots and blew it away. However, the palm tree, the flexible palm tree, gave with the wind. Instead of being uprooted and blown away, it only bent a little. It bent a little to keep from breaking. It bent with the wind and was not torn from the ground. It gave a little."

Reverend Tuney lifted his arms into the air. Tears were flowing freely down his cheeks. His voice had reached the level of shouting. "Could we think to give a little, as did our children? Or will we continue to stand rigid until we are ripped out by our roots and blown away. Will we stand rigid until our homes are destroyed, and until we rob our children of their future? Will we stand rigid until we lose all that we hold dear?"

Reverend Tuney's voice dropped to a whisper. He clenched his fist and pulled them to his chest. "So it is with our children, who could lead us! Could we not give a little?" He stretched his arms out to the people and pleaded. "For, my friends, we all have so much to give."

CHAPTER THIRTY-NINE

The Result

It was four weeks after the events on Lonesome Hill as Sheriff Tom Clark sat at his desk and held a file folder in his hands. The file folder had the name Jim Upter written on the front. He opened the file folder and thumbed through the pages inside. Then, in a fit of anger, he swept the folder and the enclosed papers onto the floor with a quick move from his hand. "Goddamn it," he yelled.

"You okay, Sheriff," Alice yelled from the outer office.

"Yeah, I'm okay," the Sheriff replied. Bending over, he started picking up the papers. His anger was due to the fact that he had made no progress in finding Jim Upter's murderer. He, also, had made no progress in finding any of the other Klan members. The frustration was beginning to get to him. No one would talk.

Other than the murder of Jim Upter, most everything else had taken its natural course. Clint Jordan had been picked up by the Federal Authorities and taken to Dallas to be held for trial. He was being charged with desertion in the face of the enemy. The army was asking for the death penalty. When they picked Clint up, Judy Cole was near hysterics. Clint had been the only parent she had ever known. The separation of the two was something the Sheriff didn't want to have to do again. He had felt like the bad guy in a movie. Judy could not understand what Clint had done wrong. To his credit, Clint had handled the situation well. He talked with Judy and tried to explain to her what was happening and why it had to happen. She finally accepted it and watched as the prison truck took him away.

Judy, herself, turned out to be a very intelligent girl. She went to live with Bob Ann and Jack. She accepted that Bob Ann was her mother and seemed to want to fit into the family. Bob Ann's prayers had been answered about Jack. He, at first, was shocked to find out about Bob Ann's past, but his great love for her and his dedication to family overcame the hurt. Judy was accepted into the family with the love and care they had for their own children. The decision was made, however, to leave Coalville and move to Dallas where Jack had accepted a job offer.

Along with Bob Ann and Jack, Reverend Tuney was moving to Dallas. He had resigned as the pastor of the Coalville Baptist Church. The congregation didn't want him to leave. In fact, they at first refused to accept his resignation. But after he took the time to explain to them that he wasn't running away from them, but going to help his daughter, they understood. They were a happy family when they left Coalville. Sheriff Clark could remember seeing them off. Most of the town was there to wish them well, including Doc Jewel. Sheriff Clark could still remember the warm feeling he had inside when he watched the two old friends hug each other and shake hands as they said their goodbyes.

Doc Jewel was genuinely happy to have Reverend Tuney as his friend again, but very sad to see him leave Coalville. The good doctor seemed to withdraw from everyone after the reverend left town. With the death of Moonbeam and losing a renewed friendship, he seemed to be very alone. There seemed to be no way to get Doc out of his slump, until Sheriff Clark hit upon an idea. Sheriff Clark smiled to himself as he remembered the conversation with Doc.

"Good afternoon, Doc," the Sheriff had said, as Doc Jewel let him into his house.

"What can I do for you, Tom? No more dead bodies, I hope."

"No, no more dead bodies," the Sheriff had laughed. "But I do have a problem you could help me with."

"What's that?"

"Well, Ruth Jordan is bein' taken to Dallas tomorrow to start her trial. They'll be holdin' her there throughout the trial. We don't know how long she'll be gone, or for that matter, if she's ever comin' back."

"How can I help you with that?" The doctor had asked sharply.

"Well, you see, it's Dick. I'm not sure what to do with that boy. He and his mother have become really close lately, but he can't stay in Dallas. He's got no kin there or anythin'. I was wondering if you could use a new handyman around your place here. Dick could work for you here and still go to school. I understand the boy is a hard worker and of good character."

"You mean you want me to take that boy on as my handyman?" The doctor had asked with uncertainty.

"It sure would help everyone out a lot, Doc. He could live out in Moonbeam's old place and, of course, he would still have his own house to use."

"I don't know, Tom. You just don't replace a Moonbeam. Old Moonbeam and I had been together for thirty years. I loved that old man." Tears had formed in Doc's eyes as he talked about Moonbeam.

"Doc, you can't replace Moonbeam. I'm not askin' you to even try to do that. But I am askin' you to help a boy out who needs some help now. Anyway, I hear he plays a mean game of checkers."

Sheriff Clark found himself laughing out loud as he remembered Doc's acceptance of the idea. It had worked out great. Dick was very grateful and happy to have the work and to be able to stay in Coalville. Now, at times, he and Doc can be seen arguing over checkers.

As for himself, he had decided that Evie must leave Lou and come live with him immediately. Tom would marry her as soon as she could obtain a divorce from Lou. They wouldn't wait for the baby to be born. He had decided to face Lou with the truth now and get the inevitable over with. He needed Evie and she needed him. She didn't love Lou and never would no matter whom the baby belonged to.

After his decision, he had talked it over with Evie and she was relieved and happy. In truth, his decision had been somewhat calculated. He had reasoned that with so much turmoil going on in the town at the present, Evie's divorce from Lou and coming to live with him may not attract as much attention as it normally would. So, now was the time to take action not later when it would be the only news in Coalville. Then maybe, just maybe, he could get reelected as Sheriff.

The only difference of opinion between him and Evie was the exact time to tell Lou. Evie had wanted to tell Lou that day and be done with it, but he had convinced her that it would be smarter to go to a lawyer and plan the whole thing carefully. After convincing her, he went to a lawyer he knew in Athens and turned the legal matters over to him. Now, under instructions from the lawyer, they would tell Lou this Saturday and Evie would move out.

It was something he was not looking forward to, but he would be glad when it was over. He hated what it was going to do to Lou. Poor Lou didn't have a clue to what was going on. He felt guilty and Evie should feel guilty, although he didn't think she did. Lou was the only innocent one in the entire matter, and he was the one that was going to be hurt the most.

Sheriff Clark shook his head to bring his mind back to the present. He still had an unsolved murder. He picked up the folder again and tapped it nervously on his desk. Someone in Coalville was a cold blooded killer. The same man who killed Moonbeam probably killed Jim Upter. He had tried to piece together everything Mary Collie had told him about her last night with Lester. Lester hadn't even known who killed Moonbeam. Everyone that could help him solve this mystery was either dead or remaining quiet.

The Sheriff had been unable to shake Harry Barnett's story about being home during the deaths of both Moonbeam and Rachael. He had no proof to connect Harry with any of the Klan activities and he could find none. As far as he knew, Harry didn't know that his children suspected he was in the Klan. He hoped it would remain that way.

The Sheriff got up and walked over to his favorite spot by his office window and gazed out at the town. He seemed to never tire of watching the people go about their business. He looked at the blue sky and the general beauty of the outdoors, but somehow nothing could suppress the anger in his heart: An anger that was created by the fact that he couldn't solve the murders. But in his heart the thing he hated most, was the fact that some people in town didn't want the murders solved.

Four people in Coalville had died violently and he had no one in jail for the crimes. Lester, of course, was a suicide, and Rachael was somewhat of an accident. However, Moonbeam and Jim Upter were clear and simple murders. Silently, he continued to watch the people from his window.

Suddenly, he spoke out loud as if addressing them all. "Okay, you people don't have to talk. But be careful my friends, and watch your backs. 'Cause I don't think you understand what you're dealin' with. One of you is not just a good old boy. He's not just a secret member of the Klan. He didn't kill Moonbeam because of his color, or because he was intrudin' on the white world. And he didn't kill Jim Upter just to keep him quiet. He did those things 'cause he's a cold blooded murderer, and he likes it."

CHAPTER FORTY

Dee and Cherrie Again

June 1934

The year was 1934. The summer was just beginning and it was already getting hot. School was out for the summer and life in Coalville settled into summer vacation. The afternoon was sunny and bright as Daryl Gene Collie walked down the path at the back of the Collie land. He stopped and gazed at the empty spot where Rachael's house once stood. His father had torn down the remains of the burnt out shell and carried off the useless lumber. The land had been cleared and leveled, but, if one knew of the house before, the outline where the house had once stood could still be seen. Dee stopped and stared at the spot.

A warm summer breeze was blowing in from the south and it rustled his blond hair. The wind stirred the grass where the house once stood. Sometimes, if he concentrated hard enough, the house would appear with Rachael standing on the front porch. He lowered his head and smiled to himself. Then, he turned and started walking down the path again. He walked until he came to an old familiar oak tree. He stood and looked up into the branches of the tree. His tree house was still intact. Dee hadn't been up to his tree house since Rachael died. He didn't know why, but, for some reason, he just couldn't go back in the tree house.

Dee walked over to another tree and sat down in the shade. He leaned back against the trunk of the tree and looked around. To the south, he could see Lonesome Hill. The hill was lonesome once again. From where he was, he couldn't see the old cabin where the Klan had met. He would need his telescope for that. The wind was blowing the trees on Lonesome Hill just as always. Looking the other way, to the north, he could see the Jordan house. Again, he couldn't make out much without his telescope.

The Jordan house was in good shape. Dick Jordan had done a good job keeping it up. Dick went to school in the day, and worked for Doc Jewel in the evenings and weekends. He stayed in Moonbeam's old place, but he came every weekend and kept the house in good repair. He had promised his mother that the house would be there when she came back. Dick and Ruth had formed a strong bond since she had been sent to prison. She had been sentenced to five years in the Texas State Prison for Women.

Dick Jordan had turned out to be a strong person. With the loss of his mother and father, Clint being sentenced to life at hard labor in a federal prison, the odds were against him. Even with all the things against him, Dick held his head high. He worked hard and had gained the respect of everyone in town, and that included Dee Collie.

Dee's gaze again returned to the old oak tree. He leaned his head back against the trunk of the tree that shaded him and closed his eyes. The breeze felt good, and the afternoon was quiet. It would be easy, he thought, to just drift off to sleep.

"Hey, Dee, hey, Dee, wake up." A loud voice shouted.

Dee opened his eyes to find Cherrie looking down at him. "Stop yellin'," he said. "It was quiet here just a minute ago."

"Mom says come to lunch," Cherrie said, as she sat beside him. "What're you doin'?"

"Oh, just sittin' here thinkin'," he replied.

"Now, what could you be thinkin' about on this fine and lovely day?" She pressed.

"Nothin' much," he sighed, "Just about all that's gone on and what I'll be doin' with myself." He reached down and picked up some grass and squeezed it in his hands.

"Do you feel like you have to do somethin' with yourself?" She asked.

"Yeah, I do," he replied, as he pitched the grass up in the air and watched the wind blow it away.

Cherrie looked at Dee and then up to the tree house. "Have you been up in your tree house yet?"

"No," he stated, simply.

"Can you tell me why not or is it a secret?"

"It's not a secret," he said looking at her, "The truth is I don't know. It's kind of like I'm afraid I'll see a ghost or something. But then again, it's like I'm not a kid anymore and that tree house is for kids."

"Well, I realize we have a birthday comin' up this month and we'll be all of fourteen years old, but I wouldn't say we're all grown up yet," Cherrie said.

"Yeah, I know that too, but don't you feel like you can't really play anymore? I mean, this tree house was just playing for me. Even when I was watching the Jordan house and all, it was just playing. I never imagined how things would turn out. I thought it was fun spying on Ruth and Dick, and playing games up there in the tree house. But I was playing and other people weren't. I don't ever want to play with people's lives again. I was wrong about so many things. Look how Dick Jordan turned out! Did you know that Reverend Tuney is sponsoring him for a scholarship to Baylor? I was so much against him. And the thing is, he never really did anything wrong. I'd sure like to take some things back. Maybe if I could, things would've turned out different."

"Well, Dee, I'll tell you what I'd like! I'd like for you to show me some more of your secrets. You told me you had more, but that I couldn't see them. Well, I think now is the time. I mean, it's been almost two years now and I think I've waited long enough." Cherrie got up and started for the old oak tree.

"Cherrie, there're not any more secrets," he called after her. "I was just sayin' that."

"What do you mean?" She asked.

"I mean I was just sayin' that to make you wonder," he responded.

"Come on, Dee. There must be somethin' you're not tellin' me," Cherrie demanded.

"Cherrie, I'm tellin' you the truth. There's nothin' else up there. There're not any more secrets! There's just not anymore!"

"Yes, I know that, Dee!" she shouted, turning around to face him again. "There're not any more secrets and there's not any ghost. Things that happened just happened. They would've happened with this tree house or without it. They would've happened even if you and I were never born. They would've happened with or without your secrets. If you had never looked through your telescope, Clint Jordan would still have deserted the army, Ruth Jordan would still have cheated the insurance company, Bob Ann Jackson would still have given her child away, and Jim Upter would still have brought the Klan to Coalville. I know there're not any more secrets, Dee! Just like I know there's not anythin' else either."

"But would Moonbeam and Rachael be dead if I'd spoke up when I should've?" He asked quietly.

"I can't answer that," she said with a shrug of her shoulders. "There's no way to tell; maybe yes, and maybe no. There's no way to know unless we can go back and change history, and we can't do that. No matter if we were right or wrong in what we did. We're not the ones that killed Moonbeam and Rachael. What killed them was stupidity and hate. I know that you and I aren't stupid, and I know that we don't hate anybody."

Dee looked at his twin sister. She stood facing him with the wind blowing in her hair. She had a look of determination on her face. For some reason, he now felt he must say some things to Cherrie that he was sure he had never said before. "Cherrie," he said slowly. "Did I ever tell you I love you?" He quickly looked down at the ground so she couldn't see his face.

"No, I don't think you ever did," she replied softly. "I think you tried to the night Rachael died, but I don't think you ever did."

"I do, Cherrie. Not like a girlfriend or anythin' like that. But I love you for bein' my sister and for bein' my friend. I love you more than anyone else in the world. I guess of all the things that have happened to me, havin' you as my twin sister is the luckiest thing of them all. It hurts me inside because I can't be as good a brother as you are a sister, and that I haven't given you as much as you've given me. You're the best sister anybody could ever ask for. You stood by me when you knew I was wrong and you fought for me at the risk of your own life." He felt his voice beginning to crack so he stopped talking.

"Dee, I never needed you to say you loved me. You show it to me a hundred times every day. I don't think I ever told you I love you either, but I do. We're twins and we're alike, but we're also different. Neither of us says the word, *love*. But I know you love me, Dee, and you know I love you. You're my twin brother, and you're a good brother. You say you haven't given as much to me as I have to you. That's because you don't know what you're givin'. You see most of the time it's easy to see what you're getting', but it's not always so easy to see what you're givin'. The things you've given me, I'll carry in my heart 'til the day I die! Don't you understand, Dee? The best thing you can give other people is not somethin' you can touch and feel? Most of the time, the best thing you can give somebody is part of yourself. And it's that part that's in your heart. It's that special somethin' that you and I have given to each other every day. It'll always be there, Dee. It'll never go away."

"I don't know why you ever let me boss you around," Dee said, keeping his head down. "You're always so much smarter than me."

Cherrie walked over and knelt down by Dee, who still had not lifted his head. She placed her hands on his shoulders and shook him. "Hey, let's climb up to that old tree house and have a look around," she laughed.

Dee looked up at her with a smile on his face. His eyes were wet with tears. "No need to," he said. "We'll do it another time. Mom probably thinks you can't find me."

Cherrie smiled at him. "How long do you think those pictures of naked women will last up there?"

"Hey! You may be right," Dee laughed, as he got to his feet. "We'll come back after lunch and rescue those for sure. I can probably trade 'em at school for some new ones."

Dee grabbed Cherrie around the neck, and pulled her along the path toward the house. Cherrie laughed and reached up and put her arm around Dee's neck. They walked up the path together with their arms locked around each other's neck.

"Anyway," Dee smiled as they walked along. "What'd you mean 'bout things I'd given you to keep in your heart? What'd I ever give you, but a hard time?"

"Oh! Things you won't understand now," Cherrie replied, as they neared the house. "Girls pick up on these things quicker than boys. Remember, you said I was smarter than you so you'll just have to trust me. But it's kind of like what the Reverend Tuney said that Sunday at church. We all have so much to give."

PART TWO

The Stand

They had so much to give and they gave it all

CHAPTER FORTY-ONE

Summer Break

June 1941

Daryl Collie stood by his dorm room widow looking out at the almost empty campus of the University of Texas. It was the first week of June 1941 and most all the students had already left for summer break. Daryl was late leaving because he had to wait on his sister who was up in Waco at Baylor University. She had to finish up some work that was required to ensure her Academic Scholarship for next year. The plan was for Daryl to leave Austin on the train for Dallas and get off in Waco to join his sister. Then, together, they would take the Greyhound bus from Waco to Coalville and home.

Being fraternal twins, they were just a couple of weeks short of their twenty-first birthdays. Like his sister, Daryl's hair was a deep blonde. It had not changed much since he was a little boy. His eyes were a dark blue set on high cheek bones in a handsome and well-structured face. He had what could be called a skinny frame that stood just over six feet tall. Today he was dressed for travel wearing blue jeans, sneakers, and a University of Texas orange and white T-shirt. Also today, his face wore a troubled and worried look rather than the happy-go-lucky look it normally featured.

Daryl took a deep breath then turned from the window and started back towards his bed upon which was his completely packed suit case. When he reached the bed, he closed and latched the suit case and then sat down heavily on the bed. Normally going home for summer break was something he looked forward to; being with his parents, seeing his friends, and working with his Dad in the feed store, made for a nice relaxing summer break from school. But this summer break would be different; much different. He reached into the outer pocket of the suitcase and pulled out a neatly folded letter. He unfolded it and read it again for the hundredth time.

Mr. Daryl Collie
ROTC Building 112
Room B22
University of Texas
Austin, Texas

Dear Mr. Collie,

It is my pleasure, as well as my gratitude, to inform you that your application to join the American Eagle Squadron in His Majesty's Royal Air Force has been accepted. Due to the pressing situation here in England, we need to expedite your joining an American combat unit. Therefore, you will find enclosed a voucher for one way passage on a RAF charter aircraft leaving New York City for London on June 20th of this year. The voucher has all the directions and information needed as well as a telephone number in New York City that you can call upon arriving in that city.

Upon arriving in London, you will be met at an undisclosed airport and taken to our training facility where you will spend one month in intense training to familiarise you with RAF formations and tactics as well as the aircraft you will be assigned. When your training is complete, you will be immediately assigned to an Eagle Squadron Group and taken to the Group with highest current needs.

We realise that one month is not the desired training time. However, your background with flight ROTC and our pressing needs dictate the time allowed.

Since you are an American, your commission as a Lieutenant in the RAF is conditional on the status of the United States entering the war. Should the United States enter the war, you will be allowed to transfer to the United States Armed Forces if you so choose.

We look forward to seeing you very soon.

Yours,
Vice Air Marshall Timothy Martin
His Majesty's Royal Air Force
London, England.

Daryl refolded the letter and put in back in the suitcase pocket. He ran his hand through his long blonde hair and then stood up and again walked to the window. He was not only faced with telling his parents that he was going to war but that he only had about one week to say good-bye. He was expected to be at the airport in New York City on the 20th and it was now the 3rd. Then, there was a week of travel time from Dallas to New York City by train. That only left roughly ten days to tell everyone what he was doing and saying good-bye to all.

When he applied to the Eagle Squadron, he decided to keep it secret. He didn't want anyone unnecessarily worried just in case his application was declined. No one knew; not even his sister with whom he always shared everything. He had been going over and over in his mind how he would explain all of this to his parents and sister. They knew as well as he did the dire situation the English were in. They stood alone against the onslaught of Nazi Germany. The Battle of Britain raged at its fullest and the outcome could well determine the future of the world. He felt he had to do something, and when he was approached by one of his flight instructors in the ROTC to apply for the Eagle Squadron, he did so without hesitation. Even though his grades in school were above average and he had logged well over three hundred flying hours, including combat simulation at San Antonio's Randolph field, the quickness with which he was accepted surprised him. He knew the RAF needed flyers desperately, but he applied in February and was accepted in May. That was quick.

Since his family didn't have a lot of money, he and his sister both had to try for scholarships to get into college. His sister, Cheryl, had it somewhat easier than he did because, first she was incredibly smart and second their mother was an alumnus of Baylor University. Cheryl was able to get in on an Academic Scholarship. However, she is required to re-qualify each year, which is why they were late getting off for home. As for Daryl, he and his parents scraped together enough money to get him in for his freshman year. He then joined the ROTC flight program and made a little extra money. By studying hard and getting extra hours of flight time, he managed to qualify for the Combat Simulation Training. He became a full Flight Cadet his sophomore year, which gave him a little more money. It also allowed him to earn extra money crop dusting during the summer breaks between his freshman year and his junior year. In fact, his Dad was planning on adding crop dusting as a service offered by the feed store.

Now, he and his sister had just finished their junior year at university. They were headed home for the summer break before starting their senior year. Except now, there wouldn't be a senior year for Daryl. He would be headed for the Battle of Britain. No matter how many times he turned the explanation over in his mind, he hated having to face his parents with the news.

CHAPTER FORTY-TWO

The Journey Home

June 1941

The train ride to Waco seemed to take forever. Daryl was sure they stopped in every town, village, or water hole along the way. Finally, the train pulled into the Waco Train Depot. As the train slowed and the conductor was shouting, "Waco, Waco", Daryl got up and pulled is bag down from the overhead baggage space. As he waited for the train to stop, he gazed out the window trying to spot Cheryl, but he couldn't see her anywhere. Picking up his bag, he made his way to the exit door of the car in which he had been riding. After exiting the car, he had to wait for the conductor to put the small stair steps in place so the passengers could step down onto the depot platform.

Finally on the platform, he moved to a spot that was less crowded, set down his bag and looked around for Cheryl. He was becoming worried, but then he saw her waving at him from the far end of the platform. She started running towards him with a huge smile on her face. As she got to him, they embraced and held each other for a long moment without speaking. Then, he pushed her back and held her at arm's length. He hadn't seen her in over four months, but she looked about the same. She was tall for a girl; about five feet and seven inches. Her hair, which she had fixed into a cute ponytail, was not as blonde as his but more of a sandy blonde now. Her sparkling eyes were a lighter, more sky blue than his. She had a dainty nose and beautiful face. Although she was his sister, he couldn't help but notice her well-shaped body and the hint of nice legs peeping out at the bottom of a long skirt. She wore a green T-shirt with Baylor written across it in large gold letters. He had always wanted to think of her as his *little sister*, but there was no doubt she was a full grown woman now.

"My God, Cherrie, you look wonderful!" He exclaimed.

"Well, thank you big brother", she laughed. "You don't look so bad yourself".

"So, how'd it go with your scholarship test?"

She tilted her head to one side and A small frown crossed her face, "Okay I think. I won't know for sure until late July when they have all the test and applications in and the board has made its decisions on everyone."

"Late July!" He shouted. "Why so long?"

She didn't answer but shook free of his grip and grabbed his arm. "We can talk about all this later on the bus. Right now we have to hurry. The bus leaves in less than an hour and the bus station is three or four blocks away. I've already been there and checked my bag. So, grab your bag and let's get goin'."

Daryl didn't say anything else. He picked up his bag and followed her as she took off quickly across the platform and through the depot door.

An hour later, they were on the Greyhound bus leaving Waco. The bus was crowded but they got two seats together near the back. Everyone on the bus had their window open as it was unbearably hot. The bus had duct fans and vents in the roof but they did little good. Even though they had both dressed light for the trip, within an hour of the ride they were sweating and their T-shirts were sticking to their hot, sweaty skin. They had talked very little. Daryl was trying to be cheerful but his mind still struggled with how to tell his parents the news about the Eagle Squadron. As a result, he seemed distracted and withdrawn. Cheryl picked up on it immediately.

"Okay, Dee, what's up?" She finally asked simply.

Dee turned to look at her and put a surprised look on his face. "Whata ya mean?" He asked as he shrugged his shoulders.

"We've been through too much, Dee. You can't fool me. What's the problem?"

"There's no problem!" He cried. "I'm just kind of lost in thought." After a short pause, he tried to change the subject. "Man, it's really hot in here. We should've remembered to bring something to drink. How much longer is it to Coalville?"

"I have a couple of Cokes in my purse", she said softly. "And I know it's hot, and it's still about another hour to Coalville, and there is a problem." She stopped talking and took a bottle of Coke from her purse along with a bottle opener. She opened the Coke and passed it to Dee. He took it without saying anything. They sat quietly for several minutes as Dee sipped his Coke.

Finally her controlled silence got to Dee. "Okay, Cherrie, there's a problem", he started. "And knowin' our history I guess I should tell you and give you a heads-up before I tell Mom and Dad. So, are you ready?"

"I've been ready ever since this trip started. But, give me a sip of that Coke before you get started."

Dee handed her the half empty Coke. She took a long gulping drink.

"Okay", she said. "Let's have it, and all of it without any frills."

Dee took a deep breath and wiped the sweat from his forehead using his T-shirt tail. He looked Cherrie straight in the eyes and said, "I've joined the American Eagle Squadron. They've accepted me and I have to report to New York City the 20th of this month. There, I'll take a chartered flight to London, England where I'll undergo a month of intense trainin' and then be assigned to an Eagle Squadron group." He stopped talking and took another deep breath and continued. "That's what I've got to tell Mom and Dad when we get home. They're not going to be happy."

Cherrie's mouth dropped open. Her mouth moved but no words came out. Suddenly she got control and blurred out loudly, "You did this without talkin' to any of us first?"

Dee put his hand over her mouth, "Holy crap, Cherrie, not so loud! Does everyone on the bus have to be involved in this?"

Cherrie pulled his hand away from her mouth. Then, she asked in a much softer voice, "Why didn't you talk to any of the family?"

"I knew what I'd get", he said defensibly. "I would've gotten a firm '*no*' and that would've been the end of it. Mom and Dad wouldn't have even talked about it with me. At least now, they have no choice but to accept it. I am of age and I don't need anyone's approval." Dee noticed he was waving his hands, setting up in his seat, and that his voice had risen also. Getting hold of himself, he fell back in his seat, put his hands in his lap, and lowered his head.

Cherrie reached over and placed her hand on Dee's hands. "But, Dee", she said tenderly. "Couldn't you've talked to me? Since we were kids, when've you not been able to talk to me?"

Using his T-shirt, Dee wiped his forehead again. He pulled one hand free from Cherrie's hand and reached over and patted her on the cheek. "You're right", he said softly. "You're always right. I should've talk to you first. But it wouldn't have mattered. I believe in this, Cherrie. I believe in this with all my heart. I think it's wrong to just look the other way and continue to go to school while someone else is doin' my fightin' for me. Because that's what it is you know. They're fightin' a battle over there that we should be helpin' with. We'll have to fight eventually. We'll have to. If you remember, I stayed out of the fight against the KKK until it was too late for people we loved. I will *NOT* make that mistake again. I will *NOT* stand by while people I love are in jeopardy. I *WILL* fight this time. And this is the best way I can fight. This is somethin' I can do."

Dee finished talking with long exhale of breath. He turned his head and again looked out the window.

"I understand", Cherrie said simply. "I feel just like you do about this war and I'm sure we'll be in it sooner than later. In truth, I've been lookin' for the best way I can be a part of it. I just haven't come up with anythin' yet. But I do disagree with you about one thing. I think you're underestimating Mom and Dad. I think they would've been more understanding than you're givin' them credit for. And another thing; you have to stop carryin' around a guilt about an event that happen when we were twelve years old. I thought that was resolved years ago. That terrible business was never your fault and no matter how long you blame yourself it simply will not change anythin'."

Dee turned back from the window and looked at his sister. "I hope you're right about Mom and Dad, because I don't want to fight with them before I leave."

"Well, you know you can count on me to help you with them. I'll do everythin' I can."

"Thanks, Cherrie, "and as for what happened when we were twelve years old, it's never completely gone away. I know the things we talked about and I know the things that happened would have probably happened anyway. But I feel I have a chance to do it right this time. I don't want to miss that chance."

Cherrie leaned back in her seat and folded her hands in her lap. "Well", she said, "at least let's not hit 'em with it first thing. Let's get a day or two under our belt first, unless Dad starts makin' his plans for your crop dustin' for the store. Then, we'll have to put a stop to that and let the cat out of the bag."

"I agree", Dee said. "But we can't wait more than two days. I just don't have enough time."

The twins rode along the rest of the way to Coalville in relative silence. They made small talk but it didn't really amount to anything. It was almost dark when the bus finally pulled into the Coalville Bus Station. The bus station was actually a small service station run by a local resident that Cherrie and Dee didn't know. The twins were surprised that no one was there to meet them. However, they were extremely happy to step off the bus and on to solid ground. The weather was still hot, but there was a breeze blowing in from the south that helped evaporate the sweat and cool them down. In addition, the sun was setting low on the horizon. They got their bags and then stood and watched as the bus pulled away to continue its trip across East Texas.

"Well", Dee said putting has hands on his hips. "I guess we need to call home and see if we can get a ride."

"Let's not call," Cherrie said. "Why don't we just walk? It's only about a mile from here".

"But these bags will get heavy very fast", Dee countered.

"Oh, come on! We can stop along the way if we need to. Just think of the look on Mom and Dad's face when we show up at the door."

So, the twins started their walk home down a small street that they had walked on together a thousand times before. They stopped three or four time along the way to rest and talk and laugh. The pressure on Dee began to ease somewhat. Being with Cherrie always seemed to do that. He was glad that he had told her the whole story. He felt more secure now in what he had to do. Both, telling his parents and going to war.

Soon, they could see their home just a little ways up the street. The sun had set by now and there was a light shining through the living room window, and the front porch light was lit dimly. Dee and Cherrie looked at each other and smiled as they walked up to the front porch. They wearily placed their bags on the porch and walked up to the front door.

CHAPTER FORTY-THREE

Coalville

May 1941

Sheriff Tom Clark sat with his six foot, five inch frame squeezed behind his small desk working on his second cup of coffee. Although the sheriff had just turned forty years of age, his 240 pounds was still mostly solid with very little fat. His hair had thinned a little, but was still a dark brown with only small traces of gray at the temples. His brown eyes where still as sharp and clear as ever, as he still didn't need glasses. Sheriff Clark had not only just turned forty but he had also, two weeks ago, won his third term as Sheriff of Coalville. Now, he looked up as Alice Conner knocked on his office door. Without waiting for a reply, she opened the door slightly and stuck her head into the office. Alice worked as a general secretary to the Sheriff and several others in the court house, but she spent most of her time handling office chores for the Sheriff. She was middle-aged with sandy blonde hair that she wore in a perpetual ponytail. Being unmarried, she had a fun loving manner and was always flirting with all the men in the court house; married or unmarried. Most everyone took her flirting as just fun and games, but at the same time Alice was not an unattractive woman, and she did dress to turn heads.

"There's a guy out here says he's from the Texas Parks Board. Wants to talk with you," she said in a low voice.

"He's from where?" The Sheriff asked, looking up and putting his coffee cup down.

"The Texas Parks Board," Alice repeated.

"What in hell is the Texas Parks Board?"

Alice lifted her eyebrows and smiled, "I got no idea," she said. "But he's from Austin and he looks important."

Sheriff Clark ran his hand through his semi-thinning hair and said, "Okay, send him in and let's find out what the Texas Parks Board is and what they want with us."

"Will do," Alice chirped, pulling her head back and closing the office door.

Shortly, the door opened again and Alice came in with a large heavy-set man following her. He was short; maybe five foot, five. His waist line showed he had not missed many meals. On his head, he wore a small straw hat that he removed as he walked in. Removing the hat revealed a mostly bald head with beads of sweat bubbling up. He had a chubby face and wore a set of glasses with thick lenses. In his right hand, he carried a large briefcase. Once completely in the office, Alice stepped aside and pointed back to the man.

"Sheriff Clark," she said politely. "This is Mr. Thomas Mann of the Texas Parks Board. Mr. Mann, this is Sheriff Clark."

As they nodded to each other and grasped hands in a greeting handshake, Alice started for the door. She stopped as she opened the door and asked, again very politely, "Would you like somethin' to drink, Mr. Mann? We have fresh coffee or ice water."

"Yes, thank you," he replied with his best smile. "I think I could use some ice water. I can't believe how hot it is and it's only May. My God, I can't believe what it's going to be like when summer really gets here."

With that, Alice left the office but left the office door lightly ajar as she was expecting to be back with the ice water very shortly.

"Please be seated," the Sheriff said, pointing to a chair across from his desk and he watched as Mr. Mann maneuvered his amble body into the chair. "Well, Mr. Mann, how can the Sheriff's Department here in Coalville help the Texas Parks Board? And I must confess I didn't know there was a Texas Parks Board."

Mr. Mann looked hurt. "How do you think we get state parks?"

The Sheriff was slightly taken aback. "Oh, sorry, I guess I never thought much about it." There was a short silence and then the Sheriff asked, "Anyway, how can we help you?"

"Well, Sheriff, it's more of a guidance issue than anything else," he said as he balanced his briefcase on his lap and snapped it open. Then he continued, "The Parks Board has obtained a sizable portion of land in this area on which to establish a State Park. Over the last several years, the Parks Board has been working to get all the land required before starting any official movement to build the park. We've been very successful in obtaining the land on several of the hills just south of your little town. One of those hills has, as I understand it, somewhat of a reputation. However, this hill is an important key in our efforts. You see, it's the only hill that has a road that goes all the way around it, and there's access to that road from your town. All of this is good, except we need another access route besides the one directly from Coalville. And that is why I have come to see you."

Mr. Mann stopped talking and sat smiling at the Sheriff. At this time, Alice returned with two glasses of ice water. She handed one to the Sheriff and the other to Mr. Mann. She nodded, smiled, and walked out of the office again. This time she closed the door behind her.

Sensing that Mr. Mann was expecting some kind of response the Sheriff spread his hands palms up and asked, "Well, how can I help you?"

Mr. Mann was still smiling as he continued, "Thank you for asking Sheriff." He reached into his briefcase and pulled out what appeared to the Sheriff to be a map of Coalville. "May I spread this on your desk, sir?"

"Sure, but first let me make some more room."

After clearing some of the clutter from his desk, the Sheriff said, "Okay, spread her out."

Mr. Mann spread the map out as well as he could on the desk. The map was a bit larger than the desk and he had to fold some of it to get it to fit. Once he had it arranged the way he wanted it, he pointed to a section of the map that was near the far left side. "Here's the hill I'm talkin' about," he continued. "You can see the road that goes around it. Now here's the road that intersects with it coming up from Coalville." He used his finger to trace the path on the map of the roads. "And you can see where it has access to the Farm-to-Market road on the other side of the hill."

The Sheriff held up his hand to stop Mr. Mann. "Excuse me, Mr. Mann, but I'm aware of all of this," he said pointedly. "We call that hill, Lonesome Hill. And it does have a reputation for strange happenings. There've even been some killings up there. If you guys are goin' to make a park outa that place, well, I wish you luck. I mean that place has got old pits and shafts, and even some old cabins up there. It's also got underbrush, thick and tall pine trees, and small mesquite trees all over the place. Like I said, good luck. But I don't see what this has to do with the Sheriff's Department."

Mr. Mann looked at the Sheriff as if there had been a misunderstanding. "Well, nothing about the hill itself has anything to do with your department."

The Sheriff was getting irritated. He folded his hands behind his head and looked hard at Mr. Mann. "Well then, what?"

"Here," Mr. Mann said, pointing to a spot on the map. "We need another access road to the ring road going around the hill. The best, and maybe only good place, is this piece of land just south of the hill. We need to purchase enough of that land to build a road directly from the ring road around the hill, and back down to where the State Highway comes into Coalville. That would allow us to create a one-way road up to the hill and then another one-way road down from the hill." Mr. Mann stopped talking for a minute to allow the Sheriff time to see what he was talking about. When the Sheriff didn't say anything Mr. Mann continued. "I believe that the land we need belongs to a James Collie and his wife Mary. What I'd like is for you to come with me to their house and help me explain what we're tryin' to do and what it would mean to the State of Texas and the local area as well. I'm hoping your influence will make it easier to purchase the land from them. We can get the land one way or the other, but we would prefer to avoid taking the land via the Emanate Domain law. Can I depend on you to help us? Will you come with me to their home?"

Sheriff Clark studied Thomas Mann for a long moment. "Well, yes. I guess," he finally said. "But any decision to sell his land will be entirely up to James. I'm not goin' to try and help him make up his mind or anythin' like that."

"That would be fine, Sheriff," Mr. Mann smiled. "Just your presents will bring some comfort to the situation and some official standing."

"Okay," Sheriff Clark replied. "What we need to do is first drive by the Collie Fertilizer and Feed Store and pick up James. That's where he'll be this time of day. You see his family owns and operates the place. We can swing by and pick him up and then drive to his house and talk with both him and Mary. When we're done, we can drop him off back at his store."

"All of that sounds good to me," Mr. Mann said, smiling his big smile again.

"By the way," the Sheriff interjected. "Is there someplace I can drop you on our way back?"

"No," Mr. Mann said, as he started to struggle out of the chair. "I have my car parked out front and I need to head back towards Austin as soon as I can."

With that, the Sheriff picked up his hat from the nearby rack and, after Mr. Mann had refolded his map and secured his briefcase, escorted Mr. Mann out the door.

As they walked through the outer office, the Sheriff informed Alice where he was going and about how long he expected to be gone. Alice didn't say anything but just waved her hand.

⸻

Less than fifteen minutes later, Sheriff Clark and Thomas Mann pulled up in front of the Collie Fertilizer and Feed Store in the Sheriff's patrol car. Getting out of the car, they walked up the front steps and into the store. It was uncomfortably hot in the store even though there were several overhead fans running at full speed. The two men walked around the store looking for James but he was nowhere to be found. In fact, there was no one there at all.

"James must be in his office out back," the Sheriff said, pointing towards the back of the store. "If you'll wait here, I'll walk back and see if I can find him. While I'm doin' that why don't you get us a couple of cold Cokes out that ice chest over there in the corner?"

Mr. Mann looked around briefly to find the ice chest. Once located, he started off towards the chest to retrieve the cokes. "Where do I put the money?" He yelled back at the Sheriff.

"Not to worry, I'll take care of it."

The Sheriff turned and started towards the back of the store, but he had only taken a few steps when he saw James and Mary Collie coming towards him from the back of the store along with another woman walking alongside of Mary. James was chewing on a sandwich in one hand and holding a glass of ice tea in the other. He stood slightly over six feet tall and his frame was thin and somewhat lanky. At forty-six years of age, he still had a head full of hair but it was graying at the temples and slightly over his forehead. Mary walked beside him folding an empty brown bag as she walked. Unlike her husband, Mary was barely over five feet tall. Although she was the same age as her husband, she still had a fine figure for her age. Her sandy blonde hair had streaks of grey running from front to back. Her bright blue eyes still had a sparkle to them. The other woman was also chewing on a sandwich as she walked. They all saw Sheriff Clark at the same time. James had a month full of sandwich so he didn't speak; he only smiled and tipped his tea glass in the Sheriff's direction.

On the other hand, Mary waved the now folded paper bag at the Sheriff, smiled and shouted, "Hey, Tom what're you doin' here? I sure hope we aren't in any trouble. We haven't seen you around these parts since the election."

"No trouble, Mary," the Sheriff replied. "But we do have a stroke of luck here. I was comin' by to pick up James to take him to the house so we could all talk together."

James had finally washed down his month full of sandwich. "Why? What's goin' on?"

As James was speaking, Thomas Mann came walking up carrying two bottles of Coke. He handed one to the Sheriff and then extended his hand to James. James took his hand and started shaking it although no one had made any introductions.

"James," the Sheriff started, "I would like for you to meet Mr. Thomas Mann of the Texas Parks Board." Then turning to Mr. Mann, "Mr. Mann this is James Collie and the pretty woman beside him is his lovely wife, Mary, and the other pretty woman beside Mary is Ruth Jordan."

After shaking James' hand briskly, Thomas Mann took Mary's hand softly and gave it a gentle shake. He then smiled at Ruth and shook her hand softly as well.

Looking at James, the Sheriff said, "Mr. Mann here has some business he would like to discuss with you and Mary. If you have some time now, we would sure appreciate being able to talk with the both of you."

James looked puzzled but didn't hesitate to accept. "Sure," he said quickly. "Mary brought me and Ruth some lunch and we were just finishin' up. Mary was headed back home, but I guess we've got some time. Business isn't exactly boomin'. Why don't we all go back to the office for our talk? Its cooler back there and we can all find a seat."

"Jim, if you don't mind I'll just run to the general store while you're talkin'," it was Ruth speaking. "That'll give you time to talk. I'll be back in a little while."

James held up his hand to halt Ruth and then turned to Mr. Mann. "How long will this take, Mr. Mann," he asked? "If it's goin' to be a long draw out affair, then maybe we should go on to the house after all."

"Oh, we're probably lookin' at maybe half an hour," Mr. Mann replied continuing to smile.

"Okay, Ruth," James waved. "We'll see you a little later," then, turning to Mr. Mann. "Let's go on to the back."

Mr. Mann looked around. "Don't you need someone to watch the store?"

James looked at Mr. Mann and laughed softly. "No, we don't," he said simply. "I expect things'll be okay."

With that, they all headed towards the back of the store.

CHAPTER FORTY-FOUR

Another Journey Home

June 1941

First Lieutenant Dick Jordan sat on the bench directly outside the Post Commander's door nervously holding his hat in his hands. He turned the hat around and around in his hands as he sat straight-backed and looking intently at the opposite wall. The bench was uncomfortable as it wasn't built to hold his six foot two inch skinny frame. That in its self was frustrating because no matter how much military food he ate or how hard the training, he simply couldn't seem to gain weight. His hair, what there was of it, was sandy brown and cut military style; high and tight. It made his neck look unusually long. The long and short of it was that he wasn't much to look at. Except for the uniform he wore, he didn't look much like a United States Marine.

His journey to this spot on this particular bench had been a long and hard one. It had all started when the town doctor in his hometown of Coalville, Texas, Doctor Julius J. Jewel helped him get into Texas A&M College. That alone had been very difficult. He had had to study extremely hard for the entrance exam. Then, he had to accumulate the money. Doc Jewel had been very kind to him by supplying him with the much needed funds. But, even with Doc Jewel's help and money, it hadn't been enough. He had to use nearly all of his own savings that he had accumulated over the years while working for Doc Jewel. In the end, his Mother had to take out a mortgage on their house in Coalville. That had been the hardest thing of all to do. He had argued with his Mother about the mortgage; begging her not to do it. But it was to no avail, she had absolutely insisted on it. Now they were stuck with a home mortgage payment.

All of this happened in 1936 while his mother was still serving a five year term in the Texas State Prison for Women. She was released, that same year, one year early for good behavior. She returned home to Coalville and Dick, who had been maintaining the home while she was away. When Ruth had gone to prison, she was a full figured beautiful woman with a fine structured face. The four years in prison had not robbed her of that beauty, but her eyes had lost some of their glow and her personality had withdrawn to somewhere deep inside of her.

Coalville, like most all the country at the time, was still deep in an economic depression and there were very few jobs. Dick was fortunate to be working for Doc Jewel, but Ruth, his mother, found it hard to find a job; especially after being in prison for four years. Fortunately, her longtime friend and local business man, James Collie stepped forward to help her out and give her a job at his feed and fertilizer store. It was a small job involving keeping the store's books and doing odds and ends around the store. The pay was small, but it was enough with Dick's income.

So, Dick had gone off to college. Texas A&M was a men's only military school and Dick was required to join the Cadet Corp, and upon graduation was obligated to go into the military reserves, or he could join the regular service if he so desired. Upon graduation in the summer of 1940, Dick had opted to join the United States Marines. He had surmised that his military salary would help pay the mortgage on his Mother's house. Since Dick graduated in the upper ten percent of his class, he was immediately sent to Officer's Candidate School at Parris Island, South Carolina.

Now, after a year of training, being promoted from Second Lieutenant to First Lieutenant for exemplary performance, and being put in command of the Second Platoon of Charlie Company, he sat outside the Post Commander's office waiting to report as ordered. He had no idea what was going on. He had simply been told by his company commander to report to the Post Commander's office promptly at fifteen hundred hours and to be in his dress blues. So, here he sat and waited still nervously fumbling with is hat.

———

Finally a tall Sergeant came out of the Post Commander's door and stood before him at strict attention. He presented a smart salute and said, "The Colonel will see now, Sir. Please follow me."

Dick stood and placed his hat under his left arm and followed the Sergeant into the Colonel's office. Upon reaching the Colonel's desk the Sergeant saluted smartly again and said, "Lieutenant Jordan, Sir." The Sergeant then did an about face and walked out the door closing it behind him.

Dick was standing at attention and the Colonel said, "Stand easy, Lieutenant." Dick quickly went into an "at ease" stance. "Please have a seat, Lieutenant," the Colonel said, pointing to a chair in front of his desk. Dick seated himself being sure not to cross his legs and to set up straight. He continued to hold his hat under his left arm. "Lieutenant," the Colonel continued, "please be at ease and place your cover on my desk."

"Thank you, Sir," Dick replied, placing his hat on the edge of the Colonel's desk.

The Colonel leaned back in his large leather chair and looked intently at Dick. "You're probably wondering why you're here."

"Yes, Sir, I'm very curious and somewhat apprehensive."

"Well, it is a matter of some importance to your career. You're expecting to make the Corp your career?"

"Aye, Sir, Dick replied promptly, "one hundred percent, Sir."

"Good! That takes that off the table." The Colonel placed an index finger to his lips as though choosing his words carefully. Then, he leaned forward and placed his folded hands on his desk top. "There's no need to drag this out. With war approaching the

United States, certain moves are being made towards getting us prepared. These moves require Post Commanders, such as me, to select certain personnel, such as you, to participate in these moves. Are you following me so far, Lieutenant?"

"I think so, Sir. I gather that you've been ordered to supply a certain number of personnel to participate in some kind of secret operation."

"Yes, very good, Lieutenant," the Colonel smiled. "Of course, this particular operation is entirely voluntary. I mean it's up to you to accept or decline. If you decide to decline, there'll be no repercussions of any kind. You'll leave this office as if this conversation never took place. Do you understand that?"

"And if I accept?" Dick asked slowly.

The Colonel continued to smile. "If you accept, I am empowered to give you an immediate promotion to captain and cut your orders for an undisclosed location on the West Cost of the United States."

Dick relaxed somewhat in his chair. He leaned forward and looked directly into the Colonel's eyes. He asked, "Do I get to know anything about this operation before I make up my mind?"

"Yes, you do. But you have to make up your mind here and now, before you leave this office. Here's what I can tell you. A Marine Colonel named Wolff is forming a special battalion for training in amphibious landings. The idea is to get one battalion completely trained in amphibious warfare. Then, in turn, that battalion will disperse out to train entire divisions in this type of warfare. And so you'll know how you ended up here, your Commanding Officer speaks very highly of you, as does your quick promotion to First Lieutenant. You're the kind of man I am proud to see wearing Marine green. It's your job if you want it. But I have to know now. I know that may not seem fair, but that's the way they gave it to me and that's the way I'm giving it to you."

"I understand, Colonel," Dick said quickly, as he got to his feet at full attention. He picked up his hat and smartly slapped it under his left arm. "I'm your Marine, Colonel. When do I leave?"

The Colonel got to his feet and held out his hand to Dick. They shook hands strongly. "I'll put your promotion in immediately. You'll be a captain before you leave this base. And, before you leave this base, you'll have sealed orders with instructions on where to report and to whom. Now here's the good news. Along with all this comes a thirty day leave starting tomorrow morning. Go home, Dick. See your family and girl, if you have one. You can unseal your orders on your way home. But you're to tell no one where you're going or how long you'll be gone. Just tell 'em you're goin' for some training courses, which is true in a way. You can pick up your captain bars and your sealed orders at the Dispatch Office on your way out tomorrow. By the way, you're a Texas boy aren't you?

"Aye Sir," Dick replied, "born and raised."

"There's an aircraft plant near Dallas; Chance Vault I believe. I'll arrange for a seat on a C-47 that makes a regular run down there. That way, you want have to waste all that time on a train."

"Thank you, Sir. I appreciate that very much."

Then, in business like fashion, the Colonel said, "Well, are there any questions, Marine?" Then in a softer tone, "At least any I can answer."

"No questions, Sir, and thank you, Sir," Dick said as he stepped back and saluted. After the Colonel returned his salute, he did a sharp about face and left the office.

Dick had gone out the door and he didn't hear the colonel whisper behind him, "Good luck Marine."

Early the next morning after spending some time at the Dispatch Office getting his new captain bars and his sealed orders, Dick squeezed himself into a seat on an over crowed C-47 cargo plane. The plane had cargo strapped in place at the back and a line of four seats on each side accommodating eight passengers. All of the seats were occupied by military personnel and all the personnel were in uniform. Dick noticed that not all the personnel were marines. He recognized two navy uniforms and one army. All onboard were officers with ranks ranging from second lieutenant to major. His seat was located at the front on the left side. The seat was very uncomfortable as it was naked steel with a thin cushion as a lining.

The plane took off on time and at first the flight was fairly comfortable, or as well as could be expected. Dick tried to make small talk with the other officers onboard but after about an hour of flight the weather became very bumpy and conversation dwindled. In fact, it became so bumpy that Dick was actually becoming afraid. It seemed they bounced all the rest of the way to Dallas. Everyone seemed to be getting sick except the army guy.

When they finally landed at Chance Vault Aircraft just outside of Dallas, everyone piled off the plane holding their stomachs and stretching their legs. It turned out the army guy was in the United States Army Air Corp. He was use to this type of flying. Their duffel bags were unloaded right there on the landing strip. Each man picked around until he found his bag. Upon getting his duffel bag, Dick looked around for information on how to get a cab to the Greyhound Bus Station in downtown Dallas. It didn't take long, as an information officer had made his way to the plane. The instructions were easy enough and shortly Dick was in a cab headed for the bus station in Dallas.

As Dick walked into the bus station, he was surprised at how few people were there. He had no trouble getting a ticket but unfortunately the next bus to Coalville didn't leave for two hours. Dick toyed with the idea of finding a secluded spot and opening his sealed orders. But he fought off the urge and decided to grab something to eat and just wait until he was on the bus. He got a hamburger and a coke from the food counter and went and set down in the main waiting area to eat. He tried eating slow but two hours was a long time to kill. After eating, Dick pushed his bag under his bench seat and stretched out his long legs and slowly began to fall asleep. He kept shaking himself awake so he wouldn't miss the call for his bus. As time passed, he was losing his battle to stay awake, when suddenly he jerked upright when he heard the call, "Coalville". Jumping up, he pulled his bag from under the bench and slung it over his shoulder. He ran through the doors to the bay area and started looking frantically for his bus fearing he may have missed the first call. But, there it was setting idling in the middle bay. The rolling sign on the front of the bus didn't say Coalville because Coalville was too small a town to rate a destination sign. The sign read, "Athens", the closest town of any size to Coalville. The line to board was already forming when Dick go there. He patiently stood in line until he reached the door. There, he passed his bag off to the baggage attendant and handed his ticket to the driver, who promptly punched it and handed it back to him.

Free of his bag and carrying only his sealed orders and a book he had bought in the main waiting area, Dick weaved his way back to his seat, which was about half the way back and against the window. He sat down, loosened his tie, opened the window, took a deep breath and waited for the bus to depart. He would save his book and orders for the trip. As time ticked by, he kept checking his watch to see if they were going to leave on time. The scheduled departure time was 3:00 PM. Although Coalville was only about a hundred and twenty miles from Dallas, it would take at least three hours to get there taking into consideration all the stops the bus had to make in all the little towns; such as Coalville. But true to the scheduled departure time, the bus pulled out of the parking bay right on time.

—⊙✦⊙—

Dick was an hour deep into his trip home before he decided to open his orders. Before opening the official looking sealed envelope, he checked around him to see if it was safe to proceed. Things looked okay as most people were trying to sleep and the seat next to him was empty. Again, carefully looking in all directions, he checked his surroundings. At last, satisfied it was safe, he ran his finger along the envelope seal and quietly as he could open the orders. He unfolded the orders and read them.

June 1, 1941

1st Lt. Dick Jordan
Commanding Officer
Second Platoon
C Company
Parris Island, South Carolina

Lt. Jordan,

You are commanded by Parris Island Post Commander Colonel Josh Mandel to report directly to U.S. Marine Colonel Manfred Wolff at the Presidio Military Facility on the San Francisco Peninsula, San Francisco, California. You are ordered to report no later than June 30, 1941. Upon reporting to Colonel Wolff, you will receive farther orders that will place you directly under his command.

All travel associated with these orders will be controlled and paid for by the enclosed vouchers.

If, for any reason, you are unable to complete the orders as described in this document, you are ordered to contact the Parris Island Base Commander Colonel Mandel to make these reasons known and to await reassignment.

Until your report date, you are granted a complete and unrestricted Leave of Absence.

So signed,

Colonel Josh Mandel
Post Commander
Parris Island, South Carolina.

Dick carefully refolded the orders and put them back into the envelope. He turned and looked out the bus window at the landscape moving by. His mind was processing all the things he had just read. He guessed that California would be a perfect place to develop amphibious landing techniques. What his part would be in the whole thing, he could only guess.

Continuing to look out the window, he guessed it would be nearly dark by the time he got home. No one was expecting him. He hadn't called or written anyone since this thing had begun. His Mom was surely going to be surprised to see him. It had been almost a year since he had last seen her. That had been when he had spent a week with her getting her settled in upon returning from prison.

―◦※◦―

Dick leaned his head back on the seat head rest and let out a long breath. "Well, I guess she's goin' to really be shocked to see me," he whispered under his breath, "I don't know if the news I bring will make her happy or sad, but, in any case, she's sure as hell goin' to be surprised."

CHAPTER FORTY-FIVE

Making a Plan

May 1941

Clint Jordan stopped working as he heard the long tweet of the water break whistle. He dropped his nine pound sledgehammer to the ground and sat down heavily on a large rock. It was the same rock he had just been trying to break into smaller rocks. In fact, Clint's job was not complicated. It only involved making big rocks into little rocks. He had been doing it for the last eight or so years. So, it could be said he was an expert at his job. He looked considerably different than he did when he arrived eight years ago. His hair was now mostly pre-mature grey. The prison insisted that prisoners keep their hair short, so his was no different. It was short and cut unevenly, as the prison barbers were not the best in the world. His prison uniform was a thing of beauty. It consisted of a shirt and pants with black and white rings from shoulders to ankles. He had white socks and low top canvas white sneakers. Underneath, he had a pair of boxer shorts and sleeveless undershirt. On the left side of his shirt over his chest was stenciled his prisoner number. There was no name. The hard work every day had trimmed his body down to almost no fat. He was lean and hard and for maybe the first time in his life he had firm solid muscles in his arms, legs and stomach.

He had arrived here at Fort Leavenworth USDB (United States Disciplinary Barracks) after his conviction by a military court martial for desertion during time of war. He tried, unsuccessfully, to have his trail transferred to a civilian court. However, the United States Army retained jurisdiction and thus here he was severing a life sentence at hard labor. He didn't think it was fair because the war was practically over at the time. But there had also been other issues that didn't much help his case. In addition, the army had originally wanted the death penalty, but relented to life at hard labor because of his willingness to help on the other civilian issues. So, he could be dead by now. Instead he did the same grueling labor day-in and day-out. However, he didn't go directly to the hard labor prison when he first got to Leavenworth. Clint was first sent to the fort hospital to dry out. He had been very fond of whiskey. He had been very, very fond of whiskey. In fact, he was a solid alcoholic. So, before the army would send him to prison, they sent him for the *cure* at the base hospital. There he remained for nearly six months where he resided most of the time in a padded cell. He was almost glad when they released him to the prison. It didn't take long before he began wondering if he didn't really prefer the padded cell.

Now, as he sat there on his big rock, the water bearer brought the water bucket up to him. Client took the dipper from the hook on the bucket and dipped himself a full dipper. He drank it down thirstily. Although it wasn't really hot yet, the hard work brought out the sweat and in turn made him extremely thirsty. When he was finished, he rehung the dipper and leaned back against the rock on which he was setting. He was expecting the water bearer to move on quickly, but instead he knelt down in front of Clint pretending to work on the dipper and water bucket.

"Are you Clint Jordan?" He asked suddenly.

Clint looked up surprised. "Who wants to know?"

"I'm here to ask questions not answer them," was the sharp reply.

"Well, if you'll look at the number on my shirt, you'll see that I don't have a name. I'm number nine-six-six-four-six." As he spoke, Clint point to the number stenciled on left side of his prison uniform.

"Look wise ass, I've got a message for Clint Jordan. If you want it, fine. If not, screw you. I've got other things to do. So, speak up because I'm leavin' and the message is goin' with me." With that, the water bearer picked up his bucket and dipper and started to rise.

"Wait," Clint said urgently, holding out his hand and grabbing the bucket. "I'm sorry, but who'd have a message for me?"

"Don't know and can't say. I'm just the mailman. But, I'll ask again. Are you Clint Jordan?"

"Yeah, I'm Clint Jordan. Now what's this all about?"

The water bearer looked around and then pushed his finger into the side of his shoe and pulled out small tightly folded piece of paper. He picked up the dipper holding the paper against the bottom concealing it. He passed the dipper to Clint who took it and slipped the paper into his hand. So as to avoid suspicion, Clint dipped himself another small drink then handed the dipper back to the bearer.

"Don't try to read it now," the bearer whispered. "Slip it into your shoe just like you saw me do. Read it tonight in your cell. I'll stop by tomorrow for any reply you might have." The bearer picked up his bucket and dipper and hurried off.

Clint was pushing the small folded paper into the side of his shoe when he heard the two short tweets signaling the end of water break. He stood up and picked up his sledgehammer. Looking around but seeing nothing unusual, he started swing his hammer and breaking up big rocks into small rocks. His mind worked over and over what had just happened. He had been here near eight years and no one had ever sent him a secret message before. He had had visits from his family and friends before, but always through the normal prison channels; as well as mail through the normal prison post office. But this was different. Somebody wanted to talk to him secretly. He wondered if it was someone inside or someone outside. With each blow of the sledgehammer, he wanted desperately to read the message. But he told himself to wait; just wait a little longer.

That evening, Clint suffered through the security check on the way back to the prison from the rock quarry. During his shower, he had to be careful to keep the message concealed when he took off his shoes. Then, he waited through the evening meal. Finally, he was returned to his small cell, but still he waited. Lights out would be ten PM. He had to read the message before that. After being in his cell for nearly an hour, he took off his shoes and carefully slipped the small folded message under the leg of his bunk.

As things quieted down and everyone relaxed into their own world in their cells, and as he lay in his bunk, he reached down and pulled the message from under the bunk leg. The lights in the cell block were out now but they were still allowed to have their own cell lamps on. It was not ten PM yet. Quietly, Clint unfolded the small message. The message was written on a piece of paper from a small note pad. The writing was printed in pencil and was neat and clear. He didn't want to attract attention, so he didn't move directly under his lamp light but instead strained to read the message in the dim light around his bunk. Holding the message so he could quickly dispose of it if he had to, he read it.

WHEN FINISHED READING THIS, DESTROY IT.
I AM A FRIEND ON THE OUTSIDE.
I AM PLANING A WAY TO GET YOU OUT.
YOU MUST FOLLOW MY INSTRUCTIONS EXACTLY.
BE PREPARED FOR MORE MESSAGES WITH
STEP BY STEP INSTRUCTIONS.
DO NOT TRY TO SEND ME A MESSAGE YET.
BELIEVE IN ME. PLEASE. BELIEVE IN ME.

Clint read the message over and over again until he had it memorized. He then began to tear it into small pieces. He tore it down as small as possible, then he dropped it into the commode and flushed it away. As he watched the message disappear down the swirling commode water, he heard the loud speaker command, "Lights out. All lights should now be out." He reached over and snapped off his small cell lamp. He lay down on his bunk and watched the cell block as all the other small lights blinked off. Now, alone in the dark the strange message played with his mind. Someone on the outside wanted to get him out. Did that mean through legal channels, or did it mean they wanted to help break him out. Since it was so secret and the message said there would be step by step instructions, it must mean it's to be a breakout. But who would want to do that for him? And even if it was a full proof plan; did he want to be on the run the rest of his life? Always running and living the life of a fugitive. But then, he had to consider the life he now lived; with each day the same as the last, brutally hard work and no hope of anything changing.

He got up from his bed in the dark and stepped over to the cell door. He leaned against the door and pressed his head against the cool, steel bars. His hands took the bars in a tight clench. He squeezed them as hard as he could. His eyes were clenched shut so tight that they hurt. In the end, the decision wasn't such a hard one. The message had said, "Believe in me. Please. Believe in me." So, for the time being, that's what he would do. He would wait for the next message and the *step by step instructions*, and he would wonder who it could be that wanted to get him out of prison.

CHAPTER FORTY-SIX

The Collies

June 1941

D ee and Cherrie left their bags on the edge of the front porch and walked up to the front door. Dee turned and smiled at Cherry and then knocked heavily on the screen door. There was no immediate response so Dee knocked again but this time much harder. They smiled at each other as they saw a light come on in the living room. The sound of the door unlocking echoed in the quiet night. Finally the door opened and through the screen door there stood Mary Collie with a shocked look on her face.

"My God," she yelled! She pushed open the screen door. "You two get in here this minute!"

Laughing, Dee and Cherrie moved into the house. They both grabbed their Mother and showered her with hugs and kisses.

"James," Mary shouted. "James, get in here. Your children are here."

James came running up the hallway and into the living room. He ran over and joined in the emotional display going on. He broke away from the group and held Cherrie at arm's length and said, "Y'all could call or write or somethin' to let us know you were comin'."

"But, Dad, we did," Cherrie responded. I wrote you a letter tellin' you what Dee and I were plannin' and that we'd be late due to my scholarship test. Didn't you get it?"

"No, I don't recall any letter," James said, thoughtfully. "But so much has been goin' on around here that we may have missed it."

Then, turning to Mary he asked, "Did you get a letter from these two?"

"No," she said. "I'm sure I would have remembered that."

"Well, never mind that now," James said, as he ushered them all into the room. "We've got a lot of catchin' up to do."

"I'll be right with you, Dad," Dee said. "But let me get our bags first. I'll be right back." Dee quickly went out on the porch and picked up the bags and was struggling with them when James came out to help.

"Give me some of those," James laughed. Together they moved the bags into the house. "You know where they go. Your rooms are all ready for you this summer."

When Dee and Cherrie were young kids, they shared the same room down the hall. The house was much smaller back then and there was no room for them to have separate rooms. As they grew older, James had decided it was time to expand. He took out a mortgage on their house to finance the expansion. Being a good businessman, James was careful to only mortgage his house; he kept the rest of his ten acres clear. With the money from the mortgage, he expanded the hallway and added three new rooms. One of the rooms became a library for Mary, another became Dee's room, and the third became a guest room. Cherrie took over her and Dee's old room. Their parents had seen to it that their rooms were ready for them upon their return home each and every summer they had been in college.

While the others were enjoying each other, Dee carried his bag to his room near the end of the hallway. He dropped his bag onto his bed. Switching on the light, he gazed around the room he'd not been in for nearly six months; not since Christmas. As per his Mother's ways, the room was absolutely clean. All of his books were in place and all of his model planes were still hanging from the ceiling. He smiled to himself and turned and went back out into the hallway to rejoin the others. On his way, he ran into Cherrie struggling with her two bags. Dee ran up to her and relieved her of the larger bag. Together, they got her bags into her room and onto her bed. As with Dee's room, it was spotlessly clean. All of Cherrie's books, dolls, and even a medium sized doll house were exactly as they should be. Then, as he used to do years ago, he grabbed Cherrie around the neck and pulled her along with him down the hallway. They emerged into the living room laughing and wrestling with each other. Mary Collie had already gotten ice tea for everyone and she and James were sitting on the couch waiting for them.

"Why don't you kids grab a seat and we can get caught up," James said, in a somewhat serious tone. "We've got several things to tell you."

Both Dee and Cherrie sensed something might be wrong. "Is there somethin' wrong, Dad?" Dee asked with a frown. He turned and looked at Cherrie who frowned back at him.

"No, nothin' serious for us," James said quickly. "It's just several things have happened that you should know about. So, if everyone has their tea and we're all settled, can we begin?"

"Sure," Dee said with a nod.

Cherrie said nothing but nodded.

"Okay, first for the bad news." As soon as he said bad news, James knew it was the wrong way to start the conversation. Both Dee and Cherrie's faces took on a worried look and they both started to stand. James quickly held up his hand to stop them. "No, no," he said with urgency. "It's not concernin' us. We're all fine. We're just fine."

When things had calmed down, he continued slowly and with broken words. "Last week...old Doc Jewel passed on. He...went in his sleep. We just had his funeral today. That's why...that's why we're kind of disorganized right now."

"Why didn't someone call us?" Cherrie asked in a hurt tone. "We would've changed our plans and hurried home."

Quickly, Mary broke in. "We couldn't have you come home now! Not during test and exams and everythin'. That would've done no good for anyone."

"Damn!" Dee exclaimed. "I've known Old Doc since I was born. He's taken care of us for as long as I can remember. He's goin' to be missed…missed a lot."

"Who's goin' to take his place?" Cherrie asked quietly.

"Well, it's kind of up in the air," James said. "Right now there is a Doctor Barnes over in Athens that's taking Old Doc's calls. That's a long drive but at least we have someone we can see and he's associated with the hospital in Athens. There's an active search goin' on as we speak by the town council to find a new local doctor."

"Is anyone taking over Old Doc's house and office?" Dee asked.

"No, not yet," Mary answered. "The Sheriff has closed and locked the house and office until a next of kin can be found or a will of some kind. So, for now, all of Old Doc's records, files, and personal things are locked up. I don't guess Old Doc ever remarried after his wife died. And I'm unaware of any children. We just don't know if Old Doc had any other livin' relatives."

Dee took in a deep breath and let it out slowly. "Well," he said, "I hope that's the worst of the news."

"It is," James said with a soft smile. "The rest of it is mostly just catch up stuff."

"Okay, then," Cherrie said, "let's have the rest of it."

"Well," Mary said smiling, "Captain Dick Jordan is home on leave from the United States Marines."

"Captain," Dee exclaimed. "Dick's already a captain? He's barely been in the Marines a year; maybe a little more than a year. How do you get to be a captain in that length of time?"

Mary laughed, "I've no idea. But it's a fact."

"I guess I'll just drop by and see how Captain Dick is doing these days," Cherrie said smiling a wicked smile.

"Oh no," Dee moaned. "Here we go again with the Dick and Cherrie thing. We don't have to start that again, do we?"

Cherrie laughed and got up and walked over to the fireplace. She looked at herself in the mirror above the fireplace. She primped her hair and checked her lipstick. "I don't know," she said teasingly, "a girl could do a lot worse than a captain. I'm thinking a lot worse."

Dee found a magazine on the table beside his chair. He picked it up and threw it at Cherrie hitting her on the back of the head. "Okay Miss Prissy, you're not so hot."

Cherrie turned around with a pout on her lips. "Mom, Dad, are you two goin' to let Dee do the big brother thing again?"

"He's only your big brother in size, my dear," Mary said. "If you remember he's only one minute and ten seconds older than you."

"Yeah, but he thinks he's my big brother," Cherrie smiled. "But, it's okay as long as we all know the truth."

"All right, all right," James interrupted, "we need to move on to the big news."

"You mean there's bigger news still to come," Dee joked.

"Oh, yes, there is," James said looking at Mary. "Do we tell'm now?"

"Now would be good."

"Well, I'll make this as short as I can so it won't be dragged out," James started. "A man from the Texas Parks Board came to talk to us last month. He offered us a nice bit of money for some of our property and the right-of-way across our land to the road that rings Lonesome Hill. The reason for this is that they're goin' to build a state park on the old coal mining hills north of town. The theme of the park will be based on the old coal mining days. They need to build a road from Coalville to the ring road around Lonesome Hill. That is so they can have one road going up to the ring road and another road coming down. There's already one road going up to the ring road but that road starts at the Farm-to-Market road on the other side of the hill. The new road will actually start in Coalville." James stopped for a moment but no one said anything so he continued. "The money they offered us will allow us to pay off the mortgage on our house and pay for the final year of college for both of you." James stopped talking again and waited for a response.

Dee and Cherrie looked at each other and then back to their parents. Dee spoke first, "By the way you talk I get the feelin' you've already accepted this offer?"

"Yes, we have, and I can tell you the money has already changed hands. Moreover, we've already cleared our mortgage and have set aside the money for both of your tuitions in September."

"How much property does this right-of-way take and where does it go?" Dee asked.

"It runs mostly between our land and the Jordan's land. Ruth Jordan also got some money out of it because the right-of-way took a small piece of her land. But mostly it runs right along the boundary until it reaches the ring road."

"Sounds like it'll take my treehouse," Dee said looking down at the floor.

"Yes," James said slowly. "The road will take down the entire tree."

"What all are we left with?" Dee asked carefully.

James could sense Dee's discomfort. He turned his head slightly to catch Cherrie's expression and he read the same thing on her face. "We have the house and the land it sets on, of course. Then, we still have the four acres behind the house all the way to the ring road."

"So, we sold off about six acres. Is that It?"

"That's it." Then after a long silence James pressed, "I get the feelin' that you two don't approve of what your Mom and I did."

"Oh, that's not it at all," Dee shot back quickly. "I just hate to see you have to do that. It's just a surprise and I guess I'm not dealin' with it as good as I should."

"Same here," Cherrie interjected. "But, I'm glad you got the house cleared. I think it's all goin' to work out fine."

"And," James continued, "You both should remember that the State of Texas could have used the Emanate Domain law and taken the land anyway and gave us whatever they felt like. By selling, we got a much better deal."

"We understand, Dad," Cherrie said.

"Yeah, we do, Dad," Dee said sounding cheerful. "After paying the mortgage and setting aside our tuitions, did you and Mom have anything left over?"

Mary, who had been silent through the entire right-of-way conversation, now spoke up. She chose her words carefully and she spoke softly but forcibly. "We did what James and I have always done. We did what we thought was right for our family. What we have left over is what we have left over. It's that simple. As for me, I don't need a *lot left over*. I've got my family and my home. My kids are gettin' a good education. What I've got I'm happy with. And as long as I've got those things, I've got no problems. But try and take any or all of those things from me, and there'll be *hell to pay*."

When she finished speaking her eyes burned a hole through Dee and Cherrie. The entire family was taken aback. There was a long silence and the quiet in the living room was as loud as a clash of thunder.

The silence was ended by Dee clearing his throat. He stood up and said, "Well said, Mom." He walked over and sat down beside her and wrapped his arms around her and squeezed her until he was afraid he was going to hurt her.

"No one could've said it better," said Cherrie as she walked over and kissed her Mother on the top of her head.

That night after his parents had gone to bed Dee walked out into the backyard shirtless and in his bare feet. He stood looking at the stars and then at the old path he used to take to his treehouse. Looking over to his right, he saw where Rachael's house used to be. He guessed that would go in the right-of-way deal as well. Well, things have to keep changing he thought to his self. They just have to keep moving and changing.

"Penny for your thoughts," a soft whisper came from behind him.

He turned to see Cherrie standing behind him in her short little nightie. "You'd be gettin' a bad deal. I'm not sure anythin' I think is worth a penny." He turned back and crossed his arm over his chest.

Cherrie walked up and stood beside him. She folded her arms behind her back. "Aren't we a bit cynical?" She asked.

"Yeah, I guess," he said. Then, after a short pause, "Mom and Dad are great aren't they?"

"They don't come any better."

They stood quietly for several minutes then Dee said, "You know you once told me we ought to go up into my old treehouse and see if those pictures of naked women are still there. Do you remember that?"

"I remember that very well. I also remember we never did. We were goin' to go after lunch as I recall. But we never did."

"No we never did," he said as he looked at her with a twinkle in his eyes.

"What're you thinkin'?" She laughed.

"I'm thinkin' that tomorrow we sneak off and go climb that old tree and go in that treehouse and just see what's still there. Maybe the telescope is still there. Who knows? And maybe pictures of naked women."

"Aren't we a little old to be climbin' trees and explorin' treehouses? And as I remember you didn't think girls should climb trees."

"Naw," he exclaimed, "I think we're just the right age. Come on, whata ya say? And, as I've gotten older, I've changed my mind about a lot of things concernin' girls."

"Oh, you have," Cherrie responded. "Maybe I should hear some of these new ideas you have about girls."

Dee waved her off and changed the subject back to the treehouse. "You know with this right-of-way deal, the old treehouse'll be gone soon. We may never get another chance to have a look."

Cherrie rocked back and forth on her heels and toes. "Okay, I guess I can give it a shot. I guess we can see what we can see."

"Yep, let's go see what we can see." He hooked his arm around her neck and started pulling her back into the house.

CHAPTER FORTY-SEVEN

A Step Back in Time

June 1941

The next morning Cherrie walked into the kitchen still wearing her short nightie. She was rubbing her eyes trying to make the sleep go away. As her eyes focused, she could see her Mother and Dee drinking coffee and talking softly.

Before she could say anything her Mother barked at her sharply, "Get back into your room and put some cloths on, girl."

She stopped and looked down at herself. Smiling, she quickly turned around and went back down the hall to her room. Shortly she returned to the kitchen wearing rolled up jeans, sneakers, and a Baylor T-shirt. By now, her Mother was spooning up large helpings of scrambled eggs on plates with beacon and toast. She went to the cabinet, got a cup, then sat down at the table and began pouring herself a steaming hot cup of coffee. "Where's Dad?" She asked matter-of-factly.

"He had to go into the store this morning," her Mother replied, "but he'll be back around noon."

She looked at Dee who was already wolfing down his breakfast. "Did you sleep okay?" She asked between sips of coffee.

"Like a log," he said through a full month.

Mary walked over and gave him a firm rap on the head with her spoon. "No talkin' with your mouth full." Things were quiet for a few minutes and then Mary continued, "What're you two up to today?"

"We thought we'd go down by the old treehouse for one last look around," Dee said pushing back from the table. "Then, I think I'll head on down to the store and see what Dad's got goin' on." Then turning to Cherrie he asked, "How long before you'll be ready to go."

"Christ, give me a minute. I can't inhale my food like you do."

Before she could say anything else, she felt a firm rap on her head. "No swearin' in this house, young lady."

"Come on, Mom, that's not swearin'!"

"It is as far as I'm concerned."

Dee gave a chuckle, "I'll be waitin' out back. Come on out when you're finished."

"Hey, wait a minute," Mary called after him. "Why on earth are you two goin' to that old treehouse? What could be of any interest there after all these years?"

Dee just smiled at her. "We just want to check it out one last time. It's goin' ta be gone before you know it." Like always, ever since he was little, he let the screen door slam as he went out.

"Oh! Christ, Dee," Mary yelled after him.

"Mom," Cherrie shouted as she jumped up to follow Dee, "no swearin' in this house!"

⸻

As Dee and Cherrie approached the old treehouse, a foreboding came over them as if they expected something bad to happen. For it was here that their disastrous adventure with Lonesome Hill had begun. Old memories came flooding back as they stood silently and looked up into the tree. The treehouse was still there, but, somehow, it looked smaller. The day was a beautiful summer day and the sun was shining bright dancing its light through the leaves and branches of the tree. But, as with the treehouse, the tree seemed smaller. Dee walked up and placed his hand on the trunk of the tree. Leaving his hand on the trunk, he walked around the tree continuing to look up at the treehouse.

Finally, Dee spoke, "Everything looks so much smaller." His voice was almost in a whisper.

"That's probably because we're so much bigger," Cherrie answered. "And why are we whisperin'?" She said laughing loudly. "Are we expectin' a ghost or somethin'?"

"You never know," Dee said in a mockingly sinister voice.

Cherrie shaded her eyes and looked up at the lower branches. She saw the old knotted rope they used to climb up into the tree. She walked over, took hold of it and gave it a yank. The rope snapped and fell to the ground. She picked it up and it crumbled in her hands. "I'd say this old rope is completely rotted out."

"Good observation," Dee joked. "You see what a college education can do for you."

"Very funny, Dee, but how do we get up there without it."

"It shouldn't be too hard, sister dear. I can almost reach the lower branch." Then looking at Cherrie, "All I need is a little boost."

"Little me, give big you a boost! You gotta be kiddin'."

"Well, if I boost you, can you reach down and pull me up?"

"Probably not," she answered simply. "Somehow I always end up with the dirty job." Without waiting for Dee's replay, she walked over and positioned herself under the lowest branch. She took a deep breath, slapped her hands together, and then configured her hands into a stirrup. "Okay, big guy, step into this stirrup and let's get this over with."

Dee hurried over and put his right foot into her hand stirrup. He then pushed off and launched himself up. It wasn't far to go so he was able to grab the branch on the first try. Quickly, he had himself sitting a straddle the branch. Sliding himself back a little, he leaned forward and down. From this position, he reached his hand down to Cherrie. She still had to make a small jump to reach his hand. He grabbed her hand and pulled her up. After a short struggle, they were both sitting on the branch.

"See," Dee said with a big smile, "that worked out fine."

Cherrie didn't say anything. She only gave him a disgusted look.

"Okay, follow me and be careful."

Dee carefully maneuvered himself to his feet. He was surprised at how close he already was to the treehouse. It only took him a few minutes to climb through several branches and reach the entrance to the treehouse, which was a trap door on the floor. He positioned himself just under the trap door and then waited for Cherrie to catch up. Soon she was standing on a branch just below him and slightly behind him.

"Well, are we ready to go in?" He asked looking down at her.

"I'm ready," she replied.

Dee was about to push on the trap door when he realized that the pad lock was still in place. "Damn," he yelled down to Cherrie. "My pad lock is still on the door!"

"God, it's got to be rusted by now," she yelled back. "Can you break it?"

"I'll see what I can do."

Dee grabbed the lock and jerked it as hard as he could but it wouldn't give. He was about to give up when he noticed that the screws connecting the latch to the floor were rusty and loose. He repositioned himself and worked his fingers around the latch until he had a good grip on it. Then, using his weight, he pulled down on the latch. It gave and fell off into his hands. But the sudden giving of the latch caused him to lose his balance and he nearly fell of the branch. He was able to grab the branch that Cherrie was standing on to regain his balance.

"Shit," he mumbled. "I nearly fell out of the damn tree."

"You okay, Dee"

"Yeah, yeah, I'm okay."

Dee got back into position and pushed the trap door open. He wasn't a child anymore so working his way through the opening took some effort. Once in, he offered his hand to Cherrie. She waved his hand away and worked her way into the treehouse. When she was in, Dee closed the trap door. Again, the treehouse was not designed for adults, but they finally got situated. Dee was too tall to stand completely up. The roof of the treehouse was only about six feet from the floor. So, Dee knelt in one corner and Cherrie sat on top of the trap door with her legs folded underneath her. Once comfortably located, they looked silently around the inside of the treehouse, which had not been visited for almost seven years.

The treehouse had no windows. In the corner behind Cherrie, was an old cardboard box that was covered in water stains and had large tears on all sides. One side was completely rotted away and the contents were spilled out onto the floor. Near the south wall was an old cigar box. It seemed to still be intact although weather beaten. Against the north wall was an old wooden box. It was empty except for some broken soda bottles. On the east wall several pictures were still stuck in place. Other pictures were lying scattered on the floor. The pictures that remained on the wall were mostly of the moon and planets. However, there was one picture that was of a different nature. It was stained yellow by the elements and it had a corner missing, but it was plain to see it was a picture of a naked woman. Above them, the roof had a hole in it. The hole was about three feet across. The wood around the hole was rotted and broken making for jagged edges. Up against the west wall and lying on the floor was a telescope. There was a tripod next to it with its legs folded. The telescope had a lens cover on each end. The body of the telescope was still in good shape as it showed no signs of rust. It looked as though the telescope and tripod had been carefully packed away. Next to the telescope and standing on its end, was another wooden box; except this one was closed by a lid and was latched by a pad lock.

The twins silently and in awe gazed all about them. After a while, Dee took his hand and pushed firmly against the floor. The wood bent and there was a disturbing cracking sound. "We need to be very careful," Dee said, "this floor could give way at any time."

"I'm not goin' to move until we leave," Cherrie replied, "or until you say to."

"This place is just like I left it as best as I can remember."

"To bad about the naked girl pictures," Cherrie said smiling. "It seems there's only one left."

"Yes, and I'm goin' to save it." Dee reached over and very carefully pulled the tack from the wall and the picture dropped into his waiting hand. For fear the picture would crumble, he didn't close his hand but let the picture lay flat in his palm. "I need something to put this in," he said looking around.

"Try that cigar box," Cherrie said pointing in the direction of the box.

"Good idea, but I can't use both hands can you reach it?"

Carefully and without getting up, Cherrie scooted close enough to the cigar box to reach it. She picked it up and opened it. Inside were two pencils, a rubber eraser, several sets of keys, and a small note pad. The note pad appeared to be blank. She held the box open and held it out so Dee could see inside.

"Good job, Cherrie," Dee smiled as he moved his hand over the cigar box and let the picture gently float inside.

Cherrie closed the cigar box and scooted back to her original position on the trap door. "I'll hold on to this while you scout around. Is there anythin' else you want to look at? What's in that box with the pad lock on it?"

"I don't think there's anythin' in it. I only used it to stand on so I could get through the hole in the roof to use my telescope."

"Oh yeah, I remember that now," Cherrie said laughing. "That's how you saw Dick give me that little kiss and that's how you saw all the Lonesome Hill events."

"Yep, that's how it all got started."

"Well, are we done?" Cherrie asked hopefully.

"Just about," Dee said as he started moving carefully around the walls of the treehouse.

"What're you doin'?" Cherrie asked alarmed.

"I want to take the telescope and tripod back with us."

"How're we goin' to do that?" She pressed.

"Here's the plan," he said seriously. "Once I get over there and can get the telescope and tripod, you hand me the cigar box. Then, you move off the trap door and open it. You move out the door and onto the branch below. When you have yourself in a good and safe position, let me know. Now, remember, you have to leave enough space for me on the branch. I will then start handing stuff down to you. You either hold on to the stuff or stack it somewhere on the tree branches, or both. When you feel good about everything, tell me and I'll start down. I'll pull the door shut behind me and join you on the branch. Then, we split up the stuff and climb down." Dee paused for a couple of seconds and then finished by saying, "It's a fool proof plan. Don't you agree?"

Cherrie just looked at him. "Sure, it's fool proof", she finally said handing him the cigar box.

The plan didn't get off to a good start. As Cherrie move off the trap door and opened it, it opened towards Dee. So, once Cherrie got out and was ready to receive the items, Dee had to first shut the door, and then move all the items to the other side. He then scooted around and reopened the door. After that, things went as planned until they got to the lower branch. There had been no part of the plan to get from the lower branch to the ground. After a short discussion, Dee swung off the branch and dangled by his hands. Then, he let go and dropped the remaining short distance to the ground. Cherrie dropped the items down to him. She then did as Dee had done and swung off the branch and dangled by her hands. She let go and fell into Dee's waiting arms. Mission accomplished.

"I think that went well," Dee said with a laugh. "Don't you?"

"Better than I thought it would," Cherrie said looking around. "What're you goin' to do now?"

"I thought we'd drop this stuff off at the house and then I want to head down to the store and see how things are goin' there and have a visit with Dad. What about you?"

"Can you carry all that stuff by yourself?" She asked stuffing her hands into her pockets.

"Why?"

"Well, since I'm already here, I thought I'd go back down the path to the Jordan place and say hello to Ruth and Dick. You know just kind of stop in for a short visit."

"Say hello to Ruth and Dick, uh," Dee said thoughtfully. "Just stop in for a short visit?"

"Sure, why not?" Cherrie challenged.

"Well, it's nothin' really big. But I was just thinkin' that Captain Dick will probably be there all by his lonesome. Ruth is more-than-likely at the store with Dad. Don't ya think?"

"Could be," Cherrie said slowly. "That very well could be."

As Dee began to pick up all the items he looked at Cherrie and said mockingly, "Yeah, it very well could be." Finally, Dee stood there with the telescope over his shoulder, the tripod under his arm, and the cigar box in his left hand. He shifted his weight from side to side as he stood there looking at her.

Cherrie put her hands on her hips and nodded her head. "Well," she said, "it looks like you can handle all that stuff okay. So, I guess I'll just head off down the path. I'll see you later at home."

"Okay, little sister," Dee said as he saluted with his free hand. "See you later at home."

With that, Cherrie turned and started walking back down the opposite path towards the Jordan house. Dee watched her as she went. Her ponytail swung as she walked sweeping against her green Baylor T-shirt, and her body moved gracefully under her jeans that were rolled up to just below her knees. She had her hands in her pockets as she walked. In another week, she would be twenty-one years old, but she could easily pass for sixteen.

—⊗⚬—

Dee took a deep breath and let it out slowly. My God, he thought, she's such a pretty thing and as sweet and true as they come. There's no doubt that she's the best of all of us; the very best. With his thoughts still occupying his mind, he turned and started walking back up the path towards the house, but suddenly he stopped and turned back. He looked again down the opposite path as Cherrie slowly disappeared from view. The last he saw of her she had reached back and taken her hair out of the ponytail and was shaking her hair free. It now hung lose around her shoulders as her head disappeared below the horizon. Then he said out loud to himself, "Dick Jordan better not hurt her. God help him if he ever hurts her."

Cheryl Jean Collie – June 1941

CHAPTER FORTY-EIGHT

Cherrie and Dick

June 1941

Dick was dressed in a pair of jeans and an olive-green T-shirt with US Marines printed across the front in large black letters. He was barefoot and, although it was cut Marine short, his hair was a matted mess. He carried a large monkey wrench in his hand as he walked back to the kitchen sink from the tool box that set on the kitchen table. For the last hour, he had been trying in vain to stop a slow leak dripping out of the piping underneath the sink. He was about to apply the monkey wrench to the large nut that connected two pieces of copper piping, when a soft knock came at the front door. The knock was so soft that, at first, he wasn't sure he heard it. He pulled his head out from under the sink and strained to hear. Then the knock came again; this time a little louder. Quickly, he jumped to his feet and started for the front door, dropping the monkey wrench into the tool box on his way. Without looking through the small door window to see who was knocking, he opened the door and stared through the screen door at the figure standing there.

After a short silence, he said, "Why, I could be mistaken, but I believe I see Cheryl Jean Collie before me and she looks all grown up."

"Well, I am Cheryl Jean Collie," Cherrie answered smiling. "But bein' all grown up is another thing all together."

Dick pushed the screen door open, stepped back, and signaled her to come in. "You certainly look all grown up to me."

"I'll take that as a compliment," Cherrie responded as she stepped into the house.

"A compliment is exactly how it was intended." Dick let the screen door slam shut, but he let the door continue to stand open. The sound of the screen door slamming seemed to bring him back to his senses, as he noticed how he looked. "Holy crap, Cherrie," he stuttered, "I look like somethin' the cat dragged in. Can you give me a minute to make myself a bit more presentable?"

"Take your time."

"Okay, I'll just be a minute. In the meantime, get yourself something cold out of the icebox and have a seat in the living room." Dick was talking as he hurried off to his room.

Cherrie went to the icebox and opened the lower door where perishable items were stored. She found a nice cold coke and took it out. There was a bottle opener attached to the side of the icebox. She opened her coke and calmly wandered into the living room. There, she took a seat on the couch. As she sipped her coke she looked around the room. Even though the furniture was old and in bad repair, the room was nicely kept. Everything was clean and in its place. The hardwood floor was well cleaned and polished. Shortly, Dick made his way back into the living room. He was now wearing a highly polished pair of black shoes and his T-shirt had been replaced by a well starched short sleeved kaki shirt. His short cut hair was now combed into place.

"I'm sorry about how I looked. I've been tryin' to fix a stubborn leak under the kitchen sink. It's been kickin' my butt for most of the mornin'."

"No apology required, Dick. I just dropped in. I wanted to see how you and your Mom are doin'. I don't guess I've seen you since you joined the Marines. Every summer I've been home, you've been off to school or doin' some kind of special trainin'. I could almost get the feelin' you're tryin' to avoid me."

Dick sat down in an old rocking chair across from Cherrie. His face took on a very deep hurt look. "Cherrie," he began, "of all the feelings you could have, that would be the most untrue. You and your family are instilled in my heart. Your Dad has been so kind to my Mom. You know Coalville is a small town and too many people know too much about each other. When Mom came home from prison, she had a really hard time gettin' back into this town. Lots of people just plain and simple shunned her. Even the good Christians at church would have little to do with her. But your Dad stepped up and helped. He gave her a job so she could be off government relief. He treated her like the old friend she is. So, Cherrie, don't you ever think I'm tryin' to avoid you. And of all your family, you're the one I treasure the most. Still to this day, I treasure you the most."

Cherrie leaned forward and clasped her hands together. She tilted her head to one side and struggled with the words she wanted to say. His short little speech and taken her aback. She wasn't prepared for the raw emotion that came forth. "We've been separated for several years," she started slowly. "This is a little hard for me and somewhat embarrassin', but I'll tell you the truth. You've never been out of my thoughts. I've dated several guys at college but nothin' of a serious nature. I guess since I was twelve years old, you've been the one and only boy I've really let into my heart. I'm sorry if that puts you under any pressure, but it shouldn't. I understand how things are and you certainly aren't required to feel the same way about me. But I would like for us to be good friends. I don't want to go another two years without seein' you. We can be good friends can't we?" When she finished her voice was breaking up and she looked at him with eyes that seemed to be pleading.

Dick pushed himself out of the rocking chair and stood up. He towered over her. His first impulse was to go over grab her and hold her, but he fought off the urge. Instead, he simply looked down at her. She had dropped her head and was now starring at the floor. "Look at me, Cherrie," he said quietly.

Slowly, she raised her head and looked up at him. There were tears in her eyes. "I'm sorry, Dick. I didn't mean for this to happen. I'm really, really sorry. I guess I better leave now."

She got to her feet and turned to leave, but he reached over and put his hand on her shoulder and gently pushed her back down on the couch. "The answer is NO," he said emphatically.

"What?" She asked puzzled.

"I said the answer is NO. I don't want to just be your *good friend*." He stopped for a moment to let that sink in, and then he continued. "When you were twelve and I was fourteen, you asked me to be your boyfriend and I said yes I would. And we were boyfriend and girlfriend through the rest of school. Then, we both went off to college and we got separated. But you never asked me to stop bein' your boyfriend and I never did." Dick stopped talking and there was a long silence. He seemed to be trying to gather up courage to continue. Finally, he continued in a halting voice, "the truth is that I'm the one that's embarrassed because you see, Cherrie, the fact is I've been in love with you from that night I went to your house and saw you with that busted lip and black eye. I don't think anythin' has every broken my heart like the sight of you lying in that bed with that beat up face. And on that same night I saw what bein' a family really means. The way your brother came at me to protect you. I was two year older than him and much bigger, but he never hesitated. He just charged right at me. I learned a lot that night from you, your brother, and your parents. You and your family have been my guide. I'm tryin' to put my family back together to have the same dedication and love that your family has. No, Cherrie, I don't want to just be your friend. I want to be your boyfriend again and maybe, someday, somethin' more than that."

Cherrie was stunned. She got to her feet and looked at Dick. Now, he was the one looking down at the floor. He nervously shifted from one foot to the other and he subconsciously wrung his hands together. "Now, you look at me, Dick Jordan!" She commanded.

He raised his head until his eyes met hers. His eyes were clear but his face was flushed red. He didn't say anything.

"You've got to be very careful when you throw around words like *love*," she said in a shaking voice, "especially with someone like me. Lots of times people use that word when they don't really mean it. They use it when what they really want to do is pacify someone, or to avoid hurtin' them. Believe me, Dick; I would much prefer that you be truthful with me. I can deal with the truth. But it would really hurt me if you misused the word *love*."

Dick stopped his nervous shifting round and the wringing of his hands. He stepped over to Cherrie and placed his hands on her shoulders and gripped her tightly. He pulled her close to him and looked into her eyes intently. "I know what the word *love* means," he said very softly, "I know what it means to me and I feel sure I know what it means to you. Cheryl Jean Collie, you can believe me when I tell you that I have never meant anythin' that I've said in my life more than what I just said; that I love you. There're not any hidden meanings or misunderstandings. It's just simple; I love you. Now, you see, it's up to you. The pressure is on you. Do you want to just be good friends, or do you want what I want, and that's for us to be together?"

Cherrie was breathing heavily and tears were streaming down her cheeks but she didn't take her eyes away from his. "I guess I want what I've wanted since I was twelve years old. And in that childish way, I want you to be my boyfriend. But now, I'd like to put that childish way aside and I want us to be a part of each other. Where ever that may lead, that's where I want to go."

Dick released her shoulders and wrapped his left arm around her waist. He pulled her tightly to him and at the same time he placed the finger on his right hand under her chin and tilted her head back. Cherrie made no resistance. Dick then bent down and placed his lips on hers and kissed her. It was not a childish kiss like the one of many years ago, but a passionate kiss. The kiss was a mixture of hot passion and of tender love.

Cherrie's mind reeled with all that was happening and how fast it was happening. But she shut her brain off and let her emotions react to his touch. The love of a childhood romance that had occurred nearly nine years before had now bloomed into a real romance between two young and loving people.

And as Cherrie had desired, where ever this romance may lead, that's where they would go.

CHAPTER FORTY-NINE

Dee meets an old Friend

June 1941

Dee walked down Main Street headed for the family fertilizer and feed store. He had dropped off the telescope and other items from the treehouse in his room at home. The walk to the store was nearly two miles but the day was nice and Dee was enjoying the exercise. His walk was nearing its end as he could see the store a few blocks away. It was almost lunch time and he hoped he would catch his Dad at the store before he took his lunch break. With that in mind, he picked up his pace and hurried along at a near trot. As he got closer to the store, he could see his Dad outside talking to Ruth Jordan. He slowed his pace and slowly walked up to where they were standing.

"Well, look at who's showed up," he Dad said smiling. "You better be careful there might be some work around here."

"Nope, didn't come to work," Dee replied, "came to talk." Then, turning to Ruth, "Hello, Ruth. I hope things are goin' well."

"Can't complain," she said. "Probably wouldn't do any good even if I did."

Ruth was not as Dee remembered her. She still had a nice figure and well developed breasts. But her once dark hair was overly grey for her age and her pretty face was drawn and wrinkled in places. However, her deep brown eyes still had the hint of a twinkle. Dee surmised that four years in prison was bound to change anyone.

"Ruth and I were just goin' to flip a coin to see who goes on lunch break first," James said. "But I think I'll let her go first and I'll spend time with you."

"Fair enough for me, James," Ruth said.

As she started to leave, Dee call after her, "Ruth, I hear Dick is home on leave from the Marines, and that he's Captain Dick Jordan now!"

"That's all true," she said looking back with a big smile. "Why don't you drop by for a visit? I know he'd love to see you."

"I might just do that. And watch out for Cherrie, I think she said somethin' 'bout droppin' by to see you two."

"Okay, I'll keep a watch out. You two enjoy your talk. I'll be back in about an hour, James." She waved her hand and then continued walking.

After about a minute, Dee asked his Dad, "How's she doin', Dad?"

James shrugged his shoulders, "As well as can be expected I guess. The town hasn't been a lot of help. I've been very disappointed in how they've acted. But at least around here she seems alright. She does a damn good job and helps me out a lot. And Dick is a big help when he's home, which isn't a lot." James then clapped his hands together to change the subject, "Did you have somethin' special you wanted to talk about? If not, I got somethin'."

"No, mostly I just wanted to see the store and shoot the breeze with you for a while. Why, what do you want to talk about?"

"Well, I know it's early in the summer, but I'd like to work out our crop dustin' schedule. I've already got at least three jobs lined up and I'm feelin' real good about two more. We can go out back to my office and go over a few things, if that's okay with you?"

Dee dropped his eyes down to the ground and shoved his hands into his jeans pockets. "Dad, if it's okay with you, I'd like to wait and do that tonight at home."

James picked up on a problem immediately. "Is there somethin' I should know about, Dee?"

Dee wouldn't lie to his father. "Yeah, Dad, there's somethin' you and Mom both need to know."

"Can you tell me how bad it is? Maybe I should hear it before your Mom."

"No, no, Dad, it's nothin' like that. I'm okay and it's nothin' that's goin' to hurt anyone. It's just somethin' I'd like to tell you and Mom at the same time. Cherrie already knows, so you see it can't be anythin' really bad."

"Ummm," James moaned. "That's no measure of anythin'. Cherrie always knows these types of things before your Mom and me."

Dee said nothing but smiled at his dad.

James looked at his son carefully. "Okay," he finally said. "We'll go over things tonight at home." Then slapping his son on the back he led Dee into the store.

⊶⊷

Ruth had returned to the store and his Dad had gone on his lunch break leaving Dee to do a few heavy chores for Ruth. Dee was busy filling hundred pound bags with a fertilizer mixture that had a heavy content of very thin residue which caused a large fog of dust in the back of the store. As a result, he had put on a baseball cap to cover his head, wore welder's goggles to protect his eyes, and was wearing a wet bandana over his nose and mouth. He had just finished filling the last bag when a pretty girl walked into the store. He turned off the mixer machine that mixed the fertilizer and then ran it through a funnel to fill the bags. He pushed the last bag aside and looked at the girl intently. She was a tall girl; maybe five foot ten. She had bright natural blonde hair that was arranged in a peek-a-boo haircut much like the movie star Veronica Lake. She was wearing a very pretty light sun dress that came down to her mid-calf. On her feet, she wore a pair of simple black sandals. To Dee, her face was a work of absolute beauty. Her face, he thought. He searched his brain because he was sure he should know that face. And if he didn't know her, he surely wanted to.

The girl walked deeper into the store and appeared to be looking around for someone to help her. Ruth was back in the office so Dee walked over to her dusting himself off as he walked. As he approached, he saw the most beautiful pair of light green eyes he had ever seen. The girl saw him coming out of the dusty fog but she continued to simply stand near the store door and look around.

As Dee walked up to her he asked, "Can I help you, Ma'am?" As he spoke, he removed his baseball cap, googles, and bandana. Removing the googles left him appearing to be wearing a mask as the dust covered face except for were the googles and bandana had been.

"Yes, I think maybe you can," she answered. "I'm looking for someone to help me fill this order." As she spoke, she handed Dee a small piece of paper with writing on it.

Dee read the short note and then handed it back to her. "Yes, Ma'am," he said, "we have that brand in stock. Accordin' to the note you have, you need ten one hundred pound bags of Kelly Quick Grow Field Fertilizer. I can get that for you right now. Do you have a means to transport the order?"

"Oh, no," she answered quickly. "I'm only to ask you to stack it out front and my brother will come by in his truck to pick it up. I'm also supposed to pay you. Can you tell me how much it'll be?"

"Yes, I can," Dee answered. "Those hundred pound bags are two dollars and seventy-five cents each and that includes tax. That means you'll owe us twenty-seven dollars and fifty cents. Do you have an account with us?"

"No, no account," she said opening a small purse she was carrying. "I'll just pay cash if that's okay."

"Cash is always okay," Dee smiled as he continued to look at her closely. "Who do I make the invoice out to?"

She had opened her purse and was carefully counting the money out into his open hand. "Just make it out to Bill Barnett if you would."

Dee's face changed to an expression of total surprise. He stepped back before she had finished counting out the money.

"Is there somethin' wrong?" She asked with a worried look on her face.

"Would that name be Billy Bob Barnett?"

"Yes, it would. Again, I'll ask, is there a problem?"

A large smile broke on Dee's face. "And you simply couldn't be Sue Ann Barnett?"

She stepped forward and forced the remaining money into his hand, which he was still holding out. "Yes, that's exactly who I am," she answered and she stepped even closer to him. She looked into his eyes and then studied him up and down. "My God, you're Daryl Collie," she breathed. "That's you under all that mess isn't it?"

"It is indeed," he laughed. "You and I have got to talk. Please tell me you can spend a little time with me. I mean after I've gone to the back and cleaned up. Please say you can."

She put a smile on her face that simply melted Dee's heart. "Sure, I can spend some time talkin'. Where can I wait for you?"

"Please go outside and sit on the bench out in front of the store. I'm goin' to move your order out to the dock and then I'm goin' in the restroom and clean up. All of that should only take me about twenty minutes. Don't you dare leave?"

"I won't leave," she said continuing to smile that wonderful smile.

In less than twenty minutes, Dee walked out the front door of the store, and to his relief, he saw Sue Ann sitting on the bench waiting for him. He walked over and extended his hand. "Thank you for waiting," he said.

"No, problem," she replied accepting his hand.

She stood up but didn't release his hand. "What about the store?" She asked. Are you goin' to leave it alone?"

"No," he said. "Ruth is there. I told her I was leavin'. I didn't come here to work anyway. I was just helpin' Dad out a little. Come on let's walk and talk."

"Okay," she said, again with that beautiful smile.

They walked along for a while not talking but still holding hands. Then Dee asked, "Why're you buyin' fertilizer for your brother? I don't see a car? How'd you get here?"

"My goodness, that's a lot of questions," she laughed.

"Well, I guess we got a lot of catchin' up to do."

"Like you, I'm just helpin' out," she said. "I'm in town for a few days and I came into town with Bill to look around the old place. So, I just took the fertilizer order while he ran some errands. He'll be back to pick me up in about an hour. So, I need to be back at your store here in a little bit."

"So it's Bill and not Billy Bob now," he laughed.

"Oh, yes. He's all grown up now and doesn't like Billy Bob."

Dee stopped walking and turned to face her; still holding her hand. "You said you're in town for a few days, where do you live now? You're not on the farm with your family anymore?"

See looked at him nervously and said, "No, I haven't been on the farm since I got out of high school. I moved to Dallas and got a job at Chance Vault. I share a rent house with a roommate that I met through an ad in the paper. I had some free days comin' so I jumped on a Greyhound and came home. I have to go back the day after tomorrow."

"What do you do for Chance Vault?" He asked.

"You won't believe it but I'm trainin' to be a riveter. Now, with the war scare they're hiring female trainees."

"A riveter," Dee exclaimed! "I'll be damned!"

"The money's good and I've got a lot of freedom now, but I come home to visit when I can."

Dee reached down and took her other hand and squeezed them as he spoke. "So, how're things on the farm now? I know things were rough for you durin' school, and Cherrie and I weren't allowed to be around you and Billy Bob after everythin' that happened. I felt bad about that back then and I still feel bad about it now."

Sue Ann's green eyes clouded over and dampness made them shine. "No one's to blame," she said softly continuing to look into his eyes. "My parents were the same way. You Collies were off limits. In a way, you still are. Bill comes to your store because it's either that are drive all the way to Athens."

"So, how're your parents doin'?"

"Not bad, really," she said. "The depression has been hard on everyone and farm life is hard. But Bill stayed on the farm and helped Dad. They get by okay. As far as what happened, well, I guess that'll never go away and people will always just be people." She stopped talking for a long minute and they both just stood there holding hands. Then she took her hands away and said, "I guess we better get back to your store. Bill should be comin' back here real soon."

"Okay," Dee responded, "but I want to see you again before you go back to Dallas. I can't stay very long in town either. I have to be somewhere and I have to leave in a few days. Please, say you'll see me again tomorrow."

"I'd like to, Dee, but I don't have any transportation without getting Bill to bring me to town."

"Not to worry, I can get my Dad's truck. Will it cause trouble if I come by and pick you up tomorrow mornin' for breakfast in town?"

"I won't let it cause trouble," she said firmly. "If you can be there by nine, I'll be waitin' and no one will stop me. I'm my own woman now."

Dee smiled at her. "Okay. Nine it is. And no one will stop me either."

They turned and started back towards the store. Dee reached over and took her hand again and she didn't resist.

Sue Ann Barnett – June 1941

CHAPTER FIFTY

Events in Dallas

May 1941

T he street car or trolley car as some called them, clicked along its route from the Oak Cliff area of Dallas to the downtown area, on a bench seat near the front of the car sat Louis Mailer. Louis was a short husky man with light brown hair and matching dark brown eyes. He wore a frown on his slightly chubby face, as he looked out the street car window at the busy traffic headed to Downtown Dallas. He had been summoned to a meeting with his biggest client at their Magnolia Building offices. There was no explanation for the meeting just that he needed to be there, and the meeting was on a short notice. He had to dress and shave quickly, then hurry to catch the street car. Not going wasn't an option as the law firm of Bitterman, Bitterman, and Levi was his largest client. They easily accounted for seventy-five percent of his income. Louis was dressed neatly in a well fitted dark blue suit with a double breast. On his feet, he wore highly polished black wing tipped dress shoes. A smart grey felt hat fit perfectly on his head. The frown on his face intensified as he rode along pondering what this quickly called meeting could be about.

When Louis left Coalville in 1933, he had only a little money that he was able to get from his divorce. His ex-wife Evie had taken most everything else including the baby boy he thought was his. However, blood test showed the baby didn't have his blood type. It was generally accepted that the baby belonged to Sheriff Clark; his best friend at the time. The whole thing was a terrible mess and Lou resigned as the Sheriff's deputy, left town and went to Dallas to put the whole experience behind him.

Upon arriving in Dallas, his first thought was to use his experience as a Deputy Sheriff and get a job in law enforcement. But he changed his mind when seeing what was required of police during the depression. He didn't like it. So, the question was what to do. He had to do something fast as his small funds were running out quickly. Then, one day while reading a man's magazine, he saw an ad for a Private Investigator school that was located not far from his small apartment in Oak Cliff. Instead of calling them, he went by the school in person. They interview him, liked his background as a Deputy Sheriff, and accepted him into their training school. The only problem was money. But he managed to scrap up the money for the tuition, books, and supplies. Over the next two years things were hard. He labored as a dish washer, a ditch digger, a messenger, and many other odd jobs, but he never faltered and kept going to classes. Finally, in the summer of 1936, Louis graduated from the school near the top of his class. He got his PI license and he was ready to start work. Several PI Agencies offered him a job but he turned them all down. He wanted his own agency.

His own agency meant more hard times and working at jobs he hated. But in two more years it all paid off. Using money he had earned and getting a small loan from a bank, he was able to open LM Private Investigators. Again, the first year was hard and lean. It was a one man office and he handled mostly divorces and various surveillance cases. Then, in early 1940, he had a real stroke of luck. One of his divorce cases involved doing some surveillance work for the law firm of Bitterman, Bitterman, and Levi; one of the largest law firms in Dallas. The results of his work lead to a big oil contract for Bitterman, Bitterman, and Levi and a winning judgment on oil rich real estate. From that point on, LM Private Investigators became the exclusive investigators for Bitterman, Bitterman, and Levi.

The business became so heavy that Louis was able to add two junior investigators to his agency. He was able to recruit them directly from his old school. LM Private Investigators was now a three man office.

⸻

Louis was lost in thought when he suddenly noticed that the street car had just passed his stop. Quickly, he reached up and pulled the cord. The street car stopped at the next scheduled stop causing him to have to walk back two blocks. When he reached the Magnolia Building, he went in through the revolving doors. The inside of the building was magnificent. It was principally occupied by the Mobil Oil Company, but many of the largest and most important firms in Texas had their offices here. Louis' client had their offices on the twenty-second floor.

The elevators were all located in one long hallway. There was a row of five elevators on each side of the hallway. They were tall with heavy and highly polished brass doors. Louis approached and entered one that was open and the operator was standing at the ready. There were several other people in the large elevator. He positioned himself against the back wall. He held his briefcase in his arms and against his chest to have more room.

"Goin' up," the operator yelled, as the door silently slid closed and he felt the gentle lurch as the elevator started up. The ride up was a short one. In fact, Louis' stop turned out to be first. "Twenty-second floor, sir," the operator said as the elevator slowly came to a stop. Again, very quietly, the doors opened.

"Thank you," Louis said as he stepped out.

From the experience of being here many times before, Louis turned left and headed to office number 2220. Soon he arrived at a large oak door with the highly polished brass name of Bitterman, Bitterman, and Levi Attorneys at Law on it. Like the lettering on the door, the door knob was highly polished brass as well as being highly ornate. Louis turned the door knob and pushed the heavy door open and walked in. There was a very large desk that dominated the entrance to the office. One lone and very attractive secretary sat at the desk.

"Oh, hello, Mr. Mailer," she said in a high and polite voice. "Everyone is already here and waiting for you in conference room four. I am sure you know the way. You can go right in".

"Thank you, Miss Holland," Louis replied just as politely. Louis showed no expression but he didn't like the sound of, "Everyone is already here and waiting for you."

When Louis reached conference room four he didn't knock but went directly in. Closing the door behind him, he looked around the room. He recognized Mr. Jacob Bitterman and Mr. Lawson Levi immediately. Mr. Bitterman was a distinguished looking elderly man in his middle sixties. His hair was all grey but his eyebrows were still dark. He had a boyish face that hid his age. On the other hand, Mr. Levi was much younger. He had dark hair that was slicked back and dark brown eyes. His face was hawkish with a nose that looked more like a bird's beak. It was easy to see that he was short, as the large chair he set in nearly swallowed him. However, Louis didn't recognize the other man who was dressed in some kind of law enforcement uniform. He was youngish; maybe in his middle thirties. He had a handsome face and a well-built body. Louis couldn't tell much more about his size because he was sitting down, but his chair didn't swallow him. Mr. Bitterman was sitting at the head of a long oval conference table. Mr. Levi and the unidentified law officer were sitting on opposite sides of the table across from each other.

Upon seeing Louis enter, Mr. Bitterman signaled for him to take a seat next to Mr. Levi. "Come in, come in, Louis," he said smiling. When Louis was seated, he continued, "Now that we're all here I guess we can get started. First I'd suppose that introductions are in order." Pointing to himself he said, "I, of course, am Jacob Bitterman the senior officer of this law firm. I generally handle all of our criminal law cases." Then, pointing to Mr. Levi, "This is Lawson Levi the junior officer of our law firm and he generally handles our civil law cases." He continued around the table, "This is Louis Mailer; he's the head of LM Private Investigations. His organization handles nearly all of the investigative operations for our law firm." Then, turning to the other side of the table and pointing to the law officer, "And last but not least is Captain Timothy Borden of the Texas Rangers. He is here at our request and he is partly the reason for this meeting." Mr. Bitterman took a short pause and looked around the table. "So, before we begin, if anyone needs a nature break, or needs coffee or the like, please do it now because I don't want any interruptions once we get started." No one spoke but nodded their heads in the negative. "Very well," Mr. Bitterman said as he took his seat. "Let's get started."

Mr. Bitterman cleared his throat and took a short drink of water from the glass setting in front of him. "Our law firm," he began, "has been retained by the State of Texas to handle all of the legal issues that have, or might, arise from the acquisition of land in the creation of a Texas State Park in a specific area of East Texas. Most of the land needed has already been acquired from owners throughout the state. We've been overseeing representatives from the state as they go about obtaining the other land needed for various things such as access and roads. All of this is preceding very nicely under the guidance of Mr. Levi our civil law expert." Mr. Bitterman paused for a few seconds to gather his thoughts. "However," he continued, "we do have a couple of issues. One is a civil matter and the other is a criminal matter. First, I'll let Lawson go over the civil issue with you." He turned and pointed to Mr. Levi, "If you please, Lawson?"

Lawson Levi stood up and nervously straightened a stack of papers in front of him on the desk. Straightening his tie and clearing his throat, Lawson Levi began, "We have what could be a possible issue with one area of the proposed state park. I say possible because at this time no one has brought this issue up and therefore it may not be a real issue at all. Now---"

"Excuse me, Lawson," it was Mr. Bitterman interrupting, "I don't mean to get into your business but I think we need to proceed in the simplest terms available. I mean let's make this as uncomplicated as we can. If you could just layout the issue in layman's terms I think all of us present would appreciate that."

"Sorry, Sir," Lawson said nodding his head. "Let me see if I can just define the possible issue." Lawson again straightened his papers and took one sheet out and laid it on top. He looked down at it and continued speaking, "There is a hill in the area that is central to the creating of the park. This hill is referred to locally as Lonesome Hill. In our acquisition efforts we discovered that this hill has no owner. That is to say when the last owner of that property died in 1916, he died with no will and he had no living relatives that we could find. Thus, in essence, he died Intestate with no one to inherit the property. Therefore after a short time, the property reverted back to the state. As a result, no acquisition is required since the state already owns the property."

"If the state already owns the land, what's the issue?" It was Louis Mailer asking the question. "Am I the only one confused?"

Lawson looked at Louis with an ugly stare. "If I may continue, Mr. Mailer, maybe I clear up your confusion."

"By all means," Louis responded, leaning back in his chair.

Returning his eyes to his notes, Lawson continued. "The last owner was a Mr. Mason. He obtained the property from the East Texas Consolidated Mines Corporation which went out of business in June of 1910. When they went out of business they liquidated all their holdings. Thus, Mr. Mason got the property for almost nothing. Mr. Mason never did anything with the property. It seems he just forgot about it and let it just set there. After he died and the state took the property, they did pretty much the same thing. So, in short, the property has been held by the state in an unimproved condition; almost!"

At the word, *"Almost"*, everyone moved in their chairs.

"Almost," repeated Louis. "How's it almost?"

"Good question, Mr. Mailer," Lawson said smiling. "As you all may or may not be aware, Texas has the Homestead Law. Any land in the state that is not being used by the state or improved by the state, theoretically, can be homesteaded. Since the property in question was obtained by the state in 1916, it has not been used by the state or improved by the state. That's been roughly twenty-five years. However, a man named Clint Jordan occupied a cabin on the property and, according to public records, lived there for over fourteen years. During that time, he made improvements to the cabin and the surrounding land. These improvements could possibly constitute an act of homesteading."

At this point, Lawson stopped talking and looked around the table at the puzzled faces. He continued his silence to let all he had said sink in.

"Excuse me, Mr. Levi," it was Captain Borden speaking.

"Yes, Captain."

"Are you tryin' to say that this Clint Jordan may have a legal claim on the property?"

"Yes, Captain, that is the civil issue we would like to clear up so that the state will not run into any unexpected challenges to their acquisition of the land for the State Park."

"Wait a minute. Everyone just hold on and wait a minute here," Louis interrupted. "I know about Clint Jordan and the whole story about him livin' on that hill. But that's been over eight years ago. Clint Jordan's been in Leavenworth prison all that time serving a life at hard labor sentence. How can he own any land? Why ain't that property gone back to the state?"

Lawson smiled at Louis with that *I know it all smile.* "All very good points, Mr. Mailer," Lawson said. "And you're correct that Clint Jordan can't own that property at this time. However, there is an heir involved. Mr. Jordan has a son named Dick Jordan and he's alive and well and isn't in prison. In fact, he's an upstanding member of the United States Marines."

Louis started to speak again, but Lawson held up his hand to stop him. "What we need to do here," Lawson quickly continued, "is to investigate the possible homestead rights of Clint Jordan and ascertain if there's any problem facing us at all. There may be no issue at all but we need to have it made very clear and presented to our representatives in Austin in a legal document. What we need from you, Mr. Mailer is to go to Coalville, get all the documents pertaining to Clint Jordan's case, go up on that hill and take photographs of the cabin and the surrounding area. Then, bring all that back to this office and we will prepare the necessary documents to clear the acquisition process."

Louis rubbed his hands together and leaned forward on the table. "You understand that I left Coalville those many years ago in a less than friendly situation."

Mr. Bitterman stood up and held up his hands to get everyone's attention. "Your situation in Coalville, Louis, isn't our concern," he said. "If you don't want the case, we can employ someone else. It's up to you. And you might want to think about it because, as I said when we started this meeting, there are two issues here and they both involve Coalville. We've only discussed the civil issue. We still have the criminal issue to discuss. So, I guess we need to know if you want to handle the investigation side of these cases or not. If you don't, you needn't continue to be here."

"I'll handle the investigations, Jacob," Louis said quickly. "I just wanted everyone to know that there may be some hostility issues between me and some people in the town; including the Sheriff. But it's nothin' I can't manage. Now, if it's okay, I'd like for us to continue to the second issue."

"Fine," Jacob said firmly. "Since the criminal issue is in my area, I'll explain the issue and what we need." He shuffled some papers until he found the one he wanted and laid it in front of him. He didn't set down but remained standing. "The criminal issue," he began, "is related to the same case as the civil issue but it presents a different perspective. It involves a murder on the same property as the civil issue. The murder was never solved and, the records we have, show it as by a person or persons unknown. The victim was a man named Jim Upter from New Orleans. It occurred during some Klu Klux

Klan uprising in Coalville. Mr. Upter seems to have been the leader of the uprising. Now, as stated, that is the crime. Now, you ask, what is our issue with this? In reality, it is much like the civil case in that it may or may not have any effect on our acquisition process. But what we have is an unsolved crime on a property owned by the state upon which we are trying to create a State Park. This probably wouldn't be an issue at all if it weren't for the civil issue. So, what needs to be done? We, the firm, asked the state for some investigation help. They were kind enough to loan us Captain Borden of the Texas Rangers. Now, Louis, we know you have firsthand knowledge of this murder as you were a Deputy Sheriff in Coalville at the time. What needs to happen now is for you, Louis, and Captain Borden to go to Coalville and complete your own in-depth investigation of this murder. Like the civil issue, we want to be able to send a legal document to our state representatives. That document needs to clarify why the murder was never solved. That doesn't mean it has to be solved. That may be impossible at this time eight years after the fact. What we need is for the document to make clear what happened as exact as can be ascertained. Also, the document must be authored by both of you. We *DO NOT* want two different documents. You need to work together and come up with one comprehensive report." Jacob took a breath and finished his talk with, "That's how the firm sees it. Do we have any comments?"

Everyone was quiet. No one spoke for several long minutes. "In that case," Jacob finally said, "when can you two gentlemen start for Coalville?"

"Well," Louis began, "this is the last week in May and I have some things I'll have to get organized before I go. But I think I could be ready to go by the second week in June," then turning to Captain Borden, "how'd that suit you, Captain?"

"I'll be available when you are, Mr. Mailer."

Jacob clapped his hands together loudly. "Good!" He exclaimed. "I'd like to meet with you before you leave, so just give me a call when you're ready to go. And good luck gentlemen; good luck to all of us."

CHAPTER FIFTY-ONE

Dee and Sue Ann

June 1941

The Collie Family had just finished their evening meal and Cherrie and her Mother were clearing the table. Dee had not eaten well. He had picked at his food through the entire meal leaving most of his food on his plate.

James had already moved into the living room and had started to turn on the radio but thought better of it. He watch as his son came into the room with him. James took a seat on the couch leaving the easy chair for Dee. However, Dee didn't sit down but walked over to the front widow and looked out at the night. It was quiet and they could hear the women in the kitchen talking softly as they washed and dried the dishes.

"Did you want to talk about the crop dusting now?" James asked carefully.

Dee jumped as if startled. "Oh, I'm sorry, Dad. I guess my thoughts were a million miles away."

"Yea, I guess they were, and during dinner as well. You hardly ate anythin'. I bet your Mom's worried." After a short pause James continued, "Why don't you tell me about it? I think you want to but you don't know how."

"You're right as always. I've got somethin' I need to tell you and Mom. Cherrie already knows.

"You're not in any trouble are you, Dee?" James asked with a worried voice.

"No, Dad. It's nothin' like that. Please don't worry."

"Okay," James said easily, "give it to me straight."

"Let me get Mom and Cherrie. This is for everyone." With that, Dee hurried into the kitchen. Shortly he was back with Mary and Cherrie in tow.

As everyone got seated Mary looked at Dee and said, "Well, I guess we're goin' to find out what's goin' on with you. Since you only picked your way through dinner."

After everyone was seated, they all stared at Dee waiting for him to speak. Cherrie had gotten up and walked over behind Dee's chair. She stood there looking at her parents as if it were a means of support.

"Well, there's no easy way to break this news so I'm just goin' ta say it," Dee said hurriedly. "I've joined the American Eagle Squadron. I've been accepted and I have to report for duty in New York City in eighteen days. From there, I'll be flown to England where I'll train for about a month and then be assigned to an Eagle Fighter Group."

Dee stopped talking and there was a dead silence in the house. His parents simply stared at him dumb-founded. No one spoke.

Mary finally found her voice. "You did this without even speakin' to us first?" She asked. "What about your senior year of university?"

At first Dee was taken aback and didn't respond immediately. Before he could gather himself to speak, his Mother was on her feet waving her hands.

"You're goin' to a shooting war?" She yelled. "This is insane. It's totally insane."

Dee got to his feet and tried to step in front of his Mother but she turned her back on him and continued to walk around the room. "Mom," he pleaded, "You have to try and understand. Please give me a chance to explain."

Mary spun on her heels and turned to face him. "Oh! I have to understand do I!" Then turning to James she yelled, "How about that James? I have to understand. Do you understand? I guess I must be stupid because I sure as *hell* don't understand."

"Mary, please sit down and let's all stay calm." It was James speaking. He had gotten to his feet also and now everyone was standing.

"Calm, you want us all to remain calm!" She exclaimed.

"Yes," James yelled raising his voice above hers. "Now please set back down and let's hear what Dee has to say.

Mary looked into James' eyes. Her eyes were blazing but were wet with tears. Without saying another word, she folded her arms across her breast and flopped heavily back down on the couch. She dropped her head so no one could see her face.

"Thank you," James said softly to his wife. He then retook his seat next to her. He put his arm around Mary's shoulders and looked up at Dee who was still standing. "Okay, Dee," he said in frustration, "explain."

Dee slowly sat back down in the easy chair. He clasped his hands together to keep them from shaking. His Mother's outburst had shaken him very badly. He glanced over at Cherrie who had move from behind him and seated herself on the arm of the couch next to her father. She smiled at him and gave him a thumbs-up sign unseen by their parents.

"The first thing I want to say," Dee started, "is that I'm very, very sorry for doin' this the way I did. I know y'all are shocked and, most of all, you're afraid for me. When I applied for the Eagle Squadron, I never really expected to get accepted. That's why I didn't tell anyone. I didn't want to worry anyone if nothin' came of it. But I did get accepted. And I want you all to know that I'm not sorry I got accepted. I'm very proud of it. I want to be a part of this fight for freedom. I think it's wrong for America to set on the sidelines while a terrible evil is castin' its shadow all over the world. And one small little island county is not only fightin' for its life, but the life of the rest of the world. I wanted to help but there was nothin' I could do. Then, the Eagle Squadron came along. That was somethin' I could do. I could fly. And I can fly really well. I want to go over there and help make a difference. I don't want to set this one out. I want to fight for what's right, which is exactly what my parents have taught me since I can remember. And I know, in my heart, that this family wouldn't expect it to be any other way. Because, in your hearts, it's exactly what you would expect of me."

The room fell silent as Dee leaned back in his chair and closed his eyes. Then another voice made itself heard. Cherrie said, "I've only known about this myself since Dee and I were on the bus comin' home. And, at first, I had just about the same reaction as you, Mom. But I think Dee is right. And I'm goin' to support him one hundred percent. In fact, I'm lookin' for a way to get involved myself. But, not to worry, I'm goin' back to Baylor to finish and get my degree. But after that, I'm goin' to do somethin' so y'all need to be prepared for that. Anyway, the good ole U S of A is goin' to be in this damn war in the very near future. And you better believe it's goin' to be a fight to the finish. So everyone might as well get their minds around it; it's comin'.'"

Cherrie got up and went over to Dee's chair and sat down on his lap and wrapped her arms around his neck.

"God in Heaven, what would I do without you, Cherrie," Dee said hugging her back.

Mary slowly raised her head and looked at her twins. Tears streamed down her cheeks. Her eyes were bloodshot red and her body shook as she tried not to cry. Struggling, she pushed herself up from the couch and stood. She was unsteady and wobbled on her feet. James immediately jumped up and grabbed her to steady her. She steadied herself and reached back and patted James on the cheek and smiled at him. Then, she pushed herself away from him and walked over to her twins. She looked down at them there in the chair holding each other. Reaching deep down within herself, she said with a strong, firm voice, "I don't like this even one little bit. But what's been done is done. And what has to be done will be done. And believe you me; this family will do whatever has to be done together. Just like we always have and just like we always will. If we have to go to war, then we'll go as one. If we have to fight, then God have mercy on those that come against us, because where my children are concerned I'll show no mercy."

⸻

The next morning a complete calmness had settled over the Collie household. The details of when Dee had to leave and how long he could stay and what he wanted to do with his remaining time had all been resolved. Mary had set a breakfast table for four but Dee explain that he had a breakfast date and would not be there. Of course, everyone wanted know with whom he had his date. Dee didn't lie. There had been enough drama without adding to it.

"Sue Ann Barnett!" Cherrie exclaimed. "You've gotta be kiddin' me."

"You haven't seen her in a long time, Cherrie, and believe me she's a walkin' talkin' dream. What's more she's as sweet as Mom's pecan pie."

"So, Dad's lettin' you use the truck for this date?"

"He is indeed. I can't talk now. I gotta run."

"Well, what about her family," Cherrie yelled after him. "You can't be one of their favorite people."

Dee looked back as he ran for the truck. "That's just another problem to solve," he yelled smiling.

⸻

As Dee maneuvered the truck on the route to the Barnett farm, he thought to himself how well things had turned out last night. After the initial shock and his Mother's first reaction, things had gone fairly well. They had spent the rest of the night talking and planning. Dee explained his schedule about when he was due in New York City, when he was to fly to England, and his training schedule. The hard part for everyone was the fact that he only had seven days left in Coalville. Because of the long train ride and his reporting date, they just couldn't squeeze in anymore days. In the end, it was decided by all that Dee would have the freedom to do what he wanted, when he wanted to do it, and for as long as he wanted. At first, his Mother had wanted him to spend all his time with the family, but she finally relented and agreed to go along with everyone else. It was after midnight before they all started for their respective rooms to go to bed. Dee had lay in bed and struggled to get to sleep, which was made harder because he could hear his Mother softly crying into her pillow. She was still crying when he finally drifted off to sleep.

Dee was jarred out of his thoughts as the truck bounced over some very large and deep chug holes. While he had been deep in thought, he had lost track of exactly where he was. He slowed down to get his barring's and discovered he was less than a mile from the Barnett house. Driving on, he soon came to the road that led to the Barnett house. He turned right onto the road and immediately stopped as the entrance gate was closed. Leaving the truck running, Dee got out and walked up to the gate. It wasn't locked. He pushed it open wide enough to allow for the truck. After driving the truck through the gate, he got back out and pushed the gate closed. Soon he was back in the truck driving down the sandy road towards the house. Shortly he could see the house and Sue Ann was standing on the porch. He slowed down so as not to stir up too much sandy dust. He had stopped in front of the house as close to the porch as possible and with the passenger door facing the porch. Getting out of the truck again, he walked slowly around the front of the truck and stopped as Sue Ann walked towards him. She was wearing jeans rolled up to her knees. They fit snugly showing off her soft curves. She wore a sleeveless white blouse and a pair of white sneakers on her feet without socks.

"Sorry I'm a little late," Dee said shrugging his shoulders.

"You're not late," Sue Ann said as she approached the truck. "I'm embarrassed because I must look anxious."

"The only way you look is beautiful," Dee said with his best smile.

Before she could speak again, Dee quickly opened the passenger side door and indicated for her to get in.

Sue Ann laughed, "Are they tryin' to teach you manners down there at the University of Texas." She climbed into the truck and Dee slammed the door firmly. He stopped to look at her before he started around the truck. The passenger side window was rolled down and she stuck her head out slightly and gave him that heart melting smile.

Dee had just started around the truck when a voice from the porch asked, "Excuse me boy, could we have a word?" Dee froze in his tracks and turned to look back at Harry Barnett.

"Dad," Sue Ann yelled, "you promised." She started to open the door but Dee hurried around and pushed it back closed.

"Hang on Sue Ann," Dee whispered. "Let me handle this."

"But he promised," she insisted.

"It's okay. You're his daughter. I'd been expectin' it."

Dee turned from Sue Ann and faced Harry. "Yes, Sir," he said, "of course, Sir."

"In private up here on the porch if'n you don't mind."

"No, Sir, I don't mind," Dee responded as he walked up the steps and onto the porch.

Harry took him by the arm and directed him to the end of the porch away from Sue Ann's hearing. "Sue Ann's a big girl now and she's got her own job and place. So, I can't be sayin' what she can do and what she can't do. But I can say who comes on my place and who don't. Now, if you and Sue Ann have to see each other, then, ya need to meet someplace else; not here. What I'm sayin', boy, is that I don't want you on my place again. Is that clear? You goin' ta have to find someplace else to get together with my girl."

Dee stared into Harry's eyes. "That's fine, Sir. We'll make other arrangements."

"See that ya do," Harry said and spun around and went quickly into the house.

Dee had turned and just started down the steps when someone grabbed his shoulder. He spun quickly knocking the hand off his shoulder. He was surprised to see Billy Bob Barnett standing there.

"Billy Bob," he breathed. Dee squared his body away just in case of trouble.

"Hold on, Dee," Billy Bob said. "I ain't here to do ya no harm."

"Sure, Billy Bob, it's good to see you."

Billy Bob looked over at Sue Ann and said, "I'm sorry Sue. I tried to stop'im. But it wasn't any use. He had to have his say."

Sue Ann held her hand out the window to Billy Bob. "It's okay Bill. I guess I knew it would happen. Thanks anyway."

Turning back to Dee, Billy Bob said, "Just so ya know, Dee, I ain't got any hard feelin's toward you or yours. You treat my sister right and we ain't goin' ta have any problems at all. But if you hurt her, Dee, you'll have to deal with me."

Dee placed his hand on Billy Bob's shoulder and said, "You got my word, Billy Bob, I'm goin' to treat your sister right. I'd never hurt her; never in this whole wide world. And anybody that would hurt her will have to deal with me first. On this I swear."

"That's good enough for me, and we all know that a swear is a swear." Billy Bob said with big smile on his face and holding out his hand.

Dee took his hand and shook it vigorously. "We need to visit sometime."

"We will," Billy Bob nodded. "We sure will."

Dee turned and walked around the truck and got in on the driver's side. He put the truck and gear and waved a good-bye to Billy Bob and drove off up the sandy road toward the gate.

After they had gone through the gate and were headed towards Coalville, Sue Ann spoke softly, "I'm sorry about all that back there."

"Let's forget it for now and save it for another time."

They drove a long quietly for a distance when Dee pointed to the seat next to him. Sue Ann knew the meaning immediately and slid across the seat pressing herself tightly against him. Dee freed one arm from driving and put it around Sue Ann pulling her even closer.

"So, where is this breakfast we're goin' to? Sue Ann asked laughing.

Dee looked at her with a knowing look. "I have it on good authority," he said, "that the Hill Road Café has an outstandin' breakfast and it's cheap."

"Well, cheap's the key word," Sue Ann laughed. "Drive on, my good man, drive on."

The Hill Road Café was nothing more than an old house that had been converted into a café. It was located at the intersection of the main highway that went through Coalville and the ring road that went around Lonesome Hill. Being an old house, it sat almost a hundred yards off the intersection. A sandy road ran from the ring road, just a little south of the intersection, to the café. What was once a yard, now served as a parking area. Inside, the living room walls had been knocked out to form the dining area. The kitchen had been expanded to include what used to be the old dining area. All in all it was a nice place. It had a fire place on one wall and the décor was old and rustic.

Dee and Sue Ann had been seated near a window at a table for two. They spent little time going over the menu. Both had picked coffee, scramble eggs, bacon, biscuits and gravy.

"Boy, I sure miss biscuits and gravy," Dee said. "You can't get'em down at the university cafeteria."

"Same here," Sue Ann laughed. "The cafeteria at Chance Vault has awful food. Not like home at all."

Turning serious, Dee asked, "Is it true you have to leave tomorrow?"

"Yeah, I gotta get back to work. I can't afford to lose this job. I mean they're trainin' me and all. Plus, it gives me freedom. I wish I could stay a little longer but I just can't. Why don't you come up for a visit? I could show you a good time!"

"I have no doubt you could," Dee replied. "But I have my own complications."

"What do you mean *complications*?" She asked puzzled.

Before he could answer, the waitress came over with their food. She put it all down on the table and freshened up their coffee. "Anything else I can do ya for?" She asked smiling."

"Yeah," Dee said quickly. "Do you have a pencil and paper I could use?"

"Sure," she answered, "I'll bring you a pencil and one of our order pads. Will that do?"

"That'll do fine. And thanks."

Without speaking, Dee and Sue Ann started eating. While they ate, the waitress came by with the pencil and order pad. She placed it on the table, smiled, and walked away. As they ate, Dee slowly started picking at his food as he had done the night before when worrying about talking to his parents.

Sue Ann picked up on it. "Dee, is there somethin' wrong?"

Dee looked up at her and put his utensils down. He leaned back in his chair and cleaned his mouth with his napkin. Then, without looking at her but staring down into his plate, he said, "I'd like to tell you somethin' but you have to promise not to laugh."

"What?" She laughed. "Is it a secret or somethin'?"

"Just promise you won't laugh."

"Okay," she said turning a bit more serious.

Dee cleared his throat and looked up into those beautiful eyes. "Sue Ann, I think in just two days you've stolen my heart. I hate the thought of you goin' back to Dallas so soon. I don't have much time myself and I want a chance to try and steal your heart away."

Sue Ann dropped her fork and she choked on the food she was swallowing. Grabbing her napkin, she covered her month and tried to keep from choking. She picked up her water glass and took a sip to clear her throat. After she was able to get herself under control, she looked over at Dee who was staring at her intently. Her mind was working very fast but she couldn't get words to come out of her mouth.

Dee saw he had stunned her. "I'm sorry," he said. "I guess this was a bad time and I guess I really put you on the spot. I know you can't possibly feel that way about me in two days. I'm embarrassed. Please forgive me, Sue Ann. But don't let me scare you off. Can we still be friends? I don't want to ruin that." Dee noticed he was rambling on so he quickly stopped talking. He tried to pick up his coffee cup to take a sip but his hand was shaking so much he was afraid he was going to spill it. Carefully, he set his coffee cup back down and was about to release it, when he felt something very soft touch is hand and then hold it so as to steady it. He nervously looked at his hand and saw Sue Ann holding it gently. Finally, he dared to look up into her eyes. Those beautiful eyes were watering with tears.

Not taking her eyes from his, she said softly, "You can't steal my heart away, Daryl Gene Collie, because you've already got it. You stole my heart away when I was eleven years old and I followed you up Lonesome Hill. But I was just a little girl then and you had no place in your heart for little girls. Now that you have a place in your heart for little girls, I would be happy for that place to be filled with my heart."

Dee allowed a small smile to spread across his lips. "When you were eleven years old, I must've been the dumbest twelve year old boy on the planet."

"No," she smiled gently, "I think twelve year old boys have other things besides little girls on their minds. And, then, after all that happened our parents kept us apart. But I still watched you at school. You still had my heart even when you left Coalville for university."

"And here we are," Dee said as he reached up and took both of her hands in his. "And I don't want you to go."

"I have to go," she said with frustration. "Why can't you come up to Dallas?"

"Okay, here goes," he said tightening his grip on her hands and continuing to look into her eyes.

Dee spent the next ten minutes explaining to Sue Ann about the Eagle Squadron, his time limitations, his remaining schedule at home, and why he was doing the whole thing. She listened intently without interrupting a single time. Dee then finished his explanation by saying, "That's why my time is limited. I have to be in New York City by the twentieth of this month. To manage that, I have to be on a train headed north in no more than seven days."

"The Eagle Squadron," Sue Ann breathed with her expression changing from love to fear. "You're goin' to war?"

"Yes," he answered simply.

The water that had been welling in her eyes now began to run down her cheeks as tears. "Well, I gotta say this has been a hell of a couple of days. What a roller coaster ride! We find each other again after almost eight years and now you want to leave again and go fight a war! What am I supposed to do?" Her voice had risen and people were beginning to look at them.

Dee continued to hold her hands tightly and said, "I want you to be here for me while I'm gone and I want you to be here for me when I come back. I want you to allow me to write you letters and I want you to write to me. I don't want to lose you, Sue Ann. Can you do all of that for me? Please?"

She pulled her hands free of his and reached up and cupped his face in her hands. Letting out a long sigh, she said, "You know I will." And then again, "You know I will." She straightened up in her chair and wiped her eyes with her napkin. "But there'll need to be a change in your plans." Her voice had become firm and assertive.

"What?"

"You leave Coalville two days earlier than you planned. You come to Dallas to stay with me those two days. You can catch your train from Dallas Union Station. That should give you time to do what you need to do here at home and still spend some time with me. In fact, it'll be much easier than tryin' to get to Union Station from here on such short notice. If you're already in Dallas, it should be a lot quicker." She finished speaking and looked at him as if there could be no argument.

Dee picked up the pencil and order pad and handed them to her. "I'll need your address and telephone number, if you have one," he said smiling.

"I have one," she replied as she started to write. "Call me and let me know how you're comin'; by bus or catchin' a ride with someone. You might try Bill. I'll talk to him. If by bus, I'll pick you up at the station. If you get a ride, just come on out to my place. I'll give you directions."

"I've just got a couple of questions," Dee said smoothly.

"Yes."

"First, how is your family goin' to handle me stayin' with you in an unmarried situation? And, second, how about your roommate? What's she goin' to do?"

"Not to worry. I'll handle everythin'. You just be there." Then she gave him that heart melting smile and said, "Generally I'm a very understandin' woman. But if you don't show up, you don't want me comin' back here to get you."

"You won't have to come and get me. I'll be there." Then, looking down at the table, Dee laughingly said, "Looks like our food is cold. I hate missin' those biscuits and gravy."

CHAPTER FIFTY-TWO

The Second Message

June 1941

Almost a month had passed since Clint had gotten the strange message smuggled in via the prisoner underground. The message played games with his mind as he tried to figure out who could have sent it and who would want him out of prison. As days turned into weeks and weeks into almost a month, he decided to stop worrying about it. It had obviously been a mistake. Whoever sent the message was either teasing him, or playing games with him, or had simply got the wrong Clint Jordan. It seemed strange to him that there could be some kind of mistake, but who knew what could happen with the underground mail. He told himself a hundred times to stop worrying about it and just let it go, but no matter how hard he tried the message continued to go around and around in his head. After all, there was very little to do in his small cell at night except lay in his bunk and think.

Then one hot miserable day, he was taking his usual water break when the water bearer lingered near him. There were several other prisoners nearby who were also waiting on the water bearer. The water bearer took them all water and held Clint until the very last. As he handed Clint the dipper, there was a small tightly folded note on the bottom of the dipper. Clint took the note and carefully placed it in his shoe as before.

"Remember," the water bearer whispered, "don't try and read it until you're in your cell tonight. I'll be by tomorrow if you have a reply." Clint didn't say anything so he picked up his water bucket and dipper and started to leave but stopped. He sat down across from Clint and pretended to empty rocks out of his shoes. He took his time putting his shoes back on. "There's goin' ta be some changes in the mail delivery," he whispered while working on his shoes. "I'm bein' taken off water bearer next week. I don't know who's goin' to take my place yet. We've not been able to find anyone we're sure of yet. I'll keep you informed." He stood up and stomped his feet as it checking out his shoes. Then he grabbed his water bucket and dipper and hurried off.

Now Clint had a new worry; a new mailman. Damn what a bad time for this to happen he thought. It was hard for Clint to go back to breaking rocks with this problem hanging over him. Finally the hard day ended, and again Clint went through the anxiety of the security checks, the evening meal, and the disrobing for the shower. But, once again, he managed it. The strain of waiting for ten minutes before lights out at ten PM was almost unbearable. Finally the time arrived. It was quiet in the cell block as lights out approached. Carefully, he took out the small tightly folded piece of paper and unfolded it. Moving to where he could see better, he read the little note.

WHEN FINISHED READING THIS, DESTROY IT.
THERE HAS BEEN A DELAY.
I T WILL TAKE A LITTLE LONGER.
I NEED TO SECURE MORE RESOURCES.
BE PATIENT
DO NOT TRY TO SEND ME A MESSAGE YET.
BELIEVE IN ME. PLEASE. BELIEVE IN ME.

There it was again, *Believe in Me.* Why should he believe in someone who keeps him or herself secret? In frustration, he wadded the note up and threw it against the cell wall. The note fell to the floor behind his bunk. He pushed himself against the cell bars. He wanted to cry out but knew better. An outcry would bring guards and he didn't need guards.

He sat down on his bunk and slowly got control of the anger and frustration he was feeling. Letting the note upset him so much made him angrier than the note itself. Soon he was in control of himself again. He got down on his hands and knees and searched for the note. At first he couldn't find it and panic set in. My God, he thought, what if it went out of his cell and onto the cell block walkway. The guards would find it. Frantically he crawled under his bunk and searched with his hands because he couldn't see in the darkness under the bunk. He was beside himself with fear and his breathing was coming fast. Then, his right hand touched something. He grabbed at it. "Thank God," he whispered to himself. It was the wadded up note.

Quickly, he un-wadded the note and carefully torn it into tiny pieces. When he was satisfied he had torn it as small as he could, he dropped the pieces into the commode and flushed it. It disappeared down the commode in the swirling water. Breathing a sigh of relief, he stood there and watched until the commode had completed its cycle and all was clear. While he was standing there he heard the command for lights out. He was still standing there when the lights went out and darkness filled the cell block.

He could hear the guards starting the cell checks to make sure everyone was in bed. He hurried to his bunk and lay down. In the hot summer, no blanket was needed so he simply lay on his bunk in his boxer shorts. The guard walked by and continued on his route with no problems. Now he tried to go to sleep, but his mind would not turn off. He imagined all kinds of scenarios, but none of them emerged as a good escape plan. Whoever the person was that was sending the notes must have some kind of plan; some idea as to how to get him out of here. The note had said more resources were needed and that it would take a *little longer*. What could *resources* mean? And how long is a *little longer*? He was asked to be patient. What else could he do except be patient?

He toyed with the idea of sending a response. But the note had said not to do that. But he couldn't help wondering what would happen if he did send a response. He had no idea how the prisoner's underground mail system worked. He wasn't even sure how to send a response. How would he address it? He would need help from the underground mailman. But now there was going to be a new mailman. At least he thought so. According to the current mailman, a new one had not been selected yet. He could only dream about how a new mailman was selected.

All of these things turned over and over in his mind. But there was really nothing he could do except follow the instructions in the note. So, for now, he just needed to get some sleep before tomorrow's hard day. As the note said, he just needed to be patient and wait and see what happened next.

CHAPTER FIFTY-THREE

Dick and Ruth

June 1941

Dick was in the kitchen closing up his tool box when he heard the front door open. Although he couldn't see who had come in, he assumed it was his Mother coming home for lunch break. "Hey, Mom, is that you?" He yelled.

"Yeah, it's me," she replied as she walked through the living room to the kitchen entrance. "What're doin'?" She asked leaning against the kitchen door frame.

"Oh, I finally got that damn drip under the sink fixed. It fought me for a while but I finally beat it. I was just puttin' up the tools."

Ruth pushed off the kitchen door frame and walked over and opened the ice box door. "I'm goin' to make me a sandwich," she said. "Do you want one?"

"Yeah, I'll join you."

Shortly Ruth and Dick were eating baloney sandwiches and drinking ice tea. They ate in silence for a little while and finally Ruth said, "I saw Dee Collie today at the store. He's really grown up. Just like you I guess." She was smiling as she talked. "He said Cherrie might drop by and see us today." She finished off her sandwich and picked up her glass of tea. "I bet she's all grown up to."

Dick looked at her suspiciously. "Yeah, she is all grown up," he said slowly. "As a matter of fact, she was by here earlier; maybe just an hour or so ago."

"Damn!" Ruth exclaimed mockingly. "I hate that I missed her." Then after a long pause she continued, "What'd she have to say? Did you two get all caught up?"

"Yes, we did, Mom. We got all caught up."

Ruth leaned back in her chair and tilted her head to one side. "How far up did you get caught up?" She asked in a suspicious tone.

The frustration inside of Dick grew quickly. He raised his hands to stop her from talking. "You know, Mom," he said in a voice laced with frustration, "we've been pretty damn lucky." She started to speak but he stood up and silenced her with a hard look. He leaned forward and braced himself on the kitchen table. "You severed your time in prison and even got out a year early. So, you've paid your debt. You come home and no one will help you except your old friend James Collie, who gave you a job just to help you out. So, now you have a job and an income when millions of people are out of work livin' through this God awful depression. Then, out of the blue, the State of Texas wants to build a State Park and use some of your land for an access road. They give you enough money to pay off the home mortgage you took out so I could get into Texas A and M. And that's just you, how about me. I get into Texas A and M on money from a very nice guy named Dr. Jewel. I get good grades and when I graduate I get into the United States Marine Corp as a second lieutenant. Through hard work and some good breaks I get an early promotion to First Lieutenant. Then, a special job comes along, I volunteer for it and now I'm a very, very young captain. All of this has happened to us. I mean all of these good things. And now, here you are, playin' cat and mouse with me over a sweet, kind girl like Cheryl Collie." He stopped talking and slammed his hands down on the table with a loud crashing sound. "Tell me, Mom," he continued, "tell me what that is all about."

Ruth could not speak. She was completely dumb struck by his outburst.

"Come on, Mom; tell me what you find so wrong with Cheryl Collie. Of all the things that have gone right for us over these years, what could possibly be bad about Cheryl Collie? To me, she's just another item to add to the list of good things that's happened to us."

Ruth was finally able to get a word in. "I'm sorry, Dick," she stammered. "I had no idea you felt so deeply about Cherrie. I had no idea."

"Well," he said in a much softer voice, "I do. I really do." He sat back down in his chair and buried his head in his hands. "I'm sorry, Mom," he moaned, "I shouldn't have yelled at you like that. I'm sorry."

Ruth walked around the table and stood over her son. She placed her hand on his shoulder and said, "I'm the one who should be sorry. Everythin' you said is completely true. We have been lucky; damn lucky. And there's nothin' in this world wrong with Cheryl Collie." She reached down and put her hand under his chin and lifted his head up to face her. "But could you tell me how deep this thing for Cheryl goes?"

He took a deep breath. "It's deep, Mom. It's really deep."

"Are we talkin' love here?" She asked softly.

"Yes, Ma'am, we are."

"And I guess she feels the same way?" She pressed.

"Yes, she does."

Ruth turned and walked back around to table to her chair. Slowly she sat back down. "Well, I guess I shouldn't be all that surprised. This has been goin' on since you were fourteen. It's been off and on, and you've been separated by school and the Marines, but it's always been there. I just thought it was young puppy love that would fade away after a time. But I guess I was wrong."

Dick looked at her with a deep longing she had seen before. Back when Dick first learned the truth about his Father. She could see it now.

"I've never forgotten her, Mom," he said. "That night of the Klan attack when I sat beside her bed has been with me all this time. She's been with me all this time. I know how young we were and how young we still are. But she's a grown woman now and I'm a grown man. So, I have to prepare you, Mom. I love Cheryl and she loves me. I know things will be hard with her in school and me in the Marines. But we've got to make it work out. There's just no one else for me. I guess there never has been. I need you to help us, Mom. Please don't fight me on this. I really need you to help us. Could you do that? Could you please just help us?"

A small smile crossed Ruth's face. She picked up her tea glass and took a long deep drink. She put the glass down and looked at her son. "Of course," she said, "I'll help you two in any way I can. And I guess we can start with James and Mary Collie. I am assumin' of course, but is Cherrie goin' to talk to her parents?"

"Holy shit," Dick breathed. "You know, I don't know. We never talked about it before she left. How stupid can I be?"

"Stupid and Love many times go together," Ruth laughed. "I think you need to get Cherrie back over here right away so we can all be on the same page before we talk to James and Mary."

Dick jumped up. "I'll go right now. But, damn, she's been gone nearly an hour. There's no tellin' what's happen in that time."

"Just go," Ruth said waving him out the door.

Dick ran out the door letting it slam behind him. Ruth walked over and stood at the door and watched him disappear down the road at a full run. "Well," she whispered to herself, "this should be very interestin'."

CHAPTER FIFTY-FOUR

Wings over Kansas

June 1941

Judy Jackson was a tall lovely young lady with a beautiful structured face. She had a nice full figure all though it didn't show very well through her flight pants and her leather flight jacket Her dark black hair wasn't very long as she kept it cut short enough so she could push it up under her flight cap. But, then, it wasn't short either as it was long enough to be attractive. She slowly ran her hand along the bright red fuselage of the freshly painted airplane. She still marveled at the fact that she had actually gotten a sponsor for the race at her young age of twenty-one. The plane was a beauty. It had been completely overhauled from an old 1938 single engine Meteor. It had a new powerful engine and all new instrumentation, and, of course, the red paint job. The red paint was a requirement from her generous sponsor; Mobil Oil Company out of Dallas, Texas. In addition to the red paint, the Mobil Oil logo, a flying red Pegasus, was painted on the tail section. But Judy didn't mind the red paint or the Pegasus, because this plane was hers to fly in the first ever all women's Lawrence, Kansas Aero Exhibition Race. She dreamed of the four thousand dollar first place prize money, but most of all she dreamed of the glory and the excitement.

Her Grandfather, the retired Reverend John Tuney, had told her many times that she was exceptionally blessed by God. And she believed that to be true. In her short life, she had had two exceptional fathers. The first was Clint Jordan who had raised her from a baby to twelve years of age. He was the only father she had known for all of those years. He had raised her in a lonely cabin on a lonely hill outside of Coalville, Texas. She had been home schooled and taught right from wrong, and above all else she had been loved. It was the wild events of the Klu Klux Klan uprising that had changed everything for her. The results of those events had introduced her to her real and long lost mother, Bob Ann Jackson. Along with that came a whole new family. Jack Jackson became her new father and he was as kind and loving as Clint had been. When events caused them to have to leave Coalville for Dallas, Jack took control of the family completely and made a good home for everyone. That included her two half-brothers and her grandfather. Jack was a skilled pharmacist and he became the chief pharmacist for the Skillern's Drug Store chain. So, during the darkest days of the Great Depression, she had a nice home and a loving family. Jack had even taken out the papers and officially adopted her. While living with Clint, her name had been Judy Cole. It was a name given to her by Clint himself. After the adoption, it was decided that she would keep the name Cole as her middle name and her new name became Judy Cole Jackson.

In 1936, when she was sixteen years old and a sophomore in high school, a meeting would take place that would completely change Judy's life. She met the great female aviation pioneer Amelia Earhart. Amelia had been in Dallas to promote Women in Aviation. She had spoken at Judy's high school and had spoken to Judy personally after the program had finished. Judy was completely infatuated and thereafter could think of nothing except flying.

Judy begged Jack to help finance her flying lessons, which Jack did with the condition that she work at one of his drug stores each summer and after school to help with the cost. This she did without hesitation. And in one years' time, Judy would solo and continue on to get her pilot's license just after she turned seventeen. Then a tragedy struck that would devastate her. On July 2, 1937, Amelia Earhart went missing somewhere in the Pacific Ocean while attempting an around-the-world trip. Although she had hardly known Amelia personally and had only spoken to her that one time, Judy felt as if she had lost one of her own family.

Judy's mother, Bob Ann, took this opportunity to try and discourage her from pursing the dangerous life of a female pilot, but it was useless. Judy doubled and tripled her efforts spending every penny she earned and every bit of money that Jack could afford to give her. By the time she graduated from high school, Judy had accumulated over sixty solo hours.

Disregarding her mother's pleading for her to go to college, she got a job flying for Journeyman's Air Cargo Company. Journeyman's main client was Chance Vault in Dallas. And their main job was to fly special cargo and secret communications between Chance Vault and Washington D.C. Since the federal government would only hire men pilots to fly the mail, it was about the only good paying job she could get that involved flying. She worked steady, flying rotations with other pilots that allowed her to continue to build up solo hours as well as cross country solo hours. The work and flying hours increased as the war scare continued to grow. While all of this was going on, Judy set her sights on the airplane racing circuit. She wanted to race in, and win, a major racing event. But she didn't have the money for her own plane and she couldn't ask Jack to sacrifice the care of the rest of the family to help her anymore. So, in all her spare time, she spent hours and days going from big company to big company looking for a sponsor to get her into a major race. She was turned down so many times that she was finally giving up hope.

Then in February of 1941, she happened to approach the Mobil Oil Company. She met a nice young man name Jimmy Orland. Jimmy was the youngest member of the Mobil Board of Directors. He was attracted to Judy immediately as she was to him. They talked for hours about the sponsorship before Jimmy would take it to the board. But when he finally did take it before the board; he sold it. Judy had her sponsor. However, she still had to qualify for the race. At first she was worried, but her job had given her all the solo hours she needed as well as the cross country solo hours. Next she worried about her age. But in June of 1941 she turned twenty-one and that got her over that obstacle. Once she reached twenty-one and was conformable with all the procedures, she obtained her annual sporting license. Now she was ready.

She was deep in thought when a familiar voice came from behind her.

"Hey, penny for your thoughts," it was Jimmy Orland speaking.

Judy spun around quickly and saw him walking towards her from the other side of the hanger. He was tall, maybe over six feet, three inches. He carried his tall frame with a well-developed and husky body. His hair was neatly cut and was a sandy brown color. He had a handsome, youthful face. He covered the distance from the other side of the hanger quickly using long quick strides.

"Oh, I was just tryin' to put all this together in my head," she said waving to him. "I still have a lot to do before the qualifying run. I understand there's already twenty-three women signed up."

Jimmy smiled at her and said, "That's true and we expecting as many as forty before the actual race. I mean we are getting a lot of big names in women's aviation signing up."

Judy looked at him with a frown. "Do you have the schedule of events yet?"

"Yes, I do," he replied but didn't say anything else.

"Well, could you maybe share it with me?' She laughed as she punched him in the chest lightly.

"Sure," he said punching her back, "the first qualifying run is tomorrow at noon. There'll be ten contestants in that first run. You're signed up for the run, so be sure you're ready. In all there'll be six qualifying runs starting tomorrow, as I said, and going on through October 15th. By then the field will be set. The contestants finishing in the top three of each run will qualify for the race. One important thing you must know is that once you have raced in your qualifying run you're done. If you don't make one of the first three places in your run, you don't get another chance."

Judy didn't say anything she just turned and looked at the plane again. She looked back at Jimmy and said, "So tomorrow is it, uh? If I don't make it, I'm done?"

"That's how it works," he said seriously. Then, he took her by the shoulders and spun her around to face him. He shook her gently and said, "That plane sitting there is one of the best, if not the best, machine in the entire race. It'll do its part. The rest is up to you, Judy. You have to be good enough."

He was still holding her as she looked up into his face. Her lips formed a small smile and her eyes twinkled a little bit. "Well, hell," she shrugged, "thanks for not puttin' any pressure on me."

The both laughed and he released his grip on her. "Pressure, what pressure," he grinned, "I sold you to the board as the best young woman pilot in this country. And I'm sure all of that is true."

"Yes, I may be the best *young* woman pilot, but I may not be the best overall woman pilot."

"That's why they have these races!" He exclaimed, "To see who the best is."

Changing the subject slightly she asked, "If the field won't be set until the middle of October, when is the actual race goin' to be held?"

"Not 'til December 10th," he replied.

"What! Why so long?" She shouted.

"They need time to accumulate all the money. Lawrence is a relatively small town. It is, however, getting a lot of support from their nearby big brother, Topeka. They hope to bring on some more race sponsors as well as getting in all the entrance fees and selling as many tickets as possible. So, it's just a money thing. But the good news is you'll have a lot of time to really get to know the plane and how to handle it." He stopped talking and pointed his finger at her. Then, he said firmly, "But put all that and everything else out your mind. At this point, you have only one thing to worry about and one thing only. And that is qualifying tomorrow. Nothing else counts for anything now; just qualifying!"

"Understood," she replied in a soft voice. "I read you load and clear."

⊲⦁⊳

The next day, after the qualifying run, Judy and Jimmy sat at a small table in the hanger looking that the plane. They were both sipping on bottles of beer.

"The good news is that you qualified," Jimmy said tilting his head back and taking a long drink of beer.

"Barely," Judy said disgustedly and slamming her beer down on the table. "I came in third and I just barely did that!"

"Careful or you'll break that beer bottle and get a nasty cut," Jimmy said softly.

Judy looked at him with a worried look. Her forehead wrinkled and her face was a deep red. "You realize," she yelled at him, "that I probably had the best plane in the group. To put it plain and simple, I got my ass out flown. The course was simple as it could be. We flew from here to Oklahoma City and then turned north to Omaha. Then, we turned back south and came back here. I was fortunate to have the fastest plane because I over shot the turn at Oklahoma City and I flew almost ten miles passed Omaha. I didn't use the right fuel to air mixture in the engine and my landing here at Lawrence stunk up the place. Now! Where's there any good news in all that?"

"You qualified," Jimmy said simply.

"Yeah, I qualified," she repeated and turned up her beer and finished it. "What do I do now? How do I fix this mess? If the race were tomorrow, I'd get humiliated."

Jimmy stood up and put down his beer bottle. "You look at me," he said angrily.

She looked up at him surprised at his outburst.

"We don't have time for this self-pity bullshit!" He barked. "You've got a lot of work to do. We didn't invest all our money in a plane and a pilot just to see the pilot go all mushy because she got her ass beat her first time up to bat. The good news is we have five months to get ready. Being in the first qualifying run was a real stroke of luck. We don't have to wait around. Whether you looked like shit while qualifying or not doesn't mean a damn thing now. You're in and now we fix things. And here's what you're goin' to do. You're goin' to quit that job at your Dad's drug store and dedicate all your time to this project. Then, you're goin' to make that qualifying run over and over again until you have it down so tight your ass will squeak when you walk. You'll have to schedule your flights so they don't interfere with the official qualifying runs or any other activity being held for the race. So, you've got to be careful but you'll do it and you'll do it right. Is all of that clear?"

She continued to stare at him with wide eyes. She had never seen Jimmy act this way, as if he were totally in charge, which she guessed he probably was. "I can't quit my job," she shuddered. "And I can't ask my Dad for any more money. So, my job is my only source of income."

"Not anymore," he shot back. "You'll go on the Mobil payroll. I'll decide what your job will be and let you know." He reached in his hip pocket and took out his wallet. He thumbed through it and pulled out a handful of bills. He counted out five one hundred dollar bills and laid them on the table. "Now, take that in the meantime."

She looked down at the money but was reluctant to pick it up. "Is this legal?" She asked. "I mean being on the payroll of your sponsor."

"That's my problem," he said putting his wallet back in his pocket. "I'll make it work. That's my job. That's what I do for Mobil. I make things work. That's why I'm on the board. I make things work. So, to make things perfectly clear for you, losing this race in a Mobil sponsored plane is absolutely *NOT* an option."

Things were clear for her now. Now she knew how she was able to get the sponsorship; a girl as young as she was in a major race with a major sponsor. Yes, it was clear that she was no longer in control. At this point, she still had an option. She could leave the money on the table and walk away from the whole thing, or she could take the money and do as she was told. In the end, the desire to be another Amelia Earhart was simply too strong for her to resist. She picked up the money and shoved it into her flight pants pocket.

"But before I commit to this all the way, there is one minor thing I'd like for you to help me with."

"And what would that be?" He asked suspiciously.

She smiled her best smile and said, "I think we could discuss it best over a nice dinner. I might even wear a dress and some heels."

"Why, Judy, are you trying to seduce me?"

"Maybe," she replied. "Would you like to be seduced?"

"Maybe," he smiled. "But whatever happens between us won't change what you've got to do and what I'm required to make happen. I hope you understand that."

"Oh, I understand that," she said moving close to him and putting her face close to his. He could feel her breath and see the beauty in her face and eyes. "What I need help with has nothin' to do with the race. It's a personal thing," she continued softly.

"There must be a really nice restaurant somewhere here in Lawrence," he said without taking his eyes from hers. "I'll find it and get us a reservation. I'll pick you up at your motel about eightish?"

"Eightish will be fine," she said as she turned and started walking away.

"And don't forget the dress and heels," he yelled after her.

"I won't forget," she answered without turning around. He couldn't see the smile on her face as she walked away.

Judy Cole Jackson – June 1941

CHAPTER FIFTY-FIVE

The Investigation Starts

June 1941

I t was after three PM on Friday and Sheriff Tom Clark was hurrying around his office trying to get things done so he could leave. His wife Evie and their two children, the nine year old boy Tyson and the six year old girl Macy, were expecting him at the elementary school playground sharply at five. Evie was to prepare a picnic basket and the family was to have a nice evening outside. His preparations were going well as the entire week had been very slow and today had been no exception. He was about to call Alice into the office to go over some final items, when she poked her head through the door and said in a disgusted tone, "There's a Texas Ranger out here to see you and someone else of your acquaintance." Since she was also hoping to leave early, this was not good news to her either.

"Did you say a Texas Ranger?" Tom asked, stopping his preparations.

"Yes," she replied simply.

"And who is the person of my acquaintance?"

"I'll let you find out yourself. Do you want me to let them in?"

The Sheriff hurried over and sat down behind his desk. "Sure, send them in."

Alice pushed the door open and in walked Captain Timothy Borden and Louis Mailer. Tom couldn't help from showing the surprise on his face to see Louis Mailer walk into his office.

"Hello, Sheriff," Captain Borden said, holding out his hand in greeting.

Alice quickly left the office pulling the door closed behind her.

Tom slowly rose from his chair and took the Captain's hand and shook it.

Pointing to Louis, the Captain said, "This is Louis Mailer a Private Investigator from Dallas. I understand you two are acquainted."

"Yes, we are," Tom said taking Louis' outstretched hand and shaking it.

"Nice to see you, Tom," Louis said plainly.

"Yeah, nice," Tom said releasing Louis' hand. Then, seating himself once again in his chair, he pointed to the other chairs across from his desk. "Please take a seat and tell me what a lowly Town Sheriff in Coalville, Texas can do for the Texas Rangers."

Once they were seated, Captain Borden started the conversation, "Well, this may take a little time to explain."

"Well," Tom said, "I hope it's not too long, because I have somewhere to be at five and I can't be late."

"Okay," the Captain said somewhat irritated. "Why don't I give it to you as quickly as I can?"

"Why don't you," Tom said shrugging his shoulders.

———◦◦◦———

It took Captain Borden about twenty minutes to explain the entire situation about the State Park, the homestead issue, and the unsolved murder. In the end, he asked the Sheriff for permission to go up onto Lonesome Hill to do some investigating and to have access to all the documents concerning the murder of Jim Upter.

The Sheriff was quiet for several minutes after Captain Borden stopped talking. Then, he placed his hands palms down on his desk. "There's good news and bad news," he finally said. "Which one do you want first?"

"We'll take the good news first," the Captain said smiling.

"Okay, the good news is that you don't have to have my permission to go up on that hill. Go up there anytime you like and investigate to your heart's content. My only request is that you keep me informed on any conclusions you might reach. As for me, I will make myself available to you just about any time you need; excluding today at five of course."

"Thank you, Sheriff," the Captain said, "and now the bad news?"

"It's the documents you see," the Sheriff said standing up. He crossed over to the office door and opened it a crack. "Alice, can you step in here for just a minute."

In few seconds, Alice walked into the room.

"Alice," the Sheriff asked seriously, "if I wanted to find all the documents that have to do with the Jim Upter murder, how would I go about it?"

"My goodness," Alice laughed lightly, "that might take some doin'."

"Why is that?" The Sheriff pressed.

Alice took a deep breath. "Well, first off, it's been about eight years. Secondly, the documents are divided between the Sheriff's Department's investigation and the city court documents. Of course, one is for the investigation itself and the other is for all the court rulings. We'd need to go into the courthouse basement, locate all the boxes for the investigation and then all the boxes for the court rulings and combine them."

The Sheriff turned to the two seated men and smiled. "You see our problem here is time and effort. It is goin' to take a lot of both."

Louis held his hand up as if to be recognized. "Excuse me," he said, "I may have a solution to our problem."

"By all means," the Sheriff said pointing to Louis.

"Since I'm familiar with the filin' system down in basement, I think if you, Sheriff, were to give the Captain and I access to the basement over this weekend, we could probably get all the information we needed. If I recall correctly, the boxes are marked by year and the only year we really need is 1932."

"That's true," Alice spoke up. "All the boxes are marked by year. And that would be both the Sheriff's Department and the City Court boxes."

Captain Borden stood up with a smile on his face. "So, all we need," he said, "is access to the basement over this weekend. Is there a problem with you givin' us that access, Sheriff?"

Tom sat back down in chair with a thoughtful look on his face. Things were quiet as he rubbed his chin and thought the question over. After a short while, he looked up at Alice. "Alice, is there a procedure in place to allow documents to be removed from their filin' place down in the basement? I mean can they be checked out so to speak?"

"Yes," she replied, "we have a form that we use but it has to be signed by someone with the proper authority to remove the documents."

"I'm certain that the papers I have from the State of Texas to reopen the investigation will give me that authority," Captain Borden said.

"I agree," the Sheriff said. "I'll have Alice give you the keys to the storage room in the basement as soon as you've filled out the form to her satisfaction."

"Good!" Captain Borden exclaimed. "When can we get started on the form?"

"Right now," the Sheriff said. "I will turn this entire matter over to Alice so I can get to my five o'clock appointment."

With that, the meeting broke up. Captain Borden and Louis Mailer followed Alice out to her desk and Sheriff Clark finished up his work and left his office locking the door behind him. On his way out, Sheriff Clark stopped at Alice's desk and asked if he could speak to Louis in private for a moment. There was no objection from Captain Borden so Louis and Sheriff Clark walked a short distance down the hall and stopped to talk.

Sheriff Clark started to speak but Louis held up his hand to stop him. "Before you say anythin', Tom, let me make somethin' clear." When the Sheriff didn't speak, Louis continued. "I'm here on business. This has nothin' to do with you and me or Evie. As far as I'm concerned our issue is over and done with. I hope you feel the same way."

Sheriff Clark looked straight into Louis' eyes. "That's good to hear, Lou," he said tightly. "I'll go along with that. Let's just make sure that while you're in town you stick to the business at hand. You're not to see or go near Evie. Can we agree on that?"

Louis smiled a smile at the Sheriff that appeared to be more of a smirk and simply said, "Agreed."

CHAPTER FIFTY-SIX

Dee Says Good-bye

June 1941

Dee felt as though something was very wrong as he carried his suit case out the front door and sat it down on the porch. There standing in the front yard was his Mother and Father, his sister Cherrie, and Ruth and Dick Jordan. Parked by the curb was a pickup truck belonging to Billie Bob Barnett. Sue Ann had arranged for Billie Bob to drive him to her rented house near Dallas. Dick was standing next to Cherrie with his arm around her shoulders. All of the women were crying. Mary Collie was beside herself with grief and foreboding. Her only son was going off to fight in someone else's war. She had accepted that it was happening but she had a terrible feeling deep inside that haunted her. Cherrie had tears streaming down her face and she pushed herself against Dick, but she didn't cry out loud. Ruth stood with wet eyes next to her son, Dick. She had a terrible feeling that her day of good-bye was not far away.

James Collie had already said his good-byes to his son. He was now more concerned with comforting Mary than saying anything else to Dee. Everything that could be said had been said. Dee walked into the yard and went to each person and gave them a big hug and, sometimes, a kiss. When he reached Cherrie and Dick, he pulled them to one side. He held Cherrie's hand but he looked directly into Dick's eyes.

"This is my sister," he said with a shaking voice, "There is no one in this world I love or care for more. I leave her in your care. Promise me here and now that you'll take care of her and treat her with the love, honesty and dignity she deserves. For if you hurt her in any way, know that I will come back and find you and I will make you sorry you were ever born."

Cherrie said nothing but looked up at Dick. Dick straightened himself and stood tall in his Marine uniform. "Daryl Collie," he said firmly, "I swear to you on my honor as a United States Marine that I will care for and honor your sister. And I also swear that anyone that would do her harm will have to come over me first. All of this I swear to you."

Dee grasped Dick's hand and shook it firmly. Then he turned to Cherrie and grabbed her and pulled her to him and held her tightly. "You take care, little sister," he whispered into her ear.

She pulled away from him and looked up at him. "Please be careful and don't try and be a hero. And damn it you better write!"

"I hate to be the one to break this up, but we gotta get goin', Dee," Billy Bob yelled from the truck. Then, he hurried over and helped Dee carry his bag over and put it in the back of the truck. Billy Bob then got into cab of the truck behind the wheel and waited for Dee.

Dee hesitated briefly and then decided he couldn't say anything else. He hurried around and got into the cab of the truck without looking back. "Okay, Bill," he said softly, "I'm ready. Let's go."

⚬⚬⚬

The drive to Sue Ann's rented house took almost three hours. It was late afternoon when they finally arrived. Both Billy Bob and Dee were tired as they had driven straight through with only a couple of breaks and Billy Bob had done all the driving. Sue Ann's rent house was not actually in Dallas but in a small area next to Dallas called Grand Prairie. It was Grand Prairie where the aviation plant Chance Vault was located. The rent house was located less than a mile from the entrance to the plant. As they pulled up into the drive way of the house, Dee observed that the house, while not big, was larger than he had expected. It was a nice looking place with fresh paint and a white picket fence around the front yard. It had a small front porch that over looked a well maintained yard. Standing barefooted on the porch and leaning again a porch column was Sue Ann Barnett. She was wearing a pair of white shorts that ended at mid-thigh and a long white T shirt with Chance Vault stenciled on it in bright red letters. Her hair looked as if it had been freshly done and, as most of the time, it covered her left eye. To Dee, if there ever was really a dream girl, then she was standing on a porch in Grand Prairie, Texas.

———

The two days with Sue Ann in her little rented house were some of the most amazing days of Dee's life. They had begged Billy Bob to stay the night with them and rest up after the long drive, but he wouldn't hear of it. He insisted on leaving them alone and took a room in a motel near the highway. He would return home the next morning. Sue Ann's roommate had gone somewhere, Dee didn't know where, and they had the place all to themselves. Sue Ann had taken the entire two days off from work and they had been together the whole time. They ate together, they went to the movies together, and they did everything else together. Much of their time was spent in the little house just making love. Their love making was wild and passionate, but at the same time was gentle and tender. At night, they would simply lay on the floor together holding each other and listening to music on the radio. When the two days had to come to an end, Dee found that he was wishing he had never heard of the Eagle Squadron. But, he had, and he had to go. Now, he sat with Sue Ann waiting for his train at Union Station in Downtown Dallas. They had gotten there early and they sat together in the station lobby. Dee's bags were stacked beside them.

Dee reached over and put his hand under Sue Ann's chin and lifted her face to look into his eyes. Although she fought hard not to cry, her eyes were damp and clouded over. "Now," Dee started, "you know you have to write to me at least once a week. And above all else, you have to swear to me that you'll wait for me. Losin' you would be worse than gettin' killed."

Sue Ann jerked her hand away and jumped to her feet. "Don't talk like that," she screamed. "Do you hear me? Don't you ever talk like that to me again?" She could no longer hold back the tears and they came streaming down her cheeks. Her body jerked in spasms to her crying. She struggled to get her breath. "Don't you ever, ever mention gettin' killed. Do you understand me? Do you?"

Dee quickly got to his feet and pulled her to him. "I'm sorry, Sue," he whispered to her, "I wasn't thinkin'. I'll never say anythin' like that again."

She buried her face into his chest and clung to him as if he were going to disappear. "Don't do that," she cried as she continued to hold on to him tightly.

"Never again," he said quietly as he noticed people were beginning to look at them. Gently, he pulled her back down onto the bench. When they were seated again, he took his hand and began wiping the tears from her cheeks and her eyes. "Hey, now, you gotta stop cryin' or I'm not goin' ta be able to leave."

"Would that be so bad?" She asked feebly. "You don't have to go. You could still stop all this." She looked up at him and immediately knew it was the wrong thing to say. Before he could say anything, she playfully punched him in the chest and said, "I'm sorry, that was as bad a thing to say as you said."

He was about to say something else when the PA system announced, "The New York Limited is now boarding on Track 22. All aboard please. The train will depart in twenty-five minutes. Please have your tickets available at boarding. If you have a ticket for the New York Limited, please go to Track 22 now. The train is boarding."

"Well, that's me," he said standing up. "I guess I better head out to the track."

"Yeah, I guess you better," she said softly standing up also.

Dee gathered up all his bags and turned to her one last time. "Remember, you belong to me now and you have to swear to me that you'll be here for me when I get back." Then smiling, he said, "And you know how we Collies hold to swears."

"Yeah, I remember that very well," she forced a laugh. "And I'll be here when you get back; I swear it. Now, you swear somethin' for me. You swear that you'll take care of yourself and not do anythin' stupid. And that you'll not fall for any of those girls over there, because I'm not only yours now, but you're mine."

Dee stood there holding his bags with a lost look on his face. Then, he started slowly backing away. "You're mine, Sue Ann, and I swear I'm yours. And don't you worry. I'm comin' back. I *AM* comin' back." With that he quickly turned and started running toward Track 22 without looking back.

Sue Ann watched him go. She was waving good-bye but he didn't see her. After he had disappeared through the tunnel to the tracks, she dropped her hand and lowered her head. Her hair dropped down and covered her entire face. The tears had started again and ran down her cheeks. She stood there for a long time. People walked around her and even bumped into her, but she didn't seem to notice. Then, finally, she looked up and seemed to awaken from her daze and noticed all the people hurrying about her. But even with all the people around her she felt truly alone. She thought that somehow it seemed terribly wrong that she had found her love again after eight years and now he was gone after just two days. Now the waiting and worrying would begin. She reached up and wiped the tears from her eyes and slowly turned and started walking toward the entrance of Union Station. As she reached the entrance, she turned and looked back at the tunnel to the tracks. She lifted her head and tossed her hair back as if in a defiant challenge, declaring to herself, and to the whole world, that she was ready for what lay ahead. Her face was stained with tears but a smile crossed her face. Then, she lifted her right arm high above her head and clenched her hand into a hard fist and shouted loudly enough for everyone in the lobby to hear, "I'll be here when you come home, Daryl Gene Collie. You can believe it, I'll be here. And you give them sons of bitches hell for all of us! You give 'em hell!"

CHAPTER FIFTY-SEVEN

Dick Says Good-bye

June 1941

The Collie household was somewhat normal even with Dee gone. James was sitting in the living room reading the latest war news in the Dallas Times Herald. Mary was in Dee's room putting things away and making sure it would stay ready for Dee when he came home. Cherrie was in her room with the door closed. She had been quiet all evening, even though dinner.

At just about eight o'clock, a knock came at the door. Since no one else was near enough to hear it, James put down his paper and went to the door. There, standing on their porch, was Ruth and Dick Jordan.

"Hey, you two," James said surprised, "come on in here." He held the door open wide and Ruth and Dick walked in. "Is somethin' wrong?" James inquired with a worried look on his face."

"No, Sir," Dick replied, "we would just like a little of your time to discuss somethin'."

"Why sure. Have a seat and we can go over whatever you want."

"Actually James," Ruth said uneasily, "it involves Mary and Cherrie also. Could you ask them to join us, please?"

James looked at them uncomfortably. "Ruth, this is makin' me kind of nervous."

"No need to be nervous, Mr. Collie," Dick said. "It's just that I'll be leavin' in a couple of days and there's a matter I would like to clear up before I leave."

Mary had heard the talking and had come into the living room to see what was happening.

"Oh, Mary, Ruth and Dick have come over to discuss somethin' with us before Dick leaves in a few days. Could you ask Cherrie to join us?"

Mary turned slowly and walked back down the hall to Cherrie's room. She knocked gently on Cherrie's door. "Cherrie, Ruth and Dick are here and they want to discuss something with us as a family. Can you please come out and join us?"

After a short delay, Cherrie's door opened. Mary looked into her face and knew something was wrong. She could read her daughter like a book. Cherrie came out without speaking and walked directly into the living room and walked over and stood by Dick. Ruth and Dick were both still standing by the door.

"Can everyone please come in and have a seat?" James asked with a trace of anger.

"If you don't mind, Sir, I'll remain standin'," Dick answered.

Ruth and Mary took seats on the couch but Cherrie remained standing by Dick.

"Okay, now." James said impatiently. "Can someone tell me what is goin' on?"

Before anyone could speak, a smile crossed Mary's face and she turned to look at Ruth who smiled back. James picked up on the smiling and became angry. "I need to know what the hell is goin' on and I need to know *NOW*."

"I'm sorry, Sir, this whole thing is my fault," Dick said nervously. "You see I have to leave in a couple of days for an assignment in California."

"Okay!" James shrugged.

"Well, before I go I want to ask you for Cheryl's hand in marriage."

James was stunned. He backed up and dropped down into his easy chair sitting down on his newspaper. "You want to what?"

"I want---, Dick started but he was cut off in mid-sentence by James.

"It's okay, I heard you the first time."

Cherrie quickly stepped up and took Dick's arm. "Dad, please," she pleaded. "I've already said yes. But Dick and I both want yours and Mom's blessin'. We have to have it, Dad. We just have to."

"Well, you certainly have my blessin'," Mary said still smiling.

"Mary, don't you think----," before he could finish Cherrie had run over to his chair and knelt down in front of him.

"We just have to have your blessin' Dad. We just have to." Tears were pooling in her eyes. "I love 'im, Dad. You know I always have. But we can't have anythin' without your blessin'."

There was a short pause as James gathered his thoughts. "What about school?" He asked feebly.

Dick jumped in quickly. "I'd never ask Cheryl to quit school. What I'm askin' for here and now is an engagement. I have the ring right here in my pocket, Sir. When Cheryl graduates in June of next year, I'll get leave and come home. And we can be married right here in your home."

"I'll be married right here in our home, Dad," Cherrie said softly taking her Dad's hand. "And you will walk me down the aisle and give me away. Just like I've always dreamed it would happen."

James knew anymore discussion was useless. The issue was already decided before any of the discussion took place. He stood up and reached down and helped Cherrie to her feet. Taking her by the shoulders, he guided her to one side and went and stood in front of Dick. "Before he left, I know my son made you swear to take care of Cherrie and treat her with love, honesty and dignity. I heard him ask you and I heard you take that swear. It's now obvious that Dee must have known somethin' I didn't. Now you've gone one step farther and asked to marry her. So, I'll be honest with you. You must know that I, like my son, will hold you responsible for my daughter's happiness. Don't you dare hurt her, Dick Jordan, don't you dare hurt her."

As he had done with Dee, Dick stood straight and looked into James' eyes. "Mr. Collie, I swear to you that as long as I take breath I will honor and love your daughter and I will allow no one to harm her. This I swear before God in Heaven."

James smiled and looked down at Mary who had stopped smiling and was now crying. She and Ruth were holding on to each other.

"Okay, Dick," James said looking back up, "let's see that engagement ring."

⊙

That night James and Mary sat together out on the front porch. Cherrie had gone home with the Jordan's so she could spend more time with Dick. They were all alone.

"Well, June has been one hell of month," James said.

"It has indeed," Mary replied. "Our only son has gone off to fight in a war that, I guess, we all will be in sooner than later. Our only daughter has gotten engaged to be married to a Marine who I suppose will be goin' off to war sooner or later."

James chuckled and said, "I wonder what's goin' to happen next."

"I can tell you," Mary said.

"What?"

"Don't be surprised if Dee and Sue Ann want to get married."

"No, I don't believe it," James said amazed. "Not a Barnett!"

"Don't be surprised," Mary repeated.

James looked at her. "I'm gettin' too old for this."

"But aren't you glad in a way," she said.

"In what way would that be?" He asked.

"Well, Cherrie could have brought home someone from college or someone from who knows where. Someone we didn't know. But instead she wants to marry a boy we know to be a nice, honest boy. Oh, hell, I guess he's a man now. He has to be man to wear the uniform of a United States Marine. And if Dee wants to marry Sue Ann, I say all the better. I know we have our problems with the Barnett's, but that's got nothin' to do with Sue Ann or Billy Bob.

They were always good kids. We had 'em over to spend the night with Dee and Cherrie more than once. I'm not goin' to hold those kids responsible for Harry Barnett. Anyway, our kids seem to be makin' good choices. I mean we may not agree with some of them; such as the Eagle Squadron thing. But they're good, honest, and well thought out decisions; decisions that I'm very proud of. I have to tell you. Tonight, I'm one proud mom. I'm one damn proud mom."

James lowered his head and then spoke softly and slowly. "It's not the people involved that I worry about."

"Then what is it, James?"

"It's this damn war," he replied angrily. "Dee's already over there. And when America gets into it, you know Dick, being a Marine, will be one of the first to go. I just worry how everyone is goin' to handle all of this and if we're goin' to be lucky enough to make it through without gettin' hurt. "

"It scares me also, James. But we have to trust our kids and pray to God that they all come through. God's our only way."

"You're right, Mary, as you always are. But I'm afraid. I'm really afraid."

CHAPTER FIFTY-EIGHT

Wings over the Channel

August 1941

F light Lieutenant Daryl Collie sat in the cockpit of his Spitfire. He was finally going to be allowed to go on a combat mission. His training had been longer than planned. It was now late August and he was supposed to have been flying missions around the first of August. The reason for the delay was the availability of aircraft, and another reason had been his stupidity. In fact, he was lucky to be here at all because of his discipline issues. He had been called before the Group Commander twice for not following proper engagement protocol. Dee found it difficult to stay in formation when his instincts told him to freelance. The RAF didn't like freelancing. Dee on several occasions had taken off on his own leaving his wingman all alone with no cover and putting himself in danger with no backup. The last time he had stood before the Group Commander he was offered a ticket home.

But that was then and this was now. Now he was assigned to No. 71 Squadron and was given the newest Supermarine Spitfire Mk V. He had spent the last two weeks getting familiar with the plane. It was a beauty and was far above anything he had trained in. It had a powerful Rolls-Royce Merlin 45 engine that would generate up to 1,515 Horse Power and hit speeds close to four hundred miles per hour, and a ceiling of just over 37,000 feet. It carried two twenty millimeter cannons and four machine guns on each wing. This Spitfire would perform as well or better than its German counterpart the Messerschmitt ME-109; especially at high altitudes. Dee knew he was going into battle with as good, if not better, airplane than his enemy.

The flight briefing had been short and to the point. Intelligence had given Fighter Command the information on a large German effort that was headed for London. Fighter Command had scrambled two full fighter groups of which one of the groups contained Dee's No.71 Squadron. The intercept mission was broken into three divisions. The first division was to meet the oncoming German attack over the channel and concentrate specifically on the bombers. They were to bring down as many bombers as possible. This was a hard thing to do because their orders were to only go after the bombers, which left them open to fighter attack. The second division was to engage the fighters over the channel and keep on engaging them all the way to London. The third division was to loop out wide of the action and come up behind the attacking Germans and catch them on their way back across the channel. It was hoped that by the time the third division engaged the attackers; they would be low on fuel and, hopefully, chopped up by the first two divisions. Dee's squadron was assigned to the third division.

Ground Control had given the command to start all engines. Dee closed his cockpit, put down his check list, and started his engine. The engine roared to life and the Spitfire vibrated with the power. Dee's stomach was doing flip flops and his month was dry as he taxied out on the runway. He held the powerful plane in place on the runway until he was given the command to go. His call sign was Fox Two. He was part of a six plane squad in which he was the wingman for the leader.

"Fox Two, you are cleared for takeoff," came the command over his headset.

This was it. This was the real thing. Dee fought down his nervousness and pushed his throttle forward and the plane started down the runway. When he reached the right speed and power output, he pulled back on his stick and he was airborne. Quickly, he found his squad in the air and formed up into formation. He settled in just behind the tail and little below his leader's plane.

"All little Foxes this is Fox Leader," the voice over his headset said. "Okay, boys let's relax and do some flying. As per our orders, we have a bit of a ways to go. So, stay with me and hold formation.

When we near our attack point, we'll get some altitude and put the sun at our backs. We'll try and jump the Krauts before they see us. Now, settle back for some flying. Fox Leader out."

Dee knew that Fox Leader was Flight Captain Jamie Willis from Long Island, New York. Captain Willis had been with No. 71 Squadron almost since its inception back in 1940. He was the old man of the Eagle Squadron. Dee felt very lucky to be flying with him. Dee took a deep breath and settled back into his cockpit seat. It would take them a while to make their long loop around. He knew that the other two divisions were probably already engaged and a disparate air battle was raging. But for him and the rest of No.71 Squadron, their time would come a little later on.

⊰⊷⊶⊷⊱

The time it took to reach the attack point was much less than Dee had calculated. It seemed only about twenty minutes had passed when Captain Willis was again calling them. "All little Foxes this is Fox Leader. We are nearing our attack point. I will be grabbing some altitude up to 30,000 feet. Once there, I'll be swinging about fifteen degrees to the south to get the sun at our backs. When we're in position, we'll orbit there until the Krauts show up. Now everyone remember that our mission is the fighters. Someone else is to get the bombers. So, no matter how juicy a beat up bomber may look leave it alone! Okay I'm starting our climb. Everybody stay with me."

Dee waited until the leader started his climb and then fell into position on his wing. As they climbed passed 10,000 feet, Dee put on his oxygen mask. Once at their assigned altitude, they leveled off and made their turn to get the sun behind them. Then, they started circling waiting for the Germans to show up. It didn't take long. The German formations came from London heading back across the channel. They looked in bad shape. Their formations were straggly and some planes were clearly not keeping up. Their fighters were flying about 1,000 feet above the bombers. But there were big holes in their coverage. It was obvious that the other two divisions had torn them up pretty bad. They waited until the Germans were completely out over the channel.

"All little Foxes this is Fox Leader. It looks like they haven't seen us yet. So, let's make ourselves known. TALLY-HO! I said again, TALLY-HO!"

With that, the leader peeled to the left and pushed his nose over into a power dive. Dee followed suit and pushed his nose over and opened his throttle. Soon, the entire squad was in a full power dive heading straight for the German fighter formations. There was no time for Dee to think about anything. The distance between the German formations and the diving Spitfires closed at a rapid rate. Dee stayed with his leader as he was trained to do. Then, suddenly, Dee could see the leader's guns blazing away. Quickly, Dee found a fighter and put it in his sights. He pressed the firing trigger on his joy stick and his cannons and machine guns began to chatter. He kept his dive and he kept his finger on the trigger until he saw the German fighter begin to come apart before his eyes. The German fighter, which he identified as a ME-109, lost one wing and began spiraling down to the channel. Dee was transfixed but he saw his leader pulling up out of the dive and he pulled back on his stick to follow. The leader banked right and so did Dee.

"All little Foxes this is Fox Leader, BREAK, BREAK!" That was the command to break formation and go after targets of opportunity. The dog fight was on.

Dee didn't waste a second wondering what to do. He jerked his stick to the left and back. At the same time, he opened his throttle more. The Spitfire responded beautifully by climbing out of the initial cluster of planes. He found himself just above the bombers and in a hole in the fighter coverage. He resisted the urge to take down a crippled bomber just below him and searched the sky for fighters. Suddenly he felt his plane bounce hard as a rake of machine gun fire ripped into it. His canopy cracked but didn't break. His engine wasn't hit. He knew immediately that he had a German fighter on his tail. His training had taught him that the ME-109 could probably out maneuver him at low altitude. So, he pulled back on this stick and opened the throttle to reach for higher sky. Again, the Spitfire responded quickly and went into a steep climb. The German pilot was good and stayed on this tail and cut loose with another blasted from his machine guns. He felt the bullets hitting the tail section of his plane but he kept up his steep climb. His mind was telling him if he could just holdout until he got a little more altitude. He glanced down at his altimeter and it read 25,000 feet. That would have to do. The ME-109 was still on this tail but couldn't get a good shot because Dee had started dipping and rolling his plane. Just as the ME-109 let loose with another burst from his guns, Dee pulled back hard on his stick and went into a high loop and at the same time slammed the plane into tight barrel roll. The ME-109 tried to stay with Dee in the loop but fell badly behind. As Dee came out of the barrel roll, he cut his throttle and applied his flaps, which acted as airbrakes. The Spitfire almost stalled but managed to keep from dropping. The ME-109 went screaming by him. As the ME-109 shot by him, Dee opened his throttle again and jumped on the German's tail. At this altitude, Dee had the advantage.

The German pilot must have immediately realized what was happening because he pushed his plane into a steep dive to get down to a lower altitude. But it was too late. Dee opened up with his cannons and machine guns and at the same time he kicked the rudder pedals to make his plane pivot from left to right spraying his fire across the sky. He watched as the German pilot tried desperately to get out of the hail of bullets, but the cannon fire hit the engine and the prop of the ME-109. Its engine burst into flames and the prop spun off the engine and started spinning uselessly through the sky. The German pilot was trying to bailout of the ME-109 when it exploded all over the sky.

Dee didn't have time to take stock of his plane. He banked to the left and looked down to see what he could do next. It appeared that the action was just about over as the German planes were making best speed to the safety of the French coast. A few Spitfires were in pursuit but not with much effort. They knew that the Germans could send more planes at them from bases in France.

"All little Foxes this is Fox Leader. Disengage and form up on me at angels twenty-five. I say again form up on me at angels twenty-five."

Angels twenty-five meant 25,000 feet. Dee was already at that altitude or near it. Dee searched the sky and saw other planes coming up to his altitude. Then, he saw Fox Leader cruising just ahead and slightly below him. He gently nudged his Spitfire down and up to his position on the wing of the leader. It was during this maneuver that he felt his plane shudder. He tried to evaluate what was wrong with his plane but he couldn't see anything except the cracked canopy. Every few minutes the plane would shudder and he would have to hold the stick tightly and make flight corrections. He checked all his instruments but nothing read out of the ordinary. He did notice that his rudder control was very sluggish when he tried to use the rudder pedals.

"All little Foxes this is Fox Leader. All little Foxes sound off for me."

"Fox One here."

"Fox Two here," Dee sounded off.

"Fox Three here."

"Fox Four here."

Then there was a long silence.

"Fox Five are you out there?" Fox Leader asked.

"I said again, Fox Five are you out there?" Fox Leader repeated.

There was another long silence.

"Roger that little Foxes," Fox Leader finally responded. "Everybody check each other's plane to see if you can see any damage."

There was a short pause while everyone looked at the planes around them.

"Fox Two this is Fox Four, you have some pretty good damage to you tail section. Your rudder is shot up to hell and back. It's flopping around back there. You need to take it easy and nurse that baby home."

"Roger that and understood," Dee replied. "And thanks Fox Four."

"Okay, little Foxes lets go home," Fox Leader said in a tired voice. "Fox Two, when we start to land you go first and we'll give you any visual help we can."

"Roger that, Fox Leader," Dee replied.

They flew all the way back home without any other chatter. No one said anything about Fox Five.

Dee got his Spitfire down safely. As he walked around his shot up plane, he was amazed that the plane made it down. The rudder was hanging on to the tail section by some wire and a small hinge. As he started walking away to the debriefing room, the ground crew was already working on all the damage to the plane.

The debriefing took almost an hour as each pilot went over everything that happened during the air battle. Dee found out three things during the debriefing, first he had been credited with two kills. Second, they had lost two Eagles. One was their own Fox Five, who was a young kid from Panama City, Florida. He had been with No. 71 Squadron one week. It was his second combat mission. The second was a guy from Tiger Squad. The third thing was that they had given the Germans a real ass kicking. The Germans lost more than half of their bombers and over a third of their fighters. On the other hand, RAF losses were described as very light and the damage to London and its people were described as acceptable.

Later, Dee and the rest of Fox Squad were at the officers club sitting around a large table drinking beer. There was talk about the air battle and what had happened and who did what. But all-in-all the talking was light and not very exuberant.

Shortly two RAF pilots walked over to the Eagle table. They were each carrying a pint of beer in each hand. They were not large men but had the look of hardened veterans of air battles. As they approached the largest of the two asked, "Which of you Yanks is Flight Officer Daryl Collie?"

Dee looked up tiredly, "I guess that would be me."

The pilot smiled a large somewhat drunken smile. "Well, me and my mate here have been assigned the duty of seeing that you get the full traditional treatment."

Dee leaned back in his chair and looked carefully at the two pilots. "Dare I ask what the traditional treatment entails?"

"Well, it involves us RAF Brits, as it were, buying the Yanks that get their first kill a couple of beers."

"Truthfully," Dee said carefully, "I'm not sure we're in the mood. You see, I may have gotten two, but then we lost two Eagles. One of them was from our own squad. That kind of takes the wind out of it."

The RAF pilot blinked his eyes and swayed a little drunkenly. "My mate and I have lost a lot of our mates," he said solemnly. "We been doin' this since the summer of forty. "Ya have ta learn, Yank, that when one of your mates goes down ya honor 'im, ya don't morn 'im."

Dee didn't know what to say. The guy made him feel small and it angered him at first. But before he could say anything Captain Willis stood up and spoke. "He's right, Collie. This job isn't goin' to get any easier. Not tomorrow or the next day or the next. All of us here have lost friends and fellow Eagles. You can't morn every time one us goes down. Feel regret, yes, but you got to honor them for who they were and what they did. So, the RAF boys have a tradition of celebrating and honoring all tied into one. Why don't you think it over, Collie?"

Dee felt the anger melt away. "Yes, Sir," he said. Then turning to the RAF pilots holding the beers he said, "I guess I could drink a couple of pints."

The drunken RAF pilot smiled a stupid smile and said, "Who said anythin' about drinkin' 'em." With that, he poured one of the pints of beer over Dee's head.

Dee jumped up out of his chair totally surprised. His first reaction was to be angry again, but then he saw all the guys at the table laughing and slapping the table, and, once again, the anger melted away.

The RAF pilot slapped Dee on the back. "Good flyin', Yank. Now here, the second pint is for drinkin'." He handed Dee the second pint of beer.

Dee laughed and took the beer and started chugging it down.

CHAPTER FIFTY-NINE

A Surprise Visitor

August 1941

It was Sunday and a day off from breaking big rocks into little rocks, and Clint Jordan lay on his cell bunk staring at the ceiling. He had the option of spending time in the prison court yard or staying in his cell; he chose to stay in his cell. As it was hot, so he lay on the bunk in only his boxer shorts and sleeveless undershirt. He had obtained a book to read from the prison library, but it rested unopened on his small metal desk. It was now late August and he had not heard anything else from his mysterious note sender. He guessed the underground mail had been disrupted because now there was no permanent water bearer but a different bearer each week. He didn't know how one became a water bearer because he had never been asked to perform the task.

He thought it best to put the notes out of his mind. Thinking about them only caused him undue apprehension. Over the last week in his bunk each night, he had reached a decision. He decided that he must find something to do with his time or he was going to go crazy. He had been here, in this one cell, for over eight years now and had not completed a single book and had not done any projects. As the inmates said, he was a real candidate to become 'stir crazy'. Just what he wanted to do, or would be allowed to do, he had not clarified in his mind as yet. But it had to be something.

As he lay in his bunk pondering this dilemma, a guard came to his cell and beat on the bars with his night stick. Clint came out of his dream world immediately.

"Hey, Jordan, you got a visitor."

Clint looked dumb-founded. "I've got a visitor?" It was a question; not a statement. He swung his legs off the bunk and onto the floor. He stood up and stared at the guard.

"Yeah, and she's a cute little thing," the guard said cocking his head to one side. "You might want to put on some clothes."

Clint jump into action. He pulled on his pants and shirt. He decided to wear socks with his prison sneakers. As he dressed, he asked, "Do you know who it is?"

The guard simply tapped the side of his leg with his night stick and said, "They don't tell me these things. I'm just here to get you." Then, smiling he continued, "But, like I said, she's a cute little thing."

Clint finished dressing and then took a minute to try and comb his rumbled hair.

"Come on," the guard said irritably. "I got other things to do. Let's get movin'."

Clint finished up and then stood by the cell door while the guard signaled to the control room to release the door. Once the door was released, he unlocked it and pushed the bolt back. Then, he swung the door open and stepped back to allow Clint to exit the cell. Clint stepped out of the cell but waited for the guard's command before he moved any farther.

"Okay, you know the way," the guard said pointing his night stick.

They walked down the cell block, through the cell block door, and down the administration hall until they came to the visitor's area. There, several booths with telephones were set up in a straight line. The booths were about five feet wide and contained a desk top and a chair. There was a thick sheet of glass that separated one side of the booth from the other. The glass was messed with chicken wire so that it couldn't be shattered. The visitor set on one side of the glass and the prisoner on the other. The only way they could hear each other was via the telephone earpiece. With his night stick, the guard indicated booth five to Clint.

"Okay, Clint, since its Sunday and you've been good; you can have thirty minutes instead of the usual twenty."

Clint nodded to the guard and sit down in booth five. He was surprised to see Judy Cole Jackson sitting across from him. She was already holding the telephone earpiece to her ear.

Quickly, he picked up the earpiece and put it to his ear. "Hey, Judy," he shouted into the mouthpiece. "It's really good to see you! You're lookin' great!"

"Thank, you," she laughed. "And you're lookin' good yourself."

"Well, I guess as good as I can in here," he replied. "This is a real surprise. A nice surprise you understand. Does this visit have a reason, or do I just get to enjoy your company?"

"My, but you're a suspicious kind of guy."

He shrugged, "You get that way in here."

"Well, the truth is," she said in a matter-of-fact tone, "I'm out here in Lawrence, Kansas for an airplane race. I've been out here since June qualifying for the race. I qualified back in June but I've been practicin' and workin' on my skills these last two months. I'm gettin' ready to fly back to Dallas to do some more work with the plane there. The race is scheduled for the middle of December so I'll be back after Thanksgiving to put the final touches on my flight plan for the race. I wanted to take this opportunity to see you while I was out here, and I'll try and get back to you before the race."

"Well, I'll be damned!" He exclaimed. "Airplane races yet! Who would've thought little Judy Cole would grow up to do race airplanes? And be so pretty at the same time."

Then, she lowered her head and spoke softly into the mouthpiece. "It's important for you to know that I still love you, Pa. Nothin' has changed for me along those lines. Jack has been a good father to me and I love him for it. But you're the one I remember teachin' me and lovin' me. You're the one that's in my heart and always will be."

Clint looked at her through the glass shield. His eyes clouded over and became damp but no tears came forth. "Of all the things you could've said to me, nothin' could mean so much. I mean nothin'."

She straightened up and lifted her voice, "You don't give up on me. You keep the faith because you never know what'll happen. If

I win this race, I'm goin' to have a little money and I've made some friends that're in powerful places. I'm goin' to get you the best lawyer anywhere. We're goin' ta get you outa here; sooner or later. So, don't you quit on me."

"Oh, I won't quit," he replied. "In fact, I've been workin' on a project to keep me busy."

"What kind of project?" She asked.

"I haven't got it all worked out yet. But I'm working on it."

Things were silent while both of the thought of what to say. He wanted to tell her about he notes but he thought better of it. In his heart, he wondered if she was the one sending the notes. If she wasn't, it could make things worse. Anyway, the guard could hear everything they were saying.

Just as he was about to break the silence a strong and loud voice said, "Okay, Clint, start winding it up. We gotta get done here."

Clint looked at the guard and nodded, and then he turned back to Judy. "Well, I guess we gotta get done here. I'm goin' to look forward to seein' you around Thanksgiving, right?"

"That's my plan," she smiled at him.

"You take care," he said. "And good luck with that airplane."

"And you remember what I said. Keep the faith."

She stood up but continued to hold the telephone to her ear. He remained seated looking up at her through the meshed glass shield. Looking down at him, her faced turned hard and then with an icy coldness in her voice that he had never heard before she said, "I mean it, keep the faith."

Without another word, she hung up the telephone, turned around, and walked hurriedly away.

CHAPTER SIXTY

The Investigation Report

August 1941

Captain Borden and Louis Mailer sat patiently in conference room four in the offices of Bitterman, Bitterman, and Levi Attorneys at Law. They had been requested to be there at one PM. It was now almost two PM so they had been waiting nearly an hour. Louis paced the floor drinking a cup of stale coffee. Captain Borden simply leaned back in his cushioned chair and waited.

It had been over a week since they had turned in their investigation report to Jacob Bitterman. In it they explained their findings and, in a special section, they outlined their recommendations. The report itself, which had acquired the strange name of *The Coalville State Park Inquiry*, was only forty-seven pages long. However, there were several addendum sections that contained photographs, recommendations, and copies of official documents. Although the report seemed self-explanatory, Jacob Bitterman wanted a face-to-face meeting to go over everything and make sure there were no misunderstandings.

Just before two PM, Jacob Bitterman finally entered the conference room. He was followed by Lawson Levi and Nancy Caper. Nancy was Mr. Bitterman's private Executive Secretary. He walked in hurriedly and went directly to the head of the conference table, which was his customary place. As in the previous meeting, Captain Borden was in the chair directly across from Mr. Levi and Louis was located next to Mr. Levi. Nancy took her seat at a special small desk behind and to the left of Mr. Bitterman. The small desk had a typewriter and several note pads and pencils, as well as other office materials.

"Okay," Mr. Bitterman started, "I guess we all know each other here so there's no need for a lot of introductions." Pointing to Nancy, "Nancy is here to take down any important notes we might need to record and to make a list of any actions we might want to take." Mr. Bitterman pulled out a copy of the report from his briefcase and laid it on the table in front of him. Everyone else already had their copy of the report and all of its addendums in front of them.

"First, I would like to say that Lawson and I have read the report in depth and studied it closely. And we are both very pleased with the results. The main purpose of this meeting is to simply verify the findings and to get an official verbalization of the recommendations in the report. So, with all of that in mind, which of you gentlemen will be doing the talking."

Captain Borden held up his hand. "Mr. Mailer and I have agreed that I will do most of the talking except when there may be a subject or point which he may be needed to clarify."

"That's just fine," Mr. Bitterman said as he sat down.

"I guess the way we would like to do this," Captain Borden said pointing to Louis and himself, "is to take the civil and the criminal elements separately, if that's okay with everyone?"

"I believe that is an excellent idea," Mr. Bitterman said. "Please proceed."

Captain Borden stood up and started his address. "First, I think we should send a letter of thanks to Sheriff Tom Clark of Coalville for all his cooperation. He made all of the Sheriff Department's documents as well as the town of Coalville documents available to us. We were free to examine, research, and copy any of the documents we wanted. In addition, he accompanied us up on the hill to the cabin used by Clint Jordan and to the cabin used by the Klu Klux Klan, which is where the killing of Jim Upter took place. So, Mr. Bitterman, Mr. Mailer and I would appreciate your office getting such a letter written and delivered to Sheriff Clark."

Mr. Bitterman looked back at Nancy and said, "Nancy, please see that such a letter is written and delivered to Sheriff Clark, if you please."

Nancy didn't speak she simply nodded her head and hastily wrote notes into her shorthand pad.

"Okay, then, let's proceed to the civil issue first," Captain Borden said rubbing his hands together. "We studied all the documents about Clint Jordan's time in the cabin on the hill. There was really not much there. Since he lived there for almost thirteen years without anyone knowing it, there is very little about him during that time. The only ones that knew about him during that time kept everything very quiet and there are no documents at all about his stay on the hill. Everyone else believed him to be dead; killed in the war. It was only after the Klu Klux Klan episode that it was discovered he was still alive. And it was during the following trails in federal court that all of his time on the hill came to light."

Captain Borden stopped and took a small sip of water from a glass in front of him that he had filled earlier. Then, he continued, "As a result, what we know of Clint Jordan on the hill is from actual testimony from all of those involved in the cover up of his desertion from the army and his care and rearing of a young child know as Judy Cole, who we know today as Judy Cole Jackson. So, what do we know about what kind of improvements Clint Jordan made while living in the cabin on the hill with a young child? Well, Mr. Mailer and I went up on the hill and took a lot of pictures of the cabin and the surrounding area. The cabin today, around eight years after the fact, is in a completely dilapidated state. However, we could still see a lot of things Clint Jordan did so that he could live on that hill and support a young child. Things such as access to water, improved paths to and from the cabin, a wood burning fireplace, and many support structures. So, he did make a lot of improvements. They were simple but they were made."

Captain Borden looked around the table. "Are there any questions to this point?" He asked. No one spoke.

"Okay, then, I'll move on. Now as for the question of any heirs that Clint Jordan might have. Judy Cole Jackson is not a blood relative to Clint Jordan. She was also never adopted by him. She now lives with her natural birth mother, Bob Ann Jackson. She has been adopted by Jack Jackson, her step-father. Therefore, it seems that she would have little or no claim to any homestead awarded to Clint Jordan. Now, Clint has an ex-wife that gave him a natural son. She's his ex-wife because when they both went to prison; a divorce was granted to Ruth Jordan. As a result of that, she too can be eliminated as a possible heir. Okay, now we come to Dick Jordan. He is Clint Jordan's natural son and is alive and well today serving in the United States Marines. In our opinion, he is the only person that could possibly be an heir to anything that Clint Jordan might have."

Stopping again and looking around the table Captain Borden asked, "Again, I'll ask for questions?" Again no one spoke.

"Mr. Mailer and I aren't lawyers and don't pretend to know if Clint Jordan has any legal claim to a homestead on that hill or not. That's up to you, Mr. Bitterman, and your law office. In any case, Clint Jordan is serving a life sentence at hard labor in the Federal Prison at Fort Leavenworth, Kansas. He, himself, can't possibly claim any kind of homestead anywhere. The question is what about his legal son and heir, Dick Jordan. Mr. Mailer and I certainly can't answer that. But we do have a recommendation. We recommend that your law firm make an offer to Dick Jordan to sign a release of any possible claim for now or in the future to any homestead on that hill. By doing that, it will keep you out of court and save time and money. You probably could go to court and maybe easily win any challenge by Dick Jordan. But there's always that outside chance that a soft-hearted judge or maybe even a jury will rule for Dick Jordan. Mr. Mailer and I believe that everything would be easier and remove any outstanding problems if you simply made an offer to Dick Jordan to sign the release. The offer doesn't have to be big; just enough to get it by."

The Captain stopped talking, took another sip of water and sat down. Louis Mailer looked at him, smiled, and nodded his head in agreement.

Jacob Bitterman stood up again and looked around the table. "Excellent work, gentlemen," he said. "Lawson and I reached the same conclusion as you two did. But we did want to hear it from you personally. We have already put the plan into motion. Lawson is in the process of putting together the document needed to have Dick Jordan sign. It will be a very tight document from the legal standpoint. We will be offering Mr. Jordan three thousand dollars. Does that number sound right to you gentlemen?"

Both Louis and Captain Borden nodded in agreement.

"Good," Mr. Bitterman continued. "Now we only have to get in front of Mr. Jordan and present the document. And as I understand it, he is on duty somewhere in California. Is that correct?"

"Yes, Sir," Captain Borden answered, "that is correct. And as the report points out his exact location is at the Presidio Military Facility on the San Francisco Peninsula, San Francisco, California."

"Lawson," Mr. Bitterman said firmly, "you're on the point to get the document done and fly out to California and finish the deal by getting Mr. Jordan to sign and then transfer the money to him."

Lawson Levi looked up surprised. "Sir, you want me to fly out to California?"

"Is there a problem?" Mr. Bitterman asked mockingly.

"No, Sir," Lawson answered meekly.

"Good, then Nancy can get all the travel arrangements you may need."

Mr. Bitterman clapped his hands together loudly and smiled broadly. "Now that we have that issue out of the way, let's move on to the second issue. Will you take the floor again, Captain?" With that, Mr. Bitterman took his seat again.

Captain Borden stood again and quickly turned through several pages of the report. He found what he was searching for and placed his hand firmly on the page holding it open.

"The criminal issue was not quite so easy to come to a recommendation," the Captain said frowning. "Louis and I both decided that we couldn't solve the crime with the information we had available. So, what we decided to do was to frame the crime in the events of the time. We identified as many of the Klu Klux Klan members as we could. By identify, I mean only those we were one hundred percent sure of. But we both agree that whoever killed Jim Upter was surely one of the Klan members. Then, we set about eliminating the Klan members we knew were not involved in the killing."

Captain Borden lifted the report from the table and turned a couple of pages until he got the one he wanted. He put the report back down on the table and continued. "From testimony from Mary Collie, who talked to Lester Homes before he killed himself, we know there was a total of eight Klan members. Unfortunately, we only know two of 'em for sure. Of course, Jim Upter we know was the leader. And, also, from testimony from Mary Collie, we know that Lester Homes was one of 'em. But we also know that neither of these two men killed anyone. So, that leaves six others. We only have one other name that could possibly be one of the six; Harry Barnett. But we have no proof other than hearsay. That leaves five others that we have no clue as to who they might be. The other things we do know is that Jim Upter was killed just outside the cabin the Klan was using for meetings, and that he was killed with a long and wide bladed knife; most probably a large kitchen butcher knife. He was stabbed in the back. It looks as though he was walking away and the killer came up behind him. Unfortunately, Sheriff Clark removed the body before any crime scene photographs could be taken. As a result, all we have is the testimony of Sheriff Clark and Clint Jordan as to the disposition of the body."

Captain Borden paused for a moment and then pushed the report aside. He shrugged his shoulders and nodded toward Louis Mailer and said, "Louis and I believe that this crime will never be solved. The only recommendation that we can give is pretty much what I said at the start. We make the Klu Klux Klan event that happened in Coalville the center piece. That is what happened. The three murders that occurred as part of that event have never been resolved. Don't say *solved*, say *resolved*. And the murder of Jim Upter is just one of the three. That he was the only one killed on the hill need not be made an issue. That's our recommendation."

Everything was quiet for several long minutes. Then, Jacob Bitterman slowly stood. He looked around the table and then stopped at Louis Mailer. "And you're in agreement with everything the Captain has said?"

Louis sat up straight in his chair, cleared his throat and said, "Yes, Sir. I'm in complete agreement. I think Captain Borden has summed up the report as good as it could be done."

"I agree," Mr. Bitterman said nodding his head in the positive. "Then, that's how we'll approach it. The Jim Upter murder will be down played to be one of three murders that took place during an unfortunate series of events that took place during a Klu Klux Klan episode in Coalville some eight years ago. There will be no mention made of the fact that Mr. Upter was actually the only one killed on the hill. We won't hide this fact if ask, we just won't put it in any of our documents. Is everyone in agreement with this?"

Everyone around the table nodded their heads in agreement.

Jacob Bitterman began putting things back into his briefcase. "Okay, I guess we can close this meeting. Lawson, you need to get ready to leave for California. I want that part of this whole thing taken care of quickly. Nancy, please help Lawson with anything he needs for the trip." As he finished cleaning up the table in front of him, he looked over at Captain Borden and Louis Mailer. "I would say you two did a nice job and you'll be paid accordingly. But keep in mind that as things go forward with the State Park, I may need to call on you again. Because both the Dick Jordan and the homestead issue have a resolution and shouldn't trouble us again, but the Jim Upter murder is being handled with smoke and mirrors. Depending on how things proceed with the State, I may or may not need your services again. Do we all understand that?"

"I understand," Captain Borden said nodding his head.

"Yes, and so do I," Louis said simply.

In a few minutes everyone was gone and conference room four was once again empty, except for Nancy Caper. She took her time picking up her note pads and other material. She had taken two complete shorthand pads full of notes. Carefully she placed the pads in her bag. Once she was organized, she looked around the room once more and then walked to the door. She walked out of the room and pulled the door closed behind her. After closing the door, she leaned back against it looked up at the ceiling. There was no one else around to see the smile on her face.

CHAPTER SIXTY-ONE

Battle in the Sky

October 1941

By the time Dee got to the Officer's Club, it was almost empty. There were a few RAF pilots having beers but there was no one at the Eagle table. He was late because he had spent the last two hours at the Flight Surgeon's office at the hospital. There was a gash in his forehead just above his left eye. The surgeon had taken five stiches to close it up properly. Slowly, he walked over to the bar, or more-or-less staggered. The Sergeant tending bar was one of RAF ground crew.

Dee placed his hands on the bar and ordered. "I think I'll have a double scotch with a beer chaser, if you please, Sergeant."

While the Sergeant was getting his drinks, Dee lowered his head and gently fingered the bandage on his head. It hurt like hell. Soon the drinks were in front of him and he was reaching into his pocket for the money to pay. But the sergeant held up his hand to stop him. "Your money ain't no good here today, Sir," he said in a low voice. "Today was a bad one and everyone earned a drink today." He gave a quick little salute and moved on down the bar.

He was right, today was a bad one. The worst in Dee's two months with the Eagle Squadron. In fact, he had heard at the hospital that it was one of the worst days for the RAF since the Battle of Britain had started back in the summer of 1940. They had lost twenty-six Spitfires today; four of them from the Eagle Squadron. Today's mission had been an ambitious one. They had gone all the way to the French coast in hopes of drawing out the German fighters all along the channel coast line. That had worked but they also drew out a swarm of fighters from farther inland away from the coast. Among these fighters from the inland bases was the German fighter the Focke-Wulf FW-190. This fighter had been seen off and on since August, but now the latest version was coming out in full force. All RAF pilots had been briefed on it but no briefing could substitute for the real thing. And the real thing was a fearful airplane. It could outclass anything the RAF was flying now. Gone were the days when the Spitfire pilot could reach for high altitude and out maneuver the ME-109. They couldn't out maneuver the FW-190. As a result, the mission ran into trouble immediately. A hailstorm of FW-190 came at the unprepared RAF pilots.

Dee had gotten firsthand experience in combat with a FW-190. The dogfight had only been engaged for a few minutes when one got on his tail. He tried to out climb it and engage it at a higher altitude but the FW-190 stayed with him all the way. When Dee tried to roll out of a sharp turn the FW-190 was right there and cut loose with all its guns. The bullets hit all along his Spitfire's fuselage and then blew off his canopy. One of the bullets grazed his flight helmet and gashed his forehead. Blood flowed freely down into his left eye. He couldn't see for the blood and the cold wind hitting him in the face. In desperation, he kicked his plane over and went into a power dive. The FW-190 stayed right with him and was about to finish him off, when two Eagles from another squad came to his rescue. They engaged the FW-190 and freed him. Dee took his plane all the way down to about a hundred feet from the ground and skimmed the trees until he reached the channel. Then, he gained a little altitude and gunned his way back to base.

Dee's wasn't the only plane shot up badly. In addition to losing twenty-six planes, they had another twenty shot up so badly they barely got back to base. It truly was a bad day.

Dee took his beer and scotch and walked over to the empty Eagle table and sat down. He inhaled deeply and slugged the scotch down and followed it with a deep draw on his beer. Then, he exhaled and slummed back in his chair. He was about to signal the bar tender for another round, when he saw Captain Willis walking towards him. The Captain still had his flight suit on and was carrying his helmet in one hand and a pint of beer in the other. He looked very, very tired. As he approached the table, he threw his helmet into a nearby chair and flopped down next to Dee.

"I see you're still alive, Collie," he said as he took a draw on his beer.

"Thanks to a couple of Eagles from the Tiger squad. They got me out of a very bad situation just in time. A son-of-a-bitchin' one-ninety had me cold. I mean I was dead when they came divin' in to get 'im off my ass."

"I guess a lot of that was goin' on," the Captain said. Then, looking at the bandage on Dee's head, he asked, "How's the head?"

Dee tapped the bandage with his forefinger and said, "Five stiches and a possible concussion. Outside of that, I guess all my parts are still workin'. However, I can't say the same for my plane. It's shot all to hell and back."

Captain Willis signaled the bar tender and pointed to Dee and himself for another round. "You know," he said, "we were actually pretty damn lucky."

Dee looked at Captain Willis in surprise. "How could anythin' that happened out there today be construed as lucky?"

"Well, the Krauts have lost a lot of good pilots to us since last year, and now their losin' more good pilots on the Russian front. Did you ever wonder how bad this mission would have been if they could've had experienced veteran pilots to put in those one-nineties? Why, this bad mission could've been a disaster!"

Dee sat up straight in his chair just as the drinks arrived. The Sergeant put the drinks down and turned around and left before Captain Willis could pay. Captain Willis smiled and said, "He can't keep givin' us free drinks. He'll get in trouble."

"So what do we do?" Dee asked seriously. "What can we do?"

"Well, I'm just a lowly Captain but it's easy to see that the Brits have been fightin' a defensive war for almost two years now. They've had to. They had no choice, and maybe they still don't. But today we went out on an offensive mission and got our butts handed to us. There's got to be better planning if we're goin' on offensive missions. We've got to have new and better tactics to beat the one-ninety."

Dee slugged down his new scotch and chased it was a big draw on his beer. "Well, Captain," he said as he stood up, "I'd like to hear all of this good news, but I need to go out and check with the ground crew and see just how long it's goin' to take to get me back in the air."

Captain Willis signaled for Dee to sit back down. "Sit down, Collie," he said softly, "I got somethin' else to tell you."

By all accounts, Dee was still a rookie. He had only been flying missions for two months. But he could tell when something was wrong. He knew something was coming his way and he wasn't going to like it. "What's up, Skipper?" He asked as he slowly sank back down into his chair.

"Let's see," the Captain started, "you got two kills in August, then three in September. That gave you five makin' you an Ace. Now, you have three more this month. That's a total of eight kills. You're an Ace with three."

"Why are you goin' over stuff we already know? So, I'm an Ace with three. A lot of guys are Aces. What're you tryin' to tell me, Skipper?"

Captain Willis took a deep breath and looked hard at Dee. "I'm goin' to have to ground you for a while, Collie," he said with his command voice. "For two weeks to be exact."

"Why?" Dee asked. He struggled to find something else to say. But, in the end, he could only repeat himself, "Why?"

"The Doc says you'll need at least a week for that head wound to get well enough for you to fly. And your plane is just about done for. I'm goin' to have it moved over for spare parts. When you get back, in two weeks, we'll have a new plane for you; one of the upgraded fives. We'll be goin' to the six early next year and this one will be a proto type."

"But, Skipper, why me? Lots of guys are in the same boat as me."

"Truth is you got eight kills in two months and you're in the Eagle Squadron. You're big news back home." Laughing, he said, "We'd like to keep you alive for just a little longer." Then, turning serious, he said flatly, "You nearly bought it today. You need some time off. Go sightseeing. Go chase girls. Go do anything, just get out of here for two weeks."

"I can't chase girls," Dee replied smiling. "I promised my girl back home."

"Her name's Sue Ann isn't it?"

"Yeah, that's her."

The Captain stood up and finished his beer. "Come by the Op's building and I'll have your leave papers ready. Go have some fun, Collie. Because when you get back, it's goin' to be tough. I mean really tough. There're somethings comin' that I can't tell you about at this time. Just trust me that they involve you. Can you just trust me?"

"Trustin' you has never been a problem, and it never will."

"Good. I'll see at the Op's building."

With that the Captain slowly walked out of the Officer's Club. Dee watched him go. He hung his head. If anyone needed a break it was the Captain. Dee wanted to help him but he didn't know how except to follow his orders. So, Dee finished his beer and left the Officer's Club. As he walked he thought a lot could happen in two weeks.

CHAPTER SIXTY-TWO

Sue Ann's News

November 1941

It was Saturday, the weekend before Thanksgiving and Mary Collie was sitting in her living room working on Dee's scrape book. Dee had become a minor celebrity in and around the East Texas area and even up around Dallas. The Dallas Time Herald followed his exploits each time he recorded another German plane shot down. The latest headline read, "Collie Gets Number Nine". Many times the news reports used the word, "Kill", but Mary preferred, "Shot Down".

It was very quiet around the house these days. It appeared that at Thanksgiving there would only be Mary and James. Dee was in England and Cherrie was staying at Baylor to get extra hours so she could graduate early. She wanted to be out of Baylor by the middle of May so she could prepare for her wedding in June. Ruth Jordan said that she might come but she was worried about Dick and didn't want to be a wet blanket. Mary thought that was silly because who could be more worried than her. In any case, this Thanksgiving was going to be a lonely one. Adding to the gloomy atmosphere was the weather. It was cloudy, windy, cold and grey outside. Mary glanced out the window and was thankful that, at least, it wasn't raining yet.

As Mary was pasting the last entry into Dee's scrape book, a soft knock came at the front door. She closed the scrape book and pressed down on it to make sure the pages didn't wrinkle. The knock came again so Mary hurried her pace to the door. She couldn't help wondering who it could be. No one was expected.

She opened the door and there to her surprise stood Sue Ann Barnett. "Good Heavens," she said truly surprised, "Sue Ann. This is a nice surprise. Please come in out of that awful weather." Mary stood back to let Sue Ann walk through the door. Mary guided her to the living room couch and watched her sit down. She noticed that Sue Ann didn't remove her long black overcoat before she sat down. "What brings you to Coalville? Are you visiting your family?"

Sue Ann was slow to speak and the silence was becoming uncomfortable. Finally, Sue Ann said, "Yes, I'm visitin' my family. I got home last night after work. Bill picked me up at my house and brought me home. He's really has been nice doin' all that drivin' just to help me." She stopped talking and sat with her hands in her lap. She lowered her head and wrung her hands nervously.

Mary could easily see that Sue Ann was very nervous and obviously wanted to say something to her but didn't know how. Therefore, Mary started the conversation very carefully. "Sue Ann, is there somethin' you wanted to talk to me about? Is there somethin' I can help you with?"

Sue Ann looked up at Mary who was still standing. "Could you please sit down, Mrs. Collie? I would like to get some advice from you."

Mary stepped back and sat down in the easy chair across from the couch. "You want some advice from me? Sue Ann, I don't know what kind of advice I could possibly give you but I'll certainly listen and try."

"It has to do with Dee," Sue Ann said. She said it as though she were forcing it out of her mouth. "I don't know how to say this so it sounds right. I'm not good at this. I hope you don't think I'm stupid or somethin'."

Mary was taken aback. "Why on earth would you think that I could possibly think that you're stupid?"

Sue Ann waved her hands about and stood up. "No, no, that was the wrong thing to say!" She exclaimed. She stood there for a moment and seemed to get her composure back. "You know Dee once told me that sometimes there's only one way to do things. I guess this is one of those times." Having said that, she unbuttoned her coat and slipped it off. She tossed it onto the couch and turned to face Mary.

Mary could see instantly that Sue Ann was pregnant. She wasn't big yet but she was definitely showing. She was wearing a loose fitting blouse to help hide her condition.

"As you can see I'm pregnant. I'm almost five months along."

"Yes, I can see that," Mary said carefully. "Because you've come to me, I'm assuming that the baby is Dee's?"

"Yes, the baby is Dee's."

"You're sure?" Mary wanted the words back the second she said them. The hurt in Sue Ann's eyes told her the truth.

Sue Ann lowered her head and put her hands behind her back. Then, without looking up she stammered, "Yes, I'm sure. Mrs. Collie, Dee is the only man I've been with. I love him. I'm sorry you doubt me, but it's the truth."

Mary stood up and went over to Sue Ann and put her hand under her chin and lifted her head. "No," she said softly, almost a whisper, "I'm the one who's sorry. I've known you all your life and it was a stupid thing for me to say. Can you please forgive me?"

Sue Ann jumped at Mary and threw her arms around her. "Of course, I forgive you. I love you." She buried her face in Mary's breast and cried.

<hr />

It was almost thirty minutes before the two women could stop crying and could get themselves under control. Once again, it was Mary who finally asked the question to get the conversation started again. "Well, I guess there are a hundred things we need to talk about, but where would you like to start?"

Sue Ann now seemed excited to talk now that the ice had been broken. "The main thing now is Dee," she said. "I don't know what I should do. I want to tell him but I'm afraid it'll distract him. I don't want him to be worryin' about me and a baby. He has to keep his mind on what he's doin'. I'm afraid a distraction like this could get him killed! Please, can you tell me what I should do?"

The two women were sitting side by side on the couch. Mary patted Sue Ann on the shoulder and said, "Well, the first thing we're goin' to do is get James involved. He's Dee's father and he needs to know all of this and I refuse to make any kind of decision without talkin' to him first. Is that fair enough?"

Sue Ann nodded her head and said, "Yes, Ma'am. I have no problem with that at all."

"Could we stop the *Ma'am* and the *Mrs. Collie* stuff? From now on it'll be Mary or Mother; I'll answer to either one."

"Yes, Ma'am," Sue Ann started before she caught herself. "I mean *Mom*."

"Good, I'll call James now and get him home."

⊰⊱

James hurried home but it still took him a half hour to get Ruth and the store organized before he left. All James had been told was that it was important for him to come home right away. It wasn't an emergency but he needed to hurry. When he arrived at home, the women were waiting in the kitchen drinking ice tea. He was surprised to see Sue Ann, but he made no comment about it.

"Okay, here I am. What's goin' on?" He asked as he seated himself at the kitchen table.

Over the next ten minutes, Mary calmly explained the entire situation to James. He listened without interrupting. His face showed worry, but there were no signs of anger. Mary finished by saying, "That's where we are now. We need to know if it's wise to inform Dee he has a baby on the way. Sue Ann is afraid it might affect how he handles himself in combat. None of us wants that. What are your thoughts?"

James didn't say anything. He got up from the kitchen table walked over to the cabinet over the sink. He opened it and reached far into the back. After some groping around, he came out with a bottle of Jack Daniel's whiskey. He turned and started for the ice box but Mary was already standing there with a glass of ice. She had a small smile on her face. Taking the glass from her hand, he poured a large drink; more than half the glass. He sat back down and took a long, deep sip of whisky.

"Dee has to be told," he said simply. "How he handles it is his business, but he has to be told. A man needs to know what is goin' on in his family so he can take what he believes to be the best course." He paused and looked directly at Sue Ann. "That's how I see it, Sue Ann."

"Then, that's how we'll do it. I'll get a letter off to him today. I'll pay extra to send it airmail. And thank you Mr. Collie for not bein' angry with me. I know you and Mary are hurt. Dee and I both would've preferred this happenin' a different way. But it didn't. We love each other and it would've happened anyway, but not like this. I wish I could say I would've done things differently, but I wouldn't. Those two days alone with Dee will live in my heart 'til the day I die."

James nodded his head and took another deep drink. He was reaching for the bottle, but Mary was already pouring him a fresh drink. "What about marriage?" He asked quietly. He didn't address the question to anyone in particular.

"I'm thinkin' Christmas," Mary said firmly. "In Dee's last letter to me, which I think was last week; he mentioned that his Group Commander had already approved a two weeks furlough for him at Christmas. He said he wasn't sure he was goin' to take it because he just had a two week furlough in late October and the first of this month. And he didn't want the other guys to have to cover for him again. But I'm sure this'll change his thinkin' along those lines."

"Christmas would be fine with me," Sue Ann said.

"Then, that's it," James said firmly, "Christmas it is. Now, Sue Ann, what about your family? Do they know all of this?"

Sue Ann took a deep breath and folded her arms across her breast. "No," she said loudly, "they don't. Except for Bill, he knows. I haven't told Mom or Dad yet. I still have that to do, which reminds me I need to call Bill to come pick me up. He's waitin' for my call over at his friend Clay's house. I told him I didn't know how it would go here so he could expect a call at any time. Since it's been so long, he probably knows it went well."

"Do you need any help talkin' to them from us?" Mary asked.

"No, it's my problem to handle. Bill will be with me and he's been a big support for me. I don't know what I'd do without him."

"Well, no matter how it goes, there are a few things I'll insist on," James said in a hard voice. "Tell me, how long are they goin' to let you keep workin'?"

"They told me I couldn't work passed my sixth month. Then, I have to take unpaid leave. But because they've spent so much time and money trainin' me they'll keep my job open and I can go back to work three months after the baby is born."

"Okay, the first thing I insist on is that when you leave your job you come here and live with us. You can take Dee's room."

"But---," Sue Ann started.

"No, buts," James interrupted her, "that's how it's goin' to happen. And the second thing I insist on is that you're to have Thanksgiving dinner with me and Mary; your brother is welcome to. And there'll be no buts about that either. Lastly, I'm concerned about how your Dad is goin' to react to that baby bein' a Collie. Tell me the truth, Sue Ann; what do you expect to happen when you tell 'im?"

Sue Ann's face took on a sad but serious look. "I expect to be kicked out of the family. I will always have Bill. As far as my Mom goes, how far she'll go along with Dad, I don't know."

"Your Mom's name is Sally isn't it?" Mary asked.

"Yes."

"Would you like for me to talk with her?" Mary pressed.

Sue Ann thought for a short moment and then said, "No, let me see how it all goes. Like I said Bill will be with me. I'll come by and let you know how it worked out before Bill takes me back to Dallas. But thank you for the thought." Then after a short pause she said,

"If I could use your phone, I guess I better call Bill. I need to get home and get it over with."

"Sure, you know where it is," Mary said.

As Sue Ann started into the living room to use the phone, James called after her, "Remember, we're your family now to. Anythin' you need, you let us know. And promise me you'll get that letter to Dee off as quick as you can."

Sue Ann turned back and pointed to James. "That letter will be written tonight and mailed first thing Monday mornin'. You have my word on it." With that, Sue Ann started dialing.

Mary lifted James' whisky glass from his hand. It was still half full from her earlier refill. She put it to her lips and took a small sip. "What the hell," she laughed and turned the glass up and took a big swallow. The whisky took her breath away at first. But then it settled in just fine. She reached over and put her hand on James' shoulder and gave it a good pat. "Well, James," she said happily, "I guess the old house won't be so empty this Thanksgiving after all. I guess it won't be as lonely as I thought it would. How about that, James? Or should I say how about that, Grand-pa James?" She laughed out loud at her joke and finished off the glass of whisky.

CHAPTER SIXTY-THREE

WAR

December 7, 1941

It was almost seven PM as Dee sat in the ready room in full flight gear. His squad had the alert duty for the evening and up until midnight, although it was highly unlikely that they would pursue any enemy aircraft in the dark. All the pilots of Fox Squad milled around the ready room trying to keep busy and not get bored. Dee found him a nice quiet corner and took out Sue Ann's letter for what seemed like the hundredth time. The letter had arrived three days ago and Dee had read it and reread it over and over. It was the letter telling him he was to be a father. It also went into her visit with his parents and the invite to Thanksgiving dinner. It went on to talk about many things, but the thing that kept jumping out at Dee was the fact that he was going to be a father. To say he was shocked would be putting it mildly. With that, came the realization that wedding plans were being made for this Christmas. There is nothing more he wanted than to marry Sue Ann, but this is not the way he envisioned it. But it would be okay; he would make it okay. His problem now would be to get another two week furlough at Christmas. He had just finished a forced furlough a week earlier. Now he would be asking the Group Commander for another one so he could get married. Even though he had been given tentative approval for Christmas leave some time ago, things change in war. Plus, he felt somewhat guilt having his mates cover for him again so soon. He already carried the burden of becoming a Double-Ace.

Upon coming back from his forced furlough, he got his new plane; an upgraded Mk V and a proto type of the new Mk VI. It was a good plane and an improvement, but Dee still didn't think it could outperform the FW-190. But it did allow him to get his tenth kill making him a Double-Ace.

Suddenly the alert siren sounded and everyone jumped to their feet. Dee stuffed the letter back into his flight jacket and started pulling on his flight helmet. Everyone had assumed it was a scramble and had started gearing up and running for the ready room door. Then, without warning, the alert siren stopped and the Group Commander in person came through the door. Everyone stopped and went to attention.

The Group Commander waved his hand and said, "As you were. Everyone relax and gear down. Then, take a seat, and listen up."

There was a lot milling around as pilots removed their helmets and found a seat. Dee went back to his quiet corner and sat back down.

"I have some important news for everyone; especially our Eagle Squadron mates," he said seriously. He moved near the front of the room so everyone could see him and his words would carry across the room. He took a chair from one of the tables and climbed up and stood on it. Two lower ranking officers hurried to stand on either side of him. He put his hands in his pockets and then continued, "I have just received word from our American liaisons that the American Naval Base in Hawaii is under attack by naval and air forces of the Empire of Japan as we speak."

He paused while a huge murmur ran across room, and members of the Eagle Squadron shot to their feet. He held up his hands for quiet. "At this time," he went on, "we don't know very much. But we do know that the attack is doing a lot of damage to the Naval Base itself and many of the surrounding airfields. Civilian areas in the cities have also been hit. The fear is that the death toll will be high." He paused again but this time the room was quiet as the RAF pilots looked at their Eagle Squadron mates.

"By the order of the Air Command, as of now, all members of the Eagle Squadron will stand down until farther orders. Return to your quarters until you are contacted by a member of our administrative staff." He took his hands out of his pockets and took a deep breath let it out like a sigh. Then said, "I can't speak officially, but it appears that this will surely mean the United States will enter the war. Therefore the status of the Eagle Squadron is in doubt at this moment. But no matter how it turns out, all of us in the RAF and the entirety of Britain for that matter, thank you and wish you God speed where ever you have to go and for whatever you may have to do."

He stepped down from the chair, stood at stiff attention, and presented a smart and hard salute. Then, turned and hurried to the door followed by the two junior officers.

⸻⬥⸻

It was almost one-thirty PM in Lawrence, Kansas as Judy Jackson put on her prettiest dress. She was to meet Jimmy at three PM for a nice late lunch. He had kept his word and got her on the Mobil payroll and it had paid off. The last two months she had trained and trained on the airplane which now was officially name the "Mobil Bullet". She ran the qualifying course every chance she got. She and the Mobil Bullet were becoming one. She now knew how the plane would react to almost any situation. The feeling in the sky as the plane responded to her every whim was euphoric. As things stood today, she had knocked almost seven minutes off of her original qualifying run. Her confidence in the race was sky high. With the race being only three days away, she felt she could relax a little and enjoy herself with a nice afternoon with Jimmy. She enjoyed their time together as their relationship had grown and they were now certainly more than just friends.

She was primping before the mirror in the motel bathroom, when a loud knock came at her motel room door. She turned from the mirror with a puzzled looked as she didn't expect anyone. Very few people knew about her motel room in Lawrence, so she was surprised anyone would be knocking on her door. Maybe it's the motel manager she thought. Maybe something is wrong. The knock came again and louder this time. She stopped her primping and hurried for the door. She opened the door to find Jimmy standing there looking all excited.

"What're you doin' here?" She asked surprised. "I was supposed to meet you at three."

"Haven't you been listing to the radio at all?" He shouted.

"No. Why?"

"For God's sake, Judy, the Jap's have bombed Pearl Harbor. We're at war!"

She just stood there and stared at him. He pushed by her and went into the motel room. She stood there for a minute, then turned and looked at him in amazement. "What? Who bombed where?" She stammered.

"The Jap's bombed Pearl Harbor. If you don't know, it's a Naval Base in Hawaii. There've been hundreds killed maybe thousands."

She slammed the motel room door closed and walked over and flopped down on the bed. "Is this a joke?" She asked. "Are you pullin' some kind of gag before the race? Because if you are, I'm not laughin' and this is goin' to really piss me off."

"You've got to be bullshitin' me, Judy," he said in frustration. "Do you actually think I'd pull something like this? Listen to me, please! *WE—ARE—AT--WAR!*"

She could see he was not joking with her. She gathered all her thoughts but all she could say was, "Damn!"

"Okay, are you dressed enough to go? Can we get outa here?"

"Yeah, I guess so. But where're we goin'?"

"Somewhere where we can get all the current news," he said. "I'm not sure where but someplace. Come on let's go."

"Wait a minute," she yelled. "Wait just a damn minute. What about the race? What's goin' to happen to the race?"

"I'm just guessing here, but I don't think the race is going to happen. I think there's going to be higher issues, Judy."

"No, no, no, they can't call off the race," she cried. "I've worked so hard; so Goddamn hard."

He went over and sat down beside her on the bed. He took her by the shoulders and shook her and then pulled her to him. "There're about thirty-nine other women in the same boat as you," he whispered in her ear. "We just have to wait and see how things shake out. But whatever happens, I'll be with you all the way. I won't let you down."

She put her arms around him and buried her face in his shoulder. "I'm sorry," she breathed, "I'm embarrassin' myself." She pushed away from him and stood up. There were no tears in her eyes just anger on her face. "Okay," she said straightening her pretty dress, "let's go find some news."

They got up to leave but she stopped him short of the door. She put her finger in his chest and said with dedication, "But those son-of-a-bitchin' Japs have made one big mistake. Their messin' with Judy Cole Jackson and I swear to you there'll be hell for them to pay. I do mean hell to pay."

It was Sunday and Clint was lying in his bunk as usual. As nearly always, he opted not to go out into the court yard and soak up the sun. But since it was December and there was no sun to soak up it made little difference. But unlike the summer months, he was wearing a long sleeve work shirt and a pair of heavy pants. He even had a pair of heavy socks on against the cool of the afternoon. The weekend had been uneventful and he was trying to concentrate on some things he could accomplish over the next several years while wasting away in this incredible shit hole. He had acquired a pencil and paper so he could write things down, but decided against it because he considered writing things down to be too dangerous. So, he kept things in his head. However, that did little good because he never came up with anything worth writing down or remembering.

He was working on a new idea when the alarm horn started to blow. At the same time, the loud speaker system began blaring, "Lock Down. Lock Down." All of this usually indicated that someone was trying to escape. The Lock Down procedure began to be put in place, as the guards started gathering all the inmates from where ever they were, mostly the court yard, and hustling them to their cells. As the cells filled, the sound of the cell doors sliding shut and locking could be heard. The alarm horn finally stopped blowing and the loud speaker finally fell silent. The guards walked up and down the cell block making sure all the inmates were present and all were secured. Then, they took their positions at intervals along the cell block and waited.

Clint knew the guard positioned just outside his cell. "Hey, Duncan," he whispered, "what's up?"

"I don't know," he whispered back. "Be quiet, Clint, or we'll be in trouble."

"Did someone make a break for it?"

"I said be quiet, Clint, or I'll bop you with my stick."

Several minutes passed and then the loud speaker system came back to life. "This is the Warden speaking," the voice on the speaker said. "About an hour ago, the Naval Base at Pearl Harbor in Hawaii was attacked and bombed by Japanese forces. The loss of life has been very heavy. As of yet, we don't know the extent of the attack. Therefore, we will remain in Lock Down until we ascertain the level of danger. Until farther notice, food will be delivered to your cell. No one except authorized personnel will be allowed outside their cell. Needless to say, this attack is an act of war and it could be presumed that as of now the United States of America is in a state of war with the Japanese Empire. That is all we have at this point. We will keep you informed as things develop."

The speaker system fell silent.

Clint leaned against his cell bars. "Well, I'll be damned," he whispered. "Hey, Duncan, I didn't even know the Japs were pissed at us. Did you?"

Duncan turned around and looked into Clint's cell. "Yeah, I knew they were pissed," he said. "And if you'd read a little more you'd know it to."

"How long do ya think we'll be in Lock Down?" Clint asked.

"Well," Duncan smiled, "I don't know. But if I was you, I'd try and get comfortable."

It was almost one PM when James, Mary, and Sue Ann walked through the door and into the house. They had just come from church. Sue Ann was with them because the decision had been made not to wait any longer about Sue Ann leaving her job at Chance Vault. She took her leave right after Thanksgiving. Sue Ann's father had reacted just about as everyone thought he would about her pregnancy. He had gone into tirade of anger and abuse. Billy Bob had stepped in and gotten Sue Ann out of the house. Even as they left, Harry Barnett could be heard screaming vile accusations and cursing loudly. Billy Bob had taken Sue Ann back to the Collie house where she stayed until James drove her back to Dallas and her job. It was during that drive to Dallas that James convinced Sue Ann to take her leave immediately and move in with them. That Monday she spoke with her manager on the assembly line and turned in her leave. Everyone at Chance Vault had been very understanding. They gave her leave and promised to have her job available three months after delivering the baby.

Thanksgiving had gone beautifully. Mary had cooked a large dinner with the help of Sue Ann and Ruth Jordan, who had decided that it was better to be with friends than to be alone. Billy Bob had also come. Mary had been delighted to have everyone in her home. They had had the blessing and James had asked God to please watch over Dee and Dick. All in all, it had been a blessed Thanksgiving.

"Boy, that preacher they sent us from Athens was really long winded," James commented as he went to the kitchen. "Let's get these Sunday clothes off and dig up somethin' to eat. Do we still have any of that pie from Thanksgiving?"

"Nope, the pie is all gone," Sue Ann said, turning up the hall towards Dee's room where she had settled in.

"Well, there must be somethin' in here," he said, opening the ice box.

"Take it easy," Mary laughed, "I'll stir somethin' up. Just give a few minutes to change clothes."

A little later everyone had changed into their easy clothes and Mary had made some chicken salad sandwiches. Mary was working on Dee's scrape book and Sue Ann was writing another letter to Dee. James was reading the Sunday paper and, at the same time, trying to find some good music on the radio. That's when they got the news. James heard an excited newscaster and stopped to listen.

"Recapping," the newscaster said excitedly, "what we know at this point is that Air and Naval Forces of the Empire of Japan have attacked the American Naval Base at Pearl Harbor, Hawaii. Other American military installations such as airfields have also been attacked. Reports of heavy casualties are coming in. Honolulu has been hit as well as other surrounding cities and towns. Until more is known about the attack, officials in Washington are calling on the American people to remain calm. The President is schedule to speak later today as more facts come in. Stay tuned to this station for the current news as it becomes available. We now return you to the program in progress."

Music began coming from the radio again but stopped suddenly. Then, "God Bless America" began to play. It would play over and over again between news reports. James reached up turned the radio off. He looked at the two women who were in silent tears. He stood and walked to the front window and looked out. "Now it begins," he said in a sorrowful voice. "Death and destruction is comin'. We need to prepare for it. Dee will be transferred to either the Army Air Force or the Naval Air Force, and Dick will be one of the first to fight. We need to prepare."

Mary slowly got to her feet and walked over to James. "I'll try and call Cherrie at Baylor. She's probably losin' her mind about now."

"No," James said quickly. "We need to keep the line clear. She'll surely try and call us. Plus, there may be others tryin' to get hold of us. I think it would be better for now to stay off the phone and let calls come in."

"You're probably right," she said. "I guess waitin' is about all we can do now."

Mary turned to speak to Sue Ann, but she had run to Dee's room and was lying on the bed sobbing quietly.

⋗⬥⬥⬥⬤

It was just after eleven AM on Sunday morning as Dick Jordan lay on his bunk in the Officer's Quarters at the Presidio Military Facility near San Francisco. He was studying the final contract between himself, the lone heir to Clint Jordan, and the law firm of Bitterman, Bitterman, and Levi. A Mr. Lawson Levi had given him the original version of the contract back in early September along with a check for three thousand dollars. The contract wanted Dick to relinquish any possible homestead claims to parts of Lonesome Hill. On the surface, Dick had no problems doing that, but he wanted to check out all the legal ramifications before signing the final document. So, he had a Marine lawyer from the JAG (Judge Advocate Office) go over everything to make sure what Dick was signing was exactly what he thought he was signing. Everything came back as expected, so he was now signing the final document to mail back to Bitterman, Bitterman, and Levi and he was endorsing the check to deposit into his military account. He considered the money an unexpected windfall. As soon as the check cleared, he would transfer the money to his Mother back in Texas with instructions to give half of it to Cheryl Collie to help with their upcoming wedding expenses.

As Dick was stuffing the signed document into an envelope, a bugle started blaring assembly. Assembly, Dick thought. Why in hell would anyone be blowing assembly on Sunday morning? He ran to the window and looked out. From his second story window, he looked down on the parade field. He saw men scrambling from their quarters onto the parade field. They were dragging their equipment with them including fire arms. Then it dawned on him that he needed to scramble to because he could see his training company running onto the field. It would be a hell of a deal for his company to be out there without their commander. He turned and ran to his locker pulling off his leisure uniform as he went. He quickly got his combat fatigues, helmet, and boots and started pulling them on as he went out the door. He didn't have time to stop by the armory and get his weapon. He would have to do that later. He raced out onto the field and found his company, Charlie Company, forming up. He immediately took charge and got his men into formation at their designated area. Dick ordered the men to sound off to make sure all were present.

When all of his men were in position and standing at attention, Dick's second in command, First Lieutenant Lonnie Hale, snapped a smart salute and reported, "Company all present and accounted for, Sir."

Dick returned the salute. "Very good, Lieutenant, return to your assigned position.

There were four companies in the training battalion; Alpha Company, Baker Company, Charlie Company, and Delta Company. All of the companies consisted only of officers; First Lieutenants and Second Lieutenants. The idea was for all the officers to be trained in amphibious warfare techniques and then be dispersed throughout the rest of the entire First Marine Division to train others. Each company was commanded by a captain. Charlie Company was commanded by Captain Dick Jordan.

When the bugle had stopped blaring and all four companies were organized and at attention on the parade field, the Battalion Commander Colonel Manfred Wolff stepped onto the parade platform in front of the entire battalion. His aide, Major Jason Fillmore, adjusted the microphone on the parade platform. Once the adjustment was complete, the Colonel stepped forward. "Stand at ease, gentlemen," he commanded. The entire battalion assumed the at ease position. "I know you're all wondering what the hell is goin' on this fine Sunday morning. Well, as I speak to you, the United States of America is under attack by the forces of the Empire of Japan."

The entire battalion retained their discipline and didn't speak out or move out of the position. They stood as assigned and waited. The Colonel continued, "At this moment, things are in confusion. But what we know is that the Naval Base at Pearl Harbor, Hawaii has been attacked and heavily bombed. Many of the Army Air Force airfields have been destroyed along with many of the aircraft. The city of Honolulu and some surrounding cities and towns have been hit. We know that the casualty count will high; military as well as civilian. At this time we don't know the extent of this attack or what its overall objective is. It could involve an attack on the American Pacific Coast. We don't know. But the Army is organizing a defense along our coast line."

He paused for a moment and looked out over all the young men standing before him. Then his voice took on a more stern and commanding tone as he continued, "Now, you may think that we will arm you and that you will join in the fight post haste. But that's not going to happen. The Army is in charge of the coast line defense. We have our own job to do. This Battalion was organized several months ago because many of our planners wanted to be prepared just in case something like this happened. Well, Gentlemen, here we are; it has happened. And, damn it, we will be prepared. The United States First Marine Division will be ready! We are going to double and triple our efforts. And all of you are going to go out to all the companies, battalions, and regiments in the First Marine Division and give them the benefit of your training in amphibious warfare. Once that is done, The United States Marines are going to go and hit the Japs where they live. On every island they occupy in the Pacific Ocean. And I mean right up to their home islands."

The Colonel waited for all he had said to sink in. He turned and whispered something to his aide and the aide nodded and then turned and hurried off the parade field. He stepped back up to the microphone. "For now, you are to return to your quarters and standby. Keep you weapons and all other equipment at the ready. Remain on high alert. But be prepared to resume your training exercises the first thing in the morning. Be prepared for long hours and hard work, because that's what's coming. Our schedule will change. Instead of getting you out into the division by next summer, you'll be out and into the division by March."

Then, he snapped to attention and commanded, "Company Commanders, take charge of you companies. Direct orders will follow." He saluted and quickly left the platform and hurried off the parade field and back to his headquarters.

Once the Colonel was gone, Dick turned to his men and said, "Okay, guys take a knee." All one hundred and ten men in his company knelt down. "You all heard the Colonel so I don't have to repeat anythin'. Get back to your quarters and stay ready. I expect the new trainin' orders will be comin' down tonight. This is real. There's no more time for any goofin' off or horse assin' around."

Dick put his hands on his hips and looked around at his men. "One last thing I want to leave with you," he said with a steady, hard and serious tone. "I want you to remember at all times who you are. I want you to always act like who you are. You're not just anybody. You *ARE* the United States First Marine Division. Don't you *EVER, EVER* forget it!

Captain Timothy Borden of the Texas Rangers and Sheriff Tom Clark of Coalville knew nothing of the Japanese attack on Pearl Harbor. They both had been up on Lonesome Hill since nine AM this fine Sunday morning. Captain Borden had requested the trip up on the hill and the Sheriff had agreed to go with him. The Captain wanted one last look around the murder scene before the construction began on the State Park. Captain Borden had already been made aware of the construction schedule. Of course this was December in East Texas, so the accuracy of the schedule would depend heavily on the weather. Right now, the weather was sunshiny and beautiful. As of now, the surveyors had started the work of laying out the access road that would run through the Collie and Jordan land. All the access rights from both families had been acquired several months ago. The heavy equipment was in place and waiting for the construction boss to give the go ahead. As for the hill itself, no heavy construction was scheduled until the access road was in place. However, cleanup crews to tear down all the old cabins and haul off the wood and debris were scheduled to start next week. They would also mark all the old pits that would require filling. That meant that any remaining evidence of the murder would be destroyed. Thus, Captain Borden asked Sheriff Clark for one last look around.

They had been browsing around the area for several hours. Captain Borden had gone through the old cabin used by the Klu Klux Klan with a fine toothed comb. The cabin was near collapse and he had to be careful as he move boards and kicked out window frames. He had found nothing of interest. The place where the murder had actually taken place still had some markings of the original crime scene that Sheriff Clark had setup those many years ago. With permission from the Sheriff, Captain Borden scraped around the crime scene with a small hand held garden rake. He dug up loose dirt around the scene. As he was down on his hands and knees scratching around, he turned up something that looked interesting. He sat down on the ground and began to dust it off. He spit on it and rubbed it with his fingers to clean it off. It was a bullet and a live round at that.

"Hey, Sheriff," he yelled. When there was no answer, he remained sitting on the ground but turned his head around to find the Sheriff. He saw the Sheriff approaching him from the old cabin. "Come take a look at this," he said as the Sheriff arrived.

"Whata ya got there?" The Sheriff asked as he knelt beside the Captain.

"I think we've got an unspent twenty-two hollow point," was the reply.

"Really, do you think it means anythin'?" the Sheriff asked.

"Well, I don't know," the Captain said still studying the bullet. "The victim was stabbed to death; not shot. But the killer could've had a gun as well. Does this ring any bells with you? I mean I guess a lot of folks have twenty-twos."

"Yeah, they do," the Sheriff said taking the bullet from the Captain. "But I could run this by the guns we've collected over the years and see if we get any kind of match."

"How many guns have you picked up over the last eight years?" The Captain inquired.

"Oh, I'd say we got about thirty to forty and I'm sure some of 'em are twenty-twos."

"Did you notice the scratches on the shell casing?" The Captain pointed out. "This bullet looks like it came from a pistol; not a rifle."

"You're right. So that cuts things down a little bit. At least ten or so of the guns we've collected are rifles or shotguns. That means maybe we only have about twenty to twenty-five to match against."

"But even if we find some twenty-twos, how can we know this bullet came from that gun since this bullet hasn't been fired?" The Captain asked.

"We can't," was the simple answer. "But we can find out where the twenty-two came from and that might give us a lead to follow."

"Sounds like a good starting point for some work," the Captain laughed.

"Yeah, it does. But that's your department. I'll let you have our inventory of guns and documentation that goes with 'em. Then, you can follow it as far as you want. I got other things to do."

"Fair enough," Captain Borden said getting to his feet and brushing off his backside. "We'll take the rest of the day off and

I'll come in Monday morning and start looking through your gun inventory."

"All of that's okay with me," the Sheriff said standing up. "Do you want me to keep this bullet at the office or do you want to keep it for your evidence inventory?"

"You keep it at your office," the Captain said waving his hand. "I don't really have any evidence inventory. This trip was just a last ditch try."

"Okay, it'll be there when you need it. We'll start an evidence inventory for this until the State Park thing blows over." The Sheriff put the bullet into his pants pocket.

"Good enough," the Captain said. "I guess we can start down now. It's after one. Sorry about keeping you from your family and church for so long."

"It's my job. Don't worry about it."

Both men started back down the hill. The path to and from the old cabin had been well marked during their earlier trips up the hill. Whereas it used to be almost impossible to find the cabin, it was an easy matter to follow the markings now. The Captain walked ahead of the Sheriff. The Sheriff followed along behind with his hand in his pocket fingering the little twenty-two bullet. The Captain couldn't see the grimmest on the Sheriff's face, because the Sheriff knew exactly where the little twenty-two bullet came from.

CHAPTER SIXTY-FOUR

Dee Transfers

December 1941

D ee stood outside the Group Commander's office nervously holding his hat in his hand. All the Eagle Squadron men were ordered to see the Group Commander in a one-on-one interview. Dee was the last one. He had been waiting in the outer office for over an hour. The longer he waited the more nervous he became. He knew what the meeting was about. It was about him leaving the Eagle Squadron for some American unit now that the United States was in the war. So, there was no real reason for him to be nervous. He had done nothing bad. Even as he stood in the Group Commander's outer office, nervous as he was, he still thought of Sue Ann's letter. He had it in the breast pocket of his uniform. He was never without it. He had visions of Sue Ann dancing in his head when a Sergeant walked up to him briskly and came to attention.

"The Group Commander will see you now, Sir," the Sergeant said. "Please follow me." The Sergeant did a sharp about turn and walked to the Commander's office door and opened it. Dee followed him and walked through the open door into the office.

Dee walked up to the Commander's desk and stood at ridged attention. "Flight Officer Daryl Collie reporting as ordered, Sir," he said.

The Group Commander sat behind a large desk that was covered in papers and documents. He leaned back in his large office chair and said, "Be at ease Flight Officer and please take a seat."

Dee sat down in a large chair directly across from the desk. He placed his hat in his lap and waited.

The Group Commander was very deliberate as he moved some documents around his desk. He looked at Dee just as deliberately. "I have three duties I must perform for each of you Eagle Squadron boys," he started in a very monotone voice. "First, I must make you aware that after we're finished here, the Sergeant will escort you down our long hall to two small offices. In one office is Lieutenant Commander William Keys of the United States Navy and in the other is Major Benjamin Franks of the United States Army Air Corp."

The Group Commander paused briefly and smiled. Then, he continued in the same monotone voice, "Since being with the RAF these four or five months, you ascertained an impressive record of ten victories making you a Double Ace. And, since the United States has very, very few experienced combat pilots, the two gentlemen I spoke of are very anxious to enlist you into their respective services. Therefore, as I said, when we're finished here you'll be required to interview with each of them. You are of course free to do what you will. You can join one of their services or you can just go home a civilian. The choice is yours. Now, my second duty is to give you these documents."

He handed Dee a packet of documents in a folder. "These documents are merely a formality that makes your separation from the RAF official. Keep these documents because they make it clear that your separation from the RAF is honorable and that you served honorably in the highest tradition of the RAF."

Dee took the documents and placed them underneath his hat. Then, the Group Commander stood up. "Now for my third duty, if you please Fight Officer Collie," he said, "could you please stand to attention?" Dee immediately stood up, placed his hat and documents in the chair, and came to a stiff attention. The Commander picked up a small razor blade from his desk and walked around to where Dee was standing. He walked around to Dee's left side and, with the razor blade, cut away the Eagle Squadron patch from his shoulder. When he was finished, he placed the small patch on the edge of his desk and walked around and returned to his seat. "Thank you, now, please stand easy."

Dee stood easy but couldn't help from looking down at the patch that had just been removed from his uniform. It was a simple small patch. All it said was, "Eagle Squadron". It was curved a little so that it fit perfectly on the left shoulder of this uniform jacket. It may have been a simple patch but it meant the world to Dee.

"Now," the Group Commander said in a much lighter tone of voice, "I have something to say that is not my duty." He stood up again and walked back around his desk and stood next to Dee. "Whatever may be your lot in life, or however men may see you in future years? However long you may live and however many children and grand-children you may have. No matter what may come or go, know this Daryl Collie; that at a time when civilized man faced one of his darkest hours you stood to be counted. When evil filled the skies with death, you were among men of courage." Then he reached down and picked up the small patch he had just removed from Dee's uniform jacket. He held it up for Dee to see and then handed it to him. "You keep this small patch as a badge of honor. For anytime you doubt yourself or find yourself in need of courage, you take this little patch out and look at it. And know that at one time you soared with Eagles."

———

As Dee followed the Sergeant down the hallway, he couldn't keep the dampness out of eyes. Although he knew it was the only thing he could do, he felt that somehow it was terribly wrong to leave the RAF while the battle still raged. When they finally reached the first office, they stopped and the Sergeant relaxed. He held out his hand to Dee and said, "If I may, Sir?"

"You may indeed, Sergeant," Dee replied grasping the Sergeant's hand and shaking strongly.

"Thank you, Sir, and God speed." With that the Sergeant turned quickly and started back up the hall.

Dee turned and faced the door to the office and dried his eyes and straightened up his uniform. He knocked gently on the door.

"Enter," was the quick response.

Dee opened the door and walked in. Sitting at a small desk was very tall man in the uniform of a Lieutenant Commander in the United States Navy. He had dark brown hair and matching eyes. His face was young but showed lines of experience. He stood up and held his hand out to Dee. "You must be Daryl Collie," he said politely.

"Yes, Sir, that would be me. And you must be Lieutenant Commander William Keys."

"Yes, I am. But just call me Mr. Keys for now. Please set down, Mr. Collie," he said pointing to the small and only other chair in the room. "I'm sorry but they didn't give us much space."

"It's not just you," Dee replied defensively, "it's the same for everyone."

"Yes, I understand."

"I was told this was a required interview," Dee said as he seated himself.

"Well, it is I guess but it's not a formal thing. I think the government wants to get a shot at you before you get home."

"Okay, but truthfully I've been givin' this a lot of thought since Pearl Harbor and I'm leanin' toward goin' with the Navy."

"Well, that's great. This is goin' to make me look good. But can I ask what's leanin' you towards the Navy?"

"Carrier based fighters."

"So, you like the idea of flyin' off a carrier?"

"Yes, I do."

"Well, you've come to the right place. That's about all we do right now. The Jap's got most of our battlewagons. Carriers are about all we got goin' for us right now."

"What about planes?" Dee asked. "Do we have any good ones?"

"The fact is, Mr. Collie, we don't have much of anything." Mr. Keys face took on an apologetic look. "We don't have anything like that Spitfire you've been flyin'. Not just us but the Army doesn't either." He fumbled with his pencil and then said enthusiastically, "But they're on the way! We're expectin' to have new planes by early 1943. But for now, all we have is the Grumman F2F Wildcat and it's no match for the Jap Zero. So, to be blunt, the best carrier based fighter plane we have is the Wildcat. And that's what we're goin' to have until early '43."

"Then how do you expect to win the skies over the Pacific?" Dee asked bluntly.

Mr. Keys looked him squarely in the eyes and said, "We expect to out fly 'em and out fight 'em with guys like you. We already got some good guys that are fightin' their guts out at Wake Island. They're outnumbered, out gunned, and their planes are outperformed, but they're still holdin' their own. They go up every day knowin' what the odds are; but they go anyway." Mr. Keys stopped talking because he could hear his own voice rising to an almost shout. "I'm sorry, Mr. Collie. I let it get away from me. I'm sorry." He lowered his head and snapped his pencil in half.

Dee reached into his pocket and felt the little Eagle Squadron patch. He rubbed it between his thumb and index finger. Then he looked up and smiled at Mr. Keys. "I like you Mr. Keys," he said. "You got some Spitfire in you. I think I may be your man. You send me out there and we'll out fight 'em. But you promise to send me those new planes so we can outperform 'em. When we can outperform 'em and out fly 'em, we'll do a little gettin' even for Pearl Harbor."

Mr. Keys stood up and held out his hand. Dee took it and they shook.

"What do I have to do to sign up?" Dee asked smiling.

"I can help you with that after you've talk to the Army next door. Rules have it that you've got to speak to both of us. Anyway, he might have a better deal for you."

"His deal isn't goin' to matter but I'll go talk with him as ordered."

"Okay, when you're done over there come back over here and we'll get you squared away the Navy way."

"I got three questions I need answerin' before I can do anythin'," Dee said seriously.

"Hit me with it. Whata ya need to know?"

"First, I gotta be home for Christmas. I'm gettin' married and I can't miss that. Second, what rank will I be? And last, where will I learn to fly off a carrier?"

"Those are easy. I was afraid they were goin' to be hard," Mr. Keys laughed. "Okay, first, you'll be home for Christmas. Your tour of duty won't start until January 12, 1942. Second, because you were an officer in the RAF, because of your experience, and your Double Ace status, you'll come onboard as a full Lieutenant. In case you're not up on Navy rank, that's equal to an Army Captain. And lastly, you'll report to Pensacola, Florida for carrier based training. Will all of that work for you?"

"It sure sounds like it. I'll be back in a couple of minutes. Save my place here."

"Your place is safe. You just be back. Don't let that Dog Face talk you into anything."

Dee left the office and stood outside the door. He took a deep breath and turned and walked into the office next door. He felt bad in a way, but the deal was done.

CHAPTER SIXTY-FIVE

Christmas

December 1941

It was nearly Christmas, December 22nd, and the world was at war. Death and destruction swept across the entire planet. But the Collie household was full of joy. Dee was home from England and, except for a small scar on his forehead; he was physically well and in good health. He came home wearing his new United States Navy uniform complete with lieutenant's bars. Cherrie was home from Baylor for Christmas break. Her eyes sparkled because Captain Dick Jordan was home on leave from the United States Marines. Sue Ann was alive and beautiful and very pregnant in her sixth month.

Mary was completely filled with joy and happiness. It had been hard finding everyone a place to sleep but Ruth Jordan solved that problem by allowing Dick and Cherrie to stay at her place. That freed up Cherrie's old room as Mary still insisted that Dee and Sue Ann have their own rooms. She knew it was old fashioned and beside the point at this stage, but it made her feel better about the coming wedding. The date for the wedding had been set for the evening of Christmas Eve, December 24th. Mary had pulled off a major deal by getting old Reverend Tuney to come down from Dallas to preside at the wedding. The old reverend was eighty-eight years old but was unbelievably excited about doing it. James had offered to drive up to Dallas and pick the reverend up and bring him to Coalville and then take him back, but Bob Ann Jackson and her family insisted on doing the transportation if they could be invited to the wedding.

They were promptly invited. The only downside was the weather; it was not cooperating. There was a mixture of sleet and freezing rain falling and it was expected to continue through Christmas.

Mary and Sue Ann were busy setting up wedding and Christmas decorations when Cherrie and Dick burst through the door. They were covered in sleet and were wet from freezing rain. They brushed themselves off and took off their coats. Everyone was laughing and talking at the same time.

"What on earth are you two doin' out in this God awful weather," Mary shouted over the laughing and greetings.

"Well, Mom, to be honest," Cherrie started with a flush on her face, "we got somethin' we want to ask everyone."

"Hey, Dick, how about a nice shot of Jack Black," Dee shouted from the kitchen.

"Hot damn, that would really hit the spot," Dick replied as he started to push his way through the crowd to the kitchen.

But he didn't get very far as Cherrie had a hold on his Marine jacket. "Hold on there, Marine," she said. "We got business to conduct first. Then you can drink."

Dick looked at Dee and shrugged, "And we're not even married yet."

"What's up?" James asked walking in from the kitchen.

Everyone went quiet and waited for Cherrie to speak.

"Okay, now everyone gather around," Cherrie said waving her arms. "Come on guys, put down your drinks."

Soon everyone was standing in a semicircle around Cherrie and Dick. Cherrie took a deep breath and started, "Dick and I have been talkin' and we've decided we don't want to wait until June to get married." She stopped talking as everyone looked at each other. "We'd like to ask my big brother and his beautiful fiancé if we could make it a double wedding."

It was quiet again until it dawned on everyone what Cherrie was asking. "Holy shit," Dee finally shouted. "Wow, wow, wow." He was jumping up and down and he ran over and picked Cherrie up and swung her around. He sat her back down across the room. Quickly he ran to Sue Ann and dropped down on his knees in front of her. "Can we Sue Ann? Can we please?" He pleaded.

Sue Ann put her hand on Dee's head and laughed, "Of course we can. It'll be beautiful."

Cherrie ran quickly to Sue Ann and positioned herself directly in front of her. Dee was still on his knees between them. Cherrie looked directly into Sue Ann's eyes and said, "Please Sue Ann, be truthful and honest. Neither Dick nor I would want to ruin a special day for you. It's your day you know."

Sue Ann took her hand off Dee's head and reached over and put it behind Cherrie's neck. Then she pulled Cherrie's head over to her and kissed her on the forehead. "It'll be our day, Sister," she said choking back tears. "It'll be our day."

"Hey, will you two open up a little and let me up," Dee shouted.

The girls backed up and let Dee get to his feet. He grabbed Sue Ann and was hugging her when his Mother spoke up. "I certainly don't want to be a wet blanket, but what does this mean for you education, Cherrie? Are you droppin' out of college?"

Dick quickly stepped forward. "It doesn't mean that at all, Mrs. Collie. I gave you my word and I'm keepin' it. The only thing that has changed is our marriage date and times when we can be together. Cherrie will finish school. She's already got a plan in place to graduate in the middle of May. We'll spend time together when we can. But Cherrie is goin' to finish school. That still stands and it stand like a rock."

Mary walked over and reached up and patted Dick softly on the cheek. "I don't know why I asked the question, Dick. I should've known better. I guess havin' a son-in-law and a daughter-in-law is goin' to be more complicated than I thought." Mary looked around and saw that James had retreated back to the kitchen. She clapped her hands loudly several times until everyone had stopped talking and was looking at her. Then, she craned her neck and looked into the kitchen, "Well, what about you, Old Man Collie? She asked. "Don't you have anythin' to say about all this? What do you think?"

"You're askin' me?" James asked mockingly.

"Yes, I'm askin' you!" Mary demanded.

"I think," James started, "that Dee was about to pour Dick a drink when all of this got started. I think we should finish that operation and get that poor Marine his drink. At least, that's my opinion on the matter."

"And a damn good opinion, Sir," said Dick hurrying into the kitchen to join James.

"Don't forget me," Dee said pushing his way through the women to get to the kitchen.

As with most family get-togethers, somehow the men end up in a bunch and the women end up in another bunch. This gathering was no different.

—⊙※⊙—

The evening had gone beautifully. James had built a nice roaring fire in the fireplace and everyone had gathered around it. There were no more clumps of men and women but just one group of loving family members; or soon to be family members. Mary couldn't have been happier. There was a soft murmur as the group talked with each other around the fire. They avoided the war news. America was having a rough time of it. They were losing on all fronts. They all knew that Dee and Dick would soon be deeply involved but no one mentioned it.

It was getting late, when a knock came at the front door. Dee got up and started for the door. "Mom, are you expectin' someone this late?" He asked.

"No," Mary said, "I can't imagine who would be out in this weather."

Dee continued on to the door and opened it. "Billy Bob Barnett," he breathed. Dee stepped back to give Billy Bob room to come in but Billy Bob remained standing at the door. "Come on in, Billy Bob," Dee said.

Billy Bob continued to stand nervously at the door without coming in. Sue Ann saw her brother and got up and joined Dee at the door. "Bill, come on in outa that weather," she said. "We have a nice fire goin' and drinks."

"Dee and Mrs. Collie, before I come in I need to tell you that I brought someone with me."

Now Mary got up and moved over and stood behind Sue Ann. "For Heaven sakes, Billy Bob, get in here and bring your date with you. My goodness, boy, cold air is gettin' in."

Billy Bob stood back and reached over and took the arm of a woman standing on the porch away from the door. He gently guided her in through the door. The woman walked slowly and kept her head down.

"Mom," Sue Ann cried. "Oh, Mom," Sue Ann repeated running over grabbing her Mother into her arms.

"Sally Barnett!" Mary exclaimed.

"I hope you don't mind, Mrs. Collie," Billy Bob said, "but she's here to beg you to allow her to come to her daughter's wedding."

Mary tried to get her breath. "Do I mind?" She almost shouted. "Here to beg me?" Mary was exasperated. "You two get in here so we can close the door!"

Billy Bob and his Mother came into the house and they were moved over by the fire. Sue Ann continued to cling to her Mother. Sally finally looked at Mary. "I know how you feel about me and Harry," she said. "I wish there was somethin' I could do about that, but there ain't. Harry won't come or have anythin' to do with Sue Ann. I've been Harry's wife for a long time and I've tried to be a good wife. But Sue Ann is my only daughter and she's goin' ta have my grand-child. And - - -." Sally couldn't finish her sentence as she began to sob heavily. Sue Ann pulled her Mother closer to her but Sally pulled away and continued to look directly at Mary. "And," she continued, "I want to be a part of my daughter's and my grand-child's lives. So, I'm beggin' you, Mary Collie, and I'll do it on my knees if need be, to allow me to be with my daughter at her weddin' to your son." She was crying openly now, "I'm beggin' you."

Mary returned Sally's gaze. "Sally Barnett, it disturbs me greatly that you think you have to beg me to come to your daughter's wedding to my son. There'll be no beggin' goin' on here. Billy Bob will be givin' Sue Ann away in place of her Father. You, Sally, will be the Maid of Honor and stand by your daughter. Will that do?"

Sally smiled through her tears. "That'll do fine. And thank you, Mary Collie."

⸎

That night as everyone in the Collie house was sound asleep, Sue Ann silently tip toed into Dee's room. She climbed into bed with him and snuggled up close to him. Dee was sleeping lightly so he awoke easily and put his arm round Sue Ann and pulled her to him.

"I think," Sue Ann whispered, "that I may be the happiest woman in the entire world. Your Mom was so great tonight. I've been told that bringin' a child into the world at this time is crazy. But our child is goin' to be a happy child; surrounded by so much love. I just may be the happiest woman in the world tonight."

⸎

Mary couldn't sleep and had been up tending the fire when she saw Sue Ann tip toe into Dee's room. She only smiled to herself and continued tending the fire.

⸎

Because of the weather, the weddings were moved from the evenings on Christmas Eve to noon. It was nothing short of a miracle that the entire Jackson family made it down from Dallas. Jack Jackson got himself, his wife Bob Ann, his two sons, Judy Cole Jackson and the Reverend Tuney all safely to Coalville with time to spare for the weddings.

428

Since the Collie house was not by any means a large mansion and because the number of people in attendance was small, everyone had some kind of role to play in both weddings.

The first wedding was Daryl Gene Collie and Sue Ann Barnett. Sue Ann's Mother, Sally Barnett, was her Maid of Honor. Cheryl Collie, Judy Jackson, Ruth Jordan, Bob Ann Jackson and Mary Collie acted as Bride's Maids. James Collie was Dee's best man and Jack Jackson and Dick Jordan acted as Daryl's groom's men. Sue Ann's brother, Billy Bob Barnett, gave the bride away.

The second wedding was Captain Dick Ray Jordan and Cheryl Jean Collie. Cheryl's Mother, Mary Collie, was her Maid of Honor. Sue Ann Collie, Bob Ann Jackson, Sally Barnett, and Judy Jackson acted as Bride's Maids. Daryl Collie was Dick's best man. Jack Jackson and Billy Bob Barnett acted as Dick's groom's men. Cheryl's Father, James Collie, gave the bride away.

The Reverend John Tuney, retired, presided over both weddings.

When both wedding were over, there was cake and ice cream and drinks for everyone. Each bride gave away the traditional garter to their respective husbands. Each bride also tossed the traditional bridal bouquet. Since Judy Jackson and Ruth Jordan were the only single women present they each got a bouquet.

And before anyone recognized it, it was over. The Jackson family wanted to get on the road early and try and be safely home before dark, because the sleet had stopped but the rain would began to freeze again when darkness came. So they loaded up and left to the heartfelt thanks of everyone involved. Dick and Cherrie invited Dee and Sue Ann over to Ruth's house for a quiet get together before each couple had to go their own way. Dee and Sue Ann accepted and left for Ruth's house shortly after Dick, Cherrie, and Ruth Jordan had gone. Billy Bob and Sally said their goodbyes and left for home. But before she left, Sally put her arms around Mary and hugged her and cried on her shoulder. The two women stood holding each other for a long period of time. In fact, Billy Bob had to gently separate the two and tell his Mother they needed to beat the weather also.

Then there were only two; Mary and James. Both of their children were married and with the ones they loved. Mary looked around the house and determined that it was not in too bad a shape. Ruth, Judy, Bob Ann, Sue Ann, and Cherrie had all jumped in and helped pick up and clean up. Most everything was done except for some small things that only Mary could do in her own house. As she was surveying everything, she saw James standing at his favorite spot at the front window. He was looking out at the grey Christmas Eve. She wondered what he was thinking.

"Hey, penny for your thoughts," she said lightly.

"Tomorrow will be Christmas," he said forlornly. "I guess Dee and Sue Ann will be here, but I wonder where Dick and Cherrie will be."

"I don't know," she answered simply.

"I guess we need to be thankful for all we have. But I know hard times are comin'," he said softly.

Mary walked up behind him and put her head against his back. "Well, those girls are goin' to have to do exactly what I did all those many years ago. Their goin' to have wait, worry, and pray for that man they love. I did it for you."

James turned around and took Mary in his arms. "You know I don't guess I ever gave you enough credit for what you had to go through. I mean, I've never had to do that until now. Waitin' while someone you treasure has to go into harm's way; worryin' and sweatin' it out. God, Mary how'd you do it."

"That's how I did it; with God," she whispered to him. "We're goin' to spend a lot of time in church; you and me. And we're goin' to hang on to each other." She reached up and patted him on the cheek. "Come on," she said, "Let's you and me go lay down together for a while." With that, she took him by the hand and led him down the hallway to their room.

CHAPTER SIXTY-SIX

More Delays

January 1942

The lockdown after the attack on Pearl Harbor lasted twenty-four hours. After that the inmates were allowed to go outside in the courtyard and take in the cold, misty and icy air. The good news was that they didn't have to work. It seemed that new work orders were being prepared. It was now January just after New Years and still no new work orders had come down. Maybe the powers that be had decided that making small rocks from big rocks was not productive in a wartime economy. In any case, the inmates hadn't been back to the rock quarry since the lockdown. A new routine of marching to meals and going into the courtyard for exercise had been established. Visitors were still allowed but Clint had not had any. He figured the coming of the war must have changed Judy's plans about coming to see him again before Christmas. In any event, he had had no visitors and no mail of any kind; legitimate or underground. The new routine had also changed the positioning of the guards. There were fewer guards along the cell block. Even during the marching to and from meals and to and from the courtyard, there were now about half the number of guards as there used to be. Even the friendly guard who used to stand near his cell door, Duncan, was not longer around. Clint wasn't sure why there were fewer guards now. His initial take on it was because of the war and the need for men in the military. But he didn't know for sure. He didn't really know anything for sure.

Clint had just returned from the afternoon exercise hour and was sitting on his bunk, when he saw the library trustee pushing his book cart down the cell block. This was a weekly occurrence; it happened every Monday. He stopped at each cell on Clint's side of the cell block to show his goods and to discuss them briefly. It was slow process, so Clint settled back in his bunk and waited. It took almost an hour for the trustee to reach Clint's cell. He stopped his cart and looked into the cell. Clint has his little light on his small desk turned on.

Clint knew the trustee, or at least he knew what he was called. Everyone called him Baron the Librarian, or most of the time, just Baron. He was a highly intelligent middle-aged guy severing a ten year sentence for beating an officer nearly to death. The sentence would have been worst except everyone knew the officer had started the fight and had even throw the first punch. But life in the army always favored the officers. However, the relatively light sentence reflected what everyone knew. Baron had served five years and was coming up for a Board Review in another month. As a result, he was on his best behavior.

"Hello, Clint," Baron said. "I can barely see you."

"Hey, Baron," Clint replied as he got off his bunk and went to the cell door. "What'd ya got this week?"

"Well, mostly old stuff. They still won't give me any newspapers so there's no war news except what they tell me, which ain't a lot."

Clint reached over to his desk and picked up a copy of Brave New World and handed it through the bars to Baron. "I finished this last week. It was interestin'. Thanks for recommendin' it to me. But this time I think I'd like somethin' that causes less brain strain."

Baron chuckled and carefully looked up and down the cell block. There was no longer a guard stationed near Clint's cell. One guard was at the cell block entrance and another at the other end. The guard at the other end would, on timed intervals, walk all the way up one side of the cell block and then down the other side; thus, earning him the title, "The Walking Guard". Currently The Walking Guard was standing still at the end of the cell block.

"I got somethin' here that just might fit the bill," Baron said softly. He fumbled through the books and magazines as if he was looking for a particular item but in the end he picked up a book that was stuffed in a slot up near the cart push handle. "This is a Reader's Digest," he said handing it to Clint through the cell bars. "There's a really good story in there about chain gangs in the Deep South. You won't believe what they say goes on. Take a close look at it. You might like it."

"Thanks," Clint said. "I'll get it back to you next week."

Baron carefully checked the guards again. Putting his head down and straightening his books and magazines he said in an almost whisper, "I have a message for you from a friend on the outside."

"What?" Clint asked surprised.

"Just keep lookin' through your book and listen. I'll only say it once so pay attention." Clint didn't say anything he just thumbed through the Reader's Digest. Baron continued, "The life at hard labor inmates will be moved. They'll be moved to Texas to work in the oil fields to free up guys for the military. It'll happen soon. Be prepared. It means more delays."

Baron then waved and said loudly, "I'll see you next week. Be sure and read that story, you'll like it." He then pushed his cart down the block to the next cell.

Clint watched him walk away pushing his cart. He then turned and put the Reader's Digest on his desk and went back and flopped down on his bunk. It was cold in the cell block so he took off his sneakers and slipped under his blanket. He fluffed up his pillow lay down to think. The rest of the day was long and slow. He found himself almost wishing he could go back to breaking rock.

It was obvious that the underground mail was going again albeit in a different form. It appeared that the new form was going to be verbal. However, how long would this last for him? If the message from his "outside friend" was true, he would be leaving Leavenworth for someplace in Texas. That, he thought, may not be too bad. It would be closer to home and make it easier for his family to visit him, if visits were allowed. Who knows where he will be kept? Near an oil field he imagined.

But, he was getting away ahead of himself. The main thing to gather from all this is that there was another delay in any escape plan. Before anything else could be done on any type of plan, he would have to be relocated, settled into a new routine, and see if the underground mail would follow. It may not. According to the message, only those sentenced to life at hard labor will be making the move. Inmates like Baron wouldn't be moving. So, the underground mail most likely will not be moving to Texas. Just like always, all he could do was wait and see what happened.

CHAPTER SIXTY-SEVEN

The Clue

January 1942

Sheriff Tom Clark had come home for lunch today rather than meet Evie and the kids somewhere. Anyway, it was cold outside and it was best for the kids to have lunch at school. Sheriff Clark watched as Evie cleaned up the kitchen after they finished the sandwiches she had made. Evie was still a pretty woman. Her long sandy blonde hair didn't show any grey for her thirty-six years. Her body still had a nice shape even after having two children. Her face was somewhat plain but had a sexy look about it. She walked around the kitchen barefoot as she still hated to wear shoes. And though Tom Clark hated to admit it, she still had the ability to drive him to lust filled rages. At times, she still used that ability to get what she wanted.

"That was a good lunch, Evie, thanks,"

"No problem. I like us eatin' at home alone when the kids are gone. Kind of like old times."

"Before I leave to go back to the office, I was wonderin' if you could help me with somethin'," Tom asked in a matter-of-fact tone.

"Sure, if I can. What's up?"

Tom reached into his pants pocket and pulled out the little twenty-two bullet. He stood it up on the cartridge end so that the hollow point was pointing to the ceiling. "Come take a look at this and tell me what you think it is."

Evie came over and sat down at the kitchen table with Tom. She leaned over and inspected the bullet carefully.

"It looks like a bullet," she said after a while.

"Well, that's because it is a bullet," Tom said smiling. "It's a Remington center fire twenty-two caliber hollow point bullet."

Evie looked at him quizzically. "Is that supposed to mean somethin' to me?"

"I'm not sure," he replied. "That's why I'm askin'."

"Well," she shrugged, "it doesn't."

"Let's take this a little deeper," Tom said seriously. "Do you still have that twenty-two revolver that Louis gave back when you guys were married?"

"You know I do," she responded somewhat irate. "It's in the bedroom closet in a shoebox on the top shelf. I moved it there when the kids got older so they wouldn't find it."

"When's the last time you used it?" He asked.

"I guess when we last went out for you to qualify. We both take some target practice durin' your qualification." There was a short silence and then she asked in a catty tone, "Would it be possible for you let me know what this is all about?"

He reached down and picked up the bullet and held it in front of her face just a few inches from her nose. "How do you suppose that this bullet from your gun got lost up on Lonesome Hill? Say maybe eight or so years ago?

Her eyes widened and she backed away from the bullet. "How do you know that it's a bullet from my gun?"

"Well, a Texas Ranger found it up on Lonesome Hill at the crime scene where Jim Upter was killed. He gave it to me to see what I could find out. I pretty much knew where it came from when I first saw it, but I checked all the guns we've confiscated over the last ten years and there're only two twenty-two pistols among them. Now, of those two pistols neither of them used Remington center fire hollow points. But, I know that your pistol does. Doesn't it?"

"Jesus Christ," she breathed, "that bullet could come from someplace else. Who knows who else might have that kind of gun? And anyway, I got no idea what kind of bullets goes in that or any gun for that matter." There were traces of fright mixed with anger in her voice.

"That's true," he said in a soothing voice. "It might be from someone or someplace we don't know, but that's a real long shot don't you think? I mean, a bullet that fits, and is used, in our gun turns up at a crime scene that was investigated by both me and you ex-husband. What would you say the odds are for that happenin'?"

Evie leaned back across the table and put her face just inches from Tom's. "What're you tryin' to say, Tom? Or maybe I should ask, what'd you want me to say?"

Tom put his hand on her cheek and rubbed it softly. "I just want you to tell me the truth, Evie. If you don't know anythin' about this, just tell me and I'll believe you. But, if you do know somethin' about it, please tell me. Don't let me get blindsided, because I'm goin' to have to tell that Texas Ranger somethin'. And I prefer it not be a lie that can catch up to me."

Evie looked at Tom steadily. Then, she reached up and took his hand from her cheek and clasped it in her hands. Tears began to fill her eyes but she continued to stare into his eyes. "I love you, Tom," she whispered. "I always have. Even back when we were doin' things behind Lou's back, I did those things because I loved you and not just for the sex. And now we've been married for almost nine years and we got two great kids. It's been good hasn't it, Tom? It has been good hasn't it?"

Tom put his hand on hers and said, "Yes, it's been good, Evie. And it's still goin' to be good. We just need to know how to figure this out. And to figure it out, I gotta know exactly what happened. Can you please tell me exactly what happened?"

She straightened up in her chair and pulled her hands away from his. She got up and went over to the sink and got the dish towel and dried her eyes. Turning around to face him she leaned back against the sink and looked down at the floor. "Okay, Tom," she said softly, "I can tell you what I know. But that may not be what all you want. But, I swear to you, it's all I know."

"That'll be fine, Evie."

"You're still goin' ta love me won't you, Tom," she cried.

"I'm still goin' to love ya, Evie."

"Okay, here's what I know and by all that's holy I swear it's all I know and it's the gospel truth."

"To start with," she began slowly, "I knew Lou was involved with the Klan from the get go. He tried hidin' it from me but I knew. He kept his hood and robe someplace else and not at home. And the truth is, I don't know how involved he was in what they were doin' but I knew he was goin' to their meetings. And I knew he was playin' both ends against the middle. They used him for information on the Sheriff's department and what you were doin' and at the same time he was watchin' them thinkin' he might be able to make a big arrest or somethin' that would make him a big man."

"Wait a minute," Tom interrupted, "are you tellin' me he was spyin' on me!"

"Yes, that's exactly what I'm tellin' you," she said firmly. "Why do you think he made such a big deal about not bringin' in the Rangers or other State Troopers to help with the investigation? He wanted to be able to guide the investigation and he couldn't do that if the Rangers or State Troopers got involved."

Tom now chose his words carefully. "You mean you knew that Lou was makin' a fool out of me all the time that you and I were together?"

She wrung her hands together and said, "I don't know about makin' a fool out of you, but I knew what he was doin'."

"It seems like at some time or the other, you could've told me what Lou did, at least later on after we were married."

"Tom," she said in exasperation, "why do you think Lou didn't fight the divorce so hard, or why he agreed to leave town so easy?"

Tom stared at her. "You made some kind of deal with him didn't you?"

"Yes, I agreed to keep my mouth shut about everything I knew if he wouldn't fight the divorce."

"I guess I can understand that," Tom said softly. "But it hurts." They both were silent for a long time as they both seemed to trying think of what to say next. "Okay," Tom finally said looking up at her and smiling, "Let's move on. Do you know if he was with them when they went to the Collie place and Rachael ended up gettin' killed?"

"I can't swear to it but I'm almost positive that he was, because he came home all wet and muddy."

"But you saw no robe or hood?" Tom pressed.

"No, I didn't."

"What about when they kidnapped Moonbeam and took him up on the hill? Was he in on that?"

"I think so," she answered. "But, again, I can't swear to it."

"Now tell me about the gun."

"Lou wouldn't say anythin' to me about it but before he would leave the house I would see him take the gun and stuff it in his belt behind his back, and then put a hand full of bullets in his pocket."

Tom looked puzzled. "Why would he take the twenty-two when he had his service revolver?"

"I don't know," she said. "But I never saw him go with his service revolver; just the little gun."

Tom sat quietly looking up at her and drumming his fingers on the table top. "Come sit down, Evie," he said gently.

She pushed away from the kitchen sink counter and returned to the table and sat down. She kept her head down so as not to look into his eyes.

"Look at me, Evie." His voice was still gentle.

She lifted her head and looked into his eyes.

"Let's recap what we know and what we don't know, Okay?" He asked.

She nodded her head yes.

"First, and above all, we know that Lou was involved with the Klan. We know that Lou was workin' both sides. One side was to watch me and report back to Jim Upter on everything I did. The other side was to watch the Klan and see if he could make some kind of important bust. We also know that he when to most of their meetings and when he went to the meetings he took the little twenty-two and not his service revolver. Now, that's what we know for sure. Now for what we think we know. We think Lou was with the Klan when they went to the Collie house the night Rachael died. We also think Lou was there when they kidnapped Moonbeam and, maybe, was there durin' the hangin'. Now, for what we absolutely don't know. We don't know if Lou was directly involved in either killin'. And, we don't know why he took the twenty-two instead of his service revolver."

He stopped talking and continued to look into Evie's eyes. He shrugged his shoulders and asked, "Does that just about sum it up?"

"I think that covers it pretty good," she replied.

He leaned back in his chair and ran his hands through his hair. Then he reached for his hat and said, "Well, I guess I better be gettin' back to the office."

She reached over and touched his arm. "Tom, what're you goin' to do?" Her voice carried more love than fear.

"I'm not sure how I'm goin' to handle this," he said standing up and putting on his hat.

"You know if you confront Lou he's goin' to know I broke my word and talked," she said.

"No he won't," Tom said simply. "It'll be easy enough to show him what we found and convince him that I put two and two together."

"Do you really think so?" She asked softly.

"I think so," he said, "but, like I said, I haven't figured out how I'm goin' to handle it yet. But whatever I do, I'll protect you and our family."

She stood and went to him. She wanted to throw her arms around him but was afraid it would be the wrong thing to do. "Tom, are we okay," she stammered.

He put his arm around her waist and pulled her to him. He bent down and kissed her hard; hard enough for it to hurt. But she didn't care. She returned his kiss in kind. Tom could feel the lusty fire starting to burn inside him. He put his hands on her shoulders and gently pushed her away. "Not now," he said smiling, "I got a lot of things to do at the office. But keep it warm if you would."

"It'll still be burnin' when you get home," she teased. "It'll still be burnin'."

CHAPTER SIXTY-EIGHT

Billy Bob Says Goodbye

January 1942

It was late January and the Collie household had returned to a much more calm state. Cherrie had returned to Baylor to finish her senior year and get her diploma. Dee had reported to the Naval Base in Pensacola, Florida to start his Naval Aviation training. Dick Jordan had returned to his base near the Presidio in California. James and Ruth had gone back to their routine at the store. Mary had gone back to her normal household routines. Sue Ann helped Mary around the house when she wasn't writing letters to Dee. She was now in her seventh month of pregnancy and it was showing more each day.

As is the case with East Texas, the weather was completely unpredictable. Whereas Christmas had been cold and grey with sleet and freezing rain, the weather now was sunshiny and a balmy seventy-two degrees.

Mary was preparing a bag lunch to take to James and Sue Ann sat at the kitchen table watching her, while writing yet another letter to Dee, when a knock came at the front door. Both women were somewhat apprehensive because lately knocks at the door have brought surprises; some good and some bad.

"I'll get it," Sue Ann said as she started to get up.

"You will not," Mary demanded putting her hand on Sue Ann's shoulder and pushing her back down into the chair. "You just keep that big tummy were it is."

Mary started for the door while cleaning her hands with the dish towel as she went. She opened the door to find Billy Bob Barnett standing there smiling. Well, she thought, at least it must be good news. "Hello, Billy Bob," she said pleasantly, "come on in." She turned and started walking back towards the kitchen even before Billy Boy had gotten through the door. "Sue Ann, it's your brother," she shouted.

"Okay, Mrs. Collie," Sue Ann yelled back.

"Sue Ann," Mary said in frustration, "I thought we discussed this. It's either Mary or Mom, but not Mrs. Collie."

"Oops, sorry," Sue Ann replied with a chuckle as she made her way into the living room. She and Mary crossed by each other; one going back to the kitchen and the other going to the living room. "Hey, big brother, what brings you away from the farm?" As she spoke, she went up and carefully embraced him being careful not to bump him with her big tummy.

"Oh, I just got some news that I needed to tell everyone and I thought my little sister would be the best startin' place."

"You've got news?" Sun Ann asked somewhat alarmed. This day and time news was not always welcome.

Billy Bob could see by her face that he had scared her. "Oh, sorry for the scare but it's nothin' bad," he quickly corrected the situation.

"Mom," Sue Ann shouted, "my brother's got some news. Do you wanta here it?"

Mary came back into the living room carrying the lunch bag for James. "I only want to hear it if it's good news, no bad news please!"

"I think its good news," he said.

"I don't like that look on his face, Mom," Sue Ann said eyeing him closely. "I've seen that look many times before. Somethin' is goin' on here. Give it up big brother, what've you done?"

"Yeah, I've done somethin'," he said grinning. "I signed up today."

"Signed up for what?" Sue Ann asked slowly.

"For the United States Army," he replied. "I'm goin' to start trainin' to be a paratrooper."

Sue Ann was stunned. Mary only stood there speechless.

"A paratrooper," she breathed holding her tummy. "You mean paratrooper as in jumpin' out of planes?"

"Yeah, that's what it means."

"Why would you do that?" She yelled. "What about Mom and Dad? Are you just goin' to leave them alone on the farm?"

Billy Bob lowered his head and shook it. "I was hoping you'd understand, Sue Ann. Surely, you didn't expect me to do nothin'. My country's at war. All my friends are joinin' up. Dee and Dick are already gone. Tell me, did you expect me to set it out?"

Sue Ann looked at him with tears forming in her eyes. She struggled for words and her month moved but nothing came out. Finally, she got herself together and went over and put her arms around him and buried her face into his chest. "No," she said softly into his chest. "I wouldn't expect you to set it out."

Billy Bob put his hand on her head and pulled it tightly to him. "I talked it over with Mom and she's okay with it. Dad's not talkin' to me much anyway so I didn't bother askin' him. He'll have to do what millions of other Dads are goin' to be doin'. He'll have to get by. And he can. They're in pretty good shape."

Then, looking to Mary, he said, "Mrs. Collie, now that you and Mom have made up, I was wonderin' if you'd mind givin' her a little of your time now and then? She could sure use a friend."

Mary went over and put her hand on his shoulder. "She's got more than a friend, Billy Bob. She's got a family. She's welcome here with her daughter anytime day or night. And she can call on me for anythin'. If I can do it, I will."

"Thank you, Ma'am," he said with relief. Then, he pushed Sue Ann away to arm's length. "Are you okay, Sis?"

Tears were now rolling down her cheeks. "Damn you, big brother," she cried, "why'd you have to get into somethin' so dangerous? Why couldn't you just be in the army? Couldn't that be enough; why the paratroopers?"

"Come on, Sis, you know me. Anyway, I've never jumped out of an airplane."

"Well, neither have I," she laughed through her tears. "But you don't see me joinin' the paratroopers."

"You're too fat to be a paratrooper," he teased and patted her tummy.

She laughed and gave him a good punch in the gut. "Do you know where and when you'll be goin'?"

"Yep, I'll have to leave no later than Monday. I've got to report to Camp Toccoa in Georgia for paratrooper trainin'. Then, I'll be assigned to one of the two Airborne Divisions. I'll send you my address and everythin' when I get there."

"Monday," Sue Ann exclaimed, "that's only four days away." Then she broke out crying again. "Oh my God, Bill, you and Dee both gone may be more than I can take. What'll I do without you?"

"I'll tell you what you do," he said firmly, "you take care of that nephew of mine growin' in that tummy of yours. I expect to be tossin' him around when I get back."

She tried to laugh but it failed. She turned to Mary, but Mary was struggling to keep the tears back herself.

"Look, Sis," he said quickly, "I gotta get goin'. I got a ton of things to get done and at least a million things to go over with Mom and Dad. I'll stop back here before I leave."

She just looked at him with a lost look on her face. Then she simply said, "Okay."

He gave her a big hug and then when over and hugged Mary, who was still struggling to keep the tears from coming to her eyes. "Thank you, Mrs. Collie, for everythin' you're doin' for Sis. I'll always remember it."

"I think everyone needs to stop callin' me Mrs. Collie." She stammered as she choked back the tears. "Y'all are family now and as I've told Sue Ann over and over again its either Mary or Mom." Then she looked up at Billy Bob and the tears broke through. "But I'd prefer you called me Mom, Bill."

"Mom, it is," he said and kissed her on the forehead. "I gotta run, but I'll see you before I leave." With that, he walked quickly to the door and left without saying anything else.

The two women were left standing in the living room with tears in their eyes. They were silent for a few minutes and then Mary said, "Well, I guess we all knew it was comin'. Your brother's not the kind to let everyone leave him behind, and he's a good boy. The paratroopers are goin' to be glad they got him."

Sue Ann went over and put her head on Mary's shoulder and cried, "Oh, Mom, what're we goin' to do. I'm scared. I'm really, really scared."

Mary patted her on the back and stroked her beautiful blonde hair. "We're all scared, sweetheart," she said. "Believe me, we're all scared."

CHAPTER SIXTY-NINE

The Battle of Midway

June 1942

As the month of June approached, several things had happened rapidly for the Collie family. Cherrie had graduated with honors from Baylor. She immediately went to work on packing and getting things in order to move out to California to be with Dick. Dick had sent her train fare and directions on how to get to the married officer's quarters at the Presidio. Mary was glad to have her at home but knew she would be leaving very soon. It hurt her, but she knew it was only right for her to be with her husband.

There was a new member of the Collie family that arrived on March 17th. His name was Kyle Gene Collie and he weighed in at seven pounds and ten ounces. Mother and son both did very well. Dee was unable to come home to see his new son, as he had completed his Naval Aviation training and was already at sea. His family didn't know where he was or to what carrier he had been assigned, but they treasured his letters, even though they were heavily censor by the security people. But they did know he was alright and was continuing his training at sea.

As everyone expected, Billy Bob excelled in the paratroopers. He had finished all this training in Georgia and ended up a Corporal. He was now awaiting assignment to the 101st Airborne Division known as the Screaming Eagles. It was unknown to everyone at this time, but in years to come the name *Screaming Eagles* would be written into history's honor roll of courage and bravery. As with Dee, Billy

Bob was not able to come home to see his new nephew. He was on alert to move at any time.

So, the Collie house continued on as best it could. Despite the constant worry, Sue Ann concentrated on being a good mother. Sally Barnett was a constant visitor to the Collie household and spent as much time as she could with her daughter and grandson. Mary couldn't resist being a doting grandmother and James was nearly as bad as the women. There had been one issue that caused some trouble and that was the question of breast milk or baby formula. The doctor at the hospital and suggested that Sue Ann use a well-known baby formula as Kyle seemed to be rejecting her breast milk. But Sue Ann would not hear of it. She insisted on breast feeding her baby. The first two weeks were very hard as Kyle battled against her breast milk, but on about the third week he started taking her milk. Thereafter, Kyle was a breast fed baby and to everyone's relief was doing just fine.

There was always talk of the war being over shortly and that everyone could come home; especially among the women. But James knew better. He knew that this was going to be a long hard and costly fight; both on the war front and at home. He would go stand at his favorite spot looking out the front window. He didn't look at anything in particular; he just watched the changing seasons of East Texas. It was June again and, as always, it was getting hot. His twins would have another birthday soon. As he stared out the window he thought, my God their goin' to be twenty-two years old. He couldn't believe how fast the time had gone by. On occasions, he would ask Sue Ann if he could hold Kyle and she would, of course, say yes. He would take the baby and go to his spot at the window. There, he and Kyle would look out at the world from a small house in a small town in East Texas.

⊙•⊙

Upon completing his Naval Aviation training, Dee was assigned to the fighter group Fighting Six on the USS Enterprise. The

Enterprise's official designation was CV-6, thus the terms Fighting Six for fighters, Bombing Six for bombers, and Torpedo Six for torpedo planes. The same naming procedure held for the carriers such as CV-3 (the USS Yorktown) and CV-8 (the USS Hornet). Fighting Six had three squadrons of nine planes each. Dee was assigned to Angel Squadron of Fighting Six. The plane they flew was the Grumman F4F Wildcat. The Wildcat couldn't match the Spitfire he had flown with the Eagle Squadron. And it certainly couldn't match the Japanese Zero fighter. The Zero was faster, more maneuverable, and had longer range than the Wildcat. In a dog fight the Zero had all the advantages. However, the Wildcat did have one advantage over the Zero that would prove to be a big difference maker. As the flyers would say, "It's one tough little son-of-a-bitch. The Wildcat was very hard to bring down. The Zero could pump rounds and rounds of bullets into the 'little son-of-a-bitch' and it would keep flying. On the other hand, all though the Zero could outperform the Wildcat in almost every category, the Zero would explode or break apart when hit with one or two burst from the Wildcat's guns. So, the Wildcat pilots learned to bounce and weave among each other to take away the Zero's superiority. They would take some heavy hits so that one of their team members could get a clean shot. And that clean shot nearly always brought the Zero down.

Dee had been training with his squad nearly every day since he was assigned. Dee knew he was outclassed by the Zero, so he had to learn how to use his plane to the best advantage to survive. As a result, they practiced every day; day in and day out. Landing and taking off from a carrier deck hadn't been as hard to master as Dee had expected. He credited that to the short touch-and-go landings and take offs he did with the Eagle Squadron. It was now the first of June and Command had stopped the training runs and started concentrating on recognition training, which took place in the carrier Ready Room. Something big was obviously brewing.

Then, they finally got the news; the Japanese were going to try and take Midway Island and in the process destroy the remaining

American carriers. With good intelligence in hand, the American fleet went out to meet them with the carriers Enterprise, Yorktown, and Hornet. Fighting Six was alerted and all but two planes, which were under repair, were made ready. Fighting Six would put twenty-five Wildcats in the air.

Then, suddenly, the battle was on. American PBY search planes had located the Japanese fleet and radioed their position back to the Midway Command Center, which in turn got the information to the carrier commander. All available planes were launched from the carriers to attack the Japanese fleet. It was supposed to be a coordinated attacked with the fighters flying high above to cover the dive bombers and torpedo planes below. The idea was to keep the Zeros off the dive bombers and torpedo planes so they could go in and attack the carriers without being shot at by the Zeros. As with most battle plans, nothing went as it was planned. The fighters took off first, followed by the torpedo planes, and then dive bombers. As each group took off they went to the heading they were told. But as it turned out the groups from all three carriers were spread all over the sky.

Dee watched as the bombers and torpedo planes from Enterprise headed out to meet the Japanese fleet while he and the rest of Fighting Six were ordered to stay back and defend Midway. The other fighters; Fighting Three from Yorktown and Fighting Eight from Hornet were ordered to follow and cover the bombers but the Wildcat had such a limited range they could not keep up because of loss of fuel searching for the Japanese fleet. The fighters were forced to turn back or ditch in the sea. As a result, the bombers and torpedo planes went on to the attack without fighter cover. The result was a near disaster. All fifteen planes in Torpedo Eight from Hornet were shot down with all the crews being killed except for one man. The Zeros attacked them unmolested and wreaked a deadly havoc.

But the Zeros had made a mistake. Instead of sending down only what was needed to beat off the torpedo planes, they all came down in a swarm. That left the Japanese carriers with no fighter cover over them. And at just that time, Bombing Six from Enterprise and Bombing Three from Yorktown arrived on the scene. They immediately saw the opening and quickly went into their steep bombing dives. In minutes three Japanese carriers were in flames and exploding.

However, at this time Dee was unaware of what was going on with the Japanese fleet. He had his hands full with Zeros from the bombing raid on Midway. The raid had already occurred by the time Fighting Six arrived. The Zeros were in the process of supporting their bombers on the way back to their carriers after completing the raid. So Dee and Fighting Six saw the Japanese planes as they were heading away from Midway. Fighting Six immediately formed up to attack, but Dee noticed something.

"Angel Leader, this is Angel Four," he called into his microphone.

"Okay, Collie, what've you got. This ain't the Brits, no need to be so formal."

"Sir, I think those planes are nearly out of fuel. They surely see us and they haven't engaged us."

"Okay, so what? We still need to engage them," was the curt reply.

"Sir, I'm thinkin' if we let them go on by we can come in behind them and start knockin' 'em off. If there as low on fuel as they appear to be, I don't think there's much they can do about it."

There was a short silence and then a quick decision was made. "Okay, let's give it a try. Boys peel back and let 'em pass and we'll catch 'em from behind."

That's exactly what they did. The Zeros were too low on fuel to engage in a dog fight and protect the bombers at the same time. Fighter Six followed the Japanese planes for as long as they dared before they ran low on fuel themselves. By unofficial count, ten zeros went down along with as many bombers.

"Okay, guys, we're getting' low on juice ourselves. Let's head back to the Enterprise and refuel."

By the time Fighter Six got back to the Enterprise the battle was all but over. But still, Fighter Six refueled and went back up to fly cover for the Enterprise. Later on, Bombing Six would find the other Japanese carrier and sink it also. Without a carrier to land on, the Japanese planes began to run out of fuel and drop into the sea.

Much later, Dee sat all alone in the Ready Room. Everyone else had geared down and showered or gone to their quarters. But Dee had things on his mind so he found a lonely stop and simply sat there. He was not alone for long as the squad leader Lieutenant Tim Baker of Columbus, Ohio walked in.

"What's up with you, Collie?" He said looking around the empty room. "Is there something wrong? I mean you're still geared up and dirty from the battle."

"No, Sir, nothin' is really wrong."

"Come on, Collie, out with it. What's got you down after such a big victory as we got today? Hell, you got credited with two kills yourself."

"I guess that's it," Dee said in almost a whisper. "It was a great victory but I had very little to do with it. A lot of good guys died today and I just feel I let them down. I don't think Fighting Six made any difference. And as for those kills, it wasn't much of a fight. Those Zeros were practically out of fuel. If I hadn't of shot them down, they would've probably run out of fuel and crashed into the sea anyway. "

Lieutenant Baker stood looking down at Dee. "You're right about one thing; a lot good guys did die today. But you're wrong about Fighting Six. We did our job. You've got no right to sit here and second guess what we were ordered to do. We defended Midway and we kept good cover over our carrier. That's was our part. I dare you to dishonor those brave guys who gave their all. If that's going to be your attitude, I'd just as soon you transfer to a different squad!"

Dee didn't say anything but stood up to face the squad leader. "And another thing," the squad leader continued, "I know we're the same rank and you could be leading this squad. But I do have a little seniority. And it's your attitude that I'm seeing right now that's going to keep you from leading a squad. And that's a damn shame because you were good up there today. Picking up on the Jap's fuel problem was a good observation during a combat situation. It probably saved some lives and put the hurt on the Japs. You can be a good leader but you've got to quit crying and get the job done."

Dee finally found his voice. "I'm sorry, Sir," he almost shouted. "You're right. I guess I just felt terrible about those guys goin' in without fighter cover. Down deep I know it was their decision, but I just feel we let them down."

"Maybe we did," Lieutenant Baker said in frustration. He paused for a long minute to gather his words. Then he continued, "Maybe we did, but war is war and now we move on. The Japs are going to be hard pressed to get back on their feet after this beating. Our job now is to keep the pressure on, keep pressing and pushing them. You just remember that we won today because of very good intelligence from the ONI boys in Honolulu, great command leadership from Admiral Nimitz on down to the Carrier Captains and on down to all our flight commanders, some very good luck, and a lot of courageous guys that laid it all on the line. You remember that, Lieutenant Collie, where ever you may transfer to."

"Sir," Dee said looking into the squad leader's eyes, "I don't want to transfer anywhere. I want to be right here on the Enterprise when we sail into Tokyo Bay."

Lieutenant Baker smiled and said, "Good, Lieutenant Collie, and I want to see you leading a squad or the entire group when we do."

Dee and Lieutenant Baker shook hands has Dee started taking his gear off and moving towards the Ready Room door. "I think I'll have a shower and go to my quarters and write my wife. She's probably heard or is goin' to hear about this battle and is worried sick." Dee stopped as he got to the Ready Room door and looked back at the squad leader. He had a big smile on his face. He pointed at the squad leader and said, "You know, I got a kid now. I haven't seen him yet, but my wife says in her letters that he's already actin' like me. Isn't that somethin'? I can't have that. We need to get this damn thing over so I can get home and set him straight."

CHAPTER SEVENTY

Cherrie Goes West

June 1942

C herrie and Sue Ann stood back and looked at the suitcase lying on the bed in Cherrie's old room.

"I don't think you're goin' to be able to close that thing," Sue Ann said studying the suitcase. "I mean look at it. You've got stuff stacked to overflowin'. And if somehow we got it closed, how're you goin' to carry it?"

Cherrie looked at her with determination, "Carryin' it isn't my job. That's somebody else's job. I just gotta get it packed."

"Why don't you use another suitcase?" Sue Ann pleaded. "You can't move your whole life to California in one suitcase!"

"I don't want to carry too much stuff until we find out exactly where we're goin' to be quartered," Cherrie explained. "When I know that, I'll get Mom to ship me all the other stuff I need."

"Okay, okay," Sue Ann said waving her hands. "Come on and let's try and close this thing."

With great effort and some creative stuffing, they finally got the suitcase closed. It sat on the bed like a huge overstuffed cow. "Well, I think that's about got it," Cherrie exhaled.

"Hold on," Sue Ann said, "there're papers or somethin' on the floor." She reached down and picked them up just as Mary came in. "Hey, it looks like your train tickets and directions. You don't want to lose these." She was about to hand them to Cherrie when she noticed the name on the tickets. "My, my," she smiled, "these tickets are made out to Cheryl Jordan."

"Who else would they be made out to?" Mary interjected. "That's her name you know."

Sue Ann handed the tickets and directions to Cherrie. "We'll I was just wonderin'," she said slyly.

"What were you wonderin'?" Cherrie challenged.

Sue Ann smiled a wicked smile and said, "Just how much longer an old married woman like you will still be called 'Cherrie'."

The three women looked at each other trying to suppress a fit of giggling.

"You get it?" Sue Ann laughed. "You bein' Cherrie and bein' married."

"I get it," Cherrie yelled laughing as she picked up a pillow from the bed and threw it at Sue Ann.

Mary grabbed a pillow and got into the fight. The three women didn't realize it but this bit of fun and games was their first relief from war pressure in over a month.

It was now late June and Cherrie had been gone for over a week. She had called home to report to her Mother and Dad that she had made the trip fine and was settled in Dick's quarters at the Presidio. She reported that even though they were living in the married officer's quarters, the place was very small. After a while, she intended to get a job and they would move off base to their own apartment. But all of that would come later; right now she and Dick were just enjoying being together.

As she did almost every day, Sue Ann sat by the window watching for the mailman. It had become a ritual. She became excited when she saw him turn into their yard and start for the mailbox. Quickly, she jumped up and ran to the door to meet him. He smiled at her and handed her two pieces of mail. She thanked him and closed the door.

"Mom," Sue Ann yelled excitedly. "Come quick, I got two letters today; one from Dee and one from Bill."

Mary came hurrying into the living room wiping her hands on the dish towel. "Oh, I hope they're not so personal that you can't read them to me!"

"Don't worry, Mom," give me a few minutes to go over them and then we can talk about what's in them. If there's anythin' just for me, I'll keep it to myself. Is that okay?"

"That's fine, that's fine," Mary replied. "Go on, open 'em and read 'em."

Over the next ten to fifteen minutes Sue Ann read both letters. She read Bill's first; saving Dee's for last. As she finished Dee's letter, she folded it neatly and pressed it to her chest. She lowered her head to hide the tears filling her eyes.

Mary became terrified, "What's happened? Please tell me. Is Dee hurt?"

Sue Ann lifted her head. There were tears in her eyes but there was also a large smile on her face. "I'm sorry, Mom," she said quickly, "it's just Dee wrote some personal stuff that's just for me. But he's okay, he's fine."

"Oh, thank God," Mary said gasping for breath. "Okay, now tell me what you can, come on."

Sue Ann continued to hold letter pressed over her heart. "He said he was sure we had heard about the battle at Midway Island and was sure we were worried about him. And he said he was in the battle, but that he came through it just fine; not a scratch. He asked us to try and not worry so much that he was in God's hands and that he was servin' with a great crew. He said he hasn't had a letter from you or Dad in sometime and that worries him. Please write. He demanded to know where the pictures of Kyle were. He wants pictures of all of us right away. Then, there was personal stuff for me."

"I knew I should've written him," Mary said frustrated. "But I thought your letters covered most everythin'. I guess he wants personal stuff from me and James. I'll write him today, I promise.

As far as the pictures go, James should be getting' them today. It's been a whole week now. Tell you what, as soon as we're through here, we'll get Kyle and go down to store and see what the holdup is. We need to get those pictures out to Dee today. Is that okay? Do you want go down to the store with me?"

"Yes I do," Sue Ann laughed. Then, she carefully put Dee's down next to this Mother's scrapbook. "You put these letters in your scrapbook and we'll keep 'em together."

Mary smiled and said, "You can go into the scrapbook anytime you like." Then she slapped her hands together. "Now, let's hear about that brother of yours."

"Okay, here we go," Sue Ann said picking up Bill's letter. "He didn't really have much to say. It was a short letter. He said his assignment came through and he has been attached to the 101st Airborne Division, Screaming Eagles. He said he'll be shippin' out in about a week and that he'll get us a new address as soon as he can. And he's beggin' us for pictures just like Dee. He asked about our Mom and Dad. He worries about Mom. And he said to tell you thanks again for being such a great mother-in-law. Lastly, he said he can't wait to wrestle around with Kyle."

"Well, he sounds like he's doin' good," Mary said happily. But she saw something in Sue Ann's eyes that worried her. "Sue, is there somethin' you're not tellin' me? You don't look very happy about his letter."

"It's just I hate hearin' words like, 'shippin' out'," she said softly. "What does that mean? Shippin' out to where?"

"Well, Sue, I'm sure he's not allowed to tell you things like that. I'm sure he's told you 'bout all he can."

Sue Ann put Bill's letter down next to Dee's. "He's goin' to war isn't he, Mom?"

Mary looked down at her hands and said, "I would think so," she said gently. "I guess that's why they're all out there; to fight this damn war."

Sue Ann just nodded her head and didn't say anything else.

"I'll tell you somethin' I'd like to do," Mary said suddenly. "I want to make scrapbooks for both Bill and Dick to go along with Dee's. Would you help me with that?"

Sue Ann looked up and smiled. "Sure I will," she said. "That ought to keep us busy."

"It's all such a waste you know," Mary said standing up. She put her hands on her hips and spoke angrily. "Those damn Germans and Japs really messed up when they started this war with us. With boys like Dee, Dick, and Bill, well, those poor bastards don't have a snowballs chance in Hell."

Sue Ann stood up and grabbed Mary's hand. "That's the spirit," she yelled. "Now, let's get Kyle out of his crib and go down to the store and see if we can get those pictures out of James."

CHAPTER SEVENTY-ONE

The State Park

July 1942

There was a World War raging across the globe but the State of Texas still proceeded to build its State Park. With everyone preoccupied with the war, there was complete amazement in Coalville when the heavy equipment showed up to start building the access road to Lonesome Hill. The project had been delayed in the spring due to getting all the surveying done and cleared by the State and all the lawyers. But now all the papers were signed and all the surveying had been approved.

Mary watched from the kitchen window as all the men were gathered around talking and pointing. This is the same window from where she used to watched Dee and Cherrie go down the back path to Dee's old treehouse, and the same window from which they first saw the flames coming from Rachael's little house. Now, Rachael house was gone and only mounds of earth covered in grass mark were it used to be. Soon, the tree and Dee's treehouse would both be gone. She gave a deep sigh and wondered if they should've sold the land after all. But, then, they would've just taken it. As she was thinking all of this, James came into the kitchen behind her. He sneaked up and wrapped his arms around from behind.

"Jesus," she yelled, "you scared me to death! What're you doin' home? I thought you were goin' to have lunch in town."

"I was," he said letting her go, "but I heard they were goin' to get started on the access road so I just came home to see what I could see." He looked around for a moment and then asked, "Where's Sue Ann?"

"She's out walkin' with Kyle. She should be back shortly."

James pushed her to the side so he could see out the window. "Isn't that the way it always is; a bunch of guys standin' around talkin' and just a couple actually workin'."

"Well, I don't think they've really started yet," she said pushing her way back to the window.

"I think I'll go out there and talk with them," he said pointing out the window. "You see that one guy in a jacket and tie? I bet he's in charge."

"What do you expect to find out?" She asked.

"You never know. I might find out somethin' interestin'."

He patted her on her butt and then hurried out the back door. James walked casually and slowly up to where the men were standing. They watched him approach but no one said anything to him. As he got closer, James waved. "Hi," he said as he walked up to them. "My name is James Collie. I live in the house over there."

"Hello," the man in the tie and jacket said. "My name is Ben Jefferson. I'm in change of this road construction."

"Oh," James replied, "so you work for the State?"

"No, no," Ben replied smiling, "I work for Keller Construction Company. We have the contract to build this road."

"Ah, I see," James said. "Then you don't have anythin' to do with the buildin' of the rest of the park."

"No, just the road," Ben said continuing to smile. "Excuse us, guys," Ben said to the men that had been standing with him. "Mr. Collie and I need to talk a bit. Why don't you get the bulldozers in place and I'll be right with you."

"Thank you," James said as they walked a short distance from the construction site.

"Is there anythin' in particular that you're interested in, Mr. Collie?" He asked.

"Well, yes, in a way," James replied. "Lots of us folks here in Coalville are wonderin' how the State can afford to continue this State Park project with the war goin' on. Seems to us that the money goin' into this could be used best someplace else. And, anyway, it's hard for us to see why anyone would want to come to a State Park out here. I mean, I've lived here all my life and there's really not much to see."

Ben laughed and said, "I can answer only part of your question, or questions. As far as the money goes, it was allocated back in 1938 during the deepest part of the depression. It was allocated by a federal project that gave money to different states to build useful projects and put people to work. So, in reality, it's a federal project; not a state project. It is, however, managed by the state. But the money is comin' from a fund that was given to the state years ago. And the state isn't goin' to give the money back just because of the war. In fact, it's still goin' to employ a lot of people that need work."

"Well, I'll be damned," James said shaking his head.

"Now, as far as folks comin' to this park once it's built, I can't address that. That's somebody else's problem. Seein' how the coal industry operated in this area years ago might be interestin' to some people. I think I might come take a look once it's all finished."

"You know, it might work after all," James said smiling. "You see I grew up here when some of the mines were still open."

"Well, I need to get back to work, Mr. Collie. Is there anything else I can do for you?"

"No, you've been very kind to spend time with me." James was about to turn and leave but stopped and held up his hand. "One last thing Mr. Jefferson, if you find anythin' of interest while diggin' around, I would appreciate you lettin' me know. You see, my kids grew up around here and y'all are about to bulldoze down my son's old treehouse. Somethin' you might find could have some sentimental value to me and my wife. My son is overseas in the thick of the fight and we'd like to keep anythin' that he might value."

Ben looked at James and went up to him and shook his hand. "You have my word, Mr. Collie. If we find anythin', anythin' at all, I'll see you get to take a look at it."

"Thank you, Mr. Jefferson," James said as he waved and started back to the house.

"And, Mr. Collie," Ben shouted after him, "God bless you and your family and may God protect you son."

It was a little over two weeks later as James, Mary, Sue Ann, and Kyle got back from church and were all settled into their Sunday afternoon routine. Sue Ann had put Kyle in his stroller and taken him for one of her long walks. Mary was tending her scrapbooks and James was reading the Sunday paper, when there was a knock at the front door. It was Ben Jefferson the construction boss. He was dressed in his work clothes and was wearing a hardhat. In his left hand he was carrying a package that looked as though it was wrapped in old newspaper.

"Hey, Ben, what're you doin' workin' on Sunday?" James asked holding the door open wide so he could come in. "You look like you could use an iced tea."

"Yes, Sir, I sure could," he said stepping through the door.

Mary had already gotten up and was walking over to meet the new comer. "Mary, this is Mr. Ben Jefferson. He's the construction boss for the access road bein' built."

"Come in and sit Mr. Jefferson, I'll go get you nice cold glass of iced tea."

"Thank you very much, Ma'am."

Ben looked around for a seat and then located himself at the end of the couch.

"What've you got there, Ben?" James asked looking the package.

"Well, I promised you if we found anythin' that looked interestin' that I'd let you take a look at first before we got rid of it. Now, I had a guy go up into the tree house and there wasn't much there except for some rotted cardboard boxes and empty soda bottles. So, I didn't keep anythin' from there. We just torn down the little house and uprooted the tree. But when we were bulldozing that little mound of dirt and grass we dug up what looked like an old house foundation."

At this time, Mary arrived with a tall glass of iced tea and handed it to Ben. "Here you go," she said.

Ben took it and immediately took a long drink. "Oh, thank you, Ma'am, that really hits the spot."

"The foundation you found used to be a small house we had out back for our house maid," James said. "However, it burned down at the cost of her life."

"Oh, I'm really sorry to hear that," Ben said as though he were really sad. After a short pause he continued, "Anyway we didn't find much of anythin' there either except for this." He held up the package.

"Can we see it?" James asked.

"Sure, that's why I brought it by, but we should maybe take it somewhere as to not get dirt and the like on you floor or coffee table."

"We can put it on the kitchen table," Mary interjected. "I can control things in there."

They trooped into the kitchen. James moved the chairs back so everyone could stand and look down on whatever it was. Ben put the package down on the table and slowly started un-wrapping it. When he was finished, James stared down at the object.

"It looks like a shotgun," he said slowly.

"I'm pretty sure that's what it is," Ben said. "The barrel is in fairly good shape it hasn't rusted too much due to the oil and gun metal. But the stock is almost rotted away except for where the grip connects to the trigger housing. And all the mechanisms have rusted away."

"Mary," James said studiously, "can get our magnifying glass from the mail cabinet?"

"Yes, I can," she said hurrying back to the living room.

"Is it somethin' you can use, Mr. Collie?" Ben asked.

James looked up a Ben and smiled. "It just might be, Ben. It just might be."

Mary returned with the magnifying glass and handed it to James. "Now, one more thing, Mary, I need a soft cloth of some kind and a needle from your sewing kit."

"On the way," she said as she scampered off.

Quickly, Mary returned with the requested items and handed them to James. James took the soft cloth and started cleaning what was left of the wooden stock near the trigger mechanism. He brushed it carefully and then took the needle and started scraping dirt from some lettering on the stock. Alternately, he would scrap and then clean. At times, he would stop and look at the lettering through the magnifying glass. After what seemed an eternity by those watching, James stood up straight and put his hands on his hips.

"Good job, Ben," he said. "This is a very important find. I know someone who's really goin' to thank you for this."

"Who would want to thank me for this old thing?" Ben asked puzzled.

"He's known around town as Sheriff Tom Clark."

CHAPTER SEVENTY-TWO

A Murder is Solved

July 1942

Louis Mailer was at his desk in his small office working on his final report for Bitterman, Bitterman, and Levi. His office was on the third floor of an office building in the Oak Cliff section of Dallas. It wasn't big by any means. He employed two other detectives that each had a desk in the same area as Louis. So, there was no real privacy, except he had a small conference room that connected to his office. He used it for meetings and other things that required some kind of privacy. As he worked, he did have privacy because his other two detectives were out on different assignments. There was a large window behind his desk that he had open as wide as possible, because it was hot. A large fan sat in front of the window and blew air into the office. Unfortunately, the air it blew was hot. As a result, he worn no suit jacket and his tie hung open at his neck. He was happy that this report would be the end of it; the end of the Coalville investigation. He could now move on to several other investigations that Senior Bitterman had lined up for him.

Lou was just trying to end the report, when someone walked through the office door. It was Sheriff Tom Clark. Lou was stunned. The Sheriff was carrying a large brief case. "My God, Tom Clark, this is a shock," he stammered as he stood up. "What in Hell are you doin' in these parts?"

"Well, Lou, I came to put an end to our long standin' murder mystery," the Sheriff said as he walked over to Lou's desk. "I need some of your time to clear up a lot of things. Is that okay? Is this a good time?"

"Strange you'd come now, Tom. I was just puttin' the finishin' touches my last report to the law firm about our Coalville investigation."

"You might want to hold off on that 'til we've had our talk," the Sheriff said as he pulled up a chair and sat down in front of Lou's desk.

"I don't know what I can do to help beyond what's in our reports."

"Just bear with me, Lou, and let's go over a few things, Okay?"

"Okay, Tom," Lou said in a cooperative tone. "Whata got?"

Tom put his large brief case on Lou's desk and opened it. He positioned the brief case so when it was open Lou couldn't see inside. He reached in and took out the small twenty-two bullet. He, then, shut the brief case. Holding the bullet up so Lou could see it he asked, "I guess your Ranger friend, Captain Borden, told all about this little guy."

"He told me y'all found a twenty-two cartridge at the murder scene and that you were goin' to investigate it."

"That's right," Tom said nodding his head. "And I did investigate. And guess what I found out?"

"Tell me," Lou said sarcastically.

Tom sat the bullet on Lou's desk very close to the report he had been working on. Tom stood it up so that the bullet pointed to the ceiling. "I found out that this little guy came from Evie's little twenty-two revolver. Can you imagine that?"

"How on earth do you know that?" Lou asked smiling. "That bullet could've come from God knows how many revolvers."

Tom smiled back. "I guess bein' a sheriff all these years has made me very skeptical and I just don't believe in coincidences anymore. And, you know, it would be one huge coincidence if this bullet came from some other revolver than Evie's. You see, I've checked all the guns that we've confiscated over the last ten years and only two of them are twenty-twos. And neither of those two used Remington center fire hollow points."

"Did you ask Evie about it?" Lou asked in an uncomfortable voice.

"I did. I did in deed. But all she could tell me is where the gun was now. It's in our closet in a shoe box."

"Did she say anythin' else?" Lou continued to probe.

"No, just that you used the gun sometimes, but she didn't know what for."

"So, where're we goin' with this?" Lou was becoming nervous.

"I'll tell you what I think I know. I think you were in cahoots with the Klan. And…"

He never finished his sentence. Lou jumped to his feet and yelled, "You can't come in here with that kind of accusation. You got no right or authority."

Tom got to his feet slowly. He was much taller than Lou. "You sit down, Lou, and we'll see what authority I have and what authority you *want* me to have. Now, sit down and listen!"

Lou reluctantly lowered himself back into his chair. "I'll hear you out, Tom, but I'm not goin' to stand for this."

Tom sat back down and continued, "As I was sayin', I think you were in cahoots with the Klan and you went to their meetings up on the hill. I think you took the twenty-two with you instead of your service revolver because if you had to use a gun you could get rid of the twenty-two easy enough whereas your service thirty-eight would be very hard to get rid of. Nobody would know or care about Evie losing her twenty-two, but if you lost your service thirty-eight that might cause some lookin' into. I think you carried extra bullets with you in your pocket. How one of them got on the ground at the murder site, I don't know yet but we're gettin' there. And we will get there, Lou."

Tom stopped talking for a moment to reach into his briefcase and pull out the old rusted and rotten shotgun. He closed the briefcase and laid the shotgun on top of it. Then he continued, "The bullet is not the only thing I have, Lou. Look what we found while the construction guys were diggin' the access road. They bulldozed over where Rachael's old house used to be and they found it. It's what's left of a shotgun. It was buried under what we believe to be the house's old foundation. Look closely at the initials on the handle grip near the trigger housing." Tom pointed to the spot on the shotgun. Lou leaned over and stared down at it. "What does it say, Lou?"

Lou looked at it hard and then sat back down in his chair and looked back at Tom. "It says H B."

"That's right it does. H B surely stands for Harry Barnett. We suspected him for years but couldn't get anythin' on him. Now we know he was there when the Klan went to the Collie house the night Rachael died. I don't know how the shotgun got from where he dropped it at the Collie house to Rachael's house, but I'll find out." Tom paused for a moment and he and Lou just looked at each other. "And I think," Tom continued, "that you were there too."

Lou moved nervously in his chair. "You can't prove any of this," he said angrily.

"I'll grant you that it's all circumstantial," Tom said rubbing his chin. "But there're things for you to consider, Lou."

"Such as what, what things should I consider?"

"I've done some research on your agency, Lou, and I discovered that the law firm of Bitterman, Bitterman, and Levi account for just about sixty percent of your income."

"So what if they do?"

"You might consider that if I go to court with what I have, circumstantial or not, and I drag you into court, what do you think that fine law firm is goin' to do? I'll tell you what they're goin' to do, Lou. They're goin' to drop you like a hot potato!"

Lou got up again and returned to the window. He put his hands behind his back and just stared out the window without speaking for several minutes. Then, without turning around, he asked softly, "Are you offerin' me any options?"

"I have a few things I've been thinkin' about."

Lou remained at the window and still had not turned around to face Tom. "Could I hear what you're thinkin'?" He asked continuing to speak softly.

"Lou, I don't think you killed anybody. But I think you know who did or at least you have a good idea who did. So, here's the deal, if you'll come clean with me and help me clear up all three incidents; Rachael's death, Moonbeam's hangin', and the murder of Jim Upter, I'll try and work things to keep you out of court and your name out of all things possible. Why do you think I haven't called Ranger Borden about all this?"

Lou turned around to face Tom. His face had changed to a look of submissiveness. "Do you think you can do all that?"

"Yes, I think there's a good chance provided you're not involved any deeper than I think you are."

"I'm not," Lou said returning to his chair. "But I could certainly be charged as an accessory to the fact, or maybe even an accessory to murder."

"Lou, why don't we talk about it and see where we can go? You and I go back a long way and we've both done things we're not proud of. I cheated on you and took your wife. You spied on me and betrayed me to the Klan. Come on, Lou, let's talk and see where we can go? Tom was speaking gently and almost pleadingly.

"Okay, Tom, where do we start?"

"Moonbeam was first, so start with Moonbeam."

———

"Okay. I wasn't much involved in that except that I was at the meeting when they dragged Moonbeam in to the cabin all tied up. The best I know is that Barnett and some other member grabbed Moonbeam when he was leavin' Doc Jewel's late that evenin'. It had already been decided to hang him at some meeting that I didn't attended. In the cabin that night we were all in our hoods and robes. The big discussion was about who was goin' to do the actual hangin' and where. Upter made the decision to hang Moonbeam in Doc's garage but decided to draw straws to see who did the deed. I, of course, was excluded from the drawin'. They were about to begin the drawin' when one member, who for now we'll call Member X, stepped forward and took all the straws from Jim's hand, crushed them and threw them on the floor. I didn't know Member X at the time, but I would later. Member X wore tight fittin' black gloves and heavy boots, and hood and robe hung lose like it was oversized. Member X just said 'this nigger belongs to me, Jim boy'."

Tom held up his hand to ask a question. "Who was Member X?"

"Tom, let me finish first then you can ask questions, okay?"

"Sorry, you're right, go ahead."

"Well, Member X grabbed the ropes holdin' Moonbeam and started draggin' 'im out the door. It was a struggle because Member X didn't seem very strong. So, another member who I could identify as Harry Barnett went and helped. Together they took Moonbeam off and that's the last I saw of 'em. Until, of course, I went with you to see Moonbeam hangin' in Doc Jewel's garage."

"Okay, now can I know Member X's name?" Tom asked impatiently.

"Not yet," Lou said. "It'll all tie together a little later. Now, let's move on the events at the Collie house the night Rachael died."

"Things didn't go well from the get go. I was along as always just to give information and to act as a lookout. You have to understand, Tom, there was never any intention to kill Rachael Lowell. By the time we got to the Collie house, the rain was startin'. So, they hurried and set Rachael's house a fire earlier than was planned.

"Okay, then Collie came out and started for the water hose but Barnett stopped him by pointin' the shotgun at him. Then, Upter had Collie order everyone in the house outside. When they were all outside, Upter started his speech. But he didn't get very far into it before Collie blew is top and started rantin' and ravin'. About this same time, Rachael made a break to her house at a full run. Upter yelled for us to stop her. A couple of members started after her but, slow as she was, she had a lead on them and she ran into the flamin' house. Collie was screamin' for her to stop. So, Barnett got rattled and slammed the butt of the shotgun into his gut. Collie doubled over and went down. Then all hell broke loose. One of the Collie kids, the boy, lunged into Barnett. Holdin' the shotgun in one hand, Barnett grabbed the kid by the hair and slung him away, but the kid came back. This time Barnett got a good head of hair and slammed the kid to the ground. He was drawin' back his hand to hit the kid when the little girl drove into Barnett. She hit him when he wasn't lookin' and the shotgun went flyin' off into the dark. Now with both hands free, Barnett started swingin' in all directions and he caught the girl square in the jaw. She went down and didn't move. That scared me. I thought he might've killed her. I saw where Barnett's shotgun landed and I sneaked over and picked it up and hid it under my robe. I was afraid he might find it and use it. Upter yelled for everyone to regroup. I used that excuse to run over near the burnin' house and tell the members that had chased Rachael that we were gettin' out of here and to go back and get with Upter. When they turned to run, I pitched the shotgun under the front porch of the burnin' house and then I ran too. I passed Collie as he was runnin' to try and get Rachael out of the house. That's why you found the shotgun at Rachael's place. We all got together and left while Collie was draggin' Rachael out of the house. And that's what I know about that episode. Now, let's move on to the twenty-two."

"Hold on just a minute, please," Tom said as, he signaled with his hands. "You were there through all of this with kids hurt and layin' on the ground and you just ran away with the rest of 'em."

"You wanted the truth; I'm tellin' you how I saw it. I admit I was afraid for the kids, but I thought by gettin' rid of the shotgun I had helped a dangerous situation. Now, do you want to dwell on this or can we move on to the twenty-two."

"Does the twenty-two have a bearin' on Upter's murder?" Tom asked shaking his head.

"I think it does. Do I continue?"

"Yes, continue."

———⊰⊱———

"You were right about me takin' the twenty-two up on the hill with me instead of my service revolver. I took it and about ten extra bullets with me. After it was discovered that the Collie boy had seen us in the cabin with Moonbeam, and everythin' kind of went to hell at the Collie place, Upter decided to quit and run for it. He was able to tell most of the group but not all. He wanted out fast. He was goin' to take Ruth and Dick with him, so I hear, but I don't know that for sure. Now, this is where I mostly get out of everythin'. I think everyone was on their own and gettin' out. I had just walked out of the cabin, when the Member X we've been talkin' about stopped me, and asked me point blank to borrow my gun. At first I said no, but then Member X kept tellin' me about needin' protection at least to get off hill. I was promised the gun would be returned the next day. How it would be returned wasn't discussed. And I admit, at the time, I couldn't figure out how Member X knew I had a gun. I guess it was as stupid as some of the other things I'd been doin, but I handed over the twenty-two. Then I reached into my pocket and pulled out some of the bullets for the gun. During the exchange, our hands bumped and I dropped the bullets. We got down on our hands and knees and picked them up. Member X was still wearin' black leather gloves makin' it hard to pick up small bullets. As we can now see, we must've missed one."

At this point, Lou stopped talking and wiped the sweat off his forehead with the back of his hand. To Tom, Lou seemed very reluctant to continue. As Tom waited for Lou to continue, Lou suddenly asked, "Tom, would you like a little shot of whiskey? I'm gonna have one. I've got it right here in my desk drawer."

Tom wasn't quick to answer but finally said slowly, "Sure, I'll have one with you. Maybe we both can use it."

Lou reached into his top desk drawer and took out a bottle of whisky with a name on the label that Tom didn't recognize. "Can you get us a couple of glasses from over there on top of the file cabinet?"

Tom stood up and backed over to the file cabinet without taking his eyes off Lou. He reached behind him and picked up two glasses with his left hand leaving his right hand on the butt of his service revolver.

"For Christ sakes, Tom, I'm not gonna shoot you or anythin'," Lou said with a small chuckle.

"Stranger things have happened," Tom replied, as he sat back down and put the glasses on the desk.

Lou quickly poured both glasses about half full. "Sorry, no ice," he said picking up his glass and taking a large gulp.

"That's okay," Tom said, taking a small sip out of his glass. "Can we get back to it now, Lou?"

"Sure, sure," Lou said, as he finished off his drink. "That really hit the spot. Okay, where were we?"

"Y'all had just picked up the bullets you dropped," Tom prompted.

Lou nodded his head. "Yes, then Member X saluted me with the gun, turned and walked off. And outside of all the official stuff we did later, I was finished with my spy and counter spy bullshit with the Klu Klux Klan. Two days later, I found the twenty-two in the top desk drawer of my desk at the office. It didn't appear to've been used. And that's it. The rest you know."

"The rest I know?" Tom asked sarcastically. "Now, is this the time I get to ask questions?"

Lou took a deep breath, "Go ahead."

"Okay, Lou, I just want to understand a few things about this Member X. Somehow Member X knew you had a gun. How? You willingly loaned a gun to someone you didn't know. Why? Your gun gets returned to your desk drawer at our offices in the courthouse. How? You know, Lou, I think you know who Member X is don't you?"

Lou smiled at Tom and poured himself another drink. He pointed the bottle at Tom but Tom shook his head no. Lou gulped down the drink in one big swallow. "Well," he said shaking his head, "I got a pretty good idea. And I think you do too. But we can't prove it, can we?"

"You wouldn't have givin' that gun to a stranger. You had this 'pretty good idea' even back then, didn't you?"

"Your right as rain, Sheriff Tom Clark, I was pretty damn sure even back then."

"So can we stop sayin' Member X and call *her* by name," Tom challenged saying 'her' loudly.

"I guess you can if you can prove it. I can't give you anythin' positive. It's just like all the rest, it's circumstantial. I never saw *her* face. There might've been fingerprints on the twenty two but we're way passed that now."

Tom looked at Lou long and hard. "Okay, I'll keep my word. I'll try and arrest Harry Barnett and this Member X without involvin' you. I'm not sure how I'll do that, but I'm damn sure gonna try."

"Tom, you know and I know, it'll take a miracle to keep me out of it," Lou said in disgust. "But I do trust you to try."

"And if I can't?"

"Well, I'm not gonna run," Lou said sincerely. "This agency I've built up is all I got. If I lose it, I might as well go to prison. I guess I'll just have to throw myself on the mercy of the court."

Tom stood up and picked up his briefcase. He held his hand out to Lou. Lou looked up at him with terrible grief in his eyes. He stood up and took Tom's hand and shook it vigorously. "I'm sorry for everythin', Tom. But please believe that I'm not the same guy I was back then. I've grown and learned. I could never do anythin' like that today. You do believe that don't you?"

Tom gripped Lou's hand tighter and said, "Yes, I do believe that, Lou. Or I'd be takin' you with me to jail."

Less than a week later and early in the morning, James Collie was riding with Sheriff Clark in his patrol car as a Deputy Sheriff. Sheriff Clark had asked James to go with him to arrest Harry Barnett. It didn't take a lot of convincing on the Sheriff's part, as James could still remember that night long ago vividly. However, James insisted that they tell Sue Ann what they were doing and why. The Sheriff objected but James refused to go if Sue Ann was not made fully aware of everything. In the end, the Sheriff gave in and a meeting was held at the Collie house and Sue Ann was told everything.

Sue Ann didn't cry or make a scene. She told Sheriff Clark that she had been expecting it for a long, long time. She also made it clear that she held no hard feelings toward James for the part he was playing. Her only request was that they try their best not to hurt her Father. Whatever the situation may be, he was still her Father. Sheriff Clark told her he didn't want any trouble, or for anyone to be hurt. But there was a job to be done and how it turned out depended on Harry Barnett.

After all was said and done, James was sworn in as a Deputy Sheriff. Sheriff Clark had described to James his desire to keep as many people as possible out of this. That is why he hadn't called in Captain Borden. James had agreed, but reluctantly.

As the patrol car pulled up to the gate leading to the Barnett house, Sheriff Clark pulled the car to a stop. He turned to James, who was carrying his hunting rifle. "Okay, now Jim, let's go over this again. You're here as my back up. I don't expect you to have to do anythin'. I want you to open the car door on your side and stand behind it. You can place your rifle through the open window so Harry can see it. Be sure you're loaded but don't do anythin' unless I give the word or unless shootin' starts. Are we clear on all this?" James nodded his head yes but didn't say anything. "Good. Now, if you could jump out and open the gate for us we'll get to it."

Sheriff Clark pulled the patrol car to a stop about twenty yards from the Barnett porch. Sally had seen them approaching and was on the porch to meet them.

"Hello, Tom. Is that you?" Sally yelled happily.

"Yeah, Sally, it's me," the Sheriff responded as he open his car door and stepped out. James did as he had been told and got out and stood behind the car door on his side.

"Well what brings you out to see us, Tom? I don't think you've been here since the election?" Sally asked still in a happy voice.

Sheriff Clark got right to the issue at hand. "Could you ask Harry if he would step out here and speak with me?" The Sheriff's voice was all business there were no pleasantries present.

Sally stiffened and stood up straight. "What's goin' on, Tom? Why so formal?"

"Please, Sally, just ask Harry to come out."

"Sally, don't worry," Harry Barnett said as he walked out onto the porch carrying a Winchester thirty-thirty rifle.

"Harry, what's this about?" Screamed Sally in terror.

Sheriff Clark held up his left hand keeping his right on the butt of his revolver. "Please, everyone, stay calm," he said. He stepped out from behind the car door and walked a short distance away from the car. "Harry, the gun isn't necessary."

"Ain't it?" Harry hissed.

"Sally," Sheriff Clark said urgently, "please come over here and stand behind the patrol car." Sally didn't move. She was terrified and didn't know what to do. She kept looking back and forth between Sheriff Clark and her husband. "Sally, please come over here and stand behind the patrol car," Sheriff Clark repeated in a harder voice.

"Sally, go ahead. It's probably for the best," Harry yelled at her.

"But, Harry..." she started.

"Just do it, woman," he yelled again in a vicious voice. Sally hurried behind the patrol car crying in hysterics.

"Come on, Harry," Sheriff Clark pleaded. "Let's just go talk."

"I know why you're here, Sheriff Clark," Harry challenged in a mocking voice. "It took you long enough. I still can't believe how dumb you are. How could anybody vote for you as sheriff? I sure as hell didn't. You'd still be settin' on your fat ass if they hadn't found my shotgun. Oh! Don't looked so surprised, you think I wouldn't find out? Shit yeah, I knew it before you even went up to talk to that dumb shit, Louis Mailer." Harry took a step towards the end of the porch and levered a bullet into his rifle's firing chamber.

Sheriff Clark quickly pulled his revolver from the holster and leveled it at Harry. "I didn't come here for this, Harry. It doesn't have to be this way." As the Sheriff spoke, James worked the bolt action on his hunting rifle loading a bullet into the firing chamber and cocking the rifle.

"Harry, I goin' to ask you to put that rifle down now before I have to do somethin' I don't want to do and somethin' that we can't reverse, please do that for me, Harry." The Sheriff seemed to be almost begging. At the same time, James slowly put his rifle to his shoulder and put the sites on Harry's chest.

"Harry, please!" It was Sally screaming. "For God's sake, Harry, please do as the Sheriff says."

"Bullshit," Harry yelled, "my daughter has run off to that nigger lovin' Collie family, my son has gone off to get is ass killed in the damn army and my wife goes over to those nigger lovers to be with our so called, grandchild. All I can say is What-ta-shit anyway." Harry raised his rifle towards the Sheriff but before he could fire, Sheriff Clark put two thirty-eight caliber hollow point bullets through his chest. A hollow point bullet makes a small hole going in but a large hole as it exits. The two rounds slammed into Harry throwing him back up against the wall of the house. He dropped the rifle and slowly slid down the wall leaving a streak of blood as he went down. By the time he fell to the porch, he was dead.

Sally screamed over and over again and fell to the ground holding her head between her hands.

⸺◦●◦⸺

Since Coalville still didn't have a resident doctor in town, Sheriff Clark had to call Athens to get a corner. Athens was fifty miles away so it had taken over four hours for the corner to arrive and another hour to go over the scene and remove the body. All this time, James had sat with Sally in the kitchen where he had taken her to try and calm her down. Even now, almost five hours after the shooting, Sally was still shaking. She had stopped crying but she was obviously confused, scared, and disoriented. The corner had given her a small sedative that he had with him to help calm her, and it did seem to have some good effect.

Now with the shooting scene marked off and the body on its way to the Athens morgue, Sheriff Clark, James, and Sally were in the patrol car headed back to Coalville. Sheriff Clark was driving, James was in the passenger seat still holding his rifle, and Sally was seated in the back. She sat quietly with her hands in her lap.

James watched Sheriff Clark as he drove. The Sheriff seemed very tense and gripped the steering wheel extremely tight. "Tom, are you okay?" James asked in a low voice.

"Of course I'm not okay," the Sheriff shot back, "I just killed a man."

"There wasn't much else you could've done," James replied remaining calm himself. "I had him in my sites too and I would've fired if you hadn't beaten me to it."

Tom took a deep breath and let it out slowly. "I know, I know. You're right. It's just that I've never killed anyone before, and I'm tellin' you it's the shits. You've been in a war and I guess at one time or the other you've felt this way?"

"Yes, I have," James said. "It took me several years and a good woman before I could justify it. But, I did finally come to understand that what I did over there in France had to be done; there was nothin' I could've done to change it. It's the same here. You did what you had to do and you'll come to see that it was justified, or as justified as anyone can make killin'."

Tom looked over at James. "Thanks, Jim, but I just hope it doesn't happen again because this thing ain't over yet."

"What does that mean?"

"We'll talk about it after we've taken care of Sally."

The decision had been made to take Sally to James' house so that she could be with Sue Ann. When they arrived at the Collie house, James and Tom took her gently into the house. They spent over an hour going over with Sue Ann and Mary about what had happened. Sue Ann didn't cry as she had fixed her heart to expect it. She took her Mother into her and Kyle's room and talked with her gently. Mary made some hot tea that she spiked with lemon, honey, and whisky. Sally drank several cups before she finally fell asleep on Sue Ann's bed.

After things were all explained and the situation had calmed a bit, James took Tom into the kitchen. "Would you like to have a little drink of whisky, Tom?" He asked.

"Not now," Tom said looking around to make sure they were alone. Then in a low voice he said, "Like I told you, this thing ain't over yet and I'll still need you to cover my back."

"Jesus, Tom, what in hell else could there be?"

"Do you remember what Harry said about us findin' the shotgun?"

"Yeah, I remember," James answered thoughtfully.

"Well, how did he know? I'll tell you how he knew; someone told him what was goin' on, and that someone has been doin' that sort of thing for a long time."

"You're talkin' about the murders of Moonbeam and Jim Upter aren't you?" James asked.

"Yes, I am."

James looked suspiciously at Tom. "And I guess you're askin' me to come with you to finish this whole thing today. Am I right about that?"

Tom looked frustrated. "Yes, you're right and I'm sorry as hell to have to ask you, Jim. But I really don't have anyone else I trust enough. Will you please do it?"

"You know I will, Tom. Do we need to leave right away?"

"Yeah, the quicker we get goin' the better."

"Okay, you go on out to the car and I'll tell Mary where I'm goin' and what I'm doin'. Plus, I want to get somethin' else to take with me."

"Are you goin' to tell her the truth?" Tom asked worried.

"Of course I am, Tom. I'm not goin' to lie to her."

"Okay, I'm sorry for askin'. I'll see you at the car. But please make it quick."

A little later as Sheriff Clark pulled the patrol car into his parking spot at the courthouse, there was a beehive of activity going on. People were running every which way and the courthouse seemed to be emptying out. Since it was only three-thirty PM, he thought all of this to be strange. The only deputies the Sheriff had now-a-days were ones he assigned on a temporary basis such as James was doing now. Since James was the only Sheriff's Deputy currently sworn in, Tom knew it couldn't be any of his people involved.

"What the hell do you think is goin' on?" Tom asked James as they both got out of the car.

"Beats me," James responded.

As they approached the courthouse steps, Tom grabbed a man running by and pulled him aside. "Hey, what's all the commotion about?" He asked.

"Where you been?" The man shot back. "It's Alice. She's gone bananas."

Tom shook the man and yelled, "What the hell you talkin' about?"

"She's gone crazy," the man yelled back. "She's got a gun and a hostage in the Sheriff's office. She's threatin' to kill the hostage." Then the man noticed he was talking to the Sheriff. "Oh shit, I'm sorry, Sheriff, I didn't notice it was you."

Tom was stunned for a moment, but then seemed to come back to his senses. "You say she's holdin' a hostage?"

The man just nodded his head yes and stared at the Sheriff.

Tom shook the man again. "Well," he yelled in the man's face, "who's the hostage and what in God's name does she want?"

The man didn't say anything he just continued to stare at the Sheriff. He tried to pull free but Tom held him securely.

"What the hell's wrong with you? Answer me Goddamn it!"

Finally the man blurred out, "It's your wife, Sheriff. She's got your wife and she wants to talk to you."

The Sheriff was dumbfounded. He let the man go and turned and stared at James. "Evie," he whispered. "She's got Evie." The Sheriff turned away from James and ran up the courthouses steps taking them three at a time.

When Tom reached the third floor, it was completed deserted except for one man. It was the Mayor of Coalville, Jacob Long. He was at Alice's desk and was on the phone. He looked up to see Sheriff Clark walk in. He frantically waved for Tom to come over to him. Tom looked around carefully and then walked slowly over to the Mayor.

"Tom," the Mayor whispered, "Alice is in there holdin' a gun to Evie's head. I think she's gone insane. I've got the Dallas Police on the line but they've got me waitin' while they get authority to send some officers down here."

"That'll take hours," Tom said simply. "Did you try Athens?"

"Yes and they're to get the County Sheriff. They're workin' on that and'll get back to me. I've told 'em to call the Mayor's office. I have someone standin' by the phone."

"Has Alice said why she's doin' this?" Tom asked. "And how did she get Evie? Evie knew I was out on business and I wouldn't be in the office."

The Mayor looked at Tom with wonder in his eyes. "I can't answer those questions, Tom. All she's yelled through that door is 'Get the Sheriff in here'."

Tom stood up straight and looked at his office door. "Well, I guess the Sheriff better go see what she wants."

"Tom, be careful. You sure you don't want to wait for help?"

"There's no time, Jacob."

Tom walked to his office door and lightly knocked on the door. "Alice, this is Sheriff Clark. I understand we have some kind of problem."

"Come on in, Tom," came the cheerful response from the office.

Tom opened the door and slowly walked into the office. He tried not to look surprised by what he saw but it was a major effort. He took off his hat hung it on the hat rack just as he always did. His face maintained a steady unemotional expression. Without ceremony, he gently closed the office door.

James had followed Tom up to the third floor and was standing at the stairwell entrance. He heard the entire conversation between Tom and the Mayor. When Tom went into the office, James could see inside. He had a quick glance before Tom closed the door. After Tom closed the door, James turned and ran back down the stairs.

Alice was over by Tom's favorite widow. She had the widow wide open and the office fan was on the floor across from her blowing on high. She was sitting in a chair and leaning on the widow seal. Her left arm was bent and her elbow rested on the outside of the widow seal. As she sat in the chair, her legs were spread wide apart. She had her dress pulled to her waist so she could accommodate her wide spread legs. Kneeling between her legs, facing away from her, was Evie. In Alice's right hand she held a thirty-eight caliber service revolver, and the barrel was pushed tightly against the back of Evie's neck.

Evie looked up at Tom, but only with her eyes; she didn't move her head. She was on her knees facing away from Alice. Her back was pressed up against the edge of the chair between Alice's legs. On the surface, she looked calm, but Tom knew by the look in her eyes that she was terrified. However, there were no tears.

Trying to remain calm, Tom started for his desk, but Alice stopped him with a shout. "Hold it, Tom," she yelled. Her voice had a hate in it that Tom had not heard before. "Before you do anythin' else, take your gun out of the holster usin' just your index finger and thumb. Then, drop it in the trash basket by the desk."

Tom did as he was told.

"Okay, you can sit down now." Her voice was cheerful once again.

Tom went to his desk and sat down. He looked across to Alice and Evie at the window. "I have to say, Alice, this whole thing comes as a real surprise."

Alice didn't look at Tom. She looked out the window. "Oh, I think after your talk with Lou and then the thing with Harry you know what's been goin' on." Then turning her head towards Tom, she asked, "Don't you?"

"Yeah, I guess I do," Tom said matter-of-factly. "But I don't understand the why of it all and especially I don't understand why Evie is here with a gun at her head."

Alice laughed and poked Evie in the back of the head with the gun barrel. "She was just available at the time. She came into the office to leave you a bag lunch. How about that, ain't she sweet?"

Tom continued to say calm. "I guess you can let her go now that you've got me?"

Alice laughed again and pushed the gun barrel hard up again the base of Evie's skull. "I guess I really got your attention, uh?"

'Yeah, Alice, you really got my attention," Tom said with anger dripping from each word. "Earlier today I had to kill a man. It gave me a horrible feelin'. I sure was hopin' I wouldn't ever have to kill anyone ever again. But here we are, Alice. You're sittin' there with a gun to my wife's head. So, before I kill you, would you like to tell me why you did all the killin' and why you'd want to hurt my wife?"

Alice's face lost all of its cheerfulness and it drained pale. "Sure I'll tell you; you dumb hick sheriff." Her voice was vicious now and she gripped the gun tighter. Then she got hold of herself and smiled at him. "You know what the song says, 'A man was the cause of it all'. Well, the man in question here was Jim Upter."

"You mean Jim Upter, Ruth's husband?"

"Yeah, that's who I mean. They weren't really married you know. His marriage to Ruth was a joke, it wasn't even real. He was hot after me from the moment he hit town. That dumb bitch never saw it. Why, old Jim and I had several little interludes." Then she laughed and turned her head back out the window. "But like you said, Tom, here we are."

Tom was becoming more and more concerned as Alice kept poking the gun hard against Evie's neck and head. More alarming was that the gun was cocked and could off easily. He tried to get her attention back to him. "If you and Jim were havin' such a gay old time, why kill 'im?"

"Men," she said shrugging her shoulders, "after all I did for him he was goin' to leave me. Can you believe that? After I killed that nigger for 'im, of course I had a little help from Harry, but it was me mostly. And I kept a watch on you and Lou both. I knew Lou was playin' both ends against the middle so we really couldn't trust him too much. I let him know everythin' that was goin' on." She paused a moment and seem to get very agitated. "Then, after all that, when everythin' went in the shitter and everyone was goin' to get out, he said he was leavin' to go back to New Orleans with Ruth and Dick. Can you believe that ungrateful, two timin' ass? So, I fixed it so he couldn't leave. I borrowed Lou's little twenty two and used it to get him where I wanted him. Then I drove my kitchen butcher knife right between his shoulder blades. And I pushed it in as deep as I could. You should've seen the look on his face as he laid dyin'. He was as dumb as most men, he didn't even know it was me. I teased him as he died. After it was over I was mad at myself for not lettin' him know who had done it to him. But, what was done was already done; no need to fret over it." She stopped talking and stood up. She towered over Evie and began to tap her on top of the head with the barrel of the gun.

Tom became frantic. "Okay, Alice, where do we go from here? Why are we doin' this?"

"Well, Tom, to tell you the truth, I'm not sure. I'm sure I'm a goner. I guess they'll put me in jail for life or put me in the electric chair, or maybe in a funny farm somewhere. I'm tryin' to decide to go out on my own, or to take a few of you dumb asses with me."

"Evie's never done anythin' to you, Alice. In fact, she's been nothin' but good to you."

"Oh, yeah, good old Evie," Alice said sadly as she continued to tap Evie on the head. "She a sweet little thing ain't she, Tom? I bet you guys get it on real good, don't you?"

"Alice, please," Tom pleaded getting to his feet.

Evie now began to cry. "Please, Alice, Please don't."

Tom started around the desk but Alice stopped him. "Stay where you are, Tom or all blow her brains out."

Tom stopped immediately. His frustration was almost unbearable.

Alice stood over Evie and put the gun barrel straight down on the top of Evie's head. With her left hand she held on the window seal to steady herself and with her right hand she prepared to pull the trigger.

Finally, she's in clear view James thought to himself and he adjusted the scope on his hunting rifle. He congratulated himself for thinking to get the scope before he left the house with Tom. Now, the image of Alice in the third story window came in clearly, and he could see the gun with the barrel jammed against the top of Evie's head. Time was running out, he told himself. It had to be now. Calling up all the years of training with guns both in the army and hunting, James took a deep breath and held it. Then, he squeezed the trigger.

Suddenly in the Sheriff's office things exploded. The gun flew from Alice's hand and fell to the floor. Alice's hand was spewing blood everywhere. Tom moved quickly and at the same time yelled at Evie. "Run Evie, get out this office now." Evie was on her feet and running for the door. She had the door open and she was out in a few seconds.

Tom was grabbing for the wastebasket to get his gun but his hand hit it and knocked it over. He was scrambling around on the floor trying to get the gun. Just as he was about to pick it up he saw Alice standing over him. She had the gun in her left hand and it was cocked and pointed directly at his head. She held her right hand up as blood flowed freely down her arm. There appeared to be two fingers missing on her hand.

"Well, Tom boy, I guess this is it," she said smiling wickedly. Then, she put the gun barrel in her mouth and blew the back of her head off.

⸻◉⸻

When it was all over, two people were dead. In the coming months there would be an inquest and a grand jury. Witnesses would be called to the County Courthouse in Athens, Texas. Sheriff Tom Clark, James Collie, Sally Barnett, Captain Timothy Borden, and Mayor Jacob Long would all be called to testify. The Athens Corner would also testify. In the end, Harry Barnett's death would be called a justifiable shooting by a duly elected officer of the law. Alice Conner's death would be ruled a suicide.

The deaths of Thomas Jefferson Washington, alias Moonbeam, and Jim Upter were both ruled to be murder committed by Alice Conner and Harry Barnett. The cases were closed.

During all the hearings, the inquest, and the grand jury, Louis Mailer's name never came up.

CHAPTER SEVENTY-THREE

The Battle for Guadalcanal

August 1942

In the middle of July 1942, Captain Dick Jordan informed his wife Cheryl Jordan that he would be shipping out in the next couple of weeks. He couldn't tell her where but only that he had been assigned permanently to the First Marine Division. Where they went, was where he was going. He got orders to detach him from Colonel Wolff's command and to reassign him to the First Marine Division. He was to report to the San Francisco airport, along with several other officers from Colonel Wolff's old command, to be flown to an undisclosed destination.

Cheryl and Dick both knew it was coming so they were prepared, or at least almost prepared. She helped Dick pack but really all he was taking with him was his military duffel bag with his rank and name stenciled on it. But the ritual of working together to pack made Cheryl feel better.

Right after she had arrived at the Presidio back in early June, she was able to get a job in San Francisco teaching third grade at Lincoln Elementary School just off the base. It had worked out great. She got the job in the summer vacation period so she would be ready when school started in September. Quickly after that, they got a little apartment just outside the Presidio and things couldn't have been better. They made passionate love every day, they laughed, and they played. But they knew it was only for a while. In fact, as it turned out, it lasted just over a month.

As she stood at the airport with Dick, Cheryl could only feel sorrow. She tried to be brave and send her man off with a smiling face, but it didn't work out that way. They held each other until the last moment when the Military Police came and almost had to physically separate Dick from Cheryl. She watched as they escorted him across the tarmac to the waiting plane. She waved and waved until the plane was in the air and long gone from site. Then, she allowed herself to cry uncontrollably.

⊷⊶

Dick caught up with the First Marine Division at a little volcanic island called Koro in the Fiji chain. Here the division was practicing amphibious landings that he had been training for. The practices did not go well and everyone was alarmed because their first battle was coming up. But they stayed at it until July 31st when they set sail for a place called Guadalcanal. It was to be America's first offensive action of the war. Dick was put in charge of Baker Company of the 2nd Battalion 1st Marine Regiment, better known as B/2/1 (Baker Company, 2nd Battalion, 1st Regiment). He spent the entire time of the trip working with and getting to know his company.

Then the big day came. On August 7, 1942 the First Marine Division landed on Guadalcanal. The landing was mostly unopposed as the Japanese had moved back inland. After getting some organizational issues worked out, the Marines headed inland to establish defensive positions. Their principle mission on Guadalcanal was to take and hold the airstrip that the Japanese had begun to build. As the Marines headed inland, no one would know it at the time but they were about to get into one of the most brutal and bloodiest battles the Marines had yet to encounter in their gloried history.

As Dick and his men worked their way through the dense jungle, they saw things that they were not prepared for. Marines captured by the Japanese had been brutally tortured and horribly mutilated and left tied to trees for all to see. The atrocities staggered the imagination. Dick couldn't believe that human beings could do those sorts of things to other human beings. He and his men both suffered severe shock at seeing these inhuman actions. They watched as Navy Corpsmen tried to help wounded Japanese soldiers only to be blown to bits by hidden hand grenades, and surrendering Japanese would be carrying explosive charges on them and kill all the Marines attempting to accept their surrender. They saw all these things and their hearts became hardened.

To make things worse, two days later on August 9th, the U.S. Navy suffered a staggering defeat at what would become known as the Battle of Salvo Island. As a result, the Navy left without unloading all the supplies and equipment that the Marines were supposed to have and very badly needed. The Navy was gone, their supplies were gone, and now the Marines were on their own against a brutal and determined enemy. But that didn't change their orders; they were still expected to hold the airstrip.

As the defensive positions were established, the push inland stopped and the Marines set about holding what they had and defending the airstrip. During this time, Captain Dick Jordan called a meeting of all his officers. They gathered inside a small tent. There were four platoon leaders and their second in commands; totaling eight officers. Once they were gathered, Dick stood in front of them.

"Okay, men, here it is," he started. "We and all of our men have seen what the Japs are capable of. It should be a simple deduction to know that bein' capture isn't an option. You need to instill in your men that basic fact. And another thing to instill in them is that they need to get just as mean, brutal, and bad as the Japs, because if they're not, they're goin' to die. I know it's our nature to show mercy and give quarter to wounded enemy or those surrenderin', but we can't do that here. Too many good Marines and Navy Corpsmen have died tryin' to help wounded Japs or take prisoners. From now on let it be known that there'll none of that in my company. We haven't met the Japs in a stand up fight yet. But when we do, you send those sons-of-bitches straight to hell. And I mean all of 'em. Am I clear?

Every single officer in the tent shouted, "Aye, Sir."

By August 20th, Dick's regiment, the First Marines, had move up to the mouth of a river that was called Alligator Creek. They took up defensive positions on the west side of the river where it emptied into the Pacific Ocean. Dick's company, Baker Company, was given the responsibility of the left flank of the defensive line, which was nearest the ocean. From his command bunker, Dick could see both the river in front of him and the ocean on his left. There was a sandbar that ran all the way from the east bank of the river to the west bank. The sandbar was only about one foot below the surface of the river, allowing men to actually walk across the river.

All of Dick's men were dug in. During the day, Dick went from foxhole to foxhole making sure his men had plenty of ammunition and that their equipment was clean, ready, and working properly. He also made sure they got what food he could find. Since the Navy had left them, they were living mostly on captured Japanese food and old Army rations from World War One.

Baker Company consisted of four platoons with about forty-three men in each platoon. The first and third platoons were rifle platoons, but the second and fourth platoons had two mortar squads each and two machine gun squads each. Dick had ordered the machine gun squads forward of the mortar squads and positioned them to cover the left flank nearest the ocean and the sandbar. The rifle squads were scattered between the machine gun squads. Dick was pleased that his platoons were at full strength and he commanded about one hundred and seventy-three Marines. That would vary at times depending on sharing strength with other companies. But at this time, Dick had all of his platoons at full strength.

As the day neared its end and the sun was setting into the ocean, everyone tried to relax and sleep a little. That lasted until a little after midnight. During the night, a Japanese force had moved up to the east bank of the river. Sometime after one AM on August 21st, flares lit up the sky and mortar and machine gun fire rained down on Marines. The Battle of Alligator Creek had begun.

Unfortunately for the Japanese, the Marines were ready. Dick ordered his mortars into action and they rained shells down on the east bank. Small arms fire from rifles on both sides of the river echo through the night. Then, a large company of Japanese charged onto the sandbar and started for Marines on the west side. The Marine machine gun squads opened up in full force. Dick ran from his command bunker to where the machine guns covering the sandbar were. Just as he got there, he could see them firing at a rapid rate, quickly reloading as their ammunition belts ran out. It was a murderous fire, but a few Japanese soldiers actually made it across the sandbar. They engaged the Marines in the front line positions in deadly hand-to-hand combat. There was no quarter given by either side. The Japanese actually managed to take a few foxholes on the front line. But an attack by Marines from Charlie Company, which was being held in reserves, killed the Japanese and retook the frontline positions. The first attack by the Japanese had failed with heavy losses.

Dick was again out of his command bunker and running recklessly from position to position checking on his men and officers. To create a cross fire, he repositioned two of his machine gun squads on either side of the sandbar. Over the next several minutes, both sides fired at each other across the river. Dick was making his way back to his command bunker when flares lit up the sky and another wave of Japanese came charging across the sandbar. This time the Japanese sent a re-enforced company of nearly two hundred men. Dick's cross fire proved to be deadly, and once again the Japanese were stopped with heavy losses. Only a few made it back to the east side of the river.

Over the next hour, it became a slugfest between mortar and artillery fire. Then, about five AM in the early morning, First Lieutenant Jamie Mason, who commanded Dick's First Platoon, came running into the command bunker.

"Christ All Mighty, Captain," he yelled frantically, "the Japs are trying to flank us on the left."

"But that's ocean." Dick responded.

"Hell, I know that, Captain, their wading through the surf. Goddamn it they're on the beach to our left flank."

"Get to Second Platoon and order them to reposition their mortars to attack the beach and have Fourth Platoon move one of its machine gun squads passed the rifle positions and put fire directly on to the beach. And hurry it up!"

Lieutenant Mason hurriedly left the command bunker holding on to his helmet. Dick watched the beach but couldn't see much. He called for flares. Soon the sky lit up and he could see hundreds of Japanese wading through the surf. He was about to try and find out why the mortars and machine guns had not opened up yet, when mortar shells began to rain down on the beach area. The mortar fire was followed quickly by the chatter of machine gun fire. Dick tried to call the Third Platoon but the communications were obviously broken. So, once again, he left his command bunker and ran to where the Third Platoon was supposed to be. He found them exactly where they should be. He ordered them to move away from the sandbar put their rifle fire onto the beach. Shortly, the beach area was being hit with mortars, machine gun, and rifle fire. It was a murderous combination that raked death across the surf of the beach. The Japanese just kept coming until none of them were left standing.

By five PM on August 21st, the battle was over. Dick and several of his officers walked out on the beach and look at the carnage. Lying in the morning sun before them on the beach and near the sandbar were over eight hundred dead or dying Japanese. Dick found the site of such slaughter repulsive. He lingered only a short while as the men came from their foxholes and bunkers to browse around looking for souvenirs. Even though they had been warned, several more Marines were killed or wounded by dying Japanese.

The Japanese had suffered their first ground defeat of the war. But it would not be their last, and the Battle for Guadalcanal was not yet over.

CHAPTER SEVENTY-FOUR

Cherrie's News

September 1942

Mary and Sue Ann Collie were down on the floor playing with Kyle. He was struggling to make his first steps but hadn't managed as yet. Both women would laugh when Kyle would stagger and fall down. However, he didn't cry. He would just rollover and laugh to the women's delight.

Mary looked over at Sue Ann and said, "James says we can go down to the drugstore and pick up our latest pictures to send to Dee. They should be ready by now."

"That'll be great and work out perfect, because I'm finishin' a letter to Dee tonight and I'll get it in the Victory Mail tomorrow. I'll include the best pictures."

Mary smiled and was about to speak again when the telephone rang. She pushed herself to her feet and walked over and picked up the phone on its third ring.

"Hello."

"Hi, Mom," came a happy voice over the line, "it's me Cherrie."

"Oh, my goodness, it's good to hear from you after so long," Mary said happily. As she spoke she signaled Sue Ann to come over. Sue Ann quickly scooped up Kyle and went and stood by Mary at the phone.

"Well, I got a couple of news items that I'm sure all of you will be interested in," Cherrie said.

"Okay, but hold on a sec while I get Sue Ann where she can hear what you're sayin'." Mary got out of the chair by the phone and sat on the floor. Sue Ann sat now next to her holding Kyle. She then turned the receiver out so Sue Ann could hear. "Okay, go ahead and fill us in. Sue Ann and Kyle are right here with me."

"Here goes," Cherrie started. "First here's what I know about Dick. I know he's with the First Marine Division, so I'm positive he's with them on Guadalcanal. I try not to worry but all the newspapers say the fightin' there is awful. His letter's don't tell me much just that he's okay and not to worry. As if I could do that. All I can do is pray and hope that he gets out of there okay." Cherrie stopped talking and they heard clinking on the line. "Sorry," Cherrie said as she returned, "I had to drop some more money in the phone. I'm down at the drug store usin' their phone. I'm not sure how much longer my money will hold out, so here's the last bit of news." There was a short pause, then, "Mom, I've got the gene." And then silence.

"Hello, Cherrie, you still there?"

"Yes, Mom, I'm here. I've got the gene," she repeated and silence again.

"Cherrie, stop this and tell me what you mean," Mary demanded.

"Come on, Mom, I'm runnin' out of money here. Think about it. I've got the gene!"

Mary was about to get angry and yell at her daughter, but then it dawned on her. "You've got the gene," she breathed laughing.

"Sue Ann waved her hand at Mary and whispered, "What does that mean?"

Mary was beside herself. She stood up. "When did you find out?"

"Two days ago, I went to the doctor today to confirm it."

"And you're sure there's two of 'em."

"Yes, Ma'am, I am. And they're due in April of '43."

"Oh, so that's it," shouted Sue Ann jumping up and down with Kyle in her arms.

Then Cherrie's tone changed. "Mom, can I speak to Sue Ann for a moment?" She asked seriously.

Mary didn't answer she just nodded as if Cherrie could see her. She handed the phone to Sue Ann and took Kyle. Sue Ann took the phone and the first thing she heard was more clinking sounds.

"Sue Ann?" Cherrie shouted.

"Yeah, I'm here, Cherrie,"

"I just put in the last of my money so this'll be fast. I'm worried about what to do about tellin' Dick. I know you worried about the same thing with Dee. I would really like some advice, because I know Dick is in a fight for his life and I'm just not sure what to do. Can you help me?"

Sue Ann took in a deep breath and then let it out slowly. "My original idea was not to tell Dee," she said softly. "But your Dad was adamant about Dee knowin'. I lost some sleep over it for several days, but, in the end, your Dad was right. I told Dee in a letter and it really scared me. I was terrified that Dee would lose his concentration on doin' his job. But Dee wrote me back and he was ecstatic. Later when he came home for Christmas he told me that my letter really lifted him up and made him even better at what he was doin'. I can't tell you what to do, Cherrie, but I think Dick would be just like Dee in this kind of thing. I really do."

There was a long silence, then the sound of the operator asking Cherrie to deposit another fifty cents. "I gotta go, Sue Ann." Cherrie shouted quickly. "Thank you and tell Mom I love her and that I'll be back in touch just as soon as I get this all figured out. Thanks again." There was a clicking as Cherrie hung up and then silence.

CHAPTER SEVENTY-FIVE

The Escape Phase 1

September 1942

Clint was the third man in line on the chain gang. Ever since they had been transfer to the Texas oil fields, they were marched out to the fields in chains and then marched back in chains. As bad as things were, he liked it better than breaking rocks. As they reached the rig they were assigned to, the line stopped and the men assigned to that particular rig were unlocked from the chain line and released into the custody of the guard in charge of that rig. Once there, they would work the entire day in that area. They would never leave the area for any reason. Their food was brought out to them and there were portable toilet facilities in each area.

Since the transfer to the Texas oil fields took place back in March, he had little contact with the outside world. Judy had come by once right after the transfer but had not been back since. The underground mail had obviously ceased to exist, because, with the exception of Judy's short visit, he had heard nothing from anybody.

The security in the oil fields was nothing like the security back at Leavenworth. Clint saw several escape possibilities, but, for one reason or the other, they didn't pan out. They were housed in an old army barracks just south of Odessa, Texas. The barracks was inside a large double barbed wire fence compound that had razor wire coiled all across the top. There were guard towers at each corner that were manned twenty-four hours a day. Search lights were located in each tower and were sweeping the compound all night. Clint figured the odds of escaping from the compound were close to zero. Any escape would have to come out in the fields.

They were picked up at the compound gate each morning at six AM and they returned each evening at six PM. Their work week went from Monday through a half day on Saturday. They rode to and from the oil fields in a modified school bus with mesh wire over the windows and a steel door between the passengers and the driver. Sometimes the trip to the fields could take a while depending on the rig where the inmate was assigned. Some of the rigs were close together and some were miles apart. The work in the fields varied from very hard to almost nothing. Everything depended on what the objective of the day was. The work ranged from rigging drilling pipe to cleaning sludge dumps where excess oil, mud, and water were dumped during the drilling process. Sometimes, when the drilling was complete on a rig and the oil had been found and tapped off, there was some slack time and the work they did was just busy work assigned by the guards.

For Clint and the inmate with him, a guy named Markus Millburn, today wasn't too bad a day. Their rig had recently been tapped off and the guard assigned them the job of moving and restacking the left over drilling pipe into an area where a truck could pick them up, an easy job in relative terms. The rig they were assigned to was almost a mile from the next nearest rig. The sky was a bright blue and the Texas summer heat was finally beginning to break. They had just finished their lunch and the guard had given them some extra time off due to the light work load. The guard was a pretty good guy that they just called Slim because he was about six foot five but only weight about one hundred and fifty pounds.

Clint was sitting on a stack of drilling pipe when the thought he heard an airplane. He looked up into the bright sky but couldn't see anything except the bright ball that was the sun. He searched the sky for a while but gave up. It was frustrating because he could still hear the airplane but he couldn't see it. Markus had gone to the portable toilet several minutes ago and not come back yet. Clint stood up and started walking toward the small one-man guard house. Slim was resting in a chair just outside the house with his rifle across his lap. When he saw Clint approach, he picked up his rifle and leveled it at him.

Clint stopped and held up his hands and said, "Okay, Slim, I'm only walkin' around."

Slim didn't say anything he just kept the rifle trained on Clint.

The sound of the airplane got louder. Clint stopped walking and again looked up in the sky. "Hey, Slim, can you see that plane? It's crazy that I hear it so well but I can't see it."

Slim still said nothing. He just watched Clint carefully. He glanced over to the portable toilet to check on Marcus but the door to the toilet was still closed. Slim was getting a little nervous. "Clint," he yelled, "you go back and sit down while I go check on Marcus. He's been gone too long."

Clint did as he was told. He went back to where he had been sitting and sat back down. Slim carefully watched Clint and at the same time walked slowly towards the toilet. Suddenly, the sound of the airplane became very loud as if it were right over them. Then, a huge fog of smoke came down upon them. It blinded Clint. He couldn't see anything. He got to his feet in a mild panic. He could still hear the airplane engine and it sounded very near. Clint decided the best thing to do was just lay down on the ground until this whole thing was over. He started to lay down when someone grabbed him by the shirt collar and started pulling him. At first Clint figured it must be Slim, but the hand that held him was soft and not very strong. Clint could have broken away but decide he better not resist; it might get him killed.

The hand pulled him quickly through the smoky fog. They were getting closer and closer to the sound of the airplane engine. Suddenly, they stopped.

A familiar voice said, "Quick, Pa, jump in the back seat."

It was Judy. Clint stood as if frozen. He didn't know what he should do.

"Pa," Judy screamed in his face, "Get in the back seat, *NOW*. We only have a few minutes before this smoke drifts away. We gotta move, move!"

Almost on instinct, Clint turned and climbed up the wing and into the back seat. Judy had already gotten into the front seat. The engine roared loudly as Judy turned the plane and opened the throttle. Out across the oil field they went, and before he could gather his thoughts they were airborne. Looking back down he could see the smoke as it started to drift away. He could barely make out Slim aiming his rifle up at them. But it was too late; they had gained good altitude and were already flying fast through the bright blue sky.

The noise of the engine and sound of the wind prevented Clint from talking to Judy. She only looked back and smiled and gave him the thumbs up sign. He returned the signal with a huge grin on his face. He looked at the plane in which he was riding. No wonder he couldn't see it in the air; it was painted a beautiful sky blue. It blended into the bright Texas sky perfectly. He chuckled to himself and settled back to enjoy the ride.

⸰⸰⸰

Judy's route had been meticulously laid out by herself and Jimmy Orland. The route took a zigzag path that avoided towns, ranches and other oil fields. She flew at only two hundred feet so she couldn't be spotted by anyone unless they were looking for her. Even with the zigzagging, her steady course was southwest. The distance to her destination was only about two hundred and twenty miles, but that was as the crow flies. Her zigzag route added another eighty miles to the trip making it nearer three hundred miles. The best speed she could safely get out the old bi-plane crop duster she was flying was right at one hundred and twenty miles per hour. That meant her flight time would be a little less than three hours. By the time she reached her destination, she should be running out of gas. The old plane had no instrumentation save for an altimeter and a compass. As a result, she was flying by dead reckoning and landmarks.

Judy checked her watch and determined they had been flying for about two and a half hours. She looked back at Clint and saw he was calmly looking around and showed no signs of worry. She started to pay more attention to her landmarks because the one indicating her landing strip should be coming up any minute, unless she had missed something on the way. She took the chance to gain a little more altitude so she had a better view. And it was a good thing she did, because off to her left less than a mile away was the large bright red marker painted on the dessert floor. She banked left and flew around the marker checking it out. She could see a truck with several men in the back looking up at her. Things were going just fine. She circled again and then dropped altitude, lined up on the marker and made a perfect landing.

As she taxied to a stop and killed the engine, Jimmy Orland walked calmly up to the plane. She looked back at Clint and said, "Okay, Pa, this is where we get out." They both chambered out of the little cockpits and jumped to the ground. Judy immediately ran up to Jimmy and threw her arms around him and kissed him hard.

Jimmy kissed her back but separated himself from her. "I'll get caught up on that later, right now you get your Pa oriented and I'll take care of the plane. We need to get it done as fast as we can." He turned and signaled one of the men in the truck who came running over. "Okay, Juan," Jimmy shouted in a command voice, "get your guys goin' on the plane. I want it repainted to its original color with all the markings exactly as they were. You got the pictures, right?"

"See, Senor Jimmy, it will be done immediately."

"How long do you think, Juan?"

"I think maybe two hours at the most, Senor."

"Okay, get going on it. I'll take the others into town for something to eat and drink and we'll be back in two hours."

"See, Senor," Juan replied and then hurried over and got his crew busy.

Jimmy walked over to Clint and Judy who were involved in a deep conversation. "Come on, you two," he said. "We can take the truck into town for some eats and drinks. We have to be back here in two hours."

"Town," Clint said in amazement. "There's a town around here."

"Well," Jimmy laughed, "Something like a town. Come on."

A short time later all three were in a small bar with a wooden floor. It had a small wooden bar and three stools. There were four tables in the room with four chairs each. An overhead fan turned hopelessly to try and offset the heat. Even though it was late September, it was still hot in this part of Texas. They each had a cold beer in front of them and a large tray of tamales from which they all took part.

"Can I ask again where we are?" Clint asked looking round the small deserted bar room.

"You, my friend, are eating and drinking at the Tamale Casa in Terlingua, Texas."

"Never heard of it," Clint said taking a sip of beer. "But I ain't complainin'. The beers cold and these tamales are damn good."

"Well, I hope you like because you're goin' to have to stay near her for about four months," Judy said seriously.

"Where'll I be stayin'? Clint asked.

"There's an old minin' shack about three miles from here that we are goin' to use," Judy answered. "It's already been stocked and should last you about a month. I'll be back before your supplies run out and restock you. Now…"

She didn't finish her sentence before Clint interrupted her. "Don't you think it's time for me to be introduced to this gentleman? And to know why he would do all this for me?"

Judy started to speak but Jimmy held up his hand and stopped her. Being interrupted the second time in a row, she grabbed her beer and leaned heavily back in her chair.

"My name is Jimmy Orland and all the things I'm doing aren't for you it's for Judy. I love her and hope to make her my wife in the near future, if I can find a way to settle her down."

"Can I speak now?" Judy asked sarcastically.

"Please do," Jimmy said spreading his arms wide to yield the floor.

"Jimmy is on the Board of Directors of Mobil Oil in Dallas, and besides bein' loaded with money and havin' a great job, he's pretty damn good lookin' too," Judy smiled pointing her beer bottle at Jimmy. Then, turning back to Clint, "He's helped me with my flyin' and a hundred other things I won't go into. And he's the main reason we've been able to pull this caper off."

Clint stretched his hand across the table and Jimmy took it and they shook hands firmly. "Thank you. I know this is a big risk for both of you. I'll try and do whatever you two say, but why do I need to stay out here for four months?"

Judy leaned on the table and looked hard at Clint, "Now, Pa, you listen, and you listen real good. We can't have any foul ups here. One mistake and we're all in the shitter. You have to stay out where we're goin' to take you. You can't be comin' here to the bar. People, few though they may be, will notice. You gotta keep your head down and stay out of site for a while. I know it may seem just like prison, but it can't be helped right now. We need time to get you a new ID. Jimmy's knows people and we can get it done but it'll take some time. Now, tell me up front and truthfully, can you do this?"

"Yes, I can and I will. And don't think it's like prison 'cause it ain't."

"Okay, everybody, I guess we're on," Judy said slapping her hand together.

"You said you'd already stocked this shack. Do I eat cold stuff all the time or do I have the means to cook?"

Jimmy laughed, "You got lots of canned goods, bread, crackers, and water. You have a small stove to cook the canned good on. You've got a couple of cases of beer, but it'll be warm because there's no ice. You got pepper and salt and sugar. There aren't any perishables like meat or milk. But when Judy comes each month she'll bring you hamburgers and the like, and a cube of ice. And you got gas and electricity. I've got a radio out in the truck that I'll leave with you so can listen to music and the news. However, I warn you that there're only two stations you can pick up; one is from Alpine, Texas and I'm not sure where the other one comes from. Okay, if you have any more questions you can ask them on the way to the plane. We got to get going. Judy's got to fly the plane back to where we barrowed it from. I'll drop you at the shack and then I'll drive back to get my car in Alpine. That is after I've paid the Mexicans for their work on the plane. I want them back across the border before nightfall."

"Okay, let's get this show on the road," Clint said firmly slamming his hands down on the table.

As they got up, Judy put her hand on Clint's shoulder and said, "Remember, Pa, stay outa this town. Keep yourself hidden. Keep your head down. Now don't let me down. I got big plans for us. Just hang in there for a few months."

Clint leaned over and kissed her on the forehead. "I'll keep my end up, I swear to you." Then, he grabbed Jimmy's hand again and shook it hard. "I hope you can settle her down and marry her, Jimmy. I like you two together."

CHAPTER SEVENTY-SIX

Volunteers

September 1942

L t. Commander Daryl Collie and two other officers walked into
the CAG (Commander Air Group) quarters on their carrier the
USS Enterprise. They were all tired. They still worn their flight suits
and were still carrying their flight helmets when they were told to
report immediately to the CAG. They had just returned from another
sortie against the Japanese trying to take back Guadalcanal from the
Marines who were doggedly holding it against attack after attack.
The Marines on Guadalcanal didn't know why this shithole of an
island was so important but they were ordered to hold the airstrip,
now called Henderson Field in honor of a Marine pilot who died
at the Battle of Midway, on that island and that is what they were
going to do. The fact was that Henderson Field on Guadalcanal
was America's only way of keeping the supply lines to Australia
and New Zealand open. Without those supply lines, Australia
and New Zealand would fall to the Japanese and would take away
America's only staging place to fight the war in the Pacific. The
Japanese realized this maybe a little too late and began reinforcing
Guadalcanal with thousands of troops and keeping a large naval
support there. The Marines were holding on with nothing more
than what had or could steal from the enemy; and the fact that they
were United States Marines.

The three offices entered the CAG's quarters and came to
attention. The CAG immediately gave them the 'as you were'

command and everyone relaxed. The CAG's quarters were not really large so the four of them crowded the quarters. "I think the Ready Room is empty now, why don't we move there to have more room?"

They all followed the CAG to the Ready Room that was indeed empty. Once inside, he told them all to be seated. The tired officers flopped down into seats on the first row. "Okay, gentlemen, I guess you're wondering what this is all about." They all nodded in the affirmative. "I need three volunteers," the said simply. There was a long silence.

The three officers looked at each other and then Lt. Jeremy Walker asked, "For what, Sir?"

"Here's the story," the CAG started, "in February of next year Henderson Field will start getting the new F4U Corsair fighter. It's a hot new fighter made by Chance Vault that will completely outclass the Zero."

"Finally," Dee said in frustration. "It's about time we got a chance to fight those bastards on at least even terms."

"You're doin' okay, Collie," the CAG smiled, "I hear you just got number six today. Now you're an Ace in the Pacific Theater."

"Yes, I did, and so have several other guys," Dee replied in a harsh tone. "But we come back shot to hell after every sortie and we lose guys because the Wildcat can't stay with the Zero. It's tough out there, CAG."

The CAG straighten up and looked hard at Dee. "Damn right it tough out there, Mr. Collie. But, you know what, it's tough all over. Our Navy has been getting' its butt kicked tryin' to keep the Japs off those Marines on Guadalcanal. You know for every Marine that has died on Guadalcanal, four Sailors have died. Those Marines don't know that, but it's true. And speaking of those Marines, they've been fighting with no food or ammo for over a month." The CAG then slammed his fist against the wall and yelled, "So don't tell me how tough things are, Mr. Collie."

Dee jumped to his feet and stood to attention. "I'm sorry, Sir," Dee said in a completely different tone. "It's the frustration talkin', Sir, please accept my apology."

"Sit down, Mr. Collie," the CAG said in a softer voice, "we're all on edge."

"Thank you, Sir," Dee said as he retook his seat.

"Now," the CAG continued, "I'm asking for three volunteers to transfer to Henderson Field for the next six to eight months. You'll be flying land based aircraft, probably the Wildcat at first. The reason for this is to keep a high degree of combat efficiency at Henderson and to get the squadrons there ready for the Corsair. Mr. Collie, you've flow the Spitfire so you know what I mean. You other two will need to follow Mr. Collie's lead. And, Mr. Collie, since you are the ranking officer, you'll be in command of the transfers. Once you've established and organized the squadrons the way you want them, you'll take command of the Corsair squadrons." The CAG looked at all three officers and shrugged his shoulders. "You may have noticed I've been talkin' as if you've already volunteered. But, the truth is, it is a volunteer mission. But, gentlemen, I can't express strongly enough that we simply *CAN NOT* allow the Japs to take Guadalcanal and control of Henderson Field. So, we'll take a poll to see who goes and who stays."

Of course, all three officers volunteered.

"Thank you, gentlemen," the CAG said softly. "The Enterprise will be close enough to Guadalcanal by noon tomorrow for you to fly there. You'll take your Wildcats there and you'll report to the group commander. You'll fly sorties just like you do here but it goin' to be a lot busier. The Japs really want that airstrip back. They go after it every day with offshore ship bombardments and fighter and bomber attacks." After a short pause the CAG finished by asking, "Are there any questions, gentlemen?"

There were no questions and a little after noon the next day Dee was leading a group of three Wildcats from the USS Enterprise to Henderson Field on Guadalcanal.

CHAPTER SEVENTY-SEVEN

Dick Gets a Ticket Home

October 1942

Dee had been at Henderson Field for a little over a week. It was now the first of October. His mail from home had not followed him to Guadalcanal as yet. It frustrated him because he wanted to see new pictures of Kyle. He had gone to his Group Commander about it but there was nothing he could do. The CAG on the Enterprise had been right; the Japs really wanted this airstrip. He had been up on sorties every day. The air fighting was gruesome and tough. He was going up against better Zero pilots that he had on the Enterprise. The Group Commander was fully aware of the new F4U Corsairs that were coming and he allowed Dee to start the reorganization of the squadrons as he saw fit.

Intelligence had it that the Japanese were going to make another big push again the Marines guarding Henderson Field. There was an officer's call in the command tent at 1800 hours (6 PM). Dee was invited along with the Group Commander because air-to-ground support would be needed. The Marines were stretched too thin along the line and needed artillery and air support to hold, because intelligence had it that some three thousand Japanese were advancing on the defense line.

Dee and the Group Commander got to the meeting a little early because they had the shortest distance to go. Some of the Marine commanders had to come all the way from their front line positions. The Group Commander found a seat and signaled Dee to come and sit by him. Dee hurried over and sat down. Over the next half hour they watched the other officers trickle in. Then, to Dee's complete shock, Captain Dick Jordan walked in. Dee turned to the Group Commander and said, "Sir, could you please excuse me for a minute, I've just seen someone I know?"

"Okay, Mr. Collie, but don't be long, this meeting is crucial."

"Aye, Sir," Dee said jumping up and practically running across the room.

He caught Dick from behind and yelled, "Hey, I guess they let anybody be an officer in the Marines."

Dick spun around as if hit. He recognized Dee immediately and grabbed him by the shoulders and shook him. "When in hell did you get here?"

"Jesus, it's goin' on two weeks now."

"What're you doin' on this shithole?"

"I've been detached from the Enterprise and I'm here to get these outfits ready for the new F4U Corsair that should be here in February."

"Damn, Dee, it's good to see you," Dick said shaking Dee's hand. "Oops, excuse me Commander, Sir."

"Hey, stow it, Marine. And it's just Lt. Commander."

"Looks like their gettin' ready to start this show," Dick said. "But be sure and hang around later we gotta talk."

"Roger that. I'll see you after the meeting." Dee waved as he returned to his seat next to the Group Commander.

The meeting only lasted about thirty minutes. The main thrust of it was that the Marines were going to have to set up a defense on a long and very thin line up on a ridge above the airstrip. They needed all the help they could get from the 'CACTUS' Air Force. Cactus was the code name for Henderson Field, so flyers stationed at Henderson got the dubious name of the Cactus Air Force. As the meeting broke up, Dee and Dick met outside the tent.

"Have you heard anythin' new from the home front?" Dee asked. "My mail hasn't caught up to me yet."

"Well, I don't know if you've gotten this or not, I only got it in a letter two days ago," Dick teased.

"What? What is it? Come on give."

"Thing is, my dear brother-in-law, you're goin' to be an uncle."

"No shit," Dee yelped.

"No shit," Dick repeated. "But it gets better. You're goin' to be an uncle two times."

"Wow!" Dee whooped. "You dirty dog, you work fast."

"Me!" Dick countered. "If I remember you only had three days with Sue Ann. At least I had a little more than a month."

"So my little sister is goin' to have twins. I just can't believe it, my little sister." Dee shook his head and step over and grabbed Dick into a huge bear hug. The two old friends stood there hugging as others walked by. "Okay, here's the deal, Captain. No heroics. You keep your ass down. Is that understood?"

"Understood, Lt. Commander, Sir," Dick said laughing.

Then Dee turned serious. "I was in the meetin' you know," he said seriously. "It's goin' to be a bitch up on that ridge. Is there a chance if things get too bad you can pull back?"

Dick looked Dee in the eyes like they did as kids. "No pullin' back, Dee," he said solemnly. "We can't let 'em through to the airstrip. We gotta stop 'em. The ridge is where we stand."

Dee nodded his head that he understood. "Keep your guys on the line, Dick, because I'm goin' to have my guys come down on those bastards with all we got. In a deal like this somethin' is bound to go wild. I don't want to hit you guys. Stay on your line. Don't pursue them. Leave that to us."

Dick smiled at Dee. "We'll be on that line 'til hell freezes over."

Out of nowhere, a Marine Sergeant came running up to Dick. "Beg your pardon, Sir," he gushed, "you're needed at battalion immediately."

"Very good, Sergeant, I'm right behind you." Dick turned back to Dee. "Okay, flyboy, get up there and do me some good."

Dee gave Dick a salute. "I'll meet you in the officer's tent for drinks when this is over."

"See you there," Dick said and returned the salute. Then, he turned and ran after the Sergeant.

The battle for the ridge was like nearly all battles on Guadalcanal, it was horrible, vicious, and murderous. The Japanese threw three thousand hardened combat troops against the thin line on the ridge. They came in suicidal charges. The Marines wavered and they yielded some ground, but they didn't break; they held. When the depleted Japanese troops tried to retreat through the jungle, and return to their base, Dee had a squadron of nine Wildcats waiting for them. The Wildcats strafed and bombed the retreating Japanese. The Japanese sent Zeros in to stop the Wildcats, but Dee had positioned another Squadron of Wildcats high above in the sun waiting for just such a move. They roared into the Zeros in a surprise attack from on high. Only two Zeros made it back to their home base. When the battle was over, almost the entire attacking Japanese force had been wipe out.

When Dick's company was finally relieved, he came down from the ridge to the officer's tent. Dee had arrived about an hour earlier and was waiting for him with a glass of scotch at a small table. Dick looked awful. His face was covered in mud and sweat. His uniform was torn and tattered. There was blood all over the front of his shirt. He saw Dee and walked over and flopped down in a wooden foldout chair. Dee was no picture of beauty himself. His face was covered in oil and dirt. His face was clean only around the eyes where he had worn his flight goggles. They sat and looked at each other without talking. Dee pushed the scotch across the table and placed it in front of Dick. Dick picked it up and gulped in down.

"Damn," he said sheepishly, "I wish they'd get some bourbon in here. I don't really care too much for scotch."

"I hope that's not your blood there on your shirt," Dee said softly.

Dick looked down at himself. "No," he said, "That belonged to one of my Platoon Leaders. He died in my arms. He was a good kid. You know the kind, a really good kid."

"Yeah, I know the kind," Dee responded.

"Those stupid bastard Japs just keep comin'," Dick said staring into his empty glass. We mow 'em down by the hundreds and they just kept comin'."

Dee took Dick's glass out of his hands and reached down into a bag next to his chair and pulled out a half empty bottle of scotch. He poured two more stiff drinks of scotch and handed one to Dick. "Sorry," he said with a faint smile, "Scotch is all I got."

Dick took the glass and gave a slight chuckle, "At this time and place, scotch will work just fine."

<hr />

The battle for Guadalcanal raged on and the Japanese kept trying desperately to take Henderson Field, but they were stopped at each effort. The Japanese still owned a large majority of the ocean around Guadalcanal allowing them to continue to bring in more and more reinforcements while at the same time preventing the Marines from getting reinforcements and supplies. However, from time to time, the battle for the ocean around Guadalcanal began to swing in favor of the American Navy. More Marines arrived and even a regiment of army soldiers arrived to help relieve the tired Marines on the defensive line.

But the Japanese continue to bombard Henderson Field from the sea. They sent Battleships with large fourteen inch guns to pound the field. But Marine and Army Engineers would have the damage patched up in less than a day. The Cactus Air Force was slowly winning the air over and around Guadalcanal. As a result, air attack against Guadalcanal was being beaten back and the threat from air was very low. But Japanese Battleships still came up the 'Slot' to bombard the island. The Slot was a narrow stretch of ocean that ran between Guadalcanal and several other islands in the Solomon Island chain. The Japanese and American Navies had been battling for this Slot since the start of the campaign. Unfortunately for the Marines on Guadalcanal, the Japanese still owned the Slot and was therefore able to send large Battleships up the Slot to simply lay off shore by Henderson Field and shell it almost every night and some times during the day.

Dick and his company were back on the defensive line near the south side of Henderson Field, when the largest sea bombardmeny of the campaign took place on October 13th. Two large Japanese Battleships came up the Slot and lay just off Henderson Field. They unleashed a huge bombardment with their fourteen inch guns. The bombardment pounded not only Henderson Field but also went all up and down the defensive line. Marines hunkered down in their bunkers and foxholes to wait out the bombardment. It was the most prolonged and heaviest bombardment the Marines had yet seen. Many Marines lost their lives or limbs, and some lost their minds.

Dick ran from his command bunker through the barrage to check on his men to make sure they were as deep in the bunkers as possible. He ran by bunkers that had sustained a direct hit and all inside were blow to pieces. Shells exploded all around him as he started back for his command bunker. As he approached it, a shell made a direct hit on the top of the bunker and exploded sending out shrapnel, wood chips from the logs protecting the bunker, and sand. Dick was blow back several feet and landed on his chest. He tried to push himself up, but he couldn't do it. Just before he passed out, he saw two of his men grab his arms and start dragging him.

When Dick awoke, he was in the hospital tent near Henderson Field. He tried to get up but a Navy Corpsman pushed him gently back down into the bed. "Take it easy, Captain," he said, "You've had a very near miss."

"What happened?" He asked looking down at his body that was covered by a sheet.

"One of those big shells the Japs are throwing at us exploded almost right in front of you."

Dick frantically started feeling his chest, arms, and legs.

The Navy Corpsman took hold of Dick's hands and pushed them down to his sides. "Relax, Captain, you're all in one piece."

"Well, then what's wrong with me? Why am I here? I need to get back to my company."

"The doc will be here in a minute to tell you what's going to happen next. In the meantime, just close your eyes and relax."

Of course, Dick couldn't relax. He fidgeted around until the doctor finally arrived. The doctor was a full Colonel and he was doing what could be called bed checks in the tent. He got to Dick and ask the age old question, "How're doin', Captain?"

"I guess not so good if they won't let me go back to my company."

The doctor smiled and put his hands on his hips. "Okay, Captain, let me explain what happened, and what's going to happen next. What happened is that a big fourteen inch shell from a Battleship exploded maybe ten yards from you. You were lucky the logs used to fortify the bunker took most of the impact of the explosion. However, it blew you into the air about twenty feet; you turned a complete flip and landed on your chest. Now, the logs probably saved your life but they also shot about a hundred wooden splinters into your chest and legs. Again, you were lucky because they missed your balls. I took most of the splinters out of you but I don't have the facilities to see how bad your left hip is hurt. I doubt you can stand on it and I know it probably will hurt like hell if you try. Now, that's what happened. Here's what's going to happen. I'm getting you out of here to a hospital ship just as quick as we can. They'll take you to Honolulu to see what needs to be done for you. Then, you'll probably go home for some rehabilitation. At some point, you'll go back to your unit but I don't know when. And that's it; except there's a general waiting outside to talk to you."

"What? Why would a General want to talk to me?"

The doctor waved as he walked away. "I just work here," he said.

Dick was shocked to see General Vandegrift, the commander of the entire First Marine Division, walk up to his little bed. Dick didn't know what to do so he tried getting up again. The General waved to a Corpsman, "Corpsman, get this Marine on his back." The Corpsman did just that and it required very little effort.

"As you were, Marine," the General said in a commanding voice. "I have several reports on you, from the battle on the ridge to the bombardment yesterday. You've done a good job and I like the way you care for your men. I'm putting you in for a Silver Star. In addition, I'm promoting you to Major. Both, the Silver Star and the official papers for your promotion, will be waiting for you in Honolulu. After your rehab at home, you'll report to the Second Battalion, First Marines Commander for assignment. They'll be glad to have you at battalion. Are there any question, Major?"

"Yes, Sir," Dick stammered, "I guess this means I'll lose my company."

"Yes, it does. You'll be a Battalion Commander now. Before you leave this beautiful island paradise, I expect you to hand in your recommendation for the Platoon Leader you want to take your place. Can you get that done, Major?"

"Yes, Sir, it'll get done."

"Very good, Major, good luck and I'll probably be seeing you again." The General turn sharply and marched out of the tent.

—◦※◦—

Dee was standing next to Dick's stretcher as they were loading him on the Higgins boat that would take him out to the hospital ship. "Well," Dee said solemnly, "Looks like you'll see my kid before I do."

Dick looked up at Dee with hurt in his eyes. "Hang in there, flyboy. And don't let those Jap bastards get our airstrip. We've paid too high a price to let it get taken now."

"You got lots of things to worry about, *Major*, but the Japs gettin' this island isn't one 'em. I'm gonna be here to fly those new F4U Corsairs from Henderson Field. And then my friend we're really goin' to take it to 'em."

They loaded Dick onto the Higgins boat and strapped him in. Then the boat was pushed away. As the boat started to pull away Dee yelled as loud as he could, and waved frantically, "Say hello to Kyle for me. And tell 'im his old man loves him and that I'll be home soon. Tell 'im, Dick. Please tell 'im."

CHAPTER SEVENTY-EIGHT

Thanksgiving

November 1942

As Thanksgiving Day arrived on Guadalcanal, the ground fighting had slowed to an almost stop. The Japanese seemed to have given up on retaking the island and Henderson Field. The air war still continued but not in the same manner as before. Dee's squadrons now were more on the offensive. They still protected Henderson Field from Japanese air attacks, but now they reached out to cover the other small islands around Guadalcanal. As the Japanese pulled back from Guadalcanal, they left over thirty thousand dead on the island and they took home an untold number of wounded. The Marines lost a little less than two thousand dead and another four thousand wounded. On the surface it seemed to be a very one sided victory, but when the over four thousand sailors that died were counted, it was still a bitterly hard fought victory.

Thanksgiving was the best day Dee had experienced in a long time. Not only did he get two letters from Sue Ann and one from his Mother, they were treated to a hot turkey diner. It was the Navy's way of saying thanks for not giving up and sorry we were so late getting back.

His letter's contained more pictures of Kyle. He was now eight months old and had already taken his first steps. According to Sue Ann, she was showing Kyle pictures of Dee and teaching him to say Da-Da. The letter from his Mother caught him up on all the happenings in Coalville including the deaths of Harry Barnett and

Alice Conner. Like Sue Ann, he had expected that Harry would get caught sooner or later, but he was totally shocked about Alice. Sue Ann had not mentioned her Father's death in any of her letters. He would not mention it either in his replies. She also informed him that Dick had finally made it home after nearly a month in Honolulu. It seems he has a cracked bone in his hip that is very painful and will take nearly a year to heal.

After finishing his Thanksgiving Day meal, he carefully folded the letters and put them in his small foot locker he had in his tent. He kept all the letters he received. He put the pictures of Kyle and Sue Ann next to his bunk. In the cockpit of his Wildcat could be found a picture of Sue Ann. To Dee she was the most beautiful girl in the entire world. He stretched out on his bunk and let his mind wonder until he fell asleep still clutching a picture of Sue Ann holding Kyle.

Thanksgiving at the Collie house was a happy one, or, as happy as it could be. Mary cooked a big turkey and baked a delicious ham. The house was full again. Sally Barnett had joined them from her sister's house north of Dallas where she had been staying since the death of Harry. The Barnett farm was up for sale but as of now no one had made an offer. Ruth Jordan came over and brought two big Pecan Pies.

After they all had eaten, Sue Ann read the latest letters from Dee to everyone, of course leaving out the very personal stuff. She also had a nice letter from Billy Bob that she shared with everyone. Then, as the evening drew to a close, a telephone call from Cherrie and Dick capped a wonderful day.

Then, everyone in the house formed a circle and held hands. James led them in a prayer for the safety of all their loved ones and for an end to this horrible war. He thanked God for their family and friends and ended the prayer and the day with an Amen.

Cherrie and Dick had just hung up the phone from talking with the family down in Texas. It was getting late in evening and they went to the bedroom to prepare for bed. Dick had only been home for a week and he was having some trouble adjusting. He felt guilty about not being with his men back on Guadalcanal. But he was cheered by the news that the island had been held and that the Japanese were pulling back. He also had heard a rumor from his Battalion Headquarters that the First Marine Division would be taken off the island in the very near future and be replaced by Army divisions. But it was just a rumor but it was one that made Dick feel much better.

Cherrie was sitting on the edge of the bed in her nightgown when Dick came out of the bathroom drying his self with a large towel. He looked down at Cherrie and smiled. "If you were any more beautiful, I don't think I could stand it."

He had the towel wrapped around the lower part of this body leaving his chest exposed. She could see all the scars from the shrapnel and wood splinters they had taken out of his chest. She got up and walked over to him and pulled the towel loose and let it drop to the floor. She pulled herself to him and buried her head in his chest. "Make love to me, Dick," she pleaded, "please make love to me."

He put his hand on her head and pulled her tighter to him. "Is it safe in your condition?" He asked with a trace of fear in his voice. "I mean you're about five months along now." He pushed her back from him at arm's length. "And look at you. You're beginnin' to show really good. The last thing in the world I want to do is hurt you or those babies."

She smiled up at him and took his hand and led him to the bed. She climbed into the bed and moved over to one side and then patted the bed where he belonged. "Come on and don't worry, Marine, women know how to do these things."

Judy had landed her plane in the same spot as she had landed the old crop duster. She was again flying her Mobil plane. After securing the airplane, she unloaded a lot of packages and then loaded them into the truck that waited for her near the landing strip. It was still early morning and the dessert air was cool. There was no hurry so she took her time. This was her second trip to Clint's hide-a-way. This time she was bringing hot food for Thanksgiving. It was actually the day after Thanksgiving but it was close enough. She hoped to surprise Clint with this early trip and all the good food. It only took about a half hour to drive to the hideout from the landing strip. As she pulled the truck up in front of the shack, she didn't see Clint. She brought the truck to a full stop and jumped out.

"Pa," she yelled looking around.

"Over here," came a reply from behind the shack. "What're you doin' here? I wasn't expectin' you again until before Christmas."

"Well, it is Thanksgiving, and I brought you some good eats."

"Thank you, Judy; you're a blessin' if there ever was one."

"Come on and help me unload all the stuff I brought."

Together they carried the packages into the shack and placed them on the makeshift table. Judy looked around. "You've got this place nice and livable," she said smiling.

"I do what I can." Then he laughed, "We can't eat now. It's not even nine o'clock in the mornin' yet."

"Sure we can," she said. "The rich folks call it brunch."

"I've never heard of Brunch?" Clint questioned.

"Yeah, it's a combination of breakfast and lunch. Get it?"

"Oh yeah," he chuckled, "very uppity."

They spent the next hour preparing and then eating all the turkey, sauce, ham, cornbread, beans, and chocolate pie that Judy brought. They ate, laughed and made small talk. After they were done, Judy helped Clint pick everything up that they didn't eat and put it in a trash bag because it couldn't be stored. They washed the dishes together and made jokes about the shack.

"You know," Judy said thoughtfully, "this is almost like the old cabin on the hill isn't it."

Clint smiled at her and said, "I was thinkin' the same thing."

"Oh, I almost forgot, I got one more thing for you. Wait here a minute while I run out to the truck." She ran out and was back in a flash. She pulled a full bottle of bourbon out of a bag she was carrying. "I thought you might like a little holiday sip."

Clint looked at the bottle and his eyes turned dark. He looked down at the floor and then back up to Judy. "No, thank you, Judy, but I do appreciate the thought. I've been livin' without it for all these years and if I take a drink now it might start me back up. I don't want to do anything to mess up what we're tryin' to do here. The beer you bring is doin' me just fine."

Judy put the bottle back in the bag and said, "Whatever you say, Pa." Judy sat back down at the table and signaled Clint to do the same. "Okay, it's time to let you in on our plan. I'm goin' to go over it in as much detail as I can. You, of course, may not agree with what we're tryin' to do. And you've got the option to say no. But if you do say no, understand that we'll have to develop a plan B. Is all that okay?"

"It's okay, go ahead."

"The long range plan is to get you out of the country," she started. "We're goin' to get you to England." Clint's eyes widened but he didn't interrupt her. "We just about have your ID documents completed. You'll be goin' to England as a member of the United States Army Air Force. You'll have documents showin' you to be a ten year Army man and a mechanic. You'll be goin' to England to be on the ground crew of the B-17 bombers. We've already got you enlisted and back dated to 1932. For all practical purposes, you will actually be in the Army. You'll get paid and everything. Your new name will be Gerald Andrew Gaylen and you'll be a technical sergeant."

Finally Clint held up his hands in wonderment. "How in hell did you manage to do all this?" He asked. "And how am I goin' to become a mechanic?"

Judy smiled and slapped her thighs. "It's all a piece of cake. But that's for my next visit just before Christmas."

"One more thing," Clint said. "How's the search for me goin'? Are they still lookin' for me?"

The smile faded from Judy's face. "Yeah, there still lookin'. They don't know anythin' about the plane that picked you up or where it is, and they don't know who was flyin' it, but they've talked to me because they know I'm a pilot. But they've got nothin' on me, and they never will. As far as you, they think you're already in Mexico. They think you went to El Paso and crossed the border there. I don't think they're even lookin' for you here in the States. So, if we can stick to our plan, we'll have you out of here in February. I promise. Keep in mind that it's the Feds that are headin' up the search for you, not the State boys. So, again, keep out of sight. I know it's tough but just hang in there a little longer. That's all I can tell you for now, really because I don't know much more." She paused and looked at him sharply. "You know you could shave and keep yourself lookin' good. I got some scissors with me, why don't I give you a haircut before I leave?"

"Good idea, Why don't you?"

<hr>

Billy Bob Barnett settled in for his Thanksgiving Day diner at Fort Bragg, North Carolina. The 101st Airborne had been moved to Fort Bragg in October. They were in intensive training to get the airborne division up to the best of any division in the US Army. He was reading another letter from his sister, Sue Ann. She had written him earlier about their Father being killed. Like Sue Ann, he had long expected something of that nature happening. But, still, it was very sad and disquieting for a son to read of his Father's death; especially being shot by an officer of the law. But that sad news was offset by the good news about Kyle was starting to walk and trying to talk. In addition, she had sent him several pictures of Kyle. In this letter, she had included a picture of Dee leaning up against his fighter plane.

Billy Bob smiled to see his friend looking so fit, and now he was a Lt. Commander. There was also good news about his Mother. She was now staying with her sister and her husband who lived somewhere north of Dallas. The farm was up for sale but there had been no takers thus far. They were expecting her to visit for Thanksgiving. Since the letter was over a week old, he could only assume she had spent Thanksgiving with the Collie family.

Billy Bob himself had just been promoted to Buck Sergeant. He now wore three stripes on his sleeves. He was in charge of what was called a rifle squad even though they all carried Thomson Submachine Guns, which had become standard issue for airborne troops.

Billy Bob and his entire division were getting restless. The entire world was at war and it seemed everyone was fighting except them. And they could expect no action in the near future as they were headed for war games in Tennessee sometime in 1943. That meant they still had at least a year or more of training before they would go anywhere near any action. But it's what he volunteered for, so he tried not to bitch too much. After all, he was a three strip sergeant now.

He finished his meal and went back to his quarters in the barracks. He had a small desk in the quarters he shared with another sergeant. He sat down and took out pin and paper and started answering Sue Ann's latest letter. He didn't have a lot to report but he wanted to reassure Sue Ann and his Mother that he was alright and still in North Carolina.

CHAPTER SEVENTY-NINE

Dee Gets a New Plane

February 1943

In February 1943, Guadalcanal's Henderson Field finally got a squadron of the new F4U Corsairs. Dee had been waiting on this new aircraft ever since he had been transferred for temporary duty to Henderson Field. Unfortunately for Dee, it took almost a month to get the new aircraft qualified. It had failed carrier qualifications because of several reasons so the Navy dispatched it to the Marines so it could be used as a land based fighter. The Marines didn't care if it was qualified for carriers or not, they simply needed a fighter that could outperform the Zero, and the Corsair would certainly do that.

Dee had mixed feeling about this because it meant that he would be required to continue flying from ground bases rather than carriers, which meant that he would remain, for the time being, at Henderson Field. In late February, Dee finally got checked out in the Corsair and was assigned to a squadron. He remained in the Navy flying for the Marines. He out ranked his squadron leader but, in the end, it made little difference.

Dee was now resigned to the fact that unless he got killed or seriously wounded, like Dick, he was in the war for the duration. In one more month, his son Kyle would be one year old and he still had yet to see him in the flesh. Dee fought hard to keep that fact from hurting him mentally and affecting his flying. The new Corsair helped a lot because he was now able to outperform the Zero and his chances of survival had increased substantially. On the other hand, the aircraft had a greater range than the Wildcat and it could be used as a fighter bomber. As a result, he was flying many more sorties than before. They were carrying the war to the Japanese now and he prayed the whole thing would be over soon.

He was pleased to get a letter from Cherrie. She told how happy Dick was the First Marine Division had been taken off Guadalcanal and sent to Australia for rest and refitting. Dick held out hopes he could rejoin his division there before they went on to their next campaign. She admitted guilt to the fact that she hoped his wound would keep him out of the next campaign, but she knew Dick would be disappointed to the point of despair if it did. She went on to say her pregnancy was going as scheduled and the babies were still due in April.

Dee had smiled as he read her letter. It was always good to hear from Cherrie. He loved her so much that just the little short letter's she sent raised his spirits as high as his Corsair would fly. When he got down and was feeling really low, he would think of the good days that he and Cherrie had shared together. He still hoped that Dick realized what a treasure he had in Cherrie. He laughed at himself, because he knew Dick did indeed realize that. And that he realized it many, many years ago.

CHAPTER EIGHTY

The Escape Phase 2

February 1943

Clint watched through the window as a panel truck approached the shack. It was painted completely white with no markings on it of any kind. He had never seen the truck before and he was very nervous as it came to a bouncing stop in front of the shack. The door nearest the shack opened and Jimmy Orland got out and started stretching his body as if he had been driving for a long time. From the other side of the truck, came Judy and a Mexican girl Clint didn't recognize. They all met in front of the shack and stood there talking for a minute and then turned toward the shack. Clint hurried out to meet them as they approached.

"Hello, everyone," Clint yelled from the shack front door.

"Hi, Pa," Judy replied smiling broadly.

"If y'all keep sneakin' up on me like this, the Fed's won't need to kill me 'cause I'll die of a heart attack," Clint laughed patting his chest.

When they were close enough, Clint pushed the shack door open as wide as it would go and ushered them inside. He tried not to let it show, but he couldn't help but keep his eyes on the young Mexican girl. He had no idea who she was or why she was here.

Clint scurried around looking for a place for everyone to sit. "I'm not sure I got enough space for everyone," he said, looking puzzled.

"That's okay, Clint," Jimmy said. "We can't stay long. I'll let Judy go over what's happenin'." After speaking, he stepped back into a corner and took the girl with him.

The girl looked very calm and had no expression on her face that Clint could read. She was obviously young but he couldn't tell how old she might really be. She had a nice and pretty face with dark eyes to match her long black hair that reached down to the middle of her back. Clint guessed she was maybe five feet, four inches tall and her frame was slim and shapely. She wore a simple white dress that covered her from shoulders to knees. On her feet, she wore a pair of black leather sandals.

"Pa," Judy yelled.

Clint snapped his head around quickly back to Judy. "Sorry, I'm just kind of surprised by a new face in our little group."

"I'll get to her in a minute," Judy said. "We got some other things to cover first." Judy sat down in one of the three chairs in the shack and indicated for Clint to sit down across from her. Clint did just that by pulling up a rickety old chair and sat down straight across from Judy.

"Things have changed a little and we have to be fluid enough to adjust to them," Judy began. "First, and above all else, you've been in this shithole long enough. You've done really good keepin' out of site and doin' as we asked you. But it's not fair to keep you here any longer. So, were goin' to move you to someplace much more livable. The FBI is still lookin' for you, but they've stop pressin' the search. They're convinced you're long gone to Mexico, and anyway you're a lot less important than a Jap or Nazi spy. Are you with me so far?"

Clint nodded in the affirmative but didn't speak.

"Okay, then," she continued. "I've signed up for a new organization called the WASP. That means Women Airforce Service Pilots. Their job is to ferry aircraft from the production area to the point of departure for delivery overseas. The idea is to free up male pilots for combat. Now, sometime late this summer the WASP will began trainin' and graduatin' pilot classes from a small Army Airforce field in Sweetwater, Texas called Avenger Field. I hope to be in one of the first classes. Once I graduate, I'll be assigned to a base to ferry aircraft to and from. When that happens we'll move on to step three of our plan to get you to England."

Judy stopped and took a deep breath and then continued, "And now we come to what's next. Over the next month, we're goin' to change your appearance a bit and you're goin' to work on gettin' to know the engine of a B-17 Bomber. One month from today, we're goin' to move you to a nice little place just north of Sweetwater where you can wait for step three. You won't have to hide so much up there, and you'll be able to go into a nearby town and shop and buy beer. For the first time, you'll really be free. You'll have a car; not a fancy one, but one to get you around. All of this brings us to Rosa Costillo."

Judy signaled for the girl to come over. Rosa walked gently over and stood next to Judy. Looking back to Clint, she said, "You're goin' to be busy readin' and studin' the instruction manual I brought you on the maintenance of the Pratt and Whitney R-1820-39 Cyclone engine. Not only did I bring you a manual, I have a model version of the engine in the truck. You'll be able to take it apart and put it back together."

Clint stood up and stopped her. "How do you two do all this?" He stammered. "How do you get all this stuff? Ain't it secret or somethin'?"

Judy chuckled, "Some of it is. But a lot of it comes from back in the late thirties when the plane was first designed. Anyway, as I've told you, I know folks in high places."

Clint looked over to Jimmy who was smiling but not saying anything. "Okay," he said, turning back to Judy, "Suppose I can do this, where does this girl come into the picture?"

At this point, Jimmy stepped over. "She's here to do your cooking, cleaning, and other work around here to free you up to study," he said. Then after a short and nervous pause, he continued, "She's also here to be your companion, if you get my drift."

Clint looked at Judy who had lowered her head and was staring at the floor. "Judy," he challenged. What about this?"

Judy stood up quickly and looked Clint straight in the eyes. "Pa, you're a man and you've been without a woman for years. I'm not a little girl anymore, so don't treat me like one. Rosa understands her role here and she's bein' paid very well for that role. It's up to you how far you carry the companionship, but don't feel like you're bein' some kind of bad guy if you chose to bed her. She'll understand just like we all will; including me, your little girl."

There was a long silence in the shack. Then Clint slowly asked, "Just for my own piece of mind, how old is she?"

"I am nineteen years old, Senor Clint." It was the girl speaking as she stepped in front of Clint. "I am fully aware of what I am doing, Senor, and I am not afraid or ashamed. My English is good but I will still need help with some words." She reached down and took Clint's hands into hers. "I will be a good woman for this house."

Before Clint could say anything else, Jimmy clapped his hands loudly and shouted, "Okay, now that we've got that settled, let's jump in and get the truck unloaded. I need to get back to Dallas and that's a long way off."

It took them about an hour to unload all the food, water, and training supplies from the truck. Judy spent a little time going over how he needed to study and how to use the engine model. She also wanted him to start dying his hair and shaving every day. The sooner he got back into the habit of civilization; the better.

As they were preparing to pile back into the truck for the trip back, Jimmy pulled Clint aside for a private conversation. "There's one thing you should know, Clint," he said seriously, as his eyes narrow down to two small slits. "Rosa isn't a whore. She's a good kid from a nice family south of the border. I'm paying her, but she wanted to do this. She's not a virgin, so she knows the score. Now, as you know, I'm fully committed to helping Judy get you to a safe place and returning you to a functional life. But you need to understand this one thing very clearly, if you should hurt Rosa in anyway, I promise you I'll drown your sorry ass in the Rio Grande. Comprendes, Senor Clint?"

Clint looked at him and smiled. "I comprendes and I would've been very disappointed in you, Jimmy, if you hadn't put it to me just the way you did."

The two men shook hands and Jimmy ran and jumped into the truck with Judy and they drove away as Clint and Rosa watched and waved.

CHAPTER EIGHTY-ONE

Cherrie Goes to Coalville

February 1943

It was Valentine's Day and Cherrie was doing her best to cook a nice meal for Dick, but her large stomach kept getting in the way. With war rationing going full blast, it was hard to get all the things she needed to make Dick's favorite meal; meatloaf. But she had planned and managed for the last month and she had everything she needed. She smiled to herself as she sniffed the aroma of the cooking meat. "This is goin' to be good," she whispered to the empty house.

As she was coming out of the kitchen to sit down for a short break, Dick came in the door. He was at least a full hour early. He was carrying a heart shaped box of chocolate candy in one hand and a bottle of Champaign in the other. His face wore what appeared to Cherrie as a worried smile. "Hey, why're you so early?" She asked. "I don't have my surprise dinner ready yet."

Dick laughed and whent to her to give her a hug. He had to go around behind her and put his arms around her shoulders to accomplish the hug. He kissed her on the back of the neck and said, "I come bearing gifts. Although I know you're not to eat candy or drink alcohol, we can save it for another time. It's Valentines and I just felt the need to buy this type of thing."

"Okay, but why're you home so early?" Her voice had a slight level of concern in it.

Dick went into the kitchen and put the candy and Champaign into their small but fancy refrigerator. When he returned to the living room, she was standing there with a worried look on her face. "I got my orders today," he said simply.

"And?"

"And I've got a ship out date. I'm to join the First Division in Australia."

It took her a moment to form the words but then she asked, "When?"

"I leave June first," he answered. "But you shouldn't start worrin' 'cause they're holdin' me out of the next campaign." His voice had a disappointed tone to it. "I can't tell you anythin' about the next campaign or when it will come off, but just know that I'll be supportin' it from Australia."

She backed up feeling behind her as she did searching for her favorite rocking chair. Dick saw what she was doing and hurried over to her, took her arm, and escorted her to the chair and helped her sit down. He knelt in front of her and took her hands into his. "We knew it was comin' sooner or later," he said softly.

"Yes," she said harshly, "and you're happy about it. You're happy to be leavin' me."

Dick squeezed her hands tightly. "That's not true, Cherrie, and you know it. Please don't ever say anythin' like that to me again; not ever."

She looked down into his eyes and knew she had hurt him. Hurting him was not going to change anything and it was really the last thing she wanted to do. She was the wife of a United States Marine. She knew how things were when she married him. She knew that her competition for his devotion was, and always would be, The Corp. His unit was going into hell and he was being ordered to stay behind. That, in itself, was tearing him up inside. He didn't need her making it double hard for him.

Tears began to well in her eyes and then started the slow trip down her cheeks. "I'm sorry, Dick," she said haltingly, "can you please forgive me. I'm so, so sorry." She pulled his hands to her cheeks and pressed them there tightly.

He leaned forward and put his forehead against her head. He could smell the sweetness of her freshly shampooed hair and he rubbed his face in the softness of it. Gathering all his internal fortitude, he pushed himself back from her but continued to hold her hands. "I have somethin' I want to ask you to do for me," he said softly.

"You know I will if I can," she answered. "What is it?"

He stood up and released her hands. He then cupped her face into his hands and looked into her eyes pleadingly. "I want you to pack up and go home to Coalville and stay with my Mom. I know you're far along and if you think you can't do it, or if it'll put the babies in jeopardy, then, of course, don't do it. It's just I'd feel better if you had the babies back home around your family and my Mom. Plus, they're givin' me a twenty day furlough whenever I want it durin' April or May. So, my plan is to be in Coalville with you when the babies come. But until then, I'll stay here and get our stuff packed up and shipped home and I have to report to the hospital once a week all next month." Then he chuckled slightly and said, "Anyway, do we really want our kids to be Californians or Texans?"

For the first time since he had walked through the door, she was able to force a gentle smile. "There's no choice there, it's gotta be Texans for sure."

"Then, you'll do it!" He exclaimed loudly. "You'll give it a try?"

"No, I won't *try* to do anythin'. I'll just do it. I'll be safe at home waitin' for you. I promise. But you better be there when these babies come."

"I wouldn't miss bein' there when those two boys come into this world. That I promise you."

"Two boys," she shouted. "What makes you think it's gonna be two boys?"

"Well, it's just a feelin' I got."

"I wouldn't let that feelin' take hold too much," she said smiling. "My genes tell me there's gonna be one of each; a girl and a boy. And the girl is gonna be born first."

"We'll see 'bout that," he said with a twinkle in his eyes, "we'll just see about that."

"I'm tellin' you," she said seriously, "it's in my genes."

He was still cupping her face in his hands and he bent over and gave her a hard, long kiss. Then, he stepped back from her and looked at her with that smile that she loved. "You know," he said, "I feel sorry for other guys, because I got me the best woman in the entire world. And they can't have you because here and now I've got you and I'm never ever gonna let you go.

She struggled out of the rocking chair and stood in front of him. The smile left her face and it took on a very serious expression. She shrugged her shoulders and said with a sincerity that radiated throughout the room, "Like I've told you so many times before, I've been yours since I was twelve years old."

CHAPTER EIGHTY-TWO

The Home Front

April 1943

James Collie stood next to the new access road to Lonesome Hill. It had now been completed. He could see up the road to the small bridge that went over the ravine that circled the hill and connected to the ring road. He was impressed by the work. It looked much nicer than he had thought it would. His view was unobstructed as the construction crews had cut down most of the trees including the old oak tree that had held Dee's treehouse. The crews were now involved with two immediate projects. The first was fixing the ring road so that it would easily support traffic from the accesses roads and around the entire hill. That meant doing a lot of cement work. The second was to clear areas on the hill itself to locate picnic areas and nature trails. All of the work was proceeding on schedule despite the war effort that was on going.

Things seemed to be changing so fast. Just two years ago, both his children were in college and everything was going along fine. That was just two short years ago. Now, Dee was still overseas flying combat missions from Guadalcanal, or at least James thought he was still on Guadalcanal.

Last month, March, Kyle had turned one year old. Dee had still only seen his son in pictures. Kyle was walking now and being a hellion about getting into things; especially things he shouldn't be getting into. James smiled as he thought about it because it was the same thing Dee use to do.

Sue Ann was a great mother. She loved Kyle to the extreme but she also was good about discipline. She didn't allow him to use his baby charm to get away with things. She showed Kyle a picture of Dee every day and took care to explain who Da-Da was. She knew Kyle didn't understand most of what she was saying but she believed deeply that he was slowly picking up a lot of what she was trying to get across.

Kyle was no longer James' only grandchild. Cherrie had come home to Coalville in February and moved in with Ruth Jordan. She had gotten a doctor in Athens and he set her up to have her babies delivered at the Athens Memorial Hospital. Dick arrived at the end of March. He looked good and no longer walked with a limp. He was there at the hospital with the rest of the family on April 5th, as Cherrie gave birth to fraternal twins; one girl and one boy. The girl was born first just one minute and five seconds before the boy. It was just as Cherrie had predicted. They were slightly premature but they did well and went home to their parents in just two weeks. Keeping with family tradition, the girl was named Chloe Ruth Jordan and the boy Joey James Jordan. James laughed to himself as he thought about it; Chloe and Joey.

Sadly Dick only had a twenty day furlough and had to return to California before his children were even a month old. But at least, unlike Dee, he did get to see them born and spend almost two weeks with them. James had been at the train station in Dallas and witnessed the good-bye between Dick and his wife and kids. It was a scene that he hoped he never had to see again in his life time. It was hard; very, very hard. Mary had opted not to go to the train station. She had said her good-byes to Dick earlier. In the end, James was glad she didn't go. He wasn't sure she could've handled it.

Mary had her hands full with three grandchildren now. She spent as much time as she could over to Ruth's house helping Cherrie with Chloe and Joey, while still trying to balance the time she spent at home with Kyle. As a result, James missed out on the lunches that Mary used to bring him at the store and, on several occasions, he would miss out on his dinner at home. And to make matters worse, Ruth was taking more and more time off to stay home with her new grandchildren. But through it all, James didn't complain. He was so happy to have them all near him that he went along with nearly everything Mary wanted to do.

James observed that Cherrie and Sue Ann were establishing an unbreakable bond. The two girls had always been friends but now they became inseparable. There was nothing that either girl wouldn't do for the other. They set up times to work with Mary on her scrapbooks, they walked their children together, they went to church together, and they read their letters from Dick, Dee, and Billy Bob to each other. It was as if they were truly sisters. All of this made James feel better because he knew that at any time bad news could come in the form of the dreaded telegram from the War Department. He just hoped and prayed that day would never come.

⎯⎯⎰⎯⎯

For Sheriff Tom Clark, it had been a long eight months since the killing of Harry Barnett and the suicide of Alice Conner. A lot of good things had happened for the Sheriff. The main good thing that happened involved his relationship with his wife, Evie. It had been a struggle for him to overcome the feeling of betrayal he felt after everything that came out during the solving of the long ago murders. He hadn't treated Evie very well during that time. They stayed together but they were distant from each other. The distance was mostly on his part. However, Evie refused to give up on their marriage and took whatever Tom dished out. He was never physically abusive to her, but he intentionally made her feel bad and tried to humiliate her at every opportunity. This lasted over three months before Tom realized that Evie really loved him and was deeply sorry for whatever he felt she did that was wrong. He knew he loved Evie and one night, with the children away at a neighbor's house, they went to their bedroom, lay down on the bed, held each other, and talked it completely through. Now, these months later, their marriage was stronger than ever.

As bad as the war was, it had brought a boom to Coalville. The surrounding farmers couldn't produce enough crops for the demand. Everything was in demand; cotton, vegetables of all kinds, dairy products, and even beef cattle. The downtown stores found it hard to keep supplies in stock. James Collie's feed and fertilizer store was doing a booming business and was many times out of stock. Because of all this new economic income, the Sheriff was allowed to hire a replacement for Alice and to add a new deputy.

To replace Alice, he hired a young girl recommended by Cheryl Jordan. The girl had been a classmate of hers at Baylor. Her husband was serving with the 36th Division, which was a Texas National Guard unit that had recently been activated. She was highly intelligent and was quick to pick up all her duties. In fact, the Sheriff really believed she was far too intelligent to be working for him. But the girl, her name was Ellen Neeley, didn't want a professional job. She only wanted to wait for her husband to come home and he would be the bread winner in their family. The problem for the Sheriff was that Ellen Neeley was an outstanding beauty. She stood five feet eight inches tall and had an almost perfect figure. Her green eyes sparkled and stood out against her long red hair. Her face was sculptured beautifully with small lips and a cute little turned up nose. It was all the Sheriff could do to keep all the men in the courthouse away from her. But it was a job he enjoyed.

Getting a fulltime deputy was a harder issue. Most of the qualified men were already serving in the military, and the ones that were available Sheriff Clark considered them draft dodgers and wouldn't hire them. The solution finally came from an unexpected source. Louis Mailer sent the Sheriff a recommendation for one of his detectives that wanted to take his family from the the big city and settle in a nice small town. The man was over forty years old and had a wife and two children in their early teens. So, the man was no draft dodger. After Sheriff Clark interviewed him, he was very impressed and hired the man the following day. The new Deputy Sheriff was named Howard Middleton and he was happy to be in Coalville.

Now, with his marriage in good repair, a new courthouse assistant, a new Deputy Sheriff, and the new State Park coming along nicely, Sheriff Tom Clark was enjoying life. Now, if this damn war would just get itself over with!

⸻

Clint Jordan had been in his new hideout for over a month now. The hideout was a small one bedroom house located about fifty miles north of Sweetwater, Texas. It was set off to itself just outside the town limits of a place known as Sandy Mound, Texas. It had a small garage that was detached from the house. He had an old Ford truck parked out in driveway but not in the garage. Sandy Mound didn't have any sandy mounds, so Clint didn't know how the little town got its name. But he did know that the town income came from the oil fields. The little town was barely one hundred and fifty miles from the exact place where he was working when he escaped. It worried him being so close to the prison area and, more or less, out in the open.

However, there were several things that made Clint happy. The big thing was that Rosa was still with him. When they packed up to leave the old miners shack, Rosa had asked Jimmy if she could continue to be with Clint. Jimmy or Judy had no objections so Rosa was still doing his cooking, cleaning, and the companionship thing. The other thing was that Clint didn't look like Clint. He had dyed his hair a dark red and he shaved everyday so as not to have any beard stubble. Rosa's cooking had put weight on him and he was at least twenty-five pounds heavier than when he was in prison. He dressed differently. He blended in the local area by wearing jeans, boots, and a western shirt. He worn a cowboy hat sometimes, but he preferred not to cover his head so that his red hair would show easier.

He had made great progress with leaning all about the B-17 engine. The model was in the detached garage and he worked on it every day. He disassembled it one week and then reassembled it the next. He studied the manual until he knew the names of all the parts.

Judy and Jimmy visited from time to time but they no longer came at the same time. Judy would come more often than Jimmy. She would visit for a while and then spend the rest of her time in Sweetwater.

Clint was content to stay near the little house, work on learning all he could about the engine, and enjoy Rosa's companionship. And, of course, wait as patiently as he could for step three of his escape plan.

Judy Jackson sat on a wooden desk chair in her room at the Blue Bonnet Hotel in Sweetwater, Texas. She was irritated and frustrated at the same time. A little over two miles from the hotel at Avenger Field, women pilots were being trained to fly the Army way so they could ferry aircraft from the production line to the delivery points in the U.S. for shipment or ferrying by male pilots overseas. The first classes were already in progress. She had applied back in February but had heard nothing. It was frustrating to her that she had not been selected as yet. She had more hours in cross country flying than most of the ones that had been selected. With all her influence and pull, she still had not been able to break into the WAFS (Women's Auxiliary Ferrying Squadron).

Soon, maybe in August, The WAFS and the WFTD (Women's Flying Training Detachment) would be merged together to form the WASP (Women's Airforce Service Pilots) and then the WASP would take over all the ferrying services. Judy felt as though time was running out for her. She desperately wanted to be a WASP. Even Jimmy, with all his pull and influence, had not been able to help her.

The Blue Bonnet Hotel was the gathering point for new trainees. They would stay here at the Blue Bonnet until picked up by an Army Air Force vehicle and transferred to the training barracks at Avenger Field. Judy hoped that being at the hotel would help her.

She thought she might pick up some information that would help her get selected. But, so far, it had proved useless. But, since she had to stay somewhere while visiting Clint, the Blue Bonnet was as good as any place.

Since Clint's move to his new location near Sweetwater, things had been easier for Judy. The trips were not nearly as far and she could spend more time with Clint. Adding to her frustration with the WASP selection process was the fact that she and Jimmy both felt Clint was ready for the final step. He had done an amazing job getting to know the B-17 engine. On this last visit, she grilled him on his progress. He amazed her by being able to break the entire model engine down. In addition to all of that, Jimmy had Clint's new ID documents completed and ready as well as getting his phony military history inserted in all the proper places. All that was needed now was to get Clint to England. And even that had been arranged up to a point. Jimmy was only waiting for Judy to give the word so he could cut the orders with the proper dates. The hold was getting Clint from Sweetwater to Buckingham AAF in Fort Meyers, Florida, where several B-17s waited to be ferried to England by male pilots and crews. The orders would make Clint a crew member for transfer to England. Judy was still working on how to get Clint there.

Judy was also having trouble with Jimmy. Recently, he had to go before the draft board for the third time to keep his draft exemption. It was an easy enough thing to do because Mobil Oil had all his documents in order declaring him essential to the war effort at home. The problem was Jimmy himself. He didn't like not going into the military. He wanted to do his bit. She knew the only reason he was not in the service was because of her. He loved her deeply and wanted to stick it out to get Clint safely out of the country and living a new life. After that was done, she doubted even his deep love for her would keep him from joining up. Then Clint would be gone, and Jimmy would be gone. And, if she didn't get into the WASP, she didn't know what she was going to do.

CHAPTER EIGHTY-THREE

The War Front

October 1943

It was late evening in Berkshire, England and Staff Sergeant Billy Bob Barnett was seated at a long table in the chow hall. He was sipping coffee along with about twenty other sergeants of different grades. They were there to listen to a talk from their Battalion Commander. The 101st Airborne Division had been in England for over a month now and training had been intense. This talk was supposed to cover their continued training and to stress the importance of the jobs of all the sergeants (NCOs or Non Commissioned Officers).

While he waited for the commander to appear, he slipped the latest letter from Sue Ann out of his pocket and started re-reading it again for the third time. Most of the letter described all the things that she and Cherrie were doing with their children. But she updated him on his Mother and what she knew about Dee and Dick. She worried about him and begged him not to try and be a hero but just do his job. Get it done and come home.

As he was slipping the letter back into his pocket, the Battalion Commander entered the room and they all jumped to attention. The command, "As you were," was issued and they all sat back down. Billy Bob tried to pay attention because his life or the life of a member of his squad might depend on what he heard here. But it was hard as the commander droned on and on. They had still seen no action. All they had done was training, training and more training.

As the commander went from subject to subject, Billy Bob found himself wishing he could take Sue Ann's letter back out and read it again.

Dee walked into his tent that he shared with two other officers. He was exhausted. Stripping off his flight gear, he slung it into the corner of the tent. Not only was he tired, he was frustrated. This month made it a full year he had been on Guadalcanal flying sorties out of Henderson Field. His kills had reached thirteen but were climbing slowly because most of his sorties involved air-to-ground support to help the troops on the ground fighting in and around New Guinea. He was about to flop down into his cot when a head peeked into the tent.

"Beg your pardon, Sir," the head said formally.

"Yeah," Dee replied unconcerned. "Come on in."

"No need, Sir, I've been ordered to tell you to hump it over to Flight Operations on the double, Colonel Pickens wants to see you."

"What!" Dee asked in frustration. "I just now got back from a very long sortie!"

"Sorry, Sir, I'm just the messenger." With that, the head disappeared and was gone.

Dee bent over and stared at the floor. "Damn," he breathed, "what now?"

He gather himself together, reached down and picked up his soft hat and put it on, then hurried out of the tent towards the Flight Operations hut at a trot. When he got there, Colonel Pickens was sitting at his make shift desk waiting for him. Dee went up to the desk and stood at attention. He saluted smartly and said, "Lt. Commander Collie reporting as ordered, Sir."

"Take it easy, Collie," the Colonel said waving his hand and pointing to one of the two chairs in the hut. "Have a seat there."

"Thank you, Sir," Dee said removing his hat and sitting down.

The Colonel reached into his drawer and pulled out a bottle of Johnny Walker Scotch. "Would you join me in a drink?"

"I'd be pleased to, Sir."

The Colonel pulled two glasses out of the drawer and put them on his small desk. Carefully, he poured each glass about half full. "Sorry, no ice," he said as he put the bottle back into the drawer.

"This'll be fine, Sir, thank you."

The two men tapped the glasses together in a toast and then downed the whiskey in one gulp. "Oh boy, that was good," the Colonel said exhaling slowly." There was a long silence and then the Colonel seemed to come back to the present. "Well, Mister Collie, I guess you're wondering what this is all about."

"Aye, Sir, I am."

The Colonel leaned back in his chair and smiled at Dee. "First, I'd like to tell you what a good job you've done since you've been here; at least since I've been in command of the flight line." He paused and then said slowly, "And I really hate to lose you."

"Lose me, Sir?" Dee asked.

"Yes, lose you." The Colonel reached across the desk and handed Dee a two page document. "You're being ordered back to the Enterprise."

Dee took the orders from the Colonel's hand and looked at them in disbelief. "I can't believe it," he breathed, "after all this time."

Then the Colonel turned formal. "The Enterprise has just finished a refitting and major overhaul in the States. The problems with the Corsair have been addressed and fixed. It's now ready for carrier service. You'll be assigned to a Corsair flight once you rejoin the Enterprise. The Enterprise will put to sea again at the end of this month. You're to leave here immediately by a supply ship that will rendezvous with the Enterprise at an undisclosed time and place. But you can be sure you'll be back onboard before she goes back into action again." The Colonel then stood up and held his hand out to Dee, "I assume all of this meets with your approval, Mister Collie?" He asked smiling.

Dee shot to his feet and shook the Colonel's hand. "It does indeed, Sir."

"As I said," the Colonel continued, "your service here has been outstanding and I'll see to it that it's reflected in your fitness report."

"Thank you, Sir, I couldn't ask for anythin' more. It's been an honor to serve under you, Sir, a real honor."

"Well," the Colonel said quickly, "I guess you better get going, Mister Collie, and the best of luck to you."

"Thank you, Sir," Dee said saluting.

Dee turned smartly and left the hut. He stood outside and looked at the orders he held in his hand. He smiled broadly and said out loud, "I'm goin' back to the Enterprise."

—⦿—

Major Dick Jordan finally caught up the First Marine Division in Melbourne, Australia. He reported to the Headquarters of the 2nd Battalion 1st Marine Regiment where he took command. As the time neared for the First Marine Division to ship out, Dick became more and more concerned about being left behind. The doctor's had given him a go ahead for headquarters duty but not combat. Although he still had a small twinge of pain when he walked, he managed not to limp. He didn't want anyone to see him limp.

Now, he walked carefully, not limping, up to the office of the 1st Marines Regimental Commander to plead his case one last time. Standing outside the office door, Dick removed his hat and checked his self over to make sure he was spit and polish. When he was satisfied, he knocked on the office door and went in.

Colonel Cain, the Regimental Commander sat at his desk with his hands folded waiting for Dick. This was not their first meeting. Ever since Dick had gotten to Melbourne in late June, he had been trying to convince the Commander to allow him to keep his battalion and to deploy with them. The Commander had decided that this meeting would be the last one.

"Have a seat, Major Jordan," the Commander said briskly.

Dick quickly took a chair directly in front of the Commander's desk.

"Before we get started, Major Jordan, let me make a few things perfectly clear. Above all else, please understand that I am only a Regimental Commander; not a general. I take orders like everyone else. My orders come down from Division; I take those orders and pass them on down to Battalion. You know how it works; you've been a Marine for a while now. Division has given me orders concerning you. They've based those orders on the recommendations of high ranking officers in the Medical Corps. Those orders state that you'll not be completely combat ready for at least another six months. Now, with all that, what do you expect me to do?"

Dick was somewhat taken aback by the Commander's quick addressment of his situation. "Sir," Dick started slowly, "I was hoping that you could help me go directly to Division about this. I thought that, with your direct help, we could convince Division that I'm in good health and very capable of leadin' my Battalion in combat."

"But Major Jordan, it's not really Division you have to convince; it's the doctor's in the Medical Corps." The Commander's voice indicated a high degree of frustration. "And the next campaign, which will remain nameless at this time, will start soon. Even if you somehow convinced the doctor's now, there's not enough time to get all of this through Division. Can't you understand all this?"

Dick hung his head and said in a soft voice, "Aye, Sir, I guess I do."

Colonel Cain stood up and walk around his desk to stand by Dick. His attitude had softened considerably. "Look, Major Jordan, I know how you feel. If it were me, I'd be fighting the same battle you are. But it's just one campaign. You're still going to get your shots in."

Dick looked up at him. "It's not about me gettin' my shots in, Sir. I fought with those guys at Guadalcanal and I've been trainin' with them ever since I got here. It seems terribly wrong for them to go into battle without me."

"I guess I can understand that, because I was also with those guys at Guadalcanal."

"Sir, what'll I be doin' once they ship out?"

"You'll still be attached to 2nd Battalion here in Melbourne. I'll be gone so I assume you'll be answering directly to Division Intelligence. Don't worry there'll be plenty for you to do."

"I'm not much of a desk guy," Dick said sorrowfully. "I think I'd be much better on the line."

"I'm sure you would be, Major."

"Who'll be commandin' 2nd Battalion?" Dick asked not looking at the Commander.

"They've promoted a guy from 3rd Battalion. He'll take over for this campaign. But the Battalion is yours as soon as they get back and you're combat ready."

Dick stood up and saluted the Colonel. "Thank you for your time, Sir. I guess I'll go and help get the Battalion ready. The new Battalion Commander will need a lot of help. I can at least do that."

Colonel Cain held out his hand to Dick and they shook. "Well, God willing, Major Jordan, I'll be back to see you retake your command."

"You take care of yourself and my Battalion, Colonel." Dick turned sharply and left the office.

When Dick was outside, he walked slowly back to his quarters. He paid little attention to where he was going as his mind kept going over and over things. He knew a lot more than the Colonel thought he knew. For instance, he knew what the next campaign was. It was an amphibious landing on Cape Gloucester on the island of New Britain. Its purpose was to relieve the pressure on the battle for New Guinea and to help defend Northern Australia. He didn't know how long the campaign was schedule for but he did know it was scheduled to begin in late December. All of that meant he probably wouldn't see any action with his unit until late next year. In the meantime, he was to work with intelligence here in Melbourne.

Dick stopped walking and realized he had walked passed his quarters. As he turned to go back, his brain kept telling him that his chances of getting his Battalion back where close to zero.

CHAPTER EIGHTY-FOUR

The Escape Phase III

October 1943

Technical Sergeant Gerald Gaylen, alias Clint Jordan, stood beside the B-17 with his military duffle bag slung over his shoulder and holding a set of orders in his hand. His hair was no longer red. He had let that grow out and now had his original brown hair. He did, however, have it cut short. He was not the slim hard muscled man he was when he was breaking rocks. He was not fat by any means, but he did carry an extra twenty-five pounds or so thanks to Rosa.

The thought of Rosa brought sorrow to his heart. She had wanted to go with him but, of course, that was impossible. For some unknown reason, she had fallen in love with him. She had just turned twenty years old and her heart was broken at the sight of him leaving her forever. Clint tried to explain their age difference; he being forty-six and her only twenty. But like most women in love, it made no difference to her. And, in truth, Clint hated leaving her. She had been everything to him for nearly eight months. If he could love any woman, he could love Rosa.

The trip here to Buckingham Army Airforce Field in Fort Meyers, Florida had been a long and tiring trip. In the end, he came all the way by car. Since Judy couldn't arrange a safe flight that had a 'no questions asked' policy, Jimmy had had to hire a driver and car to take him from Sweetwater, Texas to Fort Meyers, Florida. It had taken them over three days to make the trip. But here he was waiting to board a B-17 for England.

"Hey, Gaylen," came a shout from inside the B-17, "get you stuff onboard we'll be leaving in about twenty minutes and give me your papers so I can sign off on them." It was Lt. Mason the pilot and commander for this flight.

"Yes, Sir," Clint responded. Clint had been grilled by Judy over and over again about military curtesy, how the ranks worked, and what all the rank emblems looked like. He was as ready to be a Technical Sergeant Third Grade as anyone could make him. He walked over to the open right waist gunner position where Lt. Mason was standing and heaved his duffle bag into the plane. Then he handed him his papers.

Lt. Mason studied the papers for a short minute and then took a pin from his breast pocket and signed them. He then handed them back to Clint. "Okay Sergeant, you need to be onboard in fifteen minutes I want to get airborne. We have to meet up with the rest of the group ten minutes after we're up. We've got to fly up the East Coast before we cut out over the ocean. You got all that?"

"Yes, Sir, I got it. I'll be onboard and ready to go."

Clint folded his orders and put them in his pants pocket. He looked across the air strip and saw Judy approaching. She had flown in two days ago. Buckingham AAF was to be one of her ferrying points. She had finally made it into the WASP. They contracted her in May and she entered her training class in mid-June. She completed her training in late September. Clint was sure he had never seen Judy as completely proud of anything as she was of those little silver wings she wore over her left breast. Those silver wings said loud and clear that she was a WASP.

As Judy approached, she was wearing her flight suit and helmet. A parachute bounced against her butt as she walked. A huge smile covered her face. As she walked up to Clint, she took off her helmet and shook her hair out. Her hair was still beautiful as it fell down to the shoulders of her flight suit.

Clint smiled at her. "My God who would've known it in that outfit, but you're a beautiful woman," he said softly. "I'll bet guys from near and far are knockin' at your door every night. Maybe even one special guy."

"Well thank you, Jerry," she replied with a wicked smile and a sparkle in her eyes. "That's what they call you isn't it? I mean Jerry for Gerald. No one would call you Gerald would they?"

"No," he said, "no one calls me Gerald. Most people just call me Sarge, but you can call me Jerry if you want, or for that matter you can call me anythin' you want. I think anythin' you call me would suit me fine."

"Well, after gettin' a close look at you, I think I'll call you Pa. Does anyone ever call you that? I realize that it does indicate an older man. So, really, does anyone ever call you Pa?"

"The fact is I once knew a girl who called me that," he said stepping closer to her. "But I haven't seen that girl in a long time. I think maybe she's gotten all grown up and moved on in life."

Judy took a deep breath and tried to hold back the tears that had begun to water her eyes. Just then the B-17 engines began to fire up and the wind blast from the propellers nearly knocked them down. She reached up and put her month to his ear and whispered, "You're as good as we can make you, Pa. From now on, you're on your own. Please be careful and take care of yourself. I hope to see you again sometime when this damnable war is over."

Clint didn't say anything. He just put his hand on her head and grabbed a hand full of hair. He pulled her head tightly to his chest and held it there of a long minute.

"Hey, Sarge," came a scream from the B-17, "come on and get in here. I've gotta close this door." The man yelling was the flight engineer. He was standing at the waist gunner position holding on to the door.

Quickly, Clint released her and jumped into the B-17. No sooner was he in the plane than the door was shut and sealed.

Judy backed up to get away from the B-17 as it started to taxi down the airstrip. There was no one left standing on the tarmac except her. She made quite a site standing alone on the airstrip in her flight suit, holding her helmet in her hand, wearing her parachute on her butt, tears streaming down her cheeks, and watching a lone B-17 get airborne.

After a while, the B-17 was gone from site but Judy remained standing there for several minutes, shifting her weight from one foot to the other. She strained to see the B-17 one last time, but it was no use; it was gone. Then, as if she had made a major life changing decision, she reached up with her free hand and dried the tears from her eyes and, using the sleeve of her flight suit, wiped the tear stains from her cheeks. She turned quickly and started walking across the tarmac towards another plane that awaited her. Her pace picked up and she hurried at almost a run. As she went, she put her helmet back on and started stuffing her hair tightly underneath it. As she approached the airplane waiting for her she touched the silver wings over her breast, and thought to herself, I'm a WASP now; I've got a job to do.

CHAPTER EIGHTY-FIVE

Anne Marie Fairchild

January 1944

Twenty-two year old Anne Marie Fairchild was hurriedly finishing up her farm chores on a dreary Friday afternoon. January on the farm was a miserable time of year. A cold misty rain fell making the cold cut to the bone. He brother used to do most of the chores that she now performed but he was currently serving in the Royal Navy. The Fairchild farm was in Hertfordshire county about five miles from Radlett nearly twenty miles mostly north and some west of London.

Anne had wanted to join her friends in the Auxiliary Territorial Service but, with her brother gone, she had to stay and help on the farm. However, on weekends, she would go into London and do volunteer work with the Women's Voluntary Service working with displaced children. During the blitz of 1940 through 1942, many children were sent away from London to live in the country and even to America. But now, as the bombing had nearly completely stopped thanks to those wonderful boys in the RAF, the children were returning home. Anne helped to get them back to their parents. She loved the job and the children.

Her parents, however, hated her job. They were constantly worried about more bombing attacks. But Anne had taken a stand and they could hardly argue because of her hard work on the farm. While in London, she stayed with a former schoolmate, Jane Morrison, in her flat. Jane had been in the Auxiliary Territorial Service since the blitz. She and Anne were as close as sisters.

Though Anne was a very pretty girl, she had no boyfriend or husband. There was just no time in her schedule for men. Anne stood only five feet, three inches tall, but her body was slender and well-shaped. Her face was somewhat plain because, like most farm girls, she worn little if any makeup. When not done up in a bun while working on the farm, her long sandy brown hair reached down to the middle of her back.

When in London on the weekends, Jane was always trying to get Anne to go out at night with her and get to know some boys. The Yanks were everywhere and were great fun. They had gotten the act of drinking and partying down to an art form. Jane had a boyfriend in the American Army Air Force and had tried many times to get Anne fixed up with one of his friends, but Anne preferred to stay in the flat at night and read. Strangely, for an English farm girl, she loved American Western novels and movies. Jane's flat was filled with the paperback westerns that Anne had read.

Getting to London on Friday evening and then getting back to the farm on Monday morning was the big challenge for Anne. Anne's only transportation was an old bicycle in bad repair. She took her bike the five miles into Radlett where she would catch the underground to London. Jane would pick her up at the tube station and they would go to the flat. On Monday morning, Anne would reverse the process to get back to the farm. For the most part, the underground still ran on schedule fairly well, considering the pounding it took during the blitz.

⸻

Now, as Anne waited at the tube stop for Jane to pick her up, she surmised that the weather in London was not any better than the weather on the farm. Her coat was wet with cold rain and her hair, even though she worn a scarf, was plastered to her forehead. She stamped her feet to keep the feeling in them. Finally Jane pulled up to a stopped and opened the car door for her. Anne jumped in and slammed the door shut.

"My God," Jane said looking her over, "you look awful. How long 'ave you been standin' there?"

"Not long," Anne replied through gritted teeth, "it was the bike ride to the underground that did most of the damage."

"'ang on, I'll 'ave ya to the flat in a flash."

"Just get me somewhere warm, if you please. I'm really, really cold."

—◁●▷—

A short time later, Anne was sitting mostly naked in front of a nice gas heater and warming herself. She sipped a steaming hot cup of tea and worn a towel on her head to dry her hair. "Jane, my love," she said dreamily, "you are a life saver"

"We 'ave ta find a better way to get you to and from London, dearie," Jane declared. "You know the weather ain't goin' ta get really bad until February."

"Don't tell me," Anne breathed as she took another sip of tea.

"Well, you just rest there for a while and get yourself together and then we'll get you ready."

"Ready," Anne said surprised, "ready for what?"

"My sweetie Ricky is on a three-day-pass and he's bringin' one of his parachute chums with him. We're to meet them at the Ugly Duckling at seven."

"Hold on, Jane, I'm not goin' anywhere. I'm stayin' right here in front of this fire and sippin' tea."

Jane put her hands on her hips and looked down at Anne. "Not this time, dearie," she said firmly. "I need some help to separate Ricky from his parachute chum. Ricky's got a nice room at the King George and I want to get him alone there. Now, I've always been fair with you. You always stay here in my flat and I can't get ya to go anywhere. Do I complain? No, I don't. This is the first time I've ask you for anything." She stopped talking for a moment to get her breath and then continued, "Now fair is fair. You got to help me this time, Anne, you just 'ave to."

Anne turned her cup up and finished her tea. "What makes you think this parachute chum will want to go anywhere with me? And what is a parachute chum anyway?"

Jane laughed. "Oh my, you really do need to get out more. These particular Yank parachute boys call themselves the Screaming Eagles and what a wild bunch they are! I got no doubt he's gonna love ya."

Anne stood up, put her cup down, shook her finger at Jane and said firmly, "Okay, Jane, "I'll do it just this one time. But please don't ask me to do somethin' like this again."

"That's my dearie," Jane said relieved. "Let's get ready."

They arrived at the Ugly Duckling Pub about a quarter before eight and Ricky and his parachute chum weren't there yet. It was Friday night and the pub was crowded but the girls were able to find a table for four. They got seated and ordered beers.

"Why are we early?" Ask Anne. "Won't that make us look anxious? And what's in that bag you're carryin'?"

"We're early so we can make a plan if need be," Jane smiled. Then, pointing to the small bag in her hand she said, "And in this bag is a very naughty nightie. A very, very naughty nightie, if you know what I mean."

Anne tilted her head and smiled at her friend. "I don't think the nightie is as naughty as you. I think you're naughty."

"You may be right," Jane giggled, "you just might be right."

"Jane," a loud voice yelled over the crowd. "Hey, Jane, we're here, girl." It was the loud gruff voice of Sergeant Ricky Northcutt. Sergeant Northcutt was crew chief of one of the C-47 cargo planes that carried the airborne troops to their drop zones.

Ricky pushed his way through the crowd to where the girls were waiting. He walked up smiling. "Hello, girls," he bellowed, "the Army Air Force has arrived along with the Screaming Eagles. May we be seated at your table?"

"Stop being silly, Ricky, and sit down and introduce your friend."

"You first," Ricky said looking at Anne as he and his friend sat down.

"This is Anne Fairchild", Jane said nodding her head towards Anne, "a very good friend of mine and ex schoolmate. She lives on a farm north of London." Then, turning to Ricky she said, "Okay, now it's your turn."

Ricky smiled broadly. "Hello, Anne Fairchild, I'm Ricky Northcutt from Columbus, Ohio and this sad looking guy with me is Billy Bob Barnett from Coalville, Texas."

Billy Bob stood up and politely shook the hand of each girl. "I'm very pleased to meet you both. It's nice of you to meet us for drinks."

"Speaking of drinks," Ricky said looking around. "I better go up to the bar and get us something."

"We've got our drinks," Jane said, "just get somethin' for you and Billy Bob."

"Please," Billy Bob said holding up his hands, "just call me Bill."

"Okay, Bill," Jane laughed.

Ricky got up and started through the crowd. "I'll be right back with the goodies," he yelled back.

So far Anne hadn't spoken. She just sat quietly taking a sip of her beer occasionally.

Jane looked at Billy Bob and then to Anne. "If you two will excuse me, I need to tell Ricky something of a private nature, so I think I'll just catch him at the bar. We'll be back in a flash with the beers." With that, she got up and started after Ricky through the crowd.

Anne watched Jane leave and then turned to Billy Bob with a smile on her face. "So, Bill, you're from Texas are you? You know I read a lot of American Western paperbacks, and many of the stories take place in Texas. Maybe you can tell me if what they say about Texas in those books is really true or not."

Billy Bob didn't answer he just looked at her. By just hearing her voice and seeing her smile, there was no doubt in his mind that cupid's arrow had just been shot straight through his heart.

CHAPTER EIGHTY-SIX

Billy Bob and Anne

May 1944

Over the last four months since Billy Bob met Anne Marie Fairchild, he had been doing two things almost exclusively. First, the training for the airborne units had intensified greatly. Now, as May began, everyone could feel the sense of urgency as the cross channel invasion grew closer. No one knew the exact date, but they knew it was near. Billy Bob had less and less free time to go visit Anne; and that was the second thing.

Every spare minute Billy Bob could get free he went directly to the Fairchild Farm. As a Staff Sergeant, he had access to a jeep, which he used freely on his weekend passes and three-day-passes. But now, security was becoming tighter and tighter and any kind of pass was getting extremely hard to come by. In his heart, Billy Bob new that his next pass was probably going to be his last one until who knows when. With that in mind, he went to his Commanding Officer and got permission to marry Anne. He had his CO's permission in one pocket and the ring in the other. Now all he needed was for Anne to say yes.

He had given it a lot thought. For the last three months, he and Anne had been together as if they were married. Her parents weren't prudes and didn't object to them sleeping together when he stayed at the farm for the weekend. When at the farm, he helped with work and, being a farm boy himself, he actually enjoyed doing it. While he was around with his jeep, she never had to use her bicycle. He took her where ever she wanted to go. Yet try as he may, he couldn't get her to give up her volunteer work in London. So, he became her chauffeur when he could.

They had spent many intimate times together and she told him many times that she was closer to him than she had been to anyone else in her entire life; excluding her immediate family. But the word *love* had never come up. Since she had never used the word, he made a point of not using it either. This worried him, but, in the end, it wasn't enough to stop him from wanting to ask her to marry him, but he needed one last pass to try and win her hand.

Rumor had it that there would be no more passes in the entire 101st Division after May 15th. So, he swallowed his pride and literally begged his CO for a three-day-pass. The CO was at first reluctant, but then seemed to understand his dilemma and granted him the pass. Now he had the pass, the permission to marry, the jeep, and the ring; the rest was all up to him.

—⊙▒⊙—

It was late in the evening as Billy Bob pulled his jeep up in front of the Fairchild House. Anne came running out to meet him as she had been waiting for several hours after his call had told her that he had gotten a pass and would be there as quick as he could. He stepped out of the jeep and she leaped up and threw her arms around his neck. He was much taller than her and she hung there smiling up at him. He put his hands under her armpits and lifted her so that their faces were at the same height, and then they engaged in a long and deep kiss.

He bent over and set her on the ground. She released his neck and took his hand and led him into the house. There inside the house, Anne's Father, Clyde, awaited them.

"Good evening, Clyde," Billy Bob said pleasantly.

"Good evenin', Bill," Clyde responded, "did you 'ave a nice motor?"

"Yes, I did, Sir, thank you for askin'."

Anne's Mother, Ellen walked into the living room wiping her hands on a towel. "Well, 'as the Yank finally arrived?" She asked smiling.

"Yes, Ma'am, I'm finally here."

"Good, now we can 'ave dinner. I've been 'olden it for a bit."

"I'm sorry, Ma'am, I drove as fast as I dared. I didn't want the MP's to stop me and take away my pass."

"Of course you didn't," Ellen smiled. Then pointing her finger at Anne she said, "Anne, make sure the places are set properly and we can set about feedin' this big Yank."

Anne hurried into the dining area and saw to the dinner placements and drinks, which consisted of a nice red table wine. Ellen followed her daughter into the dining area signaling the men to follow. "Everyone knows where they sit so just take your places and we can begin."

When everyone was seated, hands were joined and Clyde said grace, after which, Ellen got up and brought a nice pork lion to the table. "I'm sorry it's not beef, Bill, but we don't have a beef allowance until next month."

"The way you cook, Ellen, I'm sure it's goin' to be just fine, and those vegetables fresh from your farm look outstandin'."

"Thank you, Bill, you're very kind." Turning to Clyde she said, "Okay, Clyde cut and serve if you will."

※

The dinner went very well and everyone was full at the end. Ellen had prepared a delicious tapioca pudding for desert that they had with fresh brewed coffee. Everyone had pushed back from the table and was sipping their coffee when Clyde suggested returning to the living area. But before anyone could move, Billy Bob stood up quickly.

"If everyone could just stay seated for a moment, I have somethin' I would like to say."

Everyone looked at each other wondering what was happening, or what was about to happen. But they all settled back in their chairs and watched Billy Bob intently.

"First I'd like to say to you, Clyde and Ellen, how great these last four months have been for me. You've treated me with great kindness and allowed me into your home and shared your food with me although I know it's rationed and at times hard to get. I've had a home away from home and I want to thank you from the bottom of my heart. Secondly, I'm sure you know how I feel about your daughter. I love her and have since the first time I saw her at that pub in London." Billy Bob paused and looked over at Anne who had lowered her head, clasped her hands in her lap, and flushed a very dark red.

Reaching into his pocket he took out a small white satin box. He opened it up and set it down in front of Anne. Then he turned back and faced Clyde and Ellen. "I want to marry Anne," he said softly and simply. "I want to make her my wife and live with her the rest of life. I swear to you that I'll love her and protect her as long as I live." Then, turning back to Anne and knelling down on one knee, he said, "Please say yes, Anne."

Everyone seemed thunderstruck and no one said a word. Anne picked up the small box and took out the ring and looked at it. It was a beautiful but simple diamond on a gold band. It wasn't large but it sparkled brightly. Anne knelt down with Billy Bob and handed him the ring and held her hand out. Billy Bob took the ring and slid it on her finger. They leaned together and kissed softly. Slowly, Anne got to her feet and took Billy Bob's hand and pulled him to his feet. She turned to face her parents with Billy Bob at her side. Tears had formed in her eyes but she looked firmly at her Mother. "This is what I want, Mum," she said struggling to get the words out.

"I suppose I saw it comin' back a ways," Ellen said as she got to her feet. She walked around the table and up her daughter. Putting her arms around her, she hugged her until Anne as gasping for breath.

Clyde who had yet to speak finally found his voice. "What does this mean exactly?" He asked somewhat alarmed.

Ellen released Anne and turned to look at her husband. "It means that our daughter is goin' to marry this Yank."

"But does it mean she's goin' to leave the farm and go to America?" Clyde asked excitedly.

Ellen shrugged her shoulders and turned to Billy Bob. "Does it?" She asked.

"Yes, eventually when the time is right," Billy Bob answered. "But that may be a few months away dependin' on what the war does to us."

"But what about the farm," he persisted.

Ellen put her hands on her hips and cocked her head to one side. "When the time comes, we'll just 'ave to make do. And anyway, Jack'll be back from the Royal Navy someday soon; God willin'. Like Bill says, it depends on what the war does to us."

Clyde was quiet and everyone was waiting for him to speak. Time ticked by and still Clyde didn't speak. Then Anne spoke up. "I'll not do it without your blessin'," she said with emotion. "You're my Dad and you've been good to me my whole life."

"The same goes for me, Mr. Fairchild," Billy Bob said sadly. "I'd never ask Anne to go against her Father."

With tears running down her cheeks, she reached down and started to take off the ring. Clyde quickly reached across and grabbed her hand and stopped her. "You're my little girl," he said with his voice shaking. "I want you to be happy and if this will make you happy, then you've got my blessin', child. You've got it."

Anne pulled her Mother and her Father together and all three hugged each other while laughing and crying at the same time. Ellen looked up and saw Billy Bob standing by himself smiling. "Hey, Bill, you better join in on this because it's entirely your fault you know."

Much later after Anne and Ellen had cleared the table and cleaned the kitchen, they all sat around and talked about all the options that could happen. At this point, Billy Bob brought up another big concern. He stressed that they needed to get married right-a-way because he didn't know when he would get another pass anytime soon.

"Is there a preacher around here that could marry us?" Billy Bob asked.

"My God," Ellen said, "I forgot to ask if your Catholic or not."

"No, I'm a Baptist."

"Would you mind gettin' married in a Catholic church?" Ellen asked.

"No, Ma'am, I would not," Billy Bob said seriously.

"All right then," Ellen said jumping to her feet, "everyone get up and let's get goin' over to Father John's house. We'll get you two hitched tomorrow in Radlett."

"How do you know he can or will do it, Mum?" Anne asked anxiously.

"Why that old wine drinker owes me more than he can ever in a lifetime repay. He'll do it, or 'ave hell to pay; so to speak," Ellen laughed.

They all were laughing as they walked out of the house and started for Father John's house.

CHAPTER EIGHTY-SEVEN

D-Day June 6th

June 1944

Here they were again thought Staff Sergeant Billy Bob Barnett, sitting on the tarmac for the second day in a row. Yesterday the invasion had been call off due to terrible weather. D-Day, as it was called, was now due to go on June 6th. The entire 101st and 82nd Airborne Divisions were gathered out by the C-47 Cargo planes that would carry them to their drop zones over France. The day now was actually June 5th, but it would be June 6th by the time they got over their drop zones and parachuted out, which was scheduled near one AM in the morning.

Actually the delays had been good for Billy Bob. It allowed him time to write his Mother and sister and tell them about Anne. He mailed the letters yesterday thinking he was going to war that next morning. However, things changed and now he was writing a follow up letter to maybe explain things in more detail. While everyone milled around checking equipment over and over again, he sat on the tarmac using his pack for a table and wrote letters. As it was nearing eight thirty PM, he needed to hurry to get the letters finished and posted before they began to load onto the C-47s. He smiled to himself thinking what his family was going to think about him being a married man now.

He picked up his helmet and looked inside at the picture of Anne that was stuck firmly in the webbing of the helmet. He had begged Anne for a picture to carry with him and she had found one that was nearly a year old. But it didn't matter; the important thing was that he was carrying Anne with him. As he smiled down at the picture, he heard a loud commotion and saw soldiers running towards something. He put his helmet on and stood up to see what was going on. Then he heard the chant, "Ike, Ike, Ike," start up. Not to be left out, he started following everyone else at a run.

He didn't have to go far. The Allied Supreme Commander, General Dwight David Eisenhower, had come down to the assembly point to walk among the troops and talk with them before they went on their hazardous mission of parachuting behind enemy lines in the dark. Billy Bob listened as the Supreme Commander talked with many of the men, but Billy Bob didn't get close enough to speak with him. But he did hear the Supreme Commander say one thing that made all the guys feel good. He said, "One of the perks of my job is being able to talk to brave men like you."

After the Supreme Commander left, everyone hurried back to their assigned planes and prepared to start loading up. It was beginning to get dark as the men began to load onto the planes. Bill Bob stood alongside the plane and ushered his squad up the ramp and into the plane. When they were all in, he followed them in. They took their assigned seats and tried to get comfortable with all the equipment they were carrying, because it was a long flight across the English Channel and to their drop zones in France.

The flight had been long and it worn on the men's nerves, but finally the Jump Master gave the order, "Stand up and hook up." The men stood up and hooked their parachute lines to the cable that ran from front to back of the plane, so when they jumped their parachute lines would pull open their parachutes.

"Okay, guys," Billy Bob yelled above the roar of the open plane door, "you know the drill. Check the equipment of the guy in front of you. And do it good, because if his chute doesn't open, it's your fault." Quickly the men checked the equipment of the guy in front of them. Then, when all was done, they stood quietly and watched the jump light. They waited for it to turn from red to green.

The jump door was open and the noise of the rushing air and the engines filled the plane. To make it worse, they were already taking ground fire and anti-aircraft fire was bursting all around them. It seemed like an eternity went by before the jump light finally went green. The Jump Master yelled, "Okay, go, go, go." One at a time the men stepped to the door and jumped. As the line of men worked forward, Billy Bob's month went dry and his mind raced with a million thoughts at once. But his two years of intense training took over and as he stepped up to the door his body went calm. Then, without any reservations of any kind, Billy Bob jumped into the darkness of the sky over France.

CHAPTER EIGHTY-EIGHT

Making Things Right

June 1944

I t was late in the evening and Technical Sergeant Gerald Gaylen and First Sergeant Lloyd MacDonald sat in the enlisted man's club drinking a few beers. To say a few may be an understatement, as they both had lost count as the bar keeper had just refilled their glasses once again. Over the last six months, the two sergeants had become fast friends. Upon the arrival of Sergeant Gaylen at the 390th Bomber Group in Framlingham, England in late October 1943 one of the first people that he got to know was First Sergeant Lloyd MacDonald. It was the First Sergeant that had gotten him assigned to the ground crew of the 571st Squadron. It was a good assignment because he had done well on the ground crew working his way up to second technician behind the Crew Chief.

Clint Jordan was enjoying his new life as Gerald Gaylen. For the first time since the First World War, he was actually making friends and doing something useful. The guys on his crew accepted him and trusted him for his abilities. They simply knew him as Sergeant Gaylen, or Jerry when military protocol wasn't required. All of this was good but there was something missing for him, and, after much thought, he concluded that it would always be missing no matter who he pretended to be or how well he pretended. In his heart, there was still one thing that needed to be made right. And now he was hoping that his good friend, the First Sergeant, could help him make it right.

He and the First Sergeant had been making small talk when suddenly Jerry ask, "Mac, would you say that you and I are best friends?"

Mac looked at him suspiciously and said slowly, "Yeah, I think I'd say that. But the way things are between us I wouldn't think a question like that should need asking. Should it?"

Jerry smiled at him and tipped his glass at him. "No," he said, "it really shouldn't."

"Then why ask it?"

"I'm sorry, Mac. I wouldn't want to do anythin' to hurt our friendship. It's just that I've got a personal thing I need help with and you're 'bout the only guy that can do it, but I hate askin' because I feel like I'm takin' advantage of you."

"Well, you might be," Mac said looking down into his half empty beer glass, "but I guess I'll have to be the judge of that. Won't I?"

Jerry nodded, "Yeah, I guess that's the crux of it."

"Okay, so ask away."

Jerry looked around the club to see how much privacy they had. There were a couple of guys at the bar and three more occupying a table near the door about ten yards away from them. Outside of that and the bar keeper, they were alone in the club.

Mac noticed Jerry looking around as if he was afraid to be heard. "Is it that big a deal, Jerry?" Mac asked in a low voice leaning closer to Jerry.

"Yeah, Mac, I think it might be that big a deal."

"Okay, I won't know 'til I hear it. Lay it on me, Jerry."

Jerry straightened up in his chair and finished off his beer. "Please listen to me without interruptin'. I know you'll be tempted but please hear me out before you say anythin'. Is that a deal?"

"It's a deal."

Jerry paused as if he were hesitant to continue but then started. "Since D-Day I know our bombin' has been relocated from Germany to France and the Normandy area to support the troop landings and the fightin' goin' on there. But the Germans have also moved their fighter cover to France to take on our bombers. Now, I've heard that the 390th has been given a mission to go into Germany again to try and pull some of the German fighters away from France so our bombin' can be more effective. In essence, it's a bluff to try and get as many of the German fighters back into Germany as we can."

Jerry paused for a moment to let all he had said sink in. He could tell that Mac wanted to ask questions but Mac kept his word and waited for Jerry to finish. Happy that Mac was waiting, Jerry continued, "I'm pretty sure that the mission is schedule within the next few days. Now, here's what I need, Mac. I want you to help me get on that mission. I want to somehow be on one of our B-17s when they go into Germany. It can be done legally if possible or I can stow away somehow. But, I need to be on that mission. It's a personal matter, Mac. And this is the only way I can make things right within myself. Is there any way you can help me?"

Mac looked at Jerry closely and leaned back in his chair. "Wait here while I go get us a couple of more beers." Mac went to the bar and returned with two more beers and set them on the table. "I guess my first question is how do you know so much about our mission plans?"

Jerry shrugged and said, "Rumor mostly, Mac. I mean lots of guys come out of those briefings and come in here and talk to each other about it, or they talk in their bays. I know they don't take it off base but they talk about it here with each other."

"Yes, I understand that and it's all well and good, but even if I could work somethin' out, why is this particular mission so important to you?"

"Like I said, Mac, it's a personal thing that I need for my own well bein'. I can't explain it beyond that. It's really complicated and I don't want you gettin' in this deeper than I'm already askin'."

"Well, you're right about the mission and the timing. It's scheduled for the day after tomorrow. You and your ground crew should be getting the orders tomorrow morning. We'll be sending four squadrons including yours, the 571st. Now, I'm going to stop here and tell you something you don't know. If I help you, it won't be the first time I've done this. Your request isn't as original as you think it is. But in every case I've done this I've made sure of two things; one, I did *NOTHING* to put the mission in jeopardy, and two; I did *NOTHING* to put the air crew in jeopardy. Are we clear on those conditions?"

Mac's voice had begun to get louder so Jerry signaled with his hands to keep it down. "It's clear, Mac, but keep it down a bit please."

Mac looked around to see if he had attracted any attention. No one seemed to be paying them any attention at all. "Sorry, Jerry, it's just that somethings need to be firmly clarified."

"Consider it clarified," Jerry said smiling.

"So, if you want me to help you, we need to get started first thing in the morning. Are we a go or not?"

"We're a go," Jerry confirmed.

"Right, then let's finish these beers and get some sack time. You be at my office at oh six hundred hours in the morning. Roger that?"

"Roger that."

⊙⊪⊙

Jerry was waiting at Mac's office door the next morning when Mac walked up. "Kind of anxious aren't we?" Mac said sarcastically.

"Just bein' prompt," Jerry chuckled.

"Come on let's go over to the mess hall and have some coffee while we talk."

The walk over to the mess hall only took a couple of minutes. Soon they were seated at a long empty table sipping coffee. "Here's how it's going down," Mac started, "the right waist gunner on the Sugar Girl is going to be sick tomorrow morning just before the mission takes off. You're going to take his place. I assume that you're qualified on the fifty caliber waist gun? I mean I did sign your test score."

"I'm qualified. I've been goin' to the school for the past three months, which you were kind enough to get me in on a time available bases. And yes, you did sign my qualification score."

"Now, as soon as the plane gets back and parks you get out there fast. *Do Not* go to the debriefing. The regular waist gunner will be waiting there and go in your place."

"Surely someone will notice me durin' the flight," Jerry said.

"The Captain of the Sugar Girl and the entire crew know about it. It's not their first time either. And they all know you anyway. I mean the Sugar Girl is in the 571st so you're part of their ground crew."

"Wow," was all Jerry could say.

"Yeah, wow," Mac repeated. "But, Jerry, remember this is a real mission and it's going over Germany. This is really dangerous. This isn't a game. You could end up dead."

"I know," Jerry said looking down into his coffee, "which brings me to one last thing I would like for you to do for me."

"Holy shit, Jerry," Mac breathed, "what else could there possibly be?"

Jerry reached into his fatigue jacket and pulled out an envelope. "If I don't make it back, please mail this for me."

"Oh no," Mac said waving his hand and pushing the envelope away, "I don't do dead men shit. That's not part of the deal."

"Mac, listen to me, please." Jerry waited for Mac to calm down and then continued, "This is really important to me. It's to a girl that can't be seen gettin' a letter from me, that's why it's got your name on the return address. I know all of this is mysterious and I'm askin' a lot but she has to know what happen to me and why I did all this."

"Jerry, this is all starting to sound like a suicide, and if it is, I'll call the whole thing off."

"No, no, Mac," Jerry said trying to calm Mac down, "I just need this girl to read this letter if somethin' does happen. That's all. It's a just in case thing."

Mac took the envelope from Jerry and pushed it into his breast pocket. "I can't for the life of me know why I'm doing all this," he said. "I get the feeling you're leading some kind of double life and I should know about it."

"You're doin' all this, Mac, because you're not only a First Sergeant but you're a first class guy. And I've been lucky as hell to know you."

"You see," Mac said pointing at him, "there you go again talking as if this was our last conversation. Damn it, Jerry, you gotta stop doing that. It makes me very uncomfortable."

Jerry laughed and slapped Mac on the back and got up from the table. "I gotta get over to the 571st hangers and make sure those planes are ready to go; especially the Sugar Girl. Thanks again for everythin', Mac." With that, Jerry walked away waving to Mac as he walked.

"So long," Mac whispered, "whoever you really are."

The flight to Germany took longer than Jerry had anticipated. The good news was that they had fighter escort the entire way. The bomber air crews called the American fighters our 'Little Friends'. The P-51 Mustang was without question the best fighter in the world. It had the range to take the B-17s all the way to Berlin and back.

As they entered German air space, the Little Friends dropped back to avoid the anti-aircraft fire from down below, which was also called Flak. German fighters wouldn't engage the bombers while the anti-aircraft shells were bursting all over the sky, because they might get hit themselves. The fighters would jump the bombers before they entered the anti-aircraft barrage and then jump them again on their way back out.

They made their bombing run and hit their target dead on. They made their turn and headed back for home as the Flak continued to burst all around them. Two B-17s had been hit. One went down and the other was limping along but a crippled B-17 was an open invitation to the German fighters. Then, suddenly, the Flak lifted and everyone began to watch the sky for German fighters. It didn't take long before German fighters were swarming everywhere. They went straight for the crippled B-17 and it looked doomed but then the Little Friends came diving out of the sky to engage the Germans. Two German fighters went down immediately and the rest broke off the attack. Two Little Friends stayed with the crippled B-17 to escort it all the way back home.

But the German fighters continued to dive into the formation of B-17s. The Little Friends were doing their best but many of the German fighters were getting through. Jerry stood firmly at his waist gun and fired at the German fighters with machine gun bullets hitting all around him. The Sugar Girl was getting hit from all sides but all of her guns were blazing. A German FW-190 Focke Wulf came down from high above the Sugar Girl and raked her topside shattering the top ball turrent and killing the gunner. The shattered ball turrent left a huge hole in the top of the Sugar Girl. The Focke Wulf then pealed back and came straight at Jerry's right side waist gun. Jerry locked in on the Focke Wulf and clamped down on his machine gun triggers and held them down. The Focke Wulf was level in front of Jerry's gun and both the Focke Wulf and Jerry were firing at each other unrelentingly. Just as Jerry felt a machine gun bullet slam into his upper right shoulder, he saw his bullets start to tear the Focke Wulf apart. Struggling to stay on his feet, he continued to hold down his machine gun trigger. Then, to his satisfaction, he saw the left wing of the Focke Wulf break off and it went into a wild spin.

Jerry realized he was still holding down the trigger on his gun but before he could release it he ran out of bullets. He needed to load another ammo belt but he was getting dizzy from loss of blood. The left waist gunner ran over reloaded his gun for him then return to his own gun. He couldn't stop firing to give aid to Jerry's wound. Jerry was unable to stay on his feet to fire his gun. He finally passed out with the ring of machine gun fire in his ears.

The raid into Germany by the 390th Bomber Group on that day in late June was deemed a success as the Germans pulled two fighter groups away from the frontlines in France to support the German homeland. The 390th lost eight B17s that day, but the Sugar Girl was not one of them. The Sugar Girl limped back, with the help of the Little Friends, carrying extensive damage and three dead. One of those dead was Technical Sergeant Gerald Gaylen. Try as the air crew may, and they did try very hard, they couldn't stop the bleeding from the huge hole left by the bullet from the Focke Wulf's machine gun.

As they took Sergeant Gaylen's body from the Sugar Girl, he had a gentle smile on his face.

CHAPTER EIGHTY-NINE

The Letters

July 1944

The Collie house was getting ready for a big Fourth of July celebration. James had been gathering fireworks over the last two weeks. It was his intention to show his grandchildren a grand fireworks display in their own backyard. It was hard to believe that Kyle was now two years old and that Chloe and Joey were now pass their first birthday. James realized that the fireworks he had planned may very well exceed the ability of the young children to understand what they are seeing. As James was busy clearing a good spot to do the fireworks in the backyard, the women were in the kitchen making homemade ice cream. Sue Ann and Cherrie were taking turns sitting on the mixer as Mary and Ruth took turns turning the crank. All the grandchildren were fast asleep taking their noon naps. Suddenly Sue Ann jumped up from the ice cream mixer and yelled, "Mailman."

There was a mad dash for the door by all four women. The mailman coming to their front porch could very well mean a letter from Dee or Billy Bob. Dick letters usually went to Ruth's house. Sue Ann was the first one through the door and smiled at the mailman as he handed a small bundle of three envelopes to her. "Thank you, sir," she said smiling.

"Okay what'd we get?" Mary asked pushing her way through the other women.

"I got one from Bill," Sue Ann cried as she handed the other letters to Mary.

A look of disappointment came over Mary face as she saw nothing from Dee. "I just got junk," she said disgustedly.

Cherrie ran up to Sue Ann, grabbed her hand and pulled her over to the couch. "Open it up and read it," she begged. "Come on hurry up."

"I'm hurryin'," Sue Ann said, "I'm hurryin'."

Sue Ann tore the letter open and then a gloomy darkness came over her face. "What's wrong?" Cherrie asked afraid of the answer.

"It's just that it's date June 5th. We still don't have anythin' from him since he jumped on D-Day." They all knew that Billy Bob had parachuted into Normandy on D-Day but they hadn't heard anything from him. Sue Ann had hoped this might be the letter telling them he was alright. But, it wasn't.

"Well, go ahead and read it. There might be some good news in it," Cherrie urged.

"Yeah, yeah, I'm readin' it. Give me a minute. It might...," Sue Ann stopped in mid-sentence, "Oh my God," she yelled. Then she repeated, "Oh my God."

Everyone came rushing to her. "What is it, Sue Ann," Mary yelled, "don't you do this to us."

Sue Ann began jumping up and down and laughing. "Bill got married. My big brother got married."

"What?" Cherrie exclaimed. "Married to whom?"

"An English girl named Anne Fairchild. But I guess her name is Anne Barnett now." Sue Ann waved her hand for silence. "Give me a minute to read the rest of it." Everyone was politely quiet while she went through the rest of the letter. "Okay, here it is," she said breathlessly, "he met her back in January at an English Pub. They fell in love immediately and started datin' whenever Bill was free. He knew he was goin' into battle so they got married on May 15th in a Catholic church in a little town called Radlett. And he's put down her complete address so we can write her."

"We'll write her, Sue Ann," Cherrie said emotionally, "we'll all write her won't we?" Everyone nodded their heads.

The whole thing finally hit Sue Ann and tears formed in her eyes. Then she said softly, "He ends it by sayin' he wants us to love her as much as he does." She sank to her knees holding the letter to her breast. "I already love her as much as he does," she whispered. "I already do."

⊖⊣⊪⊢⊙

Judy Cole Jackson was stilled dressed in her WASP uniform as she looked out the window of her Mother's house. She was watching for the love of her life, Jimmy Orland. Judy had gotten a Fourth of July pass from the WASP to go home and visit her family. Her half-brothers were gone on a church outing but everyone else was present and accounted for; even her ninety-one year old Grandfather, the retired Reverend John Tuney.

"You're goin' to stare a hole through my livin' room widow," Bob Ann said from behind her."

"Oh, Mom," Judy said turning to recognize her Mother. "I'm sorry. I'm just so anxious to see him. It's been over two months now and this is his first leave since joinin' up. His last letter said he'd be shippin' out soon but he couldn't give me an exact date or even where because of security."

"You never did tell me how Mobil Oil took his resignation. Was it an amical separation?" Bob Ann asked.

Judy smiled at her, "No, Mom, it wasn't. They were really put out because of all the time and effort they had put into keepin' him outa the draft. Plus the fact, Jimmy did a really good job for them."

"Why did he do it, Judy? He had an important job. He could've stayed home and married you."

"You know men, Mom, he felt bad about not servin'. He just couldn't stand by and watch other guys go in his place. At least, that's the way he looked at it. He said he wasn't goin' to have to tell our kids that he was in Dallas for the entire war. And, I guess, truthfully I admire him for it. I can't help myself, but I do admire him."

"So, you two did talk about marriage?" Bob Ann's voice took on a hopeful sound.

Judy laughed, "Yeah, Mom, we did. And I was ready and willin', but he insisted on waitin' 'til after the war. I couldn't get him to change his mind, even with my wildly woman ways."

"I'm sorry if I seem dumb," Bob Ann said looking puzzled, "but tell me again what is it he does?"

"He just got out of Bombardier School. He's been commissioned a 1st Lieutenant Bombardier. It's his job to drop the bombs on the enemy, Mom."

"Really, I didn't know they had a special job for that."

"Yeah, Mom, they do. It's a very special job."

"I don't want to break up this conversation," Bob Ann said pointing out the widow, but I think someone you're expectin' is gettin' out of a cab."

Judy spun around quick enough to see 1st Lieutenant Jimmy Orland leaning over and paying the cab driver. She jumped from the couch and ran for the front door. He was walking up the walkway carrying his Army Air Force duffle bag over his shoulder. She ran up and jumped on him, knocking the duffle bag out of his grip and it tumbled to the ground. They embraced and smothered each other in kisses. He held her for a long time standing on the front walk.

"I guess we better go inside before we become a spectacle," he whispered in her ear as he still held her tight.

"Yeah," she replied, "we don't want to be a spectacle."

They stepped apart and he reached down and retrieved his duffle bag. Grabbing him by the hand, she led him into the house.

Over the next two hours a grand time was had by everyone. Her step-father, Jack, had grilled some hot dogs in the back yard. Her Mother, Bob Ann, had supplied all the trimming of onions, mustard, catsup, pickles, buns and homemade fried potatoes. Judy had gone out earlier and gotten a case of cold beer.

After everyone was full of food and sitting quietly sipping on beers, Jimmy told them that he would be shipping out at the end of July. All he could tell them was that he would be going to the European Theater assigned to the 15th Army Air Force and he would be bombing from a B-24. Judy didn't like to hear that because she had ferried a few B-24s and she didn't like the way they handled. She also knew that the B-24 had the nick name of 'The Flying Coffin'." The other thing she knew was that the 15th Air Force was based in Italy; thanks to her time in WASP, so much for security and secrecy. She knew all of these things but kept it all to herself. No one else needed to know.

Jimmy held up his beer an announced, "Being that I'm such a sensitive guy, along with being highly intelligent, I'm expecting bags and bags of mail from all of you." It was obvious that Jimmy was getting a little buzz on from the beer. "I expect a least one letter, or maybe two, each day." He smiled and guzzled down the last of his bottle of beer.

Judy couldn't help but laugh. He started to get up and go get another beer but she grabbed his uniform jacket and pulled him back down. "Hold on soldier boy, I think you may be at your limit."

Then suddenly Bob Ann jumped up and ran into the bedroom. When she returned, she was carrying a letter. "Oh my goodness, Judy, I forgot all about this letter that came for you yesterday. I put it in our bedroom and in all the excitement I forgot all about it. But all this talk about mail and letters reminded me." She walked over and handed it to Judy.

"Who would write me here?" Judy asked aloud to no one in particular.

"I don't know," Bob Ann said, "maybe someone who thinks you still live here."

Judy looked at the return address. She shrugged her shoulders and said, "I don't know anybody named First Sergeant Lloyd MacDonald."

"Well, open it up and let's find out," Jimmy said smiling. "Maybe you got a boyfriend you're not telling us about."

Judy torn open the letter being careful not to destroy the return address thinking she might want to write a response. She unfolded the letter and started reading.

Dearest Judy my little girl,

I hope you will excuse my typing. I am using the typewriter in the administration office that a sergeant friend of mine let me use. I am using the hunt and peck method so bear with any mistakes. I have a dictionary here with me so I can spell.

You are reading this because I have been killed in action over Germany. Please do not grieve for me. I died doing what I wanted to do and needed to do. For me it was a matter of balancing the scales and making things right for what happened years ago in another battle with the Germans. This time I win. I maneuvered myself on a combat mission over German knowing this could happen. Know that I died exactly as I would have wanted it.

Now I want to talk about Jimmy Orland. He is a good man Judy. I know it has been killing him inside these last few years not being in the service. I know he stayed out just to help you with me. I do not know but I bet he is already enlisted and is serving someplace. On the outside he seems like the get it done type of businessman but inside he is a compassionate good man. I've seen it over and over again. So, you marry that guy and you make sure you are good to him because he has been good to you and me.

Please know that I appreciate everything you and Jimmy did for me. This last year has been a gift from you two. And if you ever see Rosa again, tell her I did love her. She is the sweetest peach on the tree.

Now you go live your life the best you can and when you remember me please remember the good times. You know like watching those sunsets on Lonesome Hill. Those were sure pretty. Remember.

I have gone but our love will always be.

Pa

Tears welled in Judy's eyes but she didn't let them roll down her cheeks. Everyone could see it was some kind of bad news but they didn't want to ask what had happened. They all knew Judy well enough to know she would tell them when she was ready. It was quiet in the house while Judy refolded the letter and smoothed it out on her lap. Then, she looked around the room and said, "Clint Jordan is dead."

There was shock and surprise in the room. Bob Ann looked at her daughter and asked, "Did they finally catch him? Did they have to shoot him or somethin'?"

Judy smile at her, "No, nothin' like that, Mom. It's a long story and I'll tell you sometime."

Jimmy rose to his feet now completely sober. "But how can that be, Judy?" He asked. "And why? He was safe. My God he was safe!"

Judy stood up and went over and took Jimmy's hand. "Do you love me, Jimmy?" She asked simply.

"You know I do, Judy, you don't even need to ask that question."

"Then I'll ask another question. Marry me, Jimmy? Marry me now or today, but please don't make me wait. It's important to me, Jimmy. I'll beg if I have to. I will."

Jimmy took her in his arms and held her tight. "There'll be no begging. And you won't have to wait. We'll leave right here and now, this very minute and go interrupt some Justice of Piece who is probably busy celebrating the Fourth of July. But we won't take no for an answer." He reached down and lifted her face so he could look into her eyes. "You know," he said, "they'll probably kick you out of the WASP."

"Well," she said, "I've served the WASP good and faithfully for almost a year now. If they don't want me because I'm married to Lt. Jimmy Orland of the United States Army Air Force, then I'll just have to get kick out. I got other fish to fry."

Jimmy turned to the room and asked, "Who wants to go with us?"

"Count me in," Jack said jumping to his feet.

"Me too," Bob Ann said. "Can you believe it, gettin' married on the Fourth of July?"

"I guess I better stay here," Reverend Tuney said waving his hand. "But I sure wish I could perform the ceremony. Good luck anyway."

As they all headed out the door, Judy carefully put Clint's letter in the left breast pocket of her uniform jacket just under her WASP silver wings.

CHAPTER NINETY

The Battle for Peleliu

September 1944

T he chances of two old friends meeting twice during the war in the vast Pacific were almost incalculable, but it did happen. Dee Collie and Dick Jordan had met on Guadalcanal in October of 1942 and now they would meet again on the small island of Peleliu. Peleliu is one of several islands that make up the island nation of Palau. It is very small as it's only a little over five square miles in size; being just over six miles long and a little less than one mile wide. But more blood per square mile would be spilt on this little island than at any other battle in the Pacific.

———

Major Dick Jordan had suffered through the long torturous days while his battalion fought on New Britain and he lingered in Melbourne, Australia doing pointless jobs and nursing his cracked hip. His hip was declared completely healed while the division was still on New Britain. Needless to say, Dick was furious about being stuck in Australia while his battalion was fighting in New Britain and he had been declared healed and ready for combat. When the First Division was pulled off New Britain they didn't return to Melbourne but instead were sent to Pavuvu in the Russell Island near Guadalcanal for rest and refitting. Dick would meet them there in March of 1944 and be reunited with his beloved 2nd Battalion, 1st Marines. Although command of the battalion was not returned to him in full, he was given command of a small liaisons unit to work intelligence between the 2nd Battalion and Regimental Headquarters. All of this came about in June of 1944. It was just as training began for their next campaign; Peleliu.

Now, in September, Dick sat on the deck of the troopship carrying him and his men from Pavuvu to Peleliu a trip of over two thousand miles. It was evening, the sea was calm, and there was still enough light to read. He took out his latest letter from Cherrie and started to reread it again for who knows how many times. It was an old letter, dated sometime in June. He had been moving around so much his mail was still chasing him across the Pacific. With the letter were several pictures of Chloe and Joey. If was hard for him to believe they were already more than a year old. Also, enclosed with the letter, there was an exceptionally beautiful picture of Cherrie wearing a very brief nightie. He smiled down at the picture and ran his finger gently across her face. He took off his fatigue cap, kissed the picture and put it in the cap. He replaced his cap on his head and got up and started walking back to the officers' quarters above deck.

⸻

Since Dee's return to the Enterprise in November of last year, the action had been hot and heavy. There had been one heavy action after another and he had been involved in all of them. By the time he got back to the Enterprise, the F6F Hellcat fighter had replaced the Wildcat. The Zero proved to be no match for the Hellcat. The Hellcat's kill ratio against the Zero was better than seventeen to one. As a result, Dee and his Corsair squadron did mostly air-to-ground support while the Hellcat squadrons flew high cover and took on any Zeros that might try and interfere.

Still Dee was able to get his kills up to eighteen thanks to what got the nickname 'The Marianas Turkey Shoot'. It was actually the Battle of the Philippine Sea but the nickname came from the fact that the Japanese suffered the loss of over six hundred planes; the Hellcats doing most of that damage. Nearly every pilot in the American fleet got credited with at least one kill. It was a horrible defeat for the Japanese. Not only did they lose all of those planes but they lost three fleet size carriers. Since that battle, which took place in June, the Japanese didn't have the resources to mount any kind of offensive action; they were now strictly on the defense. Now, the Enterprise was to be part of the armada to assault the Japanese held island of Peleliu. They were steaming at top speed to reach the rendezvous point.

Dee was out on the flight deck as the sun began to set below the horizon. He was just enjoying the evening sea air as the Enterprise plowed through water sending sea spray up on the deck. Dee was surprised when a seaman came up behind him. "Pardon me, Commander," he said in a loud enough voice to be heard over the wind and sea.

"Yes, seaman," he replied turning around.

"The Executive Officer wants to see you in his quarters at once, Sir."

"I guess that means I need to move my ass, uh seaman."

"Aye sir, I guess that's what it means." The seaman gave him a short halfhearted salute.

Dee returned the salute and then hurried for the XO's Quarters. When he arrived, he looked down at himself before entering. He was dressed in work cloths. Not the sort of way to dress to go see the XO. But, the order was 'at once' so here he was 'at once'. He knocked on the door firmly.

"Come," said the voice from behind the door.

Dee put his cap under his left arm and entered the XO's Quarters. He moved quickly to the desk where the XO was sitting and stood to attention. "Lt. Commander Collie reportin' as ordered, Sir."

"Stand easy, Commander," the XO said.

"Thank you, Sir. And, Sir, please forgive my appearance but I came immediately as ordered. If the Executive Officer will give me fifteen minutes, I can go make myself more presentable."

"Don't worry about that, Commander," the XO said pointing to a chair. "Please take a seat we have a few things to discuss."

"Aye sir," Dee said as he seated himself in nice comfortable leather chair across from the XO's desk.

The leaned back in his chair and folded his hands on his chest. Then, he looked at Dee with a hard uncompromising look. "I'm sure you're aware that we're steaming at near full speed to join the force assaulting Peleliu."

"Aye sir," Dee replied.

The XO continued to stare a hole through Dee. "I've got a job for you that I'm pretty damn sure you're not going to like."

Dee relaxed a little and moved slightly in his chair. "Aye sir," he said suspiciously, "and what kind of job are we talkin' about?"

The XO's face broke into a large smile. "Good question, Commander, and I hope I've got a good answer for you. I'm going to ask you to volunteer but if I have to I'll make it an order, because it comes straight from the Captain and has to be done and it's been made clear to me that no one can do it better than you."

Dee just stared at him. "Okay, I volunteer," he finally said.

"Okay, then listen up," the XO said standing up. He started pacing back and forth behind his desk chair. "First, I'll need you to assign one of your guys as commander of your Corsair squadron, because you'll be somewhere else. As usual they'll be flying air-to-ground support while the Hellcat squadrons will fly high cover. Have you got somebody that you feel comfortable enough with to give him temporary command of your squadron?"

"Aye sir, Lt. Bicker is my best man. He'll do a good job." Then after a short pause, "And as for me, Sir, what'll I be doin'?"

"The main objective for taking Peleliu is its airstrip. That'll be the Marines' first major objective. You're to wait on the Enterprise until that airstrip is secured. When it is, you're to take a Corsair and fly to that airstrip and land there. You'll probably be the first American to land on that airstrip. Once there, you're to make contact with a special Marine intelligence unit that has been formed. Their job, and yours, will be to work together to coordinate our air strikes where ever they're needed. It'll be up to the Marine unit to tell you where, when, and how much support they need. You then will communicate that intelligence, not just to the Enterprise, but to the command ship The Mount McKinley so that we can get them the air support they need as quick as possible. Does that make sense to you, Commander?"

"Aye sir, it makes perfect sense. I just don't understand the part about why no one can do this job better than me. Am I missin' somethin'?"

The XO smiled his large smile again. "Damn, Commander, I like you. That's exactly the question I'd ask if I were in your shoes."

"Aye sir," Dee said nodding his head, "and the answer to the question is…?"

"The answer is Major Dick Jordan," the XO said simply.

"You mean my brother-in-law?" Dee asked in amazement.

"Yes, that's the Major Dick Jordan we're talking about. You see he's the one in command of the special intelligence unit. I was only made aware of his relationship to you today. He'd made mention of the fact that he had a relative on the Enterprise during an Officer's Call on the command ship. Our Group Air Commander was really surprised to find out it was you. He relayed the information to me and I told the Captain. Since we were going to have to get and officer for this job anyway, it just made sense to use you. I would suppose that you two know each other well and can work together in good fashion. Is that a good assumption, Commander?"

At first Dee was too stunned to speak. Finally he stammered, "Aye sir, we can work together just fine."

"Good, Commander," the XO said sitting back down in his chair, "we'll talk more about it at our Officer's Call tomorrow morning. Are there any other questions, Commander?"

Dee assumed he was being told the meeting was over. He stood up to attention and said, "No questions, Sir."

"Very good, Commander, you're dismissed and thank you for volunteering."

"Aye sir," Dee said as he saluted quickly, turned and left the room.

Once outside, Dee leaned back against the bulkhead and started laughing. "Well I'll be damned," he laughed, "I'll just be damned."

The Battle for Peleliu didn't go as predicted by the 1st Marine Division's commander, Major General William Rupertus. He had predicted the island would be secured in four days. In the end, the battle lasted two months. The Japanese had changed their tactics to be absolutely defensive. Unlike Guadalcanal where the Japanese tried to hold and then retake the island using many offensive attacks, the Japanese on Peleliu only wanted to defend the island as best they could and kill as many Marines as they could in the process. They had no intention of mounting any kind of offensive scheme.

Dee, as ordered, waited on the Enterprise while the Marines fought vicious battles to gain control of the airstrip. On the second day the Marines finally took the airstrip but then lost it to a Japanese counter attack. Then, on the third day, the Marines retook the airstrip and held it. It was declared secure at the end of the third day. Dee made preparations to depart for the airstrip the next morning. He would be escorted by his Corsair squadron now being commanded by Lt. Bicker. They would escort him there, see that he landed okay, and then return to the Enterprise.

Dee was not the first American to land on the newly secured airstrip as he had been told he would be. Upon it being declared secure, the Marines immediately started using small and light spotter planes called Grasshoppers to help them find enemy positions. These small planes were slow and had a limited altitude and were very susceptible to enemy fire; even small arms fire. That was the bad news, the good news was that Dick was waiting for him at a make shift hanger near the edge of the airstrip. After he parked his plane near the hanger, some Marines pushed the Corsair into the hanger. Dee jumped down to the ground and immediately saw Dick walking towards him smiling.

"Hey, you sure look better than the last time I saw you," Dee yelled as they approached each other.

When they met, there was handshaking, backslapping, and hugging. "I am better," Dick laughed. Then turning serious he said, "I just hope I can stay that way. There's a hell of fight goin' on out there."

"Yeah, so I hear," Dee said looking around the hanger. "Well, I'm here to see if the Navy can help out. By the way, how did you get involved in this intelligence thing anyway?"

"Before we get into all the military shit, can we take a little time to get caught up? I've been running all over the Pacific and my mail is still trying to catch up to me. I haven't had any news from home since mid-June."

"Yeah, I don't see why not. You got a place we can go and talk?"

"Well, there's really not a good place but my little intelligence unit is setup just behind what's left of the airstrip control tower. That about as good as it gets."

"Let's go," Dee said slapping Dick on the back. Dee followed and Dick took the lead as they walked over to where the intelligence unit was setup.

The intelligence unit consisted of a large tent filled with all kinds of radio equipment. There was a long table in the middle of the tent that had maps and map overlays on it. As they walked in a sergeant, the only person in the tent, started to jump to his feet from the chair he was sitting in, but Dick signaled him to keep his seat.

"Sergeant Miles, this is my brother-in-law, Lt. Commander Daryl Collie."

"Nice to meet you, Sir," Sergeant Miles said giving Dee a small salute.

Dee didn't speak but only nodded.

"Sergeant," Dick said, "could you give us some privacy for a while. We've got some catchin' up to do."

"No problem, Sir," Sergeant Miles said getting to his feet, "I'll just go out and watch for the other guys and keep them away so you won't be bothered."

"Thanks, Sergeant; I'll give you a wave when we're done here."

"Roger that, Sir," he replied and vanished through the tent flap.

Dee looked around and grabbed a chair and sat down. Dick did the same.

"Okay, where do I start?" Dee asked.

"The last I heard was just after D-Day and everyone was worried about Billy Bob. No one had heard anythin' from him since he jumped into Normandy. So, you can start from any time after that."

"Okay then, I'll start with Billy Bob," Dee started. "He made it back okay. I don't know the details but I guess he was involved in some bad stuff. They took some heavy casualties but not as many as they thought there might be. They fought for nearly a month without stopping. I think they got pulled out around the middle of July and Billy Bob went back to England and his wife. I guess…"

"Wait, wait," Dick interrupted, "wife, what's this about a wife?"

"Yeah," Dee laughed. "Old Billy Bob married himself an English lady. Last I heard he's got all the papers done and approved and he's sendin' her home to Coalville. Hell, she might be there by now I guess."

"Well son-of-a-bitch," Dick laughed. "But, you know it couldn't happen to a nicer guy. I hope they make it okay. God, I hope he makes it back."

"Me too," Dee said softly.

"Okay, now what else you got?" Dick asked trying not to get somber.

"Well, Sue Ann, Cherrie, and all the kids are doin' fine. Your Mom is fine and she's lovin' every minute of havin' Cherrie and the twins at her place."

"I knew she would," Dick smiled. Then there was a short pause as each of them tried to think of what to say next. "Has anybody heard anythin' about my Dad? Has the FBI caught him yet?"

Dee lowered his head to avoid Dick's eyes. "It's obvious that you haven't heard and I sure hate to be the one to tell you."

"Tell me what?" Dick pressed.

"Dick, your Dad is dead," Dee said straight forwardly.

Dick stood up and looked down at Dee. "How'd it happen? Did he get into it with the FBI?"

Dee remained seated but looked up at Dick. "No it wasn't the FBI. In fact, they'd given up on findin' him and moved on to bigger things. Dick, you Dad died under the name of Technical Sergeant Gerald Gaylen. He was flyin' a bombin' mission over Germany in a B-17 as a waist gunner. The plane he was in made it back but three of the crew died and Clint was one of them."

Dick looked frustrated. He walked back and forth in the tent. "But how can all of this be?" He asked exasperated. "How could he get all the way to England and be on a B-17."

Dee stood up and took Dick by the shoulders. "It's a mystery to everyone so far. And I don't know any more than I've just told you. When you get back home, you can try and find out how it all happened. But right now we got some Marines to save and that's what we need to do. But I'll leave you with one last thing I do know. Your Dad, Clint Jordan, died fightin' for his country. In fact, they want to give him, or Gerald Gaylen, an Air Metal. You see Dick, your Dad shot down the plane that got him."

Dick nodded his head. "You're right, Dee, we need to get to the issue at hand. But just one last thing, does Mom know all this?"

"Yes, she does. She knows what I know."

Dick patted Dee's hands and slowly removed them from his shoulders. He turned and walked to the tent flap and held it open. "Sergeant Miles," he shouted.

"Aye, Sir," Sergeant Miles responded running up to the tent.

"Find the rest of the unit," Dick ordered. "We've got to get busy here. I don't care what they're doin' have 'em drop it and get their asses in here on the double."

"Aye, Sir," Sergeant Miles yelled as he turned and ran away, "I'm on it."

Dick dropped the tent flap and walked back over to Dee. Smiling he said, "Thanks for the update, Dee. You're a good friend and a damn fine brother-in-law." Then, his voice changed its tone. "Okay,

Commander," he said briskly pointing to a large map on the table, "if you'll come over here and take a look at this map and I'll show you the shit we're in."

Dick and Dee worked together for the next ten days coordinating Corsair strikes from the carriers. It took a lot of time to get the Corsairs off the carrier decks and to the target. Finally, they got their own ground based Corsairs that flew their missions directly from the airstrip on Peleliu. The time to get to the target was much faster and much more effective when the sorties originated from the Peleliu Airstrip.

Dee flew several missions as a spotter. Marking the targets with red smoke and then allowing the ground based Corsairs to make the strikes using rockets and napalm. But even with strong air support, the battle was bloody and costly to the Marines. The Japanese hid, sniped, and fought from hundreds of caves in the ridges of the hills. But slowly, the air strikes were taking a heavy toll on the Japanese.

As the casualty list for the Marines grew larger and larger, the push to clear out the remaining Japanese holdouts became paramount. A battle raged at a place the Marines call Bloody Nose Ridge. The Marines were caught in a narrow canyon like passage with heavy fire raining down on them from the ridges on both sides. Dick and Dee worked out a mission to help relief some of the pressure on the Marines. Dee had his Corsair loaded with smoke bombs. The only weapons he would have were his machines guns as all regular bombs and rockets had been remove to accommodate the smoke bombs. His job would be to locate and mark the targets on the ridges with red smoke. Then the ground based Corsair squadron was to pound those mark target areas with massive rocket and napalm attacks.

Dee was circling over the target area when the attack squadron of Corsairs arrived. He saw them above him at roughly four o'clock high. "Scorpion Leader, this is Lone Eagle. Do you read me?"

"I have you loud and clear, Lone Eagle."

"Roger that Scorpion Leader. I'm goin' to start my run now on the left ridge. Then, I'll make a turn and comeback on the right ridge. Don't start your attack until I've finished my return run on the right ridge. Copy that?"

"Roger, Lone Eagle. We'll hold our position until you've make your return run."

Dee did a slow turn and lined his Corsair up with the canyon. He dropped his altitude down to just below the top of the ridge on his left. When he liked his position, he gunned his engine and the Corsair jump forward and gained speed quickly. As he approached the entrance to the little canyon, he spotted the caves and gun emplacements just where he and Dick and marked them on the map. Maintaining his speed, he banked his Corsair to the right exposing his underbelly to the left ridge. As he approached each cave and gun emplacement, he released a smoke bomb right on target. He almost made a bad mistake, because as he was watching his smoke bombs explode into bright red smoke, the end of the canyon came up on him fast and he nearly clipped his wing on the ridge top. But he managed to pull out and gain altitude.

Once high over the canyon again, he could see his smoke doing its job. He was somewhat surprised the he had received very little if any ground fire. He assumed that he had taken them by surprise. He did another slow turn and headed back for the canyon from the other direction. Again, he dropped is altitude to just below what would be the right ridge, but because he coming through the canyon from the opposite direction it was on his left. He gunned his engine to gain speed and again bank his Corsair to the right and started his run. The caves and gun emplacement were again visible just where they should be. He started releasing his smoke bombs just as before, except this time the Japanese weren't surprised. He was hit by a torrent of heavy machine gun fire. Just as he released his last smoke bomb his canopy literally exploded.

Dee fought to keep control of the Corsair. He narrowly missed slamming into the ridge. The Corsair responded and he was able to pull up and gain altitude, but the controls were sluggish and the engine was struggling.

"Lone Eagle, this is Scorpion Leader you're hit. Do you wish to abort the mission?"

"Negative. I say again negative. Start your run now, Scorpion Leader, while the smoke is still visible."

"Roger that, Lone Eagle, we're starting our run now."

Dee was too busy to watch the attack. He had gained enough altitude to be sure he was over the canyon walls, but the plane was struggling to keep the altitude. As per his training, he started looking his aircraft over as best he could. His wings seemed okay and the engine cover had holes in it but the engine itself was still running and not smoking. So, he doubted fire was an issue. He tried to turn and look back at the tail section but noticed he couldn't move his right shoulder. Glancing down at his right shoulder, gave him cause for alarm. There was a large piece of the canopy sticking all the way through his shoulder and pinning him to the back of his seat. Blood was flowing freely from his shoulder and dripping down into his lap. He took his hand off the stick to see if you could pull the piece of canopy out but when he did the plane started to drop.

Dee quickly calculated that his only chance was to get back to the airstrip and try and land the plane. He started turning the plane and was glad to feel the flaps and rudder control working okay. He got turned and headed for the airstrip. "Flight Control, this is Lone Eagle can you read me." There was only static so Dee tried again, "Flight Control, this is Lone Eagle can you read me?"

"Lone Eagle this is Flight Control go ahead."

"Flight Control, I'm shot up pretty bad and need help with a visual of my undercarriage. Can you comply?"

"Roger that, Lone Eagle, as a matter of fact I can see you now. Can you lower your landing gear?"

Dee flipped the landing gear switch but didn't feel anything happen. "Is my landing gear down?"

"No, can you go to manual and crank it down?"

"Negative on that, I've got problems of my own and only have one hand. I can't let go of the stick."

"Understood, Lone Eagle, you're going to have to belly land. The crash crews are already on the field."

"Thanks, Flight Control, you might want to make sure an ambulance is there."

"Sorry, Lone Eagle, all we got is a jeep and a stretcher."

"Understood, stand-by here I come."

Dee carefully lined up the Corsair to be headed straight for the middle of the landing strip. The plane bounced and swayed but he was able to keep control. He pulled back on his stick to pull the nose up. He held the stick in between his legs and the crook of his good arm and cut the throttle back with his hand. The plane seemed to float down with the power cut back. When he felt he was close enough to the ground, he quickly cut the throttle completely and the Corsair dropped to the ground and started skidding across the tarmac. Dee used the rudder controls to try and keep the plane straight and, for the most part, was successful. But when the plane finally stopped skidding it was setting sideways and smoking.

The crash crew was there the second the plane stopped skidding spraying foam everywhere. One of crew jumped up on the wing and started unbuckling Dee's hardness.

"Christ Almighty, Commander," he said. "How am I supposed to get you out?"

Dee drowsily looked at his shoulder and said, "Well, Sarge, I guess you're goin' to have to pull that damn thing out."

"But Sir, I think we need a Corpsman for this job."

"Do you think we got time to wait?" Dee asked. He smiled at the Sarge as he could feel himself losing consciousness.

"No, Sir, I guess not." The Sarge reached into the cockpit and took hold of the canopy section in Dee's shoulder and, being careful of his own hands, started rocking the section back and forth and pulling on it at the same time.

That was the last thing Dee remembered as he passed out.

CHAPTER NINETY-ONE

The Events of September

September 1944

T he events of September 1944 led to many changes in the Collie, Jordan, Barnett, and Jackson households. Even though the tide of the war had changed in favor of the Allies in both the European and Pacific Theaters, the war showed no signs of being over in the immediate future. Men from all of the families were fighting on different fronts. Dee Collie and Dick Jordan were in the Pacific fighting in the bloody campaign at Peleliu, Billy Bob Barnett had parachuted into Holland with the 101st Airborne and was fighting to break into Germany and end the war, and now Jimmy Orland was flying bombing missions from a base in Italy against the Nazi war machine. All of the families faced fear each and every day for their loved ones in harm's way. Their strength came from each other. They stayed in constant contact with each other and shared any news that any one of them got. They listened to the war news and worried and fretted. That's about all they could do; except go to church several times a week and pray, which they did; they prayed a lot.

———◁●▷———

Judy Orland had been very busy over the last two months. She, of course, had married Lt. Jimmy Orland three weeks before he shipped out to Italy. Those three weeks had been wonderful and fun filled. However, watching Jimmy leave on the train from Dallas Union Station had been extremely hard for her. But she didn't cry, she had promise Jimmy she wouldn't cry. Then there was her resignation from the WASP. That had been another hard thing to do. She loved the WASP but she wanted a family more than anything now. With Jimmy gone, she moved back in with her parents. Both Jack and Bob Ann were very happy to have her and needed her help with a problem they were having. Judy's half-brother, Kenny, her Mother's oldest son, had just turned eighteen and intended to enlist in the Marines with or without his parents blessing. Bob Ann was out of her mind with fear and begged him to wait a while longer. When Kenny didn't respond, Bob Ann tried to enlist Judy to help.

"Mom, I can't tell Kenny what to do. Anyway, if he doesn't enlist, they'll surely draft him."

"But, Judy, the Marines," Bob Ann cried. "Why does it have to be the Marines? I was thinkin' maybe the Coast Guard or somethin' like that."

"Kenny's not goin' to buy that, Mom." Judy watched her Mom for several minutes. Bob Ann was frustrated and didn't know what to do.

"Look, Mom," Judy said, "Kenny's a good kid. He's goin' to enlist with some of the other guys from his church club. You can't stop him. You couldn't stop me remember? Since you can't stop him you need to support him. He's a good kid that's goin' to be a good man. You gotta let him go, Mom. You gotta let him go."

A week later Kenny Jackson enlisted in the United States Marines and left for basic training at Camp Pendleton, California.

<hr />

It was a reversal in roles. On Guadalcanal, Dee had seen a wounded Dick off to the hospital ship. Now, at Peleliu, Dick was seeing a wounded Dee off to a hospital ship.

Dick held Dee's hand tightly and smiled down at him as he lay on a stretcher waiting to be place aboard the landing craft that would take him to the hospital ship.

"Well brother-in-law," Dick said grinning, "it looks like you're finally goin' to get to see that son of yours, and your nephew and niece as well."

"They tell me I'll be in a hospital in Hawaii for more than a month before I can go home. They also tell me I'm probably done for the war and that I'll have to rehab this shoulder for a year or more. Surely by then you Marines will have this damn thing over with."

"Yeah, we will," Dick assured him. "If I remember right, I think you're goin' to find that hospital in Hawaii full of beautiful nurses. I'll write Cherrie and have her make Sue Ann aware of the situation. Hell, who knows, Sue Ann just might up and go to Hawaii."

"Thank you, Major, but I'll do my own writin'."

The stretcher bearers arrived and picked Dee up and started carrying him to the landing craft. He waved at Dick and then yelled with all sincerity, "Don't let those damn Japs get you, Dick. I mean it. Don't be a hero."

Dick smiled and waved back.

The Battle for Peleliu would rage on through the month of October. Dick would survive the battle but many Marines would not. The First Division of the United States Marines would lose 1,300 killed and 5,450 wounded and there would be thirty-six missing. The suicidal Japanese would lose 10,900 killed and only 202 would be captured alive. All of that blood spilled on an island that was not six square miles in size.

⊰⊱

Anne Marie Barnett was exhausted. The trip across the North Atlantic had taken almost two weeks. She had been aboard a hospital ship that sailed from Liverpool, England to New York City. The ship had to use long zig-zag routes for security reasons. The facilities on the ship were designed to accommodate wounded American soldiers not passengers. But Bill had gotten her a small private room that was normally used by a nurse. By the time she got off the ship in

New York harbor, she could barely stand on the solid ground. She was obviously not a sailor.

Things had gone so fast when Bill got back from Normandy in July. They had a wonderful time for nearly two months. Bill was with her on the farm whenever he could get free. They spent many hours together going over the countryside. All during this time, Bill work feverishly to get her papers in order so she could go to the States as his war bride. Once everything was in order, he had to work just as hard to get her space on the hospital ship. But he had gotten it all done and at the same time spent all the extra time with her. She never realized she could love someone as much as she loved Bill. She guessed it was probably a wartime romance but, for her, she was very much in love. And this marriage was the real thing and it was for life.

He knew he had another jump coming up sometime in the near future, so he felt it was paramount to get her home to the States. He had written his sister in Texas about when to expect her. He also instructed his sister to take their farm off the market, because he was going to use it now.

After the crossing of Atlantic, she then had the long train ride to Dallas. The entire trip from its start in Liverpool to its finish at Dallas Union Station took just over three weeks. Now, she stood in the lobby of Union Station holding a bag in one hand and pulling a small cart with three more bags on it. She looked confused and completely lost. Her stomach turned over and over and she thought she was going to throw up. She struggled to not panic but she could feel she was starting to lose it.

"Excuse me, are you Anne Barnett," the person speaking was a very pretty blonde girl.

"Yes, I am," she answered in a shaking voice.

"Good, I'm Sue Ann, Bill's sister," Sue Ann announced holding out her hand.

Anne took her hand and shook in gently. Then her stomach heaved and she asked quickly, "I need to go to the loo can you tell me where it is?"

"You need to go where?" Sue Ann asked puzzled.

"The loo," Anne repeated holding her hand to her month.

"What's a loo?"

"Sorry, I mean the toilet."

"Oh, the restroom," Sue Ann smiled understanding. "It's right back behind you. I'll stay with your bags while you go."

Anne nodded her head and turned around. Spotting the restrooms, she walked quickly, almost running, to them and disappeared inside. Shortly she reappeared walking much slower and dabbing her month with a wet paper towel. When she reached Sue Ann, she looked embarrassed. "I'm so sorry; you must think I'm a dunce."

"Not at all," Sue Ann said looking at her closely. Anne continued to dab her month with the wet paper towel, and hold her stomach slightly. Her face had a slight pink flush. "But", Sue Ann continued, "I'll tell you what I do think."

"What?" Anne asked surprised.

"I think you're pregnant."

Anne looked at her and broke out into a large beautiful smile. "I think you're right."

"Come on let's sit down for a moment and get ourselves together before we start the trip home."

Sue Ann pulled the cart and the two women found an empty bench and sat down. Anne looked at Sue Ann with tears in her eyes. "I'm so glad to meet you," she said softly. "I just know we're going to be really good friends."

Sue Ann reached over and pulled Anne to her and hugged her tightly. "This is Texas sweetheart, we're already friends." Sue Ann hugged her and patted her on the back. "We're already the best of friends."

⊶•◦•⊷

CHAPTER NINETY-TWO

Christmas at War Again

December 1944

It was December 7, 1944. Three years to the day that America went to war and Daryl Collie was coming home. His stay in the hospital in Hawaii had been longer than planned. He had hoped to be home for Thanksgiving but it was not to be. The damage to his right shoulder had been worse than first thought. They had done two different surgeries on him to fix badly damaged muscle tissue and to reroute or open some blood vessels. All of this took time and, as a result, instead of being home before Thanksgiving in was now early December. But now his plane was circling Dallas Love Field waiting in a landing pattern to land. He wiggled in his seat to relieve his nervousness and to try and keep comfortable due to the large sling that immobilized his right arm. He was told he would have to wear the sling both day and night for at least another month.

His plane finally got clearance to land and started its approach. He looked out the window and saw the familiar skyline of downtown Dallas. It was a welcome site. He leaned back in his seat and counted the seconds until he felt the wheels touch the tarmac and the plane was on the ground. Everyone got to their feet and started moving into the aisle picking up what small bags they had with them. Most everyone on the plane was military except for a few business types. A sailor who had sat across the aisle from him was nice enough to help him up. Dee thanked him and got into the line of people filing out of the plane.

It was December but when he stepped out of the plane and on to the gangway it was warm and the sun was shining brightly; in fact it blinded him for a moment. When his vision adjusted to the brightness, what he saw overwhelmed him with emotion. He swayed on the gangway as if he might fall. The same sailor who had helped him out of his seat now took his good arm to steady him. It was then, to his shame, that Dee noticed the sailor had his left arm missing. He pulled his arm away from the sailor and then hooked it around the sailor's neck and pulled his head to him and whispered in his ear, "God bless you, brother."

"Same to you, brother," the sailor said, and then hurried down the gangway.

What Dee saw that overwhelmed him so, was a group of people standing on the tarmac near the gate to the terminal. There was Sue Ann with Kyle standing in front of her. Next to her stood Cherrie with Chloe and Joey standing in front of her. Standing behind his wife and sister, was his Father and Mother with Sally Barnett and Ruth Jordan on either side of them. Next to Sally stood a very pretty young girl that was clearly pregnant, who, Dee thought, had to be Anne Barnett.

When he reached the bottom of the gangway and was standing on the tarmac, Sue Ann gave Kyle and gentle push and the little towheaded boy came running to him yelling, "Daddy, Daddy." Dee knelt down and grabbed the boy with his good arm and held him tight. Sue Ann came running up and knelt down with them and they just knelt there on the tarmac hugging and crying for a long time as the rest of the family walked over and gathered around them.

Kyle was only two years old and didn't understand the situation. He turned to Sue Ann and asked, "Is Daddy okay, Mommy? Why is Daddy cryin'?"

Sue Ann wiped away the tears on her checks and told Kyle with a soft chuckle, "Daddy's fine, he's just so happy to see you."

Kyle smiled and looked back at Dee and said, "I'm happy to see you to, Daddy."

On Christmas Day, 1st Sergeant Billy Bob Barnett and the 101st Airborne Screaming Eagles were not having a Merry Christmas. Because of a huge German offensive attack on December 16th, the 101st had been called out of France where they were resting in reserve. This offensive attack would create what would be called later; The Battle of the Bulge. They had been quickly dispatched to a little town in Belgium called Bastogne. Bastogne was unique because it had eleven hard top roads that ran through it and into the mountainous terrain. The Germans wanted these roads very badly so their tanks could stay out of the boggy mud. Since the Germans wanted Bastogne very badly, then the Americans wanted to keep them from getting it very badly. The Germans had Bastogne completely surrounded but the 101st was ordered to hold the town at all cost. So the Siege of Bastogne began and the 101st was determined to hold it.

Because of the extraordinary leadership and courage he showed during their jump in Holland back in September, Billy Bob had been promoted to Company First Sergeant. Now he ran from foxhole to foxhole checking on his men. The weather was cold and it was snowing off and on. They were low on everything especially ammunition and medical supplies. The men were spread very thin along a line around Bastogne in two man foxholes. Billy Bob tried to check all the foxholes to make sure the men had ammunition and were keeping warm; neither of which was true.

As he was about to return to his own foxhole a company runner caught up to him. "Sergeant," the man said frantically, "Blake and Smitty took a direct hit on their foxhole. They're both dead, Sarge. That leaves a big gap in the line that the Krauts can come through. We gotta plug it somehow and we'll need more than just two guys."

Billy Bob knelt down and thought for a moment. "Okay, start over there at Biggs and Johnson's foxhole and work your way back to where Blake and Smitty got it. Take one man from each foxhole and plug that gap. Have the guys to fix bayonets. I'll be there as soon as I report to the HQ what's goin' on. Now go, go."

Billy Bob hurried to his foxhole and had his radioman call the HQ. Once on the line Billy Bob went over the situation and ended the call by saying, "The Krauts are comin' at us in force. If you got anybody that can come up here and help, it would be appreciated."

"We're sending you some walking wounded that volunteered to leave the aid station. That's all we got. Watch for 'em and don't shoot 'em they'll be comin' up from behind you."

"Roger that," Billy Bob replied, "I guess it's over and out."

Billy Bob pitched the receiver to the radioman. "You might keep in touch with 'em. You never know."

"Will do, Sarge, ya just never know."

Billy Bob fixed his bayonet on the end of his rifle and then turned and ran to join the other guys in the gap. When he got there, he found only fifteen men. They all had rifles; there were no machine guns. Billy Bob signaled for them to knell down. He was about to take an ammo check when the walking wounded guys showed up. They were indeed walking wounded. None of these guys needed to be on the line. But that's the kind of men he served with. There were eight of them, bring his total to twenty-three.

When the other guys saw the wounded guys taking their positions in the line, they ground their teeth and squeezed their weapons and a bitter determination filled their eyes and hearts. The advancing Germans could now be clearly seen through the cold fog.

Billy Bob looked down the line at his men. Then he simply said, "Hold your fire guys 'til you can be sure you can hit 'em because the ammo we're carryin' is all we got."

The Germans threw over a hundred and twenty men at Billy Bob's little make shift force of twenty-three. The fighting was furious. When they ran out of ammo they fought with bayonets and rifle butts. Then, it was vicious hand-to-hand combat. When it was all over, the Germans pulled back leaving eighty-five men dead on the field. Of the little force that defended the gap, sixteen lay dead. Five were too wounded to stand up. Only two would be able to walk away. Of the sixteen that lay dead in the snow, one was 1st Sergeant Billy Bob Barnett.

⚬⚬⚬

The Battle of the Bulge would rage on for another week and, in the end, the Allies would be victorious and it would lead to the end of the Nazi terror that once ruled Europe. When the smoke cleared and the Germans were in full retreat, all the important generals, German and American, looked around and found that the American 101st Airborne Division Screaming Eagles were still holding Bastogne.

CHAPTER NINETY-THREE

Two Telegrams

January 1945

Since Sally Barnett found out from Sue Ann that Bill didn't want to sell the farm anymore and since Anne's arrival, Sally took the farm off the market and moved back in and brought Anne with her. There was a lot of work to do to get the farmhouse livable again. Anne was about five months along in her pregnancy but was able to help with many tasks. Also, Sue Ann, Cherrie, Mary, and Ruth all came out and helped when they could. But many of the repairs required the strength and building skill of a man. Dee was able to help out some, but he could only use one arm. James talked Sheriff Clark into coming out on a few weekends and the two of them were able to do some of the heaver repair work. On a couple of weekends, everyone turned out including Evie and made a picnic out of the effort. However, now, it was the middle of January and the weather was not always cooperative. Such as today, as Sally and Anne sat comfortably in the farmhouse as a freezing rain and sleet fell outside.

As Anne was making her special hot cocoa, Sally was reading Bill's last letter he had sent to Anne. It was dated back before Christmas and they hadn't heard from him since. They knew he was involved in The Battle of the Budge, as the newspapers called the battle. But according to reports, that battle was mostly over and the Allies were moving again nearing the German border. They both worried and wondered why Bill had not sent them another letter. They hoped and prayed that it was because he was very busy or was somewhere that he couldn't write. In the old letter she read, Bill seemed anxious to get the war over and to come home to the farm and Anne.

Anne had sent Bill letter's telling him she was pregnant but she had no idea if he had received them yet. As Anne brought the hot cocoa into the living room, Sally put the letter down and took her cup. They sat quietly on the couch looking out the window at the sleet pelt down.

After a while, Sally narrowed her eyes and looked hard out the window. "Is that a car comin' up the road? She asked.

Anne put her head next to Sally's and followed her gaze up the road. "Yes, it is," she said softly. And turning to face Sally, "Who would be out in weather like this?" She asked with fear dripping on every word.

As the car approached, they made it out as Sheriff Clark's patrol car. It pulled to a stop near the front porch. Four people got out of the car; Sheriff Clark, Mary Collie, James Collie, and Dee Collie. They hurried to the front porch and up the steps. Sheriff Clark knocked on the door.

Sally slowly open the door and looked at the four sad faces on her front porch. "Come in out of the weather," she said holding door open.

They all walked in and stood not speaking for a long minute. Anne backed away holding her stomach and knelt down on the floor and started to cry. "No, please no," she mumbled. "God won't do this. He won't do this." She slipped from her knees and sat down on the floor still holding her stomach. Sally ran to her side and put her arms around her hand held her tight.

Sheriff Clark walked over and knelt down in front of them and tried to hand Anne a Western Union Telegram but she wouldn't take it. "Please, Anne, it has to be done. Please take it."

Anne only shook her and still refused to accept the letter. The Sheriff looked to Sally. "Sally, please help me here. I don't like doin' this. This is only makin' it harder."

Sally was crying now as well and tears were running freely down her cheeks and dropping onto her blouse. She reached out with a trembling hand and took the telegram from the Sheriff. She reached down and took one of Anne's hands and put the telegram into it. "He's my son as well as your husband," she said choking. "Now please open it, Anne, please."

Anne took the telegram and torn it open, looked at it for several minutes, then dropped it on the floor. Anne started to struggle to get up from the floor and James and Dee ran over and each took an arm and lifted her to her feet. She stood up and straightened her dress out and pushed her hair back out of her face. Using her hand, she wiped the tears off her checks. "I don't wish to be rude, but I think I would like to go and lie down for a short while."

"If you would permit me, Anne," Mary Collie said softly, "I would very much like to sit with you while you lie down?"

Anne looked at Mary and tears welled in her eyes again. "I think that would be lovely, Mary," she replied with all the dignity she could muster. "Thank you so very much." Mary took Anne's arm and the two women walked out of the living room and to Anne's bedroom.

Sheriff Clark turned and put his hand on Sally's shoulder. "I have to be goin', Sally, I hope you understand."

"Of course I do, Sheriff," she said standing up and picking up the telegram as she did.

"Sally, the Sheriff has to go but Dee and I can stay as long as you need or want us to," James said gently.

"Thank you, James, but you gentlemen go a head on. I think I just want to be alone for now."

"Sure," Dee said, "but you call us if you need anythin'. And I mean anythin' at all."

After all the men had gone and she was alone in the living room, she sat down on the couch and looked down at the telegram she held in her hand. She laid it down on the couch and then looked out the window at the sleet pelting down. "My goodness, Billy Bob, my little boy, we're sure goin' to miss you," she choked. "You know you got

a baby on the way. I sure hope he's another Billy Bob. We're surely
are goin' to miss you, Son."

She folded her arms on the back of the couch and laid her down
on them. The telegram floated to floor unseen. It simply said:

> MRS ANNE BARNETT=
> 6768 ROUTE 44=
> COALVILLE, TEXAS=
> THE SECRETARY OF WAR DESIRES ME TO
> EXPRESS HIS DEEP REGRET THAT YOUR
> HUSBAND FIRST SERGEANT BILLY BOB
> BARNETT WAS KILLED IN ACTION IN
> DEFENSE OF HIS COUNTRY ON TWENTY-SIX
> DECEMBER 1944 PERIOD LETTER FOLLOWS=
> ULIO THE ADJUTANT GENERAL.

Judy Cole Orland stared down at the telegram and read it over again.
It amazed her how simple these types of telegrams were. It simply
said:

> MRS JUDY ORLAND=
> 2714 GRAFTON STREET=
> DALLAS, TEXAS=
> THE SECRETARY OF WAR DESIRES ME TO
> EXPRESS HIS DEEP REGRET THAT YOUR
> HUSBAND FIRST LIEUTENANT JIMMY
> ORLAND HAS BEEN REPORT MISSING
> IN ACTION SINCE 30 DECEMBER 1944
> IN GERMAN OCCUPIED TERRITORY
> IF FURTHER DETAILS OR OTHR
> INFORMATION ARE RECEIVED YOU WILL
> BE PROMPTLY NOTIFIED=
> ULIO THE ADJUTANT GENERAL

The follow up letter she got from the 304th Bomber Wing in Italy simply told her that her husband's plane was shot down and four chutes were clearly seen jumping from the downed aircraft, which was the reason for him being listed as Missing In Action rather than Killed In Action.

Bob Ann stood quietly waiting for Judy to tell her something but Judy just folded the telegram and the short letter and started to walk away. "Judy," her Mother cried, "tell me somethin'. What's happened? Is Jimmy okay?"

Judy stopped and turned back to face her Mother. "I'm sorry, Mom," she said tightly. "Jimmy's plane was shot down over enemy territory on December thirtieth. He's listed as MIA, that's Missing In Action, because four parachutes were seen jumping from the plane as it went down. The B-24 carries a crew of ten, so six guys didn't make it out."

"So, Jimmy could be one of the four, couldn't he?" She asked hopefully.

"Yeah, I guess so," Judy replied, "but even if he did get out and made it to the ground, he's in enemy territory. The odds are against him, Mom."

Bob Ann looked at her daughter and asked, "Are you okay, sweetheart?"

"Well, I'm as good as I can be in this situation. But I'm not goin' to cry. Jimmy told me if somethin' happened to him for me not to cry but to get on with life. So, Jimmy wouldn't like it if I cried. So, I'm not goin' to cry. But I think I would like to just be by myself for a while."

"I understand, Judy," her Mother said, "but there's one thing I think you should always remember about Jimmy."

"What's that, Mom?"

Her Mother stepped closer to her and looked her hard in the eyes. "Jimmy's had the odds against him before," she hissed. "He's had the odds against him many, many times before."

Judy smiled at her and turned away and walked to her lonely room. She went inside and closed the door. Looking around the room she saw a picture on her chest-of-drawers. It was a picture of her and Jimmy on the night they got married; July the fourth. They had chased down a Justice of the Piece and literally dragged him away from his cookout. Her Mother had taken the picture with her little Kodak. She walked over and picked the picture up and smiled at it. They looked so happy and full of piss-and-vinegar. "I'm sorry, Jimmy," she whispered, "I'm sorry but I just can't help it." Then, she flopped down on her bed, buried her face in her pillow, and cried her eyes out.

CHAPTER NINETY-FOUR

The State Park

April 1945

James Collie left his feed and fertilizer store at noon to take a short drive. He didn't want to go home for lunch today. He took his car, a brand new Ford he had bought just last March, and drove it to the access road to the new State Park. He turned onto the road and drove passed his house and on up the road to the State Park.

The State Park and been finished and had its official opening back on March 20th. They had named it The Coal Hills Historical State Park. James thought the name was odd and miss-leading. He thought people would confuse the word 'coal' with the word 'cold', changing the intended theme of the park completely. But it was done and it was official so it didn't matter. But as he drove, he looked around and concluded that the State Park was very well done. The roads were nice and went all the way to the top of Lonesome Hill where a picnic area with nice tables and landscaping had been built. The picnic area was located exactly where the cabin used by Clint Jordan use to be. They had cut down several trees and cleared the brush out so that the view to the west was absolutely beautiful. There were signs all along the roads telling about the history of the area. They had even left the cabin that was used by the Klu Klux Klan during a darker time, and restored it back to its original condition. The signs told the history of the hills but nowhere did any sign mention the Klu Klux Klan or the murders that had occurred in these hills.

James pulled his new Ford to a stop at the very top of Lonesome Hill in the picnic area. He got out and walked over and read the sign that now stood where Clint Jordan's cabin once stood. The sign told the story of the coal mines that once dotted the area and some of the mysterious stories that were associated with Lonesome Hill. Strangely enough, the name 'Lonesome Hill' was never mentioned; it was just referred to as 'The Hill'. He went over and sat down at one of the picnic tables that allowed a grand view of the other hills to the west.

James was sitting at the picnic table alone on top of Lonesome Hill because he was in a depressed state. He felt helpless to help the ones he loved so dearly. After being the leader of his family for so many years, he now felt he was failing them. If it weren't for having Dee back at home, he knew he would be completely lost. Dee's returning home was a gift to the entire family. It was now April and the sling that held his right arm down tight had been removed. However, he still had pain when he tried to use his arm too much. However, Dee's presents couldn't prevent the devastation that Sue Ann felt at the death of Billy Bob. Everyone worry about her because she couldn't let go of her brother. To make things worse, Anne Barnett was talking about going back to England after the baby was born, and the baby was due any day now. Sally and Sue Ann were frantic to get her to stay. But, so far, Anne's mind was made up.

Then, there was his daughter Cheryl. She was beside herself with worry because Dick had landed with the First Marine Division on a Japanese island named Okinawa. Okinawa was a part of the Japanese Homeland and, from all the news reports, a horrible and bloody battle was in progress. She couldn't understand why someone who had survived the bloodbaths at Guadalcanal and Peleliu would then be sent, just five months after Peleliu, to another bloodbath. Dee tried to console her, but she was having none of it. Both Cherrie and Sue Ann, who had become like sisters, tried to bury themselves in activities with their children and with each other, but it only give them minor relief.

In March, Judy Orland had notified Dee via a long and personal telephone call, that Jimmy Orland was MIA and was not expected to be found alive. Dee then insisted on going up to Dallas to talk with her personally. He asked his Mother to watch Kyle while he and

Sue Ann spent a few days in Dallas. Dee wanted to talk with Judy face-to-face but he also wanted to spend some time with Sue Ann in Dallas going to movies and eating out. The trip was only partially successful. Judy was extremely happy to see them both and her spirits were lifted greatly, but, while at a movie in downtown Dallas, there was a newsreel about the progress of the war in Europe. That, for Sue Ann, ended any hope of enjoying the rest of their stay. But Judy's worries didn't end there, because early this month she called Dee again, this time informing him that her step-brother Kenny Jackson, who only just joined the Marines in September, landed with the First Marine Division on Okinawa. Her Mother was in near hysteria.

So, James sat in the warm spring time Texas sun on the top of Lonesome Hill pondering all of these things. The war seemed to almost to be over in both Europe and the Pacific, but it would just not end. As bad as it was when the war first started, James believed now was it darkest hour. His family, along with the others was struggling to hold on. He looked down at his watch and determined it was time to get back to the store. Slowly he got up and walked back to his new Ford. After getting in the car, he sat there for a long minute still trying work out how he could help. But he wasn't any stronger than the rest of them. He just didn't know what to do.

He took a deep breath and smiled to himself. Of all this tragedy, there was one good thing that had happened. Dee and Sue Ann had wasted little time in getting to know each other again. In the middle of March, Sue Ann had announced she was pregnant again. The pregnancy seemed to bring some life back to her and she started dealing with the loss of Billy Bob with a little more tolerance. She hoped it was another boy so that she could name it after Billy Bob. Dee had made no objection.

The time alone on the hill hadn't helped much and the drive back to the store was a lonely trip. He reasoned to himself that sitting alone on top of a hill was not going to make anything better. He just hoped he was strong enough to be the head of a family that seemed to be in desperation. The war had got to end soon, he thought. It just has to.

CHAPTER NINETY-FIVE

Cherrie Gets a Telegram

May 1945

On May 8th 1945, Germany unconditionally surrendered to the Allied Command and directly to the Supreme Allied Commander, General Dwight David Eisenhower ending the war in Europe. This day was designated VE day, Victory in Europe day. And on this day, Ruth Jordan had opened the doors of her house to all that wanted to come and listen. For just a week before, she had purchased a new Philco Radio that had shortwave on it and she could listen to the celebrations all over the world.

She attracted a nice size crowd. All of the Collie family was there along with Anne and Sally Barnett. With Anne was a brand new baby boy that she named William Clyde Barnett to honor Billy Bob and her Father. Sheriff Clark and his entire family came as well as at least twelve other people that Ruth didn't know. The size of the crowd could have been a problem because Ruth and Cherrie were only prepared to supply food and drink to maybe eight people. But it wasn't a problem because nearly all the women brought a covered dish of some sort. Others brought tea, beer, and ice cream. There were also pies and cakes. A good time was had by everyone.

Later in the day as things started to break up, Ruth asked that all those still there join hands in a prayer for the boys fighting in the Pacific and that there would soon be victory there also. To lead the prayer was the brand new pastor of the Coalville Baptist Church. His name was Reverend Lonnie Tyler. He was a middle aged man with a wife and two daughters. Everyone joined hands and Reverend Tyler led them in a prayer for piece, and then they observed a long moment of silence for everyone that was still in harm's way.

The last ones to leave were Dee and Sue Ann. They remained for a while longer to visit with Cherrie and the twins. They made small talk purposely avoiding any talk of Okinawa. They all had heard the news reports of the horrible fight going on there. The Japanese were now using suicide tactics by flying planes into American ships. They called them Kamikazes. The death toll was high and growing each day. But it did no good to dwell on it or talk about it because it only drove Cherrie into deeper depression. So they talked of things around town, the new State Park, and Su Ann's baby to come.

After a while, Dee and Sue Ann left. Ruth turned off the radio and she and Cherrie took the twins for a walk. It was early May and the weather, although starting to get hot, was nice. A nice breeze blew through their hair as they walked with the twins. They didn't talk. They both just walked with their own thoughts running through their minds.

Major Dick Jordan didn't have time to celebrate VE day. He and his intelligence team were having a terrible time getting support for the Marines fighting at a place they called Sugar Loaf Hill. Sugar Loaf Hill was a hill barely five hundred feet high but it was over three hundred yards long. All along its upper ridge there were caves and tunnels that hid the Japanese. One particular cave hidden by brush and a small entrance was hiding two, and maybe more, Japanese mortar teams that were raining death down on the Marines below. The intelligence team knew where the cave was but all their efforts to get fire on the cave had failed.

They needed close ground support planes from the carriers sitting far off shore, just like they had done at Peleliu. But here it was different because the carriers had their hands full fighting off Kamikaze attack. The Kamikazes were taking a heavy toll on the fleet in terms of ships and lives. Not being able to get air support, they turned to Marine artillery. They did get some artillery but it was not effective. The Japanese simple closed the steel doors and backed into the cave and came back out when the artillery lifted.

As the Marine casualties mounted, Dick's frustration grew. Finally it hit the breaking point. "Lt. Mackey," Dick yelled over the roar of the battle.

"Aye, Sir," the Lieutenant replied quickly. Lt. Jake Mackey was Dick's second in command. He was a tall good natured kid from New Mexico. The three enlisted men in the intelligence unit all liked him.

"Come over here and look at this map with me," Dick ordered.

"Aye, Sir." The Lieutenant hurried over to where Dick was crouched.

When Jake was crouching next to him, Dee pointed to a spot on the map. "This is where that damn cave is," he said angrily. "How far would you say that is from where we are now?"

Jake raised his head slightly above the hole they were crouched in and study the hill for a quick moment. He ducked back down and said, "I figure it's roughly a half mile, maybe a little less."

"Yeah, that's about how I see it," Dick said poking his finger angrily at the map. Dick turned to look at the others in the hole with him and Jake. It was a far cry from what they had on Peleliu. There they at least had a tent. Here they had a big hole in the ground and it was the third hole they had been in over the last two weeks. "Sergeant Miles," Dick yelled again over the roar of the battle.

"Aye, Sir," the Sergeant replied. It was the same short and wiry Long Island native, Sergeant Grayson Miles who had been with him on Peleliu. The other two men were privates and new to the team, but were both skilled radiomen.

"How's our equipment holdin' up?"

"The ship-to-shore radio is down and we'll have to replace it; it can't be repaired. The radio for Regimental HQ is still good and we got communications goin' with 'em. We have to use walkie-talkies to communicate with the lead units up near Sugar Loaf and that's strictly hit or miss."

"How many grenades do we have?" Dick asked suddenly.

Sergeant Miles looked at him in surprise for a moment and then answered, "I think we still have the twenty we reserved to blow the equipment if need be."

"Okay, Sergeant, get those grenades into a sling bag for me so I can carry 'em on my shoulder. How about weapons? Do we have a Thomson anywhere with ammo?"

Jake looked at Dick with a shocked and surprised looked on his face. "Jesus, Major, what're you thinkin' about?"

"I'm sick and tired of sittin' in this hole, not bein' able to get any kind of reasonable support and watchin' those Marines gettin' killed out there." Dick yelled in a rage. "I'm goin' to go and try and do somethin' about it."

"What?" Jake shouted. "What can we do? There're just five of us and we're supposed to be working intelligence.

Dick ignored Jake and turned to Sergeant Miles again. "What about that Thomson, Sergeant Miles?"

"Yeah, we got one, or should I say I've got one and I'm not goin' to give it to you, Sir."

Dick looked at him and smiled cocking his head to one side. "You will if I order you to."

"I don't think so, Major. Whatever you're up to, me and my Thomson are going with you."

"Sorry, Sergeant, this is a volunteer operation only."

"Then, I'm volunteering. So, Sir, what're we doing?"

Jake slumped back on his elbows and said, "Oh, well, I guess I'm going too."

"No, Jake, I need you to stay here and keep operatin' this unit as best you can. Keep tryin' to get some air support. But if you do, be careful with the napalm because the Marines are close to that hill; very close."

"Aye, Sir," Jake said getting to his knees. "How can we help?"

"The Sergeant and I are goin' to crawl out of this hole and work our way up that hill over here on the far left. We're goin' to crawl all the way usin' whatever cover is available. When we get to that cave, I'm goin' to start throwin' grenades into it. When they come up to see what's happenin' or if they try and close those damn steel door, the Sergeant here is goin' open up on them with his Thomson." Dick paused and smiled at Jake. "How does that sound for a plan?"

"With all due respect, Major, it sounds insane," Jake said with a chuckle. "But I guess you're going to do it anyway."

"Thanks, Jake, that makes me feel better."

Sergeant Miles came crawling over with the sling bag full of grenades and handed it to Dick, who slung it over his head and shoulder. Sergeant Miles then unslung the Thomson from his shoulder and checked the clip and the extra clips in his belt. "I guess we're ready, Sir." He said in a matter-a-fact tone.

"I guess we are," Dick said slapping the Sergeant on the back. "Let's go see what we can do."

⸎

It took the Dick and Sergeant Miles over an hour to crawl on their bellies over sand, rock, and brush to get to where they could even see the small cave entrance. At times, they took the chance of getting up and running from one hole to another but that was dangerous so they mostly stayed on their bellies. Another danger was friendly fire. The closer they got to the cave the more fire they encountered from the Marines down below; including some errant mortar fire.

Now they were about twenty yards from the cave entrance. The steel doors were open and they could hear the *Thump, Thump* of mortar fire coming from the cave. They could even see the mortar shells striking from the cave and arcing down on the Marines below. At this point, Dick called a halt to their advancement. "Okay," he whispered to Sergeant Miles, "I have to get to within ten yards of that little entrance to make sure I don't miss. You need to stay about this distance but move more toward the center. I'm goin' to move in a little closer before I start throwin'. When I do and they start comin' out or tryin' to move those doors, they're all yours. You got all that?"

"I got it, Major," Sergeant Miles said as he started moving away from Dick to center himself in front of the entrance.

Dick started moving forward again but staying to the left of the entrance. Being right handed, that made it easier to throw while lying on his left side. Finally he was as close as he dared tried to get. He looked back to his right but couldn't see Sergeant Miles, which was probably a good thing, because the Japs probably couldn't see him either. Dick unslung the grenades and positioned the bag just to his left. Taking a deep breath in pulled the pin on the first grenade and prepared to throw it, but then he decided to wait for the next firing of the mortars. He didn't have to wait long as the *Thump, Thump* sounded again. He heaved the first grenade and it went directly into the entrance and he heard the dull thud as it exploded. Quickly, he threw two more with the same results. Now smoke was bellowing out of the cave. Working as fast as he could, he pulled the pin on another grenade and threw it into the smoke. That did it. He heard loud Japanese talking and then several appeared out of the smoke. They were only there for a second before Sergeant Miles cut them down with his Thompson.

Dick looked but still couldn't see Sergeant Miles. But as he saw the steel doors starting to close, he heard the chatter of the Thompson again and door movement stopped. Quickly, he started pulling pins and throwing grenades as fast as he could and remain accurate. More Japanese came running from the cave firing their weapons wildly and randomly. The chatter of the Thompson became steady as Sergeant Miles sprayed the entire entrance, stopping only long enough to reload a fresh clip. Japanese were lying dead all around the cave entrance. The firing of the mortars had stopped.

Dick had one grenade left and he wanted to hold it for an emergency, which was ironic because this whole thing was an emergency. Japanese continue to pour from the cave and the Thompson continued to chatter. Dick decided to throw his last grenade. He threw it into the mist of a group of Japanese trying to run back up the hill. The explosion took them all down but one. The remaining Japanese was carrying a knee mortar, which is a hand held mortar fired by holding it again the knee and dropping the shell in the tube. Dick saw him drop the shell into tube too late. The mortar shell arched up and came down about five yards from him. He rolled over to try and shield his head. The explosion hit him in the back knocking him down the hill several yards. He rolled over stunned and sitting up. He was totally helpless as the Japanese charged him with a sword. Before he passed out, he saw the Japanese soldier's body cut into by machine gun fire.

Sergeant Miles stood guard with his Thompson machine gun resting on his hip as the stretcher bearers carried Major Dick Jordan down the hill to the aid station. When the account of what Major Jordan and Sergeant Miles did was finally made clear and written up for Regimental Command, it would show twenty-seven dead Japanese outside the entrance to the cave and another thirty dead on the inside of the cave by the steel doors. Major Jordan's grenades had set off a stack of mortar shells and the resulting explosions had gutted the cave and killed twenty-five more Japanese. In addition, the actions of Major Jordan and Sergeant Miles had stopped the rain of mortar shells on the Marines down below, at least from this one cave. Regimental Command would put in a request that the Silver Star Medal for gallantry be awarded to Marine Technical Sergeant Grayson Miles and that the Navy Cross be awarded to Marine Major Dick Jordan for action against the enemy above and beyond the call of duty.

It was now late May and the war in the Pacific dragged on. Cherrie and Ruth were sitting on the front porch making homemade ice cream. Cherrie turned the crank while Joey sat on the top of the machine. He barely had the weight to hold the cranking mechanism in place. Chloe inserted ice and salt into the bucket as needed. Ruth simply sat in her rocking chair and rocked gently. The summer heat was beginning to build and by noon it would be too hot to continue to sit outside.

Everyone was involved with what they were doing when Sheriff Clark's patrol car pull up out front. The Sheriff got out of his car and started walking towards the house. Cherrie looked up and saw the look on his face. She immediately jumped to her feet and shouted, "No, no, don't you come up here."

The Sheriff continued his slow pace up to the front porch. Cherrie turned and ran into the house yelling at her children to follow her. "What is it, Mommy," Joey asked. "What's the matter?"

"Yeah, Mommy, what's goin' on?" Chloe asked.

"Just get in here and go to your room," Cherrie ordered.

"But, Mom…," Joey started.

"Do like I tell you and do it now," she shouted. "I mean it. Do it now."

When they were all inside, she slammed the door shut.

Sheriff Clark walked up the porch steps and stood in front of Ruth. Ruth stood up with her right hand on her throat. She extended her left hand and said, "I'll take it, Tom."

The Sheriff looked down and shook his head. "You know I can't do that, Ruth. It's the law. I've got to give it to Cheryl."

Ruth nodded her head as tears started forming in her eyes. "Can you give me a minute to go in and get her? Please, Tom."

"You know I will, Ruth. Take your time."

Ruth went in the house and found Cherrie in her room sitting on the bed holding her children close to her. Cherrie looked up when Ruth came in. "Is he gone?" She asked.

"No, Cherrie, he's not gone and he's not goin' to go until you take the telegram."

Cherrie shook her head violently. "No, I won't take it, Ruth. I won't take it."

Ruth went over and put her hand under Cherrie's chin and lifted her face up so she could look into Cherrie's eyes. "He's my son, Cherrie," she said softly. "I have a right to know what's happened. I'm his Mother, I have a right."

Cherrie looked into Ruth's eyes and her defiance faded. She got to her feet and told her children, "You two stay here. Grandma Ruth and I have some business to do."

Shortly Ruth walked back out onto the porch and Cherrie was close behind her. Cherrie walked pass Ruth and held her hand out to Sheriff Clark. "Okay, Sheriff, do your duty," she said solemnly.

Without speaking, Sheriff Clark handed the telegram to Cherrie. When she had accepted it, he turned and started back to his car.

"Tom," Ruth called after him, "could you stay while we open this in case we need you?"

Tom turned and walked back to the porch. "You know I can, Ruth. I'm here for you and Cherrie if you need me."

With hands shaking, Cherrie opened the telegram and read it.

MRS CHERYL JORDAN=
1213 MAIN STREET=
COALVILLE, TEXAS=

THE SECRETARY OF WAR DESIRES ME TO EXPRESS HIS DEEP REGRET THAT YOUR HUSBAND MAJOR DICK JORDAN HAS BEEN SERIOUSLY WOUNDED IN ACTION ON 8 MAY 1945 ON THE ISLAND OF OKINAWA. HE IS IN ROUTE TO A HOSPITAL IN HAWAII VIA A NAVAL HOSPITAL SHIP. IF FURTHER DETAILS OR OTHER INFORMATION ARE RECEIVED YOU WILL BE PROMPTLY NOTIFIED PERIOD A LETTER FOLLOWS=

ULIO THE ADJUTANT GENERAL

Cherrie staggered backwards and banged into the wall of the house. She looked at Ruth with tears in her eyes but a smile on her face. "Momma Ruth," she stammered, "he's alive. He's been wounded but he's on his way to a hospital in Hawaii. Momma Ruth, he's alive."

The emotion overcame her and she slide down the wall of the house and sat down on the porch. "He's alive, Momma Ruth," she repeated.

Sheriff Clark ran over and helped Cherrie to her feet. He had a huge smile on his face. "Thank God," he mumbled.

Once on her feet, she straighten her dress and pushed her hair back then said in a kind voice, "Thank you Sheriff Tom Clark for bein' so kind and thoughtful." Using her hands, she dried the tears from her eyes and wiped the tear stains from her cheeks. Standing straight and proud she continued, "And please tell Evie that Ruth and I said hello and we wish she'd come visit more often."

PART THREE

The End

They didn't give up and they didn't surrender; they made America the greatest country on earth.

CHAPTER NINETY-SIX

What Was Gained; What Was Lost

August 1945

O n August 14th 1945, the Japanese Empire finally surrendered unconditionally to the Allied Powers. However, it took the dropping of two atomic bombs on the Japanese Islands resulting in the deaths of tens of thousands to convince them to stop the killing. August the 14th would come to be known as VJ day; Victory over Japan day. The official signing of the surrender documents would be on September 2nd, 1945 aboard the Battleship Missouri in Tokyo Bay. The horrible struggle that was World War II was finally over. Now the tally of what was gained and what was lost began.

—⊖⊛⊜—

On Sunday August 19th, the Coalville Baptist Church was full to overflowing. People had come to the small town from far and wide to hear the sermon to be delivered by the new pastor Reverend Lonnie Tyler. But they didn't come just to hear the new preacher. It was known all around the East Texas area that the wife of Congressional Medal of Honor winner, 1st Sergeant Bill Bob Barnett would be in attendance. So, people came to the little church in the little town for many reasons. Some to give thanks for the end of the war, some to give thanks that their loved ones had come home, and some to see and maybe talk to Anne Barnett. But the most of them came to worship. They felt compelled by some divine force to come to worship.

After the traditional songs had been sung and the offerings collected, Reverend Lonnie Tyler walked slowly up to the podium and looked out over the standing room only crowd. When he took the job of pastor in this small church in this small town, he never expected this. If the truth were to be known, he was nervous. He cleared his throat and laid his Bible on the podium. His prepared sermon was inside the Bible at the verses he wanted use in his sermon. But he had gotten some advice and a lot of information from someone he trusted. That advice told him to abandon his prepared sermon and just talk honestly and faithfully to the congregation and all the visitors.

"My friends," he began, "it's good to see so many at our little church this Sunday. I would be less than truthful with you if I didn't tell you I was not prepared for this level of turnout. I'm nervous and, in many ways, intimidated. This will be only my third sermon since becoming pastor here. I have a prepared sermon but, seeing this crowd today, I know in my heart it's not an appropriate sermon. A trusted colleague of mine advised me to do away with my prepared sermon and just speak to you honestly and faithfully. That's what I'm going to do. As a result, the sermon will be short but to the point. So please bear with me and I hope we'll all leave this church today with a blessing in our heart." He stopped and watched the crowd for a short moment and then moved his Bible to the side and put both hands on the podium.

"What I'd like to talk about with you today is what we've gained from this horrible war and what we've lost. As I look out over this congregation, I see many men, and some women, in the uniform of our countries military services, which brings me to what we've lost." He paused briefly to let what he had just said sink in. Then, he continued, "The little town of Coalville with a population of just over three thousand sent thirty-eight men and women to fight in the war. Of that thirty-eight, eleven would die, two are missing in action, and sixteen would be wounded. That means that only nine would come back to us whole. Think about that for a minute and realize that Coalville is a typical town in America. Many, many other towns in this county laid the same level of sacrifice, or more, at the altar of freedom; the sacrifice for good over evil, the sacrifice for truth and justice over lies and persecution, and the sacrifice for Godliness over darkness."

He now gripped the podium in both hands and held it tight. His voice had now gotten louder. "Because these things we just spoke of; freedom, good, truth, justice, and Godliness are not just words." He paused and gathered himself and then repeated slowly and forcibly, "They're NOT JUST WORDS. They're things of great value to free peoples all over the world. And many times, we're called on to defend these things and sometimes to die for them."

He paused again and picked up his Bible and held it to his chest. "And that brings me to what we've gained. The sacrifices we just discussed have allowed us to hold onto those WORDS; freedom, good, truth, justice, and Godliness. Our gain is that we still have those things that evil and darkness tried to take from us. It was put before us that if we wanted to keep those things and use those words, then we would have to fight for them and we would have to sacrifice for them. And we did. We did fight and we did sacrifice. And so we still have those things and we can still use those words."

He held the Bible up for all to see. "But we must remember that there was another sacrifice many, many years ago. It was a sacrifice for the world. You can read about it in your Bible in the book of John, chapter three, verse sixteen: For God so loved the world that He gave His only begotten Son, that whoever believes in Him shall not parish, but have eternal life."

He lowered his Bible took a deep breath and put a gentle smile on his face. "Thank you for coming today, it would be nice to see this little church filled like this every Sunday. Now if you will bow your heads for our closing prayer."

As people filed out of the little church, most everyone agreed it was a wonderful sermon and that Reverend Tyler had a real future for himself at the Coalville Baptist Church. It was almost like old home week as everyone gathered out in front of the church under the boiling Texas summer sun. Reverend Tyler gathered all the metal winners together and had them form a line so people could pass along the line and shake hands and talk.

While convalescing in Hawaii, Dick had received a promotion to Lieutenant Colonel. It seemed every time he got wounded and went to Hawaii, he got promoted. At almost the same time, the recommendation for his Navy Cross was approved. Now, he stood in the hot sun in his dress blue uniform wearing the Navy Cross from Okinawa and The Silver Star from Peleliu. He tried not to show it but he was really hot. He leaned heavily on a cane so he could stand straight and his wife, Cheryl, stood next to him and helped hold him up. The mortar shell that had blowup near him on Okinawa had re-cracked his hip and he was told he would now always walk with a limp.

Standing next to him and shaking hands as people went by was Commander Dee Collie, also in his dress blues and wearing the Distinguished Flying Cross for his actions on Peleliu. To go along with that, Dee had recently received a promotion to a full Commander. The sling on his shoulder was completely gone now and he had almost full use of his right arm. He was told that, in time, he would get full use of his arm back.

Standing next to Dee and shaking hands and receiving hugs, was Anne Barnett. Around her neck, she wore the Congressional Medal of Honor awarded to 1st Sergeant Bill Bob Barnett posthumously. On either side of her, stood Sue Ann Collie and Sally Barnett. Everyone was elated because Anne had decided to stay on the farm and not return to England. Billy Bob's military insurance of ten thousand dollars paid off the farm and it was free and clear in her name.

Next in line was Judy Cole Jackson wearing Clint Jordan's Air Medal. Although it was won under an alias, the Secretary of War agreed to have it reissued under the true name of the recipient. No investigation was initiated.

At the end of the line, smiling broadly was Reverend Tyler. He was busy talking to his trusted colleague and advisor, Reverend Tuney.

After nearly an hour in the boiling sun, Reverend Tyler decided everyone had had enough. He raised his hands and shouted loudly to get everyone's attention. When it quieted down and everyone was watching him he made an announcement. "Okay, we know it's too hot to continue to stand out here. So, this evening starting at eight PM, the Church is sponsoring a late picnic at the new State Park. There'll be cold drinks, uh, no beer I'm afraid, and snacks and ice cream for everyone. Please come if you can and we'll celebrate God's peace for the world. Please be there."

After the announcement, the gathering outside the church broke up and everyone went their separate ways promising to be at the church picnic later in the evening.

At eight PM, the picnic area in the State Park was filling up with people, but not nearly as many as were at church. The main reason was that the out of town people had to get home for work the next day and couldn't stay. But a lot of the Coalville people were there especially those that had served in the war and their families. After Reverend Tyler ask for a blessing on all of those there, he promised there would be no more preaching and everyone should just have a good time, which they set about doing.

Dee and Sue Ann wondered around until they found Dick and Cherrie. The four of them got a small picnic table and sat down. "Where're those twins of yours?" Sue Ann asked.

"They're over there near the sand boxes with Mom and Momma Ruth," Cherrie answered. "I saw Kyle was over there to. He's the oldest and he sure acts like it. Reminds me of another kid I use to know."

"I was never like that," Dee shot back. "I was kind to a fault."

"Well, you got the fault part right," Cherrie laughed.

"Okay, you two cut it out." Dick ordered. "We got some important stuff to figure out."

"Like what?" Sue Ann asked."

Dick looked at Cherrie and lowered his head. "What's up, Dick?" Cherrie demanded. "I know that look. It's just like Dee. I can read it like a book. What're you not tellin' me?"

Dick looked at Dee. "Have you told Sue Ann?" He asked.

"Told me what?" Sue Ann asked starting to get up from the table.

Dee grabbed her arm and held her down. "It's no big deal," Dee said calmly.

"If it's no big deal, why don't Cherrie and I know what the hell it is?"

"Okay, okay," Dick said. Then he paused and looked into Cherrie's eyes. "The truth is," he said slowly, "the Marines want me to stay in. That's one of the reasons they gave me Lt. Colonel. With most of the Marines musterin' out, we'll be down to a small Corp. They want me to run an NCO training school in Parris Island, South Carolina. In short, Cherrie, I've got to decide if I want to stay in the Corp or not."

Cherrie got up from the table and stood up. She put her hands on her hips. "Is this an 'I' decision or a 'we' decision?" She asked bluntly.

"It's a 'we' decision for sure," he said reaching up and taking her hand.

"So I get a vote," she replied.

"You not only get a vote, you get veto power."

She sat back down and pulled his hand to her breast. "Haven't you seen enough, suffer enough, and done enough?"

"Like I said, Cherrie, you have veto power."

"Oh, sure I do. I veto this and you mope around for the rest of our marriage doin' somethin' you'll probably hate."

"I'm a Marine, Cherrie, and in my heart I always will be. Like they say 'once in the Corp, always in the Corp', but I can be other things. I'll do anythin' for you, Cherrie; I'll walk on fire if I have to."

Cherrie let out a long breath, "Okay, Marine, when do we go to South Carolina?"

Dick grabbed her and kissed her hard and long. When they separated he smiled, "We'll talk about that later. Let's get somethin' to eat."

"Hey, hold on a minute," Sue Ann shouted. "I must be missin' somethin'. What has any of your plans have to do with us?" She turned and looked at Dee. "Tell me how we're involved in this?"

Dee shrugged his shoulders and said, "We're not involved in any of their plans."

"Then what was this 'Have you told Sue Ann' all about."

"It's simple," Dee said with his best smile. "The Navy has asked me to stay also. They want me to run a flight school in San Antonio. We need to get ready for the jets that are goin' to be comin' out real soon."

"And I guess you can't wait to fly one."

"Gee, Sue Ann, a jet. Just think about it."

"I am thinkin' about it. Do I get veto power like Cherrie?"

"I don't know," he said using his best smile again; "you might use it."

She laughed and patted him on the head. "No I won't little boy. You can play with your jets. When do we go to San Antonio?"

All four of them laughed. Dee and Dick shook hands and Cherrie and Sue Ann hugged each other. "Hey, Dick," Dee said quietly. "I sneaked some beer in the car. Come on, let's celebrate." The two of them left for the car with Dick hobbling along as fast as he could.

Judy, Bob Ann, Jack, Jake, and Reverend Tuney had a table near the tall pines. Bob Ann was living a whole new life now that the war was over. Her Kenny was safe or, at least, almost safe. He had just been sent to Okinawa as a replacement when the war ended.

He wasn't coming home just yet but at least no one was trying to kill him now.

Everyone seemed happy except Judy. She was in a gloomy mood and had been since the telegram about Jimmy. She had agreed to come mostly just to see what they had done to her hill. After a while at the table, she excused herself and walked over to the exact spot where their cabin used to be. There now were a couple of big signs that described the area and how the coal mining was done. Next to the signs was a lone cement bench that looked west towards the sunset. She tried to imagine where the bench would've fit in their cabin. She decided it is exactly where her favorite widow used to be; the one where she and Clint used to watch the sunsets; the sunsets Clint claimed where the most beautiful in the world.

It was getting on pass nine PM and the sun was beginning to set. She decided to sit and watch like she did as a little girl. She settled down on the bench and waited. A soft breeze was blowing in from the south and it felt good flowing through her hair. As the sun continue to go down it set the sky on fire and the beautiful rays shot out in all directions and bounced off the few puffy clouds that floated by. "Look at that, Pa," she said out loud to herself. "Isn't that beautiful? It just like when I was little and you used to sit with me and watch. I hope you can see it, Pa. I haven't been all over the world but I think that would be hard to beat anywhere." Her eyes began to water but the light breeze dried them quickly. "I don't know what I'm goin' to do, Pa. I've lost you and I've lost the love of my life, Jimmy. Sometimes I just wish I could get in my old plane and fly away."

"Where're you going to fly to, Fly Girl?" The voice came from behind her. She jumped to her feet and spun around. Standing a few feet away from her was Dee Collie and standing next to him was the love of her life, Lt. Jimmy Orland. He was standing on crutches and his hands were bandaged.

"Jimmy!" She shouted. Then she just stood there dumb founded.

"I found this guy wonderin' around the parkin' area while I was sneakin' a beer. I thought I'd better bring him to you." Dee patted

Jimmy on the back and said, "When you're ready to go or if you need any help just let me know." Dee waved at Judy and then turned and walked away.

All of a sudden the reality of it all hit and Judy made a mad dash for Jimmy. She nearly knocked him off his crutches when leaped on him and threw her arms around his neck. Jimmy staggered back trying to keep his balance and stay on his crutches. "What happened? She breathed as she covered his face with kisses. "How'd you get here?" She continued to shower him with kisses and then stopped at his month and kissed him as long and as hard as she could. "Tell me everythin'," she breathed.

When he could finally get a word in he said, "We can talk about all that later, but, for now, I guess you're glad to see me."

She laughed loudly and pulled his hair. "Boy, have I missed you. And boy, am I glad to see you. You wait 'til we get home and I'm goin' to show you just how much I've missed you."

"Now that's somethin' even a banged up guy like me can deal with," he said in soft husky voice, "and I surely have missed you. I'm here and I'm yours, sweetheart, but I'm not sure what I'll be doing. You're probably going to have to support me for a while. I hope you don't mind doing that."

She was still hanging on him with her arms around his neck. "I don't care what you do as long as we do it together." Then, before kissing him again, she whispered into his ear softly, "You know you're the love of my life."

As they kissed again and again, the sun went down in the west and the fire in sky went out. The park lights had not come on yet and a gentle darkness settled over the park.

CHAPTER NINETY-SEVEN

The Lives of the Greatest Generation

America's Greatest Generation lived through the worst economic depression in the history of the United States. What's not generally known is that the economic depression of the nineteen thirties was not just an American depression but a worldwide depression. It was devastating and most countries in the world turned to governments such as Nazism, Fascism, Communism, Dictatorships, Imperialism, and various forms of Socialism. But not America's Greatest Generation, they stuck by their Constitution and the elected form of government.

Then came World War II and they were called on to beat back the horror of Nazism and other forms of evil that strived to rule and subjugate the world. It called for a great sacrifice in human life and in human emotion. But they stepped forward and did it.

After a great depression and a world war, they then went on to help build a great nation by living successful lives and restoring the foundation of the United States of America.

James and Mary Collie: James would live to see six grandchildren and three great grandchildren. With Daryl staying in the military and Cheryl being married, he decided to sell his Fertilizer and Feed Store that had served him so well during the depression and the war. Strangely enough, he would sell it to Anne Barnett in 1955. He retired in 1965 and enjoyed life with his wife and family. He would die peaceably three days after his 50th Wedding Anniversary to his wonderful wife and lifelong companion, Mary, in 1967 at age 72.

Mary would out live her husband by five years and would die in 1972 at age 77. Until her death, Mary lived for her children, grandchildren, and great grandchildren. She died peaceable in her sleep in her own home. James and Mary were laid to rest next to each other in the Collie family plot in the Coalville Cemetery.

Daryl and Sue Ann Collie: Dee would stay in the Navy for twenty-three years and retire a one star Rear Admiral in 1964. He and his wife, Sue Ann, would then buy and move to a home in Coalville near his Mother. He and Sue Ann would then travel the world. He and Sue Ann would have two children, four grandchildren and five great grandchildren. He would fly jets during the Korean War. He and Sue Ann would be married for 62 years until Dee's death in 2003 at age 83. Sue Ann would die three years later in 2006 at age 85. Sue Ann and Cherrie would remain steadfast friends for their entire lives. Daryl and Sue Ann were laid to rest next to James and Mary in the Collie family plot.

Dick and Cheryl Jordan: Dick would stay in the Marines for twenty-one years and retire a one star Brigadier General. He and his wife, Cheryl, would then buy and move to a home in Coalville directly across the street from Dee and Sue Ann. Cheryl would give birth to two more children to go with the twins. Because of his wounds during World War II, Dick could not fight in the Korean War. In fact his wounds would eventually get worse and cause his death at the early age of sixty-one in 1979. At the time of his death, he and Cheryl would be married thirty-eight years. Cherrie would live to be ninety-two years old and die in 2012. Dick and Cheryl would leave four children, ten grandchildren (including a set of twins), and thirteen great grandchildren (including two sets of twins). It was as Cherrie always said, "It's in the genes". Cherrie would also say that Sue Ann was her most cherished friend and that Dee was her twin brother, her friend, her confidant, and the nicest guy, other than her husband, she ever knew. Dick and Cheryl were laid to rest next to Ruth and Clint in the Jordan family plot.

Clint and Ruth Jordan: The mystery of Clint Jordan on how he escaped and ended up in England on a B-17 raid under an alias was never resolved and those that knew said nothing. Clint's remains were removed from the grave at the American Cemetery in England and moved to the Jordan family plot in the Coalville cemetery. And, in legal terms, Ruth was still married to Clint at his death, since Clint was not dead all of those other years and since there was no divorce. But because of Clint dying under another name, Ruth never got any insurance from the government. Ruth would live in her little home in Coalville for the rest of her life enjoying her grandchildren and great grandchildren, and enjoying the friendship of James and Mary Collie. Ruth would die one year after her longtime friend James Collie in 1967 at age 73. She would be laid to rest next to Clint in the Jordan family plot.

Anne and Billy Bob Barnett: Billy Bob Barnett's remains would be returned from its temporary grave in Belgium to Coalville. He was laid to rest next to his Father in the small Barnett cemetery on the Barnett Farm. Anne stayed with her Mother-in-law on the farm and made a good success of it. She would also buy the Fertilizer and Feed store from James Collie and make it an even bigger success. She would make three trips to England so her son, William, could see where his Mum was born and so she could visit her surviving family. In 1954, she would meet retired Colonel John Barnes at a 101st Airborne Division reunion that she was attending in place of Bill. They would marry one year later. She would give him two sons. John offered to adopt William so that he could take the Barnes name, but Anne would not hear of it. She swore that William would carry Bill's name always and that he must know who his Father was and that one day William would be given Bill's Congressional Medal of Honor. Anne would grow old on the farm with her husband and three sons and, in 2001 at the age of 79, died while sitting in her rocking chair on the front porch. She was laid to rest in the Barnett cemetery.

Sally and William Barnett: Sally would stay on the farm with Anne until her death in 1965 at age 66. She was laid to rest in the Barnett cemetery next to her son Billy Bob. She enjoyed life on the farm with Anne, and her new husband and the three boys. But above all, she treasured William. He grew up to be the spit and image of Billy Bob. Sue Ann would visit when she could and grew to adore William also. In 1963, William would be admitted to West Point because of his Father's Congressional Medal of Honor. When Sally died she had no bitterness to God for Billy Bob's death, because she knew Billy Bob was doing what he wanted to do. And God had seen fit to give her William.

Tom and Evie Clark: Tom Clark would win election to the office of sheriff four more times and would serve as Sheriff of Coalville until 1956 when his son, Tyson, would replace him. Tom and Evie never had any more marital problems and grew old together in their same little house. Tom would die in 1969 at age 75 and Evie would follow him eight years later in 1977 at age 78. Tom and Evie were laid to rest next to each other in the Coalville Cemetery.

Louis Mailer: Lou would continue to work for the law firm of Bitterman, Bitterman, and Levi until 1949 when he was killed while working on a divorce case. He was outside of a house taking pictures of a cheating wife when he was shot by her lover through the window. Lou's remains would be taken to Coalville where he was buried in the cemetery.

Jimmy and Judy Orland: After his war wounds had healed, Jimmy went back to work for Mobil Oil. They took him back under the condition he would never leave again unless he was being fired or retiring, to which he agreed. Jimmy and Judy had an exciting life traveling, flying, and pursuing all manner of adventures. They had two children a boy they named Clint and a girl they name Amelia. Judy got her old plane back and taught both their children to fly. They had plenty of money thanks to Jimmy's job. They bought a little get-a-way cabin way out in West Texas near the town of Marfa. Judy would fly them out there for private little get-a-ways. In 1977 Congress passed the G.I. Bill Improvement Act giving the WASP full military status and in 1984 each WASP was awarded the World War II Victory Metal. Judy was as proud of that as she was her Silver Wings, which she carried to her death. Jimmy wound retire from Mobil Oil in 1970 and he and Judy made the best of life. Then, in 1995 Jimmy would come down with lung cancer and would die one year later in 1996 at the age of 79. Judy was devastated by the loss of the love of her life. She took her plane up just to fly around and be alone and upon landing she was crying so hard her vision was blinded. As a result, she miss judged the end of the runway and crashed. She died at the scene. It was 1996 and she was 76 years of age. Some say she committed suicide, but those that knew Judy knew nothing could be farther from the truth, and anyway, Jimmy wouldn't have like for her to do that. Jimmy and Judy were both laid to rest, side by side, in the Jordan family plot in the Coalville Cemetery. On Judy's tombstone at the very bottom in small letters was inscribed, "Jimmy will always be the love of my life."

Clint and Amelia Orland: Clint Orland would go on to become an important member of the Mobil Oil Board of Directors and help guide the merger of Mobil Oil and Exxon. Amelia Orland would join the United States Air Force and fly jets for her country, and on her uniform she always wore her Mother's WASP Silver Wings and World War II Victory Medal pinned on the left breast of that uniform.

EPILOG

Marfa, Texas is a small town in far West Texas. It's on the High Desert and is right at 4,700 feet above sea level. It is a mere sixty miles from the Mexican border. On July 25th of 1944, a young Mexican woman gave birth to a baby in a small cabin just outside the Marfa city limits. The baby was a boy and weighted in at seven pounds and eight ounces. He had black hair and dark skin denoting his Hispanic heritage, but he also had hazel colored eyes and Angelo facial features.

The little cabin where the boy was born only had three rooms; a bedroom, a bathroom, and a combined living room and kitchen. The doctor who delivered the baby was a private physician from Marfa named Dr. Leonard Martinez.

Dr. Martinez walked from the bedroom and closed the door behind him. He turned to face the young woman who was sitting in a chair near one of the two windows that were in the front wall of the cabin. "Both the Mother and her Son or doing fine, but the baby should have wet towel baths about every hour in this heat" Dr. Martinez said smiling."

"Thanks, Leonard, for comin' out here like this," the woman said in a sincere voice. "I know it was a pain in the ass."

"Not really," Leonard replied, "it was no trouble."

"How much do I owe you?" The woman asked as she pulled a wallet out of her jeans.

"Please, don't insult me," Leonard said in a discussed tone. "It's been a fine day so let's not ruin it."

The woman smiled and put her wallet back in her pocket.

"Who'll take care of her a way out here?" Leonard asked concerned. "Maybe she should come into town. I can see that she and the baby are taken care of."

"Thanks again, Leonard, but I've taken care of everythin'. She and the baby will be well cared for, and her documents are all in order."

"Speaking of documents," Leonard said, "we need names so I can fill in the blanks. I need the mother's name and the name of the baby and of the father if it's known. Once I have that, I can file the birth certificate back in Marfa."

"Why don't you go back in and ask her?" The woman asked simply.

"Okay, I will." Leonard went back into the bedroom to find the mother smiling and stroking her new son. "I'm sorry, but I'll need some names so I can file a birth certificate, he said softly."

"Okay," the mother whispered.

"Your name, if you please?"

"My name is Rosa Elaina Costillo"

"And do you know the father's name?

"The father's name is unimportant at this time," she replied continuing to smile.

"And how are you naming the baby?"

Rosa looked at her son with love in every fiber of her body. "My son will carry the name Jordan Orland Costillo."

Leonard smiled down at her, "That's quite a name for a little boy."

Rosa looked up at him with determined eyes and repeated, "My son will carry the name Jordan Orland Costillo."

"Okay," Leonard said, "I'll check in on you again before I leave."

Leonard went back into the living area and started to tell the woman about the names, but she was gone. And, in the distance, he could hear the hum of an airplane engine.

———

Whatever happened to Jordan Orland Costillo? Well, that's another story!